Data Structures Using C++

VARSHA H. PATIL

Professor

University of Pune

OXFORD

UNIVERSITY PRESS

Oxford University Press is a department of the University of Oxford.
It furthers the University's objective of excellence in research, scholarship,
and education by publishing worldwide. Oxford is a registered trademark of
Oxford University Press in the UK and in certain other countries

Published in India by
Oxford University Press
YMCA Library Building, 1 Jai Singh Road, New Delhi 110001, India

First published in 2012
Second impression 2013

ISBN-13: 978-0-19-806623-1
ISBN-10: 0-19-806623-6

Typeset in Times New Roman
by Laserwords, Chennai
Printed in India by Raj Kamal Electric Press, Haryana

Dedicated to

My parents, Ashatai and Motianna Gunjal

and

My in-laws, Sumantai and Kashiram Patil

PREFACE

The study of data structures serves as the foundation for several fields of computer science such as programming, compiler design, and database management. Almost every program or software uses data structures as an effective and efficient means of data storage and organization. Often, the success of a program or software depends upon the way the data is represented and the algorithm used to process the data. While programming, different kinds of data are required to be stored and processed in the computer. Data can be stored in a generalized format using variables. A data structure uses a collection of related variables that can be accessed individually or as a whole, and represents a set of data items with a specific relationship amongst them. Thus, choosing an effective data structure is the key to success in the design of algorithms.

For designing an effective algorithm, a programmer can choose the most efficient data structure from a variety of available ones. Some common data structures include arrays, linked lists, hash tables, heaps, trees, tries, stacks, and queues. Different kinds of data structures are suited for different kinds of applications. For example, arrays are popularly used in searching, sorting, and matrix-related operations. Stacks, on the other hand, are used for converting infix=expressions to postfix and prefix forms, reversing a string, processing function calls, parsing computer programs, and simulating recursion. Similarly, queues are most useful in simulating complex real-world problems.

The data structures course has found its way into the undergraduate curriculum due to rapid development and advances in the field of computer science. This course is taught using different programming languages such as C, C++, and Java. We shall learn this course using C++, as it has emerged as one of the leading object-oriented programming languages, and is used extensively in both academia and industry.

ABOUT THE BOOK

Data Structures Using C++ is designed to serve as a textbook for undergraduate courses in computer science and engineering and postgraduate courses in computer applications. This book seeks to inculcate a scientific aptitude in the readers by laying special emphasis on the understanding of the concepts with the help of simple language and user-friendly presentation. It also intends to develop independent thinking by focussing on real-world examples as well as the practical aspects of this course through numerous chapter-end exercises.

The book emphasizes the following aspects of studying a course on data structures:

- the skills required in defining the level of abstraction of data structures and algorithms;
- the ability to devise alternate implementations of a data structure; and
- the implementation of all the characteristics of data structures through C++.

While developing the content for this book the aim has been to make the readers understand the use of abstract data types (ADTs), classes, and various techniques for building simple data structures.

KEY FEATURES

- Each concept in this book is explained by an algorithm and a piece of program code implemented through C++, for imparting practical knowledge to the readers.
- Numerous illustrations, diagrams, and flowcharts are included to aid the understanding of concepts.
- A glossary is provided at the end of every chapter, which helps the readers assimilate the key concepts efficiently.
- A summary is given at the end of every chapter for a quick recapitulation of all the important topics discussed.
- Extensive chapter-end exercises consisting of solved multiple choice questions, review questions, and programming exercises are included to facilitate revision.

ORGANIZATION OF THE BOOK

The book is organized into 15 chapters.

Chapter 1 gives an introduction to programming, data structures, and related concepts. This chapter covers the various types of data structures, structured programming, and development of software through the software engineering approach.

Chapter 2 acquaints the reader with the concept of arrays, which is the most popular and easy-to-use static data structure. Arrays are found in almost every high-level programming language as a built-in data structure. This chapter describes arrays with respect to applications such as polynomials, strings, and sparse matrices.

Chapter 3 covers the stack and its implementation as a static data structure. Applications of stacks, such as recursion and infix expression conversion, are discussed.

Chapter 4 covers recursion and related concepts. This chapter helps us understand, evaluate, and implement recursive functions. It also elaborates on how recursion works.

Chapter 5 illustrates the concept, realization, variations, and applications of queues. A queue is a special type of data structure that performs insertions at one end called the 'rear' and deletions at another end called the 'front'.

Chapter 6 covers the basic concepts and realization of the linked list. This dynamic data structure is a powerful tool and is described with respect to applications such as polynomials, strings, and sorting.

Chapter 7 deals with trees. A non-linear data structure, the tree is a means to maintain and manipulate data in many applications. Non-linear data structures are capable of expressing more complex relationships than linear data structures. Variations, implementation, and applications of trees are covered in this chapter.

Chapter 8 introduces the graph, its representation, traversal techniques, and algorithms used to process it. In many areas of application such as cartography, sociology, chemistry, geography, mathematics, electrical engineering, and computer science, we often need a representation that reflects arbitrary relationships among the objects. One of the most powerful and natural solutions that models such relationships is the graph.

Chapter 9 explains the basic search and sort techniques that help make the search process more efficient. If the data is kept in proper order, it is much easier to search. Sorting is a process of organizing data in a certain order to help retrieve it more efficiently.

Chapter 10 discusses two variations of binary search trees (BSTs)—Adelson-Velskii–Landis (AVL) and optimal binary search trees (OBSTs). A BST is a data structure that has efficient searching as well as insertion and deletion algorithms.

Chapter 11 deals with hashing, hash functions, and related aspects. The concepts of searching techniques and search trees have already been discussed in Chapters 9 and 10, respectively. In an ideal situation, we expect the target to be searched and identified in one attempt or a minimum number of attempts. One way to achieve this is to know (or to be able to obtain) the address of the record where it is stored. Hashing is a method of directly computing the address of the record with the help of a key, by using a suitable mathematical function called the hash function.

Chapter 12 provides an overview of heaps. As discussed earlier, a BST is used for searching and an array is used for sorting data of fixed size that is already collected. On the other hand, when data must be simultaneously inserted and sorted, then the data structure that works more efficiently than BSTs is the heap.

Chapter 13 discusses multiway search trees. Binary search trees generalize directly to multiway search trees. A multiway search tree is a tree of order m, where each node has at most m children. Here m is an integer. If $k \leq m$ is the number of children, then the node contains exactly $k - 1$ keys, which partition all the keys in the subtrees into k subsets. If some of these subsets are empty, then the corresponding children in the tree are also empty.

Chapter 14 introduces files and organization. Files contain records that are a collection of information arranged in a specific manner. File organization refers mainly to the logical arrangement of data in a file system.

Chapter 15 briefly covers the standard template library (STL) and its usage. C++ classes provide information for creating libraries of data structures. The C++ class allows for implementation of ADTs, with appropriate hiding of the implementation details. The STL is a part of the standard C++ class library, and can be used as the standard approach for storing and processing data.

Chapter 16 introduces the readers to the study of algorithmic strategies and their analyses. Asymptotic notations are required to quantify the performance of a particular algorithm. The various algorithmic strategies, namely, divide-and-conquer, greedy method, dynamic programming, and pattern matching required to solve a particular problem effectively and efficiently are discussed in detail. A data structure that represents a set of strings, called tries, is discussed towards the end. It aids in pattern matching by making the process faster.

The *appendix* provides a thorough overview of the fundamentals of C++ programming. C++ has proven to be the most suitable language for the implementation of abstract data types because of the introduction of the concept of classes.

I sincerely hope that the readers will be able to make the most out of this book and apply the concepts learnt in their academic and professional tenures. If you have any comments or suggestions that can be incorporated in the future editions of this book, feel free to contact me at varsha.patil@gmail.com.

Varsha H. Patil

ACKNOWLEDGEMENTS

I would like to thank many people who encouraged and helped me in various ways throughout this project, namely, my family, my didi Megha and Arvindji jaji, my colleagues, friends, and students.

First and foremost I would like to acknowledge Dr Gajanan Kharate, Dr Shirish Sane, Vaishali Pawar, Vaishali Tidke, Seema Gondhalekar, Swati Bhavsar, Alpana Borse, Snehal Umare, and all my colleagues. Special thanks to Mr Mahesh Sanghvi for his untiring efforts in making this project successful. This book would not have been what it is, without him.

I received constant support and motivation from honourable Balasahebwagh, Narendrabhau, Kishorbhau, Laxmanbhau, and Kunal Darabe. I thank them for all the inspiration.

My husband, Hemant, encouraged me even before I started writing this book. His contagious enthusiasm and generous spirit and also the ever-smiling faces of my children Abolee and Saurabh made working on this project a pleasant experience. Finally, I would like to thank my parents, sisters, brother, and all other family members for making the experience of writing this book memorable.

Last but not the least, my acknowledgements would remain incomplete if I do not thank the editorial team of Oxford University Press, India, who supported me throughout the development of this manuscript.

Dr Varsha H. Patil

FEATURES OF THE BOOK

OBJECTIVES

After completing this chapter, the reader will be able to understand the following:

- The power of recursion and its working
- Identification of the base case and the general case of a recursively defined problem
- Comparison of iterative and recursive solutions
- The steps to write, implement, test, and debug recursive functions
- The method of implementing recursion using stacks

Objectives

Each chapter begins with a list of topics that the readers can expect to learn from that chapter.

Algorithms

All chapters contain plenty of algorithms to support the theoretical concepts. Each algorithm is depicted in a step-wise manner along with a description of its function and significance.

ALGORITHM 4.2

```
An iterative version of the algorithm to compute the factorial of a
number
1. start
2. Let n be the number whose factorial is to be computed and let
   Factorial = 1
3. for I = 1 to n do
   begin
      Factorial = Factorial * I
   end
4. stop
```

PROGRAM CODE 4.1

```
int Factorial(int n)
{
   if(n == 1)        // end condition
      return 1;
   else
      return Factorial(n - 1) * n;
}
```

Program Codes

Numerous program codes in C++ provide implementation of the concepts. Comments are provided wherever necessary thus making the code self-explanatory and easy to understand.

Flowcharts

Flowcharts are provided wherever required. They provide readers with a step-wise and clear representation of algorithms and concepts.

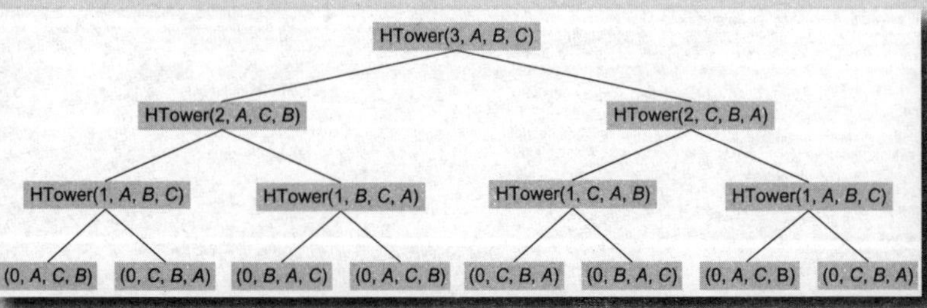

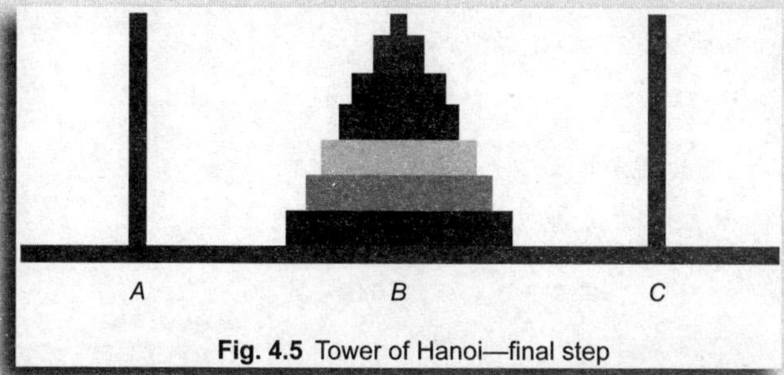

Fig. 4.5 Tower of Hanoi—final step

Illustrations

More than 400 well-labelled illustrations are provided to aid in clearer understanding of the concepts.

Recapitulation

A summary of key topics at the end of each chapter helps the readers revise all the important concepts explained in that chapter. It is provided in point-wise form for a quick grasp of the concepts learnt.

RECAPITULATION

- A function may call itself or other functions, and the called functions in turn may again call the calling function. Such functions are called recursive functions.
- Any correct iterative code can be converted into its equivalent recursive code and vice versa.
- The basic concepts and ideas involved with recursion are simple—a function that has to be solved is treated as a big problem and it solves itself by using itself

KEY TERMS

Binary recursion A simple unary recursive function calls itself once, whereas the binary recursive function calls itself twice. A factorial is a unary function, whereas Fibonacci is a binary recursion.

Depth of recursion The number of times a function calls itself is known as the recursive depth of that function.

Key Terms

All chapters provide the reader with requisite revision of key terms along with their definitions.

Multiple Choice Questions

Multiple choice questions put to test the readers' theoretical knowledge that is gained after reading the chapter. Answers to these questions are provided at the end of every chapter.

Multiple choice questions

1. Infinite recursion occurs when
   (a) a base case is omitted
   (b) a base case is never reached
   (c) both (a) and (b)
   (d) none of the above
2. Fibonacci function $\text{Fib}(n) = \text{Fib}(n-1) + \text{Fib}(n-2)$ is an example of
   (a) direct recursion
   (b) tree recursion

Review questions

1. Write a recursive algorithm to check whether a specified character is in a string.
2. Write a recursive algorithm to count all occurrences of a specified character in a string.
3. Write a recursive algorithm that removes all occurrences of a specified character in a string.

Review Questions

Numerous review questions at the end of every chapter test the readers' conceptual knowledge as well as help them think outside the box.

BRIEF CONTENTS

DETAILED CONTENTS

1 FUNDAMENTAL CONCEPTS

OBJECTIVES

After completing this chapter, the reader will be able to understand the following:

- the well-defined, clear, and simple approach of program design
- fundamental aspects of an algorithm and its characteristics
- basic concepts such as data, data type, data object, and data structure
- the power of abstract data type (ADT)
- the software development life cycle (SDLC)

Programming requires different kinds of information to be stored in the computer and the input data to be processed. The information can be stored in a generalized format using variables. In principle, one variable allows the storage of a single data entity. However, a set of single variables may not solve complex problems efficiently. A data structure uses a collection of related variables that can be accessed individually or as a whole. In other words, a data structure represents a set of data items with a specific relationship between them. In this chapter, we shall study the fundamental concepts related to programming and data structures.

1.1 INTRODUCTION TO PROGRAMMING

A computer is a programmable data processor that accepts input and instructions to process the input (program) and generates the required output as shown in Fig. 1.1. Although

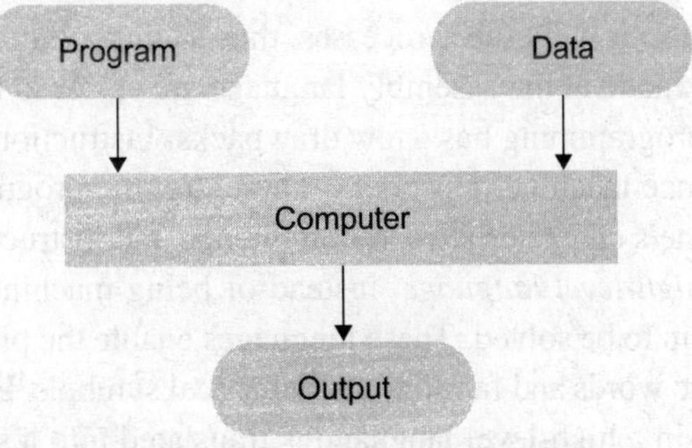

Fig. 1.1 Processing a program

computers are competent to perform complex and difficult operations, they are inherently simple and passive machines. They must be told precisely and explicitly in a language they can understand, as to what is to be done. This sequence of instructions is known as a program. A program that satisfies user needs as per his/her specifications is called *software*. The physical machinery that actually executes these instructions is known as *hardware*.

The first phase of developing a program is to define the problem statement precisely. We have to mention very clearly what a program shall do and what our expectations from the program are. After defining the problem, we have to select the best suitable algorithm to solve it. An algorithm is a stepwise description of an action that leads the problem from its start state to its goal state. An algorithm must be very clear, definite, and efficient for the problem it aims at solving. The art of programming consists of designing or choosing algorithms and expressing them in a programming language. This phase of developing a program is very important. Later the code is tested, debugged, and revised, if required.

All computer languages can be classified into the following three basic categories:

1. Machine language
2. Assembly language
3. High-level language

In most *machine languages*, binary digits (bits 0 and 1) represent everything, namely, instructions, data, and variables. Binary numbers are composed entirely of zeros and ones. Programs written in machine language can be executed very fast by computers. This is because machine instructions are directly understood by the computer and no translation program is required. However, these programs consisting of a sequence of zeros and ones are difficult to read, write, and interpret by humans.

Assembly languages are a major improvement over machine languages. In an assembly language, a short name, rather than a big binary number, defines each instruction and identifies each variable. In this language, programming numeric operation codes are substituted by mnemonics. A mnemonic is any kind of mental technique we use to help us represent numeric codes, Programs written in assembly language require a special program called the assembler that translates assembly language instructions into machine language instructions. Nowadays, programs are written in assembly language only when the speed of execution is of high priority.

Assembly language is easier to understand as it uses symbolic names for complex calculations and other processes, thus saving a lot of time and effort for the programmer. Errors made in the assembly language are easier to find and correct. However, assembly-level programming has a few drawbacks. Instructions vary from machine to machine and are hence machine-dependent. Therefore, the programmer must be aware of a particular machine's characteristics, requirements, and instruction set.

A *high-level language*, instead of being machine-dependent, is oriented towards the problem to be solved. These languages enable the programmer to write instructions using English words and familiar mathematical symbols. Every instruction that the programmer writes in a high-level language is translated into a set of machine language instructions. This is known as one-to-many translation.

Each language is considered the best to solve a particular class of problems but unsuitable to solve another class of problems. Today, there are over 200 high-level languages. Some of the most common ones are C, C++, Java, Pascal, FORTRAN, and COBOL. A system program that translates a high-level language such as C++ to a machine language is called a *compiler*. It is thus a peculiar sort of program whose input is one program and output is another program.

1.2 OBJECT-ORIENTED PROGRAMMING

Traditional structured programming has been used as algorithmic decomposition. Algorithmic or functional decomposition views software as a process. It decomposes the software/program into modules, which represent the steps of the process. These modules are implemented by language constructs such as procedures in Pascal, subroutines in FORTRAN, or functions in C++. Object-oriented programming-based (OOP-based) design represents a fundamental change from the structured programming design method. Object-oriented decomposition views software as a set of well-defined objects that model entities in the application domain. These objects interact with each other to form a software system. Functional decomposition is addressed after the system has been decomposed into objects. The basic concept in OOP is an object. Object-oriented programming is used to model the real world through objects. In our real world, everything, from an apple to a car, is an object, which can be distinguished from one another in the physical as well as the behavioural point of view. An object is an entity that performs computations and has a local state. It is also viewed as a combination of data and procedural (behavioural) elements.

The success of a software project often depends upon the choices made in the representation of data and algorithms designed to process the data. The proper choice of a data structure can be a key point in the design of many algorithms. Clearly, we need proper ways to describe and process data.

A data type consists of a collection of values together with a set of basic operations defined on these values. A data type is called an *abstract data type* (ADT) if the programmer can use it without having access to and also without knowing the details of how the values and operations are implemented.

An object-oriented language such as C++ is a programming paradigm that has a direct link to ADTs by implementing them as a class. We shall use C++ as the programming language in this book.

1.3 INTRODUCTION TO DATA STRUCTURES

Computer science includes the study of data, its representation, and its processing by computers. Hence, it is essential to study about the terms associated with data and its representation. As mentioned in Section 1.2, the success of a software project often depends upon the choices made in the representation of the data and the choice of *algorithms*, and hence we need better methods to describe and process the data. The term data structure refers to the organization of data elements and the interrelationships among them.

The field of data structures is very important and central to the study of computer science and programming. There is a clear distinction between the data structure specification and its realization. The specification comes before the programming language application and its realization comes with a specific programming language. Again, it is very important to study how these two processes can be accomplished successfully.

Specification of data structures requires explaining the functioning and overall behaviour of the data structure, whereas the implementation of the data structure requires simulating the data structure in some programming language. There is a close relationship among algorithms, data, and data structures. In this chapter, we are going to learn about the fundamental concepts of data structures, various types, programming tools, algorithms, and flowcharts.

1.3.1 Data

Data is nothing but a piece of information. Data input, data manipulation (or data processing), and data output are the functions of computers. Hence all information taken as input, processed within a computer, or provided as output to the user is nothing but data. It can be a number, a string, or a set of many numbers and strings.

Atomic and Composite Data

Atomic data is the data that we choose to consider as a single, non-decomposable entity. For example, the integer 1234 may be considered as a single integer value. Of course, we can decompose it into digits, but the decomposed digits will not have the same characteristics of the original integer; they will be four single digit integers ranging from 0 to 9. In some languages, atomic data is known as scalar data because of its numeric properties.

The opposite of atomic data is *composite data*. Composite data can be broken down into subfields that have meaning. For example, a student's record consists of Roll_Number, Name, Branch, Year, and so on. Composite data is also referred to as structured data and can be implemented using a structure or a class in C++.

1.3.2 Data Type

Data type refers to the kind of data a variable may store. Whenever we try to implement any algorithm in some programming language, we need variables. A variable may have any value as per the facilities provided by that language. Data type is a term that specifies the type of data that a variable may hold in the programming language.

Built-in Data Types

In general, languages have their built-in data types. However, they also allow the user to define his or her own data types, called *user-defined data types*, using the built-in data types; for example, in the C/C++ languages, `int`, `float`, and `char` are built-in data types. Using these built-in data types, we can design (define) our own data types by means of structures, unions, and classes.

User-defined Data Types

Suppose we want to maintain a record of 100 students with the following fields in each record: roll number, name of student, and percentage of marks of the students. Then we use the C++ class as follows:

```
class Student
{
   private:
      int roll;
      char name[20];
      float percentage;
   public:
      void GetRecord();
      void PrintRecord();
      void SearchRecord();
}
```

`Class`, `structure`, and `union` are the user-defined data types in C++.

1.3.3 Data Object

A *data object* represents a container for data values—a place where data values may be stored and later retrieved. A data object is characterized by a set of attributes, one of the most important of which is its data type. The attributes determine the number and type of values that the data object may contain and also determine the logical organization of these values.

A data object is nothing but a set of elements, say D. The data object 'alphabets' can be defined as $D = \{A, B, \ldots, Z, a, b, \ldots, z\}$ and the data object 'integers' as $D = \{\ldots, -3, -2, -1, 0, 1, 2, 3, \ldots\}$. The data object set may be finite or infinite.

A data object is a run-time instance of data structures. It is the run-time grouping of one or more data pieces. Some of the data objects that exist during program execution are programmer-defined, such as `variables`, `constants`, `arrays`, and `files`. The programmer explicitly creates and manipulates these data objects through declarations and statements in the program. System-defined data objects are ordinarily generated automatically as needed during program execution without explicit specification by the programmer.

1.3.4 Data Structure

Data structures refer to data and representation of data objects within a program, that is, the implementation of structured relationships. A data structure is a collection of atomic and composite data types into a set with defined relationships. By structure, we mean a set of rules that holds the data together. In other words, if we take a combination of data types and fit them into a structure such that we can define the relating rules, we can have data structures that consist of other data structures too.

In brief, a data structure is

1. a combination of elements, each of which is either as a data type or another data structure and
2. a set of associations or relationships (structures) involving the combined elements.

Most of the programming languages support several data structures. In addition, modern programming languages allow programmers to create new data structures for an application.

We can define *data structures* as follows:

A data structure is a set of domains D, a designated domain d ∈ D, a set of functions F, and a set of axioms A. The triple structure (D, F, A) denotes the data structure with the following elements:

***Domain* (D)** This is the range of values that the data may have.

***Functions* (F)** This is the set of operations for the data. We must specify a set of operations for a data structure to operate on.

***Axioms* (A)** This is a set of rules with which the different operations belonging to F can actually be implemented.

Let us consider an example of a data structure of an integer.

Here, the data structure d = Integer

```
Integer
Domain D = {Integer, Boolean}
Set of functions F = {zero, ifzero, add, increment}
Set of axioms A = {
                    ifzero(zero()) → true;
                    ifzero(increment(zero()) → false
                    add(zero(), x) → x
                    add(increment(x), y) = increment(add(x, y))
                    equal(increment(x), increment(y) = equal(x, y)
                   }
end Integer
```

In general, the data type of a variable is the set of values that the variable may hold. An ADT is a mathematical model that includes data with various operations defined. Implementation details of an ADT are hidden, which is why it is called abstract. To represent the mathematical model underlying an ADT, we use the data structure, which is a collection of the variables and the data types inter-related in different ways.

1.3.5 Abstract Data Type

Software engineering is very close to computer science. Software engineering is the establishment and the use of good engineering methodologies and a principle for writing reliable software. One of the most important principles in accomplishing this is the use of abstraction. Abstraction allows us to organize the complexity of a task by focussing on logical properties of data and actions rather than on the implementation details. Logical properties refer to the 'what' and implementation details refer to the 'how'. The abstraction is at the procedural and data level.

Data abstraction is the separation of logical properties of the data from details of how the data is represented. Procedural abstraction means separation of the logical properties of action from implementation. Procedural abstraction and data abstraction are closely related as operations within the ADTs are procedural abstractions. An ADT encompasses both procedural as well as data abstraction; the set of operations are defined for any data type that might make up the set of values.

An ADT is the one in which the set of operations is defined at a formal, logical level, without being restricted by the operational details. In other words, an ADT is a data declaration packaged together with the operations that are meaningful for the data type. We encapsulate the data and the operations on this data and hide them from the user. In brief, an ADT includes declaration of data, implementation of operations, and encapsulation of data and operations.

Consider the concept of a queue. At least three data structures will support a queue. We can use an array, a linked list, or a file. If we place our queue in an ADT, users should not be aware of the structure we use. As long as they can enqueue (insert) and dequeue (retrieve) data, how we store the data should make no difference.

We are aware of the importance of hiding the implementation. The user need not know the data structure to be able to use an ADT. For a queue, the application program should have no knowledge of the data structure. All references to and manipulation of the data in the queue must be handled through defined interfaces to the structure. Allowing the application program to directly reference the data structure is a common fault in many applications that prevent the ADT from being fully portable to other applications.

We want a data specification method that has the following features:

Abstract It should help the programmer organize data by focussing on its logical properties rather than on the implementation details, which in turn allows the user to hide the complexity of a task.

Safe It should control the manipulation of the representation of data so that malfunctioning can be avoided.

Modifiable It should make it relatively easy to modify the representation.

Reusable The data structure should be such that it is a reusable product for others.

Let us redefine ADT for the `Integer`.

```
Abstract data type Integer
  Operations
    zero() → int
    ifzero(int) → boolean
```

```
        increment(int) → int
        add(int, int) → int
        equal(int, int) → boolean
    Rules/axioms for operations
        for all x, y ∈ integer let
          ifzero(zero()) → true;
          ifzero(increment(zero()) → false
          add(zero(), x) → x
        add(increment(x), y) → increment(add(x, y))
        equal(increment(x), increment(y) → equal(x, y)
    end Integer
```

This is an example of the `Integer` data structure; five basic functions are defined on a set of integer data object. These functions are as follows:

1. `zero() → int`—It is a function which takes no input but generates the integer zero as result. That is, its output is 0.
2. `ifzero(int) → Boolean`—This function takes one integer input and checks whether that number is 0 or not. It generates output of type True/False, that is, of the Boolean type.
3. `increment(int) → int`—This function reads one integer and produces its incremented value, that is, (integer + 1), which is again an integer.
   For example, `increment(3) → 4`
4. `add(int, int) → int`—This function reads two integers and adds them producing another integer.
5. `equal(int, int) → Boolean`—This function takes two integer values and checks whether they are equal or not. Again, it gives output of the True/False type. So its output is of Boolean type.

The set of axioms which describes the rules of operations is as follows:

1. `ifzero(zero) → true`—This axiom says that the `zero()` function which produces an integer zero, is checked by the `ifzero()` function, and ultimately the result is true.
2. `ifzero(increment(zero())) → false`—The value of `increment(zero)` is 1 and hence `ifzero(1)` is false.
3. `add(zero(), x) → x` —This means that `0 + x = x`.
4. `add(increment (x), y) → increment (add(x, y))`—Assuming `x = 3` and `y = 5`, this means that `add(increment (3), 5) = increment(add(3, 5)) = add(4, 5) = increment(8) = 9`.
5. `equal(increment(x), increment(y)) → equal(x, y)`—This axiom specifies that if `x` and `y` are equal, then `x` + 1 and `y` + 1 are also equal.

The axioms do not specify the form of implementation of the data structure. This is why the ADT is an abstract one. An ADT can also be defined as a collection of variables together with the functions necessary to operate on those variables. Variables represent the information contained, whereas functions define the operations that can be performed on data.

In OOP, we can create an object from an ADT. In fact, C++ provides 'class' declaration precisely for the purpose of defining the ADT from which objects are created. Creating an object involves setting aside a block of memory for the variables of that object. In C++, functions that operate on variables of a class are called member functions. An ADT is a way of defining a data structure so that we know what it does but not how it does it.

1.4 TYPES OF DATA STRUCTURES

We defined a data structure as a way of organizing data that specifies

1. a set of data elements, that is, a data object; and
2. a set of operations that are applied to this data object.

These two sets form a mathematical construct that may be implemented using a particular programming language. The data structure is independent of their implementation. The various types of data structures are as follows:

1. primitive and non-primitive
2. linear and non-linear
3. static and dynamic
4. persistent and ephemeral
5. sequential and direct access

1.4.1 Primitive and Non-primitive Data Structures

Primitive data structures define a set of primitive elements that do not involve any other elements as its subparts—for example, data structures defined for integers and characters. These are generally primary or built-in data types in programming languages.

Non-primitive data structures are those that define a set of derived elements such as arrays. Arrays in C++ consist of a set of similar type of elements. Class and structure are other examples of non-primitive data structures, which consist of a set of elements that may be of different data types and functions to operate on.

1.4.2 Linear and Non-linear Data Structures

Data structures are classified as linear and non-linear. A data structure is said to be *linear* if its elements form a sequence or a linear list. In a linear data structure, every data element has a unique successor and predecessor. There are two basic ways of representing linear structures in memory. One way is to have the relationship between the elements by means of pointers (links), called linked lists. The other way is using sequential organization, that is, arrays.

Non-linear data structures are used to represent the data containing hierarchical or network relationship among the elements. Trees and graphs are examples of non-linear data structures. In non-linear data structures, every data element may have more than one predecessor as well as successor. Elements do not form any particular linear sequence. Figure 1.2 depicts both linear and non-linear data structures.

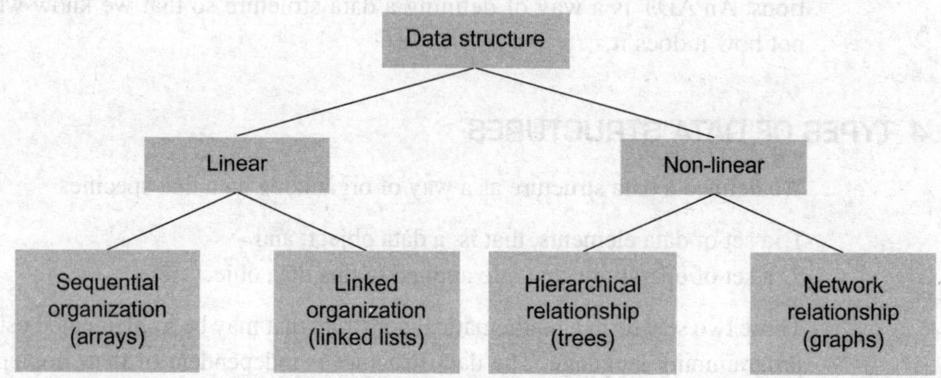

Fig. 1.2 Classification of data structures

1.4.3 Static and Dynamic Data Structures

A data structure is referred to as a *static data structure* if it is created before program execution begins (also called during compilation time). The variables of static data structure have user-specified names. An array is a static data structure.

In many applications, it is desirable to be able to start a program with the smallest amount of memory necessary and then allocate extra memory as the need arises. This facility is provided by many programming languages and in C++, through the operator `new`. These functions allow programmers to allocate memory during execution. Hence, the programmer can realize the data structure which dynamically grows and shrinks.

A data structure that is created at run-time is called *dynamic data structure*. The variables of this type are not always referenced by a user-defined name. These are accessed indirectly using their addresses through pointers.

A linked list is a dynamic data structure when realized using dynamic memory management and pointers, whereas an array is a static data structure. Non-linear data structures are generally implemented in the same way as linked lists. Hence, trees and graphs can be implemented as dynamic data structures.

1.4.4 Persistent and Ephemeral Data Structures

Data structures comprise a set of operations and a set of data to operate on. The operations that process the data may modify the data. This may create two versions of a data structure namely the recently modified (also called as updated) data structure and the previous version, which can be saved before performing any operation on it. Some languages such as ML have built-in data types such as the list. This data type has the associated operations—append and reverse. These operations preserve two copies of the data structure, list, as the recent version and the previous version.

A data structure that supports operations on the most recent version as well as the previous version is termed as a *persistent data structure*. A persistent data structure is partially persistent if any version can be accessed but only the most recent one can be updated; it is fully persistent if any version can be both accessed and updated.

An ephemeral data structure is one that supports operations only on the most recent version. The distinction between ephemeral and persistent data structure is essentially the distinction between functional (also called effect free) and conventional imperative (also called effect full) programming paradigms. The functional data structures are persistent and the imperative data structures are ephemeral.

Data structures in conventional imperative languages are ephemeral as insertion into a linked list mutates the list and the old version is lost. Data structures in functional languages are persistent as inserting an element into a list yields a new list and the old version still remains available. In addition, a stack can be implemented so that pushing yields a new stack, leaving the old stack still available. The language ML supports both persistent and ephemeral data structures.

1.4.5 Sequential Access and Direct Access Data Structures

This classification is with respect to the access operations associated with data structures. *Sequential access* means that to access the nth element, we must access the preceding $(n - 1)$ data elements. A linked list is a sequential access data structure.

Direct access means that any element can be accessed without accessing its predecessor or successor; we can directly access the nth element. An array is an example of a direct access data structure.

1.5 INTRODUCTION TO ALGORITHMS

We define computers as a data processor or as a black box. A computer acting as a black box accepts input (data and program) and generates output. A program is a set of instructions that tells the computer what to do with data. The instructions are in computer language, that is, a program is a set of instructions written in a computer language.

An algorithm, named after the ninth-century Persian mathematician Abu Jafar Mohummed bin Musa al-Khwarizmi, is simply a set of rules for carrying out some task, either by hand or, more usually, on a machine. The real world performance of any software depends on

1. the algorithm chosen and
2. the suitability and efficiency of various layers of implementation

Good algorithm design is, therefore, crucial for the performance of all software systems. Moreover, the study of algorithms provides insight into the fundamental nature of the problem. A study of the algorithms also provides insight into possible solution techniques independent of the programming language, programming paradigm, computer hardware, or any other implementation aspects.

A programmer should first solve the problem in a step-by-step manner and then try to find the appropriate instruction or series of instructions that solves the problem. This step-by-step solution is called an *algorithm*. An algorithm is independent of the computer system and the programming language.

Each algorithm includes steps for

1. input,
2. processing, and
3. output.

1.5.1 Characteristics of Algorithms

An algorithm, as defined in Section 1.5, is simply a set of rules for carrying out some task, either by hand or, more usually, on a machine. This set of rules is the idea behind a computer program. This idea is independent of implementation. An algorithm stays the same whether the program is in Pascal, running on a Cray in New York, in BASIC, running on a Macintosh in Kathmandu, or in Fortran-90, running on Param 10000 in India!

An algorithm has to solve a general, specified problem. An algorithmic problem is specified by describing the set of input instances it must work on and the desired properties that the output must have.

Let us redefine the term algorithm.

An *algorithm* is a well-defined computational procedure that transforms inputs into outputs achieving the desired input–output relationship. A computational problem is a specification of the desired input–output relationship. An instance of a problem is all the inputs needed to compute a solution to the problem. A correct algorithm halts with the correct output for every input instance. We can then say that the algorithm solves the problem.

In rather more detail, an algorithm is a finite and definite procedure for solving a problem. The finiteness is important. The definiteness is also important. We cannot accept algorithmic methods that involve making inspired guesses, such as finding a clever substitution for an integral.

Hence, an algorithm is a *finite ordered* set of *unambiguous* and *effective* steps which, when followed, accomplish a particular task by accepting *zero or more input quantities* and generate *at least one output*.

The following are the characteristics of algorithms:

Input An algorithm is supplied with zero or more external quantities as input.

Output An algorithm must produce a result, that is, an output.

Unambiguous steps Each step in an algorithm must be clear and unambiguous. This helps the person or computer following the steps to take a definite action.

Finiteness An algorithm must halt. Hence, it must have finite number of steps.

Effectiveness Every instruction must be sufficiently basic, to be executed easily.

In brief, an algorithm is an ordered finite set of unambiguous and effective steps that produces a result and terminates.

1.5.2 Algorithmics

Algorithmics is a field of computer science, defined as a *study of algorithms*. The overall goal of algorithmics is to understand the complexity of algorithms. This study includes design and analysis of algorithms.

When we set out to solve a problem, there may be a choice of algorithms available. In such a case, it is important to decide on which one to use. Depending on our priorities and on the limits of the equipment available, we may want to choose an algorithm that takes the least time, uses the least storage, is the easiest to program, and so on. The answer can depend on many factors, such as the number involved, the way the problem is presented, or the speed and storage capacity of the available computing equipment.

It may be the case that none of the available algorithms is entirely suitable so that we have to design a new algorithm of our own. Algorithmics is the science that lets us evaluate the effect of the various external factors on the available algorithms so that we can choose the one that best suits our particular circumstances; it is also the science that tells us how to design a new algorithm.

Algorithmics include the following:

How to devise algorithms Devising an algorithm is an art that can never be fully automated. By studying various techniques, that is, design strategies, it becomes easier to devise new and useful algorithms.

How to validate algorithms Once an algorithm is devised, it is necessary to show that it computes the correct answer for all possible legal inputs. The methods used for validation include contradiction and mathematical induction.

How to analyse algorithms Analysis of algorithms refers to the task of determining how much computing time and storage an algorithm requires.

1.5.3 Algorithm Design Tools: Pseudocode and Flowchart

The two popular tools used in the representation of algorithms are the following:

1. Pseudocode
2. Flowchart

Let us study each in detail.

1.6 PSEUDOCODE

An algorithm can be written in any of the natural languages such as English, German, French, etc. One of the commonly used tools to define algorithms is the *pseudocode*. A pseudocode is an English-like presentation of the code required for an algorithm. It is partly English and partly computer language structure code. The structure code is nothing but syntax constructs of a programming language (in a slightly modified format). For example, some language structure constructs such as arrays or pointers are not used in the English language, hence they are borrowed from programming languages.

1.6.1 Pseudocode Notations

Pseudocode is a precise description of a solution as compared to a flowchart. To get a complete description of the solution with respect to problem definition, pre–post conditions and return value details are to be included in the algorithm header. In addition, information about the variables used and the purpose are to be viewed clearly. To help anyone get all this information at a glance, the pseudocode uses various notations such as header, purpose, pre–post conditions, return, variables, statement numbers, and sub-algorithms. Let us discuss the details of each.

1.6.2 Algorithm Header

A *header* includes the name of the algorithm, the parameters, and the list of pre and post conditions. This information is important to know about the algorithm just by reading the header, not the complete algorithm. Therefore, the header information must be complete enough to communicate to the programmer everything he or she must know to use the algorithm. The header makes the pseudocode readable.

In Algorithm 1.1, there are two parameters, an array `A` and the total number of elements in the array, that is, its size `N`. The parameters could be called either by reference (`ref`) or by value (`val`). The type is included in pointed brackets after the identifier. The algorithm is to sort the array `A` of size `N`.

ALGORITHM 1.1

```
Algorithm sort(ref A<integer>, val N<integer>)
Pre     array A to be sorted
Post    sorted array A
Return None
1.if(N < 1) goto step (4)
2.M = N - 1
3.For I = 1 to M do
  For J = I + 1 to N do
  begin
    if(A(I) > A(J))
    then
    begin
```

```
            T = A(I)
            A(I) = A(J)
            A(J) = T
        end
        end if
    end
   4.stop
```

1.6.3 Purpose

The *purpose* is a brief description about what the algorithm does. It should be as brief as possible, describing the general algorithm processing, but should not describe all of the processing. For example, in Algorithm 1.1, the purpose just tells that this algorithm sorts the array of integers and does not need to state that the array is sorted and where the result is stored. Algorithm 1.2 searches for an element in an array.

ALGORITHM 1.2

```
Algorithm search (val list<array>,val X<integer>)
Pre list containing data array to be searched and
   argument containing data to be located
Post None
Return Location

1.Let list be the array and X be the element to be searched
2.For I = 1 to N do
  begin
       if(List(I) = X)
       then
          Return I
       end if
  end
3.Return -1
4.stop
```

1.6.4 Condition and Return Statements

The `pre` condition states the pre-requirements for the parameters, if any. For example, in an algorithm for set operations, the pre condition may state that the input should be a group of elements without duplicates. Sometimes, there are no pre conditions, in which case, we still list the pre condition with the statement `Nothing`, as shown here.

```
Pre     Nothing
```

If there are several input parameters, then the pre condition should be shown for each. For example, a simple array search Algorithm 1.2 has the following header:

```
algorithm search (val list<array>, val argument<integer>)
```

```
Search array for specific item and return index location.
Pre     list containing data array to be searched, argument containing
        data to be located in the list
Post    None
Return  Location if found else return -1 indicating that the element
        is not found
```

In this search, two parameters are passed by `value`. The `pre` condition specifies that the two input parameters, `list` and `argument`, must be initialized. If a binary search were being used, the `pre` condition would also state that the array data must be ordered.

The `post` condition identifies any action taken and the status of any output parameters. In Algorithm 1.1, the `post` condition is the array containing sorted data. If a value is returned, it will be identified by a `return` condition.

1.6.5 Statement Numbers

The statements in an algorithm are numbered sequentially. For conditional or un-conditional jumps and also for iteration statements, numbering helps identify the statements uniquely. Any label system such as the decimal or roman numbers or even alphabets can be used to label the statements. If decimal notation is used, then the statements within the iterative constructs can be numbered as 4.1, 4.2, and so on. This notation helps indent the algorithm properly.

```
4 while(i < 10) do
  begin
        4.1 x = x * y
        4.2 i = i + 1
  end
```

1.6.6 Variables

Variables are needed in algorithms. We need not define every variable used in the algorithm. The use of meaningful variable names is appreciated as the context of the data is indicated by its name. Hungarian notation is suggested for variable naming. It is suggested to use descriptive and meaningful variable names to guarantee that the meaning is understood properly.

The variable name used in an algorithm can be continued to be used when the respective algorithm is coded in a particular language. These meaningful variables make the code easier to understand, debug, and modify. It is suggested to follow a few thumb rules as:

1. It is better to use descriptive variable names instead of single character names. Often, we use variables such as `x`, `y`, `z`, `a`, or `b` and `i` or `j` for index variables of loops, matrices, and array indices. For example, instead of using `i` and `j` as index variables for a two-dimensional array, it is suggested to use `row` and `column` as index variables. In searching algorithms, the suggested variable for the element to be searched is `target` instead of `x`.

For a table of weather information, `City` and `Temperature` will be a better row index and column index variables, respectively.

2. It is suggested to avoid usage of short forms and generic names. For example, use `ListofColors` instead of `lcol` or `NumberOfStudents` instead of `nostud`. The reason being short forms do not necessarily mean what they intend. Commonly used generic names are `index`, `count`, `number`, `sum`, `total`, `row`, `column`, etc. These variables are used in various modules of a program and may have many instances. Adding a good qualifier to the generic name results in better understanding to read, debug, or modify the code.
3. It is expected to use variable names so that the data type of the variable can be indicated. For example, `fAverageMarks`, `iNumberofColors`, `bAvailability` for float, integer, and Boolean data respectively.

1.6.7 Statement Constructs

There are three statement constructs used for developing an algorithm. The objective is that an algorithm should be made up of a combination of lesser constructs, say three, as in the following:

1. sequence
2. decision
3. repetition

The use of only these constructs makes an algorithm easy to understand, debug, and modify.

Sequence

An algorithm is a sequence of instructions, which can be a simple instruction (input, output, or assignment) or either of the other two constructs. Figure 1.3 shows an example of such a sequence construct. Algorithm 1.3 computes the area of a circle.

Sequence construct	
do action 1 do action 2 . . . do action n	**Algorithm 1.3** Pre None Post None Return None 1. Read Radius 2. AreaOfCircle = 2 * 3.142 * Radius * Radius 3. Print AreaOfCircle 4. Stop

Fig. 1.3 Sequence construct

Decision

Some problems cannot be solved with the help of just a sequence of simple instructions. Sometimes, we need to test the conditions. If the result of the testing is true, we follow a sequence of instructions; if it is false, we follow a different sequence of instructions. This is called *decision* or *selection construct* (Fig. 1.4).

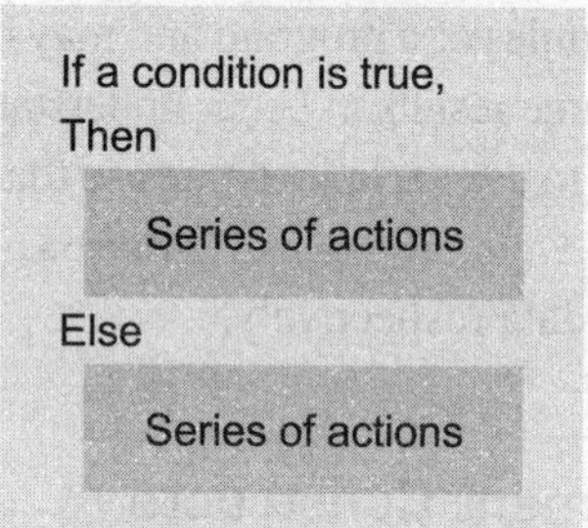

If a condition is true,
Then
Series of actions
Else
Series of actions

Fig. 1.4 Decision construct

EXAMPLE 1.1 Compare two numbers to print the maximum among them.

Solution The algorithm for comparing two numbers is listed in Algorithm 1.4.

ALGORITHM 1.4

```
    Pre None
    Post None
    Return None
1. Read two numbers Num1 and Num2
2. If Num1 > Num2
        Then Print Num1
        Else Print Num2
3. Stop
```

Repetition

In some problems, we need to repeat a set of instructions. We can use repetition construct for this purpose. Figure 1.5 shows a repetition construct and an example of computing the sum of first N numbers, $\sum N$ (Algorithm 1.5).

1.6.8 Subalgorithms

We studied three constructs—`sequence`, `decision`, and `iteration`—for developing an algorithm for solvable problems. A solvable problem is a problem that has a solution that can be described in the form of an algorithm.

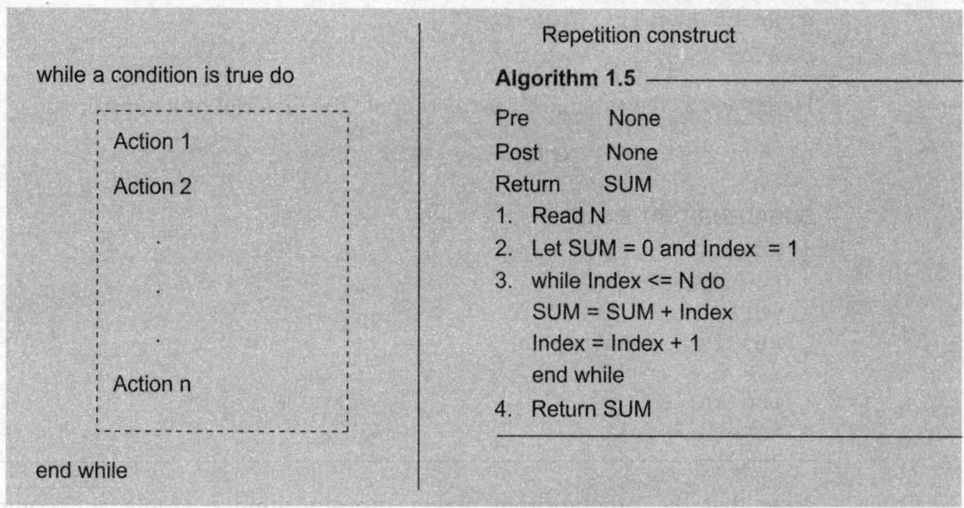

Fig. 1.5 Repetition construct

In structured programming, the problem solution is described in the form of smaller modules. This modular design breaks an algorithm into smaller units called *subalgorithms*. These units are referred by various names in programming languages such as *functions*, *subroutines*, *procedures*, *methods*, and *modules*.

The goal of modular design in algorithms is to make the complex and lengthy algorithms easy to read, write, verify, and debug. Each subalgorithm can, in turn, be divided into subalgorithms, and the process of such subdivision may continue till each step becomes effective.

EXAMPLE 1.2 Write an algorithm to compute the following:

$$P = n!/(n - r)!$$

Solution Algorithms 1.6 computes the number of possible ways of arranging any r of n elements.

ALGORITHM 1.6

```
Pre None
Post None
Return Result
1. Read n and r
2. Let
    (a) A = FACT(n) and
    (b) B = FACT(n - r)
3. Result = A / B
```

```
4. Print Result
5. Stop
```

Here FACT is the subalgorithm to compute the factorial of a number as

$$n! = n \times (n - 1) \times (n - 2) \times \ldots \times 1$$

SUBALGORITHM FACT

```
1. Read n
2. Let Result = 1
3. while(n not equal to 1) do
   Result = Result × n
   n = n - 1
   end while
4. Return Result
```

Note that the subalgorithm makes the algorithm readable and compact. A readable algorithm is the one that, at one glance, gives the reader knowledge about the overall computation process. A compact algorithm is without redundant code. You must have noted in this algorithm that the factorial computation is required twice. A subalgorithm FACT has avoided the redundancy of code to make the algorithm a compact one.

1.7 RELATIONSHIP AMONG DATA, DATA STRUCTURES, AND ALGORITHMS

There is an intimate relationship between the structuring of data and analysis of algorithms. In fact, a data structure and an algorithm should be thought of as one single unit; neither one making sense without the other. Let us consider the example of searching for a person's phone number in a directory. The procedure we follow to search a person and get his/her phone number critically depends on how the phone number and names are arranged in the directory. Let us consider two ways of organizing the data (phone numbers and names) in the directory.

1. The data is organized randomly. Then to search a person by name, one has to linearly start from the first name till the last name in the directory. There is no other option.
2. If the data is organized by sorting the names (alphabetically sorted in ascending order), then the search is much easier. Instead of linearly searching through all records, one may search in a particular area for particular alphabets, similar to using a dictionary.

As the data is in sorted order, both the binary search and a typical directory search methods work. Hence our ideas for algorithms become possible when we realize that we can organize the data as we wish. We can say that there is a strong relationship between the structuring of data (along with inter-relationship among data structures) and the operations to process the data (algorithms). In fact, the way we process our data depends on the way we organize it.

1.8 IMPLEMENTATION OF DATA STRUCTURES

A data structure is an aggregation of atomic and composite data types into a set with the relationship among them defined. As defined in Section 1.3.4, a data structure `D` is a triplet, that is, `D` = (`D`, `F`, `A`), where `D` is a set of data object, `F` is a set of functions, and `A` is a set of rules to implement the functions.

Let us consider an example of integer data type (`int`) in C++.

`D` = (0, ±1, ±2, ±3, …)
`F` = (+, –, *, /, %)
`A` = (a set of binary arithmetic rules to perform addition, subtraction, division, multiplication, and module operations)

The set of axioms `A` defines semantics of operations on `D` for `F`. An implementation of a data structure `D` is a mapping from `D` to a set of other data structures `E`. This mapping specifies how every data object of `D` is to be represented by objects of `E`. Moreover, it requires that every function of `D` must be written using the functions of the implementing data structures `E`. Thus, we may say that the integers are represented by bit strings, the Boolean is represented by 0 and 1, and an array is represented by a set of sequential locations in memory. We have also defined the term abstract data type, which is a data structure in which rules (`A`—the set of axioms) do not imply a form of representation.

Hence, another way of viewing implementation of a data structure is that it is a process of refining an ADT until all the operations are expressed effectively so that they are defined in terms of directly executable functions.

Hence, implementation of data structures can be viewed in terms of two phases: specification and implementation. Such a division of tasks is useful as it helps to control the complexity of the entire process.

Phase I: Specification At the first stage, a data structure should be designed so that we know what it does and not necessarily how it will do it.

Phase II: Implementation At this stage, we define all functions with respect to the description of how to manipulate data. This can be done with algorithms so that the details of the operation can be understood easily, and the reader can implement them easily and effectively with the help of any programming language. Either of the design tools, that is, an algorithm or a flowchart, can be used at this phase. We have already learnt about algorithms as design tools; let us now learn about flowcharts.

1.9 FLOWCHARTS

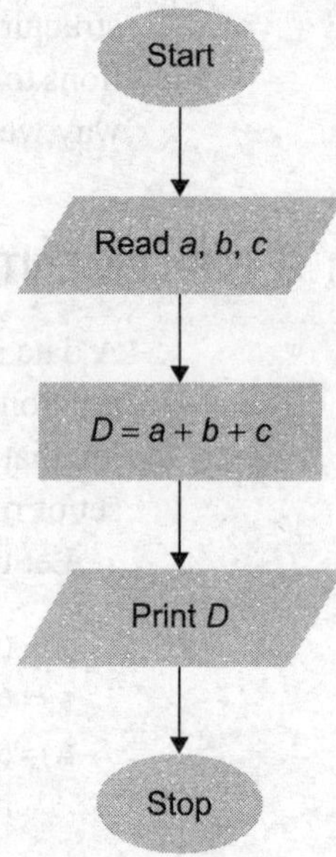

Fig. 1.6 Flowchart for adding three numbers

A very effective tool to show the logic flow of a program is the flowchart. A flowchart is a pictorial representation of an algorithm. It hides all the details of an algorithm by giving a picture; it shows how the algorithm flows from beginning to end. In a programming environment, it can be used to design a complete program or just a part of the program.

The primary purpose of a flowchart is to show the design of the algorithm. At the same time, it relieves the programmers from the syntax and details of a programming language while allowing them to concentrate on the details of the problem to be solved. This is in contrast to another programming design tool, the pseudocode, which provides a textual design solution. Both tools have their advantages, but a flowchart has the pictorial power that other tools lack. Figure 1.6 is a flowchart that describes the process of reading, adding, printing three numbers, and printing the result.

1.10 ANALYSIS OF ALGORITHMS

Algorithms heavily depend on the organization of data. There can be several ways to organize data and/or write algorithms for a given problem. The difficulty lies in deciding which algorithm is the best. We can compare one algorithm with the other and choose the best. For comparison, we need to analyse the algorithms. Analysis involves measuring the performance of an algorithm. Performance is measured in terms of the following parameters:

1. *Programmer's time complexity*—Very rarely taken into account as it is to be paid for once
2. *Time complexity*—The amount of time taken by an algorithm to perform the intended task
3. *Space complexity*—The amount of memory needed to perform the task.

It is very convenient to classify algorithms on the basis of the relative amount of time and space they require and specify the growth of time and space requirements as a function of the input size.

1.10.1 Complexity of Algorithms

Algorithms are measured in terms of time and space complexity. The *time complexity* of an algorithm is a measure of how much time is required to execute an algorithm for a given number of inputs and is measured by its rate of growth relative to standard functions.

Space complexity is similar to time complexity. The *space complexity* of an algorithm is a measure of how much storage is required by the algorithm. It is possible to design an algorithm that uses more space and less time or less space and more time.

Typically, computer scientists are interested in minimizing the time complexity of algorithms. The economics of storage versus the speed of computers is the principal factor that determines the focus on time complexity. The cost of memory has decreased at an exponential rate over the past 25 years, whereas the cost of central processing unit time has not decreased at that rate. The bottleneck is the execution time. Hence, computer scientists focus on the execution time of algorithms.

An algorithm can be characterized by a timing function $T(n)$. $T(n)$ is a measure of how much time is required to execute an algorithm with the given n data values. For example, the timing function for a sort operation specifies the time required to sort n data values. The timing function for an algorithm that solves a system of linear equations specifies the time required to solve n linear equations.

An algorithm $O(n^2)$, pronounced 'oh of n squared', indicates that its timing function will grow no faster than the square of the number of data values it processes. Let us learn more about these two measures of algorithms.

1.10.2 Space Complexity

Space complexity is the amount of computer memory required during program execution as a function of the input size. Space complexity measurement, which is the space requirement of an algorithm, can be performed at two different times:

1. Compile time
2. Run time

Compile Time Space Complexity

Compile time space complexity is defined as the storage requirement of a program at compile time.

This storage requirement can be computed during compile time. The storage needed by the program at compile time can be determined by summing up the storage size of each variable using declaration statements. For example, the space complexity of a non-recursive function of calculating the factorial of number n depends on the number n itself.

$$\text{Space complexity} = \text{Space needed at compile time}$$

This includes memory requirement before execution starts.

Run-time Space Complexity

If the program is recursive or uses dynamic variables or dynamic data structures, then there is a need to determine space complexity at run-time. In general, this dynamic storage size is dependent on some parameters used in a program. It is difficult to estimate memory requirement accurately, as it is also determined by the efficiency of compiler. Memory requirement is the summation of the program space, data space, and stack space.

Program space This is the memory occupied by the program itself.

Data space This is the memory occupied by data members such as constants and variables.

Stack space This is the stack memory needed to save the function's run-time environment while another function is called. This cannot be accurately estimated since it depends on the run-time call stack, which can depend on the program's data set. This memory space is crucially important for recursive functions.

1.10.3 Time Complexity

Time complexity $T(P)$ is the time taken by a program P, that is, the sum of its compile and execution times. This is system-dependent. Another way to compute it is to count the number of algorithm steps. An algorithm step is a syntactically or semantically meaningful segment of a program. We can determine the number of steps needed by a program to solve a particular problem instance in one of the following two ways:

1. Introduce a new variable, `count`, into the program. This is a global variable with initial value 0. Statements to increment count amount are introduced in the program at appropriate locations. This is done so that each time the statement in the original program is executed, the count is incremented by the step count of that statement. We measure the run-time of an algorithm by counting the number of steps.
2. Manually compute the number of times each statement will be executed. The number of times the statement is executed is its *frequency count*. Get the sum of frequency counts of all statements. This sum is the number of steps needed to solve a given problem.

Best, Worst, and Average Cases

The *best case* complexity of an algorithm is the function defined by the minimum number of steps taken on any instance of size n.

The *worst case* complexity of an algorithm is the function defined by the maximum number of steps taken on any instance of size n.

The *average case* complexity of an algorithm is the function defined by an average number of steps taken on any instance of size n.

Each of these complexities defines a numerical function—time versus size.

1.10.4 Computing Time Complexity of an Algorithm

The total time taken by the algorithm or program is calculated using the sum of the time taken by each of the executable statements in an algorithm or a program. The time required by each statement depends on the following:

1. the time required for executing it once
2. the number of times the statement is executed

The product of these two parameters gives the time required for that particular statement. Compute the execution time of all executable statements. The summation of all the execution times is the total time required for that algorithm or program.

In general, when we sum up the frequency count of all the statements, we get a polynomial. In an analysis, we are interested in the order of magnitude of an algorithm, that is, we are interested in only those statements that have the greatest frequency count.

1.10.5 Big-O Notation

Given the speed of computers today, we are not concerned as much with the exact measurement of an algorithm's efficiency as we are with its general order of magnitude. If the analysis of two algorithms shows that one executes 15 iterations while the other executes 25 iterations, then they are both so fast that we cannot see the difference. On the other hand, if one iterates 15 times and the other iterates 1500 times, we should be concerned.

We have shown that the number of statements executed in the function for n elements of data is a function of the number of elements, expressed as $f(n)$. Although the equation derived for a function may be complex, a dominant factor in the equation usually determines the order of magnitude of the result. Therefore, we do not need to determine the complex measure of efficiency but only the factor that determines the magnitude. This factor is the big-O, as in 'on the order of', and expressed as $O(n)$, that is, on the order of n.

The simplification of efficiency is known as the *big-O analysis*. For example, if an algorithm is quadratic, we would say its efficiency is $O(n^2)$ or on the order of n squared.

The big-O notation can be derived from $f(n)$ using the following steps:

1. In each term, set the coefficient of the term to 1.
2. Keep the largest term in the function and discard the others. The terms are ranked from the lowest to the highest as follows:

$$\log_2 n \ldots n \ldots n \log_2 n \ldots n^2 \ldots n^3 \ldots n^k \ldots 2^n \ldots n!$$

For example,

1. To calculate the big-O notation for

$$f(n) = n \times \frac{(n+1)}{2} = \frac{1}{2}n^2 + \frac{1}{2}n$$

we first remove all coefficients. This gives us

$$n^2 + n$$

which, after removing the smaller factors, gives us n^2

which, in big-O notation, is stated as

$$O(f(n)) = O(n^2)$$

2. To consider another example, let us look at the polynomial expression

$$f(n) = a_j n^k + a_{j-1} n^{k-1} + \cdots + a_2 n^2 + a_1 n + a_0$$

We first eliminate all the coefficients as follows:

$$f(n) = n^k + n^{k-1} + \cdots + n^2 + n + 1$$

The largest term in the expression is the first one, so we can say that the order of this polynomial expression is

$$O(f(n)) = O(n^k)$$

Any measure of efficiency presumes that a sufficiently large sample is being considered. If you are dealing with only 10 elements and the time required is a fraction of a second, there will be no meaningful difference between the two algorithms. On the other hand, as the number of elements being processed grows, the difference between algorithms can be staggering, for example, for n it is 10,000. Returning for a moment to the question of why we should be concerned about efficiency, consider the situation in which you can solve a problem in three ways: one is the linear method, another is the linear logarithmic method, and the third is the quadratic method. We should be able to analyse and select one among the many possible algorithms.

1.11 FROM PROBLEM TO PROGRAM

It is noticed that programmers spend most of their time in understanding what problems to solve. Initially, most problems have no simple, precise specifications. Rather, there are certain problems, such as creating a 'gourmet' recipe or preserving world peace, that may be impossible to formulate in terms of a computer solution. Even if we feel that our problem can be solved on a computer, there is usually considerable scope in several problem parameters. Often, it is only through experimentation that reasonable values for these parameters can be found.

If certain aspects of a problem can be expressed in terms of a formal model, it is usually beneficial to do so, for once a problem is formalized, we can look for solutions in terms of a precise model and determine whether a program already exists to solve that problem. Even if there is no existing program, we can at least discover what is known about this model and use the properties of the model to help construct a good solution. We shall now consider a systematic approach (or phases) to program development. Software engineering is the field that emphasises on such a systematic approach for software development. Let us now discuss software engineering, which is important for both small simple programs developed by beginners and complex software developed by a group of programmers.

1.12 SOFTWARE ENGINEERING

Software engineering is the establishment and use of good engineering methods and principles to obtain reliable software that works on real machines.

A fundamental concept in software engineering is the software development life cycle (SDLC). Software, like many other products, goes through a cycle of repeating phases. The development process in the software life cycle broadly involves four phases: analysis, design, implementation, and testing. Figure 1.7 shows these phases as part of the development process.

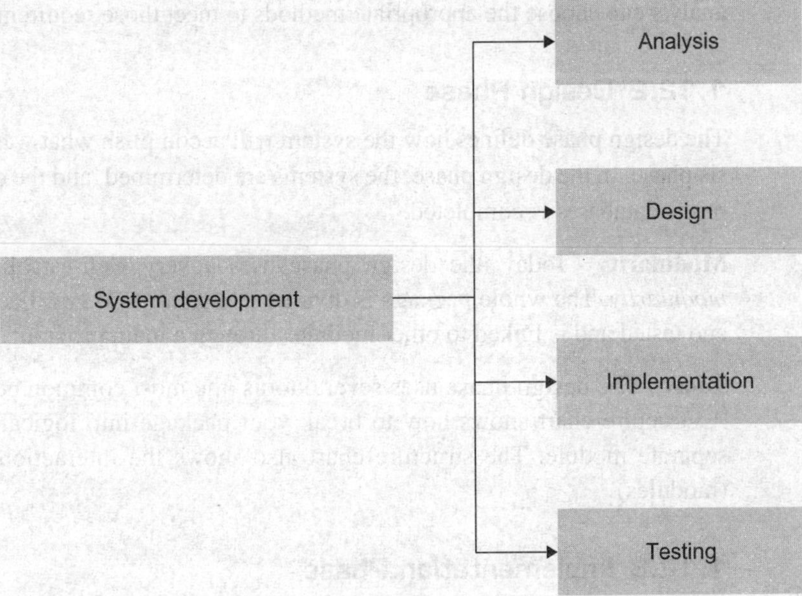

Fig. 1.7 System development phases

1.12.1 Analysis Phase

The development process starts with the *analysis phase*; the systems analyst defines requirements that specify what the proposed system is to accomplish. The requirements are usually stated in terms that the user understands. There are four steps in the analysis phase: define the user, define the needs, define the requirements, and define the methods.

Define the user A software package may be designed for a generic user or a specific user. For example, an accounting package may be created for use by any firm. On the other hand, a customized banking package may be created for a specific bank. The user of the package must be clearly defined.

Define the needs After the user has been identified, the analysts clearly define the needs. The user, or the representative of the user, clearly defines his/her expectations of the package.

Define the requirements On the basis of the needs of the user, the analyst can exactly define the requirements for the system. For example, if a package is to print cheques at the end of the month for each employee, what level of security and accuracy should be implemented needs to be clearly defined and studied. So one must study all levels of requirements of the system to be developed.

Define the methods Finally, after the requirements are defined in clear terms, the analyst can choose the appropriate methods to meet those requirements.

1.12.2 Design Phase

The design phase defines how the system will accomplish what was defined in the analysis phase. In the design phase, the systems are determined, and the design of the files and/or the databases is completed.

Modularity Today, the design phase uses a very well-established principle called *modularity*. The whole package is divided into small *modules*. Each module is designed and tested and is linked to other modules through a main program.

Tools The design phase uses several tools, the most common being a structure chart. A structure chart shows how to break your package into logical steps; each step is a separate module. The structure chart also shows the interaction among all the parts (modules).

1.12.3 Implementation Phase

In the *implementation phase*, we create the actual programs.

Tools This phase uses several tools to show the logical flow of the program before the actual writing of the code. One tool, still popular, is the flowchart. A *flowchart* uses standard graphical symbols to represent the logical flow of data through a module. The second tool used by programmers is the pseudocode. The language of the pseudocode is partly English and partly logical, which describes what the program is to do in precise algorithmic detail. This requires the steps to be defined in sufficient detail so that conversion to a computer program can be accomplished easily.

Coding After the production of a flowchart, a pseudocode, or both, the programmer actually writes the code in a language specific for the project. The choice of the language is based on the efficiency of the language for that particular application.

1.12.4 Testing Phase

Once the programs have been written, they must be tested. The testing phase can be a very tedious and time-consuming part of program development. The programmers are completely responsible for testing the system as a whole, that is, testing to make sure all the programs work properly together. There are two types of testing—black box and white box. The system test that engineers and users do is black box testing. White box testing is the responsibility of the programmer.

1.12.5 Verification Phase

Program verification is a process to prove that the program does what it is intended to do. For simpler and smaller programs, verification often consists of trying a few sample cases to see whether the results of running the code match our expectations. However, such methodology leaves certain errors undetected in the program, and hence it is avoided. Again, it is not recommended to verify the program, after the running code is available, as the defects detected are difficult to repair. It is said that 'even verification must be verified'. This means, along with the system, the tests prepared are also to be verified. In addition, the quality of every software must be verified.

RECAPITULATION

- A computer is a programmable data processing machine that accepts input, instructions to process the input (program), and generates the required output. The data and the program are stored in the computer's memory. A program is written in the computer's language.
- The art of programming consists of designing or choosing algorithms and expressing them in a programming language. An algorithm is a stepwise description of actions that lead the problem from its start state to its goal state.
- One of the common tools used to define algorithms is the pseudocode. The pseudocode is an English-like representation of the code required for an algorithm. It is part English and part structured code.
- A very effective tool to show the logic flow of a program is the flowchart. A flowchart is a pictorial representation of an algorithm. It hides all the details of an algorithm by giving the whole picture, that is, it shows how the algorithm flows from the beginning to the end.
- A data structure represents a set of data items with a specific relationship between them. The success of a software project often depends on the choices made in the representation of data and algorithms designed to

process the data. The proper choice of a data structure can be a key point in the design of many algorithms.

- Software engineering is the establishment and use of good engineering methodologies and the principle to writing reliable software. One of the most important principles in accomplishing this is the use of abstraction. Abstraction allows us to organize the complexity of a task by focusing on logical properties of data and actions rather than on the implementation details. Logical properties refer to the 'what' and implementation details refer to the 'how'. The abstraction is at the procedural and data levels.
- A data structure is a way of organizing data that specifies a set of data elements, that is, a data object, and a set of operations that are applied to this data object. These two sets form a mathematical construct that may be implemented using a particular programming language. The data structure is independent of its implementation. The various types of data structures are as follows:
    - primitive and non-primitive
    - linear and non-linear
    - static and dynamic
    - persistent and ephemeral
    - sequential and direct access
- There is an intimate relationship between the structuring of data and analysis of algorithms. In fact, a data structure and an algorithm should be thought of as a single unit, neither one making sense without the other.
- Algorithms depend heavily on the organization of data. There can be several organizations of data and/or algorithms for a given problem. The difficulty lies in deciding which algorithm is the best. We can compare the algorithms and choose the best. For comparison, we need to analyze the algorithms. The analysis involves measuring the performance of an algorithm in terms of time and space complexity.

KEY TERMS

Abstract data type Data and the operations on the data are encapsulated and hidden from the user. An abstract data type is a data declaration packaged together with the operations that are meaningful for the data type. It includes the declaration of data, implementation of operations, and encapsulation of data and operations.

Algorithm A step-by-step solution is called an algorithm. An algorithm is independent of the computer system and the programming language.

Assembler A software that translates assembly language code to machine language is called an assembler.

Compiler A software that translates higher level language code to machine language is called a compiler.

Data Data is nothing but a piece of information. Data input, data manipulation (or data processing), and data output are the themes of a computer.

Data object A data object represents a container for data values—a place where data values may be stored and later retrieved from. A data object is a run-time instance of the data structure.

Data structure Data structure refers to data and the representation of data objects within a program, that is, the implementation of structured relationships. A data structure is a set of domains D, a designated domain d ∈ D, a set of functions F, and a set of axioms A. The triple structure (D, F, A) denotes the data structure which is usually denoted as d.

Data type Data type is a term that specifies the type of data that a variable may hold in the programming language.

Flowchart A pictorial representation of an algorithm is called a flowchart.

Non-linear data structure In non-linear data structures, every data element may have more than one predecessor as well as successor. Elements do not form any particular linear sequence.

Linear data structure A data structure is said to be linear if its elements form a sequence or a linear list. In a linear data structure, every data element has a unique successor and a unique predecessor.

Program A set of instructions is called a program.

Pseudocode A pseudocode is partly English and partly programming language used for writing an algorithm.

Software engineering Software engineering is the establishment and use of good engineering methods and principles to obtain reliable software that works on real machines. Software engineering is the field that emphasizes on a systematic approach for software development.

EXERCISES

Multiple choice questions

1. The basic unit of information is the
   (a) byte
   (b) bit
   (c) block
   (d) sector
2. The order of an algorithm that finds whether a given Boolean function of n variables produces an output of 1 is
   (a) constant
   (b) linear
   (c) logarithmic
   (d) exponential
3. Software engineering primarily deals with
   (a) reliable software
   (b) cost-effective software
   (c) reliable and cost-effective software
   (d) none of the above
4. A pictorial representation of an algorithm is called
   (a) a flowchart
   (b) a structure chart
   (c) a pseudocode
   (d) an algorithm
5. An English-like representation of the code is called
   (a) a flowchart
   (b) a structure chart
   (c) a pseudocode
   (d) an algorithm
6. A subalgorithm is also known as a
   (a) function
   (b) subroutine
   (c) module
   (d) all of the above
7. A basic algorithm that arranges data according to their values is known as
   (a) inquiry
   (b) sorting
   (c) searching
   (d) recursion
8. Defining the user's needs, requirements, and methods is a part of the
   (a) analysis phase
   (b) design phase
   (c) implementation phase
   (d) testing phase
9. In the system development process, the flowchart is a tool used in the
   (a) analysis phase
   (b) design phase
   (c) implementation phase

(d) testing phase

10. In the system development process, a pseudocode is a tool used in the
    (a) analysis phase
    (b) design phase
    (c) implementation phase
    (d) testing phase

Review questions

1. What is programming? What are programming languages and how are they classified?
2. What is object-oriented programming?
3. Define the terms data, data type, data structure, and abstract data type.
4. What are the types of data structures?
5. Explain the relationship between data structure and algorithm in the process of problem solving with an example.
6. What is the formal definition of an algorithm? Write the essential properties and the performance measures of an algorithm.
7. How is a pseudocode related to an algorithm? How is a flowchart related to an algorithm?
8. Write a pseudocode to compute the sum of the first *N* integers. Draw a flowchart for the same.
9. Draw a flowchart for an algorithm that finds the smallest number among *N* numbers.
10. Draw a flowchart for an algorithm that finds the largest number among *N* numbers.
11. What is software engineering? What is software development life cycle?

Answers to multiple choice questions

1. (b) 2. (d) 3. (c) 4. (a) 5. (d) 6. (d) 7. (b) 8. (a) 9. (b) 10. (b)

2 LINEAR DATA STRUCTURE USING ARRAYS

OBJECTIVES

After completing this chapter, the reader will be able to understand the following:

- Sequential organization of data
- Linear data structure and its implementation using sequential representation in the form of arrays
- Features of arrays
- Ordered list and its representation
- Efficient use of arrays for representing and manipulating polynomials, strings, and sparse matrices

Data can be organized in a linear or non-linear form. In *linear* (or sequential) *organization*, all the elements of the data can be arranged in a particular sequence, and each element has a unique successor (and/or predecessor) in the sequence. When each element may have one or more successors (or predecessors), it is called a *non-linear data structure*. Linear list is one type of linear data structure. Linear data structures can be realized using arrays as well as linked lists. In this chapter, we shall learn about the realization of linear data structures using arrays. Almost all programming languages support the concept of arrays. It is a very common and simple means of sequential data structuring. That is why linear data structures deserve significant attention. This chapter covers linear data structure using arrays and its implementation, characteristics, and applications.

2.1 SEQUENTIAL ORGANIZATION

We have already studied that there are multiple ways to organize data (Chapter 1). Data organization heavily affects programming logic. We therefore select data structures and algorithms in such a way that the overall program proves to be efficient in terms of space and time complexities.

As the name suggests, sequential organization allows storing data a fixed distance apart. If the ith element is stored at location X, then the next sequential $(i + 1)^{th}$ element is stored at location $X + C$, where C is a constant. Linear arrays, linear stacks, and linear queues are some examples of sequential organization. Figure 2.1 shows the four elements 11, 34, 25, and 9 stored in sequential organization starting with address L, where $C = 1$.

One major advantage of sequential organization is the direct or random access to any data element of the list in constant time. As sequential organization uses continuous memory locations to store data, the data access time remains constant for accessing any element of the list, irrespective of the total length or size of the data list. When performing in-between insertions or deletions of elements in sequential organization, we have to perform data shifting to keep the organization consistent and intact. So the in-between insertions and deletions become much expensive with respect to time and space complexities.

Address	Element
L	11
$L + 1$	34
$L + 2$	25
$L + 3$	9

Fig. 2.1 Elements at sequential locations

2.2 LINEAR DATA STRUCTURE USING SEQUENTIAL ORGANIZATION: ARRAYS

To store a group of data together in a sequential manner in computer's memory, arrays can be one of the possible data structures. Arrays enable us to organize more than one element in consecutive memory locations; hence, it is also termed as *structured* or *composite data type*. The only restriction is that all the elements we wish to store must be of the same data type. It can be thought of as a box with multiple compartments, where each compartment is capable of holding one data item. Arrays support direct access to any of those data items just by specifying the name of the array and its index as the item's position (sequence number as subscript).

Arrays are the most general and easy to use of all the data structures. An array as a data structure is defined as a set of pairs (`index, value`) such that with each index, a value is associated.

`index`—indicates the location of an element in an array
`value`—indicates the actual value of that data element

Index allows the direct addressing (or accessing) of any element of an array. Most of the time, an array is implemented by using continuous or consecutive memory locations (Fig. 2.2). However, at other times, it may not necessarily be implemented by using memory locations that are a fixed distance apart.

This is internally handled by operating systems; for users, it is a sequentially arranged data at consecutive locations.

An *array* is a finite ordered collection of homogeneous data elements that provides direct access to any of its elements. Arrays can be used in any of their varied forms. A one-dimensional array is the simplest form of an array. Each word in the definition has a specific meaning:

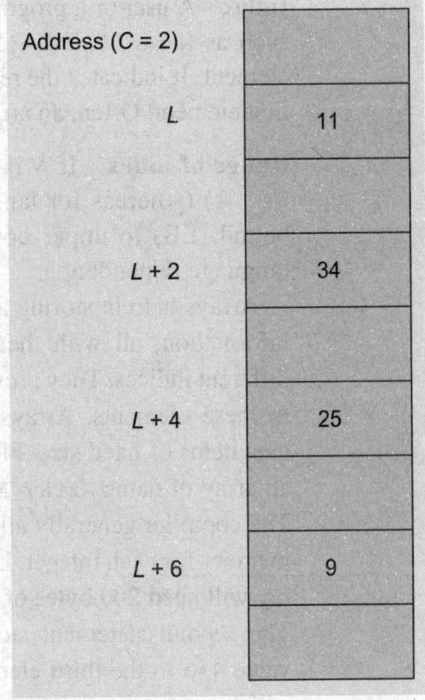

Fig. 2.2 Array elements placed a fixed distance apart

Finite The number of elements in an array is finite or limited.

Ordered collection The arrangement of all the elements in an array is very specific, that is, every element has a particular ranking in the array.

Homogeneous All the elements of an array should be of the same data type.

Let us see how to declare an array in C++.

```
int Array_A[20];
```

This statement will allocate a memory space to store 20 integer elements, and the name assigned to the array is `Array_A`.

```
char Name[20];
```

Similarly, this statement will create an array `Name` that can store 20 character data type elements in it.

The common terms associated with arrays are as follows:

Size of array The maximum number of elements that would be stored in an array is the size of that array. It is also the length of that array. Arrays are static data structures because once the size of an array is defined, it cannot be changed after compilation. For the array `Name`, the size is 20.

Base The base address of an array is the memory location where the first element of an array is stored. It is decided at the time of execution of a program. The value of this base address varies at every program execution as it is decided at the run-time. It cannot be decided or defined even by a programmer.

Data type of an array The data type of an array indicates the data type of elements stored in that array. For the array `Name`, the data type is `char`.

Index A user or a programmer can access the elements of an array by using subscripts such as `Name[0]`, `Name[1]`, `...`, `Name[i]`. This subscript is called the *index* of an element. It indicates the relative position of every element in the array with respect to its first element. Often, an array is also referred to as *subscripted variable*.

Range of index If N is the size of an array, then in C++, the range of index is $0 - (N - 1)$ (whereas for languages such as Pascal it could be some integer, say, lower bound (LB) to upper bound (UB), e.g., 2 to $n + 1$ or -3 to $n - 4$). The range is language dependent.

Arrays help in storing a large amount of information, all with the same name and different indices. They provide direct access to these elements. Arrays are suitable for data items of fixed size. Figure 2.3 declares an array of name `Array_A` of 100 integers. The compiler generally allocates 2 bytes of memory for each integer. Ultimately, the array will need 200 bytes of memory in total. The second statement stores the numeric value 456 to the third element of the array which is at `Array_A[2]`.

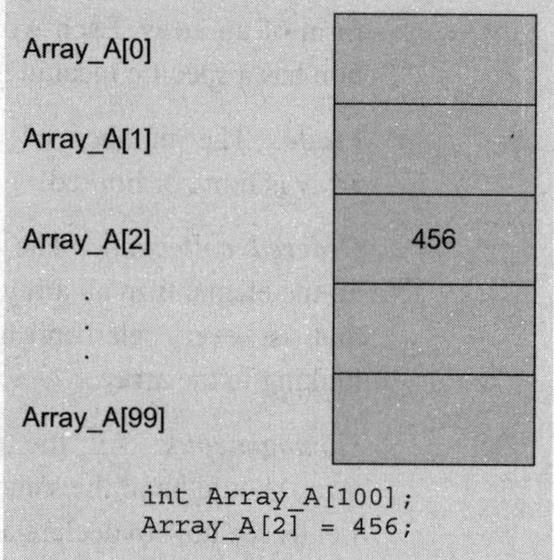

Fig. 2.3 Storing elements at any random location

The amount of storage per element depends on the data type of the array. In C++, the memory requirement for different data types is given as follows:

1. 8 bits per element for each character,
2. 16 bits per element for integer variable, and
3. 32 bits per element for each floating point number.

One kind of data type is the *generic data type* where the operations are defined but the types of the items being manipulated are not, that is, the set of operations is defined but the set of values is not. The arrays are built-in generic data type in C/C++.

2.3 ARRAY AS AN ABSTRACT DATA TYPE

As defined in Section 2.2, an array is a set of pairs, `index` and `value`. For each index, there exists one associated element of an array. For defining an array as an abstract data type (ADT), we have to define the very basic operations or functions that can be performed on it. The basic operations of arrays are creating an array, storing an element, accessing an element, and traversing the array.

The function `create()` produces a new, empty array. `Access()` takes an array and an index as input, and returns either the appropriate value or an error. `Store()` is used to enter new index–value pairs. The axiom given in line 6 of the ADT definition reads 'to retrieve the `j`th item where `x` has already been stored at index `i` in `Array_A` is equivalent to checking if `i` and `j` are equal, and if so, `x`, else search for the `j`th value in the remaining array, `Array_A`'. This axiom was originally given by J. McCarthy. Notice how the axioms are independent of any representation scheme. In addition, `i` and `j` need not necessarily be integers, but we assume that they are, so that an `equal()` function can be devised.

If we restrict the index values to be integers, then assuming a conventional random access memory, we can implement `store()` and `access()` so that they operate in a constant amount of time. If we interpret the indices to be *n*-dimensional, $(i_1, i_2, ..., i_n)$, then the previous axiom by J. McCarthy defines the *n*-dimensional arrays.

Let us specify an ADT array in which we provide specifications with operations to be performed.

```
ADT array(index, value)
1. declare create() → array
2. access(array, index) → value
3. store(array, index, value) → array
4. for all Array_A ∈ array, x ∈ value, and i, j ∈ index let
5.   access(create, i) = error
6. access(store(Array_A, i, x), j) = x if equal(i, j)
7. else access(Array_A, j)
8. end
end array
```

Formally, ADT is a collection of domains, operations, and axioms (or rules). Let us discuss each of them.

Domain A domain is the intended set of values that any array may use either as an index or as a value. We can say that a domain of an array is a collection of fixed, homogeneous elements that may be atomic or structured. The restriction is that all the elements should be homogeneous. Arrays use a set of indices or subscript values that have one-to-one correspondence with the positive integer values. In C++, the index 0 is used for the first element, index 1 is used for the second element, and so on till $N-1$, for an array of size N.

Operations As shown in the ADT, the three basic operations of an array are described as follows:

1. `create()` → `array`—This operation creates an empty, new array. Whenever a new array is created, it is initially empty.
2. `access(array, index)` → `value`—This function takes an array and index as input and accesses the data element of that position. When the array is newly created, this operation must indicate an error because initially each array is by default empty.

3. `store(array, index, value)` $\rightarrow$ `array`—This operation is used to store a value in the array at a specified index position giving the updated array as an output.

Axioms The following are the axioms which form part of the ADT:

1. `access(create, i) = error`—This is the first axiom that explains the working of the `access()` operation. If the array is newly created, it is initially empty. So if we try to access an element at the `i`th position, it will be an erroneous operation.
2. `access(store(Array_A, i, x), j) = x if equal(i, j) else access(Array_A, j)` —The second axiom states that accessing an element at index `j`, where `x` has been already stored at index `i` in `Array_A` is one of the following two:
   (a) if `i = j` then the accessed element is `x` itself.
   (b) else the operation is equivalent to the operation of accessing element at index `j`, from `Array_A`.

Usually, arrays are stored in contiguous allocation of memory as is the case of C, C++, and Java. The ADT does not specify this. Let us learn more details of the array such as its memory representation and address calculation used to facilitate direct access.

2.4 MEMORY REPRESENTATION AND ADDRESS CALCULATION

A computer's memory can be considered as one long list of bits grouped together into bytes and/or words. Each one of them can be referred to just one location so as to avoid machine-dependent details, that is, whether memory is structured with a one-byte, two-byte, or *n*-byte word. In addition, the addressing scheme varies with each computer such as byte addressable or word addressable. During compilation, the appropriate number of locations is allocated for the array. The mechanism for allocating memory is much dependant on a language. Regardless of machine and language dependency, when the space is actually allocated, the location of an entire block of memory is referenced by the base address of the first location. The remaining elements are stored sequentially at a fixed distance apart, say, by a constant C. So if the ith element is mapped into a memory location of address x, then the $(i+1)^{th}$ element is mapped into the memory location with address $(x+C)$ as shown in Fig. 2.4.

Here, C depends on the size of the element, that is, the number of locations required per element, and also on the addressing of these locations.

The address of the ith element is calculated by the following formula:

$$\text{(Base address)} + (\text{Offset of } i^{th} \text{ element from base address})$$

Here, base address is the address of the first element where array storage starts. In Fig. 2.4, the base address is `x` and the offset is computed as

$$\text{Offset of } i^{th} \text{ element} = (\text{Number of elements before } i^{th} \text{ element}) \times (\text{Size of each element})$$

$$\text{Address of } \texttt{A[i]} = \text{Base} + i \times \text{Size of element}$$

Assuming the size of the element as one memory location, the memory representation is shown in Fig. 2.4.

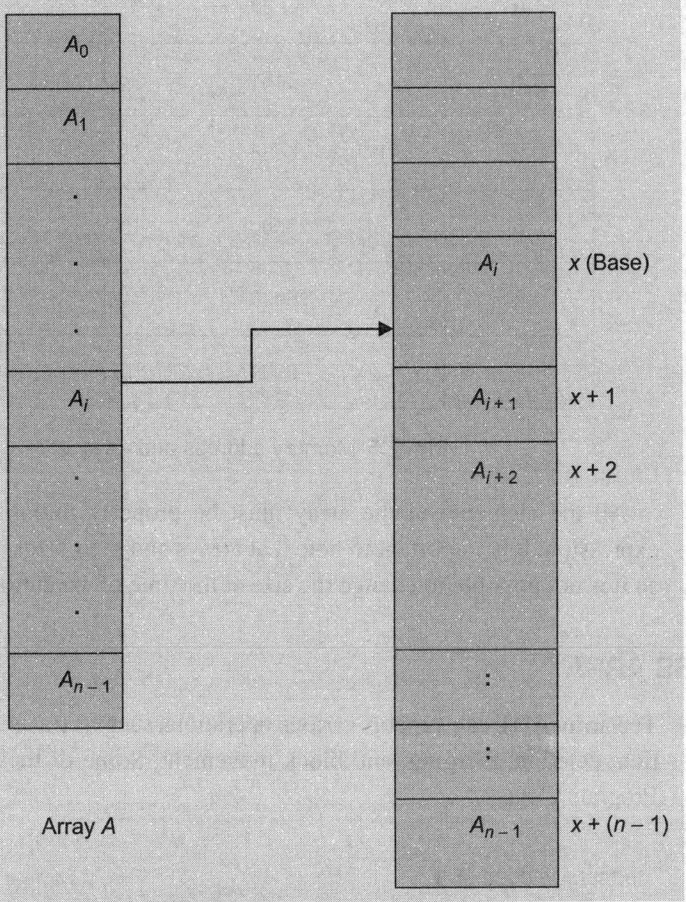

Fig. 2.4 Memory representation

Most of the languages use the base address plus offset for addressing. This way of addressing helps in direct access to an element with bounded time O(1) for access.

In brief, the `Array_A[N]` is implemented as follows:

1. `Array_A` is the name of the object/structure and is associated with a base (starting) address in memory.
2. The `[N]` notation specifies the number of array elements from the beginning (offset), which starts at zero.
3. The address of the ith element is then computed as base + $i \times$ (Size of element), where Size of element depends on the data type.

The `index`, `address`, and `values` are shown in Fig. 2.5 for an array of six real numbers.

Index[*i*]	Address	Value
0	6e80	11.56
1	6e84	34.00
2	6e88	25.65
3	6e8c	09.43
4	6e90	–67.55
5	6e94	35.12

Fig. 2.5 Memory address and array of real numbers

All the elements of the array must be properly initialized before referring in any expression. It is important to note that arrays and their sizes are mostly defined statically, so it is not possible to change the size at the time of execution.

2.5 CLASS ARRAY

The array ADT can support various operations such as traversal, sorting, searching, insertion, deletion, merging, and block movement. Some of these operations are detailed in Program Code 2.1.

PROGRAM CODE 2.1

```
class Array
{
  private:
    int MaxSize;
    int A[20];
    int Size;
  public:
    Array()        // constructor
    {
      MaxSize = 20;
      Size = 0;
    }
```

```
    void Read_Array();
    void Display();        // Traverse_Forward()
    void Traverse_Backward();
    void Insert(int Location, int Element);
    void Delete(int Location);
    int Search(int Element);
};

void Array :: Read_Array()
{
  int i, N;
  cout << "Enter size of array";
  cin >> N;
  if(N > MaxSize)
  {
    cout << "Array of this size cannot be created";
    cout << "Maximum size is" << MaxSize;
    return;
  }
  else
  {
    for(i = 0; i < N; i++)
    {
      cin >> A[i];
    }
    Size = N;
  }
}
void Array :: Display()
{
  int i;
  for(i = 0; i < Size; i++)
    cout << A[i] << "\t";
  cout << endl;
}
void Array :: Traverse_Backward()
{
  int i;
  for(i = Size - 1; i >= 0; i--)
    cout << A[i] << "\t";
```

```
    cout << endl;
}

int Array :: Search(int Element)
{
    int i;
    for(i = 0; i < Size - 1; i++)
    {
        if(Element == A[i])
        return(i);
    }
    return(-1);
}
```

2.5.1 Inserting an Element into an Array

The `insert()` operation inserts an element at a specified location into the array. A lot of data movement is involved in the `insert()` operation. To insert an element at the ith position in an array of size N, all the elements originally at positions i, $i + 1$, $i + 2$, ..., $N - 1$ will be shifted to $i + 1$, $i + 2$, $i + 3$, ..., N, respectively so that each element gets shifted to the right by one position. All the data shifting must be performed before the actual insertion. Moreover, before insertion, room must be created for the element at the ith position, and then the element is placed there.

Consider the following array:

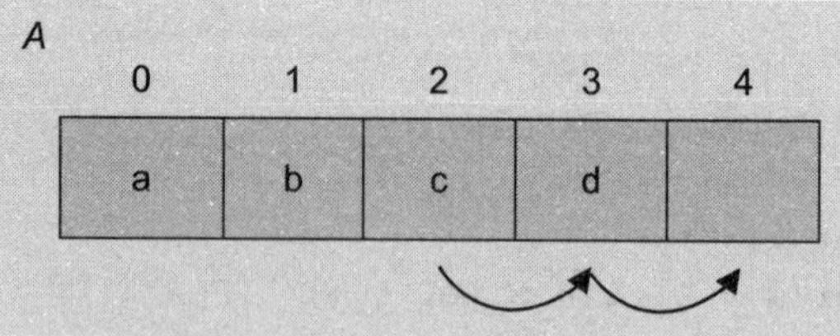

To insert 'z' at index = 2, that is at position 3, create room at 3 by data shifting.

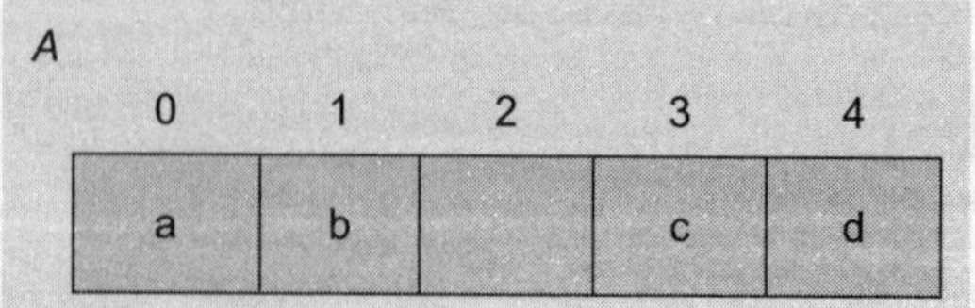

Then insert 'z' at position 3.

A

0	1	2	3	4
a	b	z	c	d

If the array is already full before the insertion of a new element, the last element of the array will be lost after insertion because of array overflow.

Now, consider the following array *A*:

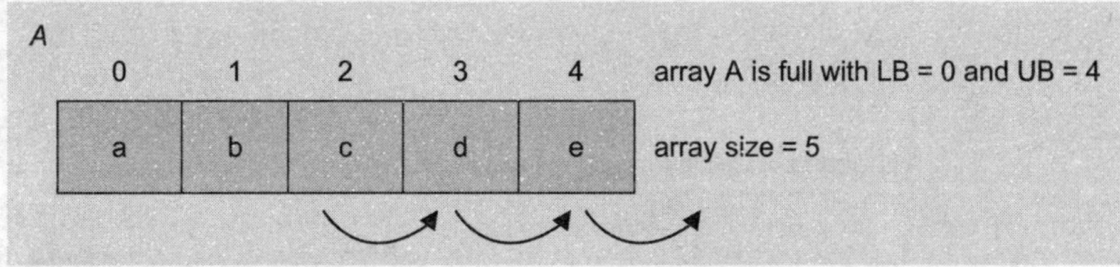

To insert 'z' at position 3, create room at the 3rd position by data shifting.

A

0	1	2	3	4	
a	b		c	d	e

Then insert 'z' at position 3.

A

0	1	2	3	4	
a	b	z	c	d	e

As the element 'e' is shifted to index 5, 'e' becomes inaccessible as the UB is crossed, and so the element 'e' may go beyond the scope of the array A. To handle such errors, appropriate checks should be made and if needed a new array of higher size should be created (when the size of the new array is double that of the original, it is known as array doubling), into which the elements are copied, and then the array renamed.

Data shifting can be performed using the following function:

```
void Array :: Insert(int Location, int Element)
{
  int i;
  if(Size >= MaxSize)
  {
    cout << "Sorry, Array Overflow";
    return;
  }
  for(i = Size - 1; i >= Location - 1; i--)
  {
    A[i + 1] = A[i]; // shifting element to right by
    1 position
  }
  A[Location - 1] = Element;
  Size = Size + 1;
}
```

2.5.2 Deleting an Element

The `delete()` operation removes the specified element from the array. Deletion of an element is achieved by overwriting the element. After one deletion operation, one location becomes empty, so all the elements should be shifted by one position after the deleted element to fill in the empty location of the deleted element. In short, deletion can be handled by simply overwriting the specified location.

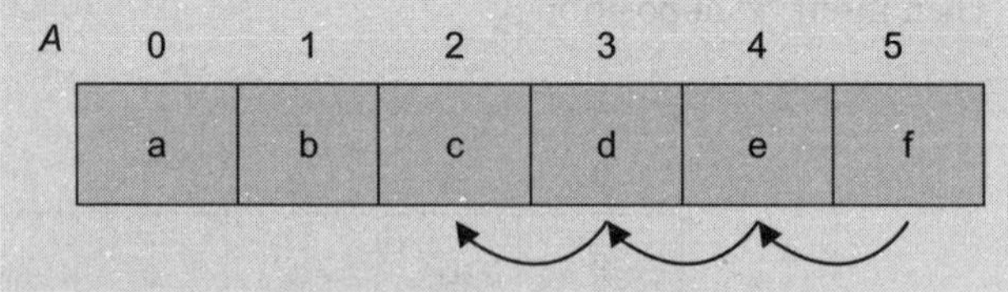

Delete 'c' from the 3rd position, that is, index = 2.

A	0	1	2	3	4	5
	a	b	d	e	f	f

Deletion can be performed using the following function:

```
void Array :: Delete(int Location)
{
   int i;
   for(i = Location; i < Size; i++)
   {
      A[i - 1] = A[i];
     // shifting elements to the left by 1 position
   }
   A[Size - 1] = 0;
   // Store 0 at the last location to mark it empty
   Size = Size - 1;
}

void main()
{
   Array A;
   A.Read_Array();
   A.Display();        // Traverse_Forward()
   A.Traverse_Backward();
   A.Insert(3, 66);    // insert at position 3
   A.Display();
   cout << endl;
   A.Delete(3);        // delete 4th element
   A.Display();
   cout << endl;
   cout << A.Search(66);
   cout << A.Search(3);
}
```

We have studied the basic operations for an array, such as reading an array and traversing it along with some common operations such as inserting an element and deleting an element in an array. Insertion and deletion operations need data shifting within the array.

The array and its operations in Program Code 2.1 are defined. To define an array of floating point data to operate on integer data, we need to change `int A[]` to `float A[]` in declaration of data members of class. This can be done each time the data type of array elements varies by editing the code using text editor and then recompiling it. C++ has a feature called *template* (also known as *parameterized type*). A template is a variable that can be instantiated to any data type. This data type could be a built-in or a user-defined type.

2.6 ARRAYS USING TEMPLATE

Program Code 2.2 is an array class using the template `T` that can be used quite easily for an array of `int`, `float`, or any user-defined data type.

The class array defined in Program Code 2.1 can be rewritten using a template in C++ as in Program Code 2.2.

PROGRAM CODE 2.2

```
template <class T>
class Array
{
  private:
  T * A;
  int Size;
  public:
  Array() { size = 20);          // default constructor
  Array(in ArraySize);          // user-defined size
  void Read_Array();
  void Display();
  void Traverse_Backward();
  void Insert(int Location, const T&Element);
  void Delete(int Location);
  int Search(const T&Element);
};

template <class T>
Array <T> :: Array(int ArraySize) : Size(ArraySize)
{
  A = new T[Size];
}

template <class T>
void Array <T> :: Read_Array()
{
  // code to read members of the array here
}
```

Other functions can be defined in a similar manner as in Program Code 2.1.

Program Code 2.2 contains a template class definition for an array and implementation of a few of its functions. The function is defined in a similar manner as in Program Code 2.1; that is, we replace `int` by `T` as the data type of the member of an array. In all member functions header, `Array()` is now replaced by `Array <T> ::`. The following statements instantiate the template class `Array()` to `int` and `float`, respectively. So `P` is an array of type `int` and `Q` is an array of type `float`.

```
Array <int> P;
Array <float> Q;
```

Similarly, we can also have an array of any user-defined data type.

2.7 MULTIDIMENSIONAL ARRAYS

The array we used till now was a one-dimensional array. Most of the times, data is organized in multiple dimensions. In such situations, a one-dimensional array proves to be insufficient, and we need two-dimensional, three-dimensional, or *n*-dimensional arrays.

2.7.1 Two-dimensional Arrays

A two-dimensional array `A` of dimension $m \times n$ is a collection of $m \times n$ elements in which each element is identified by a pair of indices $[i, j]$, where in general, $1 \leq i \leq m$ and $1 \leq j \leq n$. For the C/C++ languages this range is $0 \leq i < m$ and $0 \leq j < n$. A two-dimensional array has m rows and n columns. Figure 2.6 shows the pictorial representation of a two-dimensional array Student of size 100×9.

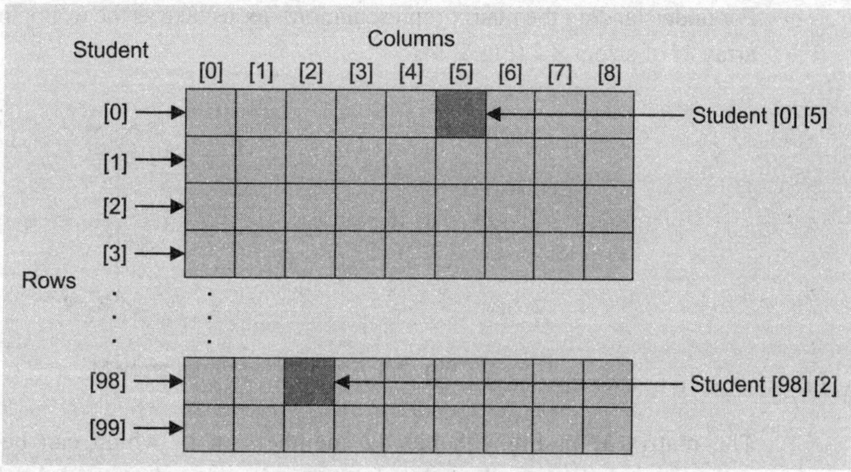

Fig. 2.6 Two-dimensional array

The best example of two-dimensional arrays is the most popular mathematical entity, matrix.

Memory Representation of Two-dimensional Arrays

Let us consider a two-dimensional array A of dimension $m \times n$. Though the array is multi-dimensional, it is usually stored in memory as a one-dimensional array. A multidimensional array is represented in memory as a sequence of $m \times n$ consecutive memory locations. The elements of a multidimensional array can be stored in the memory as

1. Row-major representation or
2. Column-major representation

Figure 2.7 shows matrix A of size $m \times n$.

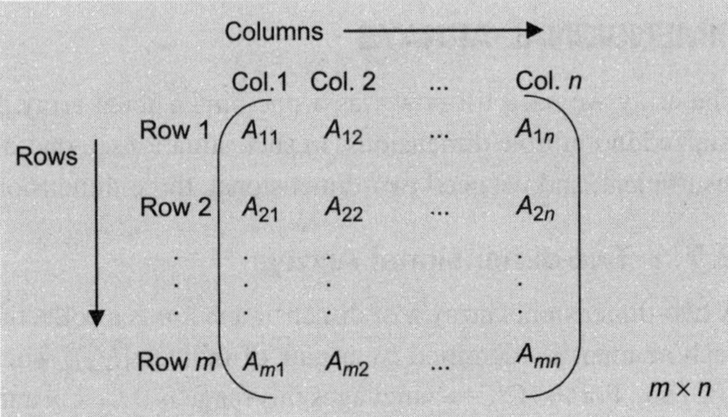

Fig. 2.7 Matrix A of size $m \times n$

For understanding the matrix representations, let us take as the example a two-dimensional array M of size 3×4 (Fig. 2.8).

$$M = \begin{pmatrix} 1 & 2 & 3 & 4 \\ 5 & 6 & 7 & 8 \\ 9 & 10 & 11 & 12 \end{pmatrix}_{3 \times 4}$$

Fig. 2.8 A two-dimensional array M

The matrix M in Fig. 2.8 has 12 members in it, which can be accessed by row and column indices such as the element in its second row, third column, is 7.

Row-major Representation

In row-major representation (Fig. 2.9), the elements of matrix M are stored row-wise, that is, elements of the 0th row, 1st row, 2nd row, 3rd row, and so on till the mth row.

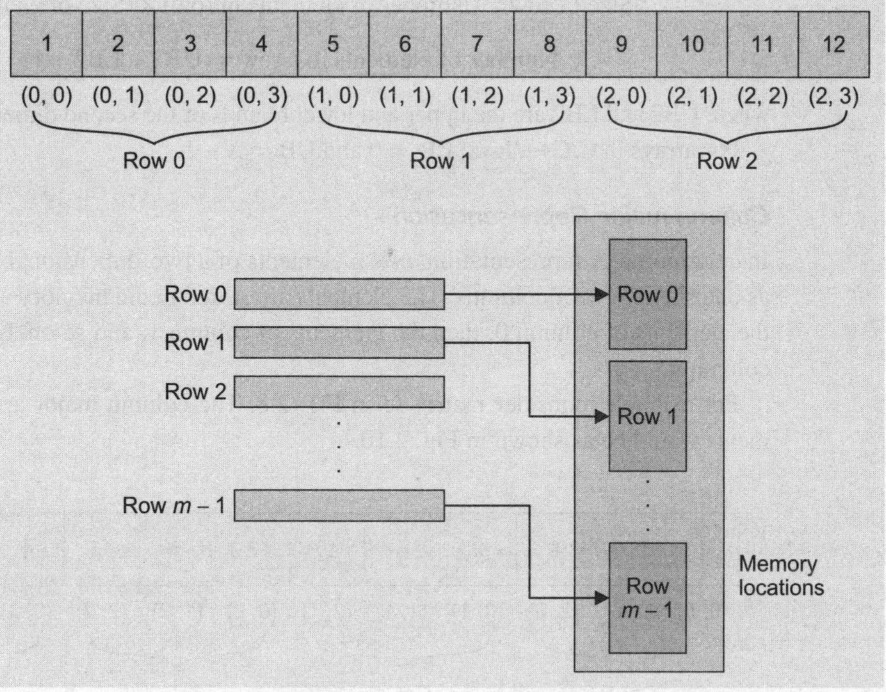

Fig. 2.9 Row-major arrangement

The address of the element of the ith row and the jth column for a matrix of size $m \times n$ can be calculated as

$$\begin{aligned}\text{Address of } (A[i][j]) &= \text{Base address} + \text{Offset}\\ &= \text{Base address} + (\text{Number of rows placed before } i^{th} \text{ row}\\ &\quad \times \text{Size of row}) \times (\text{Size of element}) + (\text{Number of elements}\\ &\quad \text{placed before in } j^{th} \text{ element in } i^{th} \text{ row}) \times \text{Size of element}\end{aligned}$$

Here, size of a row is actually the number of columns n. The base is the address of $A[0][0]$.

Address of $A[i][j] =$ Base + ($i \times n \times$ Size of element) + ($j \times$ Size of element)

As row indexing starts from 0, the index `i` indicates the number of rows before the ith row here and similarly for j. For Size of element $= 1$, the address is

$$\text{Address of } A[i][j] = \text{Base} + (i \times n) + j$$

In general,

$$\text{Address of } A[i][j] = ((i - \text{LB1}) \times (\text{UB2} - \text{LB2} + 1) \times \text{size}) + ((j - \text{LB2}) \times \text{size})$$

where the number of rows placed before the ith row = $(i - \text{LB1})$, and LB1 is the lower bound of the first dimension.

Size of row = (Number of elements in row) × (Size of element)

Number of elements in a row = (UB2 – LB2 + 1)

where UB2 and LB2 are the upper and lower bounds of the second dimension respectively.

For arrays in C/C++/Java, LB = 0 and UB = $N - 1$.

Column-major Representation

In column-major representation, $m \times n$ elements of a two-dimensional array A are stored as one single row of columns. The elements are stored in the memory as a sequence: first the elements of column 0, then the elements of column 1, and so on, till the elements of column $n - 1$.

For example, consider matrix M in Fig. 2.8. The column-major arrangement of elements would be as shown in Fig. 2.10.

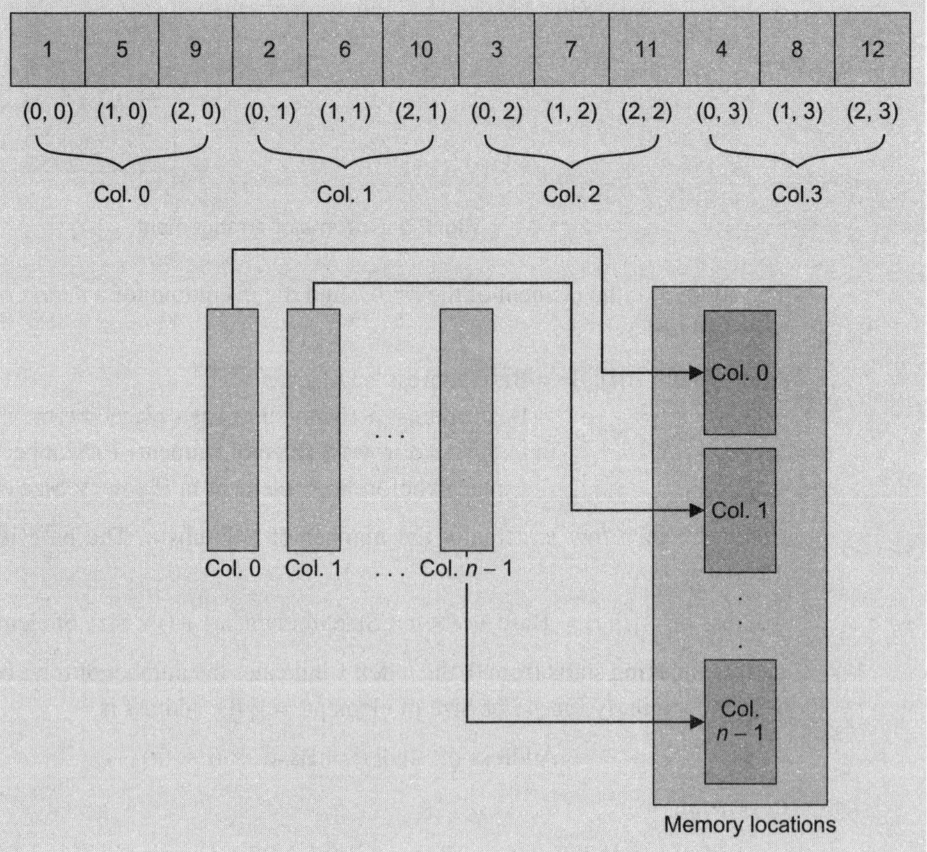

Fig. 2.10 Column-major arrangement

The address of $A[i][j]$ is computed as

Address of $(A[i][j])$ = Base address + Offset

= Base address + (Number of columns placed before j^{th} column × size of column) × (Size of element) + (Number of elements placed before in i^{th} element in i^{th} row) × Size of element

Here, the size of the column is the number of rows, that is, m. If the base is the address of $A[0][0]$, then

$$\text{Address of } A[i][j] = \text{Base} + (j \times m \times \text{Size of element}) + (i \times \text{Size of element})$$

For $\text{Size of element} = 1$, the address is

$$\text{Address of } A[i][j] \text{ for column-major arrangement} = \text{Base} + (j \times m) + i$$

In general, for column-major arrangement, the address of the element of the ith row and the jth column is

$$\text{Address of } (A[i][j] = ((j - \text{LB2}) \times (\text{UB1} - \text{LB1} + 1) \times \text{size}) + ((i - \text{LB1}) \times \text{size})$$

For arrays in C/C++/Java, LB = 0 and UB = $n - 1$ for an n-dimensional array. Example 2.1 shows the address calculation for row-major and column-major representations for a given array of integers.

EXAMPLE 2.1 Consider an integer array, `int A[3][4]` in C++. If the base address is 1050, find the address of the element `A[2][3]` with row-major and column-major representation of the array.

Solution For C++, the LB of index is 0, and we have `m` = 3, `n` = 4, and `Base` = 1050. Let us compute the address of the element `A[2][3]` using the address computation formula derived in the Section 2.7.1.

Row-major representation:

Address of `A[2][3] = Base + (i × n ) + j`

`= 1050 + (2 × 4) + 3`

`= 1061`

Figure 2.11 shows the row-major representation of the element `A[2][3]`.

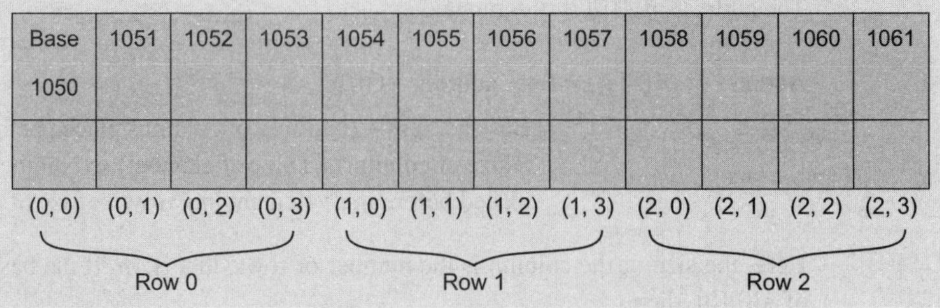

Fig. 2.11 Row-major representation of *A*[2][3]

Column-major representation:

```
Address of A[2][3] = Base + (j X m) + i
                   = 1050 + (3 X 3) + 2
                   = 1050 + 11
                   = 1061
```

Figure 2.12 represents the column-major representation of the element `A[2][3]`.

Base 1050	1051	1052	1053	1054	1055	1056	1057	1058	1059	1060	1061
(0, 0)	(1, 0)	(2, 0)	(0, 1)	(1, 1)	(2, 1)	(0, 2)	(1, 2)	(2, 2)	(0, 3)	(1, 3)	(2, 3)
Col. 0			Col. 1			Col. 2			Col. 3		

Fig. 2.12 Column-major representation of *A*[2][3]

Here, the address of the element is the same because it is the last member of the last row and the last column.

Let us compute the address of `A[1][3]`. For row-major, the address of `A[1][3]` $= 1050 + 1 \times 4 + 3 = 1057$ and for column-major, the address of `A[1][3]` $= 1050 + 3 \times 3 + 1 = 1060$.

2.7.2 *n*-dimensional Arrays

An *n*-dimensional $m_1 \times m_2 \times m_3 \times ... \times m_n$ array *A* is a collection of $m_1 \times m_2 \times m_3 \times \ldots \times m_n$ elements in which each element is specified by a list of *n* integers such as $k_1, k_2, \ldots k_n$ called subscripts where $0 \le k_1 \le m_1 - 1, 0 \le k_2 \le m_2 - 1, \ldots, 0 \le k_n \le m_n - 1$. The element of array *A* with subscripts $k_1, k_2, \ldots, k_n$ is denoted by $A[k_1][k_2] \ldots [k_n]$.

Consider the three-dimensional array $A[2][3][4]$. There are $2 \times 3 \times 4 = 24$ elements in array *A*. Its row-major arrangement is shown in Fig. 2.13.

Memory address	Array elements	$m_1 = 2, m_2 = 3, m_3 = 4$
Base	$A[0][0][0]$	
Base + 1	$A[0][0][1]$	
Base + 2	$A[0][0][2]$	
Base + 3	$A[0][0][3]$	
Base + 4	$A[0][1][0]$	Base + $m_3 \times 1$
Base + 5	$A[0][1][1]$	
Base + 6	$A[0][1][2]$	
Base + 7	$A[0][1][3]$	
Base + 8	$A[0][2][0]$	Base + $m_3 \times 2$
Base + 9	$A[0][2][1]$	
Base + 10	$A[0][2][2]$	
Base + 11	$A[0][2][3]$	
Base + 12	$A[1][0][0]$	Base + $m_3 \times 3$
Base + 13	$A[1][0][1]$	
Base + 14	$A[1][0][2]$	
Base + 15	$A[1][0][3]$	
Base + 16	$A[1][1][0]$	Base + $m_3 \times 3 + m_2$
Base + 17	$A[1][1][1]$	
Base + 18	$A[1][1][2]$	
Base + 19	$A[1][1][3]$	
Base + 20	$A[1][2][0]$	
Base + 21	$A[1][2][1]$	
Base + 22	$A[1][2][2]$	
Base + 23	$A[1][2][3]$	

Fig. 2.13 Three-dimensional array with row-major memory representation

A four-dimensional array *A*[2][3][4][2] with row-major representation would be stored in memory as shown in Fig. 2.14.

Memory address	Array elements
Base	A[0][0][0][0]
Base + 1	A[0][0][0][1]
Base + 2	A[0][0][0][2]
Base + 3	A[0][0][0][3]
Base + 4	A[0][0][1][0]
Base + 5	A[0][0][1][1]
Base + 6	A[0][0][1][2]
Base + 7	A[0][0][1][3]
Base + 8	A[0][0][2][0]
Base + 9	A[0][0][2][1]
Base + 10	A[0][0][2][2]
Base + 11	A[0][0][2][3]
Base + 12	A[0][1][0][0]
Base + 13	A[0][1][0][1]
Base + 14	A[0][1][0][2]
Base + 15	A[0][1][0][3]
Base + 16	A[0][1][1][0]
Base + 17	A[0][1][1][1]
Base + 18	A[0][1][1][2]
Base + 19	A[0][1][1][3]
Base + 20	A[0][1][2][0]
Base + 21	A[0][1][2][1]
Base + 22	A[0][1][2][2]
Base + 23	A[0][1][2][3]

Memory address	Array elements
Base + 24	A[1][0][0][0]
Base + 25	A[1][0][0][1]
Base + 26	A[1][0][1][0]
Base + 27	A[1][0][1][1]
Base + 28	A[1][0][2][0]
Base + 29	A[1][0][2][1]
Base + 30	A[1][0][3][0]
Base + 31	A[1][0][3][1]
Base + 32	A[1][1][0][0]
Base + 33	A[1][1][0][1]
Base + 34	A[1][1][1][0]
Base + 35	A[1][1][1][1]
Base + 36	A[1][1][2][0]
Base + 37	A[1][1][2][1]
Base + 38	A[1][1][3][0]
Base + 39	A[1][1][3][1]
Base + 40	A[1][2][0][0]
Base + 41	A[1][2][0][1]
Base + 42	A[1][2][1][0]
Base + 43	A[1][2][1][1]
Base + 44	A[1][2][2][0]
Base + 45	A[1][2][2][1]
Base + 46	A[1][2][3][0]
Base + 47	A[1][2][3][1]

Fig. 2.14 Four-dimensional array with row-major memory representation

Notice that the array indices are in increasing order, and hence row-major ordering is also called lexicographic order.

Address Calculation for Multidimensional Array

For a sequential single dimension row-major representation of a multidimensional array, let us try to get the address of any element $A[i_1][i_2][i_3]\ldots[i_n]$ of an n-dimensional array A. Let us consider the array $A[2][3][4][2]$. If the element $A[0][0][0][0]$ is stored at the address 0, then the element $A[0][0][0][1]$ is at address 1; the element $A[0][0][1][0]$ is at address 2; the element $A[0][0][1][1]$ is at address 3, and the element $A[1][2][3][1]$ at address 4, assuming one location per element. To derive a formula for a multidimensional array, let us first see one-dimensional (1D), two-dimensional (2D), and three-dimensional (3D) arrays and their address calculations, and further, we can generalize it for an n-dimensional array.

Address Calculation for One-dimensional Array

Let $A[m_1]$ be a one-dimensional array. Let $A[0]$ be stored at the address Base $= X$. Now, assuming one element per location, the address of $A[1]$ is $X + 1$. The address of an arbitrary element $A[i]$ is given by $X + i$, and the address of $A[m_1 - 1]$ is $X + m_1 - 1$. This is represented in Fig. 2.15.

$A[0]$	$A[1]$	$A[2]$	...		$A[i]$	...	$A[m_1 - 1]$
X	$X + 1$	$X + 2$	...		$X + i$	...	$X + (m_1 - 1)$

Fig. 2.15 One-dimensional array

Address Calculation for Two-dimensional Array

Now, consider a two-dimensional array $A[m_1][m_2]$ that has m_1 rows as Row1, Row2 ... Row($m_1 - 1$), each row containing m_2 elements as there are m_2 columns (Fig. 2.16).

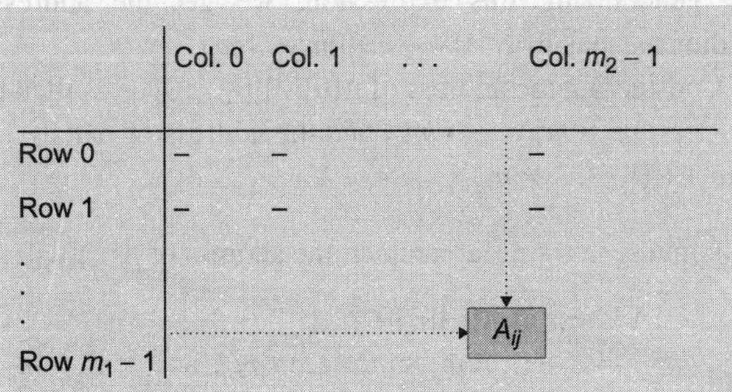

Fig. 2.16 Two-dimensional array

Now, let $A[0][0]$ be stored at address X; then $A[0][1]$ would be stored at $X + 1$; $A[0][i]$ would be at $X + i$ and so on till $A[0][m_2 - 1]$ at $X + (m_2 - 1)$. Now the address of $A[i][0]$ would be $X + (i \times m_2)$.

In general, the address of $A[i][j]$ is $X + (i \times m_2) + j$ (Fig. 2.17).

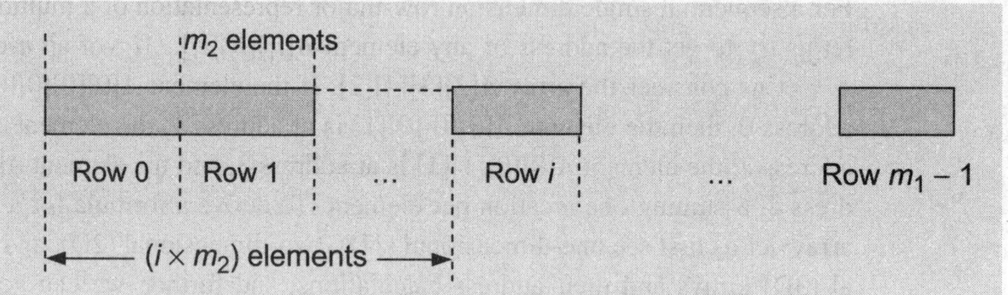

Fig. 2.17 Row-major representation of 2D array

Address Calculation for Three-dimensional Array

Figure 2.18 shows a three-dimensional array $A[m_1][m_2][m_3]$. This array is interpreted as m_1 two-dimensional arrays of dimension $m_2 \times m_3$.

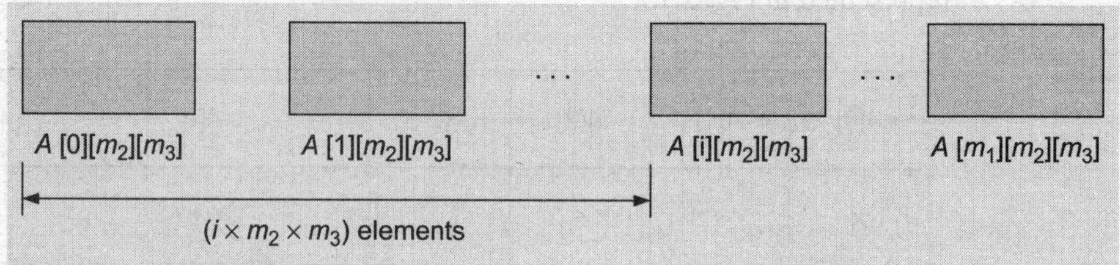

Fig. 2.18 Row-major arrangement of a three-dimensional array

The address of $A[i][0][0]$ is $X + (i \times m_2 \times m_3)$. Therefore, the address of $A[i][j][k]$ is computed as

$$\text{Addr of } A[i][j][k] = X + i \times m_2 \times m_3 + j \times m_3 + k$$

By generalizing this expression, we get the address of $A[i_1][i_2][i_3]\ldots[i_n]$ in the n-dimensional array $A[m_1][m_2][m_3]\ldots[m_n]$

Considering the address of $A[0][0][0]\ldots[0]$ as X, then the address of $A[i][0][0]\ldots[0] = X + (i_1 \times m_2 \times m_3 \times \ldots \times m_n)$ and the address of $A[i_1][i_2]\ldots[0] = X + (i_1 \times m_2 \times m_3 \times \ldots \times m_n) + (i_2 \times m_3 \times m_4 \times \ldots \times m_n)$.

Continuing in a similar manner, the address of $A[i_1][i_2][i_3]\ldots[i_n]$ will be

$$\begin{aligned}&\text{Address of } A[i_1][i_2][i_3]\ldots[i_n]\\&= X + (i_1 \times m_2 \times m_3 \times \ldots \times m_n) + (i_2 \times m_3 \times m_4 \times \ldots \times m_n)\\&\quad + (i_3 \times m_4 \times m_5 \times \ldots \times m_n) + (i_4 \times m_5 \times m_6 \times \ldots \times m_n) + \ldots + i_n\end{aligned}$$

$$= X + \sum_{j=1}^{n} i_j \times A_j \text{ where } A_j = \prod_{j=1}^{n} m_k \quad 1 < j < n \text{ and } A_n = 1$$

Similarly, we can derive the formula for column-major order too.

2.8 CONCEPT OF ORDERED LIST

Ordered list is the most common and frequently used data object. Linear elements of an ordered list are related with each other in a particular order or sequence. The following are some examples of ordered lists.

1. Odd numbers less than or equal to 15 = {1, 3, 5, 7, 9, 11, 13, 15}
2. Months = {January, February, March, April, May, June, July, August, September, October, November, December}
3. Colors of the rainbow = {Violet, Indigo, Blue, Green, Yellow, Orange, Red}

There are many basic operations that can be performed on the ordered list. The following list states them:

1. Find the length of the list.
2. Traverse the list from left to right or from right to left.
3. Access the ith element in the list.
4. Update (Overwrite) the value at the ith position.
5. Insert an element at the ith location.
6. Delete an element at the ith position.

Arrays are the most common data structures that can be used for representing an ordered list. In an ordered list, members of the list follow some specific sequence. We need to select the best suitable data structure to perform these operations efficiently. The best possible way to organize them is in an array. Let L be the list; $L = \{a_0, a_1, a_2, ..., a_{n-1}\}$ having n elements. If we store this list in an array, say list[n], then we can store the ith element at the ith location (index) of the list. This representation would store a_0 at list[0], a_1 at list[1], and so on, sequentially as a_i and a_{i+1} at the ith and $(i+1)^{th}$ locations.

The representation of an ordered list L in array form is shown in Fig. 2.19.

list[0]	list[1]	list[2]	. . .	list[n – 1]
a_0	a_1	a_2	. . .	a_{n-1}

Fig. 2.19 Ordered list stored in an array

Such representation is very efficient both to retrieve and to modify operations. It requires a constant time to retrieve the ith element from the ith array location as the computer can access randomly any word in its memory. Similar to random access, one can traverse a list in any direction by using a controlled subscript variable. Insert and delete operations will require data movement.

2.9 SINGLE VARIABLE POLYNOMIAL

A polynomial of a single variable $A(x)$ can be written as

$$a_n x^n + a_{n-1} x^{n-1} + a_{n-2} x^{n-2} + \dots \dots a_1 x + a_0 \quad \text{where } a_n \neq 0 \text{ and degree of } A(x) \text{ is } n.$$

This polynomial is a sum of terms $C.x^e$ where C is a coefficient, e is the exponent, and x is a variable. A polynomial is one of the examples of an ordered list. When we think of a polynomial as an ADT, the basic operations are as follows:

1. Creation of a polynomial
2. Addition of two polynomials
3. Subtraction of two polynomials
4. Multiplication of two polynomials
5. Polynomial evaluation

In Program Code 2.3, we have not defined the data members to represent a polynomial with coefficients and exponents. We have defined function prototypes to operate on a polynomial. To define data members that are deciding a suitable data structure for a polynomial, we have many options. For exponents and coefficients, we can use two separate one-dimensional arrays, a two-dimensional array, an array of structures, and so on. Let us analyse a few of them.

PROGRAM CODE 2.3

```
ADT Polynomial
{
  private:
    // data members here
  public:
    void Read_Poly();
    double Evaluate(double value);
    Polynomial Add_Poly(Polynomial B);
    Polynomial Mult_Poly(Polynomial B);
};
```

2.9.1 Representation Using Arrays

The polynomial of degree n represented as an ordered list of coefficients can be stored using an array of size $n + 2$. That is, $n + 1$ locations for storing coefficients of $n + 1$ terms and one location for storing the degree of polynomial. Alternatively, we can also store them by mapping each term with the index so that the ith term is at the $(n - i)^{th}$ location of the array. We store polynomials in the decreasing order of their exponents. The degree of a polynomial is the highest exponent in the polynomial. For a polynomial of degree n, we would need an array of size $n + 1$ and a store polynomial as follows:

For the term $a_i x^i$, let us store its coefficient a_i at the $[n - i]^{th}$ index in an array, that is, store a coefficient of the term with exponent i at the $[n - i]^{th}$ index.

$$\text{Poly}[n - i] = a_i \quad \text{for } i = 0 \text{ to } n$$

This is represented in Fig. 2.20.

Poly[0]	Poly[1]	Poly[2]	Poly[3]	...	Poly[n – 2]	Poly[n – 1]
a_n	a_{n-1}	a_{n-2}	a_{n-3}	...	a_1	a_0

Fig. 2.20 Storing polynomial as ordered list

```
int degree; float Poly[Max + 1];
```

Here, `degree` ≤ `Max`

This representation is very efficient with respect to operations such as `store()` and `retrieve()` as it requires constant time O(1). The conventional algorithms of addition, subtraction, multiplication, and so on can be used for this representation very efficiently.

Such representation is both time and space efficient when the polynomial is not a sparse one such as polynomial $P(x)$ of degree 3 where $P(x) = 3x^3 + x^2 - 2x + 5$ (Fig. 2.21).

Index i	0	1	2	3	...	N – 1
Coefficient	3	1	–2	5	...	0

Fig. 2.21 Polynomial of degree 3—$P(x) = 3x^3 + x^2 - 2x + 5$

Figure 2.22 shows a polynomial of degree 8.

Index i	0	1	2	3	4	5	6	7	8
Coefficient	11	0	5	1	2	0	–3	1	10

Fig. 2.22 Polynomial of degree 8—$P(x) = 11x^8 + 5x^6 + x^5 + 2x^4 - 3x^2 + x + 10$

However, when a polynomial is a sparse one such as $A(x) = x^{99} + 78$ for degree of $n = 100$, then only two locations out of 101 would be used as shown in Fig. 2.23.

Index *i*	0	1	2	3	...	99
Coefficient	1	0	0	0	...	78

Fig. 2.23 Polynomial of degree 99—$P(x) = x^{99} + 78$

In such cases, it is better to store the polynomial as pairs of `coefficient` and `exponent`. We may go for two different arrays for each, or a structure having two members as two arrays for each of `coefficient` and `exponent`, or an array of structure that consists of two data members `coefficient` and `exponent`. Let us go for the structure having two data members `coefficient` and `exponent` and its array.

2.9.2 Polynomial as Array of Structure

In Program Code 2.4, the `coefficient` and `exponent` are bound together in a structure to form one polynomial term, and then the array of ten such structures is used to represent a polynomial.

PROGRAM CODE 2.4

```
const int MaxSize = 100;
typedef struct
{
  float coefficient;
  int exponent;
} polynomial_term;

class Polynomial
{
  private:
  polynomial_term Poly[MaxSize];
  int Total_Terms;
  public:
  Polynomial() { Total_Terms = 0;}
  void Read_Poly();
  void Display_Poly();
  double Evaluate(double value);
  Polynomial Add_Poly(Polynomial B);
  Polynomial Mult_Poly(Polynomial B);
};
```

Figure 2.24 depicts such a polynomial.

Index *i*	0	1	2	3	. . .	*N* – 1
Coefficient	3	1	–2	5	. . .	
Exponent	3	2	1	0	. . .	

Fig. 2.24 Polynomial representation—$P(x) = 3x^3 + x^2 - 2x + 5$

2.9.3 Polynomial Evaluation

Polynomial evaluation is substituting the value of x and computing the result. For $x = 2$, the polynomial $P(x) = 3x^3 + x^2 - 2x + 5$ results in $3\ (2)^3 + (2)^2 - 2(2) + 5 = 29$.

Program Code 2.5 provides implementation details of polynomial evaluation for a given value of x. The functions are provided for reading and printing the polynomials.

PROGRAM CODE 2.5

```
double Polynomial :: Evaluate(double Value)
{
  int i = 0;
  double result = 0;
  while (i <= Total_Terms)
  {
    Result+=Poly[i].Coef*pow(val,Poly[i].Exp);
    // pow() is the exponential function to compute xy
    i++;
  }
  return result;
}

void Polynomial :: Read_Poly()
{
  int i;
  cout << "Let us read the polynomial now" << endl;
  cout << "Enter total number of terms in polynomial";
  cin >> Total_Terms;
  for(i = 0; i <= Total_Terms; i++)
  {
    cout << "Enter Exponent of" << i+1 << "Term";
```

```
      cin << Poly[i].Exp;
      cout<< "Enter Coefficient of" << i+1 << "Term";
      cin << Poly[i].Coef;
    }
}

void Polynomial :: Display_Poly()
{
    int i;
    for(i = 0; i <= Total_Terms; i++)
    cout << Poly[i].Coef << "x^" << Poly[i].Exp << "+";
    cout << "\b" << endl;
}

void main()
{
    Polynomial A;
    double answer;
    A.Read_Poly();
    answer = A.Evaluate(69.45);
    // Let 69.45 be the value of x
}
```

2.9.4 Polynomial Addition

Let two polynomials A and B be

$$A = 4x^9 + 8x^6 + 5x^3 + x^2 + 4x$$
$$B = 3x^7 + x^3 - 2x + 5$$

Then,

$$C = A + B = 4x^9 + 3x^7 + 8x^6 + 6x^3 + x^2 + 2x + 5$$

The polynomials A and B are to be added to get the resultant polynomial C. Here, we assume that the two polynomials are in descending order of their exponents.

Let us revise the procedure of adding two polynomials. Let i, j, and k be the three indices to keep track of the current term of the polynomials A, B, and C, respectively, being processed. Initially, it tracks the first term. The major steps involved can be listed as follows:

1. If the exponents of the two terms of polynomials A and B are equal, then the coefficients are added, and the new term is stored in the resultant polynomial C and advance i, j, and k to track to the next term.
2. If the exponent of the term indicated by i in A is less than the exponent of the current term specified by j of B, then copy the current term of B pointed by j in the location pointed by k in polynomial C. The pointers j and k are advanced to the next term.

location pointed by `k` in polynomial `C`. The pointers `j` and `k` are advanced to the next term.

3. If the exponent of the term pointed by `j` in `B` is less than the exponent of the current term pointed by `i` of `A`, then copy the current term of `A` pointed by `i` in the location pointed by `k` in polynomial `C`. Advance the pointer `i` and `k` to the next term.

   Each time a new term is generated, its `coefficient` and `exponent` fields are set accordingly. The resultant term then is attached to the end of the polynomial `C`. The current term of polynomial `C` is indicated by `k`.

Figure 2.25 shows the pictorial representation of polynomials `A`, `B`, and `C` using a two-dimensional array and indices.

Index *i*	0	1	2	3	4
Coefficient	4	8	5	1	4
Exponent	9	6	3	2	0

(a)

Index *j*	0	1	2	3
Coefficient	3	1	–2	5
Exponent	7	3	1	0

(b)

Index *K*	0	1	2	3	4	5	6
Coefficient	4	3	8	6	1	2	5
Exponent	9	7	6	3	2	1	0

(c)

Fig. 2.25 Storing polynomials in a 2D array (a) $P(x) = 4x^9 + 8x^6 + 5x^3 + x^2 + 4x$ (b) $P(x) = 3x^7 + x^3 - 2x + 5$ (c) $P(x) = 4x^9 + 3x^7 + 8x^6 + 6x^3 + x^2 + 2x + 5$

The steps involved in polynomial addition are stated in Algorithm 2.1.

ALGORITHM 2.1

```
1. Read two polynomials say A and B
2. Let M and N denote total terms in A and B respectively.
   Here, C is resultant polynomial.
4. Let i = j = k = 0
5. while (i < M and j < N) do
   begin     // repeat till one of the polynomials is copied
     if(A[i].Exp = B[j].Exp)
     begin
       C[k].Coef = A[i].Coef+B[j].Coef
       C[k].Exp = A[i].Exp;
       i = i + 1; j = j + 1, k = k + 1
     end
     else
       if(A[i].Exp > B[j].Exp)
       begin
         C[k].Coef = A[i].Coef;
         C[k].Exp = A[i].Exp;
         i = i + 1
         k = k + 1
       end
     else
     begin
       C[k].Coef = B[j].Coef;
       C[k].Exp = B[j].Exp;
       j = j + 1
       k = k + 1
     end
     end
6. while(i < m) do
   begin     // copy remaining terms
     C[k].Coef = A[i].Coef;
     C[k].Exp = A[i].Exp;
     i = i + 1
     k = k + 1
   end
7. while (j < n) do
   begin     // copy remaining terms
     C[k].Coef = B[j].Coef;
     C[k].Exp = B[j].Exp;
     j = j + 1
     k = k + 1
   end
8) stop
```

Program Code 2.6 is for the polynomial addition function based on Algorithm 2.1.

PROGRAM CODE 2.6

```
Polynomial Polynomial :: Add_Poly(Polynomial B)
{
  int i = j = k = 0;
  Polynomial C;
  while (i < A.Total_Terms && j < B.Total_Terms)
  {
    if(A.Poly[i].Exp == B.Poly[j].Exp)
    {
      C.Poly[k].Coef = A.Poly[i].Coef + B.Poly[j].Coef
      C.Poly[k].Exp = A.Poly[i].Exp;
      i++; j++; k++;
    }
    else if(A.Poly[i].Exp > B.Poly[j].Exp)
    {
      C.Poly[k].Coef = A.Poly[i].Coef;
      C.Poly[k].Exp = A.Poly[i].Exp;
      i++; k++;
    }
    else
    {
      C.Poly[k].Coef = B.Poly[j].Coef;
      C.Poly[k].Exp = B.Poly[j].Exp;
      j++; k++;
    }
  }       // end of while
  while(i < A.Total_Terms)
  {
    C.Poly[k].Coef = A.Poly[i].Coef;
    C.Poly[k].Exp = A.Poly[i].Exp;
    i++; k++;
  }
  while(j < B.Total_Terms)
  {
    C.Poly[k].Coef = B.Poly[j].Coef;
    C.Poly[k].Exp = B.Poly[j].Exp;
    j++; k++;
  }
  C.Total_Terms = k - 1;
  return C;
  }       // end of function
```

```
void main()
{
   Polynomial A, B, C;
   double answer;
   A.Read_Poly();
   B.Read_Poly();
            .
            .
            .
  C = A.Add_Poly(B);
}
```

2.9.5 Polynomial Multiplication

Let A = $4x^9 + 3x^6 + 5x^3 + 1$ and B = $3x^6 + x^2 - 2x$ be the two polynomials to be multiplied, and the resultant polynomial be C. Let us revise the paper-pencil method. The polynomial A is multiplied by each term of B. We get n partial products if B has n terms in it. Finally, we add all these partial products to get the resultant polynomial C.

This method generates partial products each of length m, where m is the length of the polynomial A. n such partial products are generated and stored and finally added to get the resultant polynomial. Here, m and n are input dependent. Let us devise a better approach where we need not generate, store, and then add all partial products. A better solution is to pick up a term of polynomial B and multiply it with each term of A. One term of B and one term of A when multiplied yield one resultant term. This term can be immediately added to the resultant polynomial C, and this process is to be repeated.

To add a resultant term to polynomial C, the resultant term is compared with each term of the resultant polynomial C. Then the new term is inserted at the appropriate location in polynomial C. If the new term with equal exponent is found, then the term is added, else it is inserted in the resultant polynomial at an appropriate position. This process is repeated for each term of B with each term of A. The major steps are listed briefly as follows:

1. Let A and B be two polynomials.
2. Let the number of terms in A be M, and number of terms in B be N.
3. Let C be the resultant polynomial to be computed as C = A × B.
4. Let us denote the ith term of polynomial B as tBi. For each term tBi of polynomial B, repeat steps 5 to 7 where $i = 1$ to N.
5. Let us denote the jth term of polynomial A as tAj. For each term of tAj of polynomial A, repeat steps 6 and 7 where $j = 1$ to M.
6. Multiply tAj and tBi. Let the new term be tCk = tAj × tBi.

7. Compare `tck` with each term of polynomial `C`. If a term with equal exponent is found, then add the new term `tck` to that term of polynomial `C`, else search for an appropriate position for the term `tck` and insert the same in polynomial `C`.
8. Stop.

Let `A` $= 4x^9 + 3x^6 + 5x^3 + 1$, `B` $= 3x^6 + x^2$, and `C` be the resultant polynomial. Initially, `C` is an empty polynomial.

1. We multiply each term of `A` with the first term of `B`. To start with, multiply $4x^9$ with $3x^6$ and the result is $12x^{15}$. Currently, `C` is empty, so there is no term in it with the exponent 15; therefore, we insert it in polynomial `C`. Now, polynomial `C` is

$$C = 12x^{15}$$

Now, continue to multiply $3x^6$ with $3x^6$, and the result obtained is $9x^{12}$. There is no term in polynomial `C` with exponent 12, so we insert it in polynomial `C` at an appropriate location. Now, polynomial `C` is

$$C = 12x^{15} + 9x^{12}$$

Continuing in a similar manner for the remaining two terms of polynomial `A`, we get polynomial `C` as

$$C = 12x^{15} + 9x^{12} + 15x^9 + 3x^6$$

2. Now, multiply each term of `A` with the second term of `B`. Initially, multiply $4x^9$ with x^2 and the result is $4x^{11}$. There is no term in `C` with exponent 11, we insert it in polynomial *C* at an appropriate location. So now we get polynomial `C` as

$$C = 12x^{15} + 9x^{12} + 4x^{11} + 15x^9 + 3x^6$$

Continue to multiply $3x^6$ with x^2 and the result is $3x^8$. There is no term in polynomial `C` with exponent 8, so we add it at an appropriate place. Now, the polynomial `C` is

$$C = 12x^{15} + 9x^{12} + 4x^{11} + 15x^9 + 3x^8 + 3x^6$$

Let us now multiply $5x^3$ with x^2 and we get $5x^5$. There is no term in `C` with exponent 5, so we insert it in polynomial `C` at a proper location. Now,

$$C = 12x^{15} + 9x^{12} + 4x^{11} + 15x^9 + 3x^8 + 3x^6 + 5x^5$$

Let us now multiply the term 1 of `A` with x^2; we get x^2. There is no term in `C` with exponent 2, so we insert it in polynomial `C` at an appropriate location. Therefore,

$$C = 12x^{15} + 9x^{12} + 4x^{11} + 15x^9 + 3x^8 + 3x^6 + 5x^5 + x^2$$

This is the resultant polynomial `C` as a result of `A` × `B`.

Program Code 2.7 includes the function for the multiplication of two polynomials as per the procedure discussed.

PROGRAM CODE 2.7

```
Polynomial Polynomial :: Mult_Ploy(Polynomial B)
{
  int flag, M, N;
  Polynomial C;
  int NewTerm_exp;
  float NewTerm_coef;
  int i = j = k = 0;
  // i and j are indices indicating the current
  // terms of polynomials A & B respectively
  // k is the index pointing to current position
  // in C where new term is to be added
  int TmpIndex;
  // TmpIndex is used to traverse polynomial C for
  // inserting new term at proper location
  M = Total_Terms;
  N = B.Total_Terms;
  while(i < M)
  {
    j = 0;
    while (j < N)
    {
       NewTerm_exp = Poly[i].Exp + B.Poly[j].Exp;
       NewTerm_coef = Poly[i].Coef * B.Poly[j].Coef;
       TmpIndex = 0;
       flag = 0;
       while(TmpIndex < k)
       // Insert NewTerm in Polynomial C
       {
         if(C.Poly[TmpIndex].Exp == NewTerm_exp)
         // search matching exponent
         {
           flag = 1;
           break;
         }
       else if(C.Poly[TmpIndex].Exp < NewTerm_exp)
       break;
       TmpIndex++;
       }
       if(flag)        // if found add coefficients
```

```
            C.Poly[k].Coef = C[k].Coef + NewTerm_coef;
        else   // else add at last location or in between
        {
           if(TmpIndex==k) // add new term at end
           {
             C.Poly [k].Exp = NewTerm_exp;
             C.Poly [k].Coef = NewTerm_coef;
             k++;
           }
           else
           {
             // insert new term
             for(p = k; p < TmpIndex; p--)
             {
               C.Poly [p].Exp = C.Poly[p].Exp;
               C.Poly [k].Coef = C.Poly[p].Coef;
             }
             C.Poly[TmpIndex].Coef = NewTerm_exp;
             C. Poly[TmpIndex].Coef = NewTerm_Coef;
             k++;
           }
           j++;
        }
        i++;
    }
 return(C);
}
void main()
{
  Polynomial A, B, C;
  B.Read_poly();
  B.Read_Poly();
  C = A.Mult_Poly(B);
}
```

2.10 ARRAY FOR FREQUENCY COUNT

We can use an array to store the number of times a particular element occurs in any sequence. Suppose we have a set of 100 non-zero values ranging between 0 and 9 and we want to know how many times 0 appeared, how many times 1 appeared, and so on up to 9.

Let these elements be placed in an array named *Numbers*. Now, we can have another array of 10 elements that will show the frequency of each value in the list *Numbers*.

```
void Frequency_Count(int Freq[10], int A[100])
{
   int i;
   for(i = 0; i < 10; i++)
     Freq[i] = 0;
   for(i = 0; i < 100; i++)
     Freq[A[i]]++;
}
```

In Fig. 2.26, Frequency[0] indicates that 0 occurred once in the array *Numbers*, 1 appeared 20 times, 2 appeared 5 times, and so on.

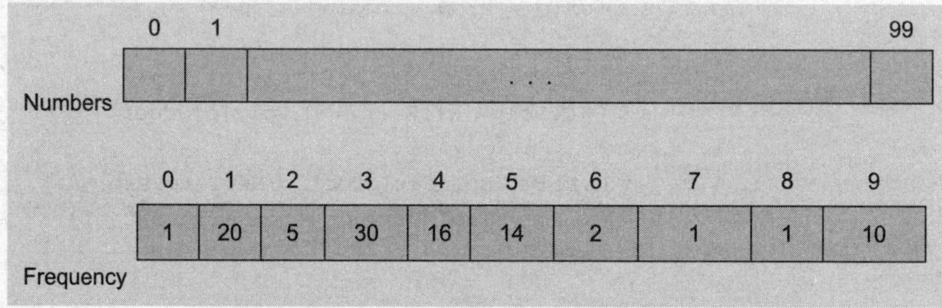

Fig. 2.26 Frequency count of numbers ranging from 0 to 9

This concept will be used in Section 2.11.3 for fast transpose.

2.11 SPARSE MATRIX

A matrix is a very commonly used mathematical object. To represent a matrix, we need a two-dimensional array with two different indices for row and column references. The representation of a matrix for operations on it should be efficient so that the space and time requirement is less.

In many applications, the crucial aspect for algorithm design is space consideration. So the developer has to take care of the representation of the matrix if it is large. In many situations, the matrix size is very large but most of the elements in it are 0s (less important or irrelevant data). Only a small fraction of the matrix is actually used. A matrix of such type is called a *sparse matrix*, as the matrix is filled sparsely by data and most of the positions are empty or contain non-relevant data. In such cases, the matrix must be represented and stored with an alternate representation to achieve good space utilization. Such representation avoids operations such as operations with 0s (addition or multiplication of 0s). Consequently, a good time complexity along with efficient storage is achieved if a sparse matrix is stored with an alternate representation rather than the conventional way.

Figure 2.27 illustrates the logical matrices ***LA*** and ***LB***.

$$LA = \begin{pmatrix} 0 & 0 & 0 & 0 & 0 \\ 0 & 1 & 0 & 0 & 0 \\ 0 & 0 & 0 & 0 & 0 \\ 0 & 1 & 0 & 0 & 0 \\ 0 & 0 & 0 & 1 & 0 \\ 0 & 0 & 1 & 0 & 0 \\ 0 & 0 & 0 & 0 & 0 \end{pmatrix}_{7\times 5} \qquad LB = \begin{pmatrix} 0 & 1 & 1 & 1 & 1 \\ 1 & 1 & 1 & 1 & 0 \\ 1 & 0 & 1 & 1 & 1 \\ 1 & 1 & 1 & 0 & 1 \\ 1 & 1 & 1 & 1 & 1 \\ 1 & 1 & 1 & 0 & 1 \\ 0 & 0 & 0 & 0 & 0 \end{pmatrix}_{7\times 5}$$

Fig. 2.27 Sparse logical matrix

In Fig. 2.27, the matrix ***LA*** is sparse with respect to 1s and dense with respect to 0s, whereas ***LB*** is sparse with respect to 0s and dense with respect to 1s.

For a matrix of *m* rows and *n* columns, if $m = n$, then the matrix is called a square matrix (Fig. 2.28).

$$A = \begin{pmatrix} 0 & 0 & 6 & 1 & 1 & 2 \\ 0 & 1 & 0 & 0 & 9 & 9 \\ 4 & 0 & 0 & 0 & 0 & 0 \\ 0 & 0 & 0 & 0 & 0 & 0 \\ 7 & 0 & 0 & 0 & 0 & 6 \\ 0 & 2 & 0 & 0 & 0 & 8 \end{pmatrix}_{6\times 6}$$

Fig. 2.28 Sparse square matrix

The matrix ***A*** in Fig. 2.28 has many 0 entries, and it may be called a sparse matrix. There is no precise definition of when a matrix is sparse and when it is not. Here, 0s may represent non-relevant data, or no change in consecutive readings of some experiment or consecutive positions.

Two general types of *n*–square sparse matrices are represented in Figs 2.29 and 2.30.

$$B = \begin{bmatrix} 10 & 0 & 0 \\ 21 & 90 & 0 \\ 45 & 28 & 15 \end{bmatrix}_{3\times 3}$$

Fig. 2.29 Sparse triangular matrix

$$C = \begin{bmatrix} 9 & 88 & 0 & 0 \\ 22 & 8 & 95 & 0 \\ 0 & 33 & 6 & 44 \\ 0 & 0 & 56 & 47 \end{bmatrix}_{4\times 4}$$

Fig. 2.30 Sparse tridiagonal matrix

In the matrix in Fig. 2.29, all entries above the main diagonal are 0. A matrix in which all non-zero entries occur only on or below the main diagonal is called a *triangular matrix*.

A matrix in which the non-zero entries can only occur on the diagonal or on elements immediately above or below the diagonal is called a *tridiagonal matrix* (Fig. 2.30).

2.11.1 Sparse Matrix Representation

A sparse matrix requires an alternate form of representation. While dealing with large matrices that are sparse, we have to think about an alternative representation to store only the non-zero elements for better space utilization.

Each element of the matrix is uniquely characterized by its row and column positions. So a triple (i, j, value) can easily represent the non-zero elements of the matrix.

In the sparse representation of a matrix, there are three columns. In the first row, we always specify the number of rows, columns, and non-zero elements (No_Of_NonZeroValues) in columns 1, 2, and 3, respectively. From the second row onwards, we store each non-zero element by its triple (i, j, value). So in a sparse matrix, there are three columns and (No_Of_NonZeroValues + 1) rows. In general, for space reliability, 3 × (No_Of_NonZeroValues + 1) should always be less than or equal to $m \times n$ where m = number of rows and n = number of columns.

No_Of_NonZeroValues = Number of non-zero elements

In brief, for the alternate representation, we should have

$$3 \times (\text{No\_Of\_NonZeroValues} + 1) \leq m \times n$$

Consider the matrix ***A*** in Fig. 2.31(a). Among the 42 elements, 8 members are non-zero. For conventional representation, we need 42 memory locations for storing the matrix (assuming one location per element), whereas for its alternate representation as in Fig. 2.31(b), we need (8 + 1) × 3, that is, 27 memory locations.

(a) 6 × 7

0	0	0	0	0	0	1	0	0	0
0	0	9	8	0					
0	3	0	0	0					
0	0	0	5	4					
0	0	2	3	0					
0	0	0	0	0					

(b) 9 × 3

Rows	Columns	Non-zero entries
6	7	8
0	0	1
1	2	9
2	3	8
3	1	3
4	3	5
4	4	4
5	2	2
5	3	3

Fig. 2.31 Sparse matrix representation (a) Sparse matrix ***A*** (b) Alternate representation of sparse matrix ***A***

In applications such as finite element analysis, image processing, simulations, and so on, matrices are of the size 2048 × 2048 or much higher. When m and n are large numbers and

No_Of_NonZeroValues is much lesser, then the alternate representation saves considerable amount of memory and time of processing.

Program Code 2.8 represents the ADT for a sparse matrix.

PROGRAM CODE 2.8

```
class Sparse_Matrix
{
  private:
  const int Max = 20
  int S_Mat[Max][3];
  public:
  void Read_SparseMatrix();
  Sparse_Matrix Simple_Transpose();
  Sparse_Matrix Fast_Transpose();
  Sparse_Matrix Add_SparseMatrix(Sparse_Matrix B);
  Sparse_Matrix Mpy_SparseMatrix(Sparse_Matrix B);
};
```

2.11.2 Sparse Matrix Addition

Along with the alternate representation, we have to think of appropriate algorithms for common matrix operations such as addition, subtraction, transpose, inverse, multiplication, and division. Let us discuss two of them—addition and transpose.

Let A and B be two sparse matrices to be added, as in Fig. 2.32.

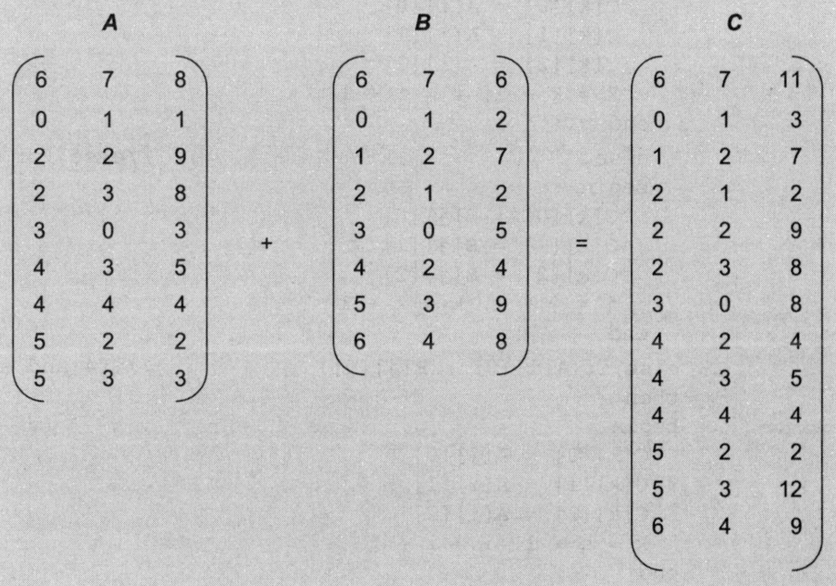

Fig. 2.32 Sparse matrix addition

Only if the size of both the matrices is the same can they be added. Let A_Row and B_Row be rows of matrix A and B respectively. M and N are the number of non-zero elements in A and B, respectively. C is the resultant sparse matrix. Algorithm 2.2 describes the procedure for adding two sparse matrices.

ALGORITHM 2.2

```
1.Let A, B be the matrices to be added and stored in C
2.Let M and N be number of non-zero entries in A and B respectively.
3.Let i, j, and k be the three index variables used for the rows of A,
  B, and C respectively.
4.Let i = j = k = 1, M = A[0][2], N = B[0][2]
5.C[0][0] = A[0][0]
  C[0][1] = A[0][1]
6.while(i ≤ M and j ≤ N) do
  begin
    if(A[i][0] = B[j][0])                          //if1
      if(A[i][1] = B[j][1])                        //if2
      then
      begin
        C[k][0] = A[i][0]
        C[k][1] = A[i][1]
        C[k][2] = A[i][2] + B[j][2]
        i = i + 1, j = j + 1, k = k + 1
      end
      else if(A[i][1] < B[j][1])                   //if3 and else for if2
      then
      begin
        C[k][0] = A[i][0]
        C[k][1] = A[i][1]
        C[k][2] = A[i][2]
        k = k + 1, i = i + 1
      end
      else                                         //else for if3
      begin
        C[k][0] = B[j][0]
        C[k][1] = B[j][1]
        C[k][2] = B[j][2]
        j = j + 1, k = k + 1
      end
    else if(A[i][0] < B[j][0])                     //if4 and else for if1
    then
    begin
      C[k][0] = A[i][0]
      C[k][1] = A[i][1]
      C[k][2] = A[i][2]
      k = k + 1, i = i + 1
    end
```

```
    begin
      C[k][0] = B[j][0]
      C[k][1] = B[j][1]
      C[k][2] = B[j][2]
      K = k + 1, j = j + 1
    end
  end while
7.  while(i < = M) do
    begin
      C[k][0] = A[i][0]
      C[k][1] = A[i][1]
      C[k][2] = A[i][2]
      k = k + 1, i = i + 1
    end
8.  while(j <= N) do
    begin
      C[k][0] = B[j][0]
      C[k][1] = B[j][1]
      C[k][2] = B[j][2]
      k = k + 1, j = j + 1
    end
9.  C[0][2] = k
10. stop
```

Program Code 2.9 includes the ADT for a sparse matrix and function for two sparse matrix additions as per Algorithm 2.2.

PROGRAM CODE 2.9

```
Sparse_Matrix Sparse_Matrix :: Add_SparseMatrix
(Sparse_Matrix B)
{
  Sparse_Matrix C;
  int i, j, k, Row1, Row2, Col1, Col2, M1, M2;
  Row1 = S_Mat[0][0];
  Col1 = S_Mat[0][1];
  M1 = S_Mat[0][2];
  Row2 = B.S_Mat[0][0];
  Col2 = B.S_Mat[0][1];
  M2 = B.S_Mat[0][2];
  if(Row1 == Row2 && Col1 == Col2)
  // checking dimensions if1
  {
    i = j = k = 1;
    C. S_Mat[0][0] = S_Mat[0][0];
    C. S_Mat[0][1] = S_Mat[0][1];
```

```
while(i ≤ M1 and j ≤ M2)        // while1
{
  if(S_Mat[i][0] == B.S_Mat[j][0])        // if2
  {
    if(S_Mat[i][1] == B.S_Mat[j][1])        // if3
    {
      C.S_Mat[k] [0] = S_Mat[i][0];
      C.S_Mat[k] [1] = S_Mat[i][1];
      C.S_Mat[k][2] = S_Mat[i][2] + B.S_Mat[j][2];
      i++; j++; k++;
    }       // end of if3
    else        // else of if3
    {
      if(S_Mat[i][1] < B.S_Mat[j][1])        // if4
      {
        C.S_Mat[k][0] = S_Mat[i][0];
        C.S_Mat[k][1] = S_Mat[i][1];
        C.S_Mat[k][2] = S_Mat[i][2];
        k++; i++;
      }       // end of if4
      else     // else of if4
      {
        C.S_Mat[k][0] = B.S_Mat[j][0];
        C.S_Mat[k][1] = B.S_Mat[j][1];
        C.S_Mat[k][2] = B.S_Mat[j][2];
        j++; k++;
      }       // end of else of if4
    }       // end of else of if3
  }       // end of if2
  else   // else of if2
  {
    if(S_Mat[i][0] < B.S_Mat[j][0])        // if5
    {
      C.S_Mat[k][0] = S_Mat[i][0];
      C.S_Mat[k][1] = S_Mat[i][1];
      C.S_Mat[k][2] = S_Mat[i][2];
      k++ ; i++;
    }       // end of if5
    else        // else of if5
    {
      C.S_Mat[k][0] = B.S_Mat[j][0];
```

```
        C.S_Mat[k][1] = B.S_Mat[j][1];
        C.S_Mat[k][2] = B.S_Mat[j][2];
        k++; j++;
        }       // end of else of if5
      }       // end of else of if2
    }       // end of while1
    while(i ≤ M1)       // while2
    {
      C.S_Mat[k][0] = S_Mat[i][0];
      C.S_Mat[k][1] = S_Mat[i][1];
      C.S_Mat[k][2] = S_Mat[i][2];
      k++; i++;
    }       // end of while2
    while(j ≤ N)       // while3
    {
      C.S_Mat[k][0] = B.S_Mat[j][0];
      C.S_Mat[k][1] = B.S_Mat[j][1];
      C.S_Mat[k][2] = B.S_Mat[j][2];
      k++; j++;
    }       // end of while3
    C.S_Mat[0][2] = k;
    return C;
  }       // end of if1 for checking dimensions
  else       //else for if1
    cout << "Sorry, matrices cannot be added because
    dimensions don't match.\n";
}       // end of function
```

2.11.3 Transpose of Sparse Matrix

In the conventional approach, by interchanging rows and columns, we get the transpose of the matrix as the elements at position `[i][j]` and `[j][i]` are swapped.

Let m and n be the number of rows and columns for matrix $\boldsymbol{A}$. The transpose of $\boldsymbol{A}$ can be obtained using the following code.

```
for(i = 1; i ≤ m; i++)
   for(j = 1; j ≤ n; j++)
      A[j][i] = A[i][j];
```

Time complexity of this technique is $O(mn)$. In addition, the conventional transpose (Fig. 2.33(a)) is not suitable for sparse matrix's alternate representation. By just exchanging the row and the column, we get the transpose of the sparse matrix as shown in Fig. 2.33(b).

$$A = \begin{pmatrix} 1 & 2 & 3 & 4 \\ 5 & 6 & 7 & 8 \\ 9 & 10 & 11 & 12 \end{pmatrix}_{3 \times 4} \qquad A^T = \begin{pmatrix} 1 & 5 & 9 \\ 2 & 6 & 10 \\ 3 & 7 & 11 \\ 4 & 8 & 12 \end{pmatrix}_{4 \times 3}$$

(a)

$$B = \begin{pmatrix} \mathbf{6} & \mathbf{7} & \mathbf{5} \\ 1 & 2 & 7 \\ 2 & 4 & 2 \\ 3 & 6 & 5 \\ 5 & 0 & 4 \\ 5 & 3 & 9 \\ 6 & 1 & 8 \end{pmatrix} \qquad B^T = \begin{pmatrix} \mathbf{7} & \mathbf{6} & \mathbf{5} \\ 2 & 1 & 7 \\ 4 & 2 & 2 \\ 6 & 3 & 5 \\ 0 & 5 & 4 \\ 3 & 5 & 9 \\ 1 & 6 & 8 \end{pmatrix}$$

(b)

Fig. 2.33 Transpose of matrices (a) Conventional matrix and its transpose (b) Sparse matrix and its transpose

The matrix in Fig. 2.33(b) is a simple sparse matrix of size 6×7 with 5 non-zero elements and its transpose.

We can notice that entries in B^T are not sorted row and column wise; we need to sort them further. Sorting further adds to time complexity. Let us learn two better approaches—the simple and fast transpose algorithms.

Simple Transpose

Let `A` be a matrix of size $m \times n$ with `T` non-zero elements and let `B` be its transpose. One of the easiest ways is to search for each column (column = 0 to $n - 1$) and sequentially place each column as a row in the transposed matrix `B` by placing the interchanged entries as row, column, and value (refer to Fig. 2.34 on page 80).

The steps to transpose a matrix are described in Algorithm 2.3 and the corresponding program is described in Program Code 2.10.

ALGORITHM 2.3

```
1. Row = A[0][0], Col = A[0][1]  and  T = A[0][2]
2. B[0][0] = Col , B[0][1] = Row  and  B[0][2] = T
```

```
3. if T = 0 goto step(5)
4. Let i = 1
   for j = 0 to Col-1 do
     for k = 1 to T do
     if(A[k][1] = j)
        begin
               B[i][0] = A[i][1]
               B[i][1] = A[i][0]
               B[i][2] = A[i][2]
               i = i +1
        end
5. stop
```

PROGRAM CODE 2.10

```
Sparse_Matrix Sparse_Matrix :: Simple_Transpose()
{
  Sparse_Matrix B;
  int Row, Col, i, j, k, T;
  Row = S_Mat[0][0];
  Col = S_Mat[0][1];
  T = S_Mat[0][2];
  if(T == 0) return;
  B.S_Mat[0][0] = Col;
  B.S_Mat[0][1] = Row;
  B.S_Mat[0][2] = T;
  i = 1;
  for(j = 0; j < Col; j++)
  {
   for( k = 1; k <= T; k++)
    {
      if(S_Mat [k][1] == j)
      {
      B.S_Mat[i][0] = S_Mat[i][1];
      B.S_Mat[i][1] = S_Mat[i][0];
      B.S_Mat[i][2] = S_Mat[i][2];
      i++;
      }
    }
  }
  return B;
}
```

In Algorithm 2.3, we first take the first row of matrix `A` as (m, n, t) and store it as (n, m, t) in matrix `B`. In the second column (the 0th column being the first), we have stored values that initially indicated columns as now indicating rows. This column is searched for using $col = 0$ to $n - 1$.

For example, in the simple transpose in the following figure, the current row of matrix `A` is initially set to 0 and no entry with column as 0. So the row is incremented and set to 1 and the process continues; the entry (2, 1, 21) in `A` is stored as (1, 2, 21) in matrix `B`, and the current row value is updated each time. The next entry (3, 1, 31) is stored as (1, 3, 31) in matrix `B`. Further, entry (1, 2, 12) is stored as (2, 1, 12) in matrix `B`. Similarly, it goes on searching for each column value.

$$A = \begin{pmatrix} \mathbf{3} & \mathbf{4} & \mathbf{5} \\ 1 & 2 & 12 \\ 2 & 1 & 21 \\ 2 & 3 & 23 \\ 3 & 1 & 31 \\ 3 & 4 & 34 \end{pmatrix} \qquad B = A^T = \begin{pmatrix} \mathbf{4} & \mathbf{3} & \mathbf{5} \\ 1 & 2 & 21 \\ 1 & 3 & 31 \\ 2 & 1 & 12 \\ 3 & 2 & 23 \\ 4 & 3 & 34 \end{pmatrix}$$

Fig. 2.34 Simple transpose

Step 4 of Algorithm 2.3 is repeated `T` times for each column. The time complexity is $O(n\mathtt{T})$ where n is the number of columns in matrix `A` and `T` is number of non-zero elements in the matrix.

In a matrix, when all data is relevant, that is, all data members are non-zero, then $\mathtt{T} = m \times n$.

Now, the time complexity will be $O(n \cdot \mathtt{T}) = O(n \cdot mn) = O(mn^2)$, which is worse than the conventional transpose with time complexity $O(mn)$. Let us learn a better approach for transpose.

Fast Transpose

Let `A` be a sparse matrix of size $m \times n$ with `T` non-zero elements. Its transpose will be stored in matrix `B`. Let `Freq` and `RowStartPos` be two one-dimensional arrays of size n. In `Freq` array, the frequency count of each column in matrix `A` is stored, and `RowStartPos` will be computed and stored at the position where each row entry of matrix `A` is to be inserted in matrix `B`. Then, the `RowStartPos` is computed using `Freq`. The corresponding algorithm is as illustrated in Algorithm 2.4.

ALGORITHM 2.4

```
1. Row = A[0][0]
   Col = A[0][1]
   M = A[0][2]
2. B[0][0] = Col
   B[0][1] = Row
   B[0][2] = M
3. if M = 0 then goto step 9
4. for i = 0 to Col - 1 do
       Freq[i] = 0 {Here Freq array stores the frequency count of each
       column, initially set to 0}
5. for k = 1 to M do
       Tmp = A[k][1]
       Freq[Tmp] = Freq [Tmp] + 1;
6. RowStartPos[0] = 1 {We shall start storing elements in B matrix
   from 2nd row that is B[1][] onwards}
7. for j = 1 to Col - 1 do
       RowStartPos[j] = RowStartPos[j - 1] + RowStartPos[j - 1];
          {Here RowStartPos n matrix gives the position to place an
           element in resultant matrix}
8. for i = 1 to M + 1 do
   begin
       k = RowStartPos[A[i][1]]
       B[k][0] = A[i][1]
       B[k][1] = A[i][0]
       B[k][2] = A[i][2]
       RowStartPos[k] = RowStartPos[k] + 1
   end
9. stop
```

This algorithm will first find the number of non-zero elements in each column and store it in an array `Freq`. The second array `RowStartPos` is used to store the starting address of each column, which will be a row in the corresponding transposed matrix. The starting address of each row in the transposed matrix is given by

`RowStartPos[i] = RowStartPos[i − 1] + Freq[i − 1]`

where,

`Freq[i − 1]` gives the number of non-zero elements in `row[i − 1]`
`RowStartPos [i − 1]` gives the starting row of `row [i − 1]`

If the starting position for any row, say 3, is 5 in a transposed matrix and there are 2 elements in row 3, then the starting position of row 4 will be $5 + 2 = 7$. Sequentially, we read the column index from matrix `A` and then get the location from the array `RowStartPos`, and we store that element in matrix `B` at the specified location in the transposed form. This is illustrated in Fig. 2.35.

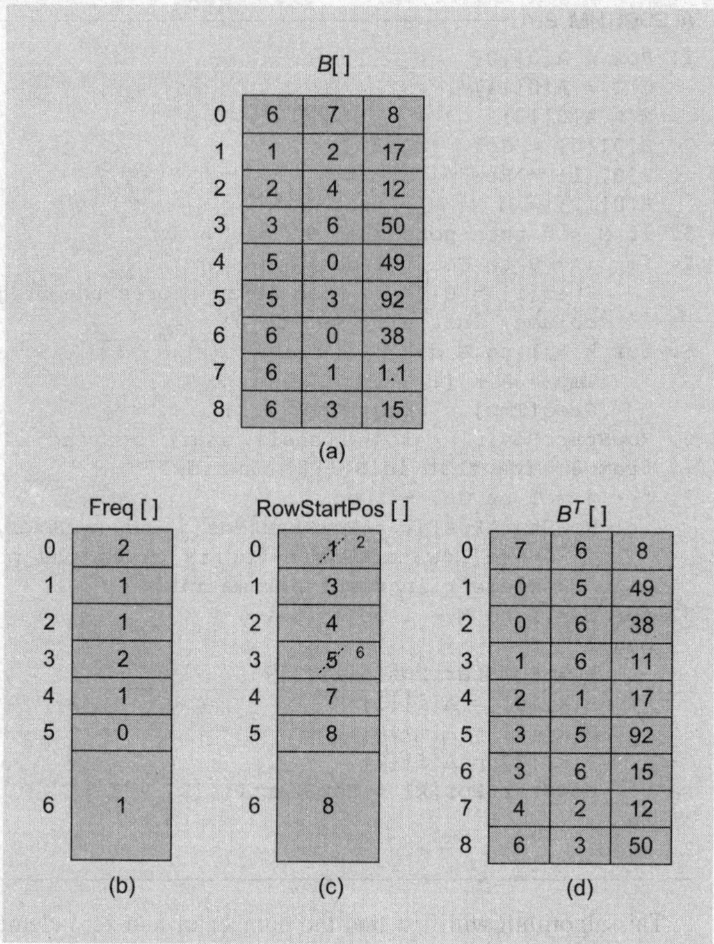

Fig. 2.35 Storing column as row in fast transpose
(a) Input matrix ***B*** (b) Freq[*i*] (c) RowStartPos[*i*] (d) $\boldsymbol{B^T}$

Time and Space Complexity Analysis of Fast Transpose

There are three loops in Algorithm 2.4, which are executed n (no. of rows), `T` (no. of non-zero members), $n - 1$, and `T` times, respectively, resulting in overall time complexity $O(n + \texttt{T})$.

In the worst case, that is, when $\texttt{T} = m \times n$ (non-zero elements), the magnitude becomes $O(n + mn) = O(mn)$, which is the same as the conventional 2D transpose. However, the constant factor associated with fast transpose is quite high. When `T` is sufficiently small compared to its maximum of $m \times n$, fast transpose works faster.

As compared to simple transpose, time is saved but an extra space for two one-dimensional arrays `Freq` and `RowStartPos` are required for the fast transpose. Program Code 2.11 implements the sparse matrix fast transpose.

PROGRAM CODE 2.11

```
Sparse_Matrix Sparse_Matrix ::Fast_Transpose()
{
  Sparse_Matrix B;
  int m, n, t, i, j, Freq[], RowStartPos[];
  Row = S_Mat[0][0];
  Col = S_Mat[0][1];
  M = S_Mat[0][2];
  B.S_Mat[0][0] = Col;
  B.S_Mat[0][1] = Row;
  B.S_Mat[0][2] = M;
  if(M == 0) return;
  else
  {
    for(i = 0; i < col; i++)
    {
      Freq[i] = 0;
    }
    for(i = 1; i <= t; i++)
    {
      T = A[i][1];
      Freq[T]++;
    }
    RowStartPos [0] = 1;
    for(i = 1; i < n; i++)
    {
      RowStartPos[i] = RowStartPos[i - 1] + Freq[i - 1];
    }
    for(i = 1; i <= M; i++)
    {
      j = A[i][1] ;
      B[RowStartPos[j]][0] = S_Mat[i][1];
      B[RowStartPos[j]][1] = S_Mat[i][0];
      B[RowStartPos[j]][2] = S_Mat[i][2];
      RowStartPos[j] = RowStartPos[j] + 1;
    }
  }
  return B;
}
```

In this program, the number of elements in each column is determined initially. These are actually going to be the number of columns in the transposed matrix. This information helps us update the array `RowStartPos`, which tells us from where we should start storing elements in the transposed array so that they are row wise sorted.

2.12 STRING MANIPULATION USING ARRAY

String is the most commonly used data object. It is usually formed from the character set of the programming language. Suppose $S = a_1\ a_2\ ...\ a_n$.

The value n is the length of the character string S, where $n \geq 0$. If $n = 0$, then S is called a *null string* or *empty string*. There are various operations that can be performed on the string:

1. Finding the length of a string
2. Concatenating two strings
3. Copying a string
4. Reversing a string
5. Performing string compare
6. Palindrome check
7. Recognizing a sub string.

These operations using arrays are discussed in detail in the sections that follow.

Basically, a string is stored as a sequence of characters in a one-dimensional character array, say A (Fig. 2.36).

	0	1	2	3	4	5	6	7	8	9
A =	S	T	R	I	N	G	\0	–	–	–

Fig. 2.36 String stored in array

The simple C++ statement for storing 'String' in an array of size 10 is as follows:

```
char A[10] = "STRING";
```

Each string is terminated by a special character, that is, null character '\0'. This null character indicates the end or termination of each string. The function `compare()` in Program Code 2.12 compares two strings to find whether they are equal.

To compare two strings, we first check whether their lengths are the same. If the lengths are the same, then there is a further possibility that the strings are the same. The lengths are to be compared if they have been precomputed or are known, else this adds to the complexity. Then, we compare each character of string `A` with string `B`. If they match, then the strings are the same; else they are not.

PROGRAM CODE 2.12

```
Class String
{
  private:
  char Str[];
  public:
  String() {}
  int Length();
  void Concat(String B);
  int Substring(String S);
};

int String :: Length()
{
  int length = 0, i;
  for(i = 0; Str[i] != '\0'; i++)
  length++;
  return(length);
}

void String :: Concat(String B)
{
  int len_A, i, j;
  // To concatenate B to A we need to traverse
  // string A till the end
  for(i = 0; Str[i] != '\0'; i++);
  len_A = i;
  // Let us concatenate B to A now
  for(i = len_A, j = 0; B.Str[j] != '\0'; j++,i++)
  {
    Str [i] = B.Str[j];
  }
  Str[i] = '\0';
}

String String :: Copy()
{
  String B;
  int i;
  for(i = 0; Str[i] != '\0'; i++)
```

```
  B.Str[i] = Str[i];
  B.Str[i] = '\0';  // Append the termination character
  return B;
}

String String :: Copy_Reverse()
{
  int i, l, Len_A;
  for(l = 0; Str[l] != '\0'; l++);
  // loop terminates after reaching end of A
  Len_A = l--
  for(i = l, j = 0; i >= 0; i--, j++)
  B.Str[j] = Str[i];
  B.Str[j] = '\0';        //Append termination character
  return B;
}

void String :: Rev_String()
{
  int i, len = 0;
  //exchange ith and jth characters till middle position
  char t;
  for(len = 0; Str[len] !='\0',len++);
  for(i = 0, j = len - 1; i != j; i++, j--)
  {
    t = Str[i]; Str[i] = Str[j];  Str[j] = t;
  }
}
int String :: Str_cmp(String A, String B)
{
  int i = 0;
  if (A.Length() != B.Length())
  return(0);
  while
  (A.Str[i] == B.Str[i] && A.Str[i] != '\0' &&
  B.Str[i] != '\0')
   ++ i;
  if(A.Str[i] == '\0' && B.Str[i] == '\0')
   return(1);
  else
   return(0);
}
```

Palindrome check Palindrome is a string that reads the same in forward and backward directions. For example, *madam* and *malayalam* are palindromes (Fig. 2.37).

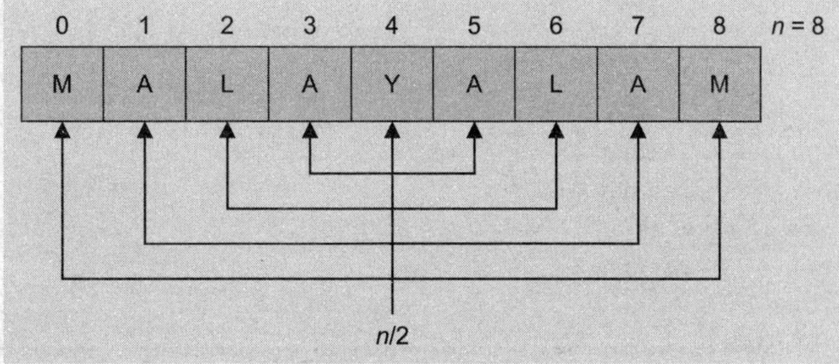

Fig. 2.37 Palindrome check

To check whether the string is a palindrome or not, there are two approaches:

1. We first find the reverse of the string and then compare it with the original string. If they match, then the string is a palindrome; otherwise, it is not. This approach needs n comparisons if the string length is n and an additional array to store the reversed string.
2. The other approach does not need n comparisons but just $n/2$ comparisons. We can compare the first character with the last. If they match, then again match the second character with the second last. Continue this process till the middle of the string. We can set two indices from both the ends and compare till the indices do not overlap. The mismatch of characters indicates that the string is not a palindrome. This approach does not need an additional data structure.

The program for checking a palindrome is given in Program Code 2.13.

PROGRAM CODE 2.13

```
int String:: Palindrome_Check()
{
   int i, j, l, flag = 0, k;
   for(l = 0; Str[l] != '\0'; l++);      //loop terminates
   l--; k = l/2;             //to avoid null char
   for(i = 0,j = l; i <= k; i++, j--)
   {
      if(Str[i] == Str[j])
      {
         flag = 1;
         continue;
      }
```

```
      else
      {
        flag = 0;
        break;
      }
    }
      if(flag == 1)
      return 0;
      else
      return 1;
}
```

Substring check For substring recognition, we will find the occurrence of string `B` in string `A`.

For example,

A = 'A B C D'

B = 'BC' or 'BCD' and so on

There are two possibilities:

1. Either `B` is a substring of `A` or
2. `B` is not a substring of `A`.

Program Code 2.14 checks if a given string is a substring or not.

PROGRAM CODE 2.14

```
int String :: substring(String B)
{
  int j = 0, flag = 0;
  for(i = 0; A.Str[i] != '\0' || B.Str[j] != '\0'; i++)
  {
    if(A.Str[i] == B.Str[j])
    {
      j++;
      flag = 1;
    }
    else
    {
      j = 0;
      flag = 0;
    }
  }
```

```
    if(flag == 1)
       return 1;
  else
       return 0;
}
```

2.13 PROS AND CONS OF ARRAYS

We have studied an array as an abstract data type and also its implementation. We have also studied and analyzed a few applications that use an array as a data structure. Let us list the characteristics, pros, and cons of an array as a data structure.

2.13.1 Characteristics

The characteristics of an array are as follows:

1. An array is a finite ordered collection of homogeneous data elements.
2. In an array, successive elements are stored at a fixed distance apart.
3. An array is defined as a set of pairs—index and value.
4. An array allows direct access to any element.
5. In an array, insertion and deletion of elements in-between positions require data movement.
6. An array provides static allocation, which means the space allocation done once during the compile time cannot be changed during run-time.

2.13.2 Advantages

The various merits of the array as a data structure are as follows:

1. Arrays permit efficient random access in constant time 0(1).
2. Arrays are most appropriate for storing a fixed amount of data and also for high frequency of data retrievals as data can be accessed directly.
3. Arrays are among the most compact data structures; if we store 100 integers in an array, it takes only as much space as the 100 integers, and no more (unlike a linked list in which each data element has an additional link field).
4. Arrays are well known in applications such as searching, hash tables, matrix operations, and sorting.
5. Wherever there is a direct mapping between the elements and their position, such as an ordered list, arrays are the most suitable data structures.
6. Ordered lists such as polynomials are most efficiently handled using arrays.
7. Arrays are useful to form the basis for several complex data structures such as heaps and hash tables and can be used to represent strings, stacks, and queues.

2.13.3 Disadvantages

Some of the disadvantages of arrays are as follows:

1. Arrays provide static memory management. Hence, during execution, the size can neither be grown nor shrunk.
2. There is a solution to handle the problem, that is, to declare the array of some arbitrarily maximum size. This leads to two other problems:
   (a) In future, if the user still needs to exceed this limit, it is not possible.
   (b) Higher the maximum, the more is the memory wastage because very often, many locations remain unused but still allocated (reserved) for the program. This leads to poor utilization of space.
3. Static allocation in an array is a problem associated with implementation in many programming languages except a few such as JAVA.
4. An array is inefficient when often data is inserted or deleted as insertion or deletion of an element in an array needs a lot of data movement.
5. Hence, an array is inefficient for the applications that often need insert and delete operations in between.
6. A drawback due to the simplicity of arrays is the possibility of referencing a non-existent element by using an index outside the valid range. This is known as *exceeding the array bounds*. The result is a program working with incorrect data. In the worst case, the whole system can crash. In C++, the powerful syntax is unfortunately prone to this kind of error. Some languages have built-in bounds checking and do not index an array outside of its permitted range.

2.13.4 Applications of Arrays

The following list indicates where arrays are most beneficial:

1. Although useful in their own right, arrays also form the basis for several more complex data structures such as heaps and hash tables and can be used to represent strings, stacks, and queues.
2. All these applications benefit from the compactness and direct access benefits of arrays.
3. Arrays can be used to store two-dimensional data when represented as matrix and matrix operations.
4. They can also be used for indexing, searching, and sorting keys, about which we shall learn in the Chapters 9 and 10.
5. In some applications where the data is the same or is missing for most values of the indices, or for large ranges of indices, space is saved by not storing an array at all. Such an application is called *sparse matrix representation*. This has an associative array with integer keys. There are many specialized data structures specifically for applications, including address translation table and routing tables.

RECAPITULATION

- Data can be organized in either a linear or a non-linear manner. In linear or sequential organization, all the elements can be arranged in a particular sequence and each element has a unique successor (and/or predecessor) in the sequence.
- Linear data organization can be realized using arrays. An array is a very common and simple means of sequential (or linear) data structuring and is supported by almost all programming languages.
- Sequential organization allows storing data at a fixed distance apart. If the ith element is stored at location X, then the next sequential $(i+1)^{th}$ element is stored at location $X + C$, where C is a constant.
- An array allows direct or random access to any data element of the list at a constant time, that is, $O(1)$ as sequential organization uses continuous memory locations to store its data. The data access time remains constant for accessing any element of the list, irrespective of the total length or size of the data list.
- For in-between insertions or deletions of elements, we need to perform data shifting to keep the organization consistent and intact, which is expensive with respect to time.
- When data is organized in multiple dimensions, a one-dimensional array proves to be insufficient, and we need two-dimensional, three-dimensional, or multidimensional arrays. A multidimensional array is an extension of a two-dimensional array to three, four, or more dimensions.
- Arrays are efficiently used for matrix, polynomial, and string operations.

KEY TERMS

Array An array is a finite ordered collection of homogeneous data elements that provides direct access (or random access) to any of its elements.

Linear and non-linear data structure In linear (or sequential) organization, all the elements can be arranged in a particular sequence, and each element has a unique successor (and/or predecessor) in the sequence. When each element may have one or more successors (or predecessors), it is called a non-linear data structure.

Memory representation of array A computer's memory can be well thought-out as one long list of bits grouped together into bytes and/or words. Each of them can be referred to as just *location* to avoid machine-dependent details about whether memory is structured with a one–byte, two–byte, or an *n*-byte word. In addition, the addressing scheme such as byte addressable or word addressable varies.

Memory representation of two-dimensional arrays Let us consider a two-dimensional array *A* of dimension $m \times n$. Though the array is multi-dimensional, it is usually stored in memory as a single-dimensional array. A multidimensional array is represented in memory as a sequence of $m \times n$ consecutive memory locations. The elements of a multidimensional array can be stored in memory as a row-major representation or a column-major representation.

Sequential organization Sequential organization allows storing data at a fixed distance apart. If the ith element is stored at location X, then the next sequential $(i+1)^{th}$ element is stored at location $X +$ C, where C is a constant.

Sparse matrix In many situations, the matrix size is very large but out of it, most of the elements are 0s (not necessarily always 0s). Only a small fraction of the matrix is actually used. A matrix of such a type is called a sparse matrix, as the matrix is filled sparsely by data and most of the positions are empty or contain non-relevant data.

EXERCISES

Multiple choice questions

1. An array is a
   (a) linear data structure
   (b) non-linear data structure
   (c) complex data structure
   (d) none of these
2. Which of the following expressions access the $(i, j)^{th}$ element of an $m \times n$ matrix stored in column-major form?
   (a) $n \times (i - 1) + j$
   (b) $m \times (j - 1) + i$
   (c) $m \times (n - j) + j$
   (d) $n \times (m - i) + j$
3. An $n \times n$ array V is defined as follows:
   $V[i, j] = i - j$ for all i, j, where $1 < i \leq n$, $1 \leq j \leq n$
   The sum of the elements of the array V is
   (a) 0
   (b) $n - 1$
   (c) $n^2 - 3n + 2$
   (d) $n^2 (n + 1)/2$
4. The smallest element of an array's index is called its
   (a) lower bound
   (b) upper bound
   (c) range
   (d) extraction
5. Pick out the correct answers from the following:
   (a) During array declaration, no storage is set aside
   (b) Array definition precedes array declaration
   (c) Array declaration precedes array definition
   (d) Initialization cannot be done during array declaration
6. The parameter passing mechanism for an array is
   (a) call by value
   (b) call by value-result
   (c) call by reference
   (d) none of the above
7. If n has the value 3, then the statement $a[{+}{+}n] = n{+}{+}$
   (a) assigns 3 to $a[5]$
   (b) assigns 4 to $a[5]$
   (c) assigns 4 to $a[4]$
   (d) produces unpredictable results
8. Let A be a two-dimensional array declared as follows:
   An array [1, ..., 10] [1, ..., 15] of integers; assuming that each integer takes one memory location, the array is stored in row-majored order, and that the first element of the array is stored at location 100, what is the address of the element $A[i][j]$?
   (a) $15i + j + 84$
   (b) $15j + i + 84$
   (c) $10i + j + 89$
   (d) $10j + i + 89$
9. To traverse an array means
   (a) to process each element in an array
   (b) to delete an element from an array
   (c) to insert an element into an array
   (d) to combine two arrays into a single array
10. A matrix is said to be sparse when
   (a) most of the elements are non-zero
   (b) most of the elements are zero
   (c) all of its elements are non-zero
   (d) None of the above.

Review questions

1. You have two arrays, A and B, each of 10 integers. Write an algorithm that tests if every element of array A is equal to its corresponding element in array B.
2. Write an algorithm that reverses the elements of an array so that the last element becomes the first, the second to the last becomes the second, and so on.
3. An $m \times n$ matrix is said to have a saddle point if some entry $A[i, j]$ is of the smallest value in row

i and the largest value in column j. Write a C++ program that determines the location of a saddle point, if one exists. What is the computing time complexity of your program?

4. Write a function in C++ called `merge_arrays()` that takes two stored arrays and merges them into one stored array. The function header should be

```
void merge_arrays()
double *a, *b, *c;
```

where `a` and `b` are pointers to the two stored arrays and `c` is a pointer to the resulting merged array.

5. Modify `merge_arrays()` of Review Question 4 so that it eliminates duplicate entries.
6. A lower triangular array a is an $n \times n$ array in which $a[i][j] == 0$, if $i < j$. What is the maximum number of non-zero elements in such an array? How can these elements be stored sequentially in memory? Develop an algorithm for accessing $a[i][j]$, where $i > j$. Define an upper triangular array in an analogous manner and do the same for such an array as for the lower triangular array.
7. Let a and b be two $n \times n$ lower triangular arrays. Show how an $n \times (n + 1)$ array c can be used to contain the non-zero elements of the two arrays. Which elements of c represent the elements $a[i][j]$ and $b[i][j]$, respectively?
8. What is meant by the terms 'row-major order' and 'column-major order'?
9. The array `data[15, 25]` is stored in memory in row-major order. If the base address is 500 and element size is 5, calculate the address of the element `data[7, 12]`.
10. Imagine N people have decided to commit suicide by arranging themselves in a circle and killing the Mth person around the circle, closing ranks as each person drops out of the circle. Find out which person is the last to die. Write a C++ program to simulate the execution sequence.
11. Write a C++ program to find out the maximum and second maximum numbers from an array of integers.
12. The mode of an array of numbers is the number m in the array that is repeated most frequently. If more than one number is repeated with equal maximal frequencies, there is no mode. Write a C++ program that accepts an array of numbers and returns the mode or an indication that the mode does not exist.
13. Write a C++ program to delete duplicate elements from an array of 20 integers.
14. There are two arrays A and B. A contains 25 elements, whereas B contains 30 elements. Write a function to create an array C that contains only those elements that are common to A and B.
15. A magic square of size 5×5 contains different elements. Write a C++ function to verify whether the sum of each individual column elements, the sum of each individual row elements, and the sum of diagonal elements are equal.
16. Write a C++ program to build a sparse matrix as an array. Write functions to check if the sparse matrix is a square, diagonal, lower triangular, upper triangular, or tridiagonal matrix.
17. Write a C++ program to subtract two sparse matrices implemented as an array.

Answers to multiple choice questions

1. (a) 2. (b) 3. (a) 4. (a) 5. (a), (b), (d) 6. (a)
7. (d) The output is compiler-dependent. 8. (a) 9. (b) 10. (b)

3 STACKS

OBJECTIVES

After completing this chapter, the reader will be able to understand the following:

- All aspects of a stack as a data type such as
  - last in first out (LIFO) data access
  - push, pop, and other stack operations
  - contiguous implementation of a stack
- Realization of a stack using arrays
- Choosing appropriate realizations for practical applications
- Implementation of multi-stacks
- Use of stacks in expression conversion, recursion, reversing data, and other applications

Stacks and queues are special data structures where insert and delete operations are performed only at specific ends rather than at intermediate or any other random positions. These are special cases of ordered lists. As we have seen in Chapter 2, linear data structures such as arrays and linked lists allow us to insert or delete an element from any position in the list; stacks and queues are linear lists with restrictions on these operations. Let us discuss these concepts in detail.

3.1 CONCEPT OF STACKS AND QUEUES

Stacks and *queues* are the two data structures where insert and delete operations are applied at specific ends only. These are special cases of ordered lists and are also called *controlled linear lists*. There is a wide variety of software applications where we need these restricted data structure operations. The following are some examples where stacks and queues are generally used:

1. Queues are widely used in applications that maintain a list of printing jobs waiting at a network printer. Here, one queue that can hold all print requests from different users is kept.
2. Handling function calls in programs very often restricts access at one end to keep track of the returning position. In such implementation, we need to use stacks. We can keep track of the return address to earlier function after furnishing/finishing a function call using stacks.

We shall discuss stacks in this chapter and queues in Chapter 4.

3.2 STACKS

In our everyday life, we come across many examples of stacks, for example, a stack of books, a stack of dishes, or a stack of chairs. The data structure *stack* is very similar to these practical examples (Fig. 3.1).

Fig. 3.1 Sample real world stacks

Consider a stack of books on a table. We can easily put a new book on the top of the stack, and similarly, we can easily remove the topmost book as compared to the books lying in-between or at the bottom positions. In the same way, only the topmost element of a stack can be accessed while direct access of other intermediate positions is not feasible. Elements may be added to or removed from only one end, called the *top* of a stack.

The linear data structures such as arrays and linked lists allow users to insert or delete an element at any position in the list, that is, we can insert or delete an element at the beginning, at the end, or at any intermediate position.

A *stack* is defined as a restricted list where all insertions and deletions are made only at one end, the *top*. Each stack abstract data type (ADT) has a data member, commonly named as *top*, which points to the topmost element in the stack. There are two basic operations `push` and `pop` that can be performed on a stack; insertion of an element in the stack is called `push` and deletion of an element from the stack is called *pop*. In stacks, we cannot access data elements from any intermediate positions other than the top position.

Given a stack S = (a_1, a_2, ..., a_n). We say that as a_1 is the bottommost element, a_n is on top of the stack, and the element a_{i+1} is said to be on the top of a_i, $1 < i \le n$.

In Fig. 3.2, S = (*A*, *B*, *C*), where *A* is the bottommost element and *C* is the topmost element.

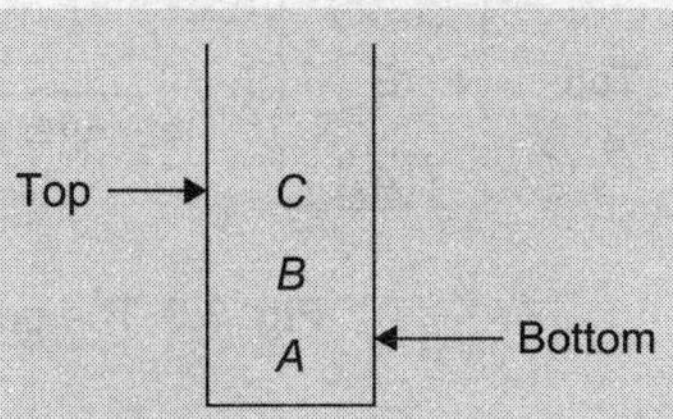

Fig. 3.2 A stack of three letters *A*, *B*, and *C*

3.2.1 Primitive Operations

The three basic stack operations are push, pop, and getTop. Besides these, there are some more operations that can be implemented on a stack such as stack_initialization, stack_empty, and stack_full. The stack_initialization operation prepares the stack for use and sets it to a vacant state. The stack_empty operation simply tests whether the stack is empty. The stack_empty operation is useful as a safeguard against an attempt to pop an element from an empty stack. Popping an empty stack is an error condition. The stack_empty condition is also termed *stack underflow*. In ideal conditions, stacks should possess infinite capacity so that the subsequent elements can always be pushed, regardless of the number of elements already present on the stack. However, computers always have finite memory capacity, and we do need to check the stack_full condition before doing push because pushing an element in a full stack is also an error condition. Such a stack full condition is called *stack overflow*.

Another stack operation is GetTop. This returns the top element of the stack without actually popping it. A few more stack operations include traversing the stack, counting the total number of elements in the stack, and copying the stack.

Let us quickly recall all the stack operations:

1. Push—inserts an element on the top of the stack
2. Pop—deletes an element from the top of the stack
3. GetTop—reads (only reading, not deleting) an element from the top of the stack
4. Stack_initialization—sets up the stack in an empty condition
5. Empty—checks whether the stack is empty
6. Full—checks whether the stack is full

Push

The push operation inserts an element on the top of the stack. The recently added element is always at the top of the stack. Before every push, we must ensure whether there is a room for a new element (Fig. 3.3).

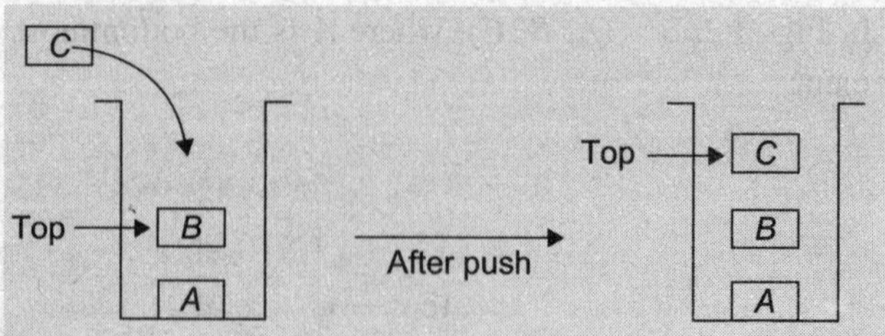

Fig. 3.3 The push operation

When there is no space to accommodate the new element on the stack, the stack is said to be *full* (Fig. 3.4). If the operation `push` is performed when the stack is full, it is said to be in *overflow* state, that is, no element can be added when the stack is full. The `push` operation modifies the *top* since the newly inserted element becomes the topmost element (Fig. 3.3).

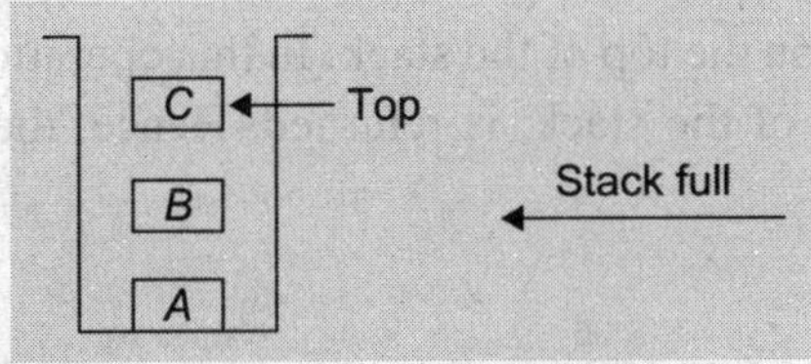

Fig. 3.4 The stack full condition (stack capacity = 3)

Pop

The `pop` operation deletes an element from the top of the stack and returns the same to the user. It modifies the stack so that the next element becomes the top element (Fig. 3.5).

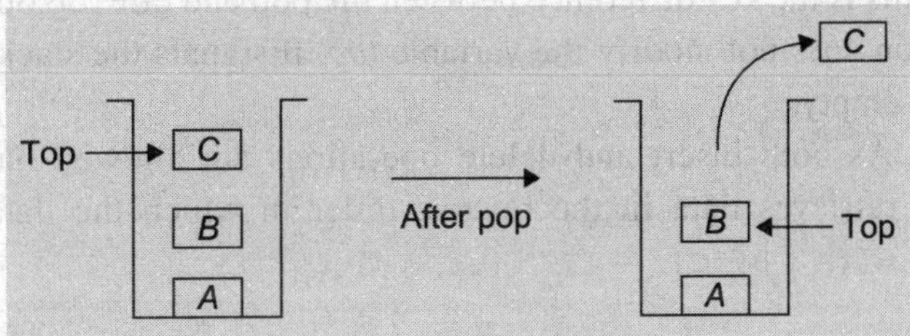

Fig. 3.5 The pop operation

When there is no element available on the stack, the stack is said to be *empty.* If `pop` is performed when the stack is empty, then the stack is said to be in an *underflow state* (Fig. 3.6).

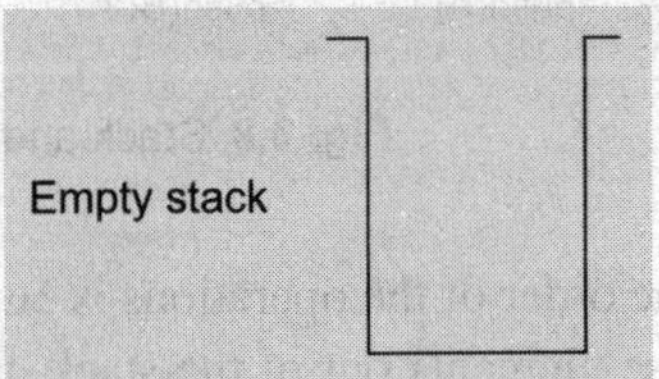

Fig. 3.6 The empty stack

The pop operation should not be performed when the stack is empty, and hence before every pop, we must ensure that the stack is not empty. After deleting the last element from the stack, the stack should be set to an empty state.

GetTop

The getTop operation gives information about the topmost element and returns the element on the top of the stack. In this operation, only a copy of the element, which is at the top of the stack, is returned. Hence, the top is still set to the same element (Fig. 3.7).

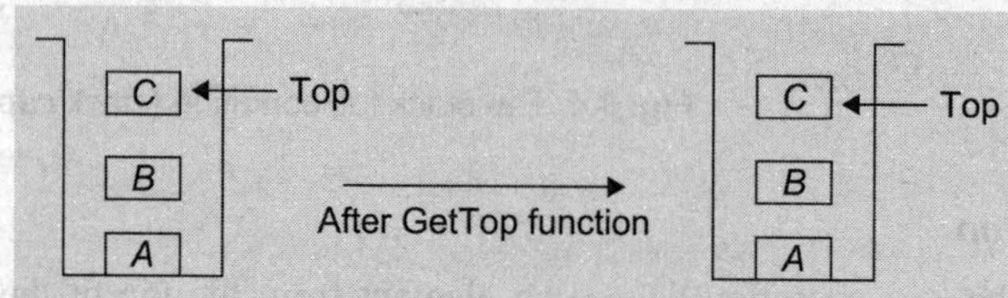

Fig. 3.7 The getTop operation

This is the key difference between the pop and getTop operations. The getTop operation does not modify the variable *top*. It signals the stack underflow error if the stack is empty.

As both insert and delete operations are allowed only at one end of the stack, it retrieves data in the reverse order in which the data is stored. In Fig. 3.8, let S = {A, B, C}.

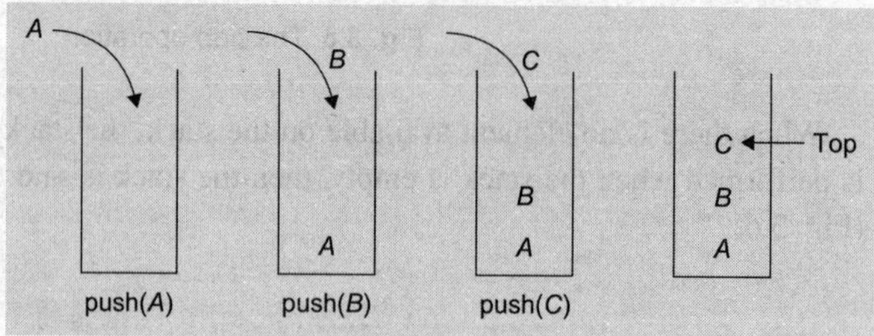

Fig. 3.8 Stack and push operations

Suppose that the order of the operations is push(A), push(B), and then push(C). When we remove these elements out of the stack, they will be removed in the order C, B, and then A. This is shown in Fig. 3.9.

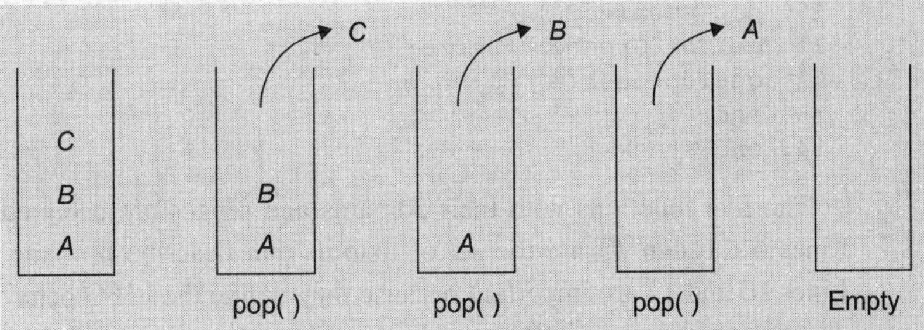

Fig. 3.9 Stack and pop operations

Elements are taken out in the reverse order of the insertion sequence. So a stack is often called *last in first out* (*LIFO*) or *first in last out* (*FILO*) data structure.

3.3 STACK ABSTRACT DATA TYPE

Let us now see the data object, operations, and axioms associated with the stack. Any sets of elements that are of the same data type can be used as a data object for stacks. The meaning of 'same data type' is that all the elements in the stack should be of the same nature, having common representational logical properties. For example, stack of integers, stack of names of students, stack of employee records, and stack of records of processes of the operating system.

The following five functions comprise a functional definition of a stack:

1. `Create(S)`—creates an empty stack
2. `Push(i, S)`—inserts the element *i* on the stack `S` and returns the modified stack
3. `Pop(S)`—removes the topmost element from the stack `S` and returns the modified stack
4. `GetTop(S)`—returns the topmost element of stack `S`
5. `Is_Empty(S)`—returns true if `S` is empty, otherwise returns false

However, when we choose to represent a stack, it must be possible to build these operations. Before we do this, let us describe formally the structure `stack`.

```
ADT Stack(element)
  1. Declare Create() → stack
  2. push(element, stack) → stack
  3. pop(stack) → stack
  4. getTop(stack) → element
  5. Is_Empty(stack) → Boolean;
  6. for all S ∈ stack, e ∈ element, Let
  7. Is_Empty(Create) = true
  8. Is_Empty(push(e, S)) = false
```

```
10. pop(push(e,S)) = S
11. getTop(Create) = error
12. getTop(push(e, S)) = e
13. end
14. end stack
```

The five functions with their domains and ranges are declared in lines 1 through 5. Lines 6 through 13 are the set of axioms that describe how the functions are related. Lines 10 and 12 are important because they define the LIFO behaviour of the stack. This description shows an infinite stack of no upper bound or roof on the number of elements specified. This will be discussed when we represent this structure using C++.

We studied the concept of ADT in Chapter 1. The ADT stack is defined in Section 3.3. To implement the ADT stack in C++, the operations are often implemented as functions to provide data abstraction. A program that uses stacks would access the stacks only through these functions and would not be concerned about the implementation.

3.4 REPRESENTATION OF STACKS USING SEQUENTIAL ORGANIZATION (ARRAYS)

A stack can be implemented using both a static data structure (array) and a dynamic data structure (linked list). The simplest way to represent a stack is by using a one-dimensional array. A stack implemented using an array is also called a *contiguous stack*.

An array is used to store an ordered list of elements. A stack is an ordered collection of elements. Hence, it would be very simple to manage a stack when represented using an array. The only difficulty with an array is its static memory allocation. Once declared, the size cannot be modified during run-time. We have already read that this leads to either poor utilization of the space or inability to accommodate all possible data elements. This is because we declare an array to be of arbitrarily maximum size before compilation.

Figure 3.10 shows the realization of a stack using arrays.

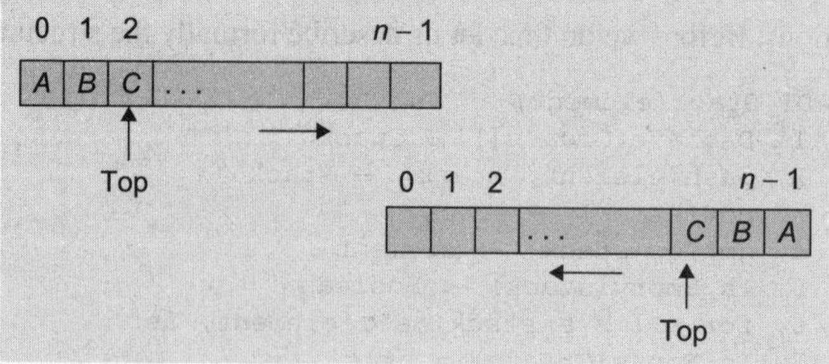

Fig. 3.10 Stack using array

Let `Stack[n]` be a one-dimensional array. When the stack is implemented using arrays, one of the two sides of the array can be considered as the top (upper) side and the other as the bottom (lower) side as in Fig. 3.10.

Let us discuss the top side, which is most commonly used. The elements are stored in the stack from the first location onwards. The first element is stored at the 0th location of the array `Stack`, which means at `Stack[0]`, the second element at `Stack[1]`, the ith element at `Stack[i − 1]`, and the nth element at `Stack[n − 1]`. Associated with the array will be an integer variable, *top*, which points to the top element in the stack. The initial value of *top* is −1 when the stack is empty. It can hold the elements from index 0, and can grow to a maximum of $n - 1$ as this is a static stack using arrays.

Program Code 3.1 gives the definition of class `Stack` and lists the function prototypes for a set of basic operations.

PROGRAM CODE 3.1

```
class Stack
{
  private:
     int Stack[50];
     int MaxCapacity;
     int top;
  public:
     Stack()
     {
        MaxCapacity = 50;
        top = -1;
        currentsize = 0;
     }
     int getTop();
     int pop();
     void push(int Element);
     int Empty();
     int CurrSize();
     int IsFull();
};
```

The simplest way to implement an ADT stack is using arrays. We initialize the variable `top` to −1 using a constructor to denote an empty stack. The bottom element is represented using the 0th position, that is, the first element of the array. The next element is stored at the 1st position and so on. The variable `top` indicates the current element at the top of the stack.

3.4.1 Create

The stack when created is initially empty. The implementation of the stack could be using an array or using a linked list implementation. For array implementation, its size should be predefined, and its implementation time should not exceed run-time. However, in case of a linked implementation, this limitation is overcome. Let us first look at a simple stack implementation. At the end of this chapter, we shall study about other better array-based implementations using C++ features such as templates and dynamic arrays.

For each and every stack, there is an operational end operator variable called the *top* which points to the element at the top of the stack. Hence, this integer variable holds the index of the array. It can also be implemented as a pointer variable. Let us currently use it as an integer variable. Even though we call it as a pointer pointing to the top element of the stack, it is an integer index variable.

The constructor must initialize the stack *top*, so as to represent an empty stack, to a value that represents the top of the empty stack. We cannot initialize it to one of the values in the range of 0 to $n - 1$ because these are the indices of the stack array. The indices 0 to $n - 1$ represent one of the locations going to hold the stack elements. However, it can be initialized to any arbitrary integer value other than 0 to $n - 1$. Each `push` operation increments *top* by one. This is to update *top* to point to a newly added element. When the element is added to the empty stack, *top* should be set to 0 as the new element will be stored at `Stack[0]`. Hence, it is suitable to initialize the *top* to –1. This is the most suitable initialization instead of any other arbitrary value.

```
int Stack[100];
int top = -1;
```

These statements create an empty stack of size 100, which will hold integer values, and the variable *top* is initialized to –1.

3.4.2 Empty

`Empty` is an operation that takes the stack as an argument, checks whether it is empty or not, and returns the Boolean value *true* or *false*, respectively.

The stack empty state can be checked by comparing the value of *top* with the value –1, because *top* = –1 represents an empty stack.

```
if(top == -1)
     return 1;
else
     return 0;
```

3.4.3 GetTop

The `getTop` operation checks for the stack empty state. If the stack is empty, it reports the 'stack underflow' error message; else it returns a copy of the element that is at the top of the stack. Here, *top* is not updated as the element is not deleted from the stack; rather, the element is still at the top location. The element is just read from the stack.

Hence, its behaviour can be described using the following statement:

```
if(top == -1)
      cout << "Stack underflow (empty)" << endl;
else
      return(Stack[top]);
```

3.4.4 Push

The `push` operation inserts an element onto the stack of maximum size `MaxCapacity`. Element insertion is possible only if the stack is not full. We have not discussed the `full` operation in ADT. The stack is practically full when the array size exceeds (or the memory is full, which can happen when we use the linked list representation of the stack). Hence, the stack full state can be verified by comparing the top with `MaxCapacity − 1`. If the stack is not full, the top is incremented by 1 and the element is added on the top of the stack. In brief,

```
if(top == MaxCapacity - 1)
   cout << "Stack overflow (full)";
else
{
   top ++;              //increment top by one
   Stack[top] = Element;          //add the element in new top position
}
```

3.4.5 Pop

The `pop` operation deletes the element at the top of the stack and returns the same. This is done only if the stack is not empty. If the stack is empty, no deletion is possible. This is checked by the `empty()` function. If the stack is not empty, then the element at the top of the stack is returned and the top is decreased by one.

This is executed as

```
if(top == -1)
      cout << "Stack underflow\n";
else
      return(Stack[top--]);
```

The stack full condition signals that more storage is needed, and in many applications of stacks, the stack empty state signals the end of processing. Program Code 3.2 illustrates the basic operations on a stack.

PROGRAM CODE 3.2

```
class Stack
{
   private:
      int Stack[50];
      int MaxCapacity;
      int top;
   public:
      Stack()
      {
         MaxCapacity = 50;
         top = -1;
      }
      int getTop();
      int pop();
      void push(int Element);
      int Empty();
      int CurrSize();
      int IsFull();
};

int Stack :: getTop()
{
   if(!Empty())
      return(Stack[top]);
}

int Stack :: pop()
{
   if(!Empty())
      return(Stack[top--]);
}

int Stack :: Empty()
{
   if(top == -1)
      return 1;
   else
      return 0;
}
```

```
int Stack :: IsFull()
{
   if(top == MaxCapacity - 1)
      return 1;
   else
      return 0;
}

int Stack :: CurrSize()
{
   return(top + 1);
}

void Stack :: push(int Element)
{
   if(!IsFull())
      Stack[++top] = Element;
}

void main()
{
   Stack S;
   S.pop();
   S.push(1);
   S.push(2);
   cout << S.getTop() << endl;
   cout << S.pop() << endl;
   cout << S.pop() << endl;
}
```

3.5 STACKS USING TEMPLATE

The stack using an array and its operations in Program Code 3.2 is defined to operate on integer data. To define stack for floating point data, we need to change `int Stack[]` to `float Stack[]` in the declaration of data members of the class. This can be done each time the data type of array elements varies, by editing the code using a text editor and then recompiling it. A *template* is a variable that can be instantiated to any data type. This data type could be of the built-in or user-defined type. Program Code 3.2 is rewritten using templates as Program Code 3.3.

PROGRAM CODE 3.3

```
template <class T>
class Stack
{
   private:
      T * Stack;                    // stack using pointer
      int top;
      int Size;
   public:
      Stack(int StackSize = 20 );          // constructor
      T& getTop();
      T& pop();
      void push(const T& Element);
      bool IsEmpty();
      int CurrSize();
};

template <class T>
Stack <T> :: Stack(int StackSize) : Size(StackSize)
{
   Stack = new T[Size];
   top = -1;
}

template <class T>
T& Stack :: getTop()
{
   if !IsEmpty()
      return(Stack[top]);
   else
      cout << "Stack is Empty" << endl;
}

template <class T>
T& Stack :: pop()
{
   if !IsEmpty()
      return(Stack[top--]);
   else
```

```
        cout << "Stack is Empty" << endl;
}
Bool Stack :: IsEmpty()
{
    if(top == -1)
        return 1;
    else
        return 0;
}

Bool Stack :: IsFull()
{
    if(top == MaxCapacity - 1)
        return 1;
    else
        return 0;
}

int Stack :: CurrSize()
{
    return(top + 1);
}

void Stack :: push(const T & Element)
{
    if(!IsFull())
        cout << "Stack is Full" << endl;
    else
        Stack[++top] = Element;
}
```

3.6 MULTIPLE STACKS

Often, data is represented using several stacks. The *contiguous stack* (stack using an array) uses separate arrays for more than one stack, if needed. The use of a contiguous stack when more than one stack is needed is not a space-efficient approach, because many locations in the stacks are often left unused. An efficient solution to this problem is to use a single array to store more than one stack. Figure 3.11 shows two stacks using one array.

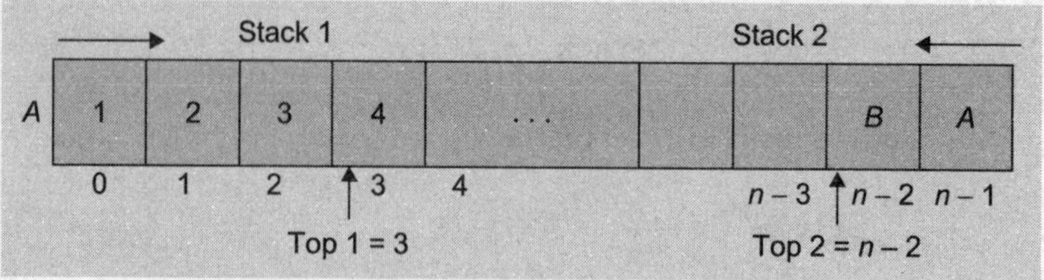

Fig. 3.11 Initial configuration for two stacks in A[0], ..., A[n – 1]

Multiple stacks can be implemented by sequentially mapping these stacks into `A[0], ..., A[n - 1]`. The solution is simple if we implement only two stacks. The first stack grows towards `A[n – 1]` from `A[0]` and the second stack grows towards `A[0]` from `A[n - 1]`.

This way, we can make use of the space most efficiently so that the stack is full only when the top of one stack reaches the top of other stack.

The difficulty arises when we have to represent *m* stacks in the memory. We can divide `A[0, ..., n – 1]` into *m* segments and allocate one of these segments to each of the *m* stacks. This initial division into segments may be done in proportion to the expected sizes of the various stacks, if the sizes are known. In the absence of such information, `A[0, ..., n – 1]` may be divided into equal segments. For each stack `i`, we shall use `s[i]` to represent a position one less than the position in `A` for the bottommost element of that stack as shown in Fig. 3.12.

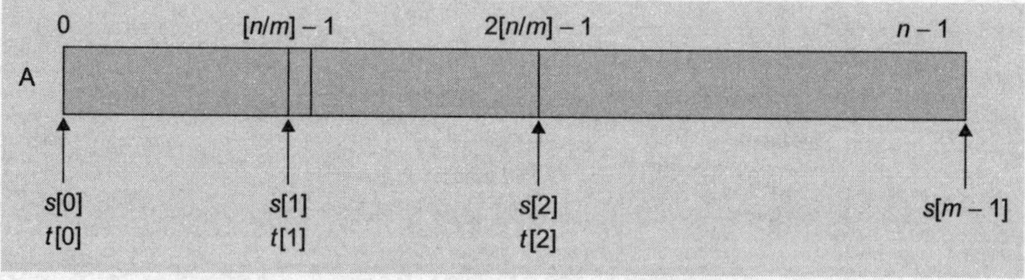

Fig. 3.12 Initial configuration for *m* stacks in A [0, ..., n – 1]

Here, `t[i]`, $0 \le i \le m - 1$ will point to the topmost element of the stack `i`. We shall use the boundary condition `s[i] = t[i]` if the `i`th stack is empty.

Initially, `s[i] = t[i] = [n/m] × (i – 1)`, $0 \le i \le n - 1$.

`Stack[i]` will grow from `s[i] + 1` to `s[i + 1]` before it catches up with the `(i + 1)`th stack. Using this scheme, the `m_push` and `m_pop` programs can be written as in Program Code 3.4.

PROGRAM CODE 3.4

```
Stack :: m_push(int i, char x)
{
   // push x to the ith stack
   if(t[i] == s[i + 1])
      Stack_full(i);
   else
   {
      t[i] = t[i] + 1;
      A[t[i]] = x;
   }
}

char Stack::m_pop(int i)
{
   // pop topmost element of stack i
   if(t[i] == s[i])
      Stack_empty(i);
   else
   {
      t[i] = t[i] - 1;
      return(A[t[i] + 1]);
   }
}
```

`Stack_full()` and `Stack_empty()` are the functions to be written depending on the strategy followed in each case. For example, if we permit the addition of elements to stacks as long as there is some free space in array `A`, the following steps may be one of the solutions to this:

1. Determine the last `i < j ≤ m`, such that there is a free space between the stacks `j` and `j + 1`, that is, `t[j] s[j + 1]`. If there is such an `A[j]`, we can move the stacks `i + 1, i + 2, ..., j` one position to the right (treating `A[n]` as the rightmost) and can create a space between the stacks `i` and `i + 1`.
2. If there is no `j` in step 1, then check the left side of stack `i`. Find the largest `j` such that `1 ≤ j ≤ i` and there is space between the stacks `j` and `j + 1`, that is, `t[j] < s[j + 1]`. If there is such a `j`, then move the stacks `j + 1, j + 2, ..., i` by one space left, creating a free space between the stacks `i` and `i + 1`.
3. If there is no such `j` satisfying the conditions of either steps 1 or 2, then all the `n` spaces of `A` are utilized, and there is no free space.

3.7 APPLICATIONS OF STACK

The stack data structure is used in a wide range of applications. A few of them are the following:

1. Converting infix expression to postfix and prefix expressions
2. Evaluating the postfix expression
3. Checking well-formed (nested) parenthesis
4. Reversing a string
5. Processing function calls
6. Parsing (analyse the structure) of computer programs
7. Simulating recursion
8. In computations such as decimal to binary conversion
9. In backtracking algorithms (often used in optimizations and in games)

3.8 EXPRESSION EVALUATION AND CONVERSION

The most frequent application of stacks is in the evaluation of arithmetic expressions. An arithmetic expression is made of *operands*, *operators*, and *delimiters*. When high-level programming languages came into existence, one of the major difficulties faced by computer scientists was to generate machine language instructions that could properly evaluate any arithmetic expression.

A complex assignment statement such as

$$X = (A/B + C \times D \; - F \times G/Q)$$

might have several meanings, and even if the meanings were uniquely defined, it is still difficult to generate a correct and reasonable instruction sequence. Fortunately, the solution we have today is both elegant and simple. Till date, this conversion is considered as one of the major aspects of compiler writing.

Let us see the difficulties in understanding the meaning of expressions. The first problem in understanding the meaning of an expression is to decide the order in which the operations are to be carried out. This demands that every language must uniquely define such an order.

For instance, consider the following expression:

$$X = a/b \times c - d$$

Let $a = 1$, $b = 2$, $c = 3$, and $d = 4$.

One of the meanings that can be drawn from this expression could be

$$X = (1/2) \times (3 - 4) = -1/2$$

Another way to evaluate the same expression could be

$$X = (1/(2 \times 3)) - 4 = -23/6$$

To avoid more than one meaning being drawn out of an expression, we have to specify the order of operation by using parentheses. For instance,

$$X = (a/b) \times (c - d)$$

To fix the order of evaluation, assign each operator a priority. Even though we write the expression in parentheses, we still query whether to evaluate (A/B) first or to evaluate $(C - D)$ first. Once the priorities are assigned, then within any pairs of parentheses the operators with the highest priority are to be evaluated first. While evaluating an expression, the following operation precedence is usually used:

The following operators are written in descending order of their precedence:

1. Exponentiation (^), Unary (+), Unary (–), and not (~)
2. Multiplication (×) and division (/)
3. Addition (+) and subtraction (–)
4. Relational operators <, ≤ , =, ≠, ≥, >
5. Logical AND
6. Logical OR

Some integer values can be assigned as priority, as in Table 3.1.

Table 3.1 Operators and their priorities

Arithmetic, boolean, and relational operators	Priority
^, Unary +, Unary – , ~	1
×, /	2
+, –	3
<, ≤, =, ≠, ≥, >	4
AND	5
OR	6

Note that all the relational operators have the same priority. Exponentiation (^) and unary operators (+, –, and ~) have the highest priority. When there are two adjacent operators with the same priority, again the question arises as to which one to evaluate first. For example, the expression, $A + B - C$ can be understood in two ways—$(A + B) - C$ or $A + (B - C)$.

This needs a decision on whether to evaluate the expression from right to left or left to right. Expressions such as $A + B - C$ and $A \times B/C$ are to be evaluated from left to right. However, the expression A ^ B ^ C is to be evaluated from right to left as

A ^ (B ^ C). For example, to compute 2 ^ 3 ^ 2, we need to represent and evaluate it as 2 ^ (3 ^ 2). When evaluated from left to right, the expression may be evaluated as ((2 ^ 3) ^ 2), which is wrong!

Hence, the operators need to decide on a rule for proceeding from left to right for all expressions except the operator exponential. This order of evaluation, from left to right or right to left, is called *associativity*. Exponentiation is right associative and all other operators are left associative. When we write a parenthesized expression, these rules can be overridden. In the parenthesized expressions, the innermost parenthesized expression is evaluated first.

Let us consider the expression

$$X = A/B \wedge C + D \times E - A \times C$$

By using priorities and associativity rules, the expression X is rewritten as

$$X = A/(B \wedge C) + (D \times E) - (A \times C)$$

For example, let X be an infix expression as = ((2 + 3) × 4)/2

We manually evaluate the innermost expression first as ((5) × 4)/2, followed by the next parenthesized inner expression (20)/2, which produces the result 10.

Still the question remains as to how a compiler can accept such an expression and produce the correct code. The solution is to rework on the expression to a form called the *postfix notation*.

3.8.1 Polish Notation and Expression Conversion

The Polish Mathematician Han Lukasiewicz suggested a notation called *Polish notation*, which gives two alternatives to represent an arithmetic expression, namely the *postfix* and *prefix* notations. The fundamental property of Polish notation is that the order in which the operations are to be performed is determined by the positions of the operators and operands in the expression. Hence, the advantage is that parentheses is not required while writing expressions in Polish notation. The conventional way of writing the expression is called *infix*, because the binary operators occur between the operands, and unary operators precede their operand. For example, the expression $((A + B) \times C)/D$ is an infix expression. In postfix notation, the operator is written after its operands, whereas in prefix notation, the operator precedes its operands. Table 3.2 shows one sample expression in all three notations.

Table 3.2 Example expression in various forms—infix, prefix, and postfix

Infix	Prefix	Postfix
(operand)(operator)(operand)	(operator)(operand)(operand)	(operand)(operand)(operator)
$(A + B) \times C$	$\times{+}ABC$	$AB + C\times$

In Example 3.1, the conversion of an expression to its postfix and prefix notati[...] cussed.

EXAMPLE 3.1 Convert the following expression to its postfix and prefix notat[...]ons:

$$X = A/B \wedge C + D \times E - A \times C$$

Solution By applying the rules of priority and associativity, this expression can be written in the following form:

$$X = ((A/(B \wedge C)) + (D \times E) - (A \times C))$$

It can be reworked to get its equivalent postfix and prefix expressions.

Postfix: $ABC \wedge / \, DE \times + \, AC \times -$

Prefix: $- + / \, A \wedge BC \times DE \times AC$

3.8.2 Need for Prefix and Postfix Expressions

We just studied that evaluation of an infix expression using a computer needs proper code generation by the compiler without any ambiguity and is difficult because of various aspects such as the operator's priority and associativity. This problem can be overcome by writing or converting the infix expression to an alternate notation such as the prefix or the postfix. The postfix and prefix expressions possess many advantages as follows:

1. The need for parenthesis as in an infix expression is overcome in postfix and prefix notations.
2. The priority of operators is no longer relevant.
3. The order of evaluation depends on the position of the operator but not on priority and associativity.
4. The expression evaluation process is much simpler than attempting a direct evaluation from the infix notation.

Let us see how postfix expressions are evaluated.

3.8.3 Postfix Expression Evaluation

The postfix expression may be evaluated by making a left-to-right scan, stacking operands, and evaluating operators using the correct number from the stack as operands and again placing the result onto the stack. This evaluation process is much simpler than attempting a direct evaluation from the infix notation. This process continues till the stack is not empty or on occurrence of the character #, which denotes the end of the expression.

Algorithm 3.1 lists the steps involved in the evaluation of the postfix expression *E*.

ALGORITHM 3.1

```
1. Let E denote the postfix expression
2. Let Stack denote the stack data structure to be used & let Top = -1
3. while(1) do
   begin
     X = get_next_token(E)  // Token is an operator, operand, or delimiter
     if(X = #) {end of expression}
        then return
     if(X is an operand)
        then push(X) onto Stack
     else {X is operator}
     begin
        OP1 = pop() from Stack
        OP2 = pop() from Stack
        Tmp = evaluate(OP1, X, OP2)
        push(Tmp) on Stack
     end
        {If X is operator then pop the correct number of operands
        from stack for operator X. Perform the operation and push the
        result, if any, onto the stack}
   end
4. stop
```

It is assumed that the last character in *E* is '#'. A procedure `get_next_token` is used to extract the next token from *E*. A token is an operand, an operator, or a #. A one-dimensional array `Stack[n]` is used as a stack.

Let us consider an example postfix expression $E = AB + C\times\#$. Now, let us scan this expression from left to right, character by character, as represented in Fig. 3.13.

This evaluation process is much simpler than the evaluation of the infix expression. Let us now devise an algorithm for converting an infix expression to a postfix notation. To see how to devise an algorithm for translating from infix to postfix, note that the operands in both notations appear in the same sequence. Let us also learn how we can manually convert an infix expression into a postfix expression.

The following are the steps for manually converting an expression from one notation to another:

1. Initially, fully parenthesize the given infix expression. Use operator precedence and associativity rules for the same.
2. Now, move all operators so that they replace their corresponding right parenthesis.
3. Finally, delete all parentheses, and we get the postfix expression.

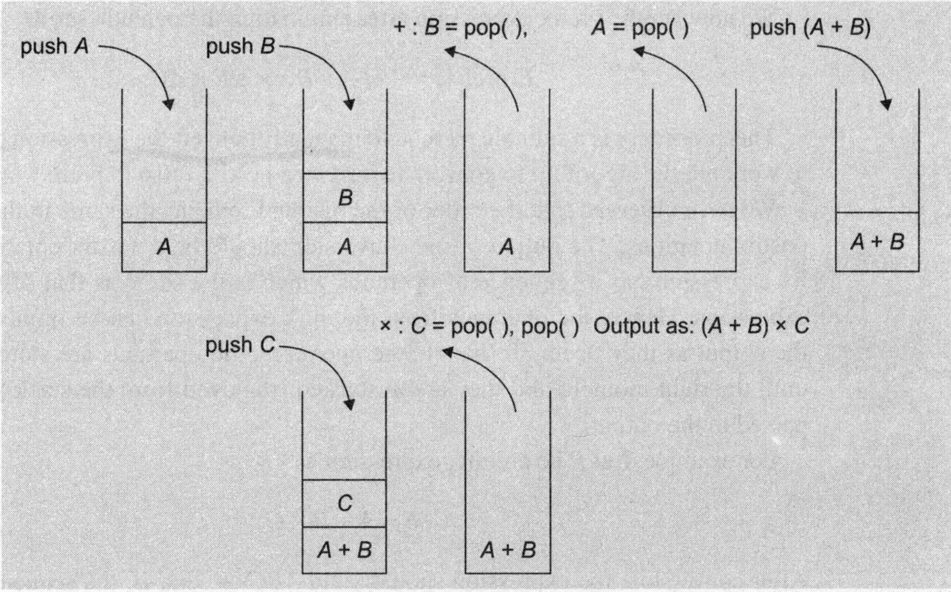

Fig. 3.13 Evaluation of postfix expression $AB + C\times$

The evaluation of a postfix expression is simple, but now we need to convert an infix expression to its postfix form. Let us consider an example $E = A/B \wedge C + D \times E - A \times C$.

Let us fully parenthesize the same as

$$E = (((A/(B \wedge C)) + (D \times E)) - (A \times C))$$

Let us move all operators to the corresponding right parenthesis and replace the same.

$$E = (((A/(B \wedge C)) + (D \times E)) - (A \times C))$$

Now let us eliminate all parentheses. We get the postfix equivalent of the infix expression.

$$E(\text{postfix}) = ABC \wedge / \; DE \times + \; AC \times -$$

This method can be used to get an equivalent prefix notation too as follows:

$$(((A/(B \wedge C)) + (D \times E)) - (A \times C))$$

We now get the prefix expression after eliminating the parentheses as

$$E(\text{prefix}) = - +/ A \wedge BC \times DE \times AC$$

This procedure is a suitable method to manually convert the expression only. Let us try to work out the algorithm to convert an infix to a postfix (also to prefix).

We have observed that the order of the operand remains the same in the infix and the postfix notations. The output of the conversion should be a postfix notation. This postfix expression has a sequence of operands which is the same as that of the input infix expression. Hence, the operands from the infix expression can be immediately sent to the output as they occur. To handle the operators, the operands are stored in the stack until the right moment and they are unstacked (removed from the stack); they are then passed to the output.

For example, Let E be an infix expression as

$$E = A + B \times C$$

After conversion, the expression should yield $ABC\times+$, that is, the sequence of stacking them should be as given in Table 3.3.

Table 3.3 Infix to postfix conversion of the expression E = $A + B \times C$

Next character	Stack	Output
A	Empty	*A*
+	+	*A*
B	+	*AB*

Now, we have to decide about the operator ×. This is illustrated in Table 3.4(a).

Here, note that the algorithm must decide whether the operator × gets placed on the top of the stack or the operator + is to be popped off. Since operator × has the highest priority, we should stack it so as to get the sequence of operations for expression X_2 as shown in Table 3.4(b).

Table 3.4 Handling and stacking of the × operator in expressions

(a) Handling of the × operator		
	Infix	Postfix
Examples	$X_1 = (A + B) \times C$ $X_2 = A + (B \times C)$	$AB + C\times$ $ABC\times+$

(Continued)

Tabel 3.4 (Continued)

(b) Stacking of the × operator		
Next character	**Stack**	**Output**
A	Empty	*A*
+	+	*A*
B	+	*AB*
×	+×	*AB*
C	+×	*ABC*
# (Pop all)	+×	*ABC* ×+

In addition, when the input is exhausted, we should output all remaining operators in the stack to get the postfix expression as *ABC*×+.

Let us consider one more example. The infix expression $A \times (B + C) \times D$, after conversion, should generate the postfix expression *ABC* +× *D*×, and hence, the sequence of operations should be as shown in Table 3.5.

Table 3.5 Infix to postfix conversion of the expression $A \times (B + C) \times D$

Next character	Stack	Output
A	Empty	*A*
×	×	*A*
(	×(	*A*
B	×(	*AB*
+	×(+	*AB*
C	×(+	*ABC*

(Continued)

At this point, unstack the corresponding left parenthesis and then delete the left and right parentheses; this should give the stack contents as follows:

Table 3.5 (Continued)

Next character	Stack	Output
)	×	*ABC*+
×	×	*ABC*+×
D	×	*ABC* +× *D*
Done	Empty	*ABC* +× *D*×

From these examples and discussion, we can say that the operators are popped out of the stack if their in-stack priority (ISP) is greater than the priority of the incoming operator that is to be added onto the stack.

Consider the infix expression $E = A \times B + C\#$. The conversion of this expression into its postfix form is shown in Table 3.6.

Table 3.6 Infix to postfix conversion of the expression $E = A \times B + C$

Next character	Stack	Output
A	Empty	A
$\times$	$\times$	A
B	$\times$	AB
$+$	$+$	$AB\times$
C	$+$	$AB \times C$
# (Pop all)	$+$	$AB \times C+$

Now, let us consider the infix expression $X = A \wedge B \wedge C$

For its equivalent postfix expression, the sequence of `push` and `pop` operations should be as given in Table 3.7.

Table 3.7 Infix to postfix conversion of the expression $X = A \wedge B \wedge C$

Next character	Stack	Output
A	Empty	A
^	^	A
B	^	AB
^		

We have decided the strategy for pushing and popping out the operator from the stack. In this example, the operator at the top of the stack and the operator to be pushed onto the stack are the same. If this rule is applied, then the output is $AB \wedge C \wedge$, which is wrong! Hence, we need to add a few more checks. We must take into account the associativity of operators and prepare a hierarchy scheme for the binary arithmetic operators and delimiters. When an operator is at the top of the stack or in an expression (current token), they are to be treated with different priorities, as shown in Table 3.8.

Table 3.8 The operator and its ISP and ICP

Symbol	In-stack priority (ISP)	Incoming priority (ICP)
)	–	–
^	3	4
×/	2	2
+–	1	1
(	0	4

Thus, we can say that when the operators are taken out from the stack, their ISP, is greater than or equal to the ICP, of the new operator.

Hence, each operator is to be assigned two priorities—the incoming priority (ICP) and the in-stack priority (ISP). Incoming priority is considered when the operator is located in the given infix expression, whereas ISP is the priority when the operator is at the top of the stack. In Example 3.1, we observed that the lower priority operators should spend more time in the stack and the higher priority operators should be popped out earlier. To achieve this, we need to assign the appropriate ICPs and ISPs to the operators. Table 3.8 shows these values. If the incoming operator is the same as that of the in-stack operator and if the operator is left associative, then the operator from the stack should be popped and printed.

For example, consider the infix expressions $X = A \times B \times C$ and $Y = A/B \times C$
The expression $X = A \times B \times C$ should yield the postfix expression as $AB \times C \times$, and $Y = A/B \times C$ should generate the postfix expression as $AB/C\times$.

If the priority of the operator on the top of stack (in-stack operator) is greater than the priority of the operator coming from the expression (incoming operator), then the incoming operator is pushed onto the stack.

In short, the following points should be taken into consideration while assigning ICPs and ISPs:

1. Higher priority operators should be assigned higher values of ISP and ICP.
2. For right associative operators, ISP should be lower than ICP. For example, $A\,^\wedge B\,^\wedge C$ should generate ABC^^, which means $(A)\,^\wedge\,(B\,^\wedge\,C)$.
3. If ICP is higher than ISP, the operator should be stacked.
4. The ISP and ICP should be equal for left associative operators.

Summing up The following are the steps involved in the evaluation of an expression.

1. Assign priorities to all operators and define associativity (left or right).
2. Assign appropriate values of ICPs and ISPs accordingly. For left associative operators, assign equal ISP and ICP. For right associative operators, assign higher ICP than ISP. For example, assign a higher ICP for '^' and for the right parenthesis ')'.
3. Scan the expression from left to right, character by character, till the end of expression.
4. If the character is an operand, then display the same.
5. If the character is an operator and if ICP > ISP

```
        then push the operator
    else
        while(ICP <= ISP)
            pop the operator and display it.
        end while
    Stack the incoming operator
```

6. Continue till end of expression

The expression could be in one of the three forms—infix, postfix, or prefix.

An expression in one form can be converted to the other two forms. Let us write algorithms for all these conversions.

1. Infix expression to postfix expression
2. Infix expression to prefix expression
3. Prefix expression to infix expression
4. Prefix expression to postfix expression
5. Postfix expression to infix expression
6. Postfix expression to prefix expression

Let *E* be the expression made of characters. Characters here include *operators*, *operands*, and *delimiters*. In addition, let '#' be the character denoting the end of the expression.

Infix to Postfix Conversion

Algorithm 3.2 illustrates the infix to postfix conversion.

ALGORITHM 3.2

```
1. Scan expression E from left to right, character by character, till
   character is '#'
      ch = get_next_token(E)
2. while(ch != '#'}
      if(ch = ')') then ch = pop()
         while(ch !=`(')
            Display ch
            ch = pop()
         end while
      if(ch = operand) display the same
      if(ch = operator) then
         if(ICP > ISP) then push(ch)
         else
            while(ICP <= ISP)
               pop the operator and display it
            end while
         ch = get_next_token(E)
   end while
3. if(ch = #) then while(!emptystack()) pop and display
4. stop
```

For this algorithm, we refer to the operators and the respective ICPs and ISPs as assigned in Table 3.8. Example 3.2 illustrates the conversion of an infix expression to its postfix form (function in Program Code 3.5).

EXAMPLE 3.2 Convert the following infix expression to its postfix form:

$$A \wedge B \times C - C + D/A/(E + F)$$

Solution Conversion of infix to postfix form can be illustrated as in Table 3.9

Table 3.9 Infix to postfix conversion of the expression $A \wedge B \times C - C + D/A/(E + F)$

Character scanned	Stack contents	Postfix expression
A	Empty	A
^	^	A
B	^	AB
×	×	AB^
C	×	AB ^ C
–	–	AB ^ C ×
C	–	AB ^ C × C
+	+	AB ^ C × C–
D	+	AB ^ C × C – D
/	+/	AB ^ C × C – D
A	+/	AB ^ C × C – DA
/	+/	AB ^ C × C – DA/
(	+/(	AB ^ C × C – DA/
E	+/(	AB ^ C × C – DA/E
+	+/(+	AB ^ C × C – DA/E
F	+/(+	AB ^ C × C – DA/EF
)	+/	AB ^ C × C – DA/EF+
	Empty	AB ^ C × C – DA/EF+/+

Infix to Prefix Conversion

For converting the infix expression to a prefix expression, two stacks are needed—the `operator Stack` and the `display Stack`. The `display Stack` stores the prefix expression. This approach is discussed in Algorithm 3.3.

ALGORITHM 3.3

```
1. Scan expression E, character by character from right to left
      ch = get_next_token(E)
2. while(ch != '#') do
      if(ch = operand) then push(ch) in display Stack
         if (ch = ')') then
            ch = pop()from operator Stack
         while(ch != '(')
            push(ch) in display Stack
            ch = pop()
         end while
         if(ch = operator) then
            if ICP(op) >= ISP(op) then
               push ch in operator Stack
            else
               ch = pop()
               while(ICP < ISP)
```

```
                ch = pop() from operator Stack and push 'ch' in
                display Stack
            end while
        ch = get_next_token(E)
    end while
3. if (ch = '#') then
      while(!emptystack(operator))
         ch = pop(operator)
         push ch on display stack
      end while
4. while(!emptystack(display))
      ch = pop(operator)
      display ch
   end while
5. stop
```

Example 3.3 illustrates the conversion of an infix expression to its prefix form.

EXAMPLE 3.3 Convert the following infix expression to its corresponding prefix form:

$$A \wedge B \times C - C + D/A/(E + F)$$

Solution The conversion to prefix notation is as given in Table 3.10

Table 3.10 Infix to prefix conversion of the expression $A \wedge B \times C - C + D/A/(E + F)$

Character scanned	Stack	Prefix expression
)	)	
F	)	F
+	)+	F
E	)+	EF
(	Empty	+EF
/	/	+EF
A	/	A + EF
/	//	A + EF
D	//	DA + EF
+	+	//DA + EF
C	+	C//DA + EF
–	+–	C//DA + EF
C	+–	CC//DA + EF
×	+–×	CC//DA + EF
B	+–×	BCC//DA + EF
^	+–×^	BCC//DA + EF
A	+–×^	ABCC//DA + EF
	Empty	+–×^ABCC//DA + EF

The corresponding program for infix to prefix conversion is illustrated in Program Code 3.5.

PROGRAM CODE 3.5

```
#include<iostream.h>
#include<conio.h>
#include<string.h>
#define Max 20
//class Stack
class stack
{
   char stack[Max];    // array of characters
   int top;
   public:
   Stack()    // constructor to initialize top
   {
      top = -1;
   }
   int isempty();  // function to check empty condition
   int isfull();  // function to check full condition
   void push(char ch);  // to push a character into stack
   char pop();  // function to pop a character from stack
   char getTop();  // function to get the top element of
stack
};

int Stack::isempty()
{
   if(top == -1)
      return 1;
   else
      return 0;
}

int Stack::isfull()
{
   if(top == Max - 1)
      return 1;
   else
      return 0;
}
```

```
void Stack::push(char ch)
{
   if(isfull())
      cout << "\nStack full";
   else
   {
      top++;
      stack[top] = ch;
   }
}

char Stack::pop()
{
   char ch;
   if(isempty())
      cout << "\n stack empty \n";
   else
   {
      ch = stack[top];
      top--;
   }
   return(ch);
}

char Stack::getTop()
{
   char ch;
   if(isempty())
      cout << "\n stack empty \n";
   else
   {
      ch = stack[top];
   }
   return(ch);
}

// Function to get in-stack priority
char isp(char ch)
{
   switch(ch)
```

```
    {
        case '+':
        case '-':return 1;
        case '*':
        case '/':return 2;
        case '^':return 3;
        case '(':return 0;
        case '#':return -2;
    }
}

// Function to get incoming priority
char icp(char ch)
{
    switch(ch)
    {
        case '+':
        case '-':return 1;
        case '*':
        case '/':return 2;
        case '^':return 3;
        case '(':return 4;
    }
}

void intopost(char infix[20],char postfix[20])
{
    int i = 0;
    char ch, x;
    stack s;
    s.push('#');
    while(infix[i]! = '\0')
    // extract character till end of expression
    {
        ch = infix[i];
        i++;
        if(ch >= 'a' && ch <= 'z')    // operand
        {
            cout << ch;
        }
        else    // operator
```

```
        {
            if(ch == '(')
            {
                while(s.getTop()! = '(')
                {
                    x = s.pop();
                    cout << x;
                }
                x = s.pop();
        }
        else
        {
            while(isp(s.getTop()) >= icp(ch))
            {
                x = s.pop();
                cout << x;
            }
                s.push(ch);
            }
        }
    }
    while(!s.isempty())
    {
        x = s.pop();
        if(x != '#')
        cout << x;
    }
}

void intopre(char infix[20],char prefix[20])
{
    int i, j;
    char ch, x;
    stack s;
    s.push('#');
    i = strlen(infix) - 1;
    j = 0;
    while(i! = -1)
    {
        ch = infix[i];
```

```
        i--;
        if(ch >= 'a' && ch <= 'z')
        {
            prefix[j] = ch;
            j++;
        }
        else
        {
            if(ch == '(')
            {
                while(s.getTop()! = ')')
                {
                    x = s.pop();
                    prefix[j] = x;
                    j++;
                }
                x = s.pop();
        }
    else
    {
        while(isp(s.getTop()) > icp(ch))
        {
            x = s.pop();
            prefix[j] = x;
            j++;
        }
        s.push(ch);
        }
    }
    }
    while(!s.isempty())
    {
        x = s.pop();
        if(x! = '#')
        prefix[j] = x;
        j++;
    }
    prefix[j] = '\0';
    strrev(prefix);
}
```

```
void main()
{
    char infix[20], postfix[20], prefix[20];
    int choice;
    do
    {
        cout << "\nMenu...........";
        cout << "\n1.Infix to postfix conversion";
        cout << "\n2.Infix to prefix conversion";
        cout << "\nEnter your choice:";
        cin >> choice;
        switch(choice)
        {
            case 1:
                cout << "\nEnter the infix expression:";
                cin >> infix;
                cout << "\nPostfix expression is:";
                intopost(infix,postfix);
                break;
            case 2:
                cout << "\nEnter the infix expression:";
                cin >> infix;
                intopre(infix,prefix);
                cout << "\nPrefix expression is:" << prefix;
                break;
        }
    }
    while(choice < 3);
}
```

Postfix to Infix Conversion

Algorithm 3.4 illustrates the postfix to infix conversion.

ALGORITHM 3.4

```
1. Scan expression E from left to right character by character
    ch = get_next_token(E)
2. while(ch !='#') do
     if(ch = operand) then push(ch)
     if(ch = operator) then
     begin
         t2 = pop() and t1 = pop()
         push(strcat['(', t1, ch, t2, ')']
```

```
        end
        ch = get_next_token(E)
    end while
3. if ch = '#', while(!emptystack()) pop and display
4. stop
```

Example 3.4 illustrates the conversion of a postfix expression to its infix form.

EXAMPLE 3.4 Convert the following postfix expression to its infix form:

$$AB \wedge C \times C - DA/EE+/+$$

Solution The conversion of the given postfix expression to its infix form is given in Table 3.11.

Table 3.11 Postfix to infix conversion of the expression $AB \wedge C \times C - DA/EE+/+$

Character scanned	Stack contents
A	A
B	AB
^	A ^ B
C	A ^ B, C
×	A ^ B × C
C	A ^ B × C, C
–	A ^ B × C – C, D
D	A ^ B × C – C, D
A	A ^ B × C – C, D, A
/	A ^ B × C – C, D/A
E	A ^ B × C – C, D/A, E
E	A ^ B × C – C, D/A, E, E
+	A ^ B × C – C, D/A, E + E
/	A ^ B × C – C, D/A/E + E
+	A ^ B × C – C + D/A/E + E

Postfix to Prefix Conversion

Algorithm 3.5 illustrates the postfix to prefix conversion.

ALGORITHM 3.5

```
1. Scan expression E from left to right character by character
     ch = get_next_token(E)
2. while(ch !='#') do
       if(ch = operand) then push(ch)
       if(ch = operator) then
```

```
        begin
           t2 = pop() and t1 = pop()
           push(strcat[ch, t1, t2]
        end
        ch = get_next_token(E)
     end while
3. if ch = '#', while(!emptystack()) pop and display
4. stop
```

Example 3.5 illustrates the conversion of a postfix expression to its prefix form.

EXAMPLE 3.5 Convert the following postfix expression to its prefix form:

$$AB \wedge C \times C - DA/EE+/+$$

Solution The conversion of the given postfix expression to its infix form is given in Table 3.12.

Table 3.12 Postfix to prefix conversion of the expression *AB* ^ *C* × *C* – *DA*/*E E*+/+

Character scanned	Stack contents
A	*A*
B	*AB*
^	^*AB*
C	^*ABC*
×	×^*ABC*
C	×^*ABC*, *C*
–	–×^*ABCC*
D	–×^*ABCC*, *D*
A	–×^*ABCC*, *D*, *A*
/	–×^*ABCC*, /*DA*
E	–×^*ABCC*, /*DA*, *E*
E	–×^*ABCC*, /*DA*, *E*, *E*
+	–×^*ABCC*, /*DA*, +*EE*
/	–×^*ABCC*, //*DA* + *EE*
+	+–^*ABCC*//*DA* + *EE*

Prefix to Infix Conversion

Algorithm 3.6 illustrates the prefix to infix conversion.

ALGORITHM 3.6

```
1. Scan expression E from right to left character by character
     ch = get_next_token(E)
2. while(ch !='#') do
```

```
      if(ch = operand) then push(ch)
      if(ch = operator) then
      begin
         t2 = pop() and t1 = pop()
         push(strcat['(', t1, ch, t2, ')']
      end
      ch = get_next_token(E)
   end while
3. if ch = '#', while(!emptystack()) pop and display
4. stop
```

Prefix to Postfix Conversion

Algorithm 3.7 illustrates the prefix to postfix conversion.

ALGORITHM 3.7

```
1. Scan expression E from left to right character by character
   ch = get_next_token(E)
2. while(ch ! ='#') do
      if(ch = operand) then push(ch)
      if(ch = operator) then
      begin
         t2 = pop() and t1 = pop()
         push(strcat [t1, t2, ch]
     end
     ch = get_next_token(E)
   end while
3. if ch = '#', while(!emptystack()) pop and display
4. stop
```

The corresponding program for postfix to infix conversion is illustrated in Program Code 3.6.

PROGRAM CODE 3.6

```
//postfix to infix conversion
#include<conio.h>
#include<iostream.h>
#include<string.h>
#define Max 20
//definition of class stack
class stack
{
   char stack[max][max];        //stack of string
   int top;
   public:
```

```
    //constructor to initialize top
    stack()
    {
       top = -1;
    }
    //function declaration
    int isempty();
    int isfull();
    void push(char str[max]);
    void pop(char str[max]);
};

//definition of isempty condition
int stack::isempty()
{
    if(top == -1)
       return 1;
    else
       return 0;
}

//definition of isfull condition
int Stack::isfull()
{
    if(top == Max - 1)
       return 1;
    else
       return 0;
}

//definition of push function
void Stack::push(char str[Max])
{
    if(isfull())
       cout << "\nStack full";
    else
    {
       top++;
       strcpy(stack[top], str);
    }
}
```

```
//definition of pop function
void Stack::pop(char str[20])
{
   if(isempty())
      cout << "\nStack empty";
   else
   {
      strcpy(str, stack[top]);
      top--;
   }
}

//definition of postfix to infix conversion
void postfixtoinfix()
{
   char postfix[20], infix[20];
   char s1[10], s2[10], s3[10], ch, temp[10];
   int i;
   Stack s;        //creating of object of class stack
   cout << "\nEnter the postfix expression:";
   cin >> postfix;
   i = 0;
   while(postfix[i]! = '\0')
   {
      ch = postfix[i];
      i++;
      s1[0] = ch;
      s1[1] = '\0';
      if(ch >= 'a' && ch <= 'z')
      {
         s.push(s1);
      }
      else
      {
         s.pop(s2);
         s.pop(s3);
         strcpy(temp,"(");
         strcat(temp, s3);
         strcat(temp, s1);
         strcat(temp, s2);
         strcat(temp, ")");
```

```
            s.push(temp);
        }
    }
    cout << "\nInfix expression is:" << temp;
}

//definition of postfix to prefix conversion
void postfixtoprefix()
{
    char postfix[20], prefix[20];
    char s1[10], s2[10], s3[10], ch, temp[10];
    int i;
    Stack s;        //creating of object of class stack
    cout << "\nEnter the postfix expression:";
    cin >> postfix;
    i = 0;
    while(postfix[i]! = '\0')
    {
        ch = postfix[i];i++;
        s1[0] = ch;
        s1[1] = '\0';
        if(ch >= 'a' && ch <= 'z')
        {
            s.push(s1);
        }
        else
        {
            s.pop(s2);
            s.pop(s3);
            strcpy(temp, s1);
            strcat(temp, s3);
            strcat(temp, s2);
            s.push(temp);
        }
    }
    cout << "\nPrefix expression is:" << temp;
}
//definition of prefix to infix conversion
void prefixtoinfix()
{
    char prefix[20], infix[20];
    char s1[10], s2[10], s3[10], ch, temp[10];
```

```
    int i;
    Stack s;        //creating of object of class stack
    cout << "\nEnter the prefix expression:";
    cin >> prefix;
    for(i = strlen(prefix); i >= 0; i--)
    {
       ch = prefix[i];
       s1[0] = ch;
       s1[1] = '\0';
       if(ch >= 'a' && ch <= 'z')
    {
          s.push(s1);
    }
    else
    {
          s.pop(s2);
          s.pop(s3);
          strcpy(temp, "(");
          strcat(temp, s2);
          strcat(temp, s1);
          strcat(temp, s3);
          strcat(temp,")");
          s.push(temp);
    }
    }
    cout << "\nInfix expression is:" << temp;
}

//definition of prefix to postfix conversion
void prefixtopostfix()
{
    char prefix[20];
    Stack s;        //creating of object of class stack
    char s1[10], s2[10], s3[10], ch, temp[10];
    int i;
    cout << "\nEnter the prefix expression:";
    cin >> prefix;
    for(i = strlen(prefix); i >= 0; i--)
    {
       ch = prefix[i];
       s1[0] = ch;
```

```
        s1[1] = '\0';
        if(ch> = 'a' && ch <= 'z')
        {
           s.push(s1);
        }
           else
        {
           s.pop(s2);
           s.pop(s3);
           strcpy(temp, s2);
           strcat(temp, s3);
           strcat(temp, s1);
           s.push(temp);
        }
     }
     cout << "\nPostfix expression is:" << temp;
}

//definition of main function
void main()
{
     int choice;
     clrscr();
     do
     {
        cout << "\n..........menu..........";
        cout << "\n1.postfix to infix.........$";
        cout << "\n2.postfix to prefix........$";
        cout << "\n3.prefix to infix..........$";
        cout << "\n4.prefix to postfix........$";
        cout << "\n5.exit.....................$";
        cout << "\n\nEnter your choice";
        cin >> choice;
        switch(choice)
        {
           //function call of functions
           case 1:
              postfixtoinfix();
              break;
          case 2:
              postfixtoprefix();
              break;
```

```
            case 3:
               prefixtoinfix();
               break;
            case 4:
               prefixtopostfix();
               break;
            default:
               cout << "\n\nSorry, wrong choice";
         }
      }while(choice < 5);
      getch();
}
```

3.9 PROCESSING OF FUNCTION CALLS

One natural application of stacks, which arises in computer programming, is the processing of function calls and their terminations. The program must remember the place where the call was made so that it can return there after the function is complete. Suppose we have three functions, say, `A`, `B`, and `C`, and one `main` program. Let the *main* invoke `A`, `A` invoke `B`, and `B` in turn invoke `C`. Then, `B` will not have finished its work until `C` has finished and returned. Similarly, `main` is the first to start work, but it is the last to be finished, not until sometime after `A` has finished and returned. Thus, the sequence by which a function actively proceeds is summed up as the LIFO or FILO property, as shown in Fig. 3.14. The output is shown in Fig. 3.15.

From the output in Fig. 3.15, it can be observed that the main program is invoked first but finished last, whereas the function C is invoked last but finished first. Hence, to keep track of the return addresses `ra`, `rb`, and `rc` the only data structure required here is the *stack*.

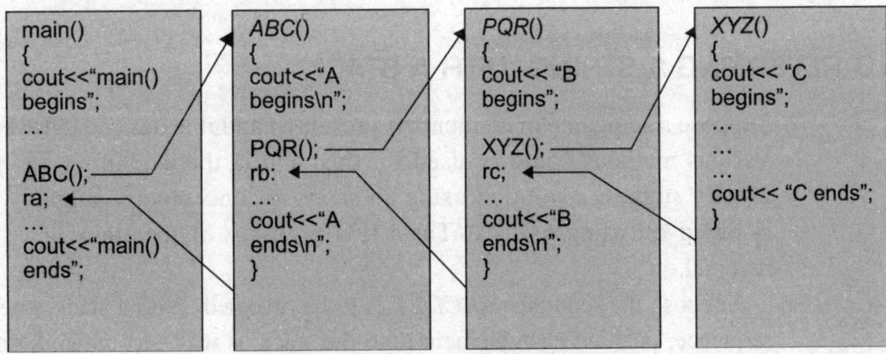

Fig. 3.14 Processing of function calls

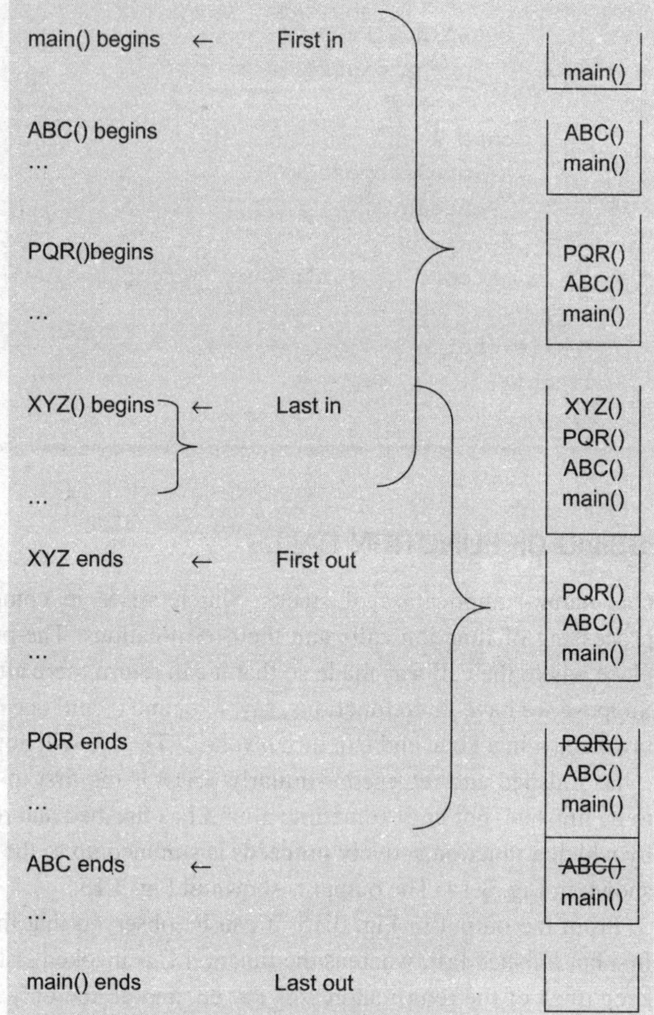

Fig. 3.15 Use of stack for processing of function calls

3.10 REVERSING A STRING WITH A STACK

Suppose a sequence of elements is presented and it is desired to reverse the sequence. Various methods could be used for this, and in the beginning, the programmer will usually suggest a solution using an array. A conceptually simple solution, however, is based on using a stack. The LIFO property of the stack access guarantees the reversal.

Suppose the sequence *ABCDEF* is to be reversed. With a stack, one simply scans the sequence, pushing each element onto the stack as it is encountered, until the end of the sequence is reached. The stack is then popped repeatedly, with each popped element sent to the output, until the stack is empty. Table 3.13 illustrates this algorithm:

Table 3.13 Reversal of a string using a stack

Input	Action	Stack	Display
ABCDEF	Push *A*	*A* ← top of stack	–
BCDEF	Push *B*	*AB* ← top of stack	–
CDEF	Push *C*	*ABC* ← top of stack	–
DEF	Push *D*	*ABCD* ← top of stack	–
EF	Push *E*	*ABCDE* ← top of stack	–
F	Push *F*	*ABCDEF* ← top of stack	–
End	Pop and display	*ABCDE* ←.top of stack	*F*
	Pop and display	*ABCD* ← top of stack	*FE*
	Pop and display	*ABC* ← top of stack	*FED*
	Pop and display	*AB* ← top of stack	*FEDC*
	Pop and display	*A* ← top of stack	*FEDCB*
	Pop and display	Stack empty	*FEDCBA*
	Stop		

Reading a string character and writing it backward can be accomplished by pushing each character on to a stack as it is read. When the string is finished, pop the characters off the stack, and they will come out in the reverse order. This process is illustrated in Program Code 3.7.

PROGRAM CODE 3.7

```
main()
{
   Stack S;        // here Stack is the character stack
   char str[], ch;
   int i;
   ch = str[0];
   i = 1;
   while(ch !='\0')
   {
      S.push(ch);
      Ch = str[i++];
   }
   while(!S.Isempty())
   {
      cout << S.pop();
   }
}
```

3.11 CHECKING CORRECTNESS OF WELL-FORMED PARENTHESES

Consider a mathematical expression that includes several sets of nested parentheses. For example, $Z - ((X \times ((X + Y/J - 2)) + Y)/3)$.

To ensure that the parentheses are nested correctly, we need to check that

1. there are equal numbers of right and left parentheses
2. every right parenthesis is preceded by a matching left parenthesis

Expressions such as $((X + Y)$ or $(X + Y))$ violate condition 1, and expressions such as $(X + Y) - ($ or $(X + Y))(-A + B)$ violate condition 2.

To solve this problem, let us define the parentheses count at a particular point in an expression as the number of left parenthesis minus the number of right parenthesis that have been encountered in the left-to-right scanning of the expression at that particular point. The two conditions that must hold if the parentheses in an expression form an admissible pattern are as follows:

1. The parenthesis count at each point in the expression is non-negative.
2. The parenthesis count at the end of the expression is 0.

A stack may also be used to keep track of the parentheses count. Whenever a left parenthesis is encountered, it is pushed onto the stack, and whenever a right parenthesis is encountered, the stack is examined. If the stack is empty, then the string is declared to be invalid. In addition, when the end of the string is reached, the stack must be empty; otherwise, the string is declared to be invalid.

3.12 RECURSION

In C/C++, a function can call itself, that is, one of the statements of the function is a call to itself. Such functions are called *recursive functions* and can be used to implement recursive problems in an elegant manner.

To solve a recursive problem using functions, the problem must have an end condition that can be stated in non-recursive terms. For example, in the case of factorials, we know that $1! = 1$. If no such condition exists, then the recursive calls will indefinitely continue until the computer runs or the program is terminated by the operating system.

Consider the recursive implementation of factorial given that

```
1! = 1  and  n! = n X (n - 1)!
```

The recursive function in C++ is given by the following statement:

```
long int factorial (unsigned int n)
{
   if(n <= 1)
```

```
        return(1);
    else
        return(n * factorial(n - 1));
}
```

As we can see, the C++ function represents the recursive mathematical definition of `n!`. To see how it works, consider the computation of 5!.

The function calls will proceed as follows:

```
factorial(5) = 5 * factorial(4)
           = 5 * (4* factorial (3))
   = 5 * (4* (3 * factorial (2)))
   = 5 * (4 *(3 * (2 * factorial (1))))
   = 5 * (4 * (3 * (2 * 1)))
   = 5 * (4 * (3 * 2))
   = 5 * (4 * 6)
   = 5 * 24
   = 120
```

As the starting number is not 1, the function calls itself with the value 5 – 1, that is, 4. Therefore, the original function call is kept incomplete and pending, and a second call is made to the factorial with value 4. This process continues until the fifth call is made, with the value 1. In this call, the function terminates without any further recursion and returns the desired value of 1!, which is 1. Subsequently, each of the pending function calls is completed upto the original factorial (5) function call, which returns the computed value as 120. In the preceding piece of code, parentheses have been used to show how the recursive calls proceed from left to right and the computations are made from right to left.

A program to print the first 15 factorials is given in the following code:

```
#include <iostream>
long int factorial(unsigned int n)
void main(void)
{
    int i;
    for(i = 1; i <= 15; i++)
        cout << "The factorial of" << i << "is =" << factorial(i);
}
```

Recursion is a technique that allows us to break down a problem into one or more sub-problems that are similar in form to the original problem. Recursive programs are most inefficient as regards their name and space complexities. Hence, there is a need to convert them into iterative ones. To achieve this conversion stacks need to be used. This is discussed in detail in Chapter 4.

3.13 PARSING COMPUTER PROGRAMS

Parsing is a special phase of compilation. While parsing a semantic expression, we need a parsing stack to hold the operands for expressions. The stack must hold both the value of the expression and its type. The purpose of the expression *value stack* is to turn infix expressions such as 1 + 2 into postfix expressions where all the required operands are saved on the stack by the parser. The operation is then performed by popping the correct number of arguments off the stack and pushing back the single result value.

3.14 BACKTRACKING ALGORITHMS

A backtracking algorithm systematically considers all possible outcomes for each decision and performs much better than an exhaustive search. To explore a solution space of the problem, depth-first traversal of the solution space can be performed. This traversal uses the stack data structure.

3.15 CONVERTING DECIMAL NUMBERS TO BINARY

To convert a number from decimal to binary, we simply divide the number by 2 until a quotient of 0 is reached. Then, use the successive remainders in reverse order as the binary representation. For example, to convert decimal 35 to binary, we perform the following computation:

Division operation

2	35	1
	17	1
	8	0
	4	0
	2	0
	1	1

If you examine the remainders from the last division to the first one, writing them down as you go, you will get the following sequence: 100011.

$$100011_{base2} = 35_{base10}$$

The division generates a one-bit result at every step. These bits are generated in the reverse order, that is, the most significant bit is generated first and the least significant bit is generated at the end. Hence, the result is the reverse of the actual resultant binary number. We need some intermediate storage that will hold the result and finally send the output as the correct result. If we store every bit generated in a stack, we will get the correct result at the end. This is because the working behaviour of the stack is LIFO. Hence, using stack operations, we can write a procedure that accepts a non-negative base 10 integer as a parameter and then write its binary representation. An example is illustrated in Example 3.6.

EXAMPLE 3.6 Convert the decimal number 254 to its binary equivalent.

Solution Divide the number by 2; then divide what is left by 2, and so on until there is nothing left. Write down the remainder (which is either 0 or 1) at each division stage. Once there are no more divisions, list the remainder values in reverse order. This is the binary equivalent.

254/2 gives 127 with a remainder of 0
127/2 gives 63 with a remainder of 1
63/2 gives 31 with a remainder of 1
31/2 gives 15 with a remainder of 1
15/2 gives 7 with a remainder of 1
7/2 gives 3 with a remainder of 1
3/2 gives 1 with a remainder of 1
1/2 gives 0 with a remainder of 1

Therefore, the binary equivalent is 11111110. The corresponding program is illustrated in Program Code 3.8.

PROGRAM CODE 3.8

```
void Dec2Bin(int DecNum)
{
   int count = 0, bit;
   Stack S;
   while(DecNum >= 0)
   {
      bit = DecNum % 2;
      S.push(bit);
      DecNum = DecNum/2;
      count++;
   }
   cout << "The binary equivalent of" << DecNum << "is =";
   while(count > 0)
   {
      cout << S.pop();
      count--;
   }
}
```

RECAPITULATION

- *A stack is* an ordered list where all insertions and deletions are made at one end, called the *top.* Adding an element is called pushing the element onto the stack. The function, which does this, is called `push`. Removing an element from the stack is called *popping* the element from the stack, and the function, which does this, is called `pop`.
- A stack can be implemented using arrays or linked lists. For array implementation, its size should be predefined, and its implementation time also should not exceed the run-time.
- A stack is used in a wide number of applications such as recursion, expression conversion, well-formed parenthesis check, and so on. The most frequent application of stack is in the evaluation of arithmetic expressions. The conventional way of writing the expression is called *infix*, because the binary operators occur in between the operands and the unary operators precede their operand.
- The Polish mathematician Han Lukasiewicz suggested a notation called *Polish notion*, which gives two alternatives to represent an arithmetic expression. The notations are *postfix* and *prefix notations*. In the postfix notation, the operator is written after its operands, whereas in the prefix notation the operator precedes its operands.
- The postfix expressions can be evaluated easily. Hence, an infix expression is converted into a postfix expression using a stack.
- In computer programming, the processing of function calls and their terminations use *stack*. A stack is used to remember the place where the call was made so that it can return there after the function is complete.

KEY TERMS

Contiguous stack The simplest way to represent a stack is by using a one-dimensional array. A stack implemented using an array is also called as a contiguous stack.

GetTop The `getTop()` function gives information about the topmost element. It returns the element on the top of the stack. In this operation, only a copy of the element, which is at the top of the stack, is returned. Hence, the top is still set to the same element.

Polish notation A Polish mathematician Han Lukasiewicz suggested a notation called Polish notation, which gives two alternatives to represent an arithmetic expression. The notations are the postfix and prefix notations.

Pop The pop operation deletes an element, which is at the top of the stack and returns the same to the user. The `pop()` function modifies the top as the element below the current topmost element becomes the top element.

Push The push operation inserts an element on the top of the stack. The recently added element is always at the top of the stack.

Recursion Recursion is a technique that allows us to break down a problem into one or more subproblems that are similar in form to the original problem.

Stack A stack is an ordered list where all insertions and deletions are made at one end, called the *top*.

EXERCISES

Multiple choice questions

1. The following sequence of operations is performed on a stack `push(1), push(2), pop, push(1), push(2), pop, pop, pop, push(2), pop`. The sequence of the popped out values is
   (a) 2, 2, 1, 1, 2
   (b) 2, 2, 1, 2, 2
   (c) 2, 1, 2, 2, 1
   (d) 2, 1, 2, 2, 2
2. In evaluating the arithmetic expression 2 × 3 − (4 + 5) using stacks to evaluate its equivalent postfix form, which of the following stack configurations is not possible?

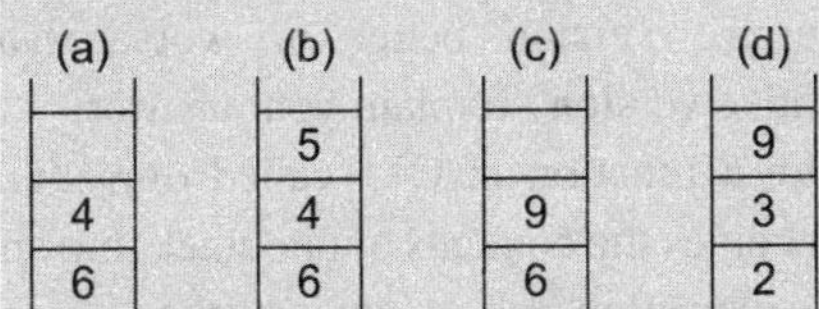

3. Stack *A* has the entries *a*, *b*, *c* (with *a* on top). Stack *B* is empty. An entry popped out of Stack *A* can be printed immediately or pushed to Stack *B*. An entry popped out of Stack *B* can only be printed. In this agreement, which of the following permutations of *a*, *b*, and *c* is not possible?
   (a) *bac*
   (b) *bca*
   (c) *cab*
   (d) *abc*
4. Which is the postfix expression for the following infix expression?
   $A + B \times (C + D)/F + D \times E$
   (a) $AB + CD + \times F/D + E\times$
   (b) $ABCD + \times F/+ DE\times+$
   (c) $A \times B + CD/F\times DE++$
   (d) $A + \times BCD/F \times DE++$
5 The infix priorities of +, ×, ^, / could be
   (a) 5, 1, 2, 7
   (b) 7, 5, 2, 1
   (c) 1, 2, 5, 7
   (d) 5, 2, 2, 4
6 The expression 1 × 2 ^ 3 × 4 ^ 5 × 6 when evaluated gives the value
   (a) 32^{30}
   (b) 162^{30}
   (c) 49152
   (d) 173458
7. The prefix form of $A - B/(C\times D\$E)$ is
   (a) $-1\times\$ACBDE$
   (b) $-ABCD\times\$DE$
   (c) $-A/B\times C\$DE$
   (d) $-A/BC\times\$DE$
8. What is the postfix form of the following prefix expression?
   $\times + AB - CD$
   (a) $AB + CD - \times$
   (b) $ABC + \times -$
   (c) $AB + \times CD-$
   (d) $AB + \times CD-$
9. The postfix form of the infix expression $(A + B) \times (C + D - E) \times F$ is
   (a) $AB + CD + E - \times F\times$
   (b) $AB + CDE + - \times F\times$
   (c) $AB + CD - EF + - \times\times$
   (d) $ABCDEF\times - + \times +$
10. Which of the following is essential for efficiently converting an infix expression to its postfix form?
   (a) An operator stack
   (b) An operand stack
   (c) An operand stack and an operator stack
   (d) A parse tree

Review questions

1. Transform the following infix expressions into their equivalent postfix expressions:
   (a) $(A - B) \times (D/E)$
   (b) $(A + B \wedge D)/(E - F) + G$

(c) $A \times (B + D)/E - F \times (G + H/K)$
(d) $(A + B) \times (C \$ (D - E) + F)/G) \$ (H - J)$

2. Transform the following infix expressions into their equivalent prefix expressions:
(a) $(A - B) \times (D/E)$
(b) $(A + B \wedge D)/(E - F) + G$
(c) $A \times (B + D)/E - F \times (G + H/K)$

3. Transform the following prefix expressions into their equivalent infix expressions:
(a) $+A - BC$
(b) $++A -\times \$ BCD /+ EF \times GHI$
(c) $+-\$ ABC \times D \times\times EFG$

4. Transform the following postfix expressions to their equivalent infix expressions:
(a) $ABC+$
(b) $AB - C + DEF -+\$$
(c) $ABCDE -+\$\times EF\times-$

5. Write short notes on
(a) The pros and cons of recursion
(b) Multi stack
(c) Infix expression evaluation
(d) Polish notation
(e) Use of stack in function calls

6. Stacks are called FILO queues because the first element pushed onto the stack is always the last one popped. Using `push()`, `pop()`, and any other functions you need, write a program that reads a line from the terminal and determines whether it is a palindrome or not. Hint: A palindrome is a string that is the same spelled forward or backward. For example, '*Madam was I pop I saw Madam.*'

7. Explain the concept of multiple stacks with an example. What are the different ways for the implementation of multiple stacks?

8. What is ADT? Give the ADT for a stack.

9. Represent two stacks in a 1D array such that the space utilization is maximum. Give the C++ declaration and also give C++ functions to perform `push` and `pop` operations on the desired stack.

10. Write a recursive version of strlen(). Is the recursive version better or worse than the iterative version? Explain your answer.

11. Write a function in C++ called `copyStack()` that copies the contents of one stack into another. The algorithm passes two stacks—the source stack and the destination stack. The order of the stacks must be identical. (Hint: Use a temporary stack to preserve the order.)

12. Write a function in C++ to check whether the contents of two stacks are identical.

Answers to multiple choice questions

1. (a)
2. (d) The postfix equivalent is $2\ 3 \times 4\ 5 + -$. For evaluating this using a stack, starting from the left, we have to scan the expression character by character. If it is an operator, pop it twice, apply the operator on the popped out entries, and push the result onto the stack. If we follow this, we can find that the configuration in option (d) is not possible.

3. (c) 4. (b) 5. (d) 6. (c) 7. (c) 8. (a) 9. (b) 10. (a)

4 RECURSION

OBJECTIVES

After completing this chapter, the reader will be able to understand the following:

- The power of recursion and its working
- Identification of the base case and the general case of a recursively defined problem
- Comparison of iterative and recursive solutions
- The steps to write, implement, test, and debug recursive functions
- The method of implementing recursion using stacks

Functions are the most basic and useful feature of any programming language. A set of instructions that performs logical operations, which could be very complex and numerous in number, can be grouped together as functions (also called *procedures*). Functions may call themselves or other functions, and the called functions in turn may call the calling function. This process is called *recursion* and such functions are called *recursive functions*. A recursive function makes the program compact and readable. This chapter covers the important aspects of recursion.

4.1 INTRODUCTION

Good programming practices emphasize the writing of programs that are readable, easy to understand, and error free. Functions are the most useful feature that accomplish this. A function is called using a function name and its parameters through instructions. Given the input–output specification of a function, the caller simply makes a call to it. This view of the function implies that it is invoked, executed, and returned (with or without results) to the place where it was called in the calling function. When a function calls itself, either directly or indirectly, it is said to be making a *recursive call.* A program becomes compact and readable with recursive functions. Recursion is extremely powerful as it enables the programmer to express complex processes easily. Recursive programs are used in a variety of applications ranging from calculating the factorial of a number to playing complex games against human intelligence.

Let us consider an example of computing the factorial of a number. *Factorial* is a mathematical term. The factorial of a number, say *n*, is equal to the product of all the integers from 1 to *n*. The factorial of *n* is denoted as

$$n! = 1 \times 2 \times 3 \times \cdots \times n \text{ or } n! = n \times n - 1 \times \cdots \times 1 \quad (4.1)$$

For example, $10! = 1 \times 2 \times 3 \times 4 \times 5 \times 6 \times 7 \times 8 \times 9 \times 10$. The simplest program to calculate the factorial of a number is by using a loop with a product variable.

Algorithm 4.1 states the iterative process of computing the factorial of `n` as $10! = 10 \times 9 \times 8 \times ... \times 1$.

ALGORITHM 4.1

```
An iterative version of an algorithm to compute the factorial of a
number
1. start
2. Let n be the number whose factorial is to be computed and let
   Factorial = 1
3. while(n > 1) do
   begin
     Factorial = Factorial * n
     n = n - 1
   end
4. stop
```

The iterative process of computing the factorial of `n` in Algorithm 4.1 can also be written as in Algorithm 4.2.

ALGORITHM 4.2

```
An iterative version of the algorithm to compute the factorial of a
number
1. start
2. Let n be the number whose factorial is to be computed and let
   Factorial = 1
3. for I = 1 to n do           // I can also be initialized to 2
   begin
     Factorial = Factorial * I
   end
4. stop
```

Algorithms 4.1 and 4.2 are iterative algorithms for computing the factorial of `n`. It is possible to give a *recursive* definition for factorial too. The mathematical function defined in Eq. (4.1) for factorial of n can also be defined recursively as

$$n! = n \times (n - 1)!, \text{ where } 1! = 1 \tag{4.2}$$

This recursive definition of factorial has two steps, as follows:

1. If $n = 1$, then factorial of $n = 1$
2. Otherwise, factorial of $n = n \times$ factorial of $(n - 1)$

Program Code 4.1 demonstrates the recursive code for Algorithm 4.1.

PROGRAM CODE 4.1

```
int Factorial(int n)
{
   if(n == 1)        // end condition
      return 1;
   else
      return Factorial(n - 1) * n;
}
```

The `Factorial()` function is an example of a recursive function. In the second `return` statement, the function calls itself. The important thing to remember when creating a recursive function is to give an *end condition*. In Program Code 4.1, the recursion stops when `n` becomes 1. In each call of the function, the value of `n` keeps decreasing. However, when the value reaches 1, the function ends. On the other hand, this function will run infinitely if the initial value of `n` is less than 1, which means that the function is not perfect. Therefore, the condition `n = 1` should be changed to `n ≤ 1`. Let us rewrite the `Factorial()` function as in Program Code 4.2.

PROGRAM CODE 4.2

```
int Factorial(int n)
{
   if(n == 1)        // end condition
      return 1;
   else
      return Factorial(n - 1) * n;
}
```

Program Code 4.2 takes advantage of the fact that the factorial of any integer `n` can be defined recursively as the product of `n` and the factorial of `n - 1`. For example, $5! = 5 \times 4!$

4.2 RECURRENCE

A *recurrence* is a well-defined mathematical function where the function being defined is applied within its own definition. The factorial we defined as $n! = n \times (n - 1)!$ is an example of recurrence with $1! = 1$ as the end condition. Take the *Fibonacci sequence* as an example. The Fibonacci sequence is the sequence of numbers

1, 1, 2, 3, 5, 8, 13, 21, 34, 55, ...

The first two numbers of the sequence are both 1, whereas each succeeding number is the sum of the preceding two numbers (we arrived at 55 as the 10th number; it is the sum of 21 and 34, the eighth and ninth numbers). Let us define a function $F(n)$ that returns the $(n + 1)^{\text{th}}$ Fibonacci number. First, we define the *base cases* as represented by the following functions:

$$F(1) = 1 \text{ and}$$
$$F(2) = 1$$

Now, we consider the other numbers. To get the $(n + 1)^{\text{th}}$ Fibonacci number, we just add the nth and the $(n - 1)^{\text{th}}$ Fibonacci numbers.

$$F(n) = F(n - 1) + F(n - 2) \tag{4.3}$$

This function F is called *recurrence* since it computes the nth value in terms of $(n - 1)^{\text{th}}$ and $(n - 2)^{\text{th}}$ Fibonacci values. The problems that can be described using recurrence are easily expressed as recursive functions in programming.

The process of recursion occurs when a function calls itself. Recursion is useful in situations where solving one or more smaller versions of the same problem can solve the problem. Computing the value of three to the fourth power can be considered as

$$3^4 = 3 \times 3^3$$

Three cubed can be defined as

$$3^3 = 3 \times 3^2$$

Three squared is

$$3^2 = 3 \times 3$$

Finally,

$$3 = 3 \times 3^0 = 3 \times 1$$

The recurrence for this computation is

$$X^Y = X \times X^{Y-1} \tag{4.4}$$

In each of these cases, the problem is reduced to a smaller version of itself. Program Code 4.3 is a recursive code for computation of Eq. (4.4).

PROGRAM CODE 4.3

```
Long int Power(int x, int y)
{
   if(y == 0)      // end condition
      return(1);
   else
      return(x * Power(x, y - 1);
      // This is the "recursive call"
}
```

The end condition in Program Code 4.3 can be `y = 1`; then the return value will be `x` (Program Code 4.6). The iterative version of the same computation is demonstrated in Program Code 4.4.

PROGRAM CODE 4.4

```
Long int Power(int x, int y)
{
   int result = 1;
   for(int i = 1; i <= y; i++)
      result = result * x;
   return(result);
}
```

4.3 USE OF STACK IN RECURSION

We have studied stack as a data structure in Chapter 3. The stack is a special area of memory where temporary variables are stored. It acts on the LIFO principle. To understand how recursive functions use the stack, let us discuss Program Code 4.2. The core steps are given in the following code:

```
if(n <= 1)
   return 1;
else
   return n * Factorial(n - 1);
```

Let n = 3; that is, let us compute the value of 3!, which is $3 \times 2 \times 1 = 6$. When the function is called for the first time, `n` holds the value 3, so the `else` statement is executed. The function knows the value of `n` but not of `Factorial(n - 1)`, so it pushes `n` (value = 3) statement is again executed, and `n` (value = 2) is pushed onto the stack as the function calls itself for the third time with the value 1. Now, the `if` statement is executed and as `n` = 1, the function returns 1. Since the value of `Factorial(1)` is now known, it reverts to its second execution by popping the last value 2 from the stack and multiplying it by 1. This operation gives the value of `Factorial(2)`, so the function reverts to its first execution by popping the next value 3 from the stack and multiplying it with the factorial, giving the value 6, which the function finally returns.

From this example, we notice the following:

1. The `Factorial()` function in Program Code 4.2 runs three times for `n` = 3, out of which it calls itself two times. The number of times a function calls itself is known as the *recursive depth* of that function.
2. Each time the function calls itself, it stores one or more variables on the stack. Since stacks hold a limited amount of memory, the functions with a high recursive depth may crash because of non-availability of memory. Such a situation is known as *stack overflow*.
3. Recursive functions usually have (and in fact should have) a *terminating* (or *end*) *condition*. The `Factorial()` function in Program Code 4.2 stops calling itself when `n` = 1. If this condition was not present, the function would keep calling itself with the values 3, 2, 1, 0, −1, −2, and so on. Such recursion is known as *endless recursion*.
4. All recursive functions go through two distinct phases. The first phase, *winding*, occurs when the function calls itself and pushes values onto the stack. The second phase, *unwinding*, occurs when the function pops values from the stack, usually after the end condition.

4.4 VARIANTS OF RECURSION

Depending on the following characterization, the recursive functions are categorized as direct, indirect, linear, tree, and tail recursions. Recursion may have any one of the following forms:

1. A function calls itself.
2. A function calls another function which in turn calls the caller function.
3. The function call is part of the same processing instruction that makes a recursive function call.

A few more terms that are used with respect to recursion are explained in the following section.

Binary recursion A *binary recursive* function calls itself twice. Fibonacci numbers computation, quick sort, and merge sort are examples of binary recursion.

Program Code 4.5 is an example of a binary recursion as the function `Fib()` calls itself twice.

PROGRAM CODE 4.5

```
int Fib(n)
{
    if(n == 1 ||n == 2)
        return 1;
    else
        return(Fib(n - 1) + Fib(n - 2));
}
```

n-ary recursion and permutations The most general form of recursion is *n-ary recursion*, where *n* is not a constant but some parameter of a function. Functions of this kind are useful in generating combinatorial objects such as permutations.

4.4.1 Direct Recursion

Recursion is when a function calls itself. Recursion is said to be *direct* when a function calls itself directly, and it is said to be *indirect* when it calls another function which in turn calls it. The `Factorial()` function we discussed in Program Code 4.2 is an example of direct recursion. The `Power()` function in Program Code 4.6 is for computing the value of Eq. (4.4) recursively. It is a slightly modified version of Program Code 4.3.

PROGRAM CODE 4.6

```
int Power(int x, int y)
{
    if(y == 1)
        return x;
    else
        return (x * Power(x, y - 1));
}
```

4.4.2 Indirect Recursion

A function is said to be indirectly recursive if it calls another function, which in turn calls it. Program Code 4.7 is an example of an indirect recursion, where the function `Fact()` calls the function `Dummy()`, and the function `Dummy()` in turn calls `Fact()`.

PROGRAM CODE 4.7

```
int Fact(int n)
{
    if(n <= 1)
        return 1;
    else
        return (n * Dummy(n - 1));
}

void Dummy(int n)
{
    Fact(n);
}
```

4.4.3 Tail Recursion

A recursive function is said to be *tail recursive* if there are no pending operations to be performed on return from a recursive call. Tail recursion is also used to return the value of the last recursive call as the value of the function. Tail recursion is advantageous as the amount of information that must be stored during computation is independent of the number of recursive calls. The `Factorial()` function in Program Code 4.2 is an example of a non-tail recursive function. The `Binary_Search()` function in Program Code 4.8 is an example of a tail recursive function.

PROGRAM CODE 4.8

```
int Binary_Search(int A[], int low, int high, int key)
{
    int mid;
    if(low <= high)
    {
        mid = (low + high)/2;
        if(A[mid] == key)
            return mid;
        else if(key < A[mid])
            return Binary_Search(A, low, mid - 1, key);
        else
            return Binary_Search(A, mid + 1, high, key);
    }
    return -1;
}
```

4.4.4 Linear Recursion

Depending on the way the recursion grows, it is classified as *linear* or *tree*. A recursive function is said to be *linearly recursive* when no pending operation involves another recursive call, for example, the `Fact()` function. This is the simplest form of recursion and occurs when an action has a simple repetitive structure consisting of some basic steps followed by the action again. The `Factorial()` function in Program Code 4.2 is an example of linear recursion.

4.4.5 Tree Recursion

In a recursive function, if there is another recursive call in the set of operations to be completed after the recursion is over, this is called a *tree recursion.* Examples of tree recursive functions are the quick sort and merge sort algorithms, the FibSeries algorithm, and so on.

The Fibonacci function FibSeries() is defined as

$$\text{FibSeries}(n) = \begin{cases} 0, & \text{if } n = 0 \\ 1, & \text{if } n = 1 \\ \text{FibSeries}(n-1) + \text{FibSeries}(n-2), & \text{otherwise} \end{cases}$$

Let $n = 5$.
FibSeries(0) = 0
FibSeries(1) = 1
FibSeries(2) = FibSeries(0) + FibSeries(1) = 1
FibSeries(3) = FibSeries(1) + FibSeries(2) = 2
FibSeries(4) = FibSeries(2) + FibSeries(3) = 3
FibSeries(5) = FibSeries(3) + FibSeries(4) = 5

Figure 4.1 demonstrates this explanation for $n = 4$.

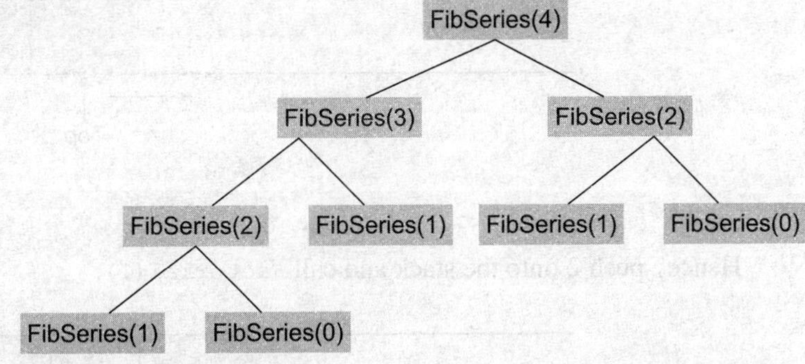

Fig. 4.1 Recursive calls in Fibonacci recursive function for $n = 4$

4.5 EXECUTION OF RECURSIVE CALLS

Let us now see how recursive calls are executed. At every recursive call, all reference parameters and local variables are pushed onto the stack along with the function value and return address. The data is conceptually placed in a *stack frame*, which is pushed onto the system stack. A stack frame contains four different elements:

1. The reference parameters to be processed by the called function
2. Local variables in the calling function
3. The return address
4. The expression that is to receive the return value, if any

Consider the following two lines from the `Factorial()` function in Program Code 4.2:

```
if(n <= 1) return 1;
else return n * Factorial(n - 1);
```

Consider the first call as `Factorial(4)`. Now,

1. $n = 4$

   Hence, statement 2, which is a recursive call, is executed.
   Push 4 onto the stack and call `Factorial(4 - 1)`.

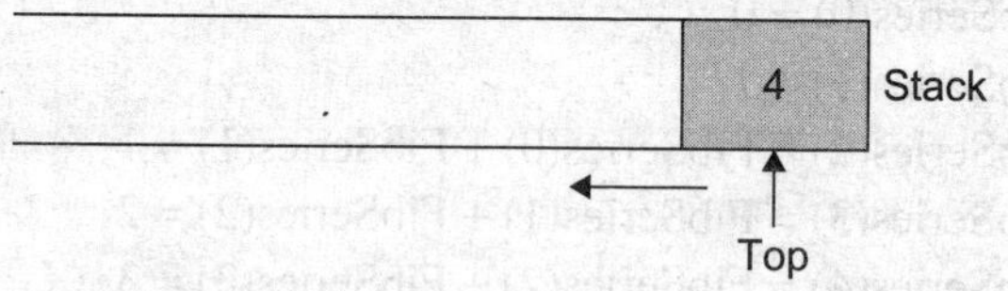

2. $n = 3$

   Hence, push 3 onto the stack and call `Factorial(2)`.

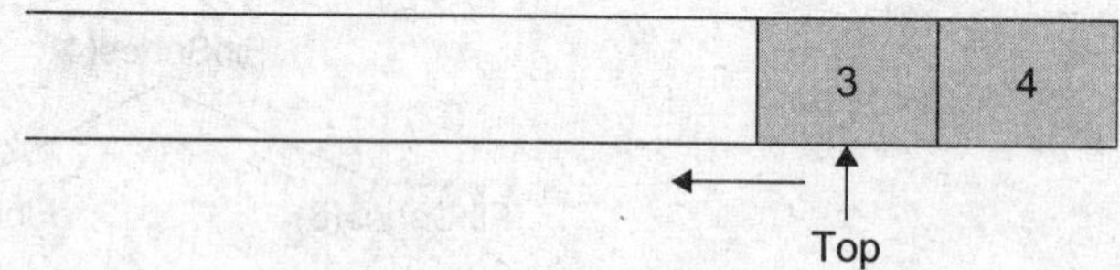

3. $n = 2$

   Hence, push 2 onto the stack and call `Factorial(1)`.

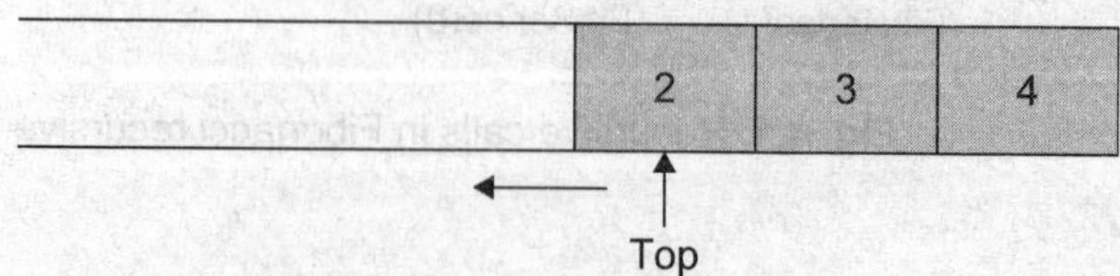

4. $n = 1$
   Now execute statement 1, which returns 1.
5. Pop the contents and $n = 2$, so now the expression becomes 2×1.
6. Now, $n = 3$ after popping the top of the stack contents.
   Therefore, the expression is $3 \times 2 \times 1$.
7. After popping the top of the stack contents applying $n = 4$, the expression is $4 \times 3 \times 2 \times 1 = 24$.
8. After popping the top of the stack contents, we get to know that the stack is empty, and the answer is $4! = 24$.

At the end condition, when no more recursive calls are made, the following steps are performed:

1. If the stack is empty, then execute a normal return.
2. Otherwise, pop the stack frame, that is, take the values of all the parameters that are on the top of the stack and assign these values to the corresponding variables.
3. Use the return address to locate the place where the call was made.
4. Execute all the statements from that place (address) where the call was made.
5. Go to step 1.

4.6 RECURSIVE FUNCTIONS

Recursion is usually viewed by students as a mystical technique that is useful only for some very special class of problems such as computing factorials or the Fibonacci series. This is not true. Practically, any function written using an iterative code can be converted into a recursive code. Of course, this does not guarantee that the resulting program will be easy to understand, but often, the program results in a compact and readable code.

Let us see when recursion is an appropriate solution. One instance is when the problem itself is recursively defined. Appropriate examples of this could be factorial and binomial coefficients.

1. $n! = n \times (n - 1)! \ \{\text{if } n = 1, n! = 1\}$
2. $\binom{n}{m} = \binom{n-1}{m} + \binom{n-1}{m-1}$
3. $\text{Fib}(n) = \text{Fib}(n - 1) + \text{Fib}(n - 2)$
4. $x^y = x \times x^{y-1}$

Recursive functions are often simple and elegant, and their correctness can be easily verified. Many mathematical functions are defined recursively, and their translation into a programming language is often easy. Recursion is natural in Ada, Algol, C, C++, Haskell, Java, Lisp, ML, Modula, Pascal, and many other programming languages. When used carelessly, recursion can sometimes result in an inefficient function. Recursive functions are closely related to inductive definitions of functions in mathematics. To evaluate whether an algorithm is to be written using recursion, we must first try to deduce an inductive definition of the algorithm.

Algorithms that are by nature recursive, such as the factorial, Fibonacci, or power, can be implemented as either iterative or recursive code. However, recursive functions are generally smaller and more efficient than their looping equivalents.

Let us consider an example. Consider a given set of cardinality $n \geq 1$. The problem is to print all the permutations of the set. For example, if the set is {1, 2, 3}, then all the permutations are as follows:

$$\{1, 2, 3\}, \{1, 3, 2\}, \{2, 1, 3\}, \{2, 3, 1\}, \{3, 1, 2\}, \text{and } \{3, 2, 1\}$$

The total number of possible permutations of a set of cardinality n is $n!$. The easiest way to generate these permutations is as follows:

$$\text{Let } S = \{a, b, c, d\}$$

Generate each permutation by printing the following:

1. a followed by the permutations of set $\{b, c, d\}$
2. b followed by the permutations of set $\{a, c, d\}$
3. c followed by the permutations of set $\{a, b, d\}$
4. d followed by the permutations of set $\{a, b, c\}$

Here, the phrase 'followed by' is the part that introduces recursion. This approach implies that we can solve the problem for a set with n elements if we had an algorithm that worked on $(n - 1)$ elements. These considerations lead to Algorithm 4.3.

ALGORITHM 4.3

```
Perm(A, i, n)
begin
   if(i = n) then
      print(A) and return
   B = A
   for j = i to n do
   begin
      Interchange(A, i, j)
      Perm(A, i + 1, n)
      A = B
   end
end
```

Moreover, recursion is also useful when the data structure that the algorithm is to operate on is recursively defined. Examples of such data structures are linked lists and trees. One more instance when recursion is valuable is when we use 'divide and conquer' and 'backtracking' as algorithm design paradigms. *Divide and conquer* is a technique where, for a function to compute n inputs, the strategy suggests splitting the inputs into k distinct subsets, $1 < k \leq n$, yielding k sub-problems. These sub-problems must then be solved and should be combined to get the final solution. If the sub-problem is still large, the technique is reapplied. The reapplication is expressed better by the recursive function. Recursion is a technique that allows us to break down a problem into one or more sub-problems that are similar in form to the original problem. Examples include binary search, merge sort, and quick sort.

4.6.1 Writing Recursive Code

The general approach to writing a recursive function is listed in the following sequence:

1. Write the function header so you are sure what the function will do and how it will be called. Identify some unit of measure for the size of the problem the function or procedure will work on. Then, pretend that the task is to write a function that will work on problems of all sizes.
2. Decompose the problem into sub-problems. Identify clearly the non-recursive case of the problem. Make it as small as possible. The function will nearly always begin by testing for this non-recursive case, also known as the *base case* or the *end condition*.
3. Write recursive calls to solve those sub-problems whose form is similar to that of the original problem.
4. Write the code to combine, enhance, or modify the results of the recursive call(s), if necessary, to construct the desired return value or create the desired side effects.
5. Write the end condition(s) to handle any situations that are not handled properly by the recursive portion of the program.

4.6.2 Tower of Hanoi: An Example of Recursion

The use of recursion often makes everything simpler. First, find out the recurring data and the essential feature of the problem that should change as the function calls itself. In the Tower of Hanoi solution, one recurs on the largest disk to be moved. That is, one has to write a recursive function that takes the largest disk as a parameter in the tower to be moved. The function should take three parameters indicating from which peg the tower should be moved (source), to which peg it should go (dest), and the last peg (spare), which is used temporarily.

Let us consider the initial position of the problem as in Fig. 4.2.

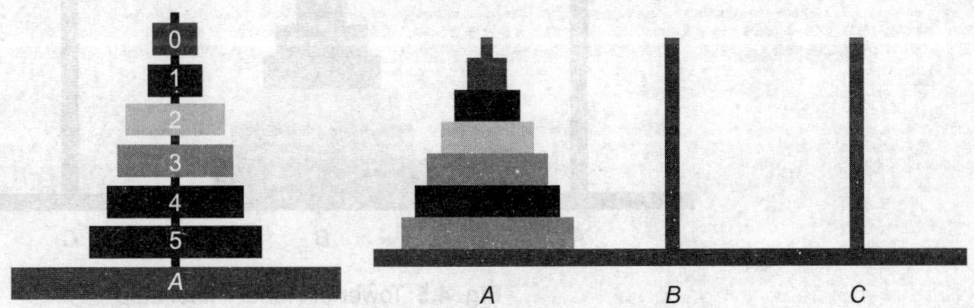

Fig. 4.2 Tower of Hanoi—initial position

We can break this into three basic steps.

1. Move the disk 4 and the ones smaller than that from the peg *A* (source) to peg *C* (spare), using peg *B* (dest) as a spare. We achieve it by recursively using the same function. After finishing this, we will have all the disks smaller than disk 4 on peg *C* (Fig. 4.3).

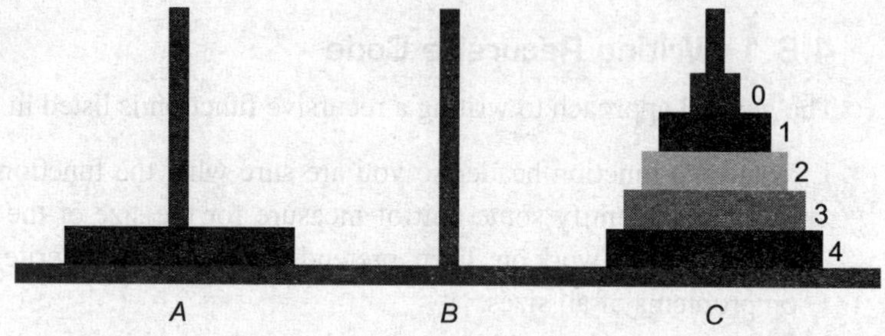

Fig. 4.3 Tower of Hanoi—step 1

2. Now, with all the smaller disks on the spare peg *C*, we can move disk 5 from peg *A* to peg *B* (Fig. 4.4).

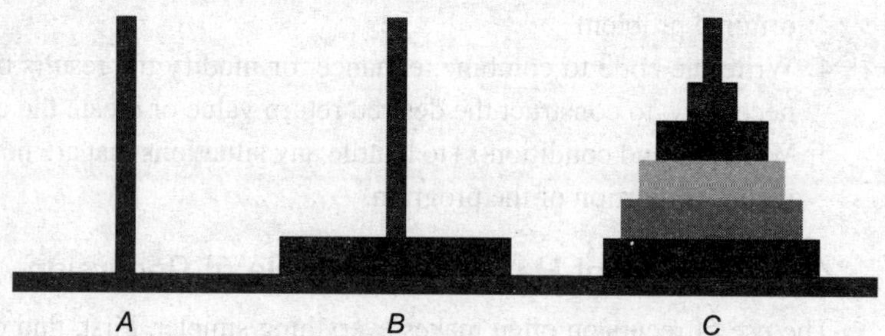

Fig. 4.4 Tower of Hanoi—step 2

3. Finally, we want disk 4 and the smaller disks to be moved from peg *C* to peg *B*. We do this recursively using the same function again. At the end, we have disk 5 and the smaller ones on peg *B* (Fig. 4.5).

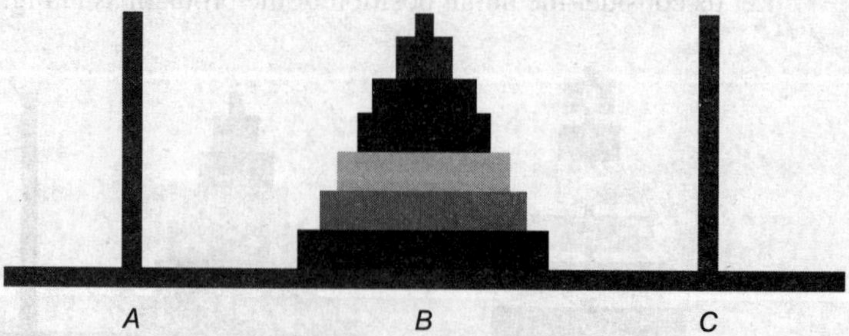

Fig. 4.5 Tower of Hanoi—final step

In Algorithm 4.4, at the caller function, a call is made to `HTower` with `disk` = 5, `source` = *A*, `dest` = *B*, and `spare` = *C*.

ALGORITHM 4.4

```
HTower(disk, source, dest, spare)
if disk == 0, then
   move disk from source to dest
else
   HTower(disk - 1, source, spare, dest)          // Step 1
   move disk from source to dest             // Step 2
   HTower(disk - 1, spare, dest, source)          // Step 3
end if
```

Note that the pseudocode adds a base case when `disk` = 0, that is, the smallest disk. In this case, we do not need to worry about smaller disks, so we can just move the disk directly. In the other cases, we follow the three-step recursive function already described for disk 5.

The tree representation of recursive calls is shown in Fig. 4.6.

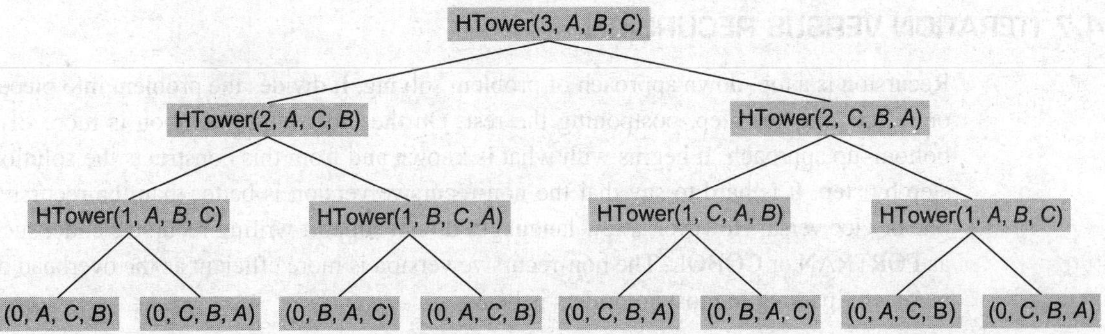

Fig. 4.6 Tower of Hanoi—Call tree for three disks

The root represents the first call to the function. The function call is represented as a node in the tree. The child nodes of the node *n* represent the function calls made by *n*. For example, HTower(2, *A*, *C*, *B*) and HTower(2, *C*, *B*, *A*) are the child nodes of HTower(3, *A*, *B*, *C*) since these are the two function calls that HTower(3, *A*, *B*, *C*) makes. The leaf nodes represent the base cases.

4.6.3 Checking for Correctness

One of the most difficult aspects of programming recursively is the process of accepting that the recursive call will do the right thing. The following checklist provides the five conditions that must hold true for recursion to work. If each of these conditions holds for a recursive function, one may conclude that the recursion will work correctly.

1. A recursive function must have at least one end condition and one recursive case.
2. The test for the end condition has to execute prior to the recursive call.
3. The problem must be broken down in such a way that the recursive call is closer to the base case than the top level call. This condition is actually not quite strong or sufficient. Moving towards the end condition alone is not sufficient; it must also be true that the base case is reached in a finite number of recursive calls.
4. The recursive call must not skip over the base case.
5. Verify that the non-recursive code of the function is operating correctly.

4.6.4 Things to Remember

The following points should be kept in mind while doing recursive programming:

1. Recursive functions call themselves within their own definition.
2. Recursive functions must have a non-recursive terminating condition; otherwise, an infinite loop will occur.
3. Recursion, though easy to code, is often but not always, memory starving.

4.7 ITERATION VERSUS RECURSION

Recursion is a top–down approach of problem solving. It divides the problem into pieces or selects one key step, postponing the rest. On the other hand, iteration is more of a bottom–up approach. It begins with what is known and from this constructs the solution step by step. It is hard to say that the non-recursive version is better than the recursive one or vice versa. However, a few languages do not support writing recursive code, such as FORTRAN or COBOL. The non-recursive version is more efficient as the overhead of parameter passing in most compilers is heavy.

4.7.1 Demerits of Recursive Algorithms

Although with many merits, recursive algorithms have their limitations. They are as follows:

1. Many programming languages do not support recursion; hence, recursive mathematical function is to be implemented using iterative methods.
2. Even though mathematical functions can be easily implemented using recursion, it is always at the cost of additional execution time and memory space. For example, let us take the case of a recursion tree for generating six numbers in a Fibonacci series. It is known that a Fibonacci series is of the form 0, 1, 1, 2, 3, 5, 8, 13, …, *n*, where each number from the third is the sum of the preceding two numbers. It can be noticed that $F(n-2)$ is computed twice, $F(n-3)$ is computed thrice, and $F(n-4)$ is computed four times.
3. A recursive function can be called from within or outside itself, and to ensure proper functioning, it has to save the return addresses in some order so that the return to the proper location will yield the desired result when the return to a calling statement is made.

4.7.2 Demerits of Iterative Methods

Although the iterative method has various merits, it has its own limitations too. They are as follows:

1. Iterative code is not readable and hence not easy to understand.
2. In iterative techniques, looping of statements is necessary and needs a complex logic.
3. The iterations may result in a lengthy code.

4.8 SIMULATING RECURSION USING STACK (ELIMINATING RECURSION)

Wherever a data object/process/relation is defined recursively, it is often easy to describe the algorithms recursively. If a programming language does not support recursion or one needs a non-recursive code, then a recursive code can be translated to a non-recursive one. Once a recursive function is written and is verified for its correctness, one can remove recursion for efficiency. This can be done using the following rules:

1. At the beginning of the recursive function, a code is inserted to create an empty stack. This stack is to be used to hold the values of parameters, the local variables, the function value, and the return address for each recursive call.
2. The jump label is attached to the first executable statement, say label_1. Now, replace each recursive call by a set of instructions that perform the following:
   (a) Push the values of all parameters and local variables on the stack.
   (b) Create the ith new label, label_*i* and store *i* in the stack. The value *i* of this label will be used to compute the return address. This label is placed in the program as described in step 2(e).
   (c) Evaluate the arguments of this call, which may be part of the expression. Assign these values to the appropriate formal parameters.
   (d) Insert an unconditional branch to the beginning of the function.
   (e) Attach the label created in step 2(b) to the statement immediately following the unconditional branch. Attach the label to a statement that retrieves the function value from the top of the stack. Then, make use of this value in whatever way the recursive program describes.
3. Once all the recursive calls have been eliminated, replace all the return statements using the following steps:
   (a) If the stack is empty, then execute a normal return.
   (b) Otherwise, take the current value of all the output parameters (explicitly or implicitly understood to be of type output or input) and assign these values to the corresponding variables that are on top of the stack.
   (c) Now, insert a code that removes the index of the return address from the stack if any has been placed there. Assign this address to some unused variable.
   (d) Remove the values of all local variables and parameters from the stack and assign them to their corresponding variables.

(e) If this is a function, insert instructions to evaluate the expression immediately following `return()` and store the result on the top of the stack.
(f) Use the index of the label of the return address to execute a branch to that label.

If all these rules are followed carefully, one can convert recursion to an iterative code.

C++ supports recursion and it is handled using a run-time stack. For each function call, all the actual parameters are pushed onto the stack. This is also called as *activation record*. This activation record contains memory for the return value—a pointer to the base of the previous stack frame in the stack. It includes the return address, that is, the address of the instruction to be executed after the function call is completed. It also includes memory for all the parameters and for all the local variables of the function. The working of recursion is as described earlier.

4.9 APPLICATIONS OF RECURSION

The following are the major areas where the process of recursion can be applied:

1. Artificial intelligence
2. Search techniques
3. Game playing
4. Computational linguistics and natural language processing
5. Expert systems
6. Pattern recognition and computer vision
7. Robotics

RECAPITULATION

- A function may call itself or other functions, and the called functions in turn may again call the calling function. Such functions are called recursive functions.
- Any correct iterative code can be converted into its equivalent recursive code and vice versa.
- The basic concepts and ideas involved with recursion are simple—a function that has to be solved is treated as a big problem and it solves itself by using itself to solve a slightly smaller problem. The recurrence relation is easily converted to recursive code.
- The working of recursion is fairly straightforward. However, to understand the working of recursion better and to be able to use it well, one requires practice. The best way to obtain this is to write a lot of recursive functions.
- Recursion can be used for divide and conquer-based search and sort algorithms to increase the efficiency of these operations.
- For most problems such as the Tower of Hanoi, recursion presents an incredibly elegant solution that is easy to code and simple to understand.

KEY TERMS

Binary recursion A simple unary recursive function calls itself once, whereas the binary recursive function calls itself twice. A factorial is a unary function, whereas Fibonacci is a binary recursion.

Depth of recursion The number of times a function calls itself is known as the recursive depth of that function.

Direct and indirect recursion When a recursive function calls itself directly, it is called direct recursion and when the function calls another function, which in turn calls the first function, it is called an indirect recursion.

End condition Recursive functions usually have and in fact should have a condition that would terminate the recursive calls. This terminating condition is called end condition. In the function factorial, when $n = 1$ the function returns 1. If this condition were not present, the function would keep calling itself with the values 3, 2, 1, 0, –1, –2, and so on till infinity. Such recursion is known as endless recursion.

Linear and tree recursion Depending on the way the recursion grows, it is classified as linear or tree. A recursive function is said to be linearly recursive when no pending operation involves another recursive call. If there is another recursive call in the set of operations to be completed after the recursion is over, then it is called a tree recursion. Factorial is an example of linear recursion and Fibonacci is an example of tree recursion.

Recurrence relation A recurrence is a well-defined mathematical function written in terms of itself; it is a mathematical function defined recursively such as $n! = n \times (n - 1)!$

Recursive functions A function may call itself or call other functions and the called functions in turn again may call the calling function. Such functions are called recursive functions.

Stack overflow in recursion Each time a function calls itself, it stores one or more variables on the stack. Since the stack holds a limited amount of memory, functions with a high recursive depth may crash because of the non-availability of memory. Such a situation is known as stack overflow.

Tail recursion A recursive function is said to be tail recursive if there are no pending operations to be performed on return from a recursive call; otherwise it is called a non-tail recursion. The factorial function is an example of non-tail recursion, whereas binary search is an example of tail recursion.

Winding and unwinding of recursion All recursive functions go through two distinct phases. The first phase, winding, occurs when the function is calling itself and pushing values onto the stack. The second phase, unwinding, occurs when the function is popping values from the stack, usually after the end condition.

EXERCISES

Multiple choice questions

1. Infinite recursion occurs when
   (a) a base case is omitted
   (b) a base case is never reached
   (c) both (a) and (b)
   (d) none of the above

2. Fibonacci function Fib(n) = Fib(n – 1) + Fib(n – 2) is an example of
   (a) direct recursion
   (b) tree recursion
   (c) linear recursion
   (d) both (a) and (b)

3. Any recursive function can be converted into an all equivalent non-recursive function
(a) always
(b) never
(c) sometimes
(d) if the function is tail recursive
4. Which of the following algorithm strategies results in an inherently recursive code?
(a) Greedy paradigm
(b) Divide and conquer paradigm
(c) Dynamic paradigm
(d) Both (a) and (c)
5. The advantage of recursion is that the
(a) code size is less
(b) time complexity is less
(c) space complexity is less
(d) none of the above
6. The data structure used for recursion is
(a) stack
(b) queue
(c) tree
(d) none of the above
7. Consider the following code:

```
void foo(int n, int sum 0)
{
    int k = 0, j = 0;
    if(n == 0) return;
    k = n % 10; j = n/10;
    sum = sum + k;
    foo(j, sum);
    printf("%d,", k);
}

int main()
{
    int a = 2048, sum = 0;
    foo(a, sum);
    printf("%d\n", sum);
}
```

What does this program print?
(a) `8, 4, 0, 2, 14`
(b) `8, 4, 0, 2, 0`
(c) `2, 0, 4, 8, 14`
(d) `2, 0, 4, 8, 0`
8. Consider the following code:

```
int f(int n)
{
    static int i = 1;
    if(n >= 5) return n;
    n = n + i;
    i++;
    return(f(n));
}
```

What would be the value returned by `f(1)`?
(a) `5`
(b) `6`
(c) `7`
(d) `8`
9. The following code is an example of ______ recursion.

```
funA()
{
    funB();
}

funB()
{
    funA();
}
```

(a) direct
(b) indirect
(c) both (a) and (b)
(d) none of these
10. The following code is an example of ______ recursion.

```
funA()
{
    .
    .
    .
        funA();
    .
    .
    .
        funA();
}
```

(a) linear

(b) tree
(c) both (a) and (b)
(d) none of these

Review questions

1. Write a recursive algorithm to check whether a specified character is in a string.
2. Write a recursive algorithm to count all occurrences of a specified character in a string.
3. Write a recursive algorithm that removes all occurrences of a specified character in a string.
4. Write a recursive algorithm that finds all occurrences of a substring in a string.
5. Write a recursive algorithm that changes an integer to a binary number.
6. In binary search, the given key is compared with the middle element of an array. If a match occurs, the search is successful; else the comparison decides whether the search would be restricted to either the upper half or the lower half of the array. Write a recursive function Binary(key, *A*, *n*), where *n* is the size of the array *A*.
7. Write a recursive function in C++ to count the number of occurrences of a given integer in an array. The function should have three parameters—an array, the number of elements in the array, and the count.
8. Write a recursive function in C++ that counts the number of occurrences of a particular digit in the decimal representation of a given integer. For example, if the parameters to the function are 8 and 382885, the function should return 3 as there are three occurrences of the digit 8 in 382885.
   [Hint: Remember that *n* % 10 will give the remainder of *n* divided by 10, whereas *n*/10 will give the integer part of *n* divided by 10.]
9. Write a recursive function in C++ to replace every occurrence of a specified character in a string with another character. The function should be a void function and should have three parameters—a string, a character to be replaced, and the character with which it is to be replaced.
10. Write a recursive function in C++ to compute the square root of a number.
11. Write a recursive function in C++ to convert decimal integers to their radix *r* representation by successive divisions.
12. Write a recursive function in C++ that takes an integer as input and displays the reverse of the number on the screen.
13. The function $F(n, r)$ can be defined recursively as $F(n-1, r) + F(n-1, r-1)$. Write a recursive program to compute $F(n, r)$.
14. Using the following recursive definitions, write a recursive function in C++.

    (a) $f(a, b)\begin{bmatrix} 1 & \text{if } b=0 \\ a \times f(a, b-1) & \text{if } b>0 \end{bmatrix}$

    (b) $f(a, b)\begin{bmatrix} 1 & \text{if } b=0 \\ a \times f(a, -b+1) & \text{if } b<0 \end{bmatrix}$
15. Write the C++ function for the recursive algorithm that prints the elements of a list in the reverse order.

Answers to multiple choice questions

1. (c) 2. (d) 3. (a) 4. (b) 5. (a) 6. (a) 7. (d) 8. (c) 9. (b)
10. (b)

5 QUEUES

OBJECTIVES

After completing this chapter, the reader will be able to understand the following:

- Restricted linear lists—queues
- Implementation of queues using arrays
- Implementation of circular queues
- Use of queues in simulations, job scheduling, and other applications

We have studied linear data structures, namely, arrays and stacks. In arrays, element insertion at and deletion from any position causes a lot of data movement. On the other hand, in stacks, these operations are performed at only one end, the *top*. A *queue* is a special type of data structure that performs insertions at one end called the *rear* and deletions at the other end called the *front*. Let us discuss the concept and functioning of queues in this chapter.

5.1 CONCEPT OF QUEUES

In our daily life, we have experienced standing in queues for various reasons such as purchasing tickets or getting admission to educational institutes. In all such places, we have to wait in a queue for our turn to get the service.

Similarly a queue is a common example of a linear list or an ordered list where data can be inserted at and deleted from different ends. The end at which data is inserted is called the *rear* and that from which it is deleted is called the *front*. These limits guarantee that the data is processed in the sequence in which they are entered. In short, a queue is a *first in first out* (FIFO) or *last in last out* (LILO) structure.

Consider an ordered list $L = \{a_1, a_2, a_3, a_4, \ldots, a_n\}$. If we assume that L represents a queue, then a_1 is the front-end element and a_n is the rear-end element. In addition, a_i is behind a_{i-1}.

Let us consider a queue Q of customers standing at a ticket counter.

Q = {Shweta, Anup, Saurabh, Vishnu, Shivadmika, Alan, Devanarayanan, Anagha}

In the queue Q, Shweta is at the front end and Anagha is at the rear end.

Queues are one of the most common data processing structures. They are frequently used in most system software such as operating systems, network and database implementations, and other areas. Queues are very useful in time-sharing and distributed computer systems where many widely distributed users share the system simultaneously. Whenever a user places a request, the operating system adds the request at the end of the queue of jobs waiting to be executed. The CPU executes the job at the front of the queue.

5.2 QUEUE AS ABSTRACT DATA TYPE

Look at the queue at the bus stop in Fig. 5.1. Here, the person to get inside the bus is the one who is at the front. The new person joining would stand at the rear end.

Fig. 5.1 Example of queue—passengers waiting at bus stop

To realize a queue as an abstract data type (ADT), we need a suitable data structure for storing the elements in the queue and the functions operating on it. The basic operations performed on the queue include adding and deleting an element, traversing the queue, checking whether the queue is full or empty, and finding who is at the front and who is at the rear ends.

A minimal set of operations on a queue is as follows:

1. `create()`—creates an empty queue, *Q*
2. `add(i,Q)`—adds the element *i* to the rear end of the queue, *Q* and returns the new queue
3. `delete(Q)`—takes out an element from the front end of the queue and returns the resulting queue
4. `getFront(Q)`—returns the element that is at the front position of the queue
5. `Is_Empty(Q)`—returns true if the queue is empty; otherwise returns false

The complete specification for the queue ADT is given in Algorithm 5.1.

ALGORITHM 5.1

```
class queue(element)
   declare create() → queue
   add(element, queue) → queue
   delete(queue) → queue
   getFront(queue) → queue
```

```
    Is_Empty(queue) → Boolean;
    For all Q ∈ queue, i ∈ element let
    Is_Empty(create()) = true
    Is_Empty(add(i,Q)) = false
    delete(create()) = error
    delete(add(i,Q)) =
       if Is_Empty(Q) then create
       else add(i, delete(Q))
    getFront(create) = error
    getFront(add(i, Q)) =
       if Is_Empty(Q) then i
       else getFront(Q)
    end
end queue
```

Since a queue is a linear data structure, it can be implemented using either arrays or linked lists. For the former, we use static memory allocation and for the latter, we use dynamic memory allocation. Let us see how a queue can be implemented using arrays.

5.3 REALIZATION OF QUEUES USING ARRAYS

We already know that an array is not a suitable data structure for frequent insertion and deletion of data elements. Another drawback of arrays is that they use static memory allocation, and so they can store only a fixed number of elements. In many practical applications, we come across a situation where the size of the data set keeps changing by such frequent insertions and deletions. Let us see the implementation of the various operations on the queue using arrays.

Create This operation should create an empty queue. Here `max` is the maximum initial size that is defined.

```
#define max 50
int Queue[max];
int Front = Rear = -1;
```

In addition to a one-dimensional array `Queue`, we need two more variables, `Front` and `Rear`. This declaration creates an empty queue of size `max`. The two variables `Front` and `Rear` are initialized to represent an empty queue. In general, it is suitable to set `Front` to one position behind the actual front of the queue and set the rear to the last element in the queue. Thus, the condition `Front = Rear` indicates an empty queue. As our array index ranges between `0` and `(max - 1)`, the front and rear are initialized to –1.

Is_Empty This operation checks whether the queue is empty or not. This is confirmed by comparing the values of `Front` and `Rear`. If `Front = Rear`, then `Is_Empty` returns true, else returns false.

```
bool Is_Empty()
{
   if(Front == Rear)
      return 1;
```

```
   else
      return 0;
}
```

Is_Full In the definition of the queue ADT, the function for checking the `Queue_Full` condition is not included. When we go in for an array implementation, due to its fixed size, we need to check the state of the queue for being full. It is recommended that before we delete an element from the queue, we must check whether the queue is empty or not. Similarly, before insertion, the queue must be checked for the `Queue_Full` state. When `Rear` points to the last location of the array, it indicates that the queue is full, that is, there is no space to accommodate any more elements.

```
bool Is_Full()
{
   if(Rear == max - 1)
      return 1;
   else
      return 0;
}
```

Add This operation adds an element in the queue if it is not full. As `Rear` points to the last element of the queue, the new element is added at the (rear + 1)th location.

```
void Add(int Element)
{
   if(Is_Full())
      cout << "Error, Queue is full";
   else
      Queue[++Rear] = Element;
}
```

Delete This operation deletes an element from the front of the queue and sets `Front` to point to the next element. `Front` can be initialized to one position less than the actual front. We should first increment the value of `Front` and then remove the element.

```
int Delete()
{
   if(Is_Empty())
      cout << "Sorry, queue is Empty";
   else
      return(Queue[++Front]);
}
```

getFront The operation `getFront` returns the element at the front, but unlike `delete`, this does not update the value of `Front`.

```
int getFront()
{
   if(Is_Empty())
      cout << "Sorry, queue is Empty";
```

```
    else
        return(Queue[Front + 1]);
}
```

Program Code 5.1 shows one way of realization of the queue ADT using arrays.

PROGRAM CODE 5.1

```
//Queue ADT
class queue
{
   private:
      int Rear, Front;
      int Queue[50];
      int max;
      int Size;
   public:
      queue()
      {
         Size = 0; max = 50;
         Rear = Front = -1 ;
      }
      int Is_Empty();
      int Is_Full();
      void Add(int Element);
      int Delete();
      int getFront();
};

int queue :: Is_Empty()
{
   if(Front == Rear)
      return 1;
   else
      return 0;
}
int queue :: Is_Full()
{
   if(Rear == max - 1)
      return 1;
   else
      return 0;
}

void queue :: Add(int Element)
```

```
{
   if(!Is_Full())
      Queue[++Rear] = Element;
   Size++;
}

int queue :: Delete()
{
   if(!Is_Empty())
      {
         Size--;
         return(Queue[++Front]);
      }
}

int queue :: getFront()
{
   if(!Is_Empty())
      return(Queue[Front + 1]);
}
```

This implementation of queues using arrays has some flaws in it. Let us discuss these flaws through Program Code 5.2.

PROGRAM CODE 5.2

```
void main(void)
{
   queue Q;
   Q.Add(11);
   Q.Add(12);
   Q.Add(13);
   cout << Q.Delete() << endl;
   Q.Add(14);
   cout << Q.Delete() << endl;
   cout << Q.Delete() << endl;
   cout << Q.Delete() << endl;
   cout << Q.Delete() << endl;
   Q.Add(15);
   Q.Add(16);
   cout << Q.Delete() << endl;
}
```

Let *Q* be an empty queue with `Front = Rear = -1`. Let `max = 5.`

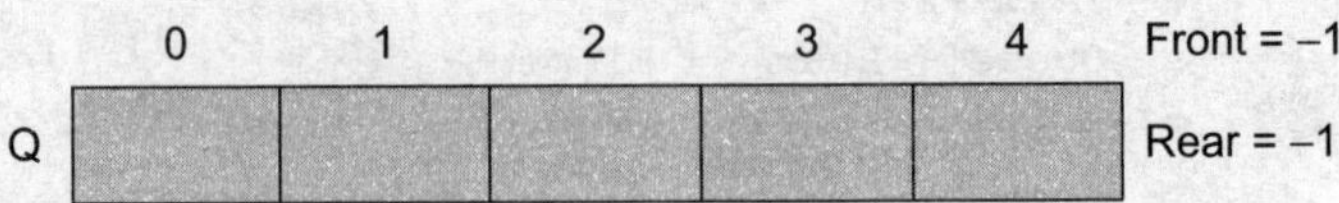

Consider the following statements:

1. `Q.Add(11)`

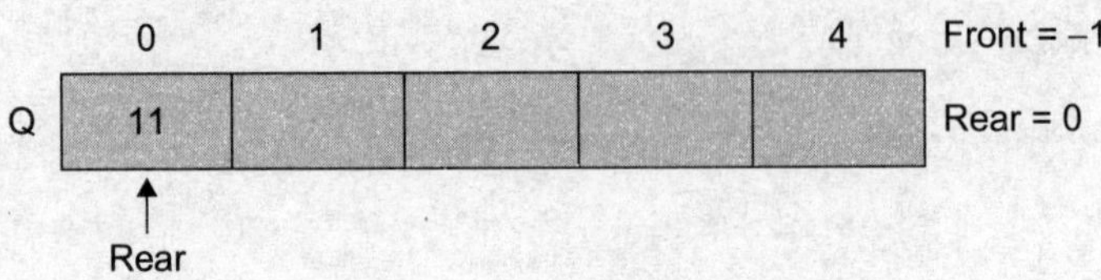

2. `Q.Add(12)`

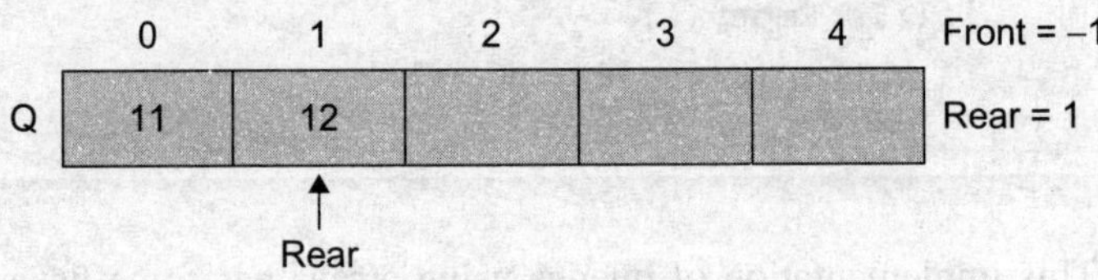

3. `Q.Add(13)`

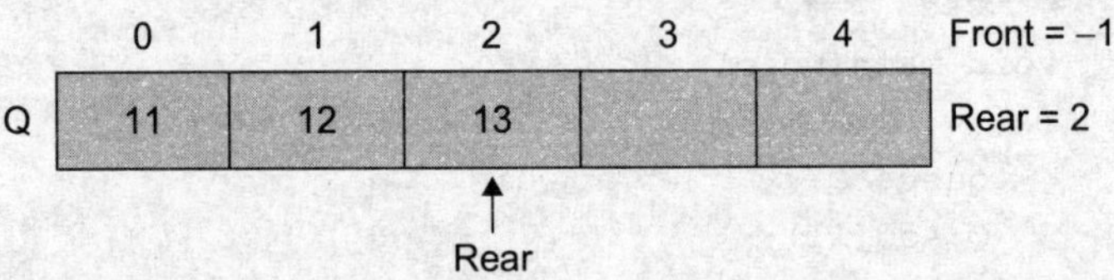

4. `A = Q.Delete()`
   Here, `A = Q[++Front] = Q[0] = 11`

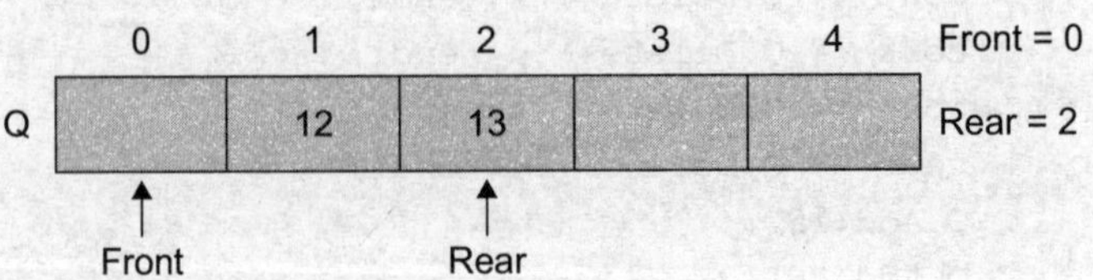

5. `Q.Add(14)`

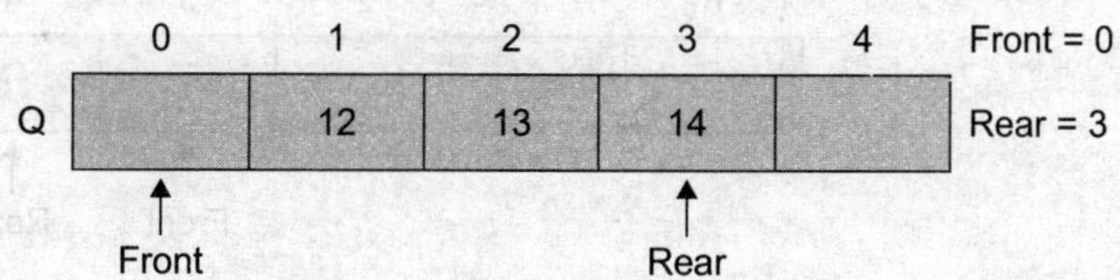

6. `A = Q.Delete()`
   `A = Q[++ Front] =    Q [1] = 12`

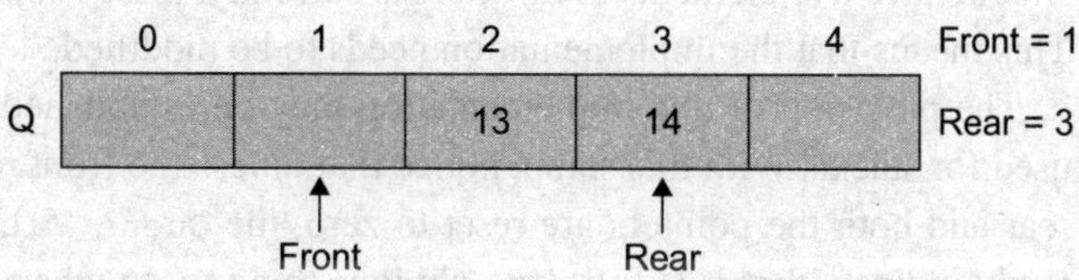

7. `A = Q.Delete()`
   `A = 13`

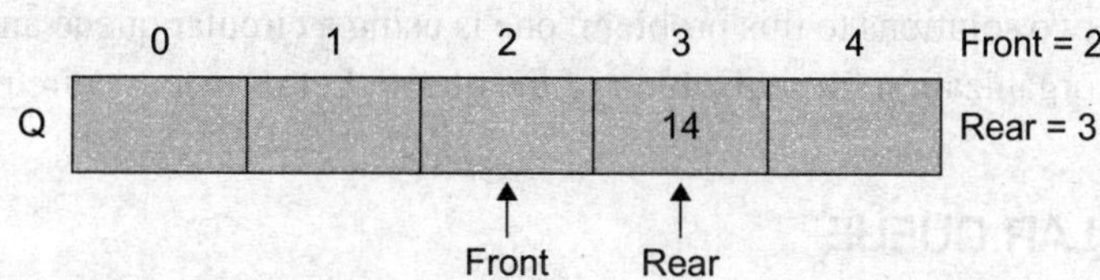

8. `A = Q.Delete()`

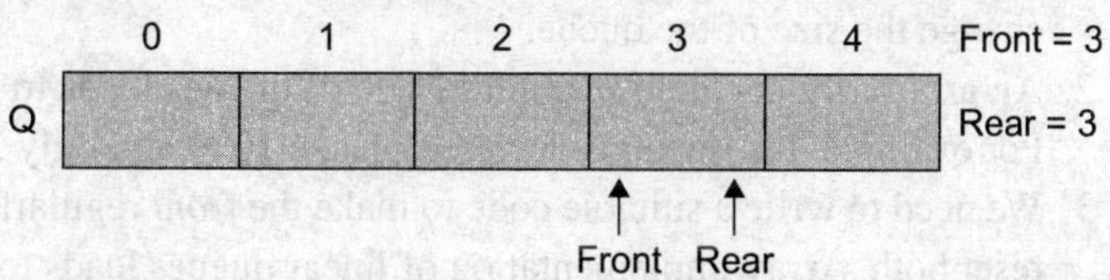

9. `A = Q.Delete()`
   Here we get the `Queue_empty` error condition as `Front = Rear = 3`
   Let us execute a few more statements.

10. `Q.Add(15)`

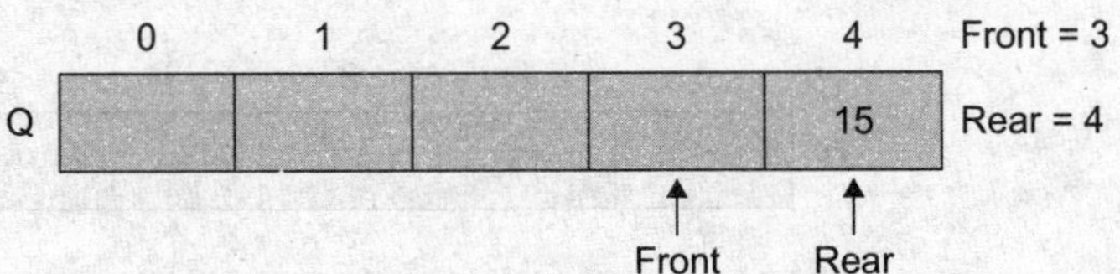

11. `Q.Add(16)`

This statement will generate the message `Queue_Full` because `Rear = 4`. If one carefully observes whether the queue is really full, it actually is not. The `Queue_Full` state should have five elements in it, whereas currently, there is only one element in the queue. This means that the implementation needs to be modified.

The precision of this implementation may be established in a manner similar to that used for stacks. With this setup, notice that unless the front regularly catches up with the rear and both the pointers are reset to zero, the `Queue_Full` condition does not necessarily indicate that it is full. One obvious thing to do when `Queue_Full` is signalled is to move the entire queue to the left so that the first element is again at the 0th location and `Front = -1`. This is obviously not a feasible solution as it is time consuming and involves a lot of data movement. This becomes impractical, especially when the queue is of a large size. The queue we have discussed so far is called the *linear queue*. There are two solutions to this problem: one is using a circular queue and the other is using a linked organization for realization of the queue. Let us discuss circular queues in Section 5.4.

5.4 CIRCULAR QUEUE

From the demonstration of the execution of a few `push` and `pop` operations it can be concluded that the linear queues using arrays have certain drawbacks listed as follows:

1. The linear queue is of a fixed size. So the user does not have the flexibility to dynamically change the size of the queue.
2. An arbitrarily declared maximum size of queues leads to poor utilization of memory. For example, the queue is declared of size 1000 and only 20 of them are used.
3. We need to write a suitable code to make the *front* regularly catch up with the *rear* and reset both. Array implementation of linear queues leads to the `Queue_Full` state even though the queue is not actually full.
4. To avoid this, when `Queue_Full` is signalled, we need to rewind the entire queue to the original start location (if there are empty locations) so that the first element is at the 0th location and `Front` is set to –1. Such movement of data is an efficient way to avoid this drawback.

The technique that essentially allows the queue to wraparound upon reaching the end of the array eliminates these drawbacks. Such a technique which allows the queues to wraparound from end to start is called a *circular queue*. Virtually, we want the insertion process and the rear to wraparound the queue.

Hence, a more efficient queue representation is obtained by implementing the array Q as circular. Here, as we go on adding elements to the queue and reach the end of the array, the next element is stored in the first slot of the array if it is empty. Suppose the queue Q is of size n. Now, if we go on adding elements in the queue, we may reach the location $n - 1$. If it is not circular, no more elements can be added even though there are empty locations at the front of the array. Instead, if there are empty locations at the front, using a circular queue we can add elements at that location rather than signalling an error as the queue is full or is shifting the data.

The empty slots will be filled with new incoming elements even though `Rear = n - 1`. Hence, the circular queue allows us to continue adding elements even though we have reached the end of the array. The queue is said to be full only when there are n elements in the queue. The pictorial representation of a circular queue is shown in Figs 5.2(a) and 5.2(b).

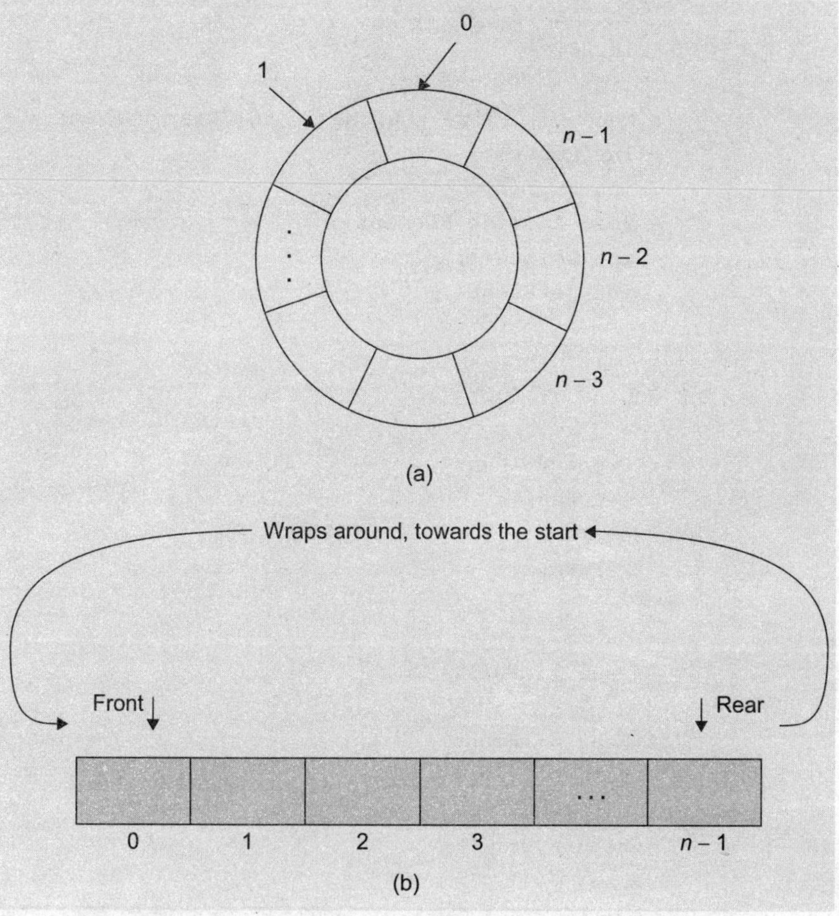

Fig. 5.2 Circular queue (a) Conceptual view (b) Physical view

Let us consider the queue Q which is of size n. We have already studied the operations on linear queues using arrays. We also studied its corresponding functions in the C++ language. Let us see whether the same functions can be used for circular queues. In a circular queue, when the *rear* is $n - 1$ and a new element is to be added, the *rear* should be set to 0.

Initially, both the *front* and the *rear* are set to −1. The value of *front* will always be one less than that of the actual *front*. The functions to add and delete elements are rewritten with a few modifications in Program Code 5.3.

PROGRAM CODE 5.3

```
#include<iostream.h>
class Cqueue
{
   private:
      int Rear, Front;
      int Queue[50];
      int Max;
      int Size;
   public:
      Cqueue() {Size = 0; Max = 50; Rear = Front = -1;}
      int Empty();
      int Full();
      void Add(int Element);
      int Delete();
      int getFront();
};

int Cqueue :: Empty()
{
   if(Front == Rear)
      return 1;
   else
      return 0;
}

int Cqueue :: Full()
{
   if(Rear == Front)
      return 1;
   else
      return 0;
}
```

```
void Cqueue :: Add(int Element)
{
   if(!Full())
      Rear = (Rear + 1) % Max;
   Queue[Rear] = Element;
   Size++;
}

int Cqueue :: Delete()
{
   if(!Empty())
      Front = (Front + 1) % Max;
   Size--;
   return(Queue[Front]);
}

int Cqueue :: getFront()
{
   int Temp;
   if(!Empty())
      Temp = (Front + 1) % Max;
   return(Queue[Temp]);
}

void main(void)
{
   Cqueue Q;
   Q.Add(11);
   Q.Add(12);
   Q.Add(13);
   cout << Q.Delete() << endl;
   Q.Add(14);
   cout << Q.Delete() << endl;
   cout << Q.Delete() << endl;
   cout << Q.Delete() << endl;
   cout << Q.Delete() << endl;
   Q.Add(15);
   Q.Add(16);
   cout << Q.Delete() << endl;
}
```

The implementation of a circular queue using an array is provided in Program Code 5.3. Let us see its working with an example. Consider `max = 5` and initially, `Front = Rear = 0`. The iterations are shown in Table 5.1.

Table 5.1 Implementation of circular queue

0	1	2	3	4	Front	Rear	Action
					0	0	`Q_Empty`
	11				0	1	Insert 11
	11	12			0	2	Insert 12
	11	12	13		0	3	Insert 13
	11	12	13	14	0	4	Insert 14
	11	12	13	14	0		Insert 15 Can't insert 15 as `Q_Full` since `Rear` = (4 + 1)%5 = 0 which is equal to `Front`
	–	12	13	14	1	4	Delete
		–	13	14	2	4	Delete
			–	14	3	4	Delete
				–	4	4	Delete Can't delete as `Front = Rear` makes `Q_Empty`

To check the `Queue_Full` and `Queue_Empty` conditions, we need to check whether the values of `Front` and `Rear` are equal. In the programming languages C/C++, the array index varies from 0 to $n - 1$, so that one location of the circular queue always remains unused. Such is not the case in languages such as Pascal. Hence, in a circular queue that uses arrays in C/C++, we can store $n - 1$ elements, where n is declared as the size of the array. Hence, for storing n elements, we should declare the array of size $n + 1$.

5.4.1 Advantages of Using Circular Queues

The following are the merits of using circular queues:

1. By using circular queues, data shifting is avoided as the *front* and *rear* are modified by using the `mod()` function. The `mod()` operation wraps the queue back to its beginning.
2. If the number of elements to be stored in the queue is fixed (i.e., if the queue size is specific), the circular queue is advantageous.
3. Many practical applications such as printer queue, priority queue, and simulations use the circular queue.

5.5 MULTI-QUEUES

If more number of queues is required to be implemented, then an efficient data structure to handle multiple queues is required. It is possible to utilize all the available spaces in a single array. When more than two queues, say n, are represented sequentially, we can divide the available memory `A[size]` into n segments and allocate these segments to n queues, one to each. For each queue i we shall use `Front[i]` and `Rear[i]`. We shall use the condition `Front[i] = Rear[i]` if and only if the ith queue is empty, and the condition `Rear[i] = Front[i]` if and only if the ith queue is full.

If we want five queues, then we can divide the array `A[100]` into equal parts of 20 and initialize *front* and *rear* for each queue, that is, `Front[0] = Rear[0] = 0` and `Front[1] = Rear[1] = 20`, and so on for other queues (Fig. 5.3).

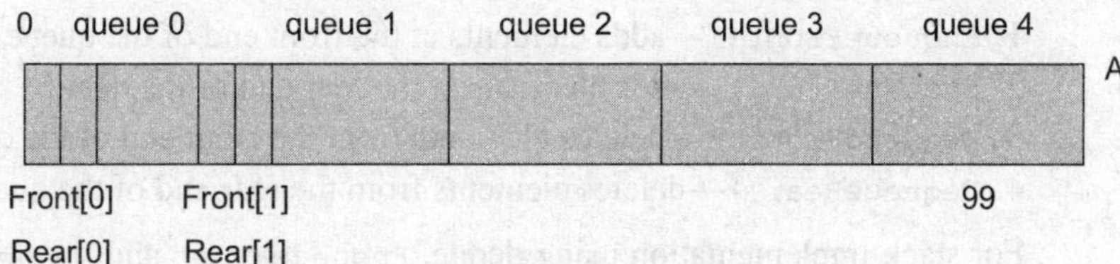

Fig. 5.3 A multi-queue

After adding elements 5 and 8 in the second queue, the resultant queue will be as in Fig. 5.4.

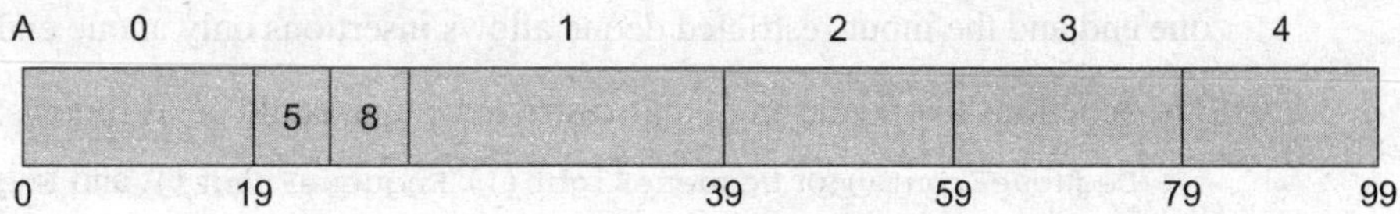

Fig. 5.4 Queue in Fig. 5.3 after addition of elements

5.6 DEQUE

The word *deque* is a short form of double-ended queue. It is pronounced as 'deck'. *Deque* defines a data structure where elements can be added or deleted at either the front end or the rear end, but no changes can be made elsewhere in the list. Thus, *deque* is a generalization of both a stack and a queue. It supports both stack-like and queue-like capabilities. It is a sequential container that is optimized for fast index-based access and efficient insertion at either of its ends. Deque can be implemented as either a continuous deque or as a linked deque. Figure 5.5 shows the representation of a deque.

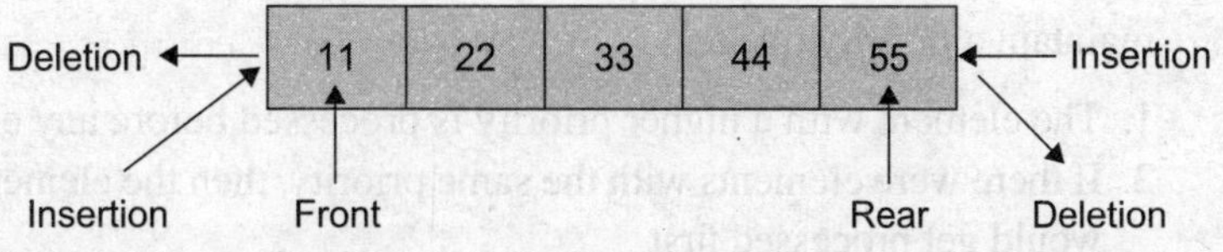

Fig. 5.5 Representation of a deque

The *deque ADT* combines the characteristics of stacks and queues. Similar to stacks and queues, a deque permits the elements to be accessed only at the ends. However, a deque allows elements to be added at and removed from either end. We can refer to the operations supported by the deque as `EnqueueFront`, `EnqueueRear`, `DequeueFront`, and `DequeueRear`. When we complete a formal description of the deque and then implement it using a dynamic, linked implementation, we can use it to implement both stacks and queues, thus achieving significant code reuse.

The following are the four operations associated with deque:

1. `EnqueueFront()`—adds elements at the front end of the queue
2. `EnqueueRear()`—adds elements at the rear end of the queue
3. `DequeueFront()`—deletes elements from the front end of the queue
4. `DequeueRear()`—deletes elements from the rear end of the queue

For stack implementation using deque, `EnqueueFront` and `DequeueFront` are used as `push` and `pop` functions, respectively.

Applications of deque Deque is useful where the data to be stored has to be ordered, compact storage is needed, and the retrieval of data elements has to be faster.

Variations of deque We can have two variations of a deque: the *input-restricted deque* and the *output-restricted* deque. The output-restricted deque allows deletions from only one end and the input-restricted deque allows insertions only at one end.

The functions to operate an output-restricted deque could be as follows:

`DequeueFront()` (or `DequeueRight()`), `EnqueueFront()`, and `EnqueueRear()`

The functions to operate an input-restricted deque are as follows:

`DequeueFront()`, `DequeueRight()`, and `EnqueueFront()` (or `EnqueueRear()`)

5.7 PRIORITY QUEUE

A *priority queue* is a collection of a finite number of prioritized elements. *Priority queues* are those in which we can insert or delete elements from any position based on some fundamental ordering of the elements. Elements can be inserted in any order in a priority queue, but when an element is removed from the priority queue, it is always the one with the highest priority.

In other words a priority queue is a collection of elements where the elements are stored according to their priority levels. The order in which the elements should be removed is decided by the priority of the element. The following rules are applied to maintain a priority queue:

1. The element with a higher priority is processed before any element of lower priority.
2. If there were elements with the same priority, then the element added first in the queue would get processed first.

Priority queues are used for implementing job scheduling by the operating system where jobs with higher priority are to be processed first. Another application of priority queues is in simulation systems where the priority corresponds to event times. The following are some examples of a priority queue:

1. A list of patients in an emergency room; each patient might be given a ranking that depends on the severity of the patient's illness.
2. A list of jobs carried out by a multitasking operating system; each background job is given a priority level. Suppose in a computer system, jobs are assigned three priorities, namely, *P*, *Q*, *R* as first, second, and third, respectively. According to the priority of the job, it is inserted at the end of the other jobs having the same priority. Consider the priority queue given in Fig. 5.6.

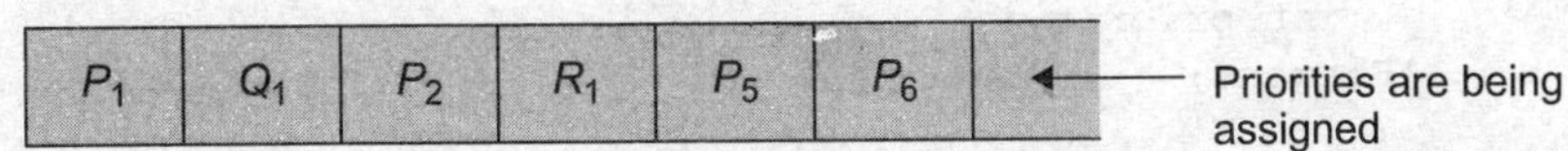

Fig. 5.6 System queue

There are two ways to implement priority queues.

Implementation method 1 The priority queue implementation in the first case can be visualized as three separate queues, each following the FIFO behaviour strictly as shown in Figs 5.7(a)–(c). In this example, jobs are always removed from the front of the queue. The elements in the second queue are removed only when the first queue is empty, and the elements from the third queue are removed only when the second queue is empty, and so on.

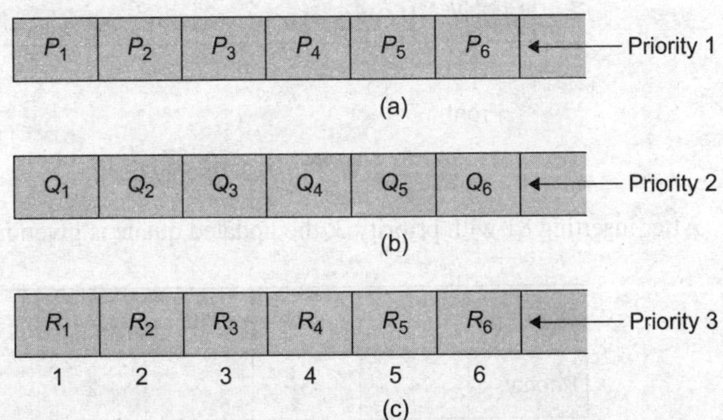

Fig. 5.7 System queues for each priority level (a) Priority 1 queue (b) Priority 2 queue (c) Priority 3 queue

Operations on a priority queue The following is the list of operations performed on the priority queue PQ:

1. Initialize PQ to be the empty priority queue.
2. Determine if PQ is empty.
3. Determine if PQ is full.
4. If PQ is not full, insert an element *X* into PQ.
5. If PQ is not empty, remove an element *X* of the highest priority.

Implementation method 2 The second way of priority queue implementation is by using a structure for a queue. This is explained in the following statement:

```
typedef struct
{
    int Data;
    int priority;
}Element;

class PriorityQueue
{
    Private:
        Element PQueue[max];
    public:
        // member functions here
}
```

Figure 5.8 represents an example of a priority queue.

Data	15	10	3	30	8
Priority	4	2	2	1	0

Front ↑ (first column) ... Rear ↑ (last column)

Fig. 5.8 Priority queue

After inserting 81 with priority 3, the updated queue is given in Fig. 5.9.

Data	15	81	10	3	30	8
Priority	4	3	2	2	1	0

Front ↑ (first column) ... Rear ↑ (last column)

Fig. 5.9 Priority queue after insertion

The highest priority element is at the front and that of the lowest priority is at the rear. Here, when element 81 of priority 3 is to be added, it is inserted in between priorities 4 and 2 as shown in Fig. 5.9. When we want to delete an element, it behaves as a normal queue, that is, the element at front, which has the highest priority, is deleted first. The elements are sorted according to their priorities in descending order.

Hence, the two ways to implement a priority queue are *sorted list* and *unsorted list*.

Sorted list A sorted list is characterized by the following features:

1. *Advantage*—Deletion is easy; elements are stored by priority, so just delete from the beginning of the list.
2. *Disadvantage*—Insertion is hard; it is necessary to find the proper location for insertion.
3. A linked list is convenient for this implementation such as the list in Fig. 5.9.

Unsorted list An unsorted list is characterized by the following features:

1. *Advantage*—Insertion is easy; just add elements at the end of the list.
2. *Disadvantage*—Deletion is hard; it is necessary to find the highest priority element first.
3. An array is convenient for this implementation.

5.7.1 Array Implementation of Priority Queue

Like stacks and queues, even a priority queue can be represented using an array. However, if any array is used to store elements of a priority queue, then insertion of elements to the queue would be easy, but deletion of elements would be difficult. This is because while inserting elements in the priority queue, they are not inserted in an order. As a result, deleting an element with the highest priority would require examining the entire array to search for such an element. Moreover, an element in a queue can be deleted from the front end only.

There is no satisfactory solution to this problem. However, it would be more efficient if we store the elements in a priority queue. Each element in an array can have the following structure:

```
typedef struct
{
    int Data;
    int priority;
    int order;
}Element;
```

where `priority` represents the priority of the element and `order` represents the order in which the element has been added to the queue.

5.8 APPLICATIONS OF QUEUES

The most useful application of queues is the simulation of a real world situation so that it is possible to understand what happens in a real world in a particular situation without actually observing its occurrence.

Queues are also very useful in a time-sharing computer system where many users share a system simultaneously. Whenever a user requests the system to run a particular program, the operating system adds the request at the end of the queue of jobs waiting to be executed. Now, when the CPU is free, it executes the job that is at the front of the job queue. Similarly, there are queues for shared I/O devices too. Each device maintains its own queue of requests.

Another useful operation of queues is the solution of problems involving searching a non-linear collection of states. A queue is used for finding a path using the *breadth-first search* of graphs.

5.8.1 Josephus Problem

Let us consider a problem that can be solved in an easy manner using a circular queue. The problem is known as the *Josephus problem*, and it postulates a group of soldiers surrounded by an irresistible enemy force. There is no hope for victory without reinforcements, and there is only a single horse available for escape. The soldiers form a circle and a number n is picked. The name of one of the soldiers is also picked from a hat. Beginning with the soldier whose name is picked they begin to count clockwise around the circle. When the count reaches n, that soldier is removed from the circle, and the count begins again with the next soldier. The process continues so that each time the count reaches n, another soldier is removed from the circle. Any soldier removed from the circle is no longer counted. The last soldier left takes the horse and escapes. The problem is that, given a number n, the ordering of the soldiers in the circle, and the soldier from whom the count begins, one needs to determine the order in which soldiers are eliminated from the circle and which soldier escapes.

The input to the program is the number n and a list of names, which is the clockwise ordering of the circle, beginning with the soldier from whom the count is to start. The last input line contains the string `end`, indicating the end of the input. The program should print the names in the order in which they are eliminated and the name of the soldier who finally escapes.

For example, suppose that $n = 3$ and that there are five soldiers named A, B, C, D, and E. We count three soldiers starting at A so that C is eliminated first. We then begin at D and count D, E and then back to A so that A is eliminated next. Then we count B, D, and E (C has already been eliminated), and finally B, D, and B. Now, D is the one who escapes.

Clearly, a circular list in which each node represents one soldier is a natural data structure to use in solving this problem. It is possible to reach any node from any other by counting around the circle. To represent the removal of a soldier from the circle, a node is deleted from the circular list. Finally, when only one node remains on the list, the result is determined. The algorithm for this problem is given in Algorithm 5.2.

ALGORITHM 5.2

```
1. Let n be the number of members
2. Get the first member
3. Add all members to the queue
4. while (there is more than one member in the queue)
   begin
      count through n - 1 members in the queue;
      print the name of the nth member;
      Remove the nth member from the queue;
   end
5. Print the name of the only member in the list.
```

5.8.2 Job Scheduling

In the job-scheduling problem, we are given a list of n jobs. Every job i is associated with an integer deadline $d_i \geq 0$ and a profit $p_i \geq 0$. For any job i, profit is earned if and only if the job is completed within its deadline. A feasible solution with the maximum sum of profits is to be obtained.

To find the optimal solution and feasibility of jobs, we are required to find a subset J such that each job of this subset can be completed by its deadline. The value of a feasible solution J is the sum of profits of all the jobs in J.

The steps in finding the subset J are as follows:

1. $\Sigma p_i \times i \in J$ is the objective function chosen for the optimization measure.
2. Using this measure, the next job to be included should be the one that increases $\Sigma p_i \times i \in J$.
3. Begin with $J = \varnothing$, $\Sigma p_i = 0$, and $i \in J$.
4. Add a job to J, which has the largest profit.
5. Add another job to J bearing in mind the following conditions:
   (a) Search for the job that has the next maximum profit.
   (b) See if this job in union with J is feasible.
   (c) If yes, go to step 5 and continue; else go to (d).
   (d) Search for the job with the next maximum profit and go to step 2.
6. Terminate when addition of no more jobs is feasible.

Example 5.1 shows a job scheduling algorithm that works to yield an optimized high profit solution.

EXAMPLE 5.1 Consider five jobs with profits $(p_1, p_2, p_3, p_4, p_5) = (20, 15, 10, 5, 1)$ and maximum delay allowed $(d_1, d_2, d_3, d_4, d_5) = (2, 2, 1, 3, 3)$.

Here, the maximum number of jobs that can be completed is

$$\text{Min}(n, \text{maxdelay}(d_i)) = \text{Min}(5, 3) = 3$$

Hence, there is a possibility of doing 3 jobs, and there are 3 units of time, as shown in Table 5.2.

Table 5.2 Job scheduling

Time slot	Profit	Job
0–1	20	1
1–2	15	2
2–3	0	3 cannot be accommodated
2–3	5	4
	Total profit = 40	

In the first unit of time, job 1 is done and a profit of 20 is gained; in the second unit, job 2 is done and a profit of 15 is obtained. However, in the third unit of time, job 3 is not available, so job 4 is done with a gain of 5. Further, the deadline of job 5 has also passed; hence three jobs 1, 2, and 4 are completed with a total profit of 40.

5.8.3 Simulation

Any process or situation that we wish to simulate is considered as a system. A *system* may be defined as a group of objects interacting to produce some result. For example, an industry is a group of people and machines working together to produce some product.

A powerful tool that can be used to study the behaviour of systems is simulation.

Simulation is the process of forming an abstract model of a real world scenario to understand the effect of modifications and the introduction of various strategies on the situation. It allows the user to experiment with real and proposed situations without actually observing its occurrence. The major advantage of simulation is that it permits experimentation without modifying the real solution.

A model of the system must be produced to simulate a situation. Moreover, to determine the structure of a model, the entities, attributes, and activities of the system should be determined. Entities represent the objects of interest in the simulation. Attributes denote the characteristics of these entities. An activity is a process that causes a change of system state. An event is an occurrence of an activity at a particular instant of time. The state of the system at any given time is specified by the attributes of the entities and the relation between the entities at that time. The simulation program must schedule the events in the simulation so that the activities will occur in the correct time sequence.

Let us consider an example. Suppose that a person has to deposit his telephone bill. There are four service windows that can accept the bill. A person can deposit his bill at any of the service windows. Suppose a person enters the office at a specific time ($t1$) to deposit the bill, the transaction may be expected to take a certain period of time ($t2$) before it is completed. If a service window is free, the person can immediately deposit the bill and leave the office at the time ($t1 + t2$) spending exactly the time required to deposit the bill.

If it so happens that none of the windows is free and there is a line waiting at each window, the person joins the end of the shortest line and waits until all the persons ahead have deposited their bills and have left the line. At that time, this person can deposit his bill. In this case, the time spent by the person in the bill office is t2 plus the time spent waiting in the line.

Let us try to compute the average time spent by the person in the bill office. To do this, we write a program to simulate the actions of the persons. The arrival of a person is modelled as an input of data consisting of the arrival time and the duration of the expected time to be spent in depositing the bill.

These data pairs are ordered by increasing arrival time. The four service windows are represented by four queues. Each person waiting in the line is represented by a node in that queue. The node at the front of the queue represents a person currently being served at the window.

In this case, a person is an entity. The state of the system might change whenever a person leaves or enters the bill office. We can therefore define five events that can change the status of the system—a person entering the office and the four cases of a person leaving a particular queue.

The first event to occur is the arrival of the first customer. The event list is therefore initialized by reading the first input line. All the four service windows are initially free. The first node from the event list is removed and placed in the shortest of the queues. When the person is at the front of the window, a node representing the departure of the person is added to the event list, and the next input line is read. An arrival node corresponding to the arrival of the next person is placed on the event list. As soon as one arrival node is removed from the event list, another is added to the list so that there is exactly one arrival node on the event list unless there are no more inputs.

When a departure node is removed from the event list, the amount of time spent by the departing person is computed and added to a total and the node representing the person is removed from the front of the queue. After a node has been deleted from the front of the queue, the next person in the queue becomes the first to be served by that window and a departure node is added for that person to the event list.

At the end of the simulation, when the event list is empty, the total is divided by the number of persons to get the average time spent by a person.

5.9 QUEUES USING TEMPLATE

The queue in Program Code 5.1, implemented using an array, is defined to operate on integer data. When we want to define a queue of floating point data, we need to change `int Queue[]` to `float Queue[]` in the declaration of the data members of the class. This can be done each time the data type of array elements varies, by editing the code using the text editor and then recompiling it. A *template* is a variable that can be instantiated to any data type. This data type could be of the built-in or the user-defined types. Program Code 5.4 represents a queue using templates.

PROGRAM CODE 5.4

```
template<class T>
class queue : public Queue<T>
{
   private:
      int Front;      // 1 counterclockwise from the
      Front element
      int Rear;      // position of the Back element
      int ArrayLength;      // queue capacity
      T *Queue;      // element array
   public:
      queue(int InitialCapacity = 20);
      ~ queue()
      {
         delete[] queue;
      }
      bool Empty() const
      {
         return Front == Rear;
      }
      int Size() const
      {
         return(Rear - Front + ArrayLength) % ArrayLength;
      }
      T& Front()
      {
         if(Front == Rear)
            cout << "Sorry queue empty" << endl;
            return Queue[(Front + 1) % ArrayLength];
      }
      T& Back()
      {
         // return Rear element
         if(Front == Rear)
            cout << "Sorry queue empty" << endl;
            return Queue[Rear];
      }
      void Delete()
```

```
    {
        // remove Front element
        if(Front == Rear)
            cout << "Sorry Queue Empty" << endl;
            Front = (Front + 1) % ArrayLength;
            Queue[Front].~T();
    }
    void Add(const T& Element);
};

template<class T>
queue <T> :: queue(int InitialCapacity)
{
    ArrayLength = InitialCapacity;
    Queue = new T[ArrayLength];
    Front = 0;
    Rear = 0;
}

template<class T>
void queue <T> :: Add(const T&  Element)
{
    if((theBack + 1) % arrayLength == Front)
        cout << "Sorry queue is full" << endl;
    else
        Rear = (Rear + 1) % ArrayLength;
        Queue[Rear] = Element;
}

int main(void)
{
    queue <int> Q(10);
    int Data;
    Q.Add(1);
    Q.Add(2);
    Data = Q.Delete();
    cout << Data;
    Q.Add(3);
    Data = Q.Delete();
    cout << Data;
    Q.Add(4);
}
```

A queue implemented using an array has many disadvantages, as arrays provide static declaration and hence are less flexible with respect to run-time changes in the size of the queue. We shall discuss the implementation of queues using a linked list, which overcomes these drawbacks, in Chapter 6.

RECAPITULATION

- A queue is an ordered list where all insertions are done at one end called the *rear* and deletions at another end called the *front*. These limits guarantee that the data is processed in the sequence in which it is entered. In short, a queue is a first in first out (FIFO) or last in last out (LILO) structure.
- A queue is a linear data structure as it can be implemented using with the help of arrays (using static memory allocation) or linked lists (using dynamic memory allocation). An array is not a suitable data structure for frequent insertion and deletion of data elements. In addition, it uses static memory allocation so that it can store a fixed number of elements. Hence, array implementation is not suitable for frequent insertions and deletions.
- These drawbacks can be avoided by implementing the queue using a circular array. In a circular queue, as we go on adding elements to the queue and reach the end of the array, the next element is stored in the first slot of the array if it is free.
- There are variations of queues such as circular queue, multi-queues, and deque. Deque defines a data structure where elements can be added or deleted at either the front end or the rear end but no changes can be made elsewhere in the list.
- Queues are used in many applications such as simulation, priority queue, job queue, and so on. Priority queues are those in which we can insert or delete elements from any position based on some fundamental ordering with respect to the priorities of the elements.

KEY TERMS

Add This operation adds an element at the rear of the queue if the queue is not full. This operation is also named as *enqueue* and *insert*.

Circular queue The technique that essentially allows the queues to wrap around upon reaching the end of the array is called a circular queue.

Delete This operation deletes an element from the front of the queue and returns the same. This operation is also named as *dequeue* .

Deque The word *deque* is a short form of double-ended queue. It is pronounced as 'deck'. Deque defines a data structure where elements can be added or deleted at either the front end or the rear end, but no changes can be made elsewhere in the list. Thus, a deque is a generalization of both a stack and a queue.

FIFO A queue is a first in first out (FIFO) or last in last out (LILO) structure to guarantee that the data are processed in the sequence in which they are entered.

Multi-queue If more number of queues is required to be implemented, then an efficient data structure to handle multiple queues is required. It is possible to utilize all the available space in a single array. When more than two queues, say *n*, are represented sequentially, we can divide the available memory into *n* segments and allocate these segments to *n* queues, one each.

Priority queue A priority queue is a collection of a finite number of prioritized elements. Priority queues are the queues where we can insert elements or delete elements from any position based on some fundamental ordering of the elements. Elements can be inserted in any order in a priority queue, but when an element is removed from the priority queue, it is always the one with the highest priority.

Queue A queue is a common example of a linear list or an ordered list in which the data can be inserted at one end, called the rear, and deleted from another end, called the front.

EXERCISES

Multiple choice questions

1. The initial configuration of a queue is *a*, *b*, *c*, *d* (*a* is at the front end). To get the configuration *d*, *c*, *b*, *a*, one needs a minimum of
   (a) 2 deletions and 3 additions
   (b) 3 deletions and 2 additions
   (c) 3 deletions and 3 additions
   (d) 3 deletions and 4 additions
2. A priority queue is used to implement a stack `S` that stores characters. The operation `Push(C)` is implemented as `insert(Q, C, K)` where `K` is an appropriate integer key chosen by the implementation. `Pop` is implemented as `Deletemin(Q)`. For a sequence of operations, the keys chosen are in
   (a) non-increasing order
   (b) non-decreasing order
   (c) strictly increasing order
   (d) strictly decreasing order
3. A linear list of elements in which deletion can be done from one end (*front*) and insertion can take place only at the other end is known as
   (a) queue
   (b) stack
   (c) tree
   (d) branch
4. In a queue (where `Q.rear` and `Q.front` are pointers to the ends of a queue)
   (a) the number of total elements is fixed
   (b) if `Q.rear` > `Q.front`, it is empty
   (c) the number of elements at any time is (`Q.rear` – `Q.front` – 1)
   (d) none of these
5. A queue
   (a) can be created by setting up an ordinary contiguous array to hold the elements
   (b) can take care of the delete operation automatically
   (c) needs one pointer to handle addition and deletion of an element
   (d) none of these
6. *n* elements of a queue are to be reversed using another queue. The number of `add` and `remove` operations required to do so is
   (a) $2 \times n$
   (b) $4 \times n$
   (c) n
   (d) The task cannot be accomplished.
7. A queue is
   (a) a linear data structure
   (b) a non-linear data structure
   (c) both (a) and (b)
   (d) none of these
8. The end at which a new element gets added to a queue is called the
   (a) front
   (b) rear
   (c) top
   (d) bottom
9. The end from which an element gets deleted from a queue is called the
   (a) front
   (b) rear
   (c) top
   (d) bottom

10. A queue is also called a
    (a) last in first out data structure
    (b) first in last out data structure
    (c) first in first out data structure
    (d) last in last out data structure

Review questions

1. A dequeue is a list where additions and deletions can be made at either the head or the tail. With dequeue stored as a circularly linked list, provide an algorithm to add and delete a node from either end of a dequeue.
2. What is a circular queue? Write a C++ program to insert an element in the circular queue. Write a C++ function for printing the elements of the queue in reverse order.
3. A queue *Q* containing *n* elements and an empty stack *S* are given. It is required to transfer the queue to the stack so that the element at the front of the queue is on the top of the stack and the order of all the other elements is preserved. Show how this can be done in O(*n*) time using only a constant amount of additional storage. Note that the only operations that can be performed on the queue and stack are `delete`, `insert`, `push`, and `pop`. Do not assume any implementation of the queue or the stack.
4 Suppose a stack implementation supports, in addition to `push` and `pop`, an operation `reverse`, which reverses the order of the elements on the stack.
    (a) To implement a queue using such a stack implementation, show how to implement `Enqueue` using a single operation and `Dequeue` using a sequence of three operations.
    (b) Evaluate the following postfix expression containing single digit operands and arithmetic operators + and × using a stack.

$$52 \times 34 + 52 \times\times +$$

5. Suppose we wish to have two sequentially allocated queues occupying a single vector *x*[1, 2, ..., *n*]. The front of both the queues are the end points of the array *x*, with one queue moving down whereas the other is moving up. Write a C++ program to insert a new element in each queue. In addition, find the number of elements in each queue at a given time.
6. Assume that a circular queue is stored in an array. Write down the necessary C++ language declarations to define 50 different circular queues having integer values with a maximum size of 100 each.
7. Represent a circular queue of maximum size *n* in an array `A(0, 1, ..., n - 1)`. Assume that each node in a queue contains an integer. Write the C++ declaration for the circular queue. In addition, write two C++ functions to add an element to the queue and to remove the element form the queue.
8. Write the algorithm for the job-scheduling method.
9. Solve for four jobs with profits (100, 10, 15, 27) and delays (2, 1, 2, 1).

Answers to multiple choice questions

1. (c) 2. (d) 3. (a) 4. (d) 5. (a) 6. (d) 7. (a) 8. (b) 9. (a)
10. (c) and (d)

6 LINKED LISTS

OBJECTIVES

After reading this chapter, the reader will be able to understand the following:

- The limitations of static data structures
- The need for a data structure that can dynamically shrink and grow
- Linked list as a dynamic data structure and its flexibility
- The variations in linked lists and their applications

Until now, we have studied arrays and realization of stacks and queues using arrays. One of the drawbacks of an array is that it is a static data structure, that is, the maximum capacity of an array should be known before the compilation process. Therefore, we must explicitly define its size before compilation. Practically, defining such static sizes before the compilation of a program reduces effective space utilization. Accurate predictions about data structure sizes are very difficult. Another drawback of arrays is that the elements in an array are stored a fixed distance apart, and the insertion and deletion of elements in between require a lot of data movement. The linked list is the solution to overcome all these problems. A linked list using dynamic memory management follows this principle—allocate and use memory when you need it and release it (free or de-allocate) when you are done.

A linked list is a very effective and efficient dynamic data structure for linear lists. Items may be added or deleted from it at any position more easily as compared to arrays. A programmer does not need to worry about how many data items a program will have to store. This enables the programmer to make effective use of the memory, since it works on the principle of need and supply. This reduces the maintenance of the program, as program maintenance often includes the need to increase the capacity of a program to handle larger collections.

We shall study the linked list, its variations, and its pros and cons in this chapter.

6.1 INTRODUCTION

Arrays and linked lists are examples of linear lists. Linear lists are those in which each member has a unique successor. Arrays contain consecutive memory locations that are a fixed distance apart, whereas linked lists do not necessarily contain consecutive memory locations. These data items can be stored anywhere in the memory in a scattered manner. To maintain the specific sequence of these data items, we need to maintain link(s) with a successor (and/or a predecessor). It is called as a *linked list* as each node is linked with its successor (and/or predecessor). Figures 6.1 and 6.2 show the realization of a linear list using a linked list.

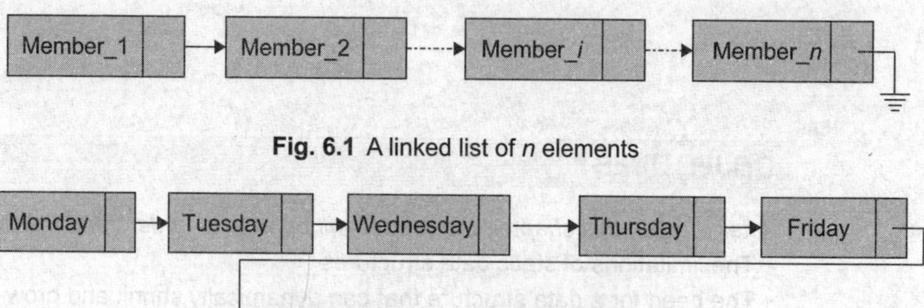

Fig. 6.1 A linked list of *n* elements

Fig. 6.2 A linked list of days in a week

The linked list, as a data structure in programming, is used quite frequently since it is very efficient. To use linked lists effectively, the concepts of pointers must be very clear to the programmer. In fact, frequent use of linked lists makes the concept of pointers very clear to the programmer. This study of the linked list will introduce us to its strengths and weaknesses. This study gives us an appreciation of the time, space, and code complexity issues. Linked list examples are a classic combination of algorithms and manipulation of pointers. Let us now learn about the linked list.

6.2 LINKED LIST

A *linked list* is an ordered collection of data in which each element (node) contains a minimum of two values, *data* and *link(s)* to its successor (and/or predecessor). A list with one link field using which every element is associated to its successor is known as a *singly linked list* (SLL). In a linked list, before adding any element to the list, a memory space for that node must be allocated. A link is made from each item to the next item in the list as shown in Fig. 6.3.

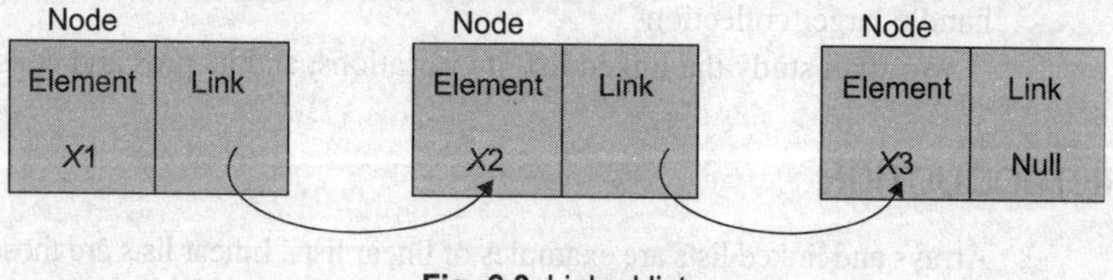

Fig. 6.3 Linked list

Each node of the linked list has at least the following two elements:

1. The data member(s) being stored in the list.
2. A pointer or link to the next element in the list.

The last node in the list contains a null pointer (or a suitable value like –1) to indicate that it is the end or tail of the list, and by suitable means we identify the first node. As elements are added to a list, memory for a node is dynamically allocated. Therefore, the number of elements that may be added to a list is limited only by the amount of memory available. To understand the linked list concept better, let us consider Examples 6.1 and 6.2.

EXAMPLE 6.1 We all are aware of the very interesting game of treasure hunt. In this game, a team member is provided the primary hint of the first locality. From the first location's hint, the participant gets the second, and so on. To reach the final target, the participant has to go through each and every location in a specific order. Even if the order of one of the locations is wrong, the participant will not obtain the clue for reaching the next location, and hence, the player will not be able to find the final destination of the treasure.

EXAMPLE 6.2 Assume that there are 10 books in a library, which form a specific sequence. This ordered set of 10 books is to be kept in a shelf. There are two ways to arrange the books. One of the arrangements is to keep all the 10 books in 10 continuous empty slots (similar to an array). The second possible arrangement is to place the books at available locations in a distributed manner (similar to a linked list) by keeping track of the various locations of the books.

Let Books = {book1, book2, book3, …, book10}

As the books form a specific sequence, both the arrangements must preserve the sequence. Let us analyse both the arrangements. Table 6.1 shows the first arrangement.

Table 6.1 Shelf and books arranged sequentially

Shelf position	S	$S + 1$	$S + 2$	$S + 3$	$S + 4$	$S + 5$	$S + 6$	$S + 7$	$S + 8$	$S + 9$
Book Number	Book1	Book2	Book3	Book4	Book5	Book6	Book7	Book8	Book9	Book10

The following are the requisites for this arrangement.

1. In a shelf, we need an empty slot that can accommodate all the 10 books.
2. We need to be aware of the position of the first book.
3. The order is maintained by keeping the books in sequence as book1, book2, and so on till book10, in successive empty locations.
4. Referring to the ith location directly with respect to the first location, one can access the ith book. In short, we have direct access to any i^{th} book.

Now, consider the following situation. An empty slot sufficient to accommodate 10 books is not available in the shelf, but 10 empty scattered locations are available.

Let us take a look at the second arrangement as shown in Table 6.2. Here, we need 10 empty locations available in the shelf. These 10 locations could be distributed and need not necessarily be a continuous block.

Table 6.2 Shelf and books arranged in a distributed manner

First book (at *S* + 2)

<table>
<tr><td>Location</td><td>S</td><td>S + 1</td><td>S + 2</td><td>S + 3</td><td>S + 4</td><td>S + 5</td><td>S + 6</td><td>S + 7</td></tr>
<tr><td>Book no.</td><td rowspan="2">Already occupied</td><td rowspan="2">Already occupied</td><td>Book 1</td><td rowspan="2">Already occupied</td><td>Book 5</td><td rowspan="2">Already occupied</td><td>Book 7</td><td>Book 2</td></tr>
<tr><td>Next book link</td><td>goto S + 7</td><td>goto S + 14</td><td>goto S + 10</td><td>goto S + 11</td></tr>
</table>

<table>
<tr><td>Location</td><td>S + 8</td><td>S + 9</td><td>S + 10</td><td>S + 11</td><td>S + 12</td><td>S + 13</td><td>S + 14</td><td>S + 15</td></tr>
<tr><td>Book no.</td><td rowspan="2">Already occupied</td><td>Book 4</td><td>Book 8</td><td>Book 3</td><td>Book 10</td><td>Book 9</td><td>Book 6</td><td rowspan="2">Empty</td></tr>
<tr><td>Next book link</td><td>goto S + 4</td><td>goto S + 13</td><td>goto S + 9</td><td>Null</td><td>goto S + 12</td><td>goto S + 6</td></tr>
</table>

Last book (at *S* + 12)

The following steps are used for this arrangement:

1. Let us use some means to preserve the sequence. Let us keep the first book in the first free location found. Do note the location of the first book. Let us keep the second book at the second empty location in the shelf. Attach a tag as a link to the first book to remember where the second book is kept. This tag has the location ID of the second book. Put the third book in the next empty location. Attach a tag to link to the second book. The second book's link stores the location ID of the third book, and so on.
2. Remember only the first book's position.
3. We cannot refer to the third book directly. Only the link attached to the second book can indicate where the third book is. The second book's position is available at the first book's link. Hence, to get the ith book, we have to go through all the books in a sequence: book1, book2, and so on till book(i – 1). The tag attached to the (i – 1)th book would tell where the ith book is.

The first arrangement is similar to arrays, a sequential organization. The second arrangement is a linked list, a linked organization. Now, let us compare both the arrangements. The first method needs continuous empty spaces to accommodate 10 books, whereas the second method can accommodate books in any of the 10 empty places, which may or may not be continuous. Hence, even if a continuous space to keep the 10 books is not available in the second method, the books can be accommodated.

In the first method, we have direct access to any i^{th} book in the sequence, whereas in the second method, until we traverse through the first i books sequentially, we cannot find where the $(i + 1)^{th}$ book is kept. In the first method, we must know well in advance how many books are to be kept so that we can reserve the space for the same. However, in the second method, we can keep every new book in the empty location found anywhere in the shelf; we need not reserve a location for the same.

The next point to be taken into consideration is the utilization of shelf space. In the first method, if the number of the books to be kept in a continuous space is not known in advance, this creates two problems. First, we reserve a continuous block say, m, of arbitrary size. In general, m denotes maximum size. Suppose the number of books to be kept is n, which is much smaller than m. Then, $(m - n)$ locations remain unused. The second problem is when the number of books n is greater than the reserved space m, we will not be able to accommodate the books in the continuous block.

The next aspect for comparison is with respect to the various operations on the data elements such as insertion and deletion of a book. In the first method, inserting a book at the ith location needs a shifting of (i to n) books to the right side, each by one position. Similarly, taking out the ith book from the shelf creates an empty space in the sequence of books. Hence, we need to shift ($i + 1$ to n) books to the left, each by one position.

The second method needs no shifting of data elements to insert or delete a data element. It only needs a few changes in the tags of the books, which are called as *links*. For the applications where the data elements to be stored are of varying sizes, that is, sequential representation, arrays are inadequate. This leads to an elegant solution, that is, linked organization.

6.2.1 Comparison of Sequential and Linked Organizations

Although linked lists are often used in computing, they are not simple to master. However, the flexibility and performance they offer is worth the pain of learning and using them. The brief features of sequential and linked organizations are described here.

Sequential organization The features of this organization are the following:

1. Successive elements of a list are stored a fixed distance apart.
2. It provides *static allocation*, which means, the space allocation done by a compiler once cannot be changed during execution, and the size has to be known in advance.
3. As individual objects are stored a fixed distance apart, we can access any element randomly.

4. Insertion and deletion of objects in between the list require a lot of data movement.
5. It is space inefficient for large objects with frequent insertions and deletions.
6. An element need not know/store and keep the address of its successive element.

Linked organization The features of this organization include the following:

1. Elements can be placed anywhere in the memory.
2. Dynamic allocation (size need not be known in advance), that is, space allocation as per need can be done during execution.
3. As objects are not placed in consecutive locations at a fixed distance apart, random access to elements is not possible.
4. Insertion and deletion of objects do not require any data shifting.
5. It is space efficient for large objects with frequent insertions and deletions.
6. Each element in general is a collection of data and a link. At least one link field is a must.
7. Every element keeps the address of its successor element in a link field.
8. The only burden is that we need additional space for the link field for each element. However, additional space is not a severe penalty when large objects are to be stored.
9. Linked organization needs the use of pointers and dynamic memory allocation.

A linked list can be implemented using arrays, dynamic memory management, and pointers. The second implementation requires dynamic memory management where one can allocate memory at run-time, that is, during the execution of a program. Linked lists are generally implemented using dynamic memory management. Each linked list has a head pointer that refers to the first node of the list and the data nodes storing data member(s). The linked list may have a *header node*, *tail pointer*, and so on.

6.2.2 Linked List Terminology

The following terms are commonly used in discussions about linked lists:

Header node A header node is a special node that is attached at the beginning of the linked list. This header node may contain special information (metadata) about the linked list as shown in Fig. 6.4.

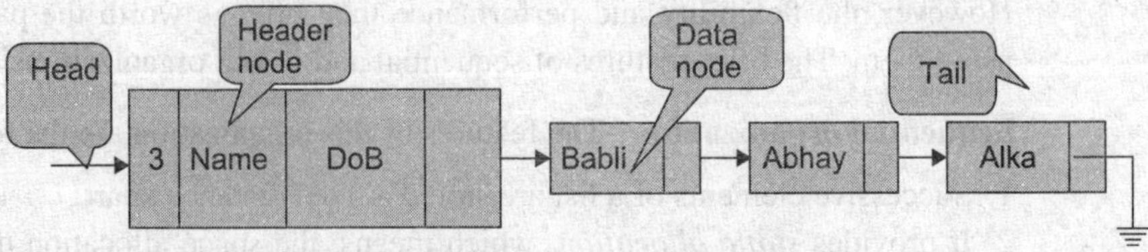

Fig. 6.4 Linked list with header node

This special information could be the total number of nodes in the list, date of creation, type, and so on. The header node may or may not be identical to the data nodes.

Data node The list contains data nodes that store the data members and link(s) to its predecessor (and/or successor).

Head pointer The variable (or handle), which represents the list, is simply a pointer to the node at the head of the list. A linked list must always have at least one pointer pointing to the first node (head) of the list. This pointer is necessary because it is the only way to access the further links in the list. This pointer is often called *head pointer*, because a linked list may contain a dummy node attached at the start position called the *header node*.

Tail pointer Similar to the head pointer that points to the first node of a linked list, we may have a pointer pointing to the last node of a linked list called the *tail pointer*.

6.2.3 Primitive Operations

The following are basic operations associated with the linked list as a data structure:

1. Creating an empty list
2. Inserting a node
3. Deleting a node
4. Traversing the list

Some more operations, which are based on the basic operations, are as follows:

5. Searching a node
6. Updating a node
7. Printing the node or list
8. Counting the length of the list
9. Reversing the list
10. Sorting the list using pointer manipulation
11. Concatenating two lists
12. Merging two sorted lists into a third sorted list

In addition, operations such as merging the second sorted list into the first sorted list and many more are possible by the use of these operations.

6.3 REALIZATION OF LINKED LISTS

In a linked organization, the data elements are not necessarily placed in continuous locations. The relationship between data elements is by means of a link. Along with each data element, the address of the next element is stored. Thus, the associated link with each data element to its successor is often referred to as a *pointer*. In general, a *node* is a collection of data and link(s). *Data* is a collection of one or more items. Each item in a node is called a *field*. A field contains either a data item or a link. Every node must contain at least one link field.

6.3.1 Realization of Linked List Using Arrays

Let L be a set of names of months of the year.

$$L = \{\text{Jan, Feb, Mar, Apr, May, Jun, Jul, Aug, Sep, Oct, Nov, Dec}\}$$

Here, L is an ordered set. The linked organization of this list using arrays is shown in Fig. 6.5. The elements of the list are stored in the one-dimensional array, `Data`. The elements are not stored in the same order as in the set L. They are also not stored in a continuous block of locations. Note that the data elements are allowed to be stored anywhere in the array, in any order.

To maintain the sequence, the second array, `Link`, is added. The values in this array are the links to each successive element. Here, the list starts at the 10th location of the array. Let the variable `Head` denote the start of the list.

$$L = \{\text{Jan, Feb, Mar, Apr, May, Jun, Jul, Aug, Sep, Oct, Nov, Dec}\}$$

	Data	Index	Link
	Jun	1	4
	Sep	2	7
	Feb	3	8
	Jul	4	12
		5	
	Dec	6	–1
	Oct	7	14
	Mar	8	9
	Apr	9	11
Head →	Jan	10	3
	May	11	1
	Aug	12	2
		13	
	Nov	14	6
		15	

Fig. 6.5 Realization of linked list using 1D arrays

Here, `Head = 10` and `Data[Head] = Jan`.

Let us get the second element. The location where the second element is stored at is `Link[Head] = Link[10]`. Hence, `Data[Link[Head]] = Data[Link[10]] = Data[3] = Feb`.

Let us get the third data element through the second element. `Data[Link[3]] = Data[8] = Mar`, and so on.

Continuing in this manner, we can list all the members in the sequence. The link value of the last element is set to –1 to represent the end of the list. Figure 6.6 shows the same representation as in Fig. 6.5 but in a different manner.

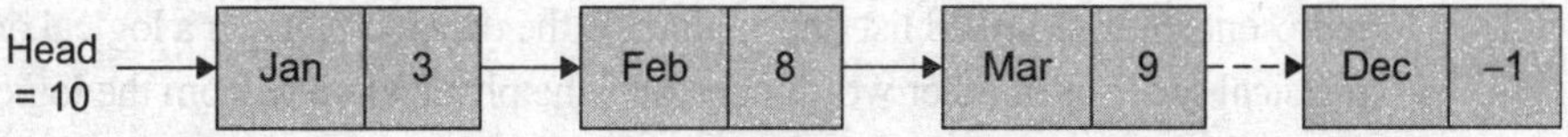

Fig. 6.6 Linked organization

The unused locations are omitted and the list is drawn in the sequence of elements in the list *L*.

Figure 6.6 shows that the first element of the ordered list *L* is at the 10th position. The link value of the first element is 3. This indicates that the second element is at `Data[3]`. The link value of the second element is 8. This indicates that the third element is at `Data[8]`, and so on. Here, –1 is stored at `link[6]`, which indicates the end of the list.

Even though `data` and `link` are shown as two different arrays, they can be implemented using one 2D array as follows:

```
int Linked_List[max][2];
```

Figure 6.7 illustrates the realization of a linked list using a 2D array where $L = \{100, 102, 20, 51, 83, 99, 65\}$, `Max = 10` and `Head = 2`.

	Index	Data	Link
	0	20	3
	1	99	7
Head ⟶	2	100	5
	3	51	6
	4		
	5	102	0
	6	83	1
	7	65	–1
	8		
	9		

Fig. 6.7 Realization of linked list using 2D arrays

6.3.2 Linked List Using Dynamic Memory Management

We learnt that unlike arrays, linked lists need not be stored in adjacent locations. Individual elements can be stored anywhere in the memory. Each data element is called a *node*. Each node contains at least two fields namely *data* and *link*. Every node holds a link to the next node in the list. During run-time (execution of a program), as per the need, a node is allocated (i.e., memory is allocated for a new node). In other words, a new node of the list will be created dynamically. We just remember the pointer to the list at the end, that is, pointer to the first node. In addition, the last node's link field can be set to 0 to mark the end of the list. The 0 here represents null. A linked list thus maintains the data elements in a logical order rather than in a physical order or in other words separates the physical view from the logical view.

Empty Linked List

An empty linked list is a head pointer with the value `Null`. An empty list is also called a *null list*. The length of a null or empty list is 0.

We should note the following facts while creating and inserting a node in a linked list:

1. The nodes may not actually reside in sequential locations.
2. The locations of nodes may change during different runs of program.
3. Therefore, when we write a program that works on lists, we should never look for a specific address except when we test for 0 (i.e., null).

We need the following for the implementation of linked list:

1. A means for allocating memory for a node that has at least one link field.
2. A mechanism to verify whether the allocation is successful.
3. A mechanism to release the allocated node and add to free pool of memory, as and when needed.

These tasks can be performed using the dynamic memory management functions in C++. To verify the memory allocation process, the address returned by the memory allocation function is compared with the value `Null`. A non-null address returned indicates that the process is successful. In C++, *new* and *delete* are the operators used for the same.

6.4 DYNAMIC MEMORY MANAGEMENT

Many languages permit a programmer to specify an array's size at run-time. Such languages have the ability to calculate and assign, during execution, the memory space required by the variables in a program. The process of allocating memory at run-time is known as *dynamic memory allocation*. Let us look at the memory allocation process shown in Fig. 6.8.

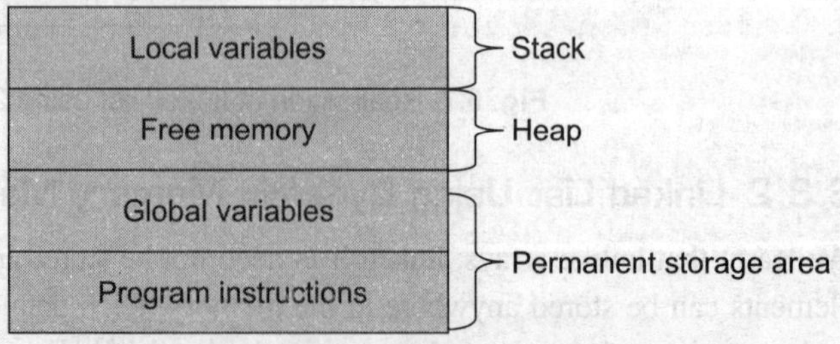

Fig. 6.8 Memory allocation process

The program instructions and global and static variables are stored in a region known as the *permanent storage area*, and the local variables are stored in another area called the *stack*. The memory space allocated between these two regions is available for dynamic allocation during the execution of the program. This free memory region is called the *heap*. The size of the heap keeps changing when a program is executed because of the creation and deletion of the variables that are local to the functions and blocks. Therefore, it is possible to encounter memory overflow during the dynamic allocation process. In such situations, the memory allocation functions as discussed in and returns a null pointer when it fails to locate enough memory requested Section 6.4.1.

6.4.1 Dynamic Memory Management in C++ with new and delete Operators

A special area of main memory, called the *heap*, is reserved for the dynamic variables. Any new dynamic variable created by a program consumes some memory in the heap. The heap is a pool of memory from which the `new` operator allocates memory. The memory allocated from the system heap using the `new` operator is de-allocated (released) using the `delete` operator. C++ enables programmers to control the allocation and de-allocation of memory in a program. The users can dynamically allocate and de-allocate memory for any built-in or user-defined data structure.

The new Operator

The `new` operator creates a new dynamic object of a specified type and returns a pointer that points to this new object (if it fails to create the desired object, it returns 0). In standard C++, a program that uses dynamic memory management should include a standard header `<new>`, which provides access to the standard version of the operator `new`. Consider the following declaration and statement:

```
MyType *ptr;
ptr = new MyType;
```

These statements create a new dynamic object of the type `MyType` of the proper size and return a pointer of the type specified to the right of the operator `new`, that is, `MyType` *.

Syntax

```
Pointer_Type_Variable = new Data_Type;
```

Note that `new` can be used to dynamically allocate any primitive type (such as `int` or `double`) or class type as follows:

1. `int *Number;`
   `Number = new int(20);`
2. `Time *timeptr; timeptr = new Time;`

3. `Date *B_Date_Ptr, *Today;`

```
B_Date_ptr = new Date(20, 1, 1969);
Today = new Date(20, 1, 2005);
```

Here in example 3, `Date` is a class. If the type is a class with a constructor, the default constructor is called for the newly created dynamic variable. Initialization can be done by calling the appropriate constructor. If the program creates too many dynamic variables, it will consume all the memory in the heap. If this happens, any additional calls to `new` will fail. Hence, we should always check to see whether a call to the `new` operator is successful or not. With earlier C++ compliers, if all the memory in the heap has been used and `new` cannot create the requested dynamic variable, then it returns a special pointer named `Null`.

The Null Pointer

`Null` is a special constant pointer value that is used to give a value to a pointer variable that would not otherwise have a value. It can be assigned to a pointer variable of any type. In earlier compliers, a check was needed by the user for the successful operation of `new`. Newer compliers do not require such a check. Current compilers throw the exception `std::badalloc` and the program automatically aborts with an error message. We need no explicit check in the code. The users can 'catch' the exception.

The delete Operator

The object created exists till it is explicitly deleted, or till the function/program runs. To destroy a dynamically allocated variable/object and free the space occupied by the object, the `delete` operator is used.

```
delete ptr;
```

The `delete` operator eliminates a dynamic variable and returns the memory that it had occupied in the heap. The memory can now be reused to create new dynamic variables. After a call to delete, the value of the pointer variable, such as `ptr`, is undefined (except when the dynamic variable is an array). These undefined pointer variables are known as *dangling pointers*. One way to avoid dangling pointers is to set any such variable as null.

If we want to free a dynamically allocated array, the following is the syntax:

```
delete[] pointer_variable;
```

Such a statement will delete the entire array pointed to by `pointer_variable`. The square brackets tell C++ that a dynamic array variable is being eliminated, so the system checks the size of the array and removes that many indexed variables.

```
double* DoubleArrayPtr;
DoubleArrayPtr = new double[array_size];
```

We can use `delete` to release the dynamic array.

```
delete[] DoubleArrayPtr;
```

Similar to other operators, `new` and `delete` operators can be overloaded. Program Code 6.1 demonstrates dynamic variables, `new` and `delete` operators, and pointers.

PROGRAM CODE 6.1

```
#include<iostream.h>
int main()
{
    int *ptr1, *ptr2;
    ptr1 = new int;
    *ptr1 = 52;
    cout << "*ptr1 = " << *ptr1 << endl;
    cout << "*ptr2 = " << *ptr2 << endl;
    *ptr2 = 63;
    cout << "*ptr1 = " << *ptr1 << endl;
    cout << "*ptr2 = " << *ptr2 << endl;
    ptr1 = new int;
    *ptr1 = 98;
    cout << "*ptr1 = " << *ptr1 << endl;
    cout << "*ptr2 = " << *ptr2 << endl;
    return 0;
}
Output:
    *ptr1 = 52
    *ptr2 = Garbage
    *ptr1 = 52
    *ptr2 = 63
    *ptr1 = 98
    *ptr2 = 63
```

6.5 LINKED LIST ABSTRACT DATA TYPE

Although a linked list can be implemented in a variety of ways, the most flexible implementation is by using pointers. To implement the same in C++, we can view the entire linked list as an object of the class `LList`. Figure 6.9 shows an abstract representation of a linked list.

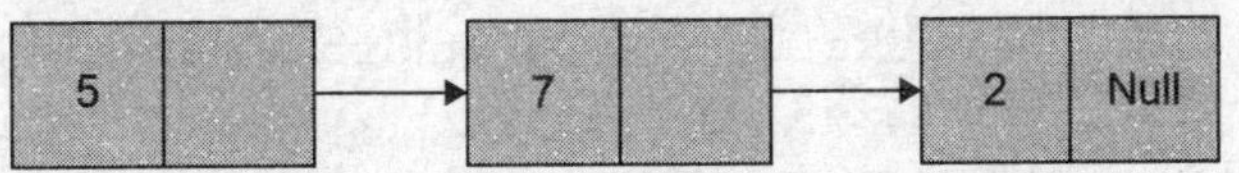

Fig. 6.9 Abstract representation of linked list

Each linked list has to have a special external link (or pointer), say, `Head`. We call it an external link because it is not stored in the list. We shall now extend the abstract notation to show the external link. Figure 6.10 illustrates the list with the external link, `Head`.

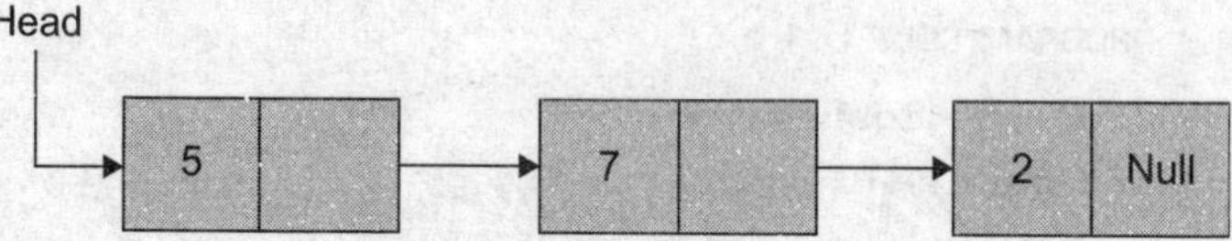

Fig. 6.10 Linked list with head pointer

To represent this linked list (Fig. 6.10), we consider it as an object of class `LList` whose definition is as follows:

```
class LList
{
   private:
      Node *Head;
   public:
      LList();
      ~LList();
      :  }
      :  } member functions here
      :  }
};
```

The `LList` class has only one data member, the `Head` pointer, which points to the first node of the list, which is used to access the list. The member functions including the constructor and the destructor are used to process the list. Note that the `Head` is private and all other member functions are public. This is because particular nodes of the list are accessible to outside objects through pointers; the nodes are made inaccessible to outside objects by declaring `Head` private so that the information hiding principle is not really compromised. This is illustrated in Program Code 6.2.

PROGRAM CODE 6.2

```
class LList
{
   private:
      Node *Head;
      Node *Tail;        // optional data members
      int Size;
   public:
      LList()
      {
         Head = Tail = Null;
```

```
            Size = 0;
        }
        void Create();
        void Traverse();
        void Insert( int data, position);
        void Append(int data);
        void Delete(int position);
        void Reverse();
};
```

6.5.1 Data Structure of Node

Each node has data and link fields. The data field holds data element(s) and the link field(s) stores the address of its successor (and/or predecessor, if any). As the link field is a pointer to its successor, it should be a pointer variable, which should hold the address of its successor. The successor node is of the same type as that of the node itself. Hence, every node has one member, which points to a node of the same type as itself. As every node is a group of two (or more) data elements which are of different data types, they are logically grouped using the data type, *object*. The link field of a node is a pointer that references to a node of the same type as itself. Hence, we need a *self-referential object*.

The declaration of the data structure of a `node` is given as follows:

```
class Node
{
   public:
      int data;
      Node *link;
};

class List
{
   private:
      Node *Head;
      public:
      . }
      . } member functions here
      . }
};
```

Here, within the class, the statement `Node *link` defines the link field of a node. Here, `Node` is a data type of the pointer variable `link`.

Consider the following piece of code:

```
class Node
{
   public:
```

```
   int data;
   Node *link;
} *first, A;
first = &A;
A.data = 10;
A.link = Null;
```

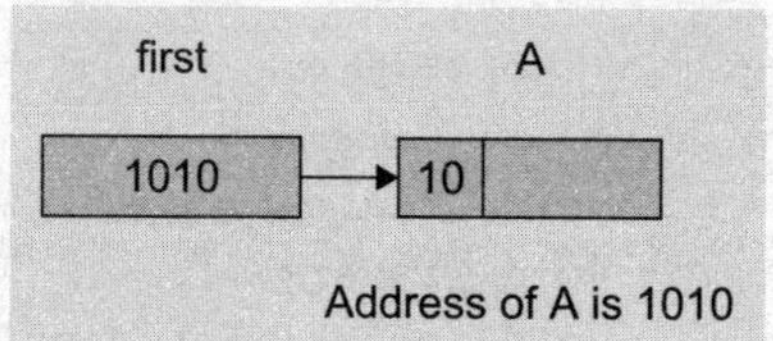

Now, the statement

```
cout << first->data;
```

will print the output 10.

We discussed the node structure of the linked list. Let us now discuss the various operations on a linked list, illustrated in Program Code 6.3.

PROGRAM CODE 6.3

```
class Node
{
   public :
      int data;
      Node *link;
};

class Llist
{
   private:
      Node *Head,*Tail;
      void Recursive_Traverse(Node *tmp)
      {
         if(tmp == Null)
            return;
         cout << tmp->data << "\t";
         Recursive_Traverse(tmp->link);
      }
   public:
      Llist()
      {
         Head = Null;
      }
      void Create();
      void Display();
      Node* GetNode();
      void Append(Node* NewNode);
      void Insert_at_Pos( Node *NewNode, int position);
```

```
      void R_Traverse()
      {
         Recursive_Traverse(Head);
         cout << endl;
      }
      void DeleteNode(int del_position);
};

void Llist :: ~Llist()
{
   Node *Temp;
   while(Head != Null)
   {
      Temp = Head;
      Head = Head->link;
      delete Temp;
   }
}

void Llist :: Create()
{
   char ans;
   Node *NewNode;
   while(1)
   {
      cout << "Any more nodes to be added (Y/N)";
      cin >> ans;
      if(ans == 'n') break;
      NewNode = GetNode();
      Append(NewNode);
   }
}

void Llist :: Append(Node* NewNode)
{
   if(Head == Null)
   {
      Head = NewNode;
      Tail = NewNode;
   }
   else
   {
```

```
        Tail->link = NewNode;
        Tail = NewNode;
    }
}

Node* Llist :: GetNode()
{
    Node *Newnode;
    Newnode = new Node;
    cin >> Newnode->data;
    Newnode->link = Null;
    return(Newnode);
}

void Llist :: Display()
{
    Node *temp = Head;
    if(temp == Null)
        cout << "Empty List";
    else
    {
        while(temp != Null)
        {
            cout << temp->data << "\t";
            temp = temp->link;
        }
    }
    cout << endl;
}

void main()
{
    Llist L1;
    L1.Create();
    L1.Display();
}
```

6.5.2 Insertion of a Node

Depending on the type of list or need of the user, insertion can be made at the beginning, middle, or at the end of the list. If the list is an ordered list, the insertion should not affect the order and this may require inserting the data at proper locations so that the order is preserved. The information about where the node is to be inserted can be decided by searching through the list, obtaining the position, and then inserting the same.

Note that the symbol ⏚ shown in all figures in this chapter indicates the end of list marker representing null. We shall use the same notation throughout the book.

Insertion of a Node at a Middle Position

Assume that a node is to be inserted at some position other than the first position. Let `Prev` refer to the node after which `NewNode` node is to be inserted.

We need the following two steps:

```
NewNode->link = Prev->link;
Prev->link = NewNode;
```

The node `NewNode` is to be inserted between `Prev` and the successor of `Prev`. The link manipulation required to accomplish this is shown in Fig. 6.11 with dotted lines.

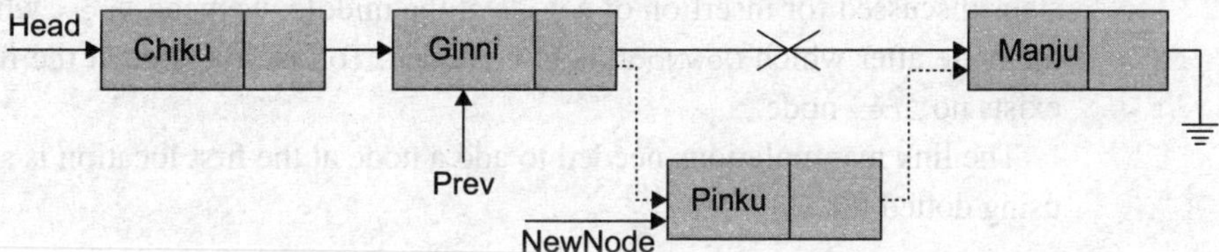

Fig. 6.11 Link manipulations for insertion of a node

The steps to perform the link manipulation are as follows:

1. `NewNode` is a node to be inserted after `Prev`. The node that is a successor of `Prev` will now become the successor of `NewNode`. Currently, `Prev->link` holds the pointer to the successor of `Prev`. Set the link field of the `NewNode` such that `Prev`'s successor node becomes the successor of `NewNode`.

   ```
   NewNode->link = Prev->link;
   ```

   In other words, `NewNode` becomes the predecessor of the node whose predecessor was `Prev`, because `NewNode` is to be placed in between `Prev` and its successor (Fig. 6.12).

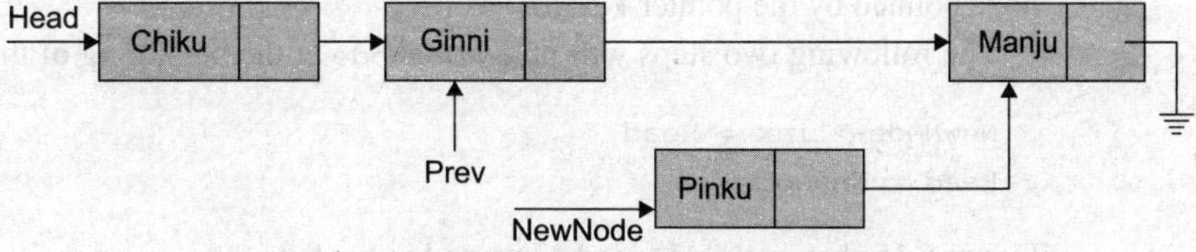

Fig. 6.12 Link manipulations for insertion of a node (Step 1)

2. Now, let us make `NewNode` the successor of `Prev`. This can be achieved by setting the link field of `Prev` to `NewNode` (Fig. 6.13).

```
Prev->link = NewNode;
```

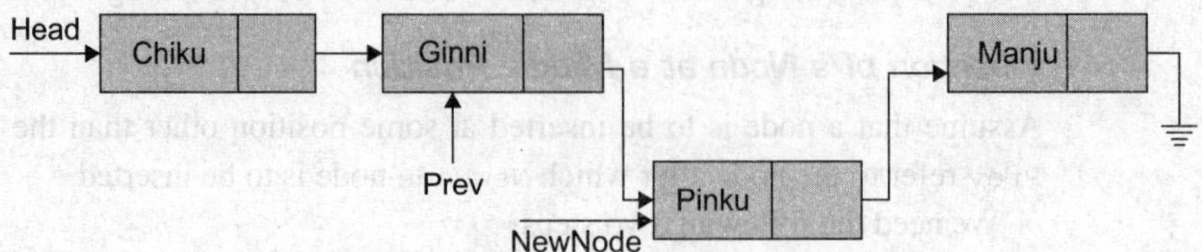

Fig. 6.13 Link manipulations for insertion of a node (Step 2)

Insertion of a Node at the First Position

Let us consider a situation when the node is to be inserted at the first position. As per the steps discussed for insertion of a node at the middle, we need `Prev`, which is a pointer to the node after which `NewNode` is to be added. To insert a node at the first position, there exists no `Prev` node.

The link manipulations needed to add a node at the first location is shown in Fig. 6.14 using dotted lines.

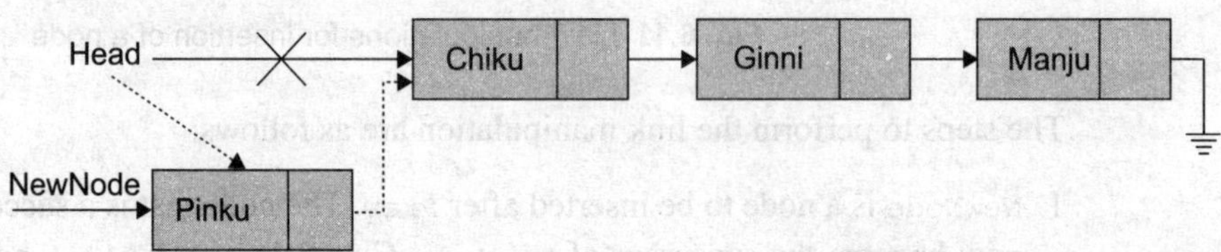

Fig. 6.14 Link manipulations for insertion of a node at the first position

`Head` is the pointer variable pointing to the starting node of the list. The insertion of `NewNode` at the first position should make `Head` point to `NewNode`, and in addition, the current node which is at the first position should become the second node of the list. Hence, the link field of `NewNode` should be set to point to the current first node, that is, the node pointed by the pointer `First`.

The following two steps will insert `NewNode` at the beginning of the linked list.

```
NewNode->link = Head;
Head = NewNode;
```

Figure 6.15 shows `NewNode` to be inserted in the list.

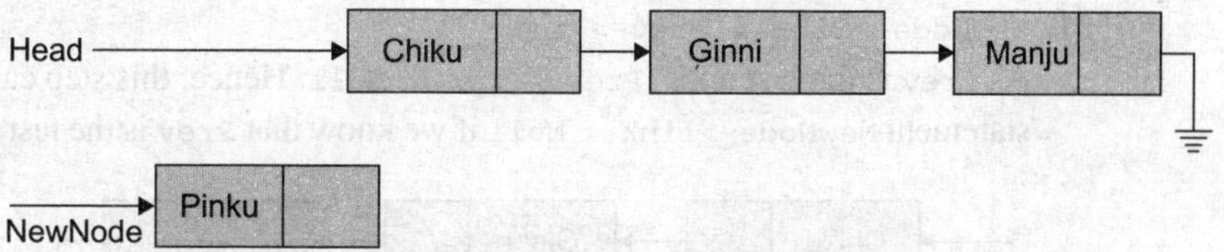

Fig. 6.15 Insertion of a node at the first position (Initial step)

Step 1 This step is represented in Fig. 6.16.

```
NewNode->link = Head;
```

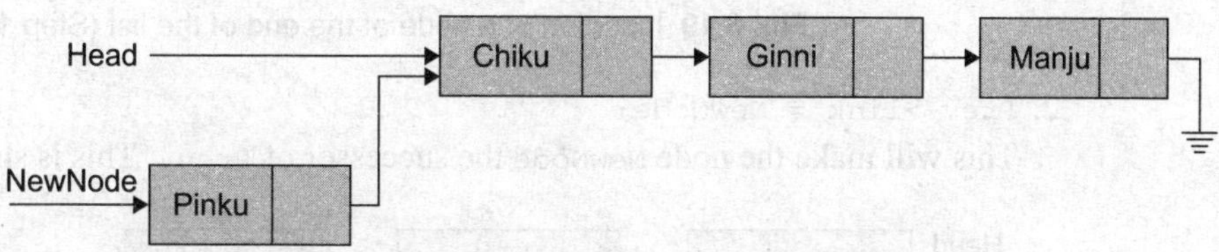

Fig. 6.16 Insertion of a node at the first position (Step 1)

Step 2 This step is represented in Fig. 6.17.

```
Head = NewNode;
```

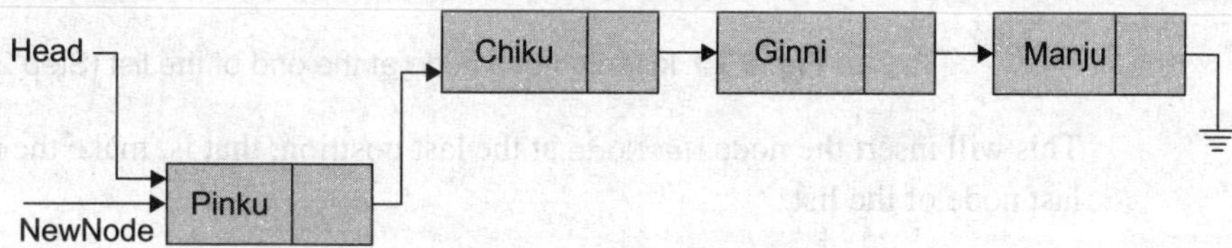

Fig. 6.17 Insertion of a node at the first position (Step 2)

Insertion of a Node at the End

The steps for inserting a node in the middle of a list also work for inserting a node at the end of the list. As the node is to be inserted after the last node, `Prev` is a pointer to the last node. Let the node to be inserted be `NewNode` as shown in Fig. 6.18.

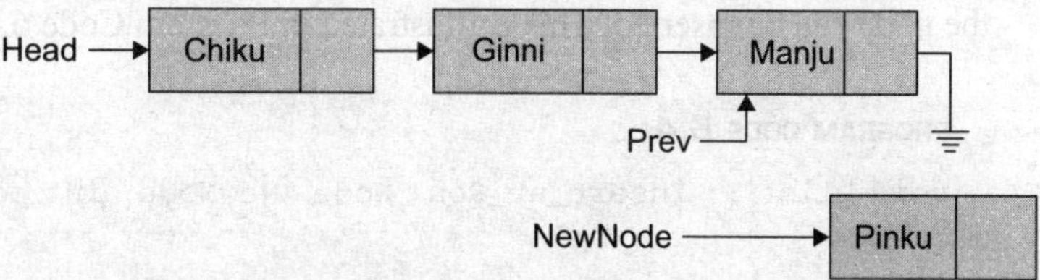

Fig. 6.18 Link manipulations for insertion of a node at the end of a list

1. `NewNode->link = Prev->link`

   As `Prev` is the last node, `Prev->link = Null`. Hence, this step can be replaced by the statement `NewNode->link = Null` if we know that `Prev` is the last node as in Fig. 6.19.

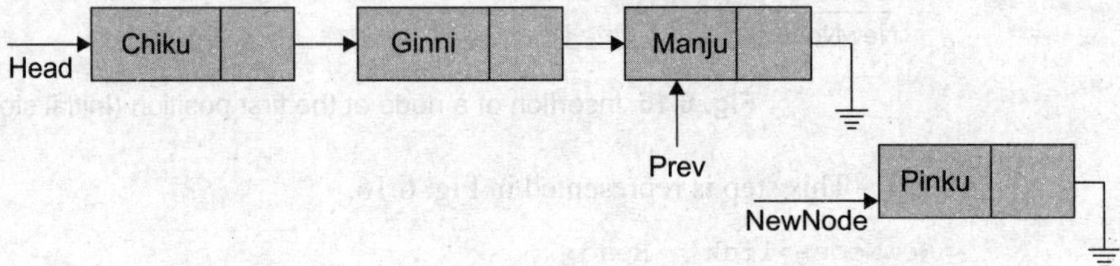

Fig. 6.19 Insertion of a node at the end of the list (Step 1)

2. `Prev->link = NewNode;`

   This will make the node `NewNode` the successor of `Prev`. This is shown in Fig. 6.20.

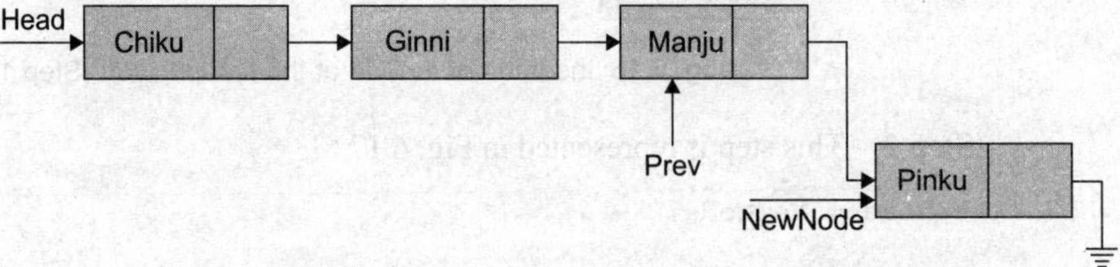

Fig. 6.20 Insertion of a node at the end of the list (Step 2)

This will insert the node `NewNode` at the last position, that is, make the node `NewNode` the last node of the list.

Generalized Insert Routine

Let us write a single insert routine which would insert a node at any random position in a list. Let us assume that the position i at which the node is to be inserted is known. We traverse the list till the $(i-1)^{th}$ node to insert a new node at the ith position. Now, let the $(i-1)^{th}$ node be the previous node referenced by the pointer `Prev`. The function can be suitably modified when instead of the position, the node before or after which the new node is to be inserted is known. In that case, the proper location can be searched and then the node can be inserted. This is illustrated in Program Code 6.4.

PROGRAM CODE 6.4

```
void Llist :: Insert_at_Pos( Node *NewNode, int position)
{
   Node *temp = Head;
   int count = 1,flag = 1;
   if(position == 1)        // inserting at first position
```

```
    {
        NewNode->link = temp;
        Head = NewNode;         // update head
    }
    else
    {
        while(count != position - 1)
        {
            temp = temp->link;
            if(temp == Null)
            {
                flag = 0; break;
            }
            count ++;
        }
        if(flag == 1)
        {
            temp->link = temp->link;
            temp->link = NewNode;
        }
        else
            cout << "Position not found" << endl;
    }
}

void main()
{
    int pos;
    Node *NewNode;
    Llist L1;       // L1 is object of list.
    L1.Create();
    L1.Display();
    NewNode = L1.GetNode();
    cout << "Enter position where node is to be inserted"
<< endl;
    cin >> pos;
    L1.Insert_at_Pos(NewNode, pos);
    L1.Display();
}
```

Program Code 6.4 demonstrates the steps involved in inserting a node at a specified position in a linked list. A similar function can be written to insert a node before or after a specified node.

6.5.3 Linked List Traversal

List traversal is the basic operation where all elements in the list are processed sequentially, one by one. Processing could involve retrieving, searching, sorting, computing the length, and so on. List traversal requires a looping algorithm (Algorithm 6.1). To traverse the linked list, we have to start from the first node. We can access the first node through a pointer variable `Head`. Once we access the first node, through its link field, we can access the second node; through the second node's link field, we can access the third, and so on, as every node points to its successor till the last node.

ALGORITHM 6.1

1. Get the address of the first node, call it `current`; `current` = `Head`.
2. if `current` is `Null`, goto step 6.
3. Process the data field of the current node (node pointed by `current`). Here, the process may include printing data, updating, and so on
4. Move to the next node–`current = current->link`
   (Now `current` should point to the next node. The address of next node is in the link field of `current`. Hence, set `current` to the link field of `current`}
5. goto step 2
6. stop

Non-recursive Method

The non-recursive function for list traversal is shown in Program Code 6.5.

PROGRAM CODE 6.5

```
void Llist :: Traverse()
// just displaying the list members
{
   Node *temp = Head;
   if(temp == Null)
      cout << "Empty List";
   else
   {
      while(temp != Null)
      {
         cout << temp->data << "\t";
         temp = temp->link;
      }
   }
   cout << endl;
}
```

This function can be called by any function. The same function can also be used to print, search, update, and count length by adding a few statements.

Here, the data element may not necessarily be just one. The node may hold more than one data element. Let us see output for list L pictorially.

$$L = \{21, 22, 23\}$$

1. `Current = Head`

2. After execution of statement 1

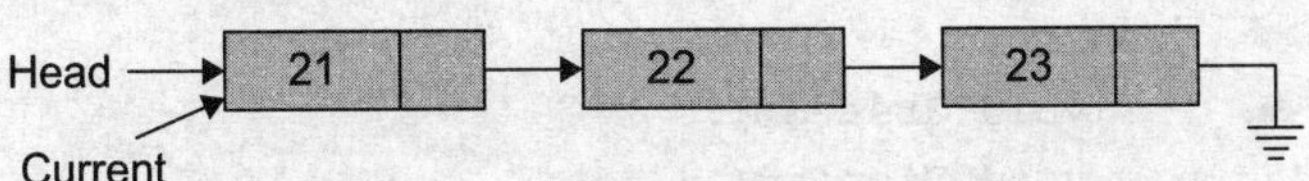

3. As `current != Null`, statements 3, 4, and 5 are executed.

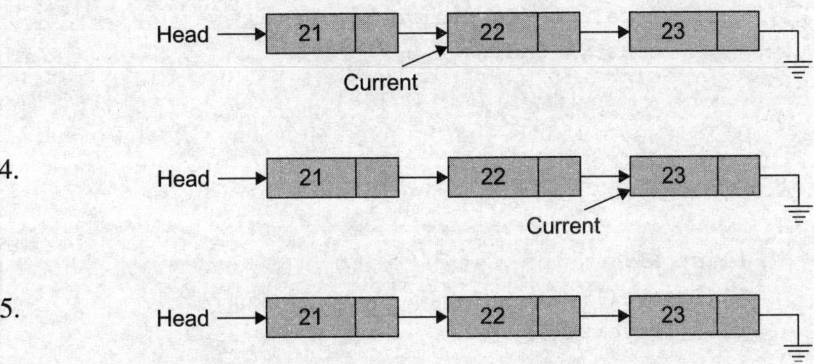

Now `Current = Null` is true, while loop condition is false; hence stop.

Output		
21		
21	22	
21	22	23

Recursive Traversal Method

Program Code 6.6 is the recursive code for traversing the linked list.

PROGRAM CODE 6.6

```
class Llist
{
   private:
      Node *Head, *Tail;
      void Recursive_Traverse(Node *tmp)
      {
         //Recursive traversal code
         if(tmp == Null)
            return;
         cout << tmp->data << "\t";
         Recursive_Traverse(tmp->link);
      }
   public:
      void Create();
      void Display();
      void R_Traverse()
      {
         Recursive_Traverse(Head);
         //call to recursive traversal
         cout << endl;
      }
};

void main()
{
   Llist L1;
   L1.Create();
   L1.R_Traverse();
}
Output:
21  22  23
```

Let us change the sequence of the last two statements in the recursive traverse function in Program Code 6.6.

```
void Llist :: Recursive_Traverse(Node *tmp)
{
   if(tmp == Null)
      return;
   Recursive_Traverse(tmp->link);
   cout << tmp->data << "\t";
}
```

What will be the output now? Will it be 21 22 23 or 23 22 21? Do verify.

6.5.4 Deletion of a Node

There may be nodes that are to be deleted from a list. Linear lists may very often require insertion and deletion of nodes. Linked lists are the most suitable data structures for this purpose. We discussed how to insert a node in a list. Let us learn about how to delete a node from a list.

Let us assume that the node to be deleted contains data *x*. We need the following steps to delete the same. Let $x = 13$ and let it be pointed to by the pointer `Curr`. To delete this node, the required link manipulations are shown in Fig. 6.21 with dotted lines.

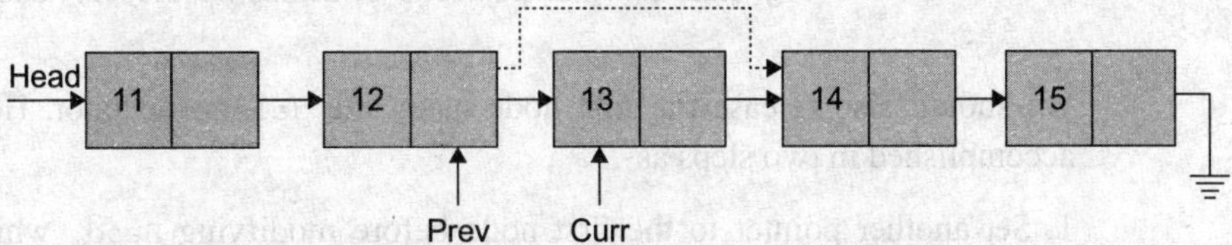

Fig. 6.21 Link manipulations for deletion of a node

To delete the node `Curr`, we need to modify the link between `Curr` and its previous node, and the link between `Curr` and its successor.

We need to modify them as shown in Fig. 6.21. The `Prev` is pointing to `Curr` as its current successor. As the `Curr` is to be deleted, the Prev's link should be modified such that it points to the successor of `Curr`. This makes the successor of `Curr` the successor of `Prev`. This deletes the node `Curr` from the linked list.

Note that we need the address of the node to be deleted as well as its predecessor to modify the links such that the node is deleted.

This can be achieved by the following steps shown in Algorithm 6.2.

ALGORITHM 6.2

1. Let both `Curr` and `Prev` be set to `Head`.
2. Traverse the list and search the node to be deleted.
3. Let `Curr` point to the node to be deleted and `Prev` be its previous node.
4. Modify the link field of `Prev` so that it skips `Curr` and points to its next.
   `Prev->link = Curr->link`
5. Free the memory allocated for the node `Curr`.
6. Stop

The node to be deleted can be at any position. It could be the first, middle, or last node.

Deleting the First Node

Deleting the first node is also referred to as deleting a header node. If the node at the first position is to be deleted, then we need to modify the pointer pointing to the first node (also called as the head pointer), say `Head`.

Deletion of the first node needs the link manipulations shown in Fig. 6.22 with dotted lines.

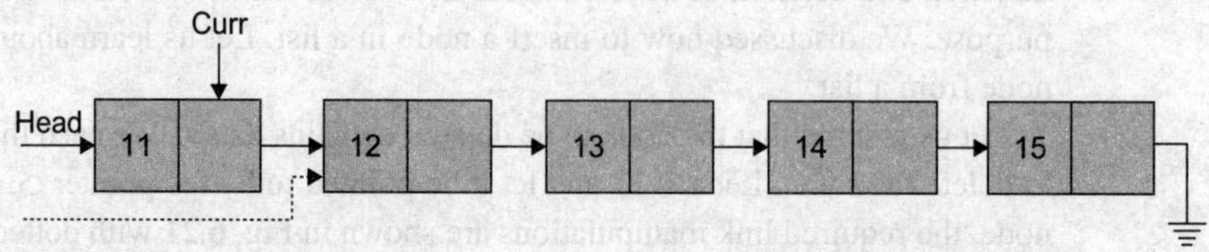

Fig. 6.22 Link manipulations for deletion of the first node

We should also release the first node using the `delete` operator. Hence, this can be accomplished in two steps as

1. Set another pointer to the first node before modifying `Head,` which is the pointer pointing to the first node. Set `Head` to point to the second node. This can be accomplished by the statements,

```
Curr = Head;
Head = Head->link;
```

2. Now, release the memory allocated for the first node.

```
delete Curr;
```

These two statements will delete the first node, and `Head` will point to the second node so that the second node becomes the first node. Later, the memory allocated for the first node is freed.

Deleting a Middle Node

Let `curr` point to the node to be deleted, and `prev` be the predecessor of `curr`. Then, the following statements will delete the node `curr`.

```
prev->link = curr->link;
delete curr;
```

These two statements will also delete the last node of the list. Let us work out a function for the deletion of a node that may be at any position (Program Code 6.7).

PROGRAM CODE 6.7

```
void Llist :: DeleteNode(int pos)
{
    int count = 1, flag = 1;
    Node *curr, *temp;
```

```
    temp = Head;
    if(pos == 1)
    {
       Head = Head->link;
       delete temp;
    }
    else
    {
       while(count != pos - 1)
       {
          temp = temp->link;
          if(temp == Null)
          {
             flag = 0; break;
          }
          count++;
       }
       if(flag == 1)
       {
          curr = temp->link;
          temp->link = curr->link;
          delete curr;
       }
       else
          cout << "Position not found" << endl;
    }
}

void main()
{
    int pos,del_position;
    Llist L1;       // L1 is object of list.
    L1.Create();
    L1.Display();
    cout << "Enter position of the node to be deleted"
    << endl;
    cin >> del_position;
    L1.DeleteNode(del_position);
    L1.R_Traverse();
}
```

6.6 LINKED LIST VARIANTS

The basic idea of a linked list serves as the starting point for many useful variations. There are some variants of linked lists. In the following sections, we shall look at a few of them which have proven to be essential tools for computer scientists and software engineers.

6.6.1 Head Pointer and Header Node

A linked list must always have at least one pointer pointing to the first node of the list. This pointer is a must because otherwise, we have no way to access the linked list. This pointer is many times called a *head pointer*, because a linked list may contain a dummy node (exam) attached at the start position called *header node*. A *header node* is a special node that is attached at the front of the linked list. This header node may contain special information in data fields. The information could be the total number of nodes in the list.

Note that the header node may be of the same type as the node of the linked list or it may have a different data type with some special (additional) fields in it. A linked list with header node is called *header-linked list*.

Figure 6.23 is a header-linked list where the header node is of the same data type as that of the other nodes of the list.

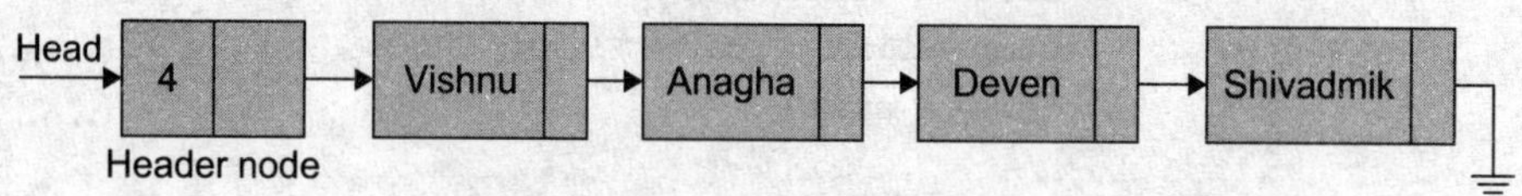

Fig. 6.23 Header-linked list

Here, the data field of the header node stores 4, which indicates that the linked list contains 4 records ahead. For example, suppose there is an application where the number of items in a list is often calculated. Usually, we need to traverse the whole list to count the length. However, if the current length is maintained in the header node, the information can be accessed easily. Figure 6.24 has a special header node whose data type is not the same as that of the other nodes of the list.

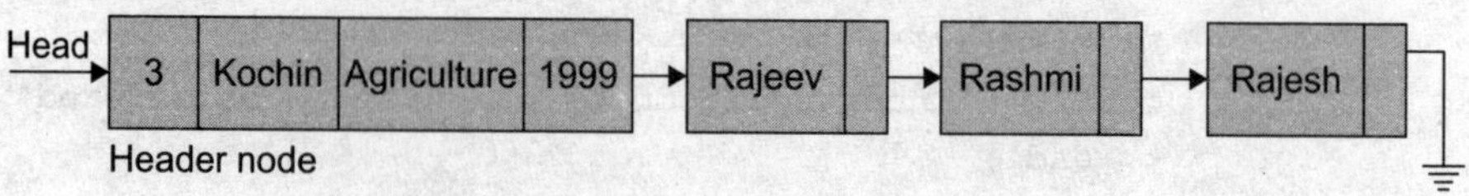

Fig. 6.24 Header-linked list with header node different from other nodes

In this list, the header node has some special fields such as length, city, department, year, and so on. Such a node will have the link field that points to the node of the linked list, as illustrated in Program Code 6.8.

PROGRAM CODE 6.8

```
class Head_Node
{
   public:
      int count;
      char City[15];
      char Dept[30];
      int Est_Year;
      .
      .
      .
      Node *link;
      // header node links to first node of the list
};
class Node
{
   public:
      emp_name[20];
      Node *link;
      // every node links to its successor of the same
      type
};
```

The most popular convention is to call the pointer that points to the first node of the list as head pointer no matter whether the header node is present or not.

6.6.2 Types of Linked List

We studied that in a linked list, every node must have at least one linked field. Thus, each node provides information about its predecessor and/or successor in the list. It may also have the knowledge about where the previous node lies in the memory. Thus, linked lists can be classified broadly as follows:

1. Singly linked list
2. Doubly linked list

The list and operations we discussed so far had only one link pointing to its successor and is called as singly linked list.

Singly Linked List

A linked list in which every node has one link field, to provide information about where the next node of the list is, is called as *singly linked list* (SLL). It has no knowledge about where the previous node lies in the memory. In SLL, we can traverse only in one direction. We have no way to go to the ith node from $(i + 1)^{th}$ node, unless the list is traversed again from the first node (Fig. 6.25).

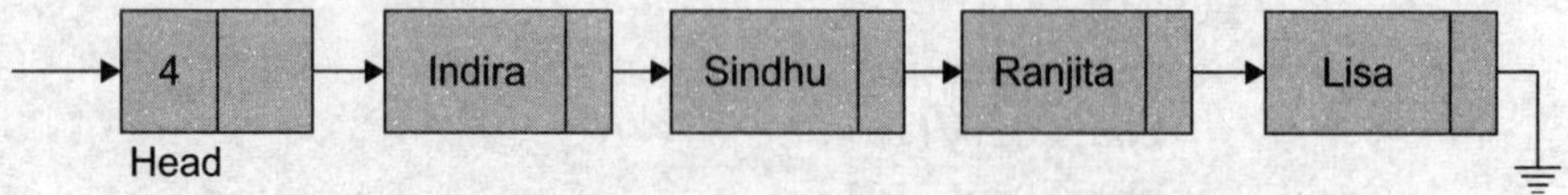

Fig. 6.25 Singly linked list

Often SLL is just referred to as a linked list.

Doubly Linked List

In a doubly linked list (DLL), each node has two link fields to store information about the one to the next and also about the one ahead of the node. Hence, each node has knowledge of its successor and also its predecessor. In DLL, from every node, the list can be traversed in both the directions (Fig. 6.26).

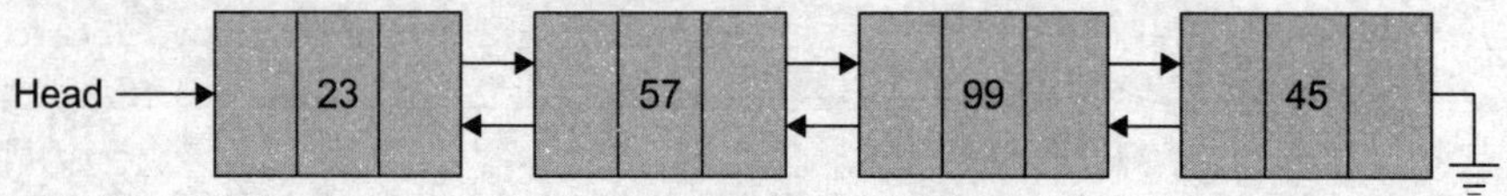

Fig. 6.26 Doubly linked list

Both SSL and DLL may or may not contain a header node. The one with a header node is explicitly mentioned in the title as a header-SLL and a header-DLL.These are also called as singly linked list with header node and doubly linked list with header node.

6.6.3 Linear and Circular Linked Lists

The other classification of linked lists based on their method of traversal is as follows:

1. Linear linked list
2. Circular linked list

Linear Linked List

The linked lists that we have seen so for are known as *linear linked lists*. All elements of such a linked list can be accessed by traversing a list from the first node of the list.

Circular Linked List

Although a linear linked list is a useful and popular data structure, it has some shortcomings. For example, consider an SLL. Given a pointer *A* to a node in a linear list, we cannot reach any of the nodes that precede the node to which *A* is pointing. This disadvantage can be overcome by making a small change. This change is without any additional data structure. The link field of the last node is set to `Null` in a linear list to mark the end of the list. This link field of the last node can be set to point to the first node rather than `Null`. Such a linked list is called a *circular linked list* (Fig. 6.27).

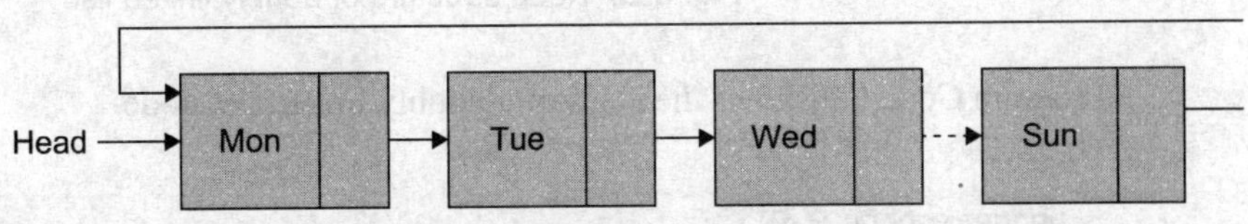

Fig. 6.27 Circular linked list

From any node in such a list, it is possible to reach any other node in the list. A circular list could be singly circular or doubly circular list and with or without a header node. Circular lists have many applications. We shall study those in further topics.

Linear lists are also called *non-circular* or *grounded lists*. The last node's link field of a linear list is set to `Null`. It is pictorially denoted using the 'ground' symbol used in electronic circuits. Let us discuss the DLL and its operations.

6.7 DOUBLY LINKED LIST

In SLL, each node provides information about where the next node is. It has no knowledge about where the previous node is. For example, if we are at the ith node in the list currently, then to access the $(i - 1)^{th}$ node or $(i - 2)^{th}$ node, we have to traverse the list right from the first node. In addition, it is not possible to delete the ith node given only a pointer to the ith node. It is also not possible to insert a node before the ith node given only a pointer to the ith node (there are other ways that are without link manipulations such as using data exchange).

For handling such difficulties, we can use DLLs where each node contains two links, one to its predecessor and other to its successor (Fig. 6.28).

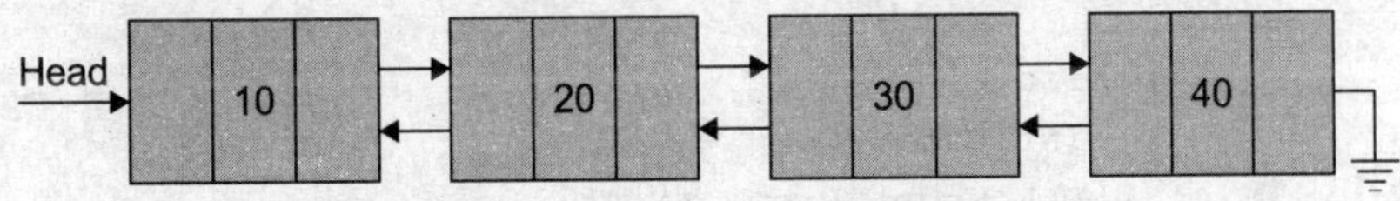

Fig. 6.28 Doubly linked list of four nodes

Each node of a DLL has three fields in general but must have at least two link fields (Fig. 6.29).

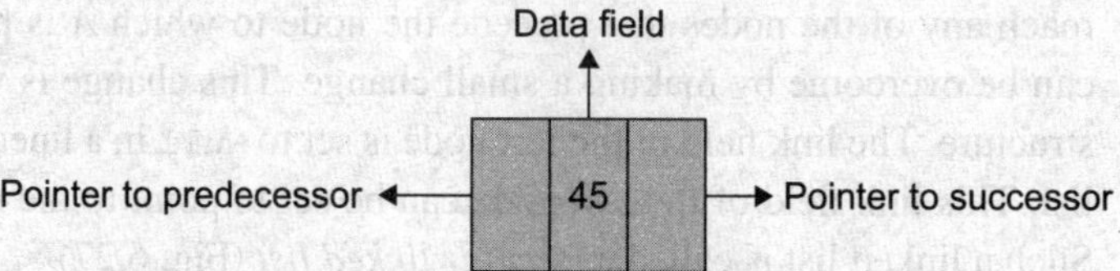

Fig. 6.29 Node structure of doubly linked list

Program Code 6.9 shows the class of a doubly linked list node.

PROGRAM CODE 6.9

```
class DLL_Node
{
   Public:
      int Data;
      DLL_Node *Prev, *Next;
      DLL_Node()
      {
         Prev = Next = Null;
      }
};
```

A DLL may either be linear or circular and it may or may not contain a header node. DLLs are also called *two-way lists*.

6.7.1 Creation of Doubly Linked List

Creation of DLL has the same procedure as that of SLL, as shown in Program Code 6.10. The only difference is that each node must be linked to both its predecessor and successor.

PROGRAM CODE 6.10

```
class DLL_Node
{
   public:
      int Data;
      DLL_Node *Prev, *Next;
      DLL_Node()
      {
         Prev = Next = Null;
```

```
      }
};

class DList
{
   private:
      DLL_Node  *Head, *Tail;
   public:
      DList()
      {
         Head = Tail = Null;
      }
      void Create();
      DLL_Node* GetNode();
      void Append(DLL_Node* NewNode);
      void Traverse();
      void DeleteNode(int val);
      void Delete_Pos(int pos);
      void Insert_Before(int val);
      void Insert_After(int val);
      void Insert_Pos(DLL_Node *NewNode, int pos);
};

DLL_Node* DList :: GetNode()
{
   DLL_Node *Newnode;
   Newnode = new DLL_Node;
   cout << "Enter Data";
   cin >> Newnode->Data;
   Newnode->Next = Newnode->Prev = Null;
   return(Newnode);
}

void DList :: Append(DLL_Node* NewNode)
{
   if(Head == Null)
   {
      Head = NewNode;
      Tail = NewNode;
   }
```

```
    else
    {
        Tail->Next = NewNode;       //Attach to last node
        NewNode->Prev = Tail;
        Tail = NewNode;
    }
}

void DList :: Create()
{
    char ans;
    DLL_Node *NewNode;
    while(1)
    {
        cout << "Any more nodes to be added (Y/N)";
        cin >> ans;
        if(ans == 'n') break;
        NewNode = GetNode();
        Append(NewNode);
    }
}

void DList :: Traverse()
{
    DLL_Node *Curr;
    Curr = Head;
    if(Curr == Null)
        cout << "The list is empty \n";
    else
        while(Curr != Null)
        {
            cout << Curr->Data << "\t";
            Curr = Curr->Next;
        }
        cout << endl;
}

void main()
{
    DList L2;
    L2.Create();
    L2.Traverse();
```

6.7.2 Deletion of a Node from a Doubly Linked List

Deleting from a DLL needs the deleted node's predecessor, if any, to be pointed to the deleted node's successor. In addition, the successor, if any, should be set to point to the predecessor node as shown in Fig. 6.30.

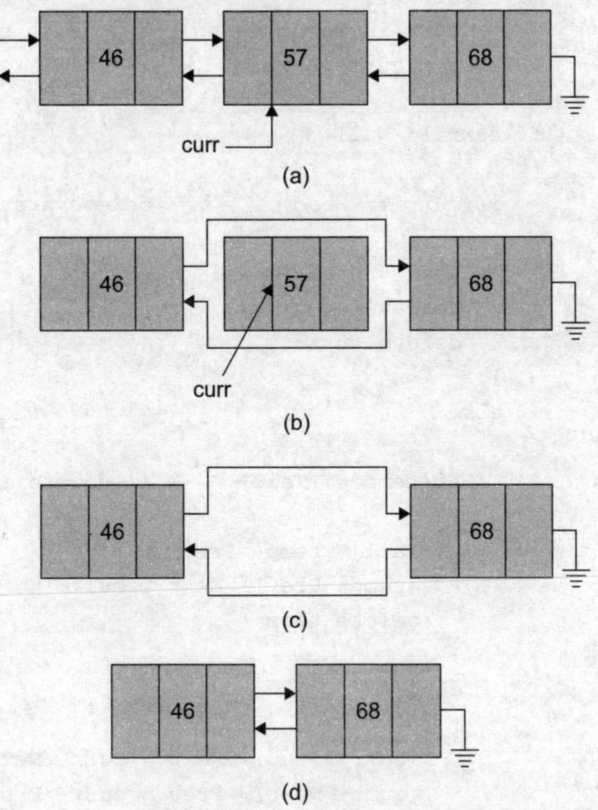

Fig. 6.30 Deletion node in doubly linked list (a) Links modified on deletion of node (b) Memory of the deleted node freed (c) Realignment of nodes (d) After node deletion

The core steps involved in this process are the following:

```
(curr->Prev)->Next = curr->Next;
(curr->Next)->Prev = curr->Prev;
delete curr;
```

The C++ code for the same is as shown in Program Code 6.11.

PROGRAM CODE 6.11

```
void DList :: DeleteNode(int val)
{
   DLL_Node *curr, *temp;
```

```
    curr = Head;
    while(curr!=Null)
    {
       if(curr->Data == val)
          break;
       // curr is pointing to the node to be deleted
       curr = curr->Next;
    }
    if(curr != Null)
    {
       if(curr == Head)         // delete first node
       {
          Head = Head->Next;
          Head->Prev = Null;
          delete curr;
       }
       else
       {
          if(temp == Tail)        // delete last node
          {
             Tail = temp->Prev;
             (temp->Prev)->Next = Null;
             delete temp;
          }
          else
          {
             (curr->Prev)->Next = curr->Next;
             (curr->Next)->Prev = curr->Prev;
             delete curr;
          }
       }
       if(Head == Null)
       {
          Tail = Null;
       }
    }
    else
       cout << "Node to be deleted is not found \n";
}
void DList :: Delete_Pos(int pos)
{
    DLL_Node *temp = Head;
```

```
    {
       if(pos == 1)       // delete header node
       {
          Head = Head->Next;
          Head->Prev = Null;
          delete temp;
       }
       else
       {
          while(count != pos)
          {
             temp = temp->Next;
             if(temp != Null)
                count++;
             else
             break;
          }
          if(count == pos)
          {
             if(temp == Tail)      // delete last node
             {
                Tail = temp->Prev;
                (temp->Prev)->Next = Null;
                delete temp;
             }
             else
             {
                (temp->Prev)->Next = temp->Next;
                (temp->Next)->Prev = temp->Prev;
                delete temp;
             }
          }
          else
             cout << "The node to be deleted is not
             found" << endl;
       }
    }
}

void main()
  int count = 1;
   if(Head != Null)
```

```
{
    int val,pos;
    DList L2;
    L2.Create();
    L2.Traverse();
    cout << "Enter Node Data to be deleted-->";
    cin >> val;
    L2.DeleteNode( val);
    L2.Traverse();
    cout << "Enter Node position to be deleted-->";
    cin >> pos;
    L2.Delete_Pos(pos);
    L2.Traverse();
}
```

6.7.3 Insertion of a Node in a Doubly Linked List

Now, let us discuss inserting a node in DLL. To insert a node, say `Current`, we have to modify four links as each node points to its predecessor as well as successor. Let us assume that the node `Current` is to be inserted in between the two nodes say `node1` and `node2`. We have to modify the following links:

`node1->Next`, `node2->Prev`, `Current->Prev`, and `Current->Next`

When the `Current` node is inserted in between `node1` and `node2`, `node1`'s successor node changes. Hence, we need to modify `node1->Next`. For the node `node2`, its predecessor changes. Therefore, we need to modify `node2->Prev` This is shown in Fig. 6.31.

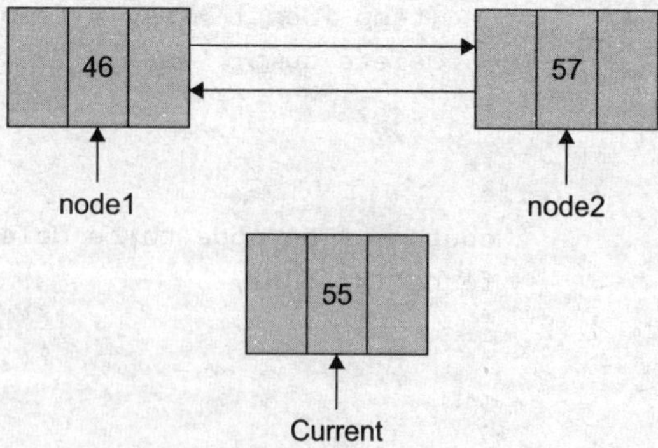

Fig. 6.31 Inserting a node current

`Current` is a new node to be inserted. We need to set both its predecessor and successor by setting the links as `Current->Prev` and `Current->Next`

After the insertion of `Current`, the resultant modified links should be shown as in Fig. 6.32.

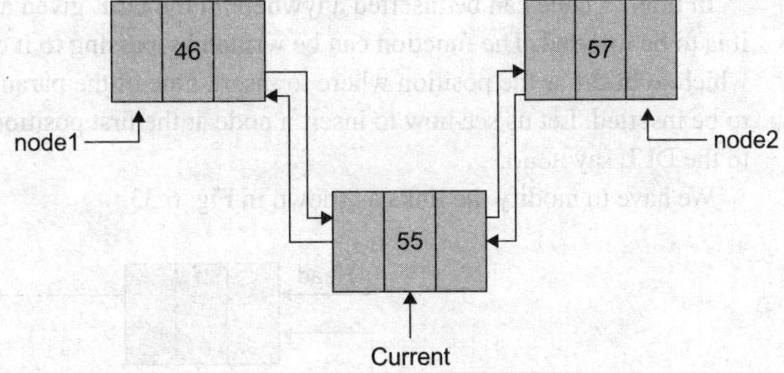

Fig. 6.32 Link modification for insertion of a node in a DLL

Hence, to modify the links, the statements would be

1. To modify `node1->Next` we use the operation
   ```
   node1->Next = Current;
   ```
2. To modify `node2->Prev` we use the operation
   ```
   node2->Prev = Current;
   ```
3. To set `curr->Next`, we use the operation
   ```
   Current->Next = node2;
   ```
4. To set `curr->Prev`, we use the operation
   ```
   Current->Prev = node1;
   ```

In brief, the statements to insert a node in between `node1` and `node2` are as follows:

```
node1->Next = Current;
node2->Prev = Current;
Current->Next = node2;
Current->Prev = node1;
```

These statements are with respect to Fig. 6.32, where we considered that the node is to be inserted in between `node1` and `node2`.

Though the new node is to be inserted between `node1` and `node2`, we need to know only about `node1`. The `node2` is the successor of `node1`, which can be accessed through `node1->Next`. Practically, the node can be inserted in DLL given only one node after which (or before which) the node is to be inserted.

Let us consider the insertion of a node given one node before or after which the node is to be inserted, say before `node2`. Then, the four statements could be

```
(node2->Prev)->Next = Current;
Current->Prev = node2->Prev;
```

```
Current->Next = node2;
node2->Prev = Current;
```

In brief, a node can be inserted anywhere in the DLL given a node after/before which it is to be inserted. The function can be written by passing to it either a node after/before which to insert or the position where to insert. One of the parameters would be the node to be inserted. Let us see how to insert a node at the first position. We are given a pointer to the DLL say `Head`.

We have to modify the links as shown in Fig. 6.33.

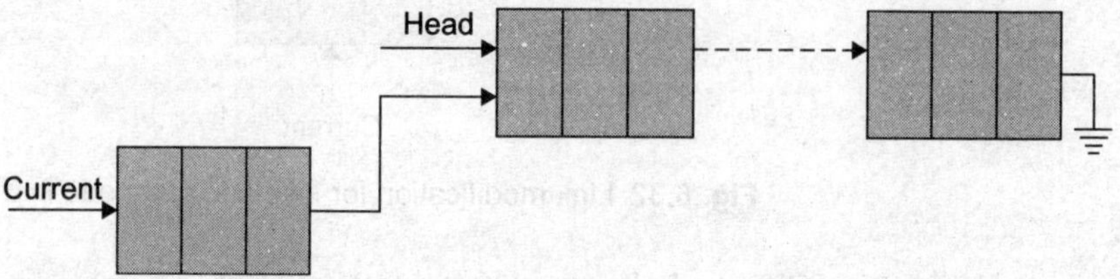

Fig. 6.33 Inserting a node before first node

This is represented by the following statements:

```
Current->Next = Head;
Head->Prev = Current;
Head = Current;
Current->Prev = Null;
```

6.7.4 Traversal of DLL

Given a head pointer to the DLL; traversal is the same as that of an SLL. The advantage of DLL over SLL is, given a pointer *P* pointing to any of the nodes of list, the list can be traversed only in one (forward) direction in SLL, whereas the list can be traversed in both (forward and backward) directions in DLL. Again, if we have a circular DLL, it has more advantages. It helps us keep the traversal procedure an unending one. Program Code 6.12 shows the traversal of a DLL.

PROGRAM CODE 6.12

```
void DList :: Insert_Pos(DLL_Node* NewNode, int pos)
{
   DLL_Node *temp = Head;
   int count = 1;
   if(Head == Null)
      Head = Tail = NewNode;
```

PROGRAM CODE 6.12

```
void DList :: Insert_Pos(DLL_Node* NewNode, int pos)
{
   DLL_Node *temp = Head;
   int count = 1;
   if(Head == Null)
      Head = Tail = NewNode;
   else if(pos == 1)      // insert before head
   {
      NewNode->Next = Head;
      Head->Prev = NewNode;
      Head = NewNode;
   }
   else
   {
      while(count != pos)
      {
         temp = temp->Next;
         if(temp != Null)
            count++;
         else
            break;
      }
      if(count == pos)
      {
         (temp->Prev)->Next = NewNode;
         NewNode->Prev = temp->Prev;
         temp->Prev = NewNode;
      }
      else
       cout << "The node position is not found" << endl;
   }
}
```

6.8 CIRCULAR LINKED LIST

The linked lists that we have seen so far are known as linear linked lists. All elements of such a linked list can be accessed by first setting up a pointer pointing to the first node in the list and then traversing the entire list. Although a linear linked list is a useful data structure, it has some drawbacks. For example, consider an SLL. Given a pointer `Current` to a node in an SLL, we cannot reach any of the nodes that precede the Current node (this is not the case with DLL as DLL has two, one backward and one forward, links). This drawback can be overcome by making a small change, and this change is without any additional data structure. In a singly linear list, the last nodes link field is set to `Null`. Instead of that, store the address of the first node of the list in that link field. This change will make the last node point to the first node of the list. Such a linked list is called *circular linked list* , shown in Fig. 6.34.

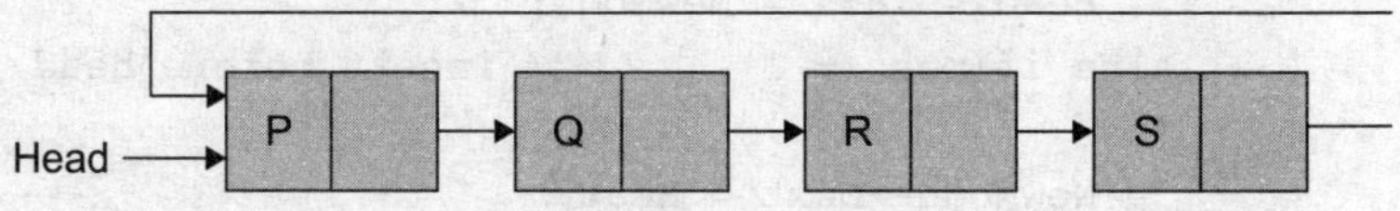

Fig. 6.34 Circular linked list

From any node in such a list, it is possible to reach to any other node in the list. We need not traverse the list again right from the first node. Circular linked list is used in many applications. Circular linked list is used to keep track of free space (unused nodes) in memory. In a circular list, traversal can be continued from `current` node. It helps us to keep the traversal procedure an unending one. The two primary applications of circular list is time slicing and memory management.

We can have a circular SLL or DLL. Both alternatives are possible. Similarly, circular linked lists could be with or without header nodes.

6.8.1 Singly Circular Linked List

Let us consider an SLL without a header node as shown in Fig. 6.35.

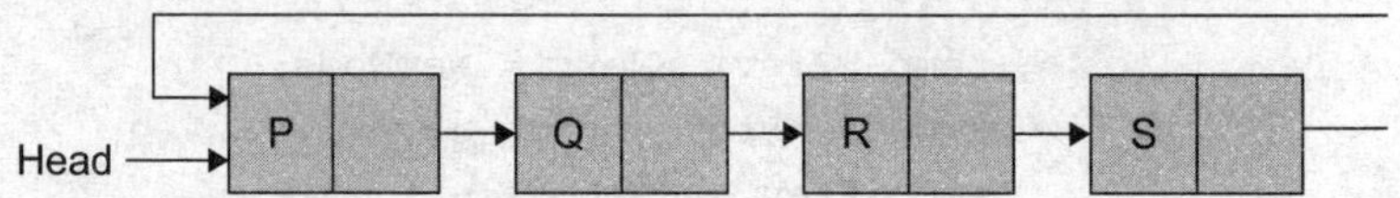

Fig. 6.35 Singly circular linked list

In a singly circular list, the pointer head points to the first node of the list. From the last node, we can access the first node. Remember that we cannot access the last node through the header node; we have access to only the first node. We need to traverse the whole list to reach to the last node. An elegant solution to this is set the pointer `Head` to point to the last node instead of the first node. This is illustrated in Fig. 6.36.

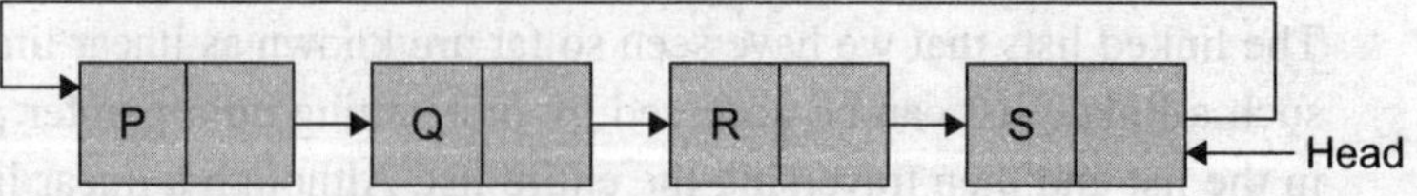

Fig. 6.36 Singly circular linked list

Now, through `Head` we have access to the last node, and it also (`Head->next`) gives us the address of the first node.

6.8.2 Circular Linked List with Header Node

Consider a circular list with a single node in the list (Fig. 6.37).

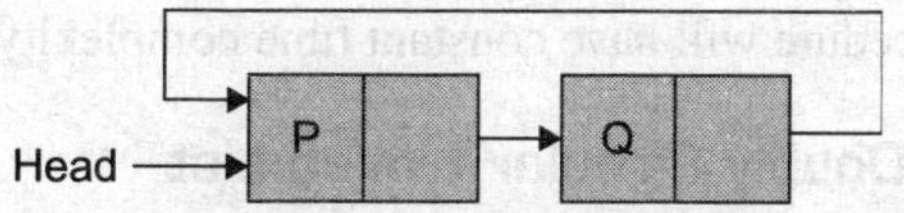

Fig. 6.37 Singly circular linked list with two nodes

Circular list with a single node has a problem of checking end of traversal as

```
(while(x->link != Head));
```

This would enter an infinite loop.

So, we can use a circular linked list with header node as shown in Fig. 6.38.

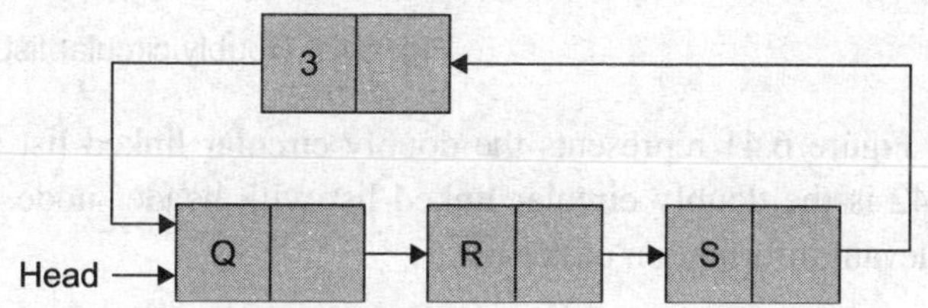

Fig. 6.38 Singly circular linked list with header node

The circular list with header node drawn in Fig. 6.38 can be redrawn as in Fig. 6.39.

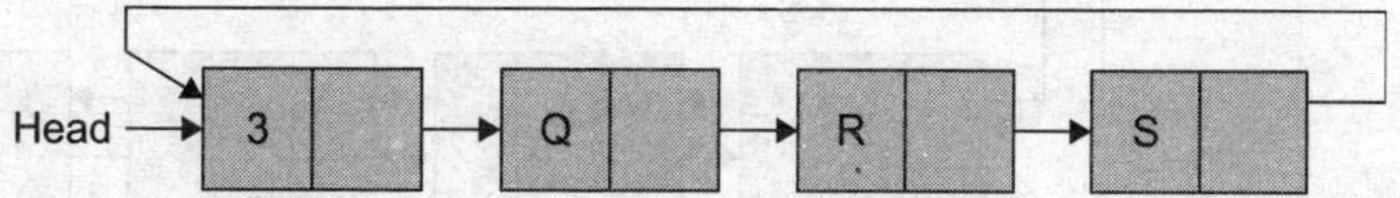

Fig. 6.39 Singly circular linked list with header node—representation 2

Suppose we want to insert a new node at the front of this list. We have to change the link field of the last node. In addition, we have to traverse the whole list to reach till the last node as the link field of the last node is also to be updated. Hence, it is convenient if the head pointer points to the last node rather than the header node, which is the first node of the list.

If the singly headed circular linked list has a head pointer as shown in Fig. 6.40, then a node can easily be inserted at the front and also at the rear of the list.

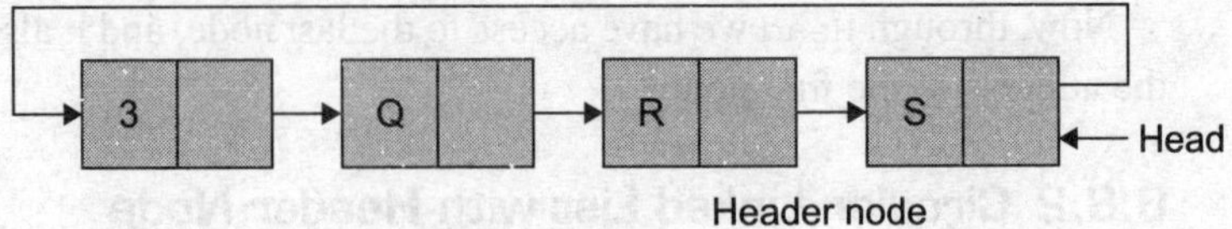

Fig. 6.40 Singly headed circular linked list with head pointing to last node

This procedure will have constant time complexity for both insert at front and at rear.

6.8.3 Doubly Circular Linked List

In doubly circular linked list, the last node's next link is set to the first node of the list and the first node's previous link is set to the last node of the list. This gives access to the last node directly from the first node (Fig. 6.41).

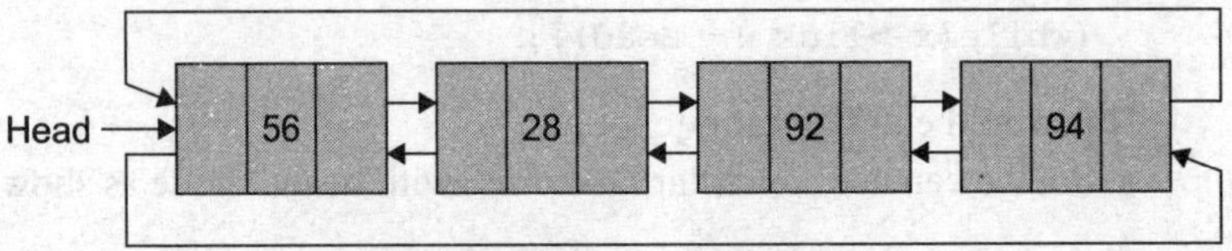

Fig. 6.41 Doubly circular list

Figure 6.41 represents the doubly circular linked list without a header node. Figure 6.42 is the doubly circular linked list with header node. Header node may store some relevant information of the list.

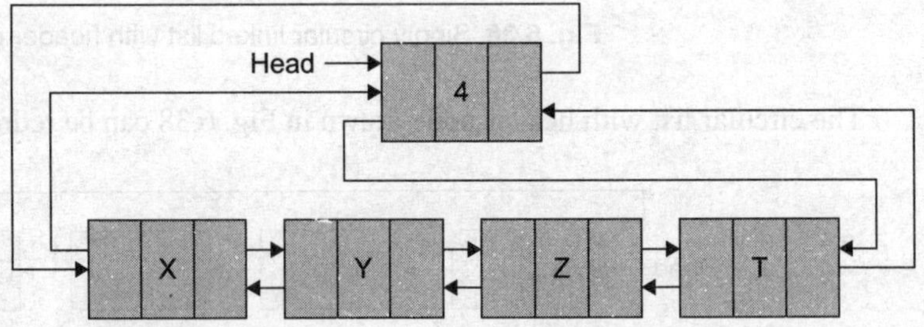

Fig. 6.42 Headed doubly circular list

The operations on circular linked list—`insert`, `delete`, `create` and `traverse`—follow the same method as that of linear list except for a few changes. We can redraw the circular list with header node as in Fig. 6.43.

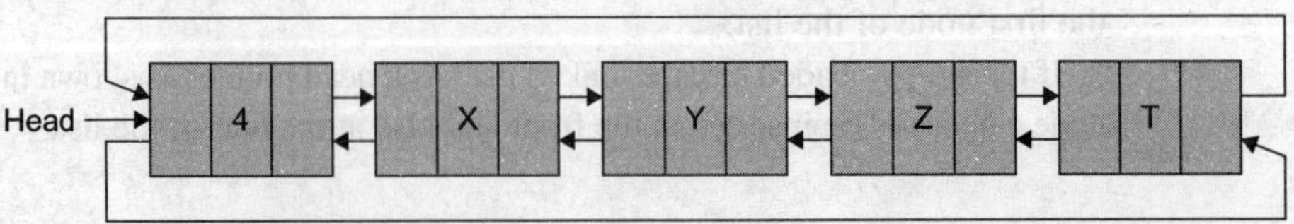

Fig. 6.43 Headed doubly circular list—representation 2

6.9 POLYNOMIAL MANIPULATIONS

We have already studied the representation and operations of polynomials using arrays. Let us now learn the representation of single variable polynomials using linked list. The manipulation of symbolic polynomials is a good application of list processing. Let the polynomial we want to represent using a linked list be $A(x)$. It is expanded as,

$$A(x) = k_1x^m + \ldots + k_{n-1}x^2 + k_nx^1$$

where k_i is a non-zero coefficient with exponent m such that $m > m - 1 > \ldots > 2 > 1 \geq 0$. A node of the linked list will represent each term. A node will have 3 fields, which represent the coefficient and exponent of a term and a pointer to the next term (Fig. 6.44).

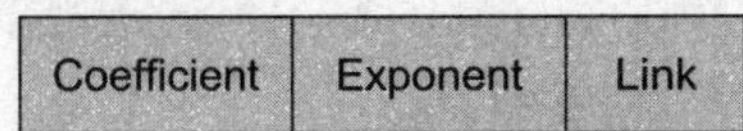

Fig. 6.44 Polynomial node

For instance, the polynomial, say $A = 6x^7 + 3x^5 + 4x^3 + 12$ would be stored as in Fig. 6.45.

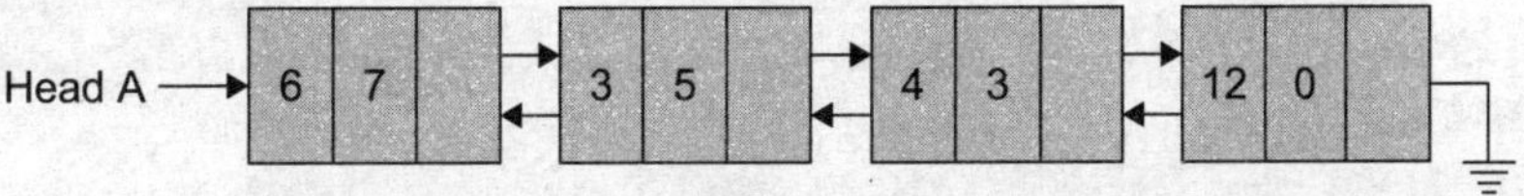

Fig. 6.45 Polynomial $A = 6x^7 + 3x^5 + 4x^3 + 12$

The polynomial $B = 8x^5 + 9x^4 - 2x^2 - 10$ would be stored as in Fig. 6.46.

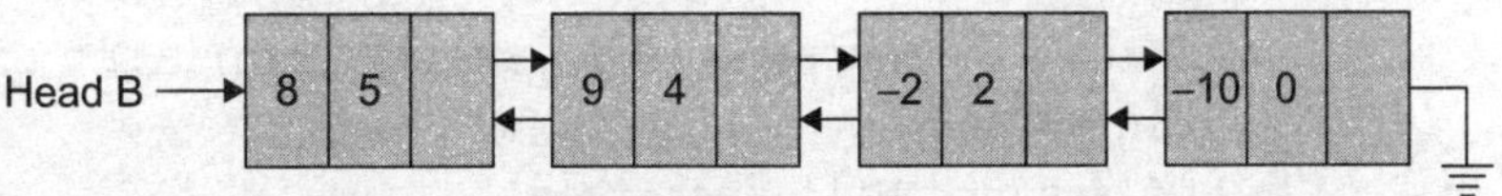

Fig. 6.46 Polynomial $B = 8x^5 + 9x^4 - 2x^2 - 10$

The function for the creation of a polynomial can be written as follows. Here, as the polynomial is stored in the SLL, the `create` procedure remains the same as that of the linked list we studied before. The difference is the data field we used earlier had single integer data fields, whereas here, we have two data fields and one linked field. The two data fields are the exponent and the coefficient of each term of the polynomial. Program Code 6.13 shows the creation of a polynomial.

PROGRAM CODE 6.13

```
class PolyNode
{
   public:
      int coef;
     int exp;
```

```
        PolyNode *link;
};

class Poly
{
    private:
        PolyNode *Head, *Tail;
    public:
        Poly() {Head = Tail = Null;}        // constructor
        void Create();
        PolyNode *GetNode();
        void Append(PolyNode* NewNode);
        void Display();
        Poly PolyMult(Poly A);
        Poly PolyAdd(Poly A);
        void Insert(PolyNode*);
        int Evaluate(int val );
};

void Poly :: Create()
{
    char ans;
   PolyNode *NewNode;
    while(1)
    {
        cout << "Any term to be added? (Y/N)\n";
       cin >> ans;
       if(ans == 'N'|| ans == 'n')
           break;
        NewNode = GetNode();
        if(Head == Null)
        {
           Head = NewNode;
           Tail = NewNode;
        }
        else
           Append(NewNode);
    }
}

void Poly :: Append(PolyNode* NewNode)
{
    if(Tail == Null)
        Head = Tail = NewNode;
```

```
    else
    {
        Tail->link = NewNode;
        Tail = NewNode;
    }
}

PolyNode* Poly :: GetNode()
{
    PolyNode *NewNode;
    NewNode = new PolyNode;
    if(NewNode == Null)
    {
        cout << "Error in memory allocation \ n";
        // exit(0);
    }
    cout << "Enter coefficient and exponent";
    cin >> NewNode->coef;
    cin >> NewNode->exp;
    NewNode->link = Null;
    return(NewNode);
}
```

6.9.1 Polynomial Evaluation

The function traversal of SLL can be used with a few modifications for polynomial evaluation. Given a value of x, we have to evaluate the polynomial as shown in Program Code 6.14.

PROGRAM CODE 6.14

```
int Poly :: Evaluate(int val)
{
    int j, result = 0,Power;
    PolyNode *tmp = Head;
    while(tmp != Null)
    {
        Power = 1;
        for(j = 1; j <= tmp->exp; j++)
            Power = Power * val;
        result += (tmp->coef) *Power;
        tmp = tmp->link;
    }
    return result;
}
```

6.9.2 Polynomial Addition

Let two polynomials A and B be

$$A = 4x^9 + 3x^6 + 5x^2 + 1$$
$$B = 3x^6 + x^2 - 2x$$

The polynomial A and B are to be added to yield the polynomial C. The assumption here is the two polynomials are stored in linked list with descending order of exponents.

The two polynomials A and B are stored in two linked lists with pointers `ptr1` and `ptr2` pointing to the first node of each polynomial, respectively. To add these two polynomials, let us use the paper–pencil method. Let us use these two pointers `ptr1` and `ptr2` to move along the terms of A and B.

Paper–Pencil Method

If the exponents of the two terms are equal, then their coefficients are added and a new term is created for the resultant polynomial C. If the exponent of the current term in A is less than the exponent of the current term of B, then a duplicate of the term in B is created and attached to C. The pointer `ptr2` is advanced to the next term. Similar action is taken on A if the exponent of the current term of A is greater than the exponent of the current term of B.

Each time a new node is generated, its exponent and coefficient fields are set accordingly, and the resultant term is attached to the end of the resultant term C. For polynomial C, we have `ptr3` to move along the resultant polynomial C. It always points to the newly appended term, that is, points to the last term of C. This avoids traversal of list C to append to the node each time. Attaching a node to a polynomial is the same as that of inserting a node at the end of a list. Only when the first node is added, the appropriate steps are carried out to initialize `ptr3`.

An algorithm to attach the term `NewTerm` to a polynomial, say C, with pointer `ptr3` is as follows:

```
1. if(c_ptr = Null)
      then c_ptr = NewTerm;
   else
      c_ptr->link = NewTerm;
   c_ptr = NewTerm;
2. stop
```

Polynomial Addition Algorithm

The following are the steps to add two polynomials A and B to yield the polynomial C.

```
1. Let A_ptr and B_ptr be pointers to polynomials A and B, respectively
2. Let C_ptr = Null, be a pointer to C
3. while(A_ptr != Null and B_ptr != Null)
   begin
      allocate node say NewTerm
```

```
        NewTerm->link = Null
        if(A_ptr->exponent = B_ptr->exponent)
        then
        begin
           NewTerm->exponent = A_ptr->exponent
           NewTerm->coefficient = A_ptr->coefficient + B_ptr->coefficient
           A_ptr = A_ptr->link
           B_ptr = B_ptr->link
        end
        else if(A_ptr->exponent > B_ptr->exponent)
        begin
           NewTerm->exponent = A_ptr->exponent
           NewTerm->coefficient = A_ptr->coefficient
           A_ptr = A_ptr->link
        end
        else
        begin
           NewTerm->exponent = B_ptr->exponent
           NewTerm->coefficient = B_ptr->coefficient
           B_ptr = B_ptr->link
        end
     attach NewTerm to C
4. while(A_ptr != Null)
     begin
        allocate new node
        NewTerm->link = Null
        NewTerm->exponent = A_ptr->exponent
        NewTerm->coefficient = A_ptr->coefficient
        A_ptr = A_ptr->link
        Attach NewTerm to C
end
5. while(B_ptr != Null)
     begin
        allocate new node
        NewTerm->link = Null
        NewTerm->exponent = B_ptr->exponent
        NewTerm->coefficient = B_ptr->coefficient
        B_ptr = B_ptr->link
        Attach NewTerm to C
     end
6. stop
```

Program Code 6.15 illustrates the code for polynomial addition.

PROGRAM CODE 6.15

```
poly Poly :: PolyAdd(Poly P2)
{
   PolyNode *Aptr = Head;
   PolyNode *Bptr = P2.Head;
```

```
Poly C;
PolyNode *NewTerm;
while(Aptr != Null && Bptr != Null)
{
   NewTerm = new PolyNode;
   NewTerm->link = Null;
   if(Aptr->exp == Bptr->exp)
   {
      NewTerm->coef = Aptr->coef + Bptr->coef;
      NewTerm->exp = Aptr->exp;
      C.Append(NewTerm);
      Aptr = Aptr->link;
      Bptr = Bptr->link;
   }
   else if(Aptr->exp > Bptr->exp)
   {
      NewTerm->coef = Aptr->coef;
      NewTerm->exp = Aptr->exp;
      C.Append(NewTerm);
      Aptr = Aptr -> link;
   }
   else
   {
      NewTerm->coef = Bptr->coef;
      NewTerm->exp = Bptr->exp;
      C.Append(NewTerm);
      Bptr = Bptr -> link;
   }
}       // end of while
while(Aptr != Null)
{
   NewTerm = new PolyNode;
   NewTerm->link = Null;
   NewTerm->coef = Aptr->coef;
   NewTerm->exp = Aptr->exp;
   C.Append(NewTerm);
   Aptr = Aptr->link;
}
while(Bptr != Null)
{
   NewTerm = new PolyNode;
```

```
        NewTerm->link = Null;
        NewTerm->coef = Bptr->coef;
        NewTerm->exp = Bptr->exp;
        C.Append(NewTerm);
        Bptr = Bptr->link;
    }
    return C;
}
```

6.9.3 Polynomial Multiplication

Let $A = 4x^9 + 3x^6 + 5x^3 + 1$ and $B = 3x^6 + x^2 - 2x$ be the two polynomials to be multiplied and the resultant polynomial be *C*. Let us revise the paper–pencil method. Polynomial *A* is multiplied by each term of *B*. We get *n* partial products if *B* has *n* terms in it. Finally, we add all these partial products to get the result.

This method generates partial products each of length *m*, where *m* is the length of the polynomial *A*. Such *n* partial products are generated, stored, and finally added to get the resultant polynomial. Here, *m* and *n* are input-dependent. Let us devise a better approach where we need not generate, store, and then add all partial products. Hence, a better solution is to pick up a term from the polynomial *B* and multiply it with each term of the polynomial *A*. One term of *B* and one term of *A* when multiplied yield one resultant term. This term can be immediately added to the resultant polynomial *C*, and this process is repeated.

To add a resultant term to polynomial *C*, it is compared with each term of the resultant polynomial *C* to insert the new term at the appropriate location in polynomial *C*. If the new term with equal exponent is found, then the term is added, else it is inserted in the resultant polynomial at the appropriate position. This process is repeated for each term of *B* with each term of *A*. The major steps can be listed as follows:

1. Let *A* and *B* be two polynomials.
2. Let the number of terms in *A* be *M* and number of terms in *B* be *N*.
3. Let *C* be the resultant polynomial to be computed as $C = A \times B$
4. Let us denote the ith term of the polynomial *B* as tB_i. For each term tB_i of the polynomial *B*, repeat steps 5 to 7 where $i = 1$ to *N*.
5. Let us denote the jth term of the polynomial *A* as tA_j. For each term of tA_j of the polynomial *A*, repeat steps 6 to 7 where $j = 1$ to *M*.
6. Multiply tA_j and tB_i. Let the new term be $tC_k = tA_j \times tB_i$.
7. Compare *tCk* with each term of the polynomial *C*. If a term with equal exponent is found, then add the new term *tCk* to that term of the polynomial *C*, else search for the appropriate position for the term *tCk* and insert the same in the polynomial *C*.
8. Stop.

Program Code 6.16 shows the multiplication of two polynomials.

PROGRAM CODE 6.16

```
poly Poly :: PolyMult(Poly P2)
{
   PolyNode *Aptr = Head;
   PolyNode *Bptr = P2.Head;
   Poly C;
   PolyNode *NewTerm;
   while(Bptr != Null)
   {
      Aptr = Head;
      while(Aptr != Null)
      {
         NewTerm = new PolyNode;
         NewTerm->link = Null;
         NewTerm->coef = Aptr->coef * Bptr->coef;
         NewTerm->exp = Aptr->exp + Bptr->exp;
         C.Insert(NewTerm);
         Aptr = Aptr->link;
         cout << "\n C \n";
         C.Display();
      }
      Bptr = Bptr->link;
   }
   return C;
}

void Poly :: Insert(PolyNode *NewTerm)
{
   PolyNode *prev = Head, *Curr = Head;
   if(Head == Null)        // if 1
      Head = Tail = NewTerm;
   else
   {
      Curr = Head;
      while(Curr != Null)
      {
         if(Curr->exp == NewTerm->exp)        //if 2
         {
            Curr->coef += NewTerm->coef;
```

```
                    break;
                }
                else       // else2
                {
                    if(Curr->exp < NewTerm->exp)       //if 3
                    {
                        if(Curr == Head)       //if 4
                        {
                            NewTerm->link = Head;
                            Head = NewTerm;
                            break;
                        }
                        else       // else 4
                        {
                            prev->link = NewTerm;
                            NewTerm->link = Curr;
                            break;
                        }
                    }     // end if 3
                }     // end else 2
               prev = Curr;
               Curr = Curr->link;
            }    // end of while
            if(Curr == Null)       // add at end
            {
               prev->link = NewTerm;
               Tail = NewTerm;
            }
        }     // end of else
}     // end of function

void main()
{
   Poly P1, P2, P3;
   P1.Create();
   P1.Display();
   P2.Create();
   P2.Display();
   P3 = P1.PolyMult(P2);
   P3.Display();
   getch();
}
```

6.10 REPRESENTATION OF SPARSE MATRIX USING LINKED LIST

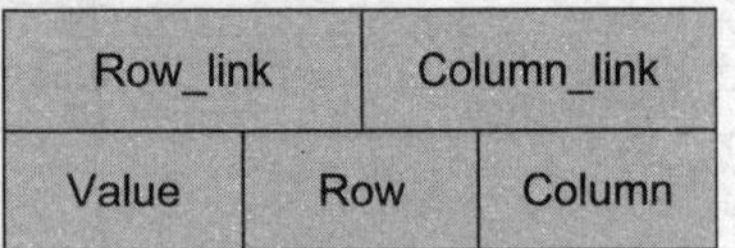

Fig. 6.47 Node structure for linked sparse matrix

We have studied the sparse matrix representation using arrays, which is a sequential allocation scheme. Representing a sparse matrix sequentially allows faster execution of matrix operations, and it is more storage efficient than linked allocation schemes. However, it has many shortcomings. The insertion and deletion of elements need the movement of many other elements. In applications with frequent insertions and deletions, a linked representation can be adopted. A basic node structure as shown in Fig. 6.47 is required to represent each matrix element.

The value, row, and column fields contain the value, row, and column indices, respectively, of one matrix element. The fields row_link and column_link are pointers to the next element in a circular list containing matrix elements for row and column, respectively.

Here, row_link points to the next node in the same row and column_link points to the next node in the same column. The principle is that all the nodes, particularly in a row (or column), are circularly linked with each other; each row and column contains a header node. Thus, for a sparse matrix of order $m \times n$, we have to maintain m header nodes for all rows and n header nodes for all columns, plus one extra node, the header node.

Header nodes for each row and column are used such that more efficient insertion and deletion algorithms can be implemented. The header node of each row contains 0 in the column field, and that of each column contains 0 in the row field. During the implementation in any programming language, 0 can be replaced by any other suitable value such as −1. *Header* is one additional header node that points to the starting address of the sparse matrix.

Header Nodes

1. Row field contains the number of rows.
2. Column field contains the total number of non-zero entries.
3. Row_link field contains pointer to the header node of the first row.
4. Column_link field contains pointer to the header node of the first column.

We may have arrays of pointers A Column[] and A Row[] that contain pointers to the header nodes of each column and row, respectively. In Fig. 6.48, both the header nodes pointing to the first header node of row and column and the array pointers are shown. The header node can provide the pointer to the header nodes linked list of both rows and columns, but it is through sequential traversal. However, arrays of pointers A Column and A Row can provide direct access to each row header node and column header node. Further element access will be obviously through sequential traversal. Hence, we may implement both or either of A Row/A Column and header node.

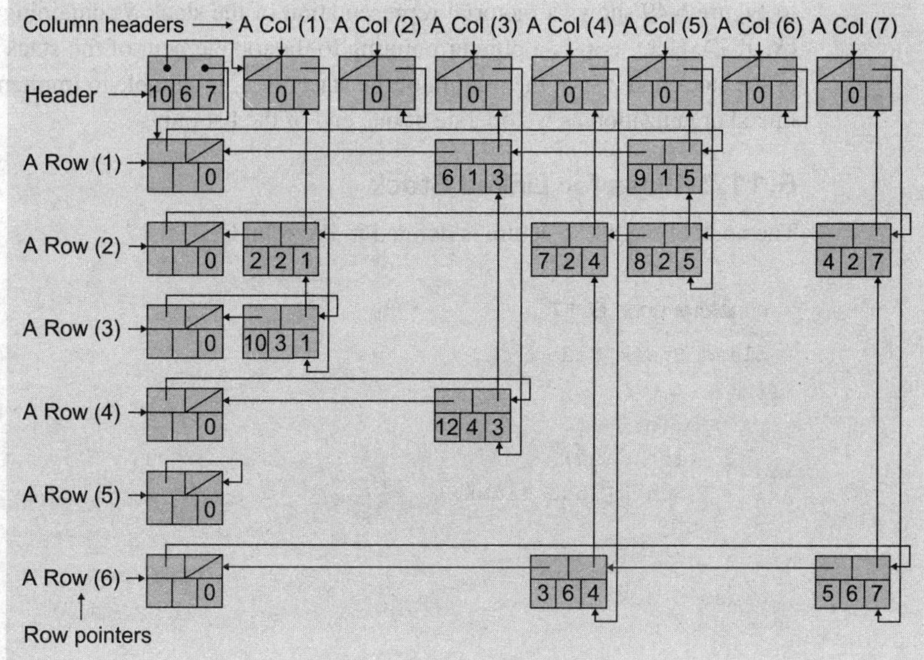

Fig. 6.48 Multilinked sparse matrix

6.11 LINKED STACK

In Chapter 3, we have implemented stacks using arrays. However, an array implementation has certain limitations. One of the limitations is that such a stack cannot grow or shrink dynamically. This drawback can be overcome by using linked implementation. We have studied linked list implementation of a linear list. Let us study the same linked list with restriction on addition and deletion of a node to use it as a stack. A stack implemented using a linked list is also called *linked stack*.

Each element of the stack will be represented as a node of the list. The addition and deletion of a node will be only at one end. The first node is considered to be at the top of the stack, and it will be pointed to by a pointer called `top`. The last node is the bottom of the stack, and its link field is set to `Null`. An empty stack will have `Top = Null`. A linked stack with elements (*X*, *Y*, Z) in order (*X* on top) may be represented as in Fig. 6.49.

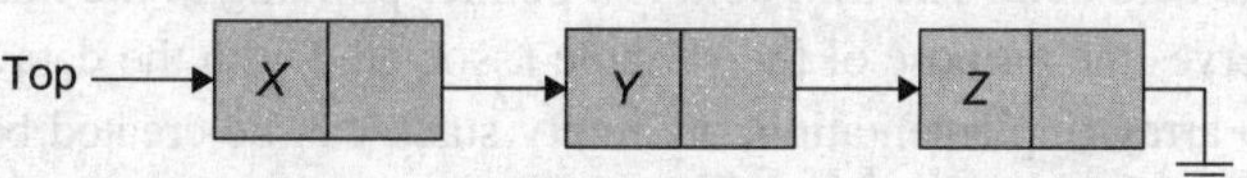

Fig. 6.49 Linked stack of elements (*X*, *Y*, Z)

Figure 6.49 shows a pictorial representation of the stack *S* containing three elements (*X*, *Y*, Z). Here, `top` is a pointer pointing to the top element of the stack. *X* is at the top of the stack and *Z* is at the bottom of the stack. SLL is suitable to implement stack using linked organization as we operate at one end of the list only.

6.11.1 Class for Linked Stack

The node of the list structure is defined in Program Code 6.17.

PROGRAM CODE 6.17

```
class Stack_Node
{
   public:
      int data;
      Stack_Node *link;
};

class Stack
{
   private:
      Stack_Node *Top;
      int Size;
      int IsEmpty();
   public:
      Stack()
      {
         Top = Null;
         Size = 0;
      }
      int GetTop();
      int Pop();
      void Push( int Element);
      int CurrSize();
};
```

Here, the stack can have any data type such as `int`, `char`, `float`, `struct`, and so on for the data field. The link field is a pointer pointing to the node below (next to) it. The `Top` serves the purpose of the variable associated with the data structure `stack` here. Similar to array implementation, an empty stack can be created by initializing the `Top`. This is going to hold the address of a node. It is a pointer rather than an integer as in contiguous stack. Hence to represent an empty stack, `Top` is initialized to `Null`. Every `insert` and `delete` of a node will be only at the end pointed by the pointer variable `Top`. Figure 6.50 represents the insertion of data in a linked stack considering the following sequence of instruction:

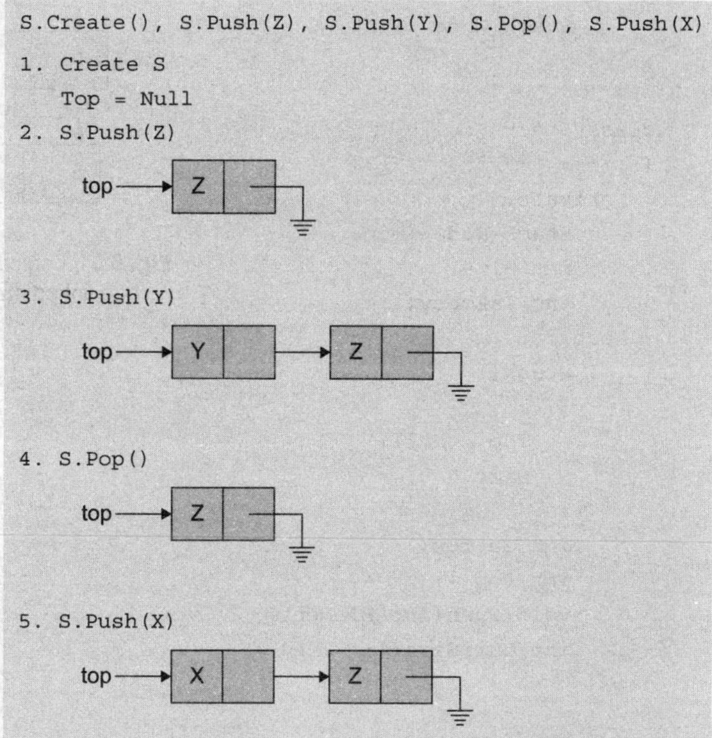

Fig. 6.50 Insertion of data in linked stack

Here, the stack grows and also shrinks at `Top`. Let us see the functions required to implement a stack using a linked list.

6.11.2 Operations on Linked Stack

The memory for each node is dynamically allocated on the heap. So when an item is pushed, a node for it is created, and when an item is popped, its node is freed (using `delete`). The only difference is that the capacity of a linked stack is generally greater than that of a contiguous stack since a linked stack will not become full until the dynamic memory is exhausted Program Code 6.18 shows operations on a linked stack. Figure 6.51 shows a logical view of the linked stack.

PROGRAM CODE 6.18

```
class Stack_Node
{
   public:
      int data;
      Stack_Node *link;
};

class Stack
{
   private:
      Stack_Node *Top;
      int Size;
      int IsEmpty();
   public:
      Stack()
      {
         Top = Null;
         Size = 0;
      }
      int GetTop();
      int Pop();
      void Push(int Element);
      int CurrSize();
};

int Stack :: IsEmpty()
{
   if(Top == Null)
      return 1;
   else
      return 0;
}

int Stack :: GetTop()
{
   if(!IsEmpty())
      return(Top->data);
}
```

Fig. 6.51 Logical view of a linked stack

```
void Stack :: Push(int value)
{
   Stack_Node* NewNode;
   NewNode = new Stack_Node;
   NewNode->data = value;
   NewNode->link = Null;
   NewNode->link = Top;
   Top = NewNode;
}

int Stack :: Pop()
{
   Stack_Node* tmp = Top;
   int data = Top->data;
   if(!IsEmpty())
   {
      Top = Top->link;
      delete tmp;
      return(data);
   }
}
```

We have designed the functions for operations on stack, where the stack is implemented using linked organization. The `Top` is initialized to `Null` to indicate empty stack. The `Push()` function dynamically creates a new node. After creating a new node, the pointer variable `Top` should point to the newly added node in the stack.

```
void main()
{
  Stack S;
  S.Push(5);
  S.Push(6);
  cout << S.GetTop()<<endl;
  cout << S.Pop()<<endl;
  S.Push(7);
  cout << S.Pop()<<endl;
  cout << S.Pop()<<endl;
}
```

```
Output
  6
  6
  7
  5
```

6.12 LINKED QUEUE

We studied about how to represent queues using sequential organization in Chapter 5. Such a representation is efficient if we have a circular queue of fixed size. However, there are many drawbacks of implementing queues using arrays. The fixed sizes do not give flexibility to the user to dynamically exceed the maximum size. The declaration of arbitrarily maximum size leads to poor utilization of memory. In addition, the major drawback is the updating of `front` and `rear`. For correctness of the said implementation, the shifting of the queue to the left is necessary and to be done frequently. Here is a good solution to this problem which uses linked list. We need two pointers, `front` and `rear`. Figure 6.52 shows a linked queue which is easy to handle.

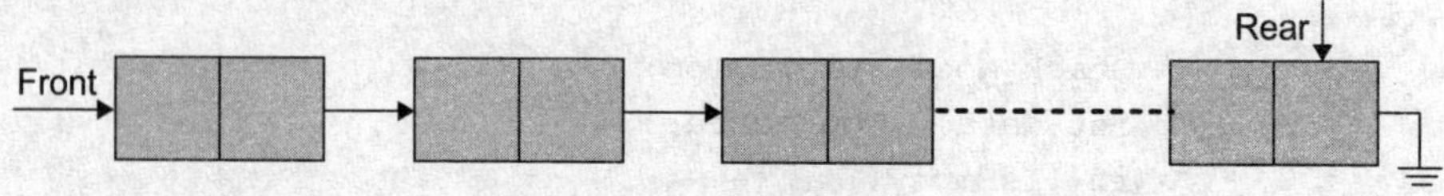

Fig. 6.52 The linked queue

Notice that the direction link for nodes is to facilitate easy insertion and deletion of nodes. One can easily add a node at the `rear` and delete a node from the `front`.

One of the node structures could be as in Program Code 6.19.

PROGRAM CODE 6.19

```
class Student
{
   public:
      int Roll_No;
      char Name[30];
      int Year;
      char Branch[8];
      Student *link;
};
class Queue
{
   Student *front, *rear;
   public:
      Queue()
      {
         front = rear = Null;
      }
};
```

Let us consider the following node structure for studying the linked queue and operations:

```
class QNode
{
   public:
      int data;
      QNode *link;
};

class Queue
{
   QNode *Front, *Rear;
   int IsEmpty();
   public:
      Queue()
      {
         Front = Rear = Null;
      }
      void Add( int Element);
      int Delete();
      int FrontElement();
      ~Queue();
};

int Queue :: IsEmpty()
{
   if(Front == Null)
      return 1;
   else
      return 0;
}
```

The queue element is declared using the class `QNode`. Each node contains the data declaration and the link pointer to the next element in the queue. This declaration creates an empty queue and initializes the pointers `front` and `rear` to `Null`. Here, `front` always points to the first node of queue and `rear` points to the last node of queue.

`Queue empty` condition is simply checked by comparing the `front` with `Null`. The function `IsEmptyQ` returns 1 (i.e., true) if the queue is empty and returns 0 (i.e., false), otherwise.

```
int Queue :: IsEmpty()
{
   if(Front == Null)
      return 1;
   else
      return 0;
}
```

FrontElement() returns the data element at the front of the queue. Here, the front is not updated. FrontElement() just reads what is at front.

```
int Queue :: GetFront()
{
   if(!IsEmpty())
      return(Front->data);
}
```

Note that if the NewNode is a node getting added in an empty queue, then along with the rear, the front should also be set to point to the newly added node, which is at the front of the queue. Hence, as both the front and the rear may get updated. Program Code 6.20 shows the addition of an element to a linked queue.

PROGRAM CODE 6.20

```
void Queue :: Add(int x)
{
   QNode *NewNode;
   NewNode = new QNode;
   NewNode->data = x;
   NewNode->link = Null;
   // if the new is a node getting added in empty queue
   //then front should be set so as to point to new
   if(Rear == Null)
   {
      Front = NewNode;
      Rear = NewNode;
   }
   else
   {
      Rear->link = NewNode;
      Rear = NewNode;
   }
}
```

Delete() function first verifies if there is any data element in the queue. If there is an element, Delete() gets and returns the data at the front of the queue to the caller function. Then, the front is set to point to the new queue front node, which is next to the node being deleted. If the last node is being deleted, then the deleted node's next pointer is guaranteed to be Null. Note that if the current deletion of a node results in queue empty state, then along with the front, the rear should also be set to Null.

```
int Queue :: Delete()
{
```

```
    int temp;
    QNode *current = Null;
    if(!IsEmpty())
    {
        temp = Front->data;
        current = Front;
        Front = Front->link;
        delete current;
        if(Front == Null)
            Rear = Null;
        return(temp);
    }
}

int Queue :: FrontElement()
{
    if(!IsEmpty())
        return(Front->data);
}

void main()
{
    Queue Q;
    Q.Add(11);
    Q.Add(12);
    Q.Add(13);
    cout << Q.Delete() << endl;
    Q.Add(14);
    cout << Q.Delete() << endl;
    cout << Q.Delete() << endl;
    cout << Q.Delete() << endl;
    Q.Add(15);
    Q.Add(16);
    cout << Q.Delete() << endl;
    cout << Q.Delete() << endl;
}
Output
11
12      // due to FrontElement
12
13
14
15
16
```

6.12.1 Erasing a Linked Queue

The following function in Program Code 6.21 traverses through the whole queue and also releases the memory allocated for each node. This task is handled by a destructor.

PROGRAM CODE 6.21

```
void Queue :: ~Queue()
{
    QNode *temp;
    while(Front! = Null)
    {
        temp = Front;
        Front = Front->link;
        delete temp;
    }
    Front = Rear = Null;
}
```

The linked queue may have the first node on a queue as a header node where the data field may hold some relevant information. In such a list, the first node, that is, the header node, is ignored (i.e. skipped) during `Delete()` operation. Similarly, the `Add()` function and `queue empty` condition will be changed accordingly.

6.13 GENERALIZED LINKED LIST

We have defined and represented linear list, which contains series of data elements, all of which had the same data type. In this topic, we shall extend the notion of list even further. We shall study generalized lists, which may be a list of lists.

Generalized lists are defined recursively as lists whose members may be single data elements or other generalized lists. Generalized lists are the most flexible and useful structures. We can use such lists to represent virtually all of the data structures. In addition, generalized lists provide the key data structure for several programming languages, such as LISP. Other languages, such as T and Miranda, include generalized lists and their operations as built-in capabilities. This widespread inclusion of generalized lists in many languages and environments attests the value of such lists in many applications.

6.13.1 Definition

A generalized list is a linear list (non-indexed) of zero or more data elements or generalized lists. In other words, a generalized list is a finite sequence of $n \geq 0$ elements, α_1, α_2, ... α_n, which we write as list $A = (\alpha_1, \alpha_2, ..., \alpha_n)$, where a_i is either an atom or the list. The elements of α_i, where $1 \leq i \leq n$, which are not atoms are said to be the sub-lists of the list. Here A is the name of generalized list and n is its length.

Thus, a generalized list may be made up of a number of components, some of which are data elements (atoms) and others are generalized lists.

Let us use the common terms being referred to with respect to the generalized list, Head and Tail. These terms refer to parts of the generalized list, that is, Head is the first component in the generalized list, and Tail is the list with the first component removed. If $n \le 1$, then a_1 is the *head of list* whereas $(\alpha_2, \ldots \alpha_n)$ is the *tail of list*.

Some examples of generalized lists are the following:

1. $A = ()$	The empty (or null) list.
2. $B = (a, (b, c), d)$	List of three elements—the first element is a, the second element is list (b, c), and the third element is d.
3. $C = (B, B, A)$	List of length 3 with the first and the second element as list B and the third element as list A, which is a null list.
4. $D = (a, b, D)$	List of length 3 which is recursive as it includes itself as one of the elements. It can also be written as $D = (a, b, (a, b, (a, b, \ldots)\ldots$

In example 2, *A* is a list made up of three components. The first component is an atom, the second component is a list made up of two atoms, and the third component is the atom *d*.

One of the better approaches to visualize the generalized lists is using a header node. In this approach, each generalized list has a header node labelled Head. Figure 6.53 shows the pictorial representation of list *B*.

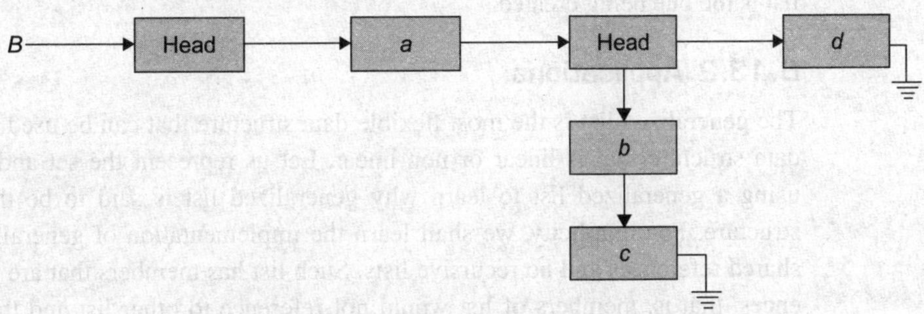

Fig. 6.53 Representation of $B = (a, (b, c), d)$

In example 3, the list *C* has three components: the first component is list *B*, the second component is again list *B*, and the third component is list *A*. This can be pictorially viewed as in Fig. 6.54.

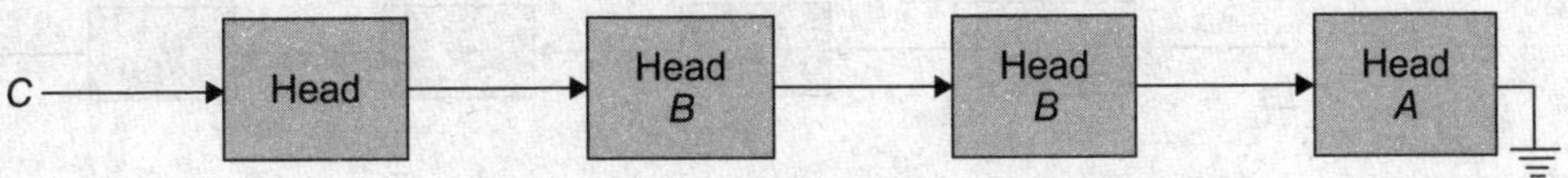

Fig. 6.54 Representation of $C = (B, B, A)$

The list *D* in example 4 can be viewed as Fig. 6.55.

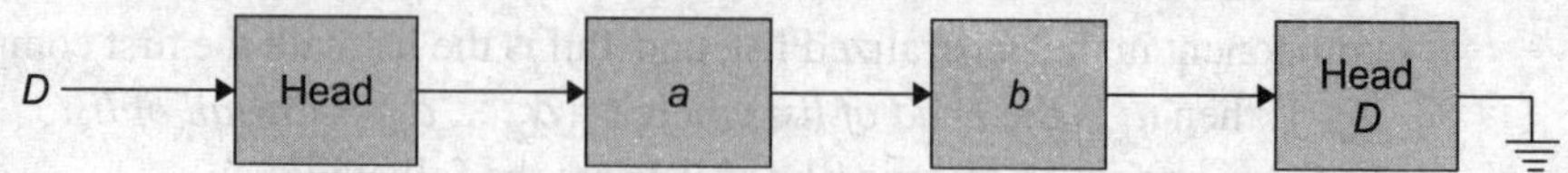

Fig. 6.55 Representation of *D* = (*a*, *b*, *D*)

These cases represent the categories of generalized lists in the order of implementation complexity. The lists could be one of the following categories:

1. Lists with no shared references—The components of one list are not members of any other list. In example 2, *B* is a list with no shared references.
2. Lists with shared references—The components of one list can be the members of another list. The logical interpretation of lists leads to two categories as the following:
   (a) *Static interpretation*—The current status of the referenced list is anticipated. The referenced list is copied into the referencing list.
   (b) *Dynamic interpretation*—The list itself is anticipated. Any future changes in the referenced list should be reflected in the referencing list.
3. Recursive list—A recursive list is the one that directly or indirectly references itself. Here *D* is a recursive list.

Here, the referenced list is the one that is a member of the other list, and the referencing list is the one being created.

6.13.2 Applications

The generalized list is the most flexible data structure that can be used for almost every data structure that is linear or non-linear. Let us represent the set and the polynomial using a generalized list to learn why generalized list is said to be the supreme data structure. For simplicity, we shall learn the implementation of generalized list with no shared references and no recursive lists. Such list has members that are not shared references, that is, members of list would not reference to other list and the list would not have the member that directly or indirectly refers itself. The popular implementation of such lists uses the linked list with a header node as in Figs. 6.56–6.58. Let us consider three lists *L*1, *L*2, and *L*3 as *L*1 = (*a*, *b*, *c*, *d*), *L*2 = (*a*, (*b*), (*c*,*d*), *e*), and *L*3 = (*a*, ((*b*)), *c*). The pictorial representation of these lists using header node is shown in Figs 6.56–6.58, respectively.

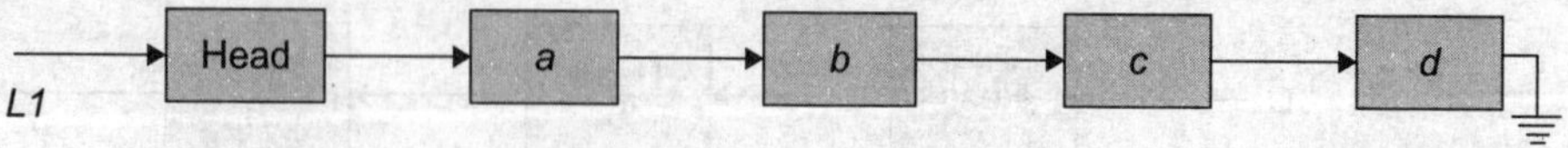

Fig. 6.56 GLL with header nodes for *L*1 = (*a*, *b*, *c*, *d*)

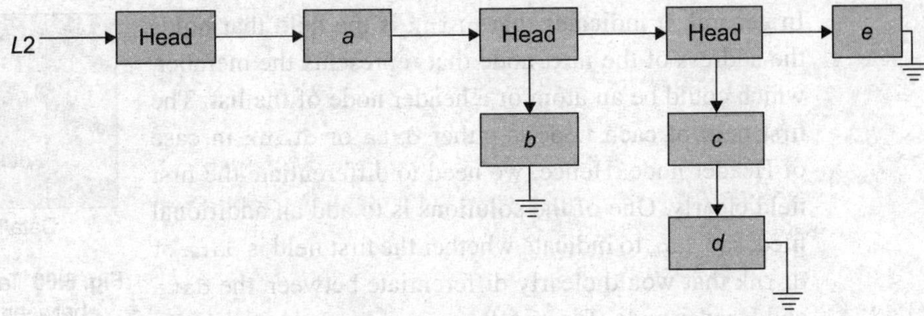

Fig. 6.57 GLL with header nodes for $L2 = (a, (b), (c,d), e)$

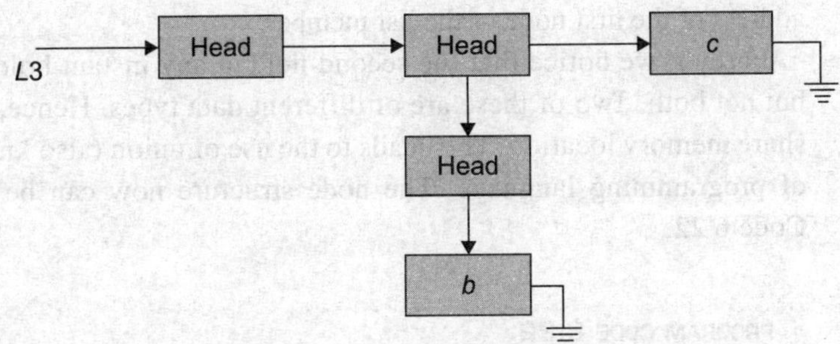

Fig. 6.58 GLL with header nodes for $L3 = (a, ((b)), c)$

Here, *L*1 has four members which are atoms, *L*2 too has four members but two of them are lists, and *L*3 has three members in it one of which is a list that has the list as a member again. The pictorial representation very clearly reveals it. Now, we need to reflect this data type and implement the code for the generalized linked list. We need to clearly distinguish between a member that is an atom and a member that is a list. In a linked representation of the generalized list, each node has fields as either

1. Data and `nLink`—the data field(s) would store data and the `nLink` field refers to the next member node which could be an atom or a list or
2. Header node that has two links `dlink` and `nLink`, where `dlink` is used to refer to the first node of the list member (which could be an atom or a list) and the `nLink` refers to the next member node (which could be an atom or a list) (Fig. 6.59).

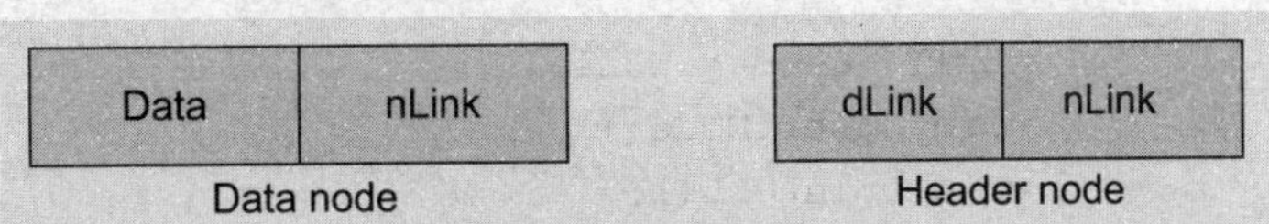

Fig. 6.59 Node structure of a generalized list

In general, it indicates that `nLink` is the field that holds the address of the next node that represents the member, which could be an atom or a header node of the list. The first field of each node is either `data` or `dLink` in case of Header node. Hence, we need to differentiate the first field clearly. One of the solutions is to add an additional filed, say `tag`, to indicate whether the first field is `data` or `dLink` that would clearly differentiate between the `data` and Header node (Fig. 6.60).

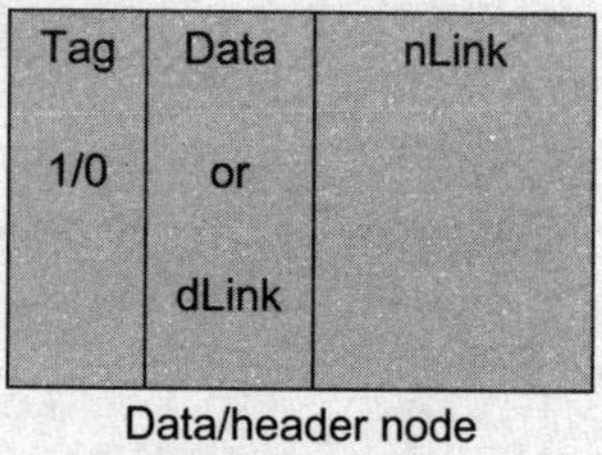

Tag	Data	nLink
1/0	or dLink	

Data/header node

Fig. 6.60 Tag for differentiating between data node and header node

Here, when `Tag = 1,` it indicates that the second field is data, and `Tag = 0` indicates that it is the header node where the second field holds the address of the first node of the list member.

Further, we notice that the second field at any instant holds either `data` or `dLink` but not both. Two of these are of different data types. Hence, it would be efficient to share memory location. This leads to the use of union (also known as *variant records*) of programming language. The node structure now can be defined as in Program Code 6.22.

PROGRAM CODE 6.22

```
class GNode
{
   int Tag;
   union
   {
      <data type> Data;
      GNode *dLink;
   }
   GNode * nLink;
};

class GLL
{
   private:
      GNode * Head;
   public:
      GLL() {Head = Null;}
      void InsertNode();
      void PrintGLL();
};
```

Let us now see how we can use the generalized linked list to efficiently represent multi-variable polynomials and sets.

6.13.3 Representation of Polynomials Using Generalized Linked List

We have learned the use of linked list for the representation and operations of polynomial with a single variable. In practice, we often need to process a polynomial with more than one variable. Consider the following polynomial *P* with three variables *x* ,*y*, and *z*. Consider the two-variable polynomial *Q* of *x* and *y*.

$$Q(x, y) = 5x^4y^3 + 6x^6y^5 + 3x^5y^2 + xy$$

Now, similar to a single variable polynomial, we can represent this polynomial $Q(x,y)$ as a sequential organization with four fields: coefficient, Exp_X, Exp_Y, and nLink as in Fig. 6.61.

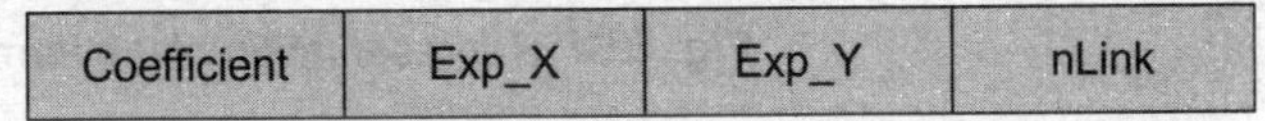

Fig. 6.61 Two-variable polynomial

Similarly, for $P(x, y, z) = 9x^8y^2z + 4x^4y^3z^3 + x^6y^5z^4 + 8x^5y^2z + 7x^4y^6z + 4xyz + 3xz$ we can represent this polynomial $P(x, y, z)$ as a sequential organization with five fields: coefficient, Exp_X, Exp_Y, Exp_Z, and nLink as in Fig. 6.62.

Coefficient	Exp_X	Exp_Y	Exp_Z	nLink

Fig. 6.62 Three-variable polynomial

However, such representations denote that the polynomials in different number of variables would need a different number of fields. These nodes would have to differ in size depending on the number of variables. Such representations would lead to complexity in storage management for the polynomials with two, three, or more variables. We need to devise an efficient representation of multiple variable polynomials. An elegant solution is to go for a generalized list with fixed size nodes, which would represent the polynomial with any number of variables. Let us see how can we achieve it.

Consider the following polynomial:

$$P(x,y,z) = 5x^9y^4z^3 + 6x^7y^4z^3 + 3x^8y^2z^3 + 3x^5y^3z + 8x^3y^3z + 2y^2z$$

This polynomial can be rewritten as

$$((5x^9 + 6x^7)y^4 + (3x^8)y^2)z^3 + ((3x^5 + 8x^3)y^3 + 2y^2)z$$

We can write such a polynomial as one with a single variable whose each term node would be as in Fig. 6.63.

Tag	Coefficient or dLink	Variable	Exponent	nLink

Fig. 6.63 Representation of multi-variable polynomial as single variable polynomial

For example, the term as $9z^2$ would be represented as in Fig. 6.64.

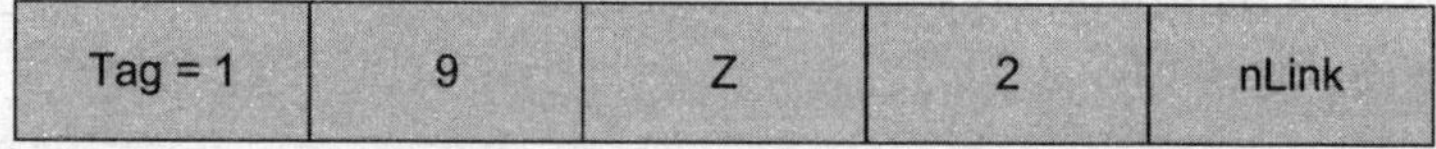

Fig. 6.64 Representation of the term $9z^2$

The term as $(2y^3 + 3x^2)z^2$ would be represented as in Fig. 6.65.

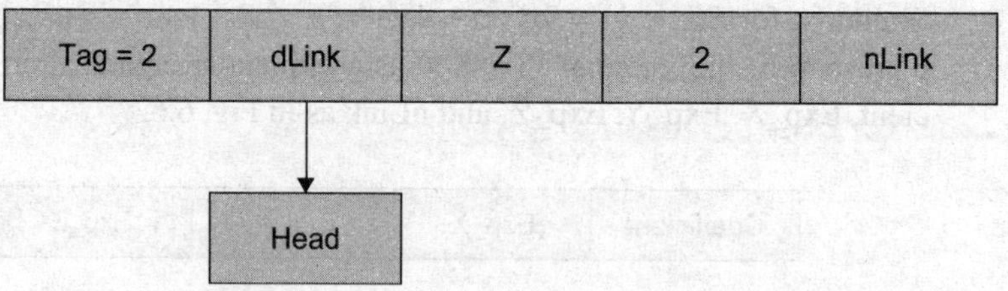

Fig. 6.65 Representation of the term $(2y^3 + 3x^2)z^2$

We notice that for a polynomial of z with 10 terms, the third field of all nodes would be set to z for all term nodes. Can we avoid storing z for all terms of a polynomial? This is possible by storing it only once using the header node. For the header node, the fields `Tag`, `nLink`, and `dLink` are used, and the remaining two fields remain unused and it can be used for storing the variable.

Now, the node structure becomes as in Fig. 6.66.

Tag = 0/1/2	Variable, coefficient, or dLink	Exponent	nLink

Fig. 6.66 Representation of multi-variable polynomial as single variable polynomial

The multi-variable polynomial that is represented as a single variable polynomial whose coefficient is either constant or another polynomial, can now be very well stored using a linked list with such a node structure.

For example, the three-variable polynomial $P(x,y,z)$ can be represented factoring out a variable z, followed by the second variable y.

$$\text{Let } P(x, y, z) \text{ be } 5x^9y^4z^3 + 6x^7y^4z^3 + 3x^8y^2z^3 + 3x^5y^3z^2 + 8x^3y^3z^2 + 6y^2z$$

This polynomial can be rewritten as

$$(5x^9y^4+ 6x^7y^4 + 3x^8y^2)z^3 + (3x^5y^3 + 8x^3y^3)z^2 + 6y^2z$$

On observation of $P(x, y, z)$, we can notice that there are two terms in the variable z, $BZ^i + CZ^j + DZ^k$, where B, C, and D are polynomials themselves of variables x and y.

Now, the polynomial can further be rewritten as

$$((5x^9 + 6x^7)y^4 + (3x^8)y^2)z^3 + ((3x^5 + 8x^3)y^3)z^2+ ((6x^0)y^2)z.$$

Now, $C(x, y)$, $B(x, y)$, and $D(x, y)$ are of the form $Ey^m + \ldots + Fy^n$, where E and F are polynomials of x. Continuing in this way, we see that every polynomial consists of a variable plus coefficient and exponent pairs, and the coefficient itself could be a polynomial.

Each node would be one of the three—the header node (Fig. 6.67), data node with constant coefficient (Fig. 6.68), and the data node whose coefficient is a polynomial (Fig. 6.69). These can be pictorially viewed as follows:

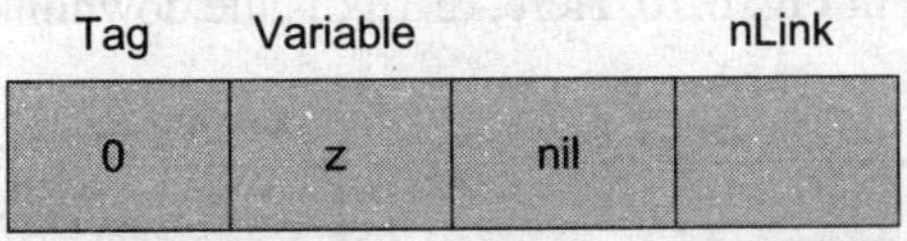

Tag	Variable		nLink
0	z	nil	

Fig. 6.67 Representation of header node

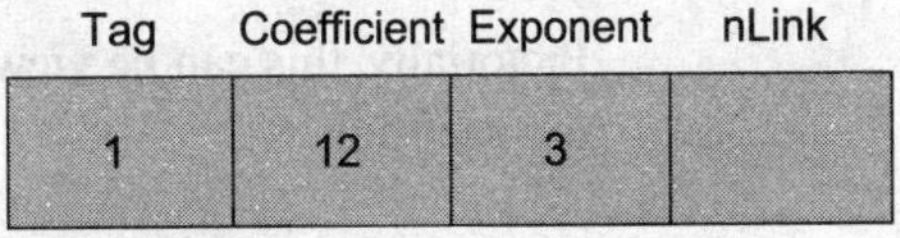

Tag	Coefficient	Exponent	nLink
1	12	3	

Fig. 6.68 Representation of data node with constant coefficient

Tag	dLink	Exponent	nLink
2		4	

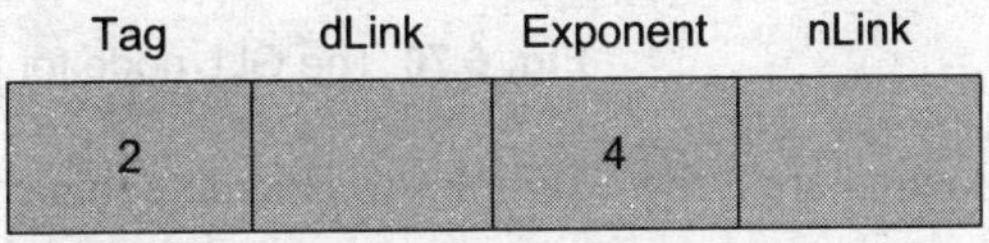

Fig. 6.69 Representation of data node with polynomial coefficient

Thus, every polynomial, regardless of the number of variables in it, can be represented using nodes. This is presented in Program Code 6.23:

PROGRAM CODE 6.23

```
class GLLPolyNode
{
```

```
        int Tag;
        union
        {
            char variable;
            float coefficient;
            GLLPolyNode *dLink;
        };
        int exponent;
        GLLPolyNode *nLink;
};

class GLLPoly
{
    private:
        GLLPolyNode *Head;
    public:
        GLLpoly() {Head = Null;}
        void InsertNode();
        void PrintGLL();
};
```

Pictorially, this can be viewed as in Fig. 6.70. Here, `dLink` is the downlink and `nLink` is the next link.

<table>
<tr><td rowspan="3">Tag
0/1/2</td><td>Variable</td><td rowspan="3">Exponent</td><td rowspan="3">nLink</td></tr>
<tr><td>Coefficient</td></tr>
<tr><td>dLink</td></tr>
</table>

Fig. 6.70 The GLL node for polynomial

The following are a few examples to elucidate this concept:

1. $P(x,y) = 9x^2y^2 + 6xy^2 + y + x^2$
   This polynomial of two variables can be rewritten as
   $$P = y^2(9x^2 + 6x) + y + x^2y^0$$
   This is represented in Figs 6.71(a) and (b).

2. $Q = 8x^3y^3z^3 + 3x^3y^2z^3 + y^2z^2 + xy^2z^2 + 8x + 9y$

   This can be rewritten as $z^3(x^3(8y^3 + 3y^2)) + z^2(y^2\ (1 + x)) + 8xz^0 + 9yz^0$. The pictorial representation of the Q is shown in Fig. 6.72.

Note that only three fields of the nodes are shown for convenience and the unused one is omitted.

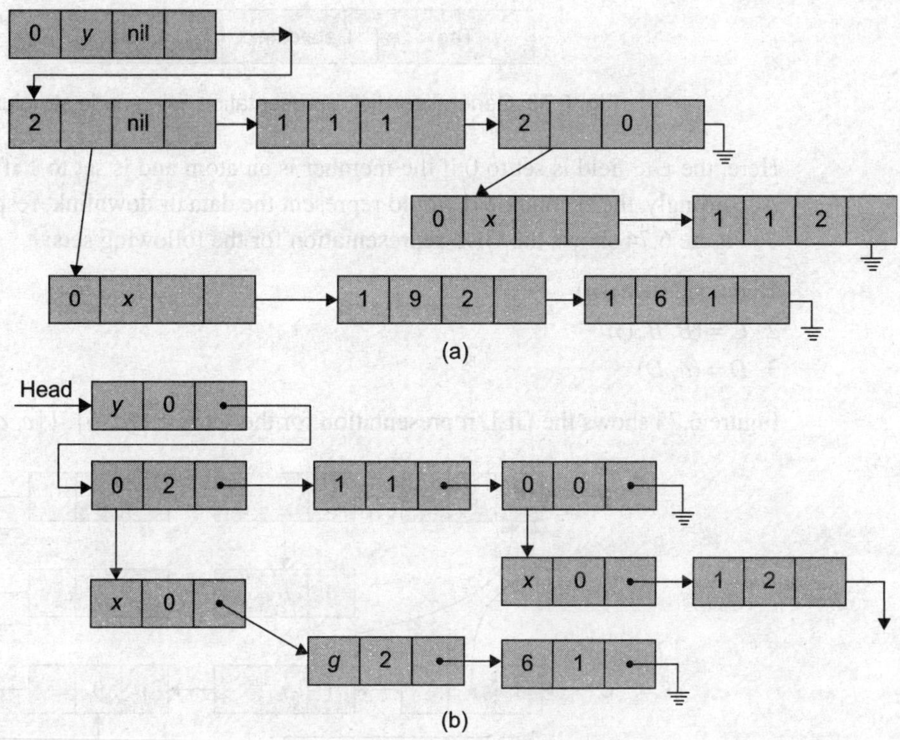

Fig. 6.71 Polynomial representation (a) The GLL for $9x^2y^2 + 6xy^2 + y + x^2$ (b) The GLL with three fields, omitting unused field

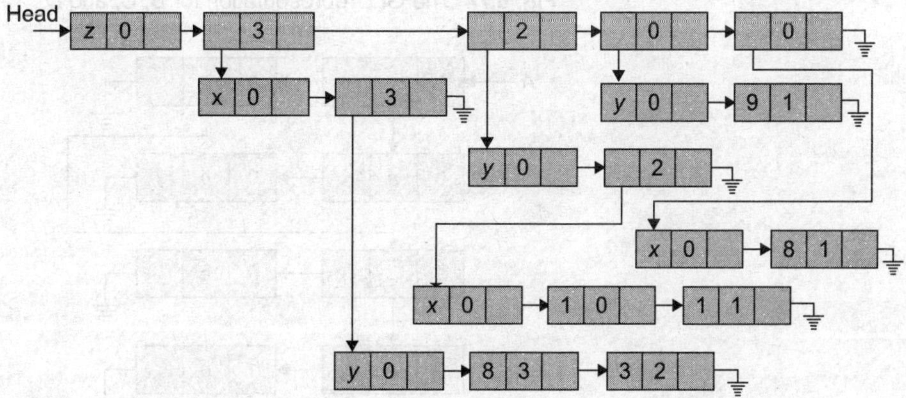

Fig. 6.72 The GLL for $8x^3y^3z^3 + 3x^3y^2z^3 + y^2z^2 + xy^2z^2 + 8x + 9y$

6.13.4 Representation of Sets Using Generalized Linked List

Let A be a set, $A = \{a, b, \{c, d, \{\ \}\}, \{e, f\}, g\}$. Here, A consists of elements that are either atoms or sets. Hence, we need a GLL node to convey whether the member of set is an atom or a set. The generalized list can be represented using the node structure as Fig. 6.73.

Tag	Data/dLink	nLink

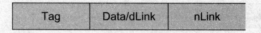

Fig. 6.73 Generalized list representation using node structure

Here, the `tag` field is set to 0 if the member is an atom and is set to 1 if it is another list. Accordingly, the second field would represent the data or downlink, respectively.

Figure 6.74 shows the GLL representation for the following sets:

1. $B = (a, (b, c), d)$
2. $C = (B, B, ())$
3. $D = (a, D)$

Figure 6.75 shows the GLL representation for the set $A = \{\{a, b\}, \{\{c, d\}, e\}\}$.

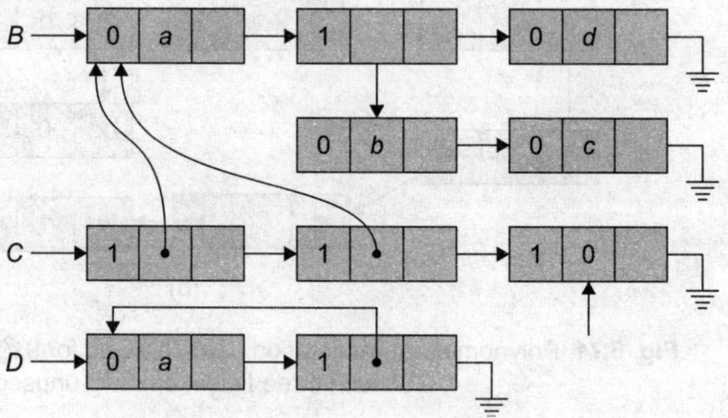

Fig. 6.74 The GLL representation for *B*, *C*, and *D*

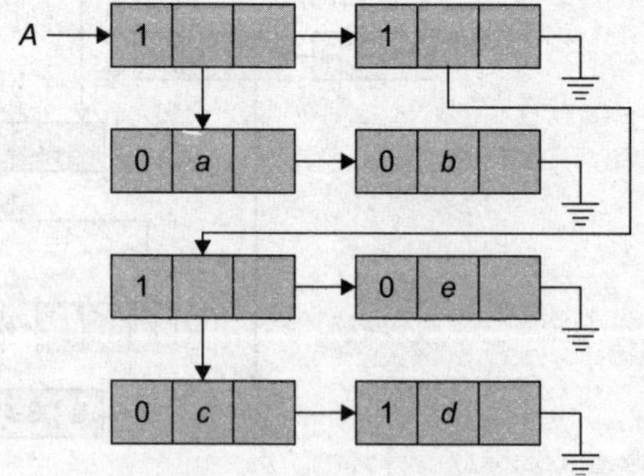

Fig. 6.75 The GLL representation for *A*

The set $X = \{L, M, \{N, \{O, P\}\}, \{Q, \{R, \{S, T\}\}, A, \{B, C\}\}$ is pictorially represented using a generalized linked list in Fig. 6.76.

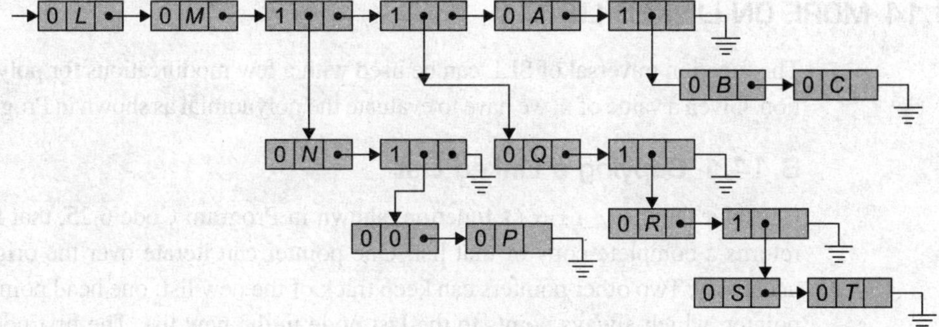

Fig. 6.76 The GLL for set *X*

We have represented the polynomials and sets using generalized linked list. Let us write the functions for traversing and printing the generalized linked list.

Printing Generalized Linked Lists

Program Code 6.24 gives the code for printing a GLL.

PROGRAM CODE 6.24

```
void GLL :: PrintGLL()
{
   Stack S;
   GLLNode *curr = Null;
   S.Push(Head);
   curr = Head;
   while(1)
   {
      if(curr == Null)
      {
         if !S.IsEmpty()
            curr = S.Pop();
         if(curr→tag == 1)
            cout << curr→data;
         curr = curr→nlink;
         else if(curr→nlink != Null)
            S.push(curr→nlink)
         curr = curr→dlink
      }        //end if
   }        // end while
}        // end print
```

6.14 MORE ON LINKED LISTS

The function traversal of SLL can be used with a few modifications for polynomial evaluation. Given a value of x, we have to evaluate the polynomial as shown in Program Code 6.14.

6.14.1 Copying a Linked List

Consider the `Copy_List()` function, shown in Program Code 6.25, that takes a list and returns a complete copy of that list. One pointer can iterate over the original list in the usual way. Two other pointers can keep track of the new list: one head pointer and one tail pointer, which always points to the last node in the new list. The first node is done as a special case, and then the tail pointer is used in the standard way for the others.

PROGRAM CODE 6.25

```
Node *Llist :: CopyList()
{
   Node *current = Head;
   Node *newList = Null;
   Node *Tail = Null;
   while(current != Null)
   {
      if(newList == Null)
      {
         newList = new Node;
         newList->Data = current->Data;
         newList->link = Null;
         Tail = newList;
      }
      else
      {
         Tail->link = new Node;
         Tail = Tail->link;
         Tail->Data = current->Data;
         Tail->link = Null;
      }
      current = current->link;
   }
   return(newList);
}
```

16.4.2 Computing the Length of a Linked List

The `Length()` function, in Program Code 6.26, takes a linked list and computes the number of elements in the list.

`Length()` is a simple list function, but it demonstrates several concepts, which will be used later in more complex list functions.

PROGRAM CODE 6.26

```
int Llist :: Length()
{
    Node *current = Head;
    int count = 0;
    while(current != Null)
    {
        count++;
        current = current->link;
    }
    return count;
}
```

Calling Length()

Program Code 6.27 is a typical code that calls `Length()`. It first calls `create()` to make a list and store the head pointer in a local variable. It then calls `Length()` on the list and catches the `int` result in a local variable.

PROGRAM CODE 6.27

```
void LengthTest()
{
    Llist myList;
    mylist.Create();
    int len = mylist.Length();
}
```

6.14.3 Reversing Singly Linked List Without Temporary Storage

The procedure for reversing a singly linked list without temporary storage is illustrated by Program Code 6.28.

PROGRAM CODE 6.28

```
void Llist :: Reverse()
{
    Node *curr, *prev, *next;
    prev = Head;
    curr = Head->link;
```

```
    prev->link = Null
    while(temp != Null)
    {
       next = temp->link;
       temp->link = prev;
       prev = temp;
       temp = next;
    }
    head = prev;
}
```

6.14.4 Concatenating Two Linked Lists

Concatenation of two linked lists is illustrated by Program Code 6.29.

PROGRAM CODE 6.29

```
void Llist :: concatanate(Llist A)
{
   Node *X, *Y;
   X = Head;
   Y = A.Head;
   while(X->link != Null)
   {
      X = X->link;
   }
   X->link = Y;
   Head = X;
}

//A call to concatenate:
{
   Llist L1, L2;
   L1.Create(); L2.Create();
   L1.Concatanate(L2);
}
```

Here, *X* and *Y* are concatenated, and *X* is the pointer to the first node of the resultant list.

6.14.5 Erasing the Linked List

The procedure for erasing a linked list and returning all nodes to the free pool of memory is illustrated by Program Code 6.30.

PROGRAM CODE 6.30

```
void Llist :: ~Llist()
{
   Node *temp;
   while(Head != Null)
   {
      temp = Head;
     Head = Head->link;
      delete temp;
   }
}
```

6.15 APPLICATION OF LINKED LIST—GARBAGE COLLECTION

Memory is just an array of words. After a series of memory allocations and de-allocations, there are blocks of free memory scattered throughout the available heap space. To be able to reuse this memory, the memory allocator will usually link the freed blocks together in a free list by writing pointers to the next free block in the block itself. An external free list pointer points to the first block in the free list. When a new block of memory is requested, the allocator will generally scan the free list looking for a free block of suitable size and delete it from the free list (relinking the free list around the deleted block).

One of the components of an operating system is the memory management module. This module maintains a list, which consists of unused memory cells. This list very often requires the operations to be performed on the list, such as `insert`, `delete`, and `search` (traversal). Such a list implemented as a linked organization is called the *list of available space*, *free storage list*, or the *free pool*.

Suppose some memory block is freed by the program. The space available can be used for future use. One way to do so is to add the blocks in the free pool. For good memory utilization, the operating system periodically collects all the free blocks and inserts into the free pool. Any technique that does this collection is called *garbage collection*. Garbage collection usually takes place in two phases. First, the process runs through all the lists, tagging those cells, which are currently in use. In the second phase, the process runs through memory, collecting all untagged blocks and inserting the same in free pool. In general, garbage collection takes place when either overflow or underflow occurs. In addition, when the CPU is idle, the garbage collection starts. Note that the garbage collection is invisible to the programmer.

Overflow Sometimes, a new data node is to be inserted into data structure, but there is no available space, that is, free pool is empty. This situation is called *overflow*.

Underflow This refers to the situation where the programmer wants to delete a node from the empty list.

The most suitable data structure for garbage collection is *circular DLL*. It allows the process of search to be unending traversal through list process as it is circular; DLL allows to traverse on both the sides.

RECAPITULATION

- Linear list is the list where each element has a unique predecessor and a unique successor. Linear lists are of two categories, namely general and restricted. General list is the one where data can be inserted or deleted anywhere in the list, whereas in restricted lists, there are a few restrictions.
- Linear list can be implemented using arrays and pointers. An implementation that uses pointers and dynamic memory allocation is called as linked list. A linked list is a very effective and efficient dynamic data structure. Items may be added or deleted from it at any position much easily as compared to arrays.
- Linked lists are useful data structures, especially if you need to automatically allocate and de-allocate space in a list. The basic operations are `create` list, `transverse` the list, `insert`, and `delete` a node.
- There are two variations of linked list, namely SLL and DLL. Both the linked lists can be circular lists. The linked list could be with or without a header node. Header node is used to store some information about the list so that it can be accessed without traversing the same. Information could be total number of nodes in the list, and similarly any other.
- Linked list is the most popular data structure used. It has many applications such as process queue, print queue, garbage collection, and so on.

KEY TERMS

Circular linked list The linked list whose link field of last node is set to point to the first node rather than `Null` is called a circular linked list.

`delete` operator To destroy a dynamically allocated variable/object and free the space for the object, the operator `delete` is used.

Doubly linked list In doubly linked list, each node has two link fields to store information about the one next to and also about the one ahead of the node. Hence, each node has knowledge of its successor and also its predecessor. In doubly linked list, the list can be traversed in both the directions from every node.

Dynamic memory allocation The process of allocating memory at run-time is known as dynamic memory allocation.

Generalized lists Generalized lists are defined recursively as lists whose members may be single data elements or other generalized lists. A generalized list is a linear list (non-indexed) of zero or more data elements or generalized lists. In other words, a generalized list is a finite sequence of $n \geq 0$ elements, $\alpha_1, \alpha_2, \ldots \alpha_n$, which we write as list $A = (\alpha_1, \alpha_2, \ldots, \alpha_n)$, where α_i is either an atom or a list. The elements of α_i, where $1 \leq i \leq n$, which are not atoms are said to be the sub-lists of list.

Linear linked list The linked list that we have seen so far are known as linear linked lists. All elements of such a linked list can be accessed by traversing the list from the first node of the list.

Linked list A linked list is an ordered collection of data where each element contains minimum two values, data and link(s), to its successor (and/or predecessor).

Linked stack and queue A stack implemented using a linked list is called a linked stack and implementation of queue using a linked list is called as a linked queue.

new operator The new operator creates a new dynamic object of a specified type and returns a pointer that points to this new object.

Null Null is a special constant pointer value that is used to give a value to a pointer variable that would not otherwise have a value. Null can be assigned to a pointer variable of any type.

Singly linked list A linked list where every node has one link field, to provide information about where the next node of the list is, is called as singly linked list.

EXERCISES

Multiple choice questions

1. The concatenation of two lists is to be performed in O(1) time. Which of the following implementations of a list should be used ?
   (a) Singly linked list
   (b) Doubly linked list
   (c) Circular doubly linked list
   (d) Array implementation of list
2. Which of the following operations is performed more efficiently by a doubly linked list than by a linear linked list?
   (a) Deleting nodes whose location is given
   (b) Searching an unsorted list for a given item
   (c) Inserting a node after the node with a given location
   (d) Traversing the list to process each node
3. Consider the linked list of n elements. What is the time taken to insert an element after an element pointed by some pointer?
   (a) O(1)
   (b) $O(\log_2 n)$
   (c) $O(n)$
   (d) $O(n \log_2 n)$
4. In a linked list, the logical order of elements
   (a) is the same as their physical arrangement
   (b) is determined by their physical arrangement
   (c) cannot be determined from their physical arrangement
   (d) none of these
5. Underflow condition in a linked list may occur when attempting to
   (a) insert a new node when there is no free space for it
   (b) delete a non-existent node in the list
   (c) delete a node in empty list
   (d) none of these
6. Overflow condition in a linked list may occur when attempting to
   (a) create a node when free space pool is empty
   (b) traverse the nodes when free space pool is empty
   (c) create a node when linked list is empty
   (d) none of these
7. Deletion of a node in a linked list involves keeping track of the address of the node
   (a) which immediately follows the node that is to be deleted
   (b) which immediately precedes the node that is to be deleted
   (c) that is to be deleted
   (d) none of these

8. Header of a linked list is a special node at the
   (a) end of the linked list
   (b) at the middle of the linked list
   (c) beginning of the linked list
   (d) none of these
9. A header-linked list where the last node points to the header node is called
   (a) grounded header list
   (b) circular header list
   (c) general header list
   (d) none of these
10. It is required to insert a node at the end of a singly connected linked list having n nodes. How many nodes are to be traversed for this insertion?
    (a) 1
    (b) $n/2$
    (c) n
    (d) none of these

Review questions

1. How is an element in an array different from the element in a linked list?
2. What are the fields of a node in a linked list?
3. What is the function of the pointer field in a linked list?
4. How do you point to the first node in a linked list?
5. What is a singly linked list?
6. In most programming languages, an array is a static data structure. When you define an array, the size is fixed. What problem will this restriction create?
7. A linked list is a dynamic data structure. The size of a linked list can be changed dynamically (during program execution). How does this feature benefit a programmer?
8. Which operation do you think is easier for the following different cases? Justify your answer.
   (a) Adding an element to an array, or adding an element to a linked list
   (b) Deleting an element to an array, or deleting an element to a linked list
   (c) Accessing an element to an array, or accessing an element to a linked list
   (d) Sorting an element to an array, or sorting an element to a linked list
9. What is a linked list? How is it represented?
10. What is a dynamic memory allocation? How does it help in building complex programs?
11. What is the principal difference between the functions `malloc` and `calloc`?
12. Why a linked list is called a dynamic data structure? What are the advantages of using linked lists over arrays?
13. Describe different types of linked lists.
14. Represent the following polynomials using GLL.
    (a) $x^3(y^3(3z^4 - yz^3 + z) - y(z^2 + z) - xyz$
    (b) $x^{10}y^3z^2 + x^4y^4z + 2yz$
    (c) $-x^3y^2z^4 + xz^2x^3y - xyz + zy^3$
15. Write a C++ program with functions for the following using a suitable variant of the linked list (singly, doubly, even, and circular with or without header node):
    (a) Compute length, Reverse list, Print in Reverse order, Insert/Delete node, Search a node, Print list, Create sorted list, Concatenate two lists.
    (b) Evaluate a polynomial of a single variable.
    (c) Compute addition, subtraction, and multiplication of two polynomials.
    (d) Read and print sparse matrix.
    (e) Store string and Compute length, Reverse string from a particular character, search and change substring, Insert/Delete character, Search a character; Sort the string without using another list, Concatenate two strings, Compare two strings.
    (f) Compute 1's complement and 2's complement of a binary number.
    (g) Add two binary numbers.

(h) Appointment scheduling for a day: Set bounds by taking starting time and ending time of a day. Display free slots. Ask for a new appointment. Check for validity and insert. Delete cancelled appointment. Display all appointments of a day.

(i) A function `move()` which would move a node forward n positions in the linked list.

(j) Sort a list using pointer manipulation.

(k) Merge two sorted lists into third.

(l) Merge second sorted list into first sorted list.

(m) Create sorted list and insert element in the same.

(n) Check whether a string stored is palindrome or not.

(o) Create two lists to store two sets. Compute intersection, union, difference, and symmetric difference of the same. Compute power set of a set.

16. Write a program that reads the name, age, and salary of 10 persons and maintains them in a linked list sorted by name.
17. There are two linked lists *A* and *B* containing the following data:
    A: 3, 7, 10, 15, 16, 9, 22, 17, 32
    B: 16, 2, 9, 13, 37, 8, 10, 1, 28
    Write a program to create
    (a) a linked list *C* that contains only those elements that are common in linked lists *A* and *B*
    (b) a linked list *D* that contains all elements of *A* as well as *B* ensuring that there is no repetition of elements.
18. A linked list contains some positive numbers and some negative numbers. Using this linked list, write a program to create two more linked lists, one containing all positive numbers and the other containing all negative numbers.
19. Write a C++ program that accepts a list implemented using linked list, traverses it, and returns the data in the node with the smallest key value.
20. Write a C++ program that traverses a list implemented using a linked list and deletes the node following a node with a negative key.
21. Create two linked lists to represent the following polynomials:
    (a) $3x^2y + 9xy^3 + 15xy + 3$
    (b) $13x^3y^2 + 7x^2y + 22xy + 9y^3$
    Write a function `add()` to add these polynomials and print the resulting linked list.

Answers to multiple choice questions

1. (c) 2. (a) 3. (a) 4. (c) 5. (c) 6. (a) 7. (b) 8. (c) 9. (b) 10. (d)

7 TREES

OBJECTIVES

After completing this chapter, the reader will be able to understand the following:

- Hierarchical representation of data using trees
- Binary search trees (BSTs) that allow both rapid retrievals by key and inorder traversals
- The use of trees as a flexible data structure for solving a wide range of problems

In computer science, a *tree* is a widely used data structure that emulates a tree structure with a set of linked nodes. Trees are used popularly in computer programming. They can be used for improving database search times (binary search trees, AVL trees, red–black trees), in game programming (minmax trees, decision trees, path finding trees), 3D graphics programming (binary trees, quadtrees, octrees), arithmetic scripting languages (arithmetic precedence trees), data compression (Huffman trees), and even file systems (btrees, sparse indexed trees, trie trees). Let us learn about trees in this chapter.

7.1 INTRODUCTION

Let us first revise the classification of data structures as *linear* and *non-linear*. A data structure is said to be *linear* if its elements form a sequence or a linear list. In a linear data structure, every data element has a unique successor and a unique predecessor. There are two basic ways of representing linear structures in memory. One way is to have the relationship between the elements by means of pointers (links), called as *linked lists*. Another way is using sequential organization, that is, *arrays*.

Non-linear data structures are used to represent the data containing hierarchical or network relationship between the elements. Trees and graphs are examples of non-linear data structures. In non-linear data structures, every data element may have more than one predecessor as well as successor. Elements do not form any particular linear sequence.

Non-linear data structures are capable of expressing more complex relationships than linear data structures. In general, wherever the hierarchical relationship among data is to be preserved, the tree is used. Well-known examples of such structures are family trees, hierarchy of positions in organization, and so on. *Tree*, a non-linear data structure, is a means to maintain and manipulate data in many applications. Consider the following example:

The operating system of a computer system organizes files into directories and subdirectories. Directories are also referred to as *folders*. The operating system organizes folders and files using a tree structure as in Fig. 7.1.

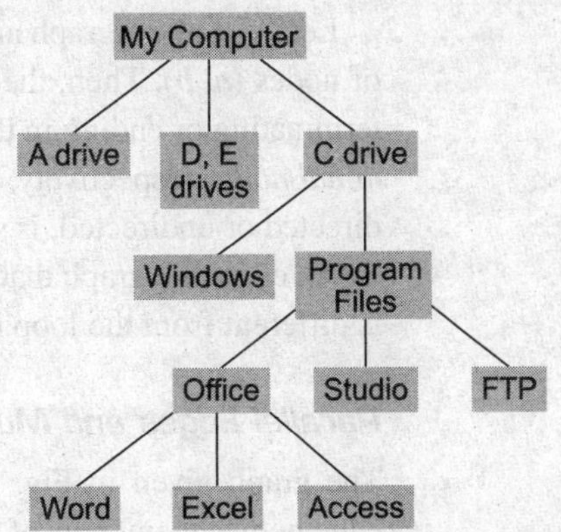

Fig. 7.1 Folder and subfolders organization

A folder contains other folders (subfolders) and files. This can be viewed as the tree drawn in Fig. 7.1. Note that the root here is desktop. The common uses of trees include the following:

1. Manipulating hierarchical data
2. Making information easily searchable
3. Manipulating sorted lists of data

A tree is a graph called the directed acyclic graph. So let us first discuss the basic terminology related to trees.

7.1.1 Basic Terminology

We should first learn about a general graph because trees can be viewed as restricted graphs. A graph G consists of a non-empty set V, a set E, and a mapping from the set E to set V. Here, V is the set of *nodes*, also called as *vertices points*, of the graph, and E is the set of edges of the graph. For *finite graphs*, V and E are finite. We can represent them as $G = (V, E)$.

Adjacent Nodes

If an edge $e \in E$ is associated with a pair of nodes (a, b) where $a, b \in V$, then it is said that the edge e joins or connects the nodes a and b. Any two nodes that are connected with an edge are called as *adjacent nodes*.

Directed and Undirected Graphs

In a graph $G(V, E)$, an edge that is directed from one node to another is called a *directed edge*, whereas an edge that has the no specific direction is called an *undirected edge*. A graph where every edge is directed is called as a *directed graph* or *diagraph*. A graph where every edge is undirected is called as an *undirected graph*. If some of edges are directed and some are undirected in a graph, the graph is called as a *mixed graph*.

A city map showing only the one-way streets is an example of a directed graph where the intersections are vertices and the edges are streets. A map showing only the two-way streets is an example of an undirected graph, and a map showing all the one-way and two-way streets is an example of a mixed graph.

Let (V, E) be a graph and let $e \in E$ be a directed edge associated with the ordered pair of nodes (a, b). Then, the edge e is said to be initiating or originating in the node a and terminating or ending in the node b. The nodes a and b are also called the *initial* and *terminal nodes* respectively, of the edge e. An edge $e \in E$ that joins the nodes a and b, be it directed or undirected, is said to be *incident* to the nodes a and b, respectively.

An edge of a graph that joins a node to itself is called a *loop* (sling). Note that this loop is different from the loop in a program. The direction of the loop has no significance.

Parallel Edges and Multigraph

The graph given in Fig. 7.2(a) has only one edge between any pair of nodes. In the directed edges, the two possible edges between the pair of nodes that are opposite in direction are considered distinct. In some directed as well as undirected graphs, there may exist more than one edge incident to the same pair of nodes, say a and b.

In Fig. 7.2(b), the edges e_1, e_2, and e_3 are incident to vertices a and b. Such edges are called as *parallel edges*. Here, e_1, e_2, and e_3 are three parallel edges. In addition, e_5 and e_6 are two parallel edges. Any graph that contains parallel edges is called a *multigraph*. On the other hand, a graph that has no parallel edges is called a *simple graph*.

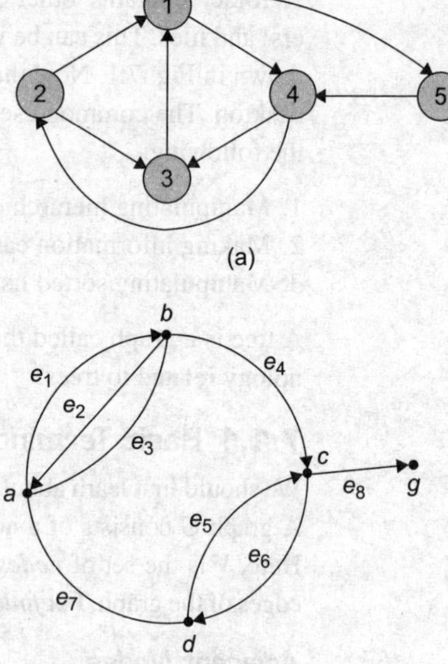

Fig. 7.2 Classification based on edges (a) Simple graph (b) Multigraph

Weighted Graph

A graph where weights are assigned to every edge is called a *weighted graph*. Weights can also be assigned to vertices. A graph of areas and streets of a city may be assigned weights according to its traffic density. A graph of areas and connecting roads may be assigned weights such that the distance between the cities is assigned to edges and area population is assigned to vertices.

Null Graph and Isolated Vertex

In a graph, a node that is not adjacent to any other node is called an *isolated node*. A graph containing only isolated nodes is called a *null graph*. Hence, the set of edges is an empty set in a null graph.

Let V = set of students, E = {there exists an edge incident to two students if they share books}. Let $V = \{a, b, c\}$. If no two students among a, b, and c shares books, then the graph $G = \{V, E\}$ is represented as shown in Fig. 7.3(a).

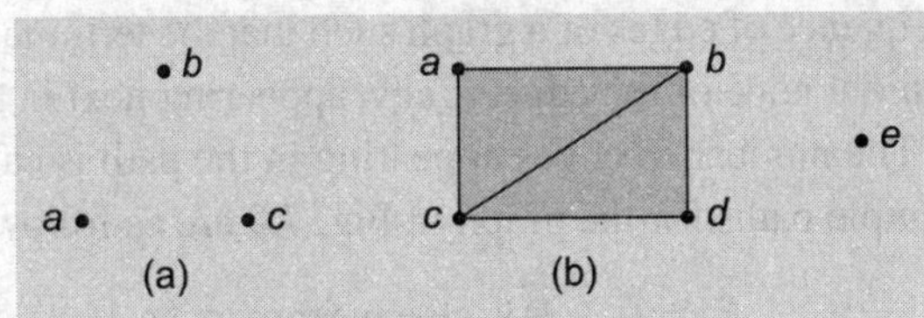

Fig. 7.3 Classification based on nodes (a) Null graph (b) Graph with isolated vertex

Here, G is a null graph, and a, b, and c are isolated vertices. In Fig. 7.3(b), $V = \{a, b, c, d, e\}$ and $E = \{(a, b), (a, c), (b, c), (c, d), (b, d)\}$, and e is an isolated vertex.

Degree of Vertex

In a directed graph, for any node V, the number of edges that have V as its initial node is called the *outdegree* of the node V. In other words, the number of edges incident from a node is its *outdegree* (*outgoing degree*), and the number of edges incident to it is an *indegree* (*incoming degree*). The sum of indegree and outdegree is the total degree of a node (*vertex*). In an undirected graph, the total degree or degree of a node is the number of edges incident to the node. The isolated vertex degree is zero. The degree of vertex a in Fig. 7.4 is 3, whereas the degree of vertex f is 1. For vertex 1 in Fig. 7.2(a), the incoming degree is 2 and the outgoing degree is 2.

Paths and Circuits

Let $G = (V, E)$ be a simple graph. Consider a sequence of edges of G such that the terminal node of any edge in the sequence is the initial node of the next edge, if any, in the sequence (Fig. 7.4).

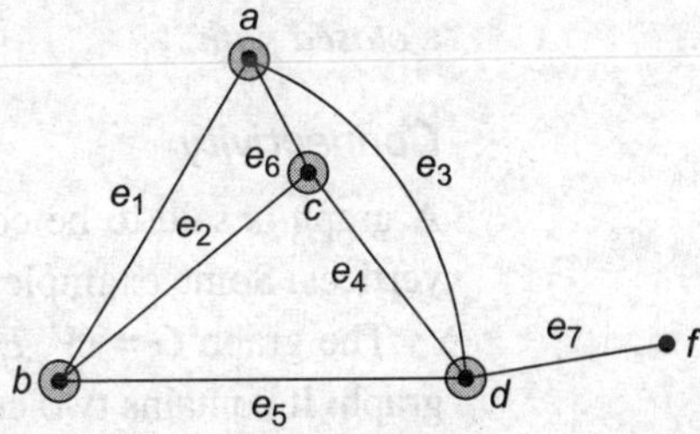

Fig. 7.4 Graph G

Here, $G = (V, E)$, $V = \{a, b, c, d\}$, and $E = \{e_1, e_2, e_3, e_4, e_5, e_6, e_7\}$.

An example of such a sequence is given by $\{e_1, e_2, e_4, e_5\}$.

The sequence $\{e_1, e_2, e_4, e_5\}$ can also be written as $\{a, b, c, d, b\}$.

In addition, $\{e_6, e_2, e_1, e_3, e_4, e_2, e_5\}$ is another sequence. Note that not all edges and nodes appearing in a sequence need to be distinct. In addition, for a given graph, any arbitrary set of nodes such as $\{a, f, b\}$ that is written in any order does not give a sequence as required. In fact, each node appearing in the sequence must be adjacent to the nodes appearing just before and after it in the sequence, except for the first and the last nodes.

Consider the graph in Fig. 7.5.

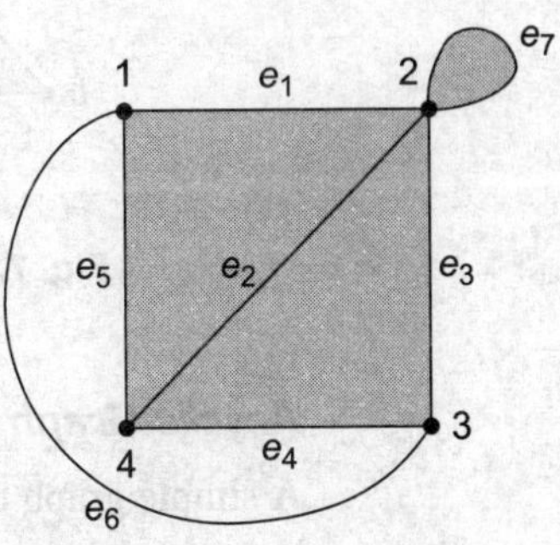

Fig. 7.5 Graph with self loop

A sequence of edges of a graph such that the terminal node of any edge in the sequence is the initial node of the edge, if any, appearing next in the sequence, defines the path of a graph. The number of edges appearing in the path is called the *length of the path*.

Example paths for the graph in Fig. 7.5 are as follows:

$P_1 = \{(2, 4)\}$, also written as $\{e_2\}$
$P_2 = \{(2, 3), (3, 1), (1, 4)\}$, also written as $\{e_3, e_6, e_5\}$
$P_3 = \{e_1, e_2, e_4, e_3, e_1, e_5\}$ or $\{(1, 2), (2, 4), (4, 3), (3, 2), (2, 1), (1, 4)\}$

A path where no edge is traversed more than once is called a *simple path* (or edge simple path). A path where no vertex is traversed (visited) more than once is called an *elementary path* (node simple path). For example, $\{e_1, e_2, e_4, e_6, e_5\}$ is a simple path but not elementary as the vertex 1 is traversed (visited) twice.

A path that originates and ends at the same node is called a *cycle* (circuit). A cycle is elementary if each node is traversed once (except origin) and is simple if every edge of the cycle is traversed once. For example, the following are the cycles for the graph in Fig. 7.5.

$C_1 = \{(2, 2)\}$, also represented as $\{e_7\}$
$C_2 = \{(1, 2), (2, 4), (4, 1)\}$, also represented as $\{1, 2, 4, 1\}$ or $\{e_1, e_2, e_5\}$
$C_3 = \{e_3, e_2, e_5, e_6\}$ or $\{3, 2, 4, 1, 3\}$

Here, the cycle $\{e_1, e_2, e_5\}$ in both simple and elementary cycles is also referred to as a *closed path*.

Connectivity

A graph is said to be connected if and only if there exists a path between every pair of vertices. Some examples are shown in Figs 7.6(a) and (b).

The graph $G = (V, E)$ drawn in Fig. 7.6(a) with $V = \{a, b, c, d, e\}$ is a disconnected graph. It contains two connected components. A connected graph has a single connected component. The graph shown in Fig. 7.6(b) is a connected graph.

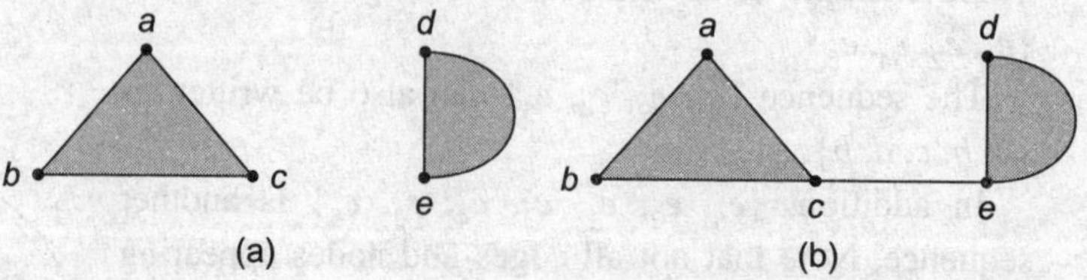

Fig. 7.6 Graph connectivity (a) Graph with two connected components (b) Connected graph with one connected component

Acyclic Graph

A simple graph that does not have any cycles is called *acyclic graph*. Such graphs do not have any loops.

Trees

A class of graphs that is acyclic is termed as *trees*.

Let us now discuss an important class of graphs called *trees* and its associated terminology.

Trees are useful in describing any structure that involves hierarchy. Familiar examples of such structures are family trees, the hierarchy of positions in an organization, and so on.

Forest and Trees

A *forest* is a graph that contains no cycles, and a connected forest is a *tree*. For example, Fig. 7.7 shows a forest with three components, each of which is a tree.

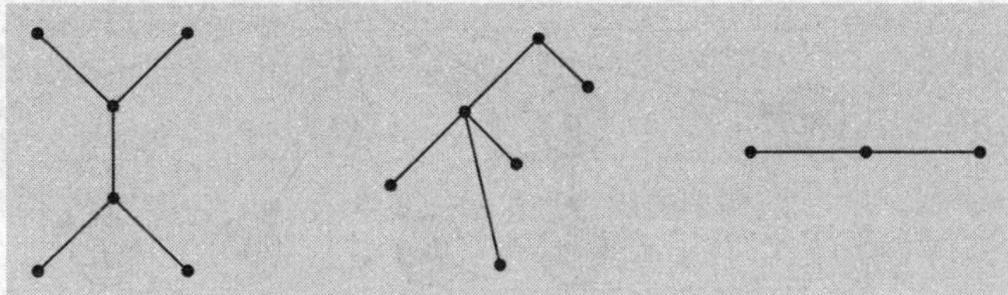

Fig. 7.7 Forest with three trees

Note that trees and forests are simple graphs. The following terminology belongs to trees.

Directed tree An acyclic directed graph is a *directed tree*.

Root A directed tree has one node called its *root*, with indegree zero, whereas for all other nodes, the indegree is 1.

Terminal node (leaf node) In a directed tree, any node that has an outdegree zero is a *terminal node*. The terminal node is also called as *leaf node* (or *external node*).

Branch node (internal node) All other nodes whose outdegree is not zero are called as *branch nodes*.

Level of node The level of any node is its path length from the root. The level of the root of a directed tree is zero, whereas the level of any node is equal to its distance from the root. Distance from the root is the number of edges to be traversed to reach the root.

7.1.2 General Tree

A tree T is defined recursively as follows:

1. A set of zero items is a tree, called the *empty tree* (or null tree).
2. If $T_1, T_2, ..., T_n$ are n trees for $n > 0$ and R is a *node*, then the set T containing R and the trees $T_1, T_2, ..., T_n$ are a tree. Within T, R is called the *root* of T, and $T_1, T_2, ..., T_n$ are called *subtrees*.

The tree in Fig. 7.8(a) is the empty tree since there are no nodes. The tree in Fig. 7.8(b) has only one node, the *root*. The tree in Fig. 7.8(c) has 16 nodes. The root node has four subtrees. The roots of these subtrees are called the *children* of the root. There are 16 nodes in the tree, so there are 15 non-empty subtrees. The nodes with no subtrees are called *terminal nodes* or more commonly, *leaves*. These are 10 leaves in the tree in Fig. 7.8(c).

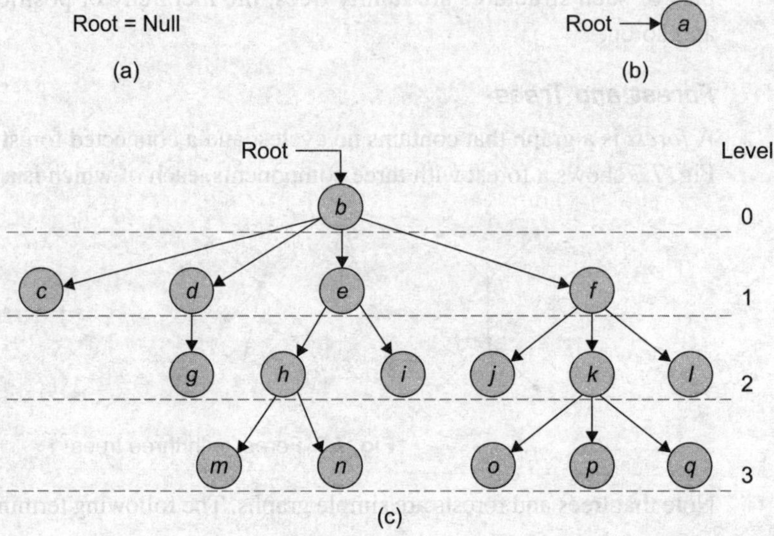

Fig. 7.8 Degree of a tree (a) Empty tree—degree undefined (b) Tree with a single node—degree 0 (c) Tree of height 3—degree 4

The degree of a node is the number of subtrees it has. Thus, the degree of the nodes in Fig. 7.8(c) ranges from zero to four. By definition, the degree of each leaf node is zero. The *degree of a tree* is the maximum degree of a node in the tree. As the tree in Fig. 7.8(a) has no nodes, there is no maximum degree of a node, and the degree of the tree is not defined. The tree in Fig. 7.8(b) has degree zero, and the tree in Fig. 7.8(c) has degree four.

Since family relationships can be modelled as trees, we often call the root of a tree (or subtree) the *parent*, and the roots of the subtrees the *children*. Consequently, the children of the same node are called *siblings*.

The advantage of the relationship between a parent and its children is that a directed edge (or, simply an edge) extends from a parent to its children. Thus, the edges connect a root with the roots of each subtree. For example, in Fig. 7.8(c), an edge extends from the root *b* to each of the nodes *c*, *d*, *e*, and *f*. Similarly, edges extend from *e* to *i* and from *d* to *g*. An undirected edge extends in both directions between a parent and a child. Thus, the undirected edges would also extend from *i* to *e* and from *g* to *d*.

A directed path (or simply path) is a sequence of directed edges $e_1, e_2, ..., e_n$, where the node at the end of one edge serves as the beginning of the next edge. An undirected path is a similar sequence of undirected edges.

For example, in Fig. 7.8(c), one path containing three edges begins at the root and extends through nodes *f*, *k*, and *p*. Similarly, the path beginning at node *h* and containing the nodes *e*, *b*, and *d* is an undirected path. In this chapter and chapters 8 and 9, *edge* refers to a directed edge from a parent to its child. Following the analogy of family hierarchies, if a path exists from one node to another, it is common to state that the first node is an ancestor of the second, and the second is a descendent of the first.

The *length of a path* is the number of edges it contains (which is one less than the number of nodes on the path). The *depth* or *level of a node* is the length of a node, which is the length of a directed path from the root to that node. The *height of a tree* is the length of the path from the root to a node at the lowest level. In other words, the height of a tree is the maximum path length in the tree. Thus, the level of the root of a tree is zero, and the level of each child of the root is one. Equivalently, the height of a tree is the largest level number of any node in the tree.

There are three common ways to symmetrically order (or list) the nodes in a tree: preorder, inorder, and postorder. For each of these orderings, an empty tree gives rise to an empty list, and the tree with one node yields the list with one node. For trees with more than one node, the following statements are true:

1. The preorder list contains the root followed by the preorder list of nodes of the subtrees of the root from left to right.
2. The inorder list contains the inorder list of the leftmost subtree, the root, and the inorder list of each of the other subtrees from left to right.
3. The postorder list contains the postorder list of subtrees of the root from left to right followed by the root.

Figure 7.9 shows a tree whose nodes are labelled with numbers rather than letters.

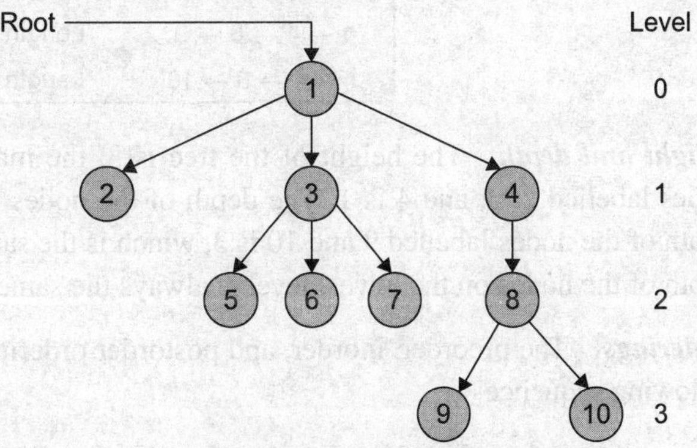

Fig. 7.9 Sample tree

The following is a list of terms for review using the example tree in Fig. 7.9.

Subtrees The nodes labelled 2, 3, and 4 are the roots of the subtrees (children) of the node labelled 1. The nodes labelled 5, 6, and 7 are the roots of the subtrees (children) of the node labelled 3. The node labelled 8 is the root of the subtree (child) of the node labelled 4. The nodes labelled 9 and 10 are the roots of the subtrees (children) of the node labelled 8.

Leaves The nodes labelled 2, 5, 6, 7, 9, and 10 are the terminal nodes or leaf nodes.

Degree The nodes labelled 1 and 3 have degree 3. The node labelled 8 has degree 2. The node labelled 4 has degree 1. All the leaf nodes have degree 0. The degree of the tree is 3, because the maximum degree of any node is 3.

Levels The level number appears on the right of the tree. The level of the root is 0, the level of the nodes labelled 2, 3, and 4 is 1, the level of the nodes labelled 5, 6, 7, and 8 is 2, and that of the nodes labelled 9 and 10 is 3.

Family relationships The node labelled 1 is the parent of the nodes labelled 2, 3, and 4. The node labelled 3 is the parent of the nodes labelled 5, 6, and 7. The node labelled 4 is the parent of the node labelled 8, which in turn is the parent of the nodes labelled 9 and 10. The nodes labelled 2, 3, and 4 are siblings similar to the nodes labelled 9 and 10. Note that the node labelled 8 is not the sibling of the nodes labelled 5, 6, and 7.

Paths and path lengths Paths exist from all parents to children. A unique path exists from the root to each leaf node as shown in Fig. 7.9. Since any sub-path is a path, all the paths are represented. This is shown in the next page:

1 → 2	Length: 1
1 → 3 → 5	Length: 2
1 → 3 → 6	Length: 2
1 → 3 → 7	Length: 2
1 → 4 → 8 → 9	Length: 3
1 → 4 → 8 → 10	Length: 3

Height and depth The height of the tree is 3, the maximum level. The depth of the nodes labelled 2, 3, and 4 is 1. The depth of the nodes labelled 5, 6, 7, and 8 is 2. The depth of the nodes labelled 9 and 10 is 3, which is the same as the height of the tree. The depth of the nodes on the lowest level is always the same as the height of the tree.

Orderings The preorder, inorder, and postorder orderings of the nodes are given in the following sequence:

1 → 2 → 3 → 5 → 6 → 7 → 4 → 8 → 9 → 10 (preorder)
2 → 1 → 5 → 3 → 6 → 7 → 9 → 8 → 10 → 4 (inorder)
2 → 5 → 6 → 7 → 3 → 9 → 10 → 8 → 4 → 1 (postorder)

We shall learn about these orderings in Section 7.7.

7.1.3 Representation of a General Tree

We can use either a sequential organization or a linked organization for representing a tree. If we wish to use a generalized linked list, then a node must have a varying number of fields depending upon the number of branches. However, it is simpler to use algorithms for the data where the node size is fixed.

For a fixed size node, we can use a node with data and pointer fields as in a generalized linked list.

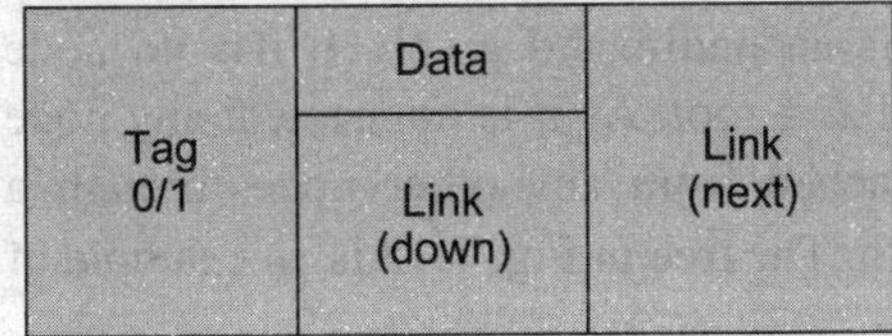

Figure 7.10 shows a sample tree.

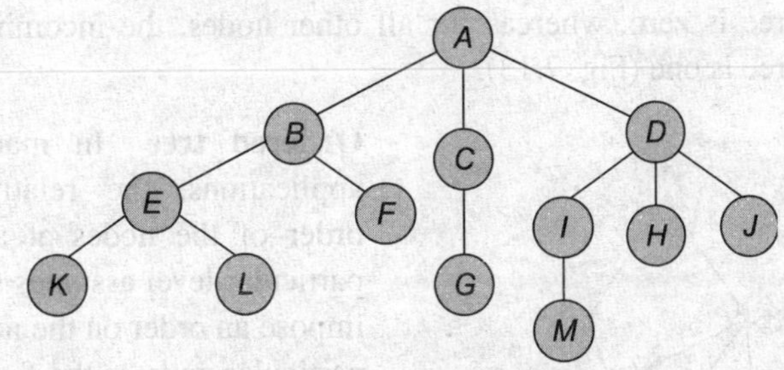

Fig. 7.10 Sample tree

The list representation of this tree is shown in Fig. 7.11.

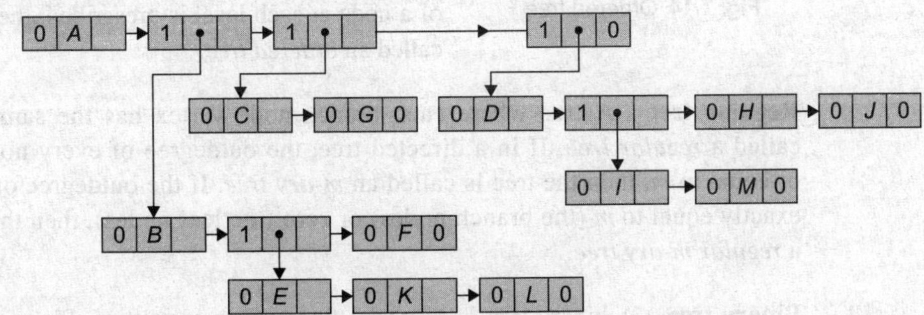

Fig. 7.11 List representation

7.2 TYPES OF TREES

In this section, we shall study some important types of trees.

1. Free tree
2. Rooted tree
3. Ordered tree
4. Regular tree
5. Binary tree
6. Complete tree
7. Position tree

Free tree A free tree is a connected, acyclic graph. It is an undirected graph. It has no node designated as a root. As it is connected, any node can be reached from any other node through a unique path. The tree in Fig. 7.12 is an example of a free tree.

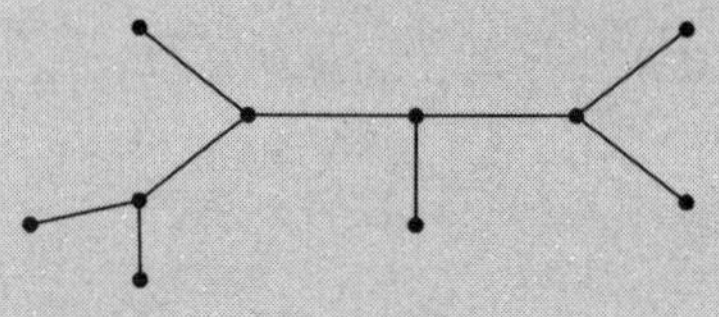

Fig. 7.12 Free tree

Rooted tree Unlike free tree, a *rooted tree* is a directed graph where one node is designated as root, whose incoming degree is zero, whereas for all other nodes, the incoming degree is one (Fig. 7.13).

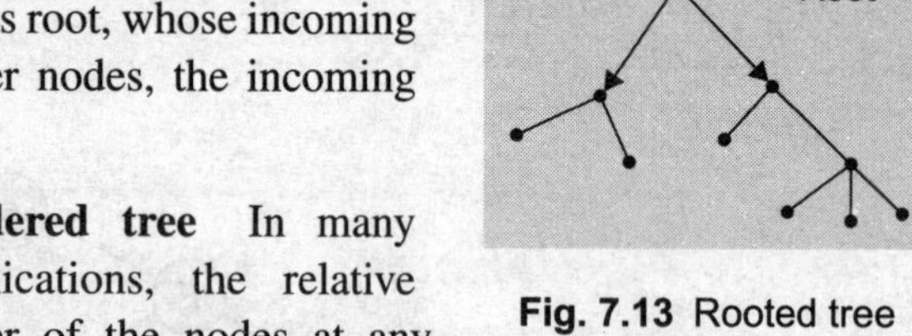

Fig. 7.13 Rooted tree

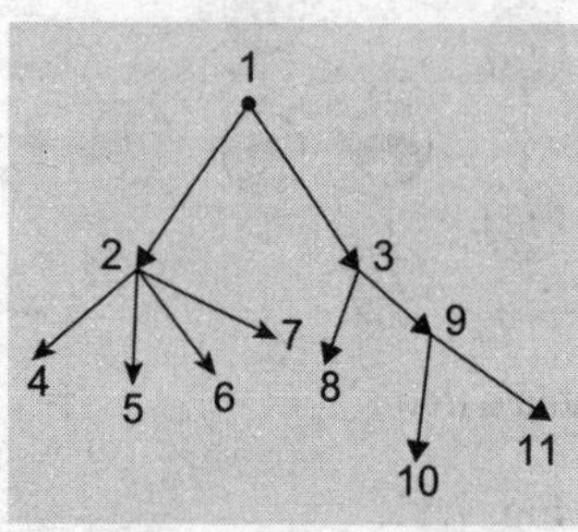

Fig. 7.14 Ordered tree

Ordered tree In many applications, the relative order of the nodes at any particular level assumes some significance. It is easy to impose an order on the nodes at a level by referring to a particular node as the first node, to another node as the second, and so on. Such ordering can be done from left to right (Fig. 7.14). Just like nodes at each level, we can prescribe order to edges. If in a directed tree, an ordering of a node at each level is prescribed, then such a tree is called an *ordered tree.*

Regular tree A tree where each branch node vertex has the same outdegree is called a *regular tree*. If in a directed tree, the outdegree of every node is less than or equal to *m*, then the tree is called an *m-ary tree*. If the outdegree of every node is exactly equal to *m* (the branch nodes) or zero (the leaf nodes), then the tree is called a *regular m-ary tree*.

Binary tree A binary tree is a special form of an *m*-ary tree. Since a binary tree is important, it is frequently used in various applications of computer science.

We have defined an m-ary tree (general tree). A binary tree is an m-ary position tree when $m = 2$. In a binary tree, no node has more than two children.

Complete tree A tree with n nodes and of depth k is complete if and only if its nodes correspond to the nodes that are numbered from 1 to n in the full tree of depth k.

A binary tree of height h is complete if and only if one of the following holds good:

1. It is empty.
2. Its left subtree is complete of height $h-1$ and its right subtree is completely full of height $h-2$.
3. Its left subtree is completely full of height $h-1$ and its right subtree is complete of height $h-1$.

A binary tree is completely full if it is of height h and has $(2^{h+1} - 1)$ nodes.

Full binary tree A binary tree is a *full binary tree* if it contains the maximum possible number of nodes in all levels. Figure 7.15 shows a full binary tree of height 2.

In a full binary tree, each node has two children or no child at all. The total number of nodes in a full binary tree of height h is $2^{h+1}-1$ considering the root at level 0.

It can be calculated by adding the number of nodes of each level as in the following equation:

$$2^0 + 2^1 + 2^2 + \cdots + 2^h = 2^{h+1} - 1$$

Figure 7.15 has $2^{2+1} - 1 = 8 - 1 = 7$ nodes.

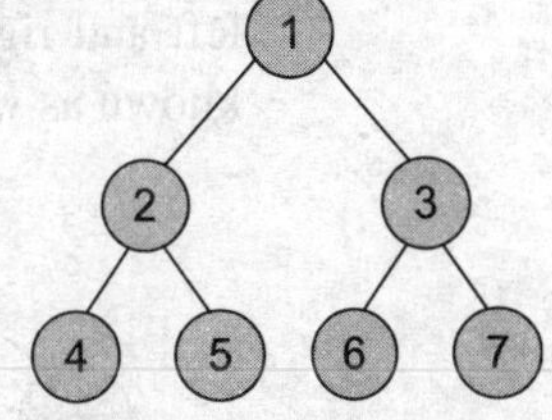

Fig. 7.15 Full binary tree

Complete binary tree A binary tree is said to be a *complete binary tree* if all its levels except the last level have the maximum number of possible nodes, and all the nodes of the last level appear as far left as possible. In a complete binary tree, all the leaf nodes are at the last and the second last level, and the levels are filled from left to right.

Figure 7.16 is a complete binary tree.

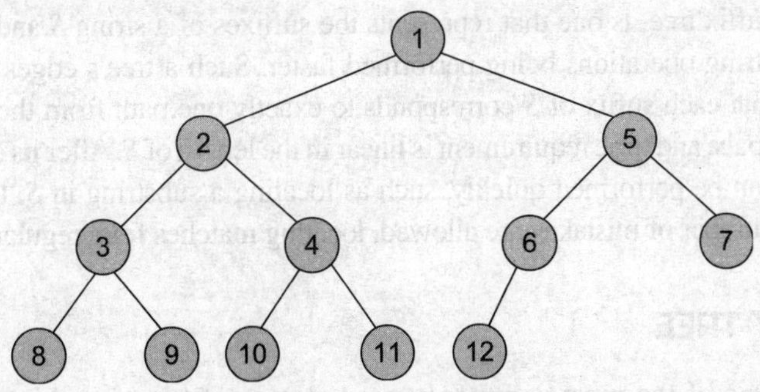

Fig. 7.16 Complete binary tree

Applications such as the priority queue and heap sort use the complete binary tree.

Left skewed binary tree If the right subtree is missing in every node of a tree, we call it a *left skewed tree* (Fig. 7.17).

If the left subtree is missing in every node of a tree, we call it as *right subtree* (Fig. 7.18).

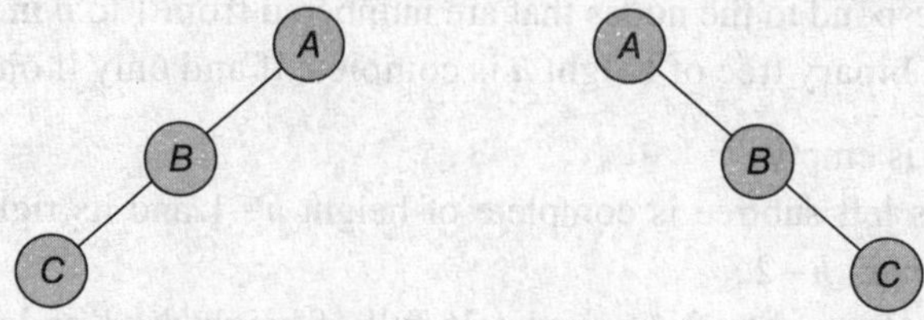

Fig. 7.17 Left skewed tree

Fig. 7.18 Right skewed tree

Strictly binary tree If every non-terminal node in a binary tree consists of non-empty left and right subtrees, then such a tree is called a *strictly binary tree.*

In Fig. 7.19, the non-empty nodes *D* and *E* have left and right subtrees. Such expression trees are known as *strictly binary trees*.

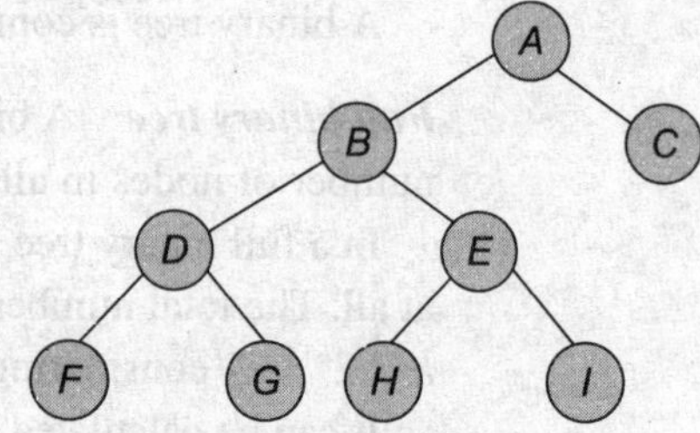

Fig. 7.19 Strictly binary tree

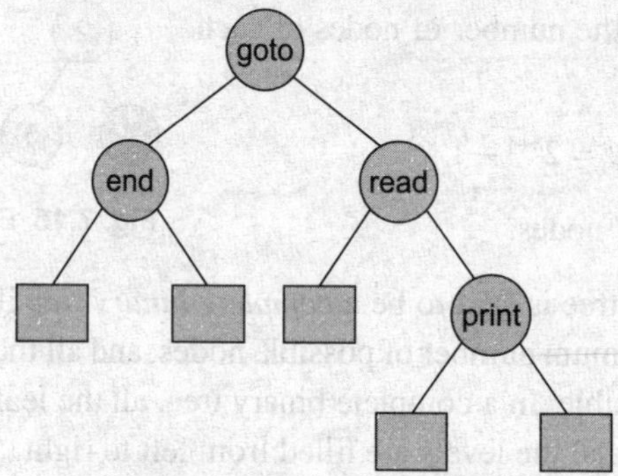

Fig. 7.20 Extended binary tree

Extended binary tree A binary tree *T* with each node having zero or two children is called an *extended binary tree*. The nodes with two children are called *internal nodes*, and those with zero children are called *external nodes*. Trees can be converted into extended trees by adding a node (Fig. 7.20).

Position tree A position tree, also known as a suffix tree, is one that represents the suffixes of a string *S* and such representation facilitates string operations being performed faster. Such a tree's edges are labelled with strings, such that each suffix of *S* corresponds to exactly one path from the tree's root to a leaf node. The space and time requirement is linear in the length of *S*. After its construction, several operations can be performed quickly, such as locating a substring in *S*, locating a substring if a certain number of mistakes are allowed, locating matches for a regular expression pattern, and so on.

7.3 BINARY TREE

One of the most commonly used classes of trees is a binary tree. A binary tree has the degree two, with each node having at most two children. This makes the implementation of trees easier. In addition, binary trees have a wide range of applications. We shall study these in this section.

Definition A binary tree

1. is either an empty tree or
2. consists of a node, called *root*, and two children, *left* and *right*, each of which is itself a binary tree.

The definition is recursive as we have defined a binary tree in terms of itself. All the internal nodes of a binary tree are themselves the roots of smaller binary trees (Fig. 7.21).

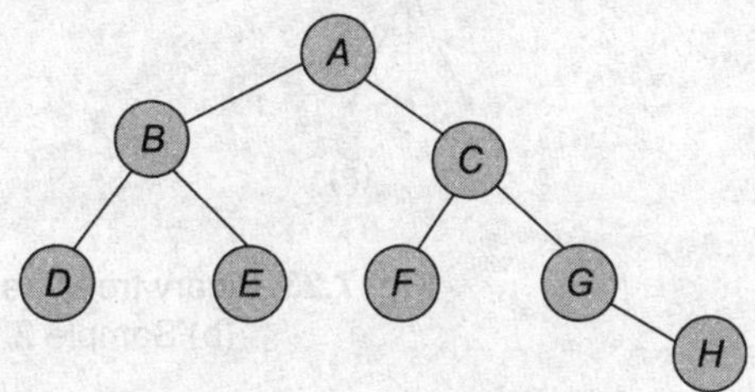

Fig. 7.21 Binary tree

Let us consider the two distinct binary trees in Fig. 7.22.

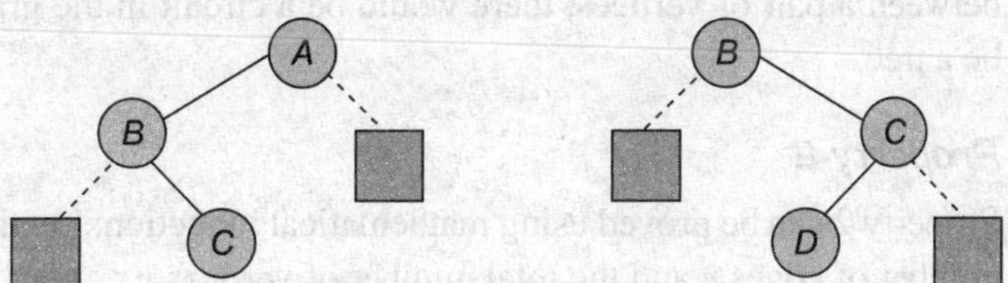

Fig. 7.22 Two binary trees

The definition implies that every non-empty node has two children, either of which may be empty. Here *A*'s right child and *B*'s left child are empty trees (represented by shaded boxes). Usually, empty trees in a binary tree are not shown.

7.3.1 Properties of a Binary Tree

A *tree* is a connected acyclic graph. In many ways, a tree is the simplest non-trivial type of graph. It has several good properties such as the fact that there exists a unique path between every two vertices. The following theorems list some simple properties of trees:

Let *T* be a tree. Then the following properties hold true:

1. There exists a unique path between every two vertices.
2. The number of vertices is one more than the number of edges in the tree.
3. A tree with two or more vertices has at least two leaves.

Let us refer to Fig. 7.23 for proving these properties.

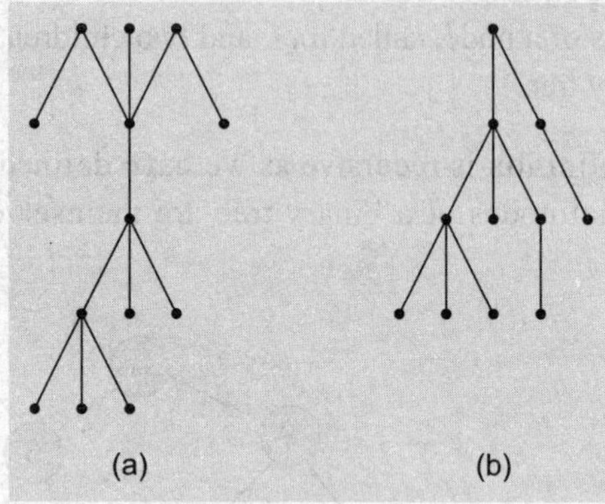

Fig. 7.23 Binary trees (a) Sample 1 (b) Sample 2

Property 1

Property 1 comes from the definition of a tree. As a tree is a connected graph, there exists at least one path between every two vertices. However, if there are two or more paths between a pair of vertices, there would be a circuit in the graph and so the graph cannot be a tree.

Property 2

Property 2 can be proved using mathematical induction. Let there be a tree T with the total number of edges e and the total number of vertices v.

Induction step A tree with one vertex contains no edge, and a tree with two vertices has one edge.

Induction hypothesis Let us consider that there is an edge $\{a, b\}$ in T such that the removal of the edge $\{a, b\}$ divides T into two disjoint trees T_1 and T_2, where T_1 contains the vertex a and all the vertices whose paths to a in T do not contain the edge $\{a, b\}$, and T_2 contains the vertex b and all the vertices whose paths to b do not contain the edge $\{a, b\}$.

Since both T_1 and T_2 have utmost $v - 1$ vertices, it follows from the hypothesis that

$$\text{for } T_1 \Rightarrow e_1 = v_1 - 1 \text{ and}$$
$$\text{for } T_2 \Rightarrow e_2 = v_2 - 1,$$

where e_1 and e_2 are the number of edges and v_1 and v_2 are the number of vertices in T_1 and T_2, respectively.

Thus $e_1 + e_2 = v_1 + v_2 - 2$

Since $e = e_1 + e_2 + 1$ and $v = v_1 + v_2$, we have $e = v - 1$, as shown in the following figure:

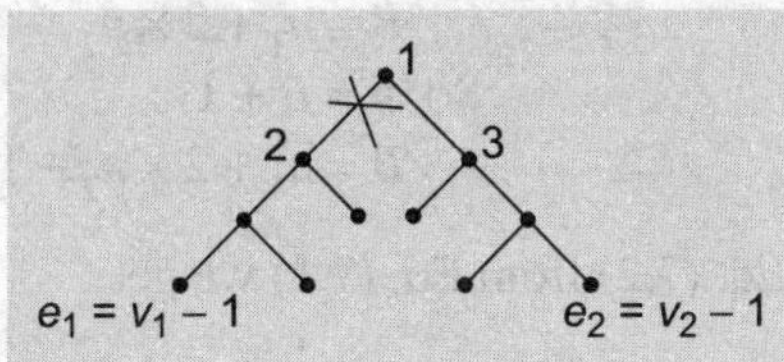

Property 3

Property 3 follows from Property 2, that is, the sum of degrees of the vertices in any graph is equal to $2e$, which is equal to $2v - 2$, in a tree. Since a tree with more than one vertex cannot have any isolated vertex, there must be at least two vertices of indegree 1 in the tree.

Other Properties

1. The maximum number of nodes of level i in a binary tree is 2^{i-1}, where $i \geq 1$.
2. The maximum number of nodes of depth d in a binary tree is 2^{d-1} , where $d \geq 1$.

Let us prove these properties using induction. Assume the root is only one node at level 1.

Hence, the maximum number of nodes is 2^{i-1}, that is, $2^{1-1} = 2^0 = 1$.

By induction hypothesis, let i be any arbitrary positive integer greater than 1. Then, the maximum number of nodes on level $i - 1$ is $2^{i-1-1} = 2^{i-2}$.

Hence, it is proved that the maximum number of nodes at level i is 2^{i-1}.

Note: If we assume the root at level 0, then the expression is 2^i.

Since each node in a binary tree has a maximum degree 2, the maximum number of nodes at level i is 2^{i-1}.

The maximum number of nodes of depth d of a binary tree is given by

$$\sum_{i=1}^{d}(\text{maximum no. of nodes at level } i) = \sum_{i=1}^{d} 2^{d-1}$$

Relation Between Number of Leaf Nodes and Degree-2 Nodes

In any non-empty tree T, if there are n_0 leaf nodes and n_2 nodes of degree 2, then

$$n_0 = n_2 + 1$$

Let n_1 be the number of nodes of degree 1 and n be the total number of nodes.
Since all nodes in T are with the utmost degree 2, then

$$n = n_0 + n_1 + n_2 + \ldots \tag{7.1}$$

If the number of branches is B, then $n = B + 1$. For a binary tree, all the branches stem out from a node of degree 1 or 2. Thus,

$$B = n_1 + 2 \times n_2$$

$$\text{So, } n = B + 1$$

$$B = n_1 + 2 \times n_2 + 1 \tag{7.2}$$

Subtracting Eq. (7.2) from Eq. (7.1) we get

$$n_0 = n_2 + 1$$

Binary Tree With n Nodes Having n + 1 External Nodes

Taking the base case of a tree with only one node, that is the root, it has two external nodes or null links. So, if $n = 1$, then the number of external nodes is $n + 1$, that is, 2.

From this base case, if there are n internal nodes where the left subtree has L nodes, then the right subtree has $n - L - 1$ internal nodes (1 for the root).

By induction hypothesis, the number of external nodes of the left subtree is $L + 1$.

The number of external nodes of the right subtree is $(n - L - 1) + 1 = n - L$. So, the total number of external nodes is $L + 1 + n - L = n + 1$.

7.4 BINARY TREE ABSTRACT DATA TYPE

We have defined a binary tree. Let us now define it as an abstract data type (ADT), which includes a list of operations that process it.

```
ADT btree
 1. Declare create()→btree
 2. makebtree(btree, element, btree)→btree
 3. isEmpty(btree)→boolean
 4. leftchild(btree)→btree
 5. rightchild(btree)→btree
 6. data(btree)→element
 7. for all l,r ∈ btree, e ∈ element, Let
 8. isEmpty(create) = true
 9. isEmpty(makebtree(l,e,r)) = false
10. leftchild(create()) = error
11. rightchild(create()) = error
12. leftchild(makebtree(l,e,r)) = l
13. rightchild(makebtree(l,e,r)) = r
14. data(makebtree(l,e,r)) = e
15. end
end btree
```

The six functions with their domains and ranges are declared in lines 1 through 6. Lines 7 through 14 are the set of axioms that describe how the functions are related.

The `create()` operation creates an empty binary tree; the `isEmpty()` operation checks whether `btree` is empty or not and returns the Boolean value true or false, respectively; `leftchild(btree)` and `rightchild(btree)` return the left and right subtrees, respectively; `data(btree)` returns the data element.

Program Code 7.1 states the class definition of the operations that process the tree ADT.

PROGRAM CODE 7.1

```
class TreeNode
{
   public:
      char Data;
      TreeNode *Lchild;
      TreeNode *Rchild;
};

class BinaryTree
{
   private:
      TreeNode *Root;
   public:
      BinaryTree(){Root = Null};
      // constructor creates an empty tree
      TreeNode * GetNode();
      void InsertNode(TreeNode*);
      void DeleteNode( TreeNode*);
;
```

Operations on binary tree The basic operations on a binary tree can be as listed as follows:

1. Creation—Creating an empty binary tree to which the 'root' points
2. Traversal—Visiting all the nodes in a binary tree
3. Deletion—Deleting a node from a non-empty binary tree
4. Insertion—Inserting a node into an existing (may be empty) binary tree
5. Merge—Merging two binary trees
6. Copy—Copying a binary tree
7. Compare—Comparing two binary trees
8. Finding a replica or mirror of a binary tree

7.5 REALIZATION OF A BINARY TREE

In this section, we shall study the basic realization of a binary tree and discuss its capabilities for supporting various operations. The implementation of a binary tree should represent the hierarchical relationship between a parent node and its left and right children. We have studied the elementary data structures such as linked list and arrays. Now, we shall extend these concepts to the binary tree structures. We shall give more emphasis to the linked implementation as it is more popular than the corresponding sequential structure due to the following two main reasons:

1. A binary tree has a natural implementation in a linked storage.
2. The linked structure is more convenient for insertions and deletions.

Let us study both the implementations.

7.5.1 Array Implementation of Binary Trees

One of the ways to represent a tree using an array is to store the nodes level-by-level, starting from the level 0 where the root is present. Such a representation requires sequential numbering of the nodes, starting with the nodes on level 0, then those on level 1, and so on.

We have defined a complete tree. A complete binary tree of height h has $(2^{h+1} - 1)$ nodes in it. The nodes can be stored in a one-dimensional array, *tree*, with the node numbered at the location *tree*(i). An array of size $2^{h+1} - 1$ is needed for the same.

The root node is stored in the first memory location as the first element in the array. The following rules can be used to decide the location of any i^{th} node of a tree:
For any node with index i, $0 \leq i \leq n - 1$,

1. Parent(i) = $\lfloor (t - 1)/2 \rfloor$ if $i \neq 0$; if $i = 0$, then it is the root that has no parent.
2. Lchild(i) = $2 \times i + 1$ if $2i + 1 \leq n - 1$; if $2i \geq n$, then i has no left child.
3. Rchild(i) = $2i + 2$ if $2i + 2 \leq n - 1$; if $(2i + 1) \geq n$, then i has no right child.

Let us consider the complete binary tree in Fig. 7.24.

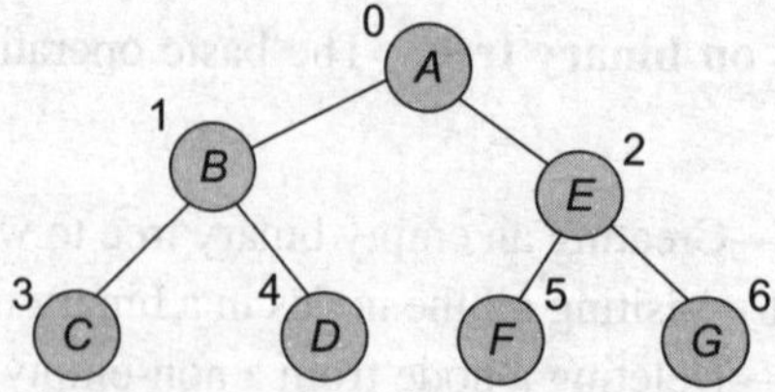

Fig. 7.24 Complete binary tree

The representation of the binary tree in Fig. 7.24 using an array is as follows:

0	1	2	3	4	5	6	7	8
A	B	E	C	D	F	G	–	–

Let us consider one more example as in Fig. 7.25.

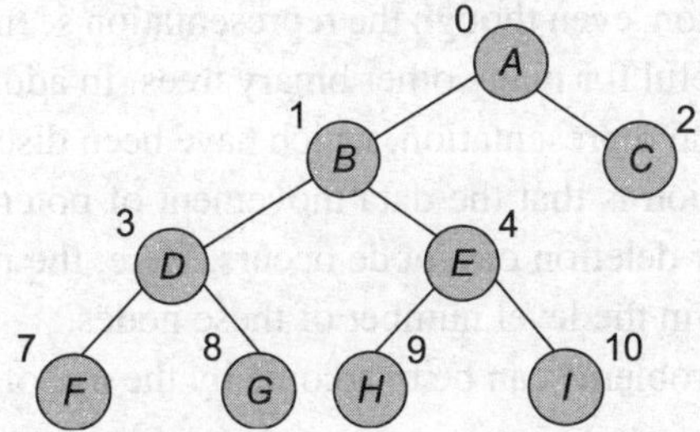

Fig. 7.25 Tree with 11 nodes

Now, the array representation of the tree in Fig. 7.25 is as follows:

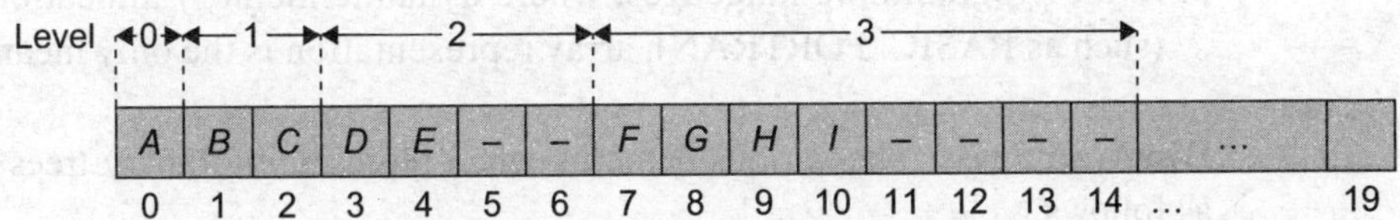

Let us consider one more example of a skewed tree as in Fig. 7.26.

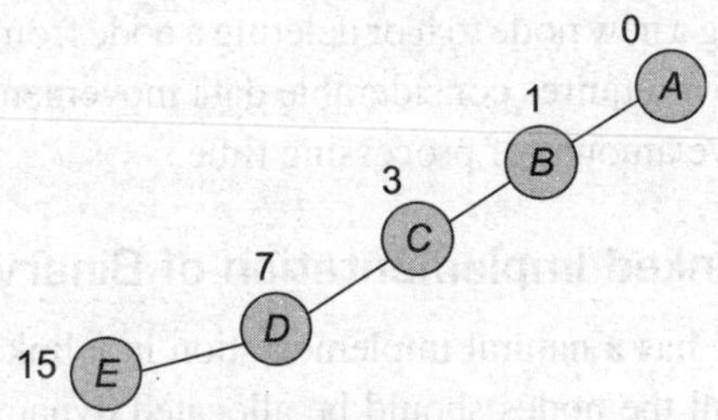

Fig. 7.26 Sample skewed tree

This tree has the following array representation:

0	1	2	3	4	5	6	7	8	9	10	11	12	13	14	15		19
A	B	–	C	–	–	–	D	–	–	–	–	–	–	–	E	...	–

This representation of binary trees using an array seems to be the easiest. Certainly, it can be used for all binary trees. However, such a representation has certain drawbacks. In most of the representations, there will be a lot of unused space. For complete binary trees, the representation seems to be good as no space in an array is wasted between the nodes. Certainly, the space is wasted as we generally declare an array of some arbitrary maximum limit. From the examples, we can make out that for the skewed tree, however, less than half of the array is only used and more is left unused. In the worst case, a skewed tree of depth k will require $2^{k+1} - 1$ locations of array, and occupy just a few of them.

In addition, even though the representation seems to be good for complete binary trees, it is not useful for many other binary trees. In addition, the representation has drawbacks of sequential representation, which have been discussed. A major drawback of sequential representation is that the data movement of potentially many nodes is needed when the insertion or deletion of a node occurs. Here, the movement of nodes is needed to reflect the change in the level number of these nodes.

These problems can be overcome by the use of linked representation.

Advantages The various merits of representing binary trees using arrays are as follows:

1. Any node can be accessed from any other node by calculating the index.
2. Here, the data is stored without any pointers to its successor or predecessor.
3. In the programming languages, where dynamic memory allocation is not possible (such as BASIC, FORTRAN), array representation is the only means to store a tree.

Disadvantages The various demerits when representing binary trees using arrays are as follows:

1. Other than full binary trees, majority of the array entries may be empty.
2. It allows only static representation. The array size cannot be changed during the execution.
3. Inserting a new node to it or deleting a node from it is inefficient with this representation, because it requires considerable data movement up and down the array, which demand excessive amount of processing time.

7.5.2 Linked Implementation of Binary Trees

Binary tree has a natural implementation in a linked storage. In a linked organization, we wish that all the nodes should be allocated dynamically. Hence, we need each node with data and link fields. Each node of a binary tree has both a left and a right subtree. Each node will have three fields—Lchild, Data, and Rchild. Pictorially, this node is shown in Fig. 7.27.

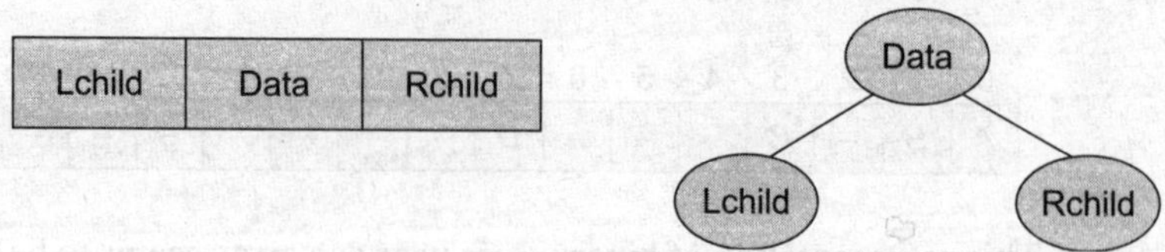

Fig. 7.27 Tree node

A node does not provide information about the parent node. However, it is still adequate for most of the applications. If needed, the fourth parent field can be included. The binary tree in Fig. 7.28 will have the linked representation as in Fig. 7.29. The root of the tree is stored in the data member *root* of the tree. This data member provides an access pointer to the tree.

Here, 0 (zero) stored at Lchild or Rchild fields represents that the respective child is not present. Let us consider one more example as in Fig. 7.29.

In this node structure, Lchild and Rchild are the two link fields to store the addresses of left child and right child of a node; data is the information content of the node. With this representation, if we know the address of the root node, then using it, any other node can be accessed.

Each node of a binary tree (as the root of some subtree) has both left and right subtrees, which can be accessed through pointers as follows.

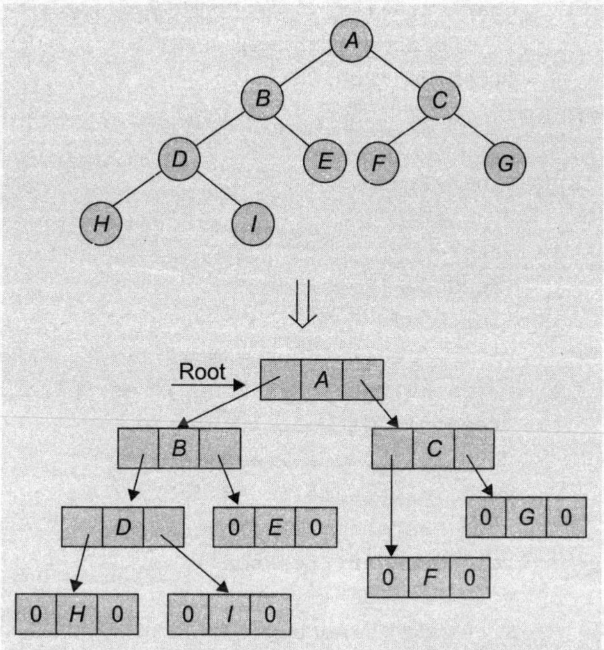

Fig. 7.28 Sample tree 1 and its linked representation

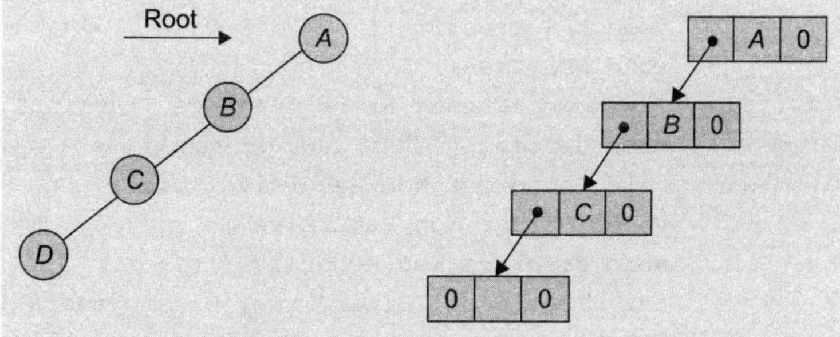

Fig. 7.29 Sample tree 2 and its linked representation

Program Code 7.1 described the ADT for a binary tree. Program Code 7.2 is a class for the binary tree that shows specifications for the ADT. Implementation of these functions is covered in the forthcoming topics.

PROGRAM CODE 7.2

```
class TreeNode
{
   public:
      char Data;
         TreeNode *Lchild;
      TreeNode *Rchild;
};

class BinaryTree
{
   private:
      TreeNode *Root;
   public:
      BinaryTree() {Root = Null;}        // constructor
      // int BTree_Equal(BinaryTree, BinaryTree);
      TreeNode *GetNode();
      void InsertNode(TreeNode*);
      void DeleteNode(TreeNode*);
      void Postorder(TreeNode*);
      void Inorder(TreeNode*);
      void Preorder(TreeNode*);
      TreeNode *TreeCopy();
      void Mirror();
      int TreeHeight(TreeNode*);
      int CountLeaf(TreeNode*);
      int CountNode(TreeNode*);
      void BFS_Tree();
      void DFS_Tree();
      TreeNode *Create_Btree_InandPre_Traversal(char
      preorder[max], char inorder[max]);
      void Postorder_Non_Recursive(void);
      void Inorder_Non_Recursive();
      void Preorder_Non_Recursive();
      int BTree_Equal(BinaryTree, BinaryTree);
      TreeNode *TreeCopy(TreeNode*);
      void Mirror(TreeNode*);
};
```

Using this declaration for a linked representation, the binary tree representation can be logically viewed as in Fig. 7.30. The physical representation shows the memory allocation of nodes.

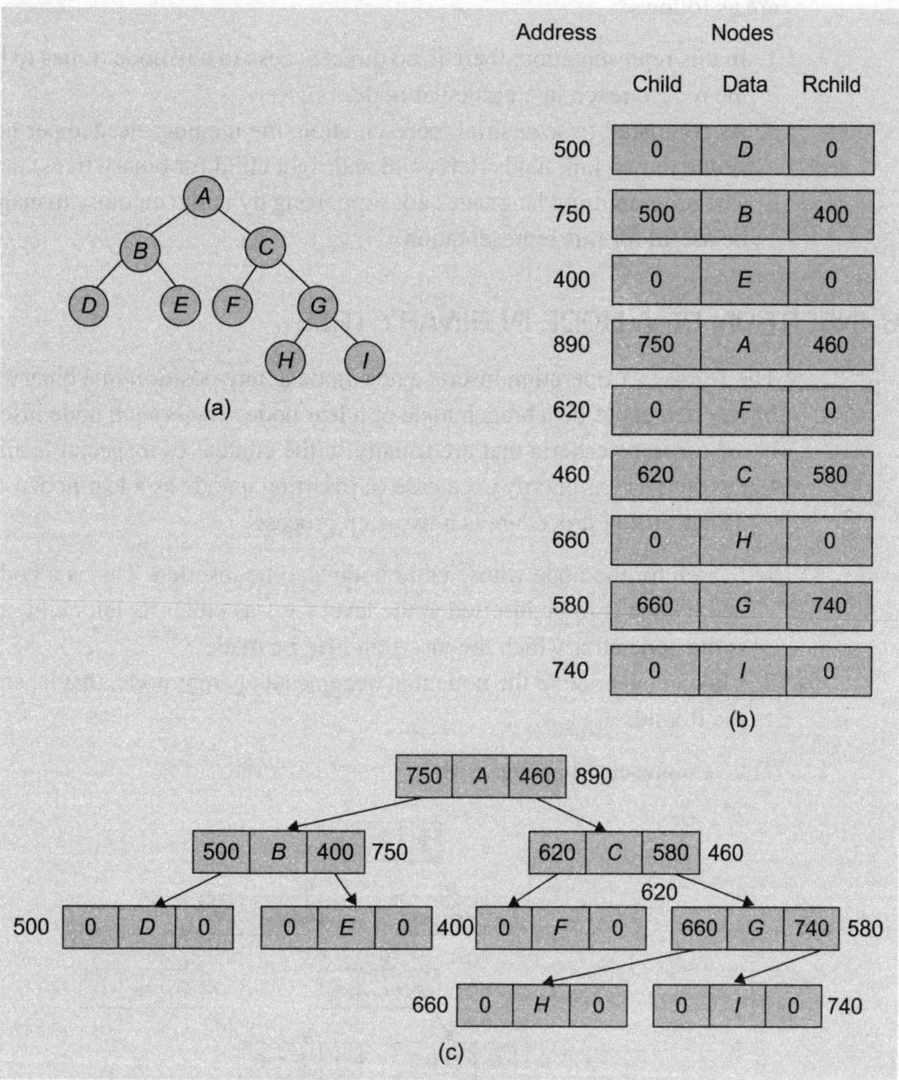

Fig. 7.30 Tree and its views (a) Binary tree (b) Physical view (c) Logical view

Advantages The merits of representing binary trees through liked representations are as follows:

1. The drawbacks of the sequential representation are overcome in this representation. We may or may not know the tree depth in advance. In addition, for unbalanced trees, the memory is not wasted.

2. Insertion and deletion operations are more efficient in this representation.
3. It is useful for dynamic data.

Disadvantages The demerits of representing binary trees through linked representation are as follows:

1. In this representation, there is no direct access to any node. It has to be traversed from the root to reach to a particular node.
2. As compared to sequential representation, the memory needed per node is more. This is due to two link fields (left child and right child for binary trees) in the node.
3. The programming languages not supporting dynamic memory management would not be useful for this representation.

7.6 INSERTION OF A NODE IN BINARY TREE

The `insert()` operation inserts a new node at any position in a binary tree. The node to be inserted could be a branch node or a leaf node. The branch node insertion is generally based on some criteria that are usually in the context of a special form of a binary tree. Let us study a commonly used case of inserting a node as a leaf node.

The insertion procedure is a two-step process.

1. Search for the node whose child node is to be inserted. This is a node at some level i, and a node is to be inserted at the level $i + 1$ as either its left child or right child. This is the node after which the insertion is to be made.
2. Link a new node to the node that becomes its parent node, that is, either the Lchild or the Rchild.

This is represented in Fig. 7.31.

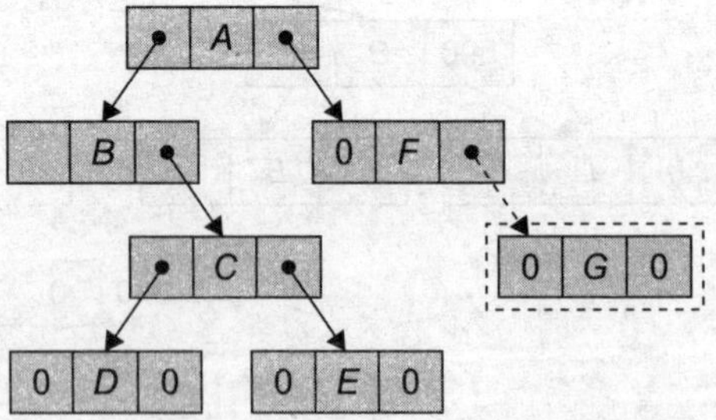

Fig. 7.31 Insertion of node *G* as the Rchild of node *F*

7.7 BINARY TREE TRAVERSAL

Traversal is a frequently used operation. Traversal of a tree means *stepping through the nodes of a tree* by means of the connections between parents and children, which is also called *walking the tree*, and the action is *a walk of the tree*. Traversal means visiting every node of a binary tree. There are many operations that are often performed on a tree such as search a node, print some information, insert a node, delete a node, and so on. All such operations need the traversal through a tree.

This operation is used to visit each node (exactly once). A full traversal of a tree visits nodes of a tree in a certain linear order. This linear order could be familiar and useful. For example, if the binary tree contains an arithmetic expression, then its traversal may give us the expression in infix, postfix, or prefix notations.

There are various traversal methods. For a systematic traversal, it is better to visit each node (starting from the root) and its two subtrees in the same way. In other words, when traversing, we need to treat each node and its subtree in the same fashion. If we let L, D, and R stand for moving left, data, and moving right, respectively (Fig. 7.32), when at a node, then there are six possible combinations—LDR, LRD, DLR, DRL, RDL, and RLD.

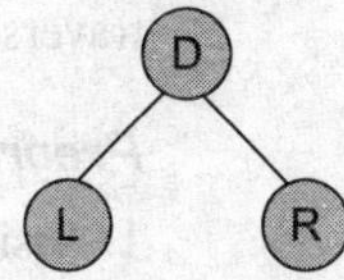

Fig. 7.32 Components of a subtree

Consider the binary tree shown in Fig. 7.33. This tree represents a binary tree. We have studied all the notations of an expression tree and its inter-conversions in Chapter 3.

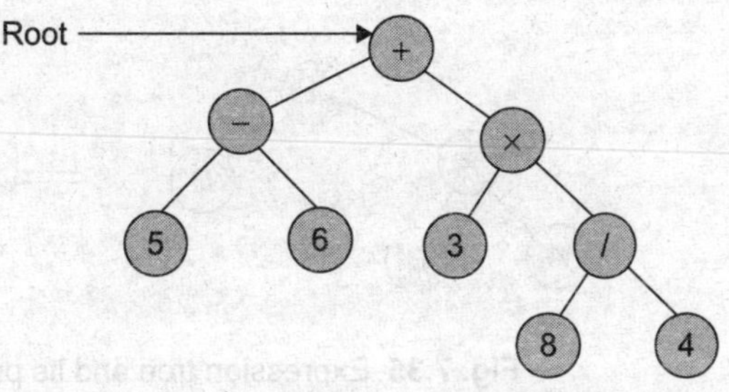

Fig. 7.33 A binary tree representing an arithmetic expression

Let us see the result of each of the six traversals.

LDR:	5 − 6 + 3 × 8 / 4
LRD:	5 6 − 3 8 4 / × +
DLR:	+ − 5 6 × 3 / 8 4
DRL:	+ × / 4 8 3 − 6 5
RDL:	4 / 8 × 3 + 6 − 5
RLD:	4 8 / 3 × 6 5 − +

We can notice that DLR and RLD, LDR and RDL, and LRD and DRL are mirror symmetric. If we adopt the convention that traversing is done left before right, only then, the three traversals, that is, LDR, LRD, and DLR, are fundamental. These are called as *inorder*, *postorder*, and *preorder* traversals because there is a natural correspondence between these traversals producing the infix, postfix, and prefix forms of an arithmetic expression, respectively.

7.7.1 Preorder Traversal

In this traversal, the root is visited first followed by the left subtree in preorder and then the right subtree in preorder. The tree characteristics lead to naturally implement the tree traversals recursively. It can be defined in the following steps:

Preorder (DLR) Algorithm

1. Visit the root node, say *D*.
2. Traverse the left subtree of the node in preorder.
3. Traverse the right subtree of the node in preorder.

Let us consider the tree in Fig. 7.34.

A preorder traversal of the tree in Fig. 7.34 visits the node in a sequence: *A B D E G C F*. For an expression tree, the preorder traversal yields a prefix expression (Fig. 7.35).

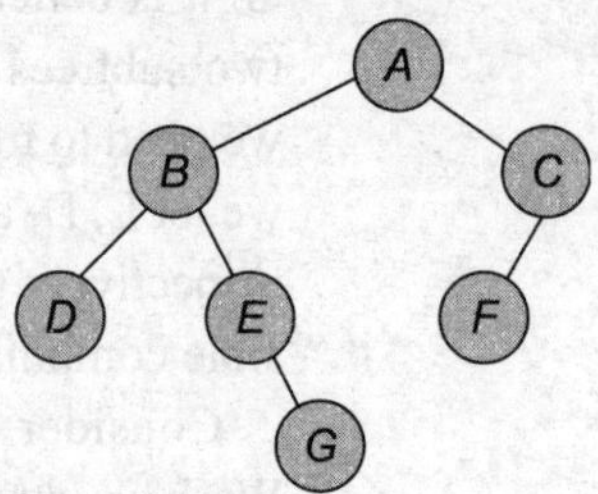

Fig. 7.34 Binary tree

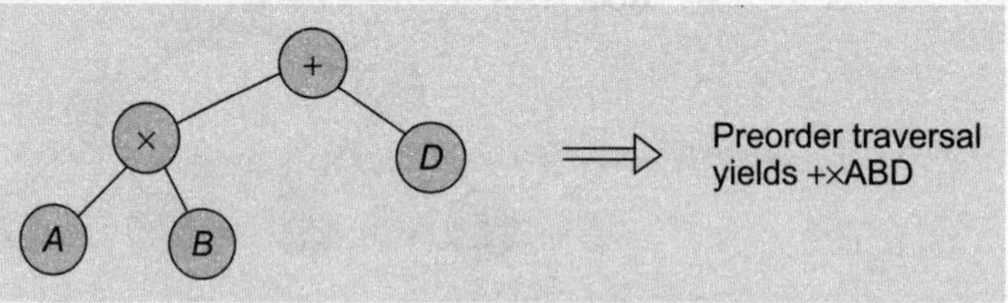

Fig. 7.35 Expression tree and its preorder traversal

The preorder traversal says, 'visit a node, traverse left, and continue moving. When you cannot continue, move right and begin again or move back, until you can move right and stop'. The `Preorder()` function can be written as both recursive and non recursive.

```
void BinaryTree :: Preorder(TreeNode*)
{
    if(Root != Null)
    {
        cout << Root->Data;
        Preorder(Root->Lchild);
        Preorder(Root->Rchild);
    }
}
```

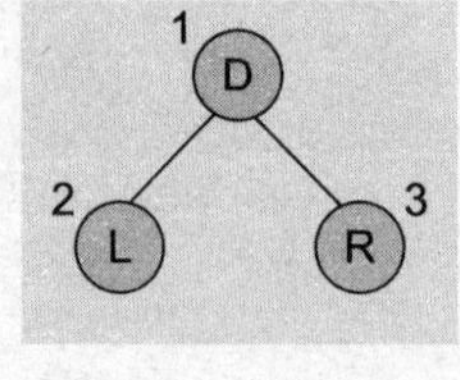

Let us consider the tree in Fig. 7.36. This tree contains an arithmetic expression with the binary operators add (+), multiply (×), divide (/), exponentiation (^), and variables *A*, *B*, *C*, *D*, and *E*.

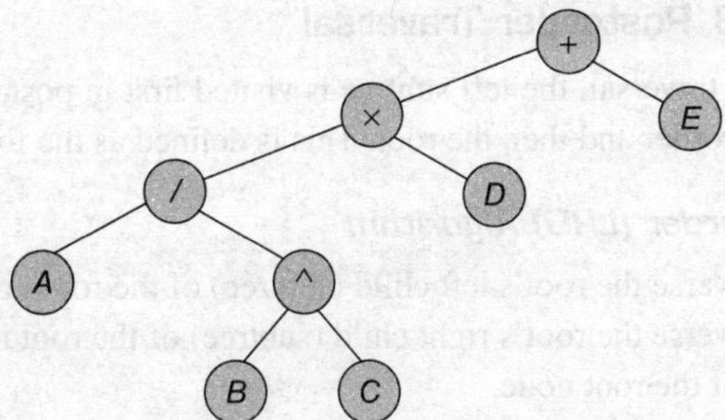

Fig. 7.36 Binary tree for expression

It gives us the prefix expression $+\times/A \wedge BCDE$. The preorder traversal is also called as *depth-first traversal*.

7.7.2 Inorder Traversal

In this traversal, the left subtree is visited first in inorder followed by the root and then the right subtree in inorder. This can be defined as the following:

Inorder (LDR) Algorithm

1. Traverse the left subtree of the root node in inorder.
2. Visit the root node *node*.
3. Traverse the right subtree of the root node in inorder.

Let us consider the binary tree in Fig. 7.34. An *inorder traversal* of a tree visits the node in the following sequence.

Inorder sequence: D B E G A F C An inorder expression traversal of the tree in Fig. 7.35, which is an expression tree, yields an inorder expression as $A \times B + D$ and for Fig. 7.36 yields an inorder expression as $((A/B \wedge C) \times D) + E$.

The `Inorder()` function simply calls for moving down the tree towards the left until it can no longer proceed. So next, we visit the node, move one node to the right, and continue again. If we cannot move, move one node to the right and continue again. If we cannot move to the right, go back one more node and then continue. The inorder traversal is also called as *symmetric traversal*. This traversal can be written as a recursive function as follows:

```
void BinaryTree :: Inorder(TreeNode*)
{
    if(Root != Null)
    {
        Inorder(Root→Lchild);
        cout << Root→Data;
        Inorder(Root→Rchild);
    }
}
```

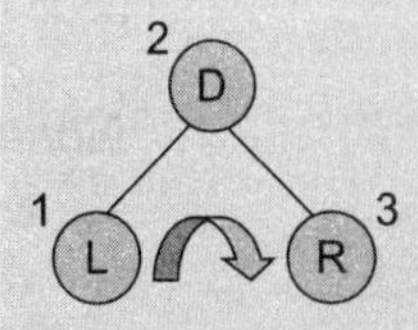

7.7.3 Postorder Traversal

In this traversal, the left subtree is visited first in postorder followed by the right subtree in postorder and then the root. This is defined as the following:

Postorder (LRD) Algorithm

1. Traverse the root's left child (subtree) of the root node in postorder.
2. Traverse the root's right child (subtree) of the root node in postorder.
3. Visit the root node.

Let us consider the binary tree in Fig. 7.34. The postorder traversal yields the following sequence:

Postorder sequence: D G E B F C A For the expression tree in Fig. 7.35, the postorder traversal yields a postfix expression as the following:

$$= A\ B \times D +$$

For the tree in Fig. 7.36, the postfix expression by the postorder traversal is *ABC××/ D×E+*. The postorder traversal says, "traverse left and continue again. When you cannot continue, move right and begin again or move back until you can move right and visit the node."

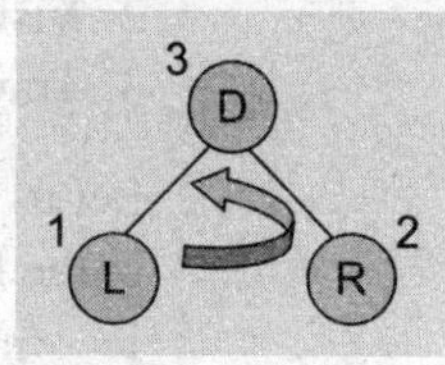


```
void BinaryTree :: Postorder(TreeNode*)
{
    if(Root != Null)
    {
        Postorder(Root→Lchild);
        Postorder(Root→Rchild);
        cout << Root→Data;
    }
}
```

7.7.4 Non-recursive Implementation of Traversals

We have defined the recursive traversals. These are easy to read and understand. However, a language translator such as a compiler will be burdened to carry out the execution. Let us go for the other non-recursive approach for these algorithms. Let us write a non-recursive implementation using stacks. Here, at the time of left or right traversal, when the left or right node is the root of the other subtree, the current node is to be stacked for further traversal.

Non-recursive Preorder Algorithm

```
1. Tmp = Root
2. while(stack not empty) do
   begin
      if(Tmp is not null) then
      begin
         visit(Tmp→Data)
         Push(Tmp→Lchild)
```

```
         Tmp = Tmp->Lchild
      else if(stack is empty)
         then exit
      else
         Tmp = Pop()
         Tmp = Tmp->Rchild
      end
   end
3. stop
```

The C++ implementation of the non-recursive preorder algorithm is given in Program Code 7.3.

PROGRAM CODE 7.3

```
void BinaryTree :: Preorder_Non_Recursive()
{
   TreeNode *Tmp = Root;
   stack S;
   while(1)
   {
      while(Tmp != Null)
      // traverse left till left is null and push
      {
         S.Push(Tmp);
         cout << Tmp ->Data;
         Tmp = Tmp->Lchild;
      }
      if(S.IsEmpty()) return;
      //if stack is not empty then pop one and go to
      right
      Tmp = S.Pop();
      Tmp = Tmp->Rchild;
      // if stack is empty stop the process
   }
}
```

We need stack and queue for tree operations such as depth-first and breadth-first traversals. Program Code 7.4 uses these two data structures:

PROGRAM CODE 7.4

```
class stack
{
   public:
      TreeNode *stk[max];
```

```
        int data,top;
        stack *S;
    public:
        stack()
        {
            top = -1;
        }
        int IsEmpty()
        {
            if(top == -1)
                return 1;
            else
                return 0;
        }
        void Push(TreeNode *x)
        {
            stk[top++] = x;
        }
        TreeNode *Pop()
        {
            TreeNode *x;
            x = stk[top--];
            return(x);
        }
};

class stack1
{
    public:
        char stk1[max];
        int data,top;
    public:
        stack1()
        {
            top = -1;
        }
        int IsEmpty1()
        {
            if(top == -1)
                return 1;
            else
                return 0;
        }
```

```
      void Push1(char x)
      {
         stk1[top++] = x;
      }
      char Pop1()
      {
         char x;
         x = stk1[top--];
         return(x);
      }
};

class queue
{
   TreeNode *que[max];
   int data, rear, front;
   public:
      queue()
      {
         rear = front = -1;
      }
      int Empty()
      {
         if(rear == front)
            return 1;
         else
            return 0;
      }
      int Full()
      {
         if(rear == max)
            return 1;
         else
            return 0;
      }
     void Add(TreeNode *x)
      {
         if(Full())
            cout << "\n Queue Overflow";
        else
          que[++rear] = x;
      }
      TreeNode *Del()
```

```
        {
            TreeNode *x;
            if(Empty())
            {
                cout << "\n Queue is empty";
                //return -1;
            }
            else
            {
                x = que[front++];
                return(x);
            }
        }
};
```

Non-recursive Inorder Algorithm

Algorithm 7.1 is for non-recursive inorder traversal of a binary tree.

ALGORITHM 7.1

```
1. Tmp = Root
2. while(1) do
   begin
      while(Tmp != Null) then
      begin
         push(Tmp)
         Tmp = Tmp→Lchild
      end
      if(stack is empty) then exit
      Tmp = Pop()
      visit(Tmp→data)
      Tmp = Tmp→Rchild
   end while
3. Stop
```

The C++ implementation of Algorithm 7.1 is stated in Program Code 7.5.

PROGRAM CODE 7.5

```
void BinaryTree :: Inorder_Non_Recursive()
{
    TreeNode *Tmp;
    stack S;
    Tmp = Root;
   while(1)
```

```
    {
       while(Tmp != Null)
       {
          S.Push(Tmp);
          Tmp = Tmp->Lchild;
       }
       if(S.IsEmpty())
          return;
          //if stack is not empty then pop one and go to
right
       Tmp = S.Pop();
       cout << Tmp->Data;
       Tmp = Tmp->Rchild;
    }
}
```

Non-recursive Postorder Algorithm

Algorithm 7.2 is for non-recursive postorder traversal of a binary tree. As compared to earlier algorithms, in postorder traversal, we require the `Pop` operation when returning from the left and right subtrees.

ALGORITHM 7.2

1. When we return from the left subtree, perform the following operations:
   (a) `Tmp = Pop`
   (b) `Tmp = Tmp→Rchild.`
2. When we return from the right subtree, perform the following operations:
   (a) `Tmp = Pop`
   (b) `Print Tmp→data` (that is, visit and process the node, if required)
   (c) `Tmp = Pop`

Hence, we need to differentiate between the `return` operation from the left subtree and right subtree. Let us use the stack that stores the status: 'L' for left, and 'R' for right. For performing the extra `Pop` operation while returning from the right subtree, we need to assign `Tmp = Null`. Program Code 7.6 demonstrates this.

PROGRAM CODE 7.6

```
void BinaryTree :: Postorder_Non_Recursive(void)
{
   TreeNode * Tmp = Root;
   stack S;
```

```
    stack1 S1;
    char flag;
    // stack S stores the node and S1 stores the flag 'L' or 'R'
    while(1)
    {
        while(Tmp != Null)
        // traverse tree left till not Null
        {
            S.Push(Tmp);
            S1.Push1('L');
            // push node in S and 'L' in S1
            Tmp = Tmp->Lchild;
        }
        if(S.IsEmpty())
            return;
        else
        {
            Tmp = S.Pop();
            //pop node
            flag = S1.Pop1();
            if(flag == 'R')
            // if flag is 'R' display data
            {
                cout << Tmp->Data;
                Tmp = Null;
            }
            else      // if flag is 'L'
            {
                S.Push( Tmp);
                // push Tmp with flag 'R'
                S1.Push1('R');
                Tmp = Tmp->Rchild;
                // move to right
            }
        }
    }
}
```

7.7.5 Formation of Binary Tree from its Traversals

Sometimes, we need to construct a binary tree if its traversals are known. From a single traversal, a unique binary tree cannot be constructed. However, if two traversals are known, then the corresponding tree can be drawn uniquely. Let us examine these possibilities and then chalk out the algorithm for the same.

The basic principle for formulation is as follows:

1. If the preorder traversal is given, then the first node is the root node. If the postorder traversal is given, then the last node is the root node.
2. Once the root node is identified, all the nodes in all left and right subtrees of the root node can be identified.
3. Same techniques can be applied repeatedly to form the subtrees.

We can conclude that for the binary tree, construction and traversals are essential out of which one should be inorder traversal and another should be preorder or postorder traversal. Alternatively, for the given preorder and postorder traversals, the binary tree cannot be obtained uniquely.

Consider the following sequences of traversal as in Example 7.1.

EXAMPLE 7.1 Construct a binary tree using the following two traversals:

Inorder : *D B H E A I F J C G*
Preorder: *A B D E H C F I J G*

Solution From the preorder traversal, it is evident that *A* is the root node. In addition, in the inorder traversal, all the nodes that are to the left side of *A* belong to the left subtree and those to the right side of *A* belong to the right subtree (Fig. 7.37).

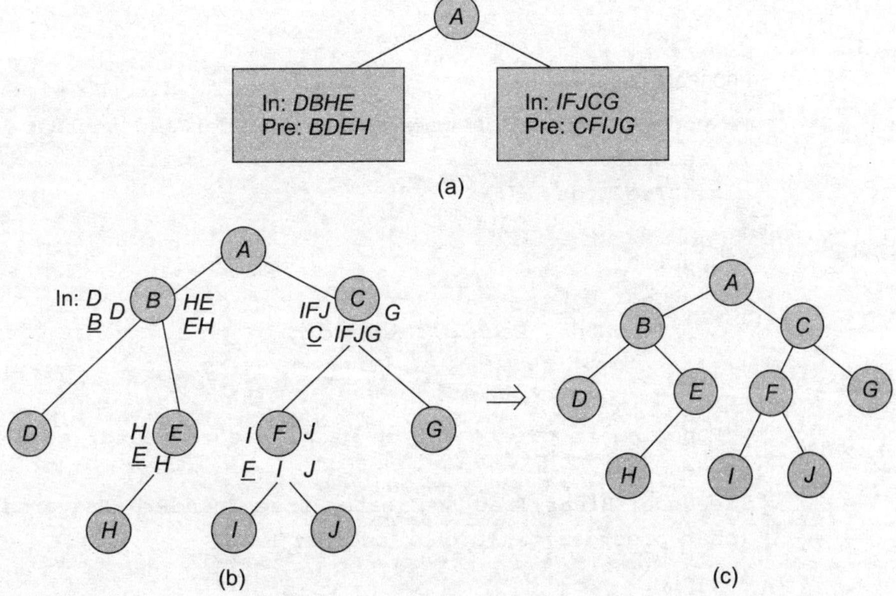

Fig. 7.37 Binary tree from inorder and preorder traversals (a) Two subtrees as a being the root from two traversals (b) Repeated application (c) Final binary tree

Example 7.2 shows the construction of a binary tree from a sequence of inorder and postorder traversals.

EXAMPLE 7.2 Construct a binary tree from its inorder and postorder traversals.

Inorder : 1 2 3 4 5 6 7 8 9

Postorder: 1 3 5 4 2 8 7 9 6

Solution As 6 is the last node traversed in postorder, 6 is the root (Fig. 7.38). The final binary tree constructed is as in Fig. 7.39.

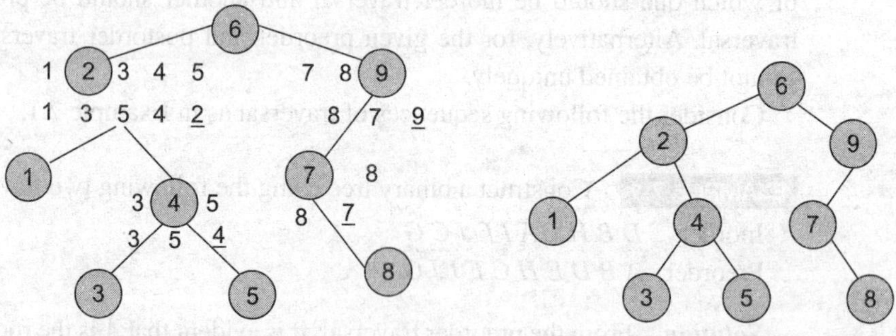

Fig. 7.38 Sample tree

Fig. 7.39 Final binary tree

Using the inorder and preorder traversals, a binary tree can be constructed. Program Code 7.7 is the implementation of the same.

PROGRAM CODE 7.7

```
// code to construct tree using preorder and inorder
// sequences
class TreeNode
{
   public:
      char Data;
      TreeNode *Lchild, *Rchild;
};

//Function to create a tree using preorder and inorder
sequences
TreeNode *BinaryTree :: Create_Btree_InandPre_Traversal
(char preorder[max], char inorder[max])
{
   //to store divided inorder and preorder sequence
   char in1[max],in2[max],pre1[max],pre2[max];
```

```
    TreeNode *Tmp;
    int i,j,k;
    if(strlen(preorder) == 0)
       return Null;
       Tmp = new TreeNode;
       Tmp->Data = preorder[0];
       //following code is for dividing inorder sequence
       for(i = 0;inorder[i] != preorder[0]; i++)
          in1[i] = inorder[i];
       in1[i] = '\0';
       i++;
       k = 0;
       for(j = i; inorder[j] != '\0'; j++)
          in2[k++] = inorder[j];
       in2[k] = '\0';
       cout << " in " << in1 << "    " << in2;
      //following code is for dividing preorder sequence
       i = j = 0;k = 1;
       for(k = 1; preorder[k] != '\0'; k++)
       {
          if(strchr(in1,preorder[k]) != Null)
          // strchr function used to check char is
          present in string or not
             pre1[i++]=preorder[k];
          else
             pre2[j++]=preorder[k];
       }
       pre1[i]='\0';
       pre2[j]='\0';
       Tmp->Lchild = Create_Btree_InandPre_Traversal
       (pre1,in1);
       Tmp->Rchild = Create_Btree_InandPre_Traversal
       (pre2,in2);
       return Tmp;
 }
```

7.7.6 Breadth- and Depth-first Traversals

As defined earlier, we know that the traversal of a tree means visiting through the nodes of a tree. A traversal where the node is visited before its children is called a *breadth-first traversal*; a walk where the children are visited prior to the parent is called a *depth-first traversal*.

Depth-first Traversal

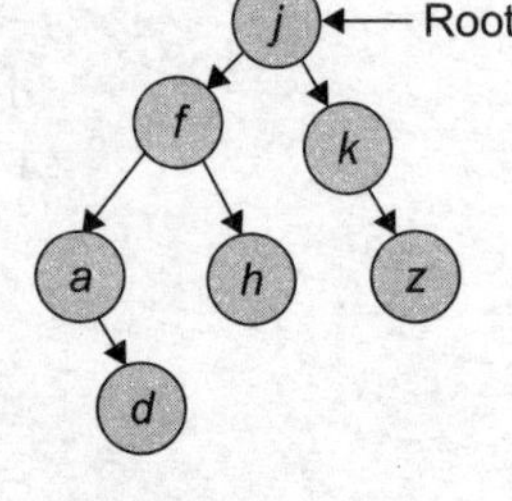

Fig. 7.40 Sample tree

A traversal where the children are visited (operated on) before the parent is called the *depth-first traversal*. We have already seen a few ways to traverse the elements of a tree. For example, look at the tree in Fig. 7.40.

A preorder traversal would visit the elements in the order: *j*, *f*, *a*, *d*, *h*, *k*, *z*.

This type of traversal is called a *depth-first traversal* as it tries to go deeper in the tree before exploring the siblings. For example, the traversal visits all the descendants of *f* (i.e., keeps going deeper) before visiting *f*'s sibling *k* (and any of *k*'s descendants).

The two other traversal orders are *inorder* and *postorder*. An inorder traversal would give us the following sequence: *a*, *d*, *f*, *h*, *j*, *k*, *z*. A postorder traversal would give us the following sequence: *d*, *a*, *h*, *f*, *z*, *k*, *j*. These traversals also try to go *deeper* first.

For example, the inorder traversal visits *a* and *d* before it explores *a*'s sibling *h*. Likewise, it visits all of the *j*'s left subtree (i.e., *a*, *d*, *f*, *h*) before exploring *j*'s right subtree (i.e., *k*, *z*). The same is true for the postorder traversal. It visits all of the *j*'s left subtree (i.e., *d*, *a*, *h*, *f*) before exploring any part of the right subtree (i.e., *z*, *k*).

Let us see how it is implemented non-recursively using stack. Program Code 7.8 is the implementation of non-recursive depth-first traversal using stack.

PROGRAM CODE 7.8

```
void BinaryTree :: DFS_Tree()
{
    stack S;
    TreeNode *Tmp=Root;
    do
    {
        cout << Tmp->Data;
        if(Tmp->Rchild != Null)
            S.Push(Tmp->Rchild);
        if(Tmp->Lchild != Null)
            S.Push(Tmp->Lchild);
        if(S.IsEmpty()) break;
        Tmp = S.Pop();
    }
    while(1);
}
```

Breadth-first Traversal

Depth-first is not the only way to go through the elements of a tree. Another way is to go through them level-by-level (Fig. 7.41). For example, each element exists at a certain level (or depth) in the tree.

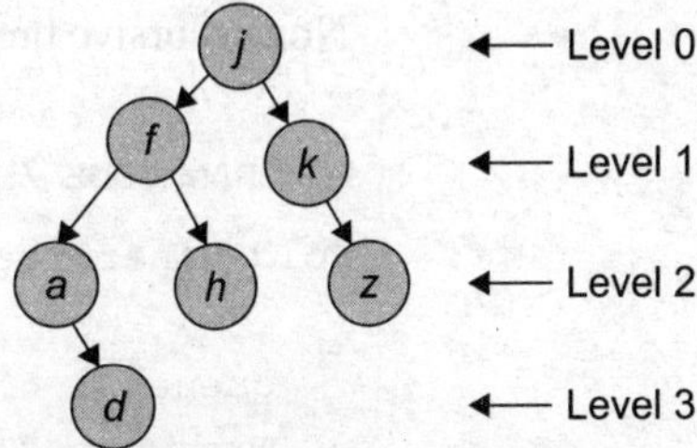

Fig. 7.41 Tree of level 3

So, if we want to visit the elements level-by-level (and left to right, as usual), we would start at level 0 with *j*, then go to level 1 for *f* and *k*, then go to level 2 for *a*, *h*, and *z*, and finally go to level 3 for *d*. This level-by-level traversal is called a *breadth-first traversal* because we explore the breadth, that is, the full width of the tree at a given level, before going deeper. One may think about why we should ever traverse a tree breadth wise. Well, there are many reasons for the same.

Tree of officers Suppose you have a tree representing some command structure as in Fig. 7.42.

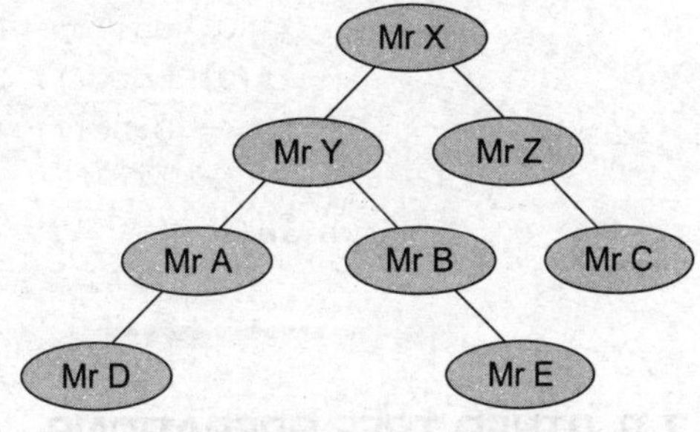

Fig. 7.42 Officers tree

This tree is meant to represent who is in charge of the lower ranking of officers. For example, Mr X is directly responsible for Mr Y and Mr Z. People of the same rank are at the same level in the tree. However, to distinguish between people of the same rank, those with more experience are on the left and those with less experience are on the right (i.e., experience from left to right). One way the command would follow to trace the path is to list the officers in the tree in the breadth-first order. This would give the following result:

Mr X at the top level, say manager; then his subordinates, say department heads as. Mr Y and Mr Z and their subordinates as Mr A, Mr B, Mr C, Mr D, and Mr E.

In this case, traversing the tree breadth-first makes more sense as we want to print the results post wise from the highest level. As we have seen, the tree traversals go deeper in the tree first using stack as a helper data structure. Instead, if we are going to implement a breadth-first traversal of a tree, we will need the queue as a helper data structure. Let us consider the tree drawn as in Fig. 7.43.

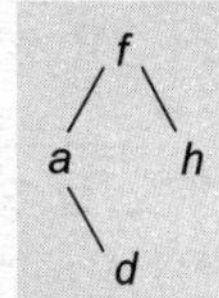

Fig. 7.43 Breadth-first traversal—sample tree

When we are at element *f*, that is the only time we have the access to its two immediate children, *a* and *h*. So, when we are at *f*, we need the data structure that holds its children. Obviously then, *f* must have been in the data structure before them, since we would have put *f* in when we were at *f*'s parent. So, if we put the parent in the data structure before its children, we need to select the data structure that will give us the order we need. A queue will give us the order we want! A queue enforces the first-in-first-out (FIFO) order, and we have to process the parent first before its descendants.

Non-recursive breadth-first traversal is implemented in Program Code 7.9 using a queue.

PROGRAM CODE 7.9

```
void BinaryTree :: BFS_Tree()
{
   queue Q;
   TreeNode *Tmp = Root;
   do
   {
      cout << Tmp->Data;
      if((Tmp->Lchild) != Null)
         Q.Add(Tmp->Lchild);
      if(Tmp->Rchild != Null)
         Q.Add(Tmp->Rchild);
      if(Q.Empty()) break;
      Tmp = Q.Del();
   }
   while(1);
}
```

7.8 OTHER TREE OPERATIONS

Using traversal as a basic operation, many other operations can be performed on a tree, such as finding the height of the tree, computing the total number of nodes, leaf nodes, and so on. Let us study a few of such operations.

7.8.1 Counting Nodes

`CountNode()` is the function that returns the total count of nodes in a linked binary tree.

```
int  BinaryTree :: CountNode(TreeNode *Root)
{
  if(Root == Null)
     return 0;
  else
     return(1 + CountNode(Root->Rchild) + CountNode(Root->Lchild));
}
```

7.8.2 Counting Leaf Nodes

The `CountLeaf()` operation counts the total number of leaf nodes in a linked binary tree. *Leaf nodes* are those with no left or right children.

```
int BinaryTree :: CountLeaf(TreeNode *Root)
{
  if(Root == Null)
     return 0;
```

```
    else if((Root->Rchild == Null) && (Root->Lchild == Null))
        return(1);
    else
        return(CountLeaf(Root->Lchild) + CountLeaf(Root->Rchild));
}
```

7.8.3 Computing Height of Binary Tree

The `TreeHeight()` operation computes the height of a linked binary tree. *Height* of a tree is the maximum path length in the tree. We can get the path length by traversing the tree depthwise. Let us consider that an empty tree's height is 0 and the tree with only one node has the height 1.

```
int BinaryTree :: TreeHeight(TreeNode *Root)
{
    int heightL, heightR;
    if(Root == Null)
        return 0;
    if(Root->Lchild == Null && Root->Rchild == Null)
        return 0;
    heightL = TreeHeight(Root->Lchild);
    heightR = TreeHeight(Root->Rchild);
    if(heightR > heightL)
        return(heightR + 1);
    return(heightL + 1);
}
```

7.8.4 Getting Mirror, Replica, or Tree Interchange of Binary Tree

The `Mirror()` operation finds the mirror of the tree that will interchange all left and right subtrees in a linked binary tree.

```
void BinaryTree :: Mirror(TreeNode *Root)
{
    TreeNode *Tmp;
    if(Root != Null)
    {
        Tmp = Root->Lchild;
        Root->Lchild = Root->Rchild;
        Root->Rchild = Tmp;
        Mirror(Root->Lchild);
        Mirror(Root->Rchild);
    }
}
```

7.8.5 Copying Binary Tree

The `TreeCopy()` operation makes a copy of the linked binary tree. The function should allocate the necessary nodes and copy the respective contents into them.

```
TreeNode *BinaryTree :: TreeCopy()
{
    TreeNode *Tmp;
    if(Root == Null)
```

```
        return Null;
    Tmp = new TreeNode;
    Tmp→Lchild = TreeCopy(Root→Lchild);
    Tmp→Rchild = TreeCopy(Root→Rchild);
    Tmp→Data = Root→Data;
    return Tmp;
}
```

7.8.6 Equality Test

The `BTree_Equal()` operation checks whether two binary trees are equal. Two trees are said to be equal if they have the same topology, and all the corresponding nodes are equal. The same topology refers to the fact that each branch in the first tree corresponds to a branch in the second tree in the same order and vice versa.

```
int BinaryTree :: BTree_Equal(Binarytree T1 , BinaryTree T2)
{
    if(Root == Null && T2.Root == Null)
        return 1;
    return(Root && T2.Root);
    &&(Root->Data == T2.Root->Data);
    &&BTree_Equal(Root->Lchild ,T2.Root->Lchild);
    &&BTree_Equal(Root->Rchild, T2.Root->Rchild));
}
```

7.9 CONVERSION OF GENERAL TREE TO BINARY TREE

A general tree is one where each node can have an outgoing degree *n*, where $n \geq 0$. Each node may have many applications such as charts, genesis, networks, and so on. In this section, we shall study that every general tree can be represented as a binary tree. We can make out from the study of representations of trees that the representation of a binary tree is easier than the general tree representation.

Binary trees are the trees where the maximum degree of any node is two. Any general tree can be represented as a binary tree using the following algorithm:

1. All nodes of a general tree will be the nodes of a binary tree.
2. The root *T* of a general tree is the root of a binary tree.
3. To obtain a binary tree, we use a relationship between the nodes that can have the following two characteristics:
   (a) The first or the leftmost child–parent relationship
   (b) Node-next right sibling relationship

Use the following steps to obtain *T* from *T*:

1. Connect (insert an arrow from) each node to its right sibling (if one exists).
2. Disconnect (remove arrows from) each node from (to) all but the leftmost child.

Examples 7.3 and 7.4 demonstrate the conversion of a general tree into a binary tree.

EXAMPLE 7.3 Convert the general tree in Fig. 7.44 into its corresponding binary tree.

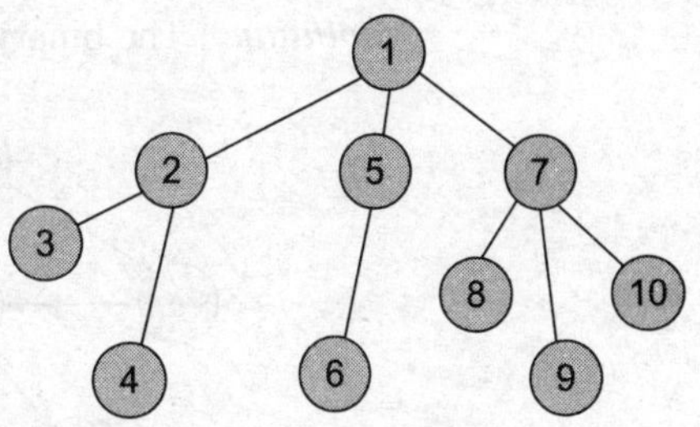

Fig. 7.44 General tree

Solution In this tree, the leftmost child of 2 is 3 and the next right child of 2 is 4. The binary tree corresponding to the tree is obtained by connecting together all siblings of each node (Fig. 7.45) and deleting all links from a node to its children except for the link to its leftmost child. The binary tree obtained is shown in Fig. 7.46.

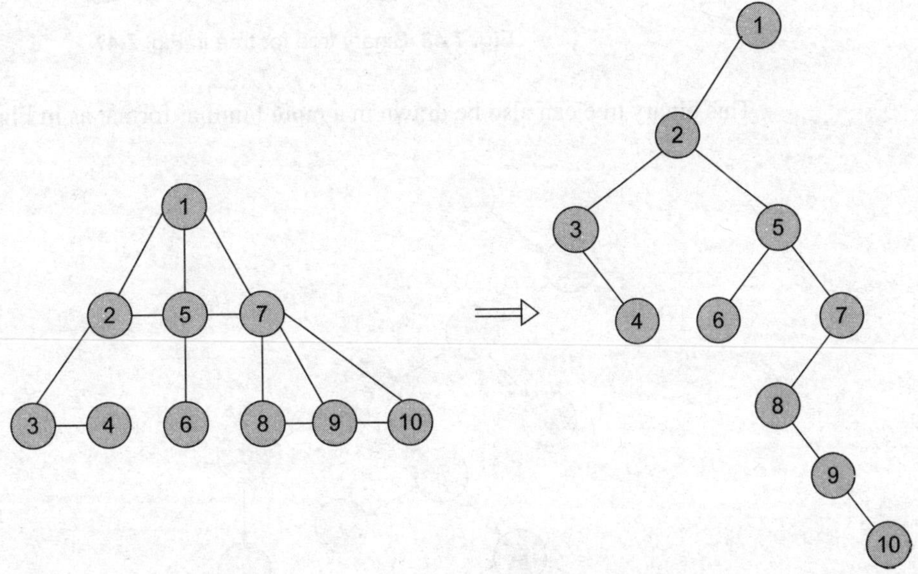

Fig. 7.45 Step 1

Fig. 7.46 Binary tree for tree in Fig. 7.44

EXAMPLE 7.4 Convert the general tree in Fig. 7.47 into its corresponding binary tree.

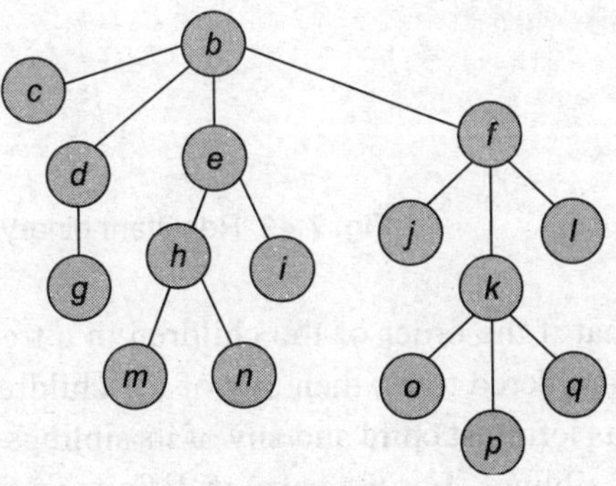

Fig. 7.47 General tree

Solution The binary tree representation of Fig. 7.47 is shown in Fig. 7.48.

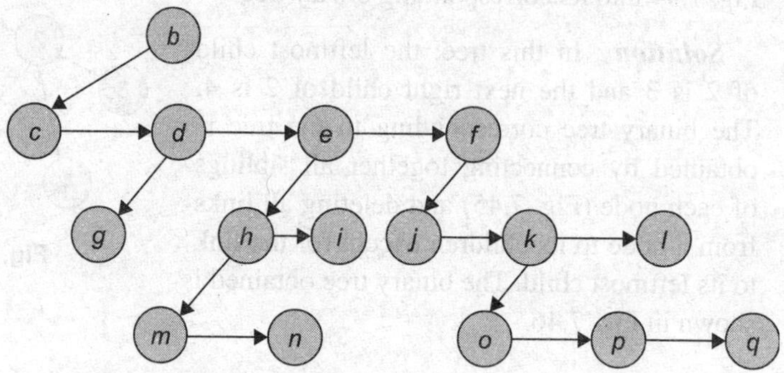

Fig. 7.48 Binary tree for tree in Fig. 7.47

This binary tree can also be drawn in a more familiar format as in Fig. 7.49.

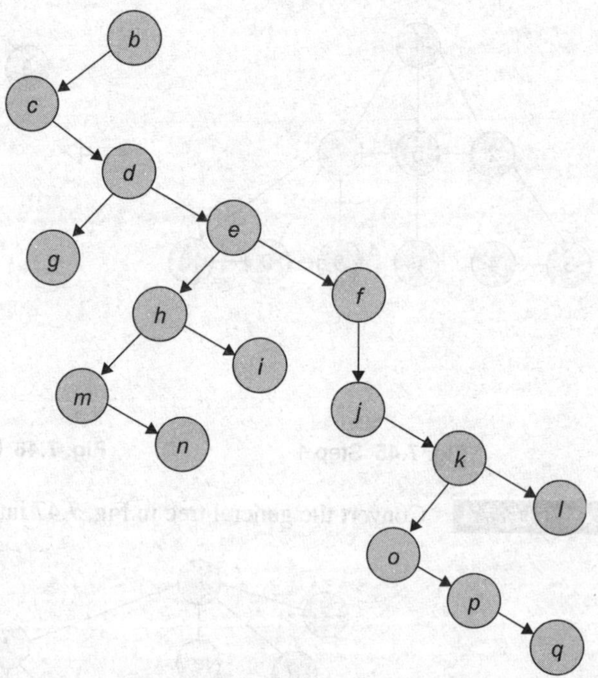

Fig. 7.49 Resultant binary tree in format 2

Note that if the order of the children in a tree is not important (unordered tree), then any of the children of a node could be its leftmost child and any of its siblings could be its next right siblings. For the sake of definiteness, we choose the nodes based upon how the tree is drawn. The node structure for a binary tree can be shown as in Fig. 7.50.

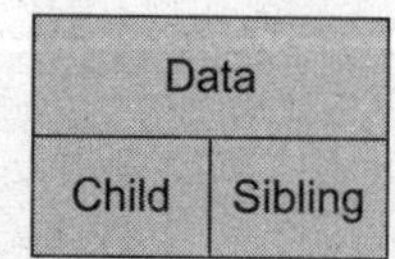

Fig. 7.50 Node structure for binary tree

In addition, notice that the transformation from the resultant binary tree to the original n-ary tree is reversible. That is, given a binary tree representation of a general tree, we can re-create the general tree. A left node is the leftmost child of its parent. A right node is a sibling of its parent

Example 7.5 illustrates the conversion of a given tree to a binary tree.

EXAMPLE 7.5 Convert the following tree in Fig. 7.51 into a binary tree.

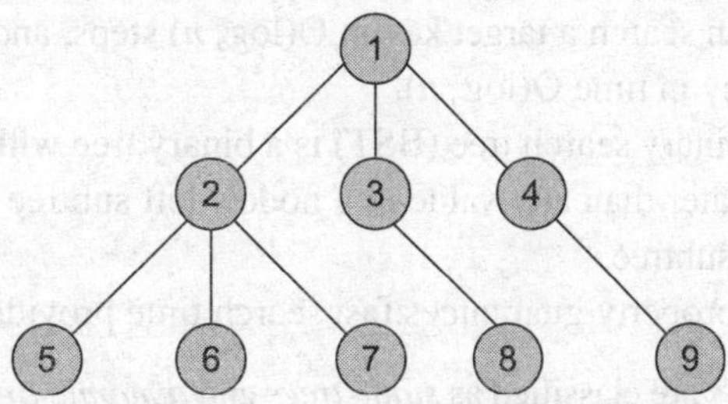

Fig. 7.51 Given general tree

Solution Let us connect the siblings and drop all the pointers from the parent to the children except to the first child as in Fig. 7.52.

Now every child becomes a left child, every sibling becomes a right child, and the resultant tree is a binary tree as in Fig. 7.53.

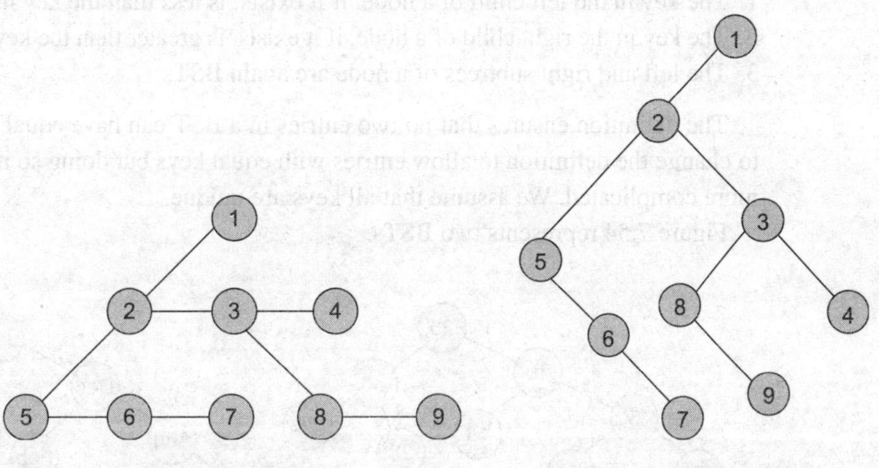

Fig. 7.52 Step 1 **Fig. 7.53** Resultant binary tree

7.10 BINARY SEARCH TREE

We know that the sequential search with O(n) searches is slower compared to the binary search with O($\log_2 n$) searches. If the list is an ordered list stored in a contiguous sequential storage, the binary search is faster. Though the list is stored, if it is stored in a linked list, the binary search cannot work as it does not support direct access. However, when we frequently need to make changes in the list, that is, inserting a new entry or deleting an old entry, then it is much slower to use a contiguous sequential list than a linked list, as `insert()` and `delete()` operations need data movement. On the other hand, in a linked organization, we need only a few pointer manipulations for insertion and deletions. If so, we can then find an implementation for an ordered list where we can search quickly (as with binary search) and insert or delete elements quickly (as with linked list). A binary tree provides an excellent solution to this problem.

1. We can make entries of an ordered list into the nodes of a binary tree. We shall see that we can search a target key in $O(\log_2 n)$ steps, and in addition, we can insert and delete the key in time $O(\log_2 n)$.
2. The binary search tree (BST) is a binary tree with the property that the value in a node is greater than any value in a node's left subtree and less than any value in the node's right subtree.
3. This property guarantees fast search time provided the tree is relatively balanced.

The BSTs are classified as *static trees* and *dynamic trees*. *Static tree* is a BST where the set of values in the nodes is known in advance and never changes. *Dynamic tree* is a BST where the values in a tree may change over time. We shall study the ways of building and balancing these search trees to guarantee that the trees remain balanced so that the search time is minimum.

Binary search tree A BST is a binary tree that is either empty or where every node contains a key and satisfies the following conditions:

1. The key in the left child of a node, if it exists, is less than the key in its parent node.
2. The key in the right child of a node, if it exists, is greater than the key in its parent node.
3. The left and right subtrees of a node are again BSTs.

The definition ensures that no two entries in a BST can have equal keys. It is possible to change the definition to allow entries with equal keys but doing so makes an algorithm more complicated. We assume that all keys are unique.

Figure 7.54 represents two BSTs.

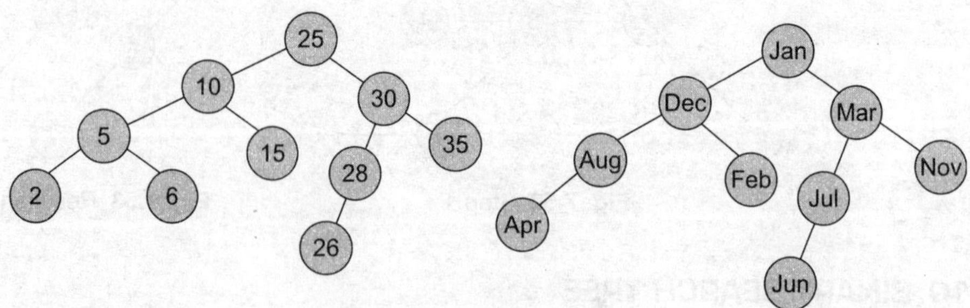

Fig. 7.54 Binary search trees

The following are the operations commonly performed on a BST:

1. Searching a key
2. Inserting a key
3. Deleting a key
4. Traversing the tree

Program Code 7.10 demonstrates the class for a BST showing the node structure and the function prototypes to operate on.

PROGRAM CODE 7.10

```
class TreeNode
{
   <data type> Key;
   TreeNode *Lchild, *Rchild;
};

class BSTree
{
   private:
      TreeNode *Root;
   public:
      BSTree() {Root = Null;}       // constructor
      void InsertNode(int Key);
      void DeleteNode(int key);
      void Search(int Key);
      bool IsEmpty();
};
```

7.10.1 Inserting a Node

To insert a new node into a BST, the keys should remain in proper order so that the resulting tree satisfies the definition of a BST.

Let us consider the insertion of the keys Esha, Beena, Deepa, Gilda, Amit, Geeta, and Chetan, into an initially empty tree in the given order as shown in Fig. 7.55.

If the tree is empty, then the first entry, Esha, when inserted, becomes the root, as shown in Fig. 7.55(a). Since Beena is less than Esha, insertion goes into the left subtree of Esha, and so on for all keys. If the tree is not empty, then we must compare the key with the one in the root. `Insert()` function can be written both recursively as well as non-recursively.

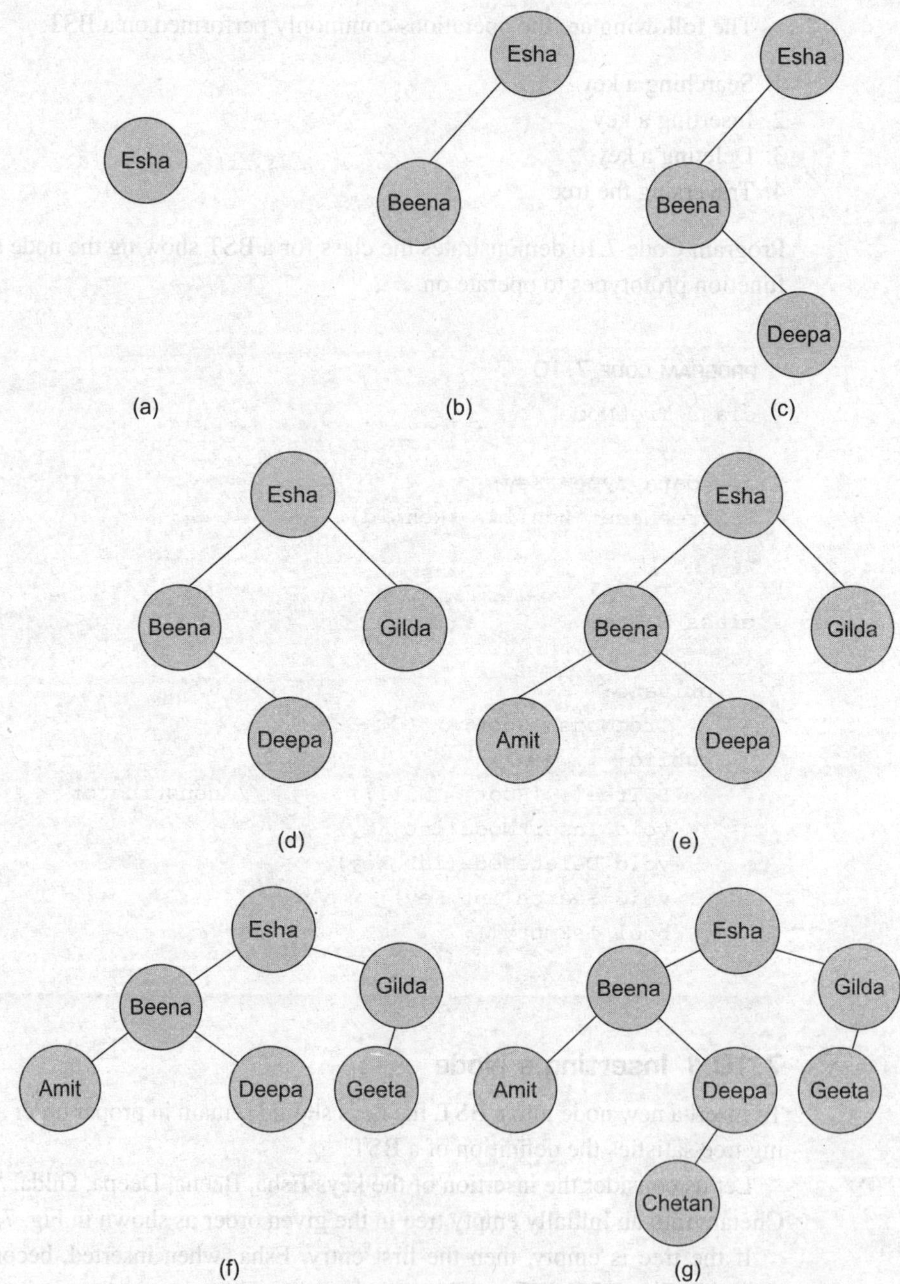

Fig. 7.55 Insertion in BST (a) Insert Esha (b) Insert Beena (c) Insert Deepa (d) Insert Gilda (e) Insert Amit (f) Insert Geeta (g) Insert Chetan

The BST ADT was given in Program Code 7.10. The code for the function to insert a node is listed in Program Code 7.11.

PROGRAM CODE 7.11

```
TreeNode *BSTree :: Insert(int Key)
{
   TreeNode *Tmp, NewNode;
   NewNode = new BSTNode;
   NewNode->Data = Key;
   NewNode->Lchild = NewNode->Rchild = Null:
   if(Root == Null)
   {
      Root = NewNode;
      return;
   }
   Tmp = Root;
   while(Tmp != Null)
   {
      if(Tmp->Data < Key)
      {
         if(Tmp->Lchild == Null)
         {
            Tmp->Lchild = NewNode;
            return;
         }
         Tmp = Tmp->Lchild;
         else if(Tmp->Rchild == Null)
         {
            Tmp->Rchild = NewNode;
            return;
         }
      }
   }
   Tmp = Tmp->Rchild;
}
```

Initially, the tree is empty. The tree is built through the `Insert()` function. Example 7.6 shows the construction of a BST from a given set of elements.

EXAMPLE 7.6 Build a BST from the following set of elements—100, 50, 200, 300, 20, 150, 70, 180, 120, 30—and traverse the tree built in inorder, postorder, and preorder.

Solution The BST is constructed through the following steps:

Step 1: Initially, `Root = Null`. Now let us insert 100.

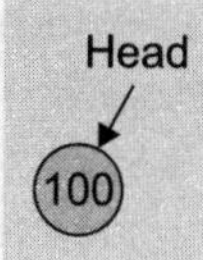

Step 2: Insert 50. As it is less than the root, that is, 100, and its left child is `Null`, we insert it as a left child of the root.

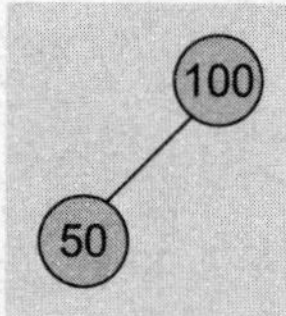

Step 3: Insert 200. As it is greater than the root, that is, 100, and its right child is `Null`, we insert it as a right child of the root.

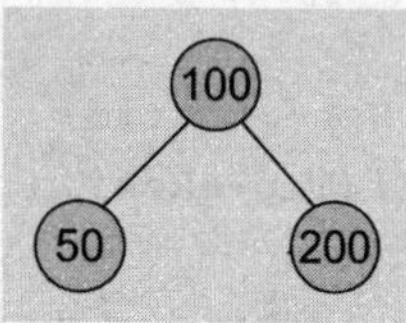

Step 4: Insert 300. As it is greater than the root, that is, 100, we move right to 200. It is greater than 200, and its right child is `Null`, so we insert it as a right child of 200.

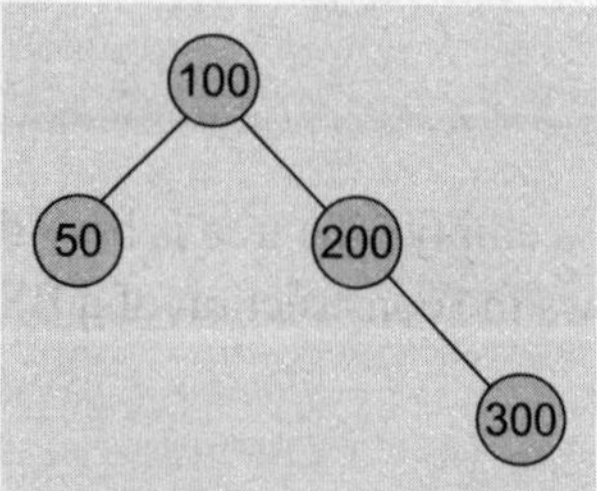

Similarly, we insert the other nodes.

Step 5: Insert 20.

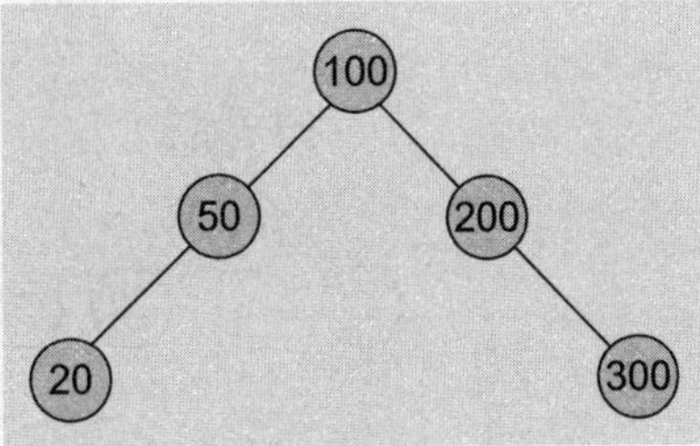

Step 6: Insert 150.

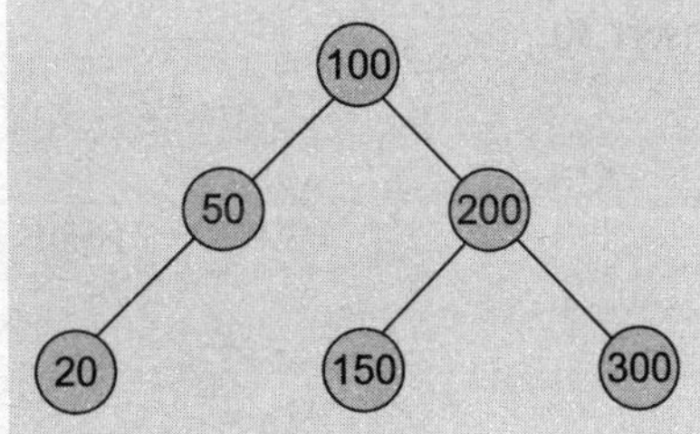

Step 7: Insert 70.

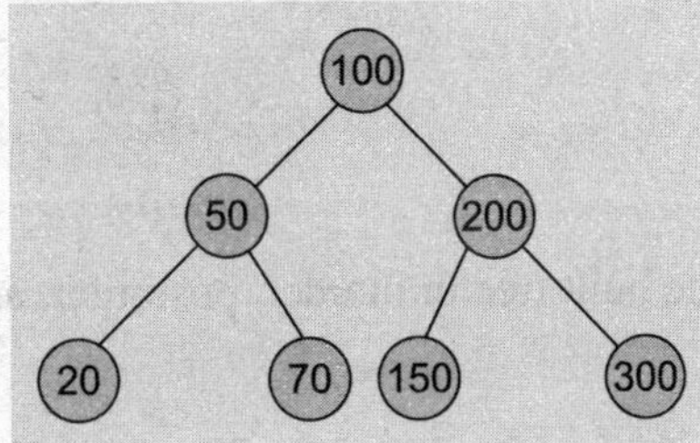

Step 8: Insert 180.

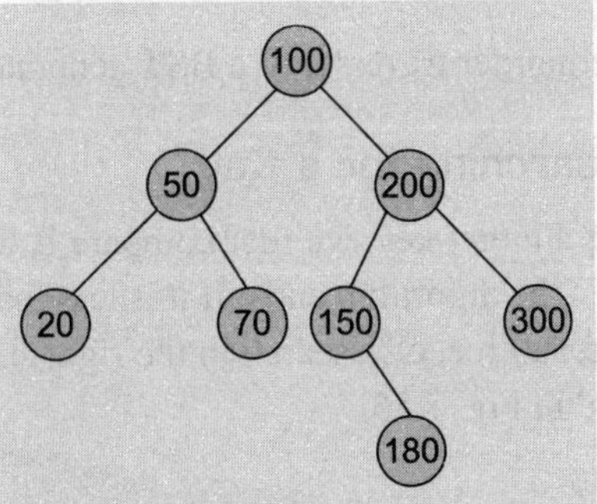

Step 9: Insert 120.

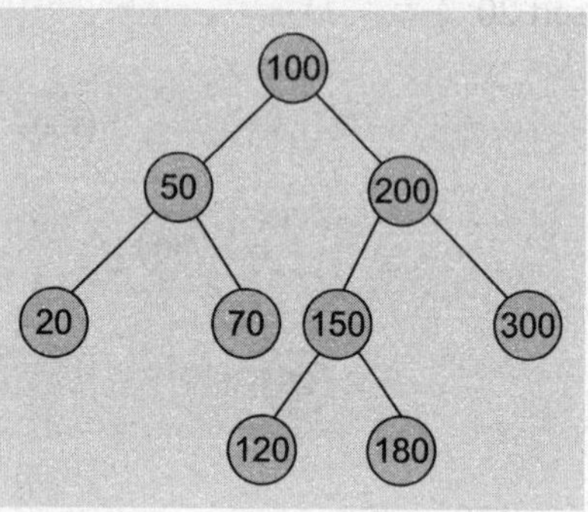

Step 10: Insert 30.

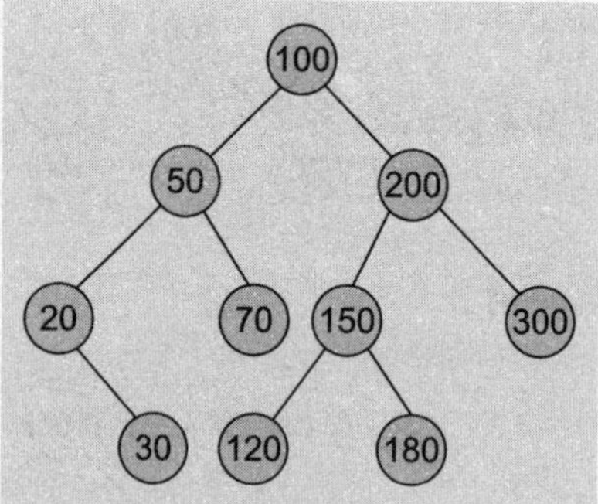

Traverse the built tree in inorder, postorder, and preorder and display the sequence of numbers.

Preorder: 100 50 20 30 70 200 150 120 180 300
Inorder: 20 30 50 70 100 120 150 180 200 300
Postorder: 30 20 70 50 120 180 150 300 200 100

Note that the inorder traversal of a BST generates the data in ascending order.

7.10.2 Searching for a Key

To search for a target key, we first compare it with the key at the root of the tree. If it is the same, then the algorithm ends. If it is less than the key at the root, search for the target key in the left subtree, else search in the right subtree. Let us, for example, search for the key 'Saurabh' in Fig. 7.56.

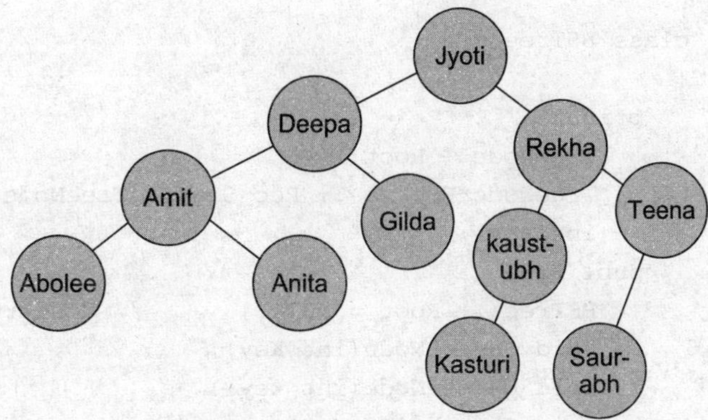

Fig. 7.56 Binary search tree

We first compare 'Saurabh' with the key of the root, 'Jyoti'. Since 'Saurabh' comes after 'Jyoti' in alphabetical order, we move to the right side and next compare it with the key 'Rekha'. Since 'Saurabh' comes after 'Rekha', we move to the right again and compare with 'Teena'. Since 'Saurabh' comes before 'Teena', we move to the left.

Now the question is to identify what event will be the terminating condition for the search. The solution is if we find the key, the function finishes successfully. If not, we continue searching until we hit an empty subtree.

Program Code 7.12 shows the implementation of `search()` function, both non-recursive and recursive implementations.

PROGRAM CODE 7.12

```
TreeNode *BSTree :: Search(int Key)
{
   TreeNode *Tmp = Root;
   while(Tmp)
   {
      if(Tmp->Data == Key)
         return Tmp;
      else if(Tmp->data < Key)
         Tmp = Tmp->Lchild;
      else
         Tmp = Tmp->Rchild;
   }
   return Null;
}
```

```
class BSTree
{
   private:
      TreeNode * Root;
      TreeNode*BSTree :: Rec_Search(TreeNode *root,
      int key);
   public:
      BSTree() {Root = Null;}       // constructor
      void InsertNode(int Key);
      void DeleteNode(int key);
      void Search(int Key);
      bool IsEmpty();
      TreeNode* BSTree:: Recursive_Search(int key)
      {
         Rec_Search(Root, int Key);
      }

};
TreeNode *BSTree :: Rec_Search(TreeNode *root, int key)
{
   if(root == Null)
      return(root);
   else
   {
      if(root->Data < Key)
         root = Rec_Search(root->Lchild);
      else if(root->data > Key)
         root = Rec_Search(root->Rchild);
   }
}
```

The class with recursive function is given in this program code.

7.10.3 Deleting a Node

Deletion of a node is one of the frequently performed operations. Let *T* be a BST and *X* be the node of key *K* to be deleted from *T*, if it exists in the tree. Let *Y* be a parent node of *X*. There are three cases when a node is to be deleted from a BST. Let us consider each case:

1. *X* is a leaf node.
2. *X* has one child.
3. *X* has both child nodes.

Case 1: Leaf node deletion If the node to be deleted, say *X*, is a leaf node, then the process is easy. We need to change the child link of the parent node, say *Y* of node to be deleted to `Null`, and free the memory occupied by the node to be deleted and then return. Consider the following tree given in Fig. 7.57. Here, 5 is the node to be deleted.

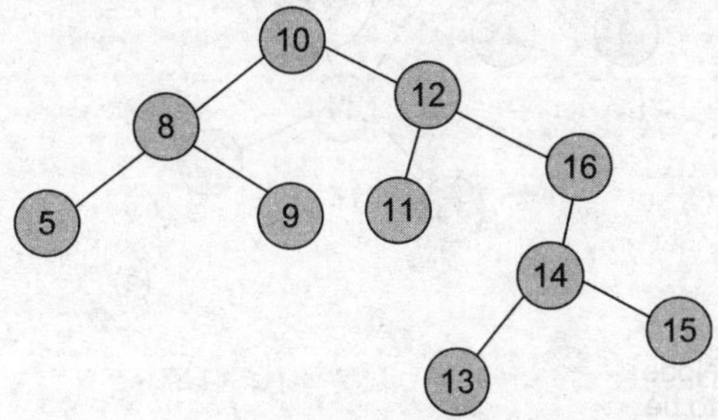

Fig. 7.57 Binary search tree

After deleting the node with data = 5, the BST becomes as in Fig. 7.58.

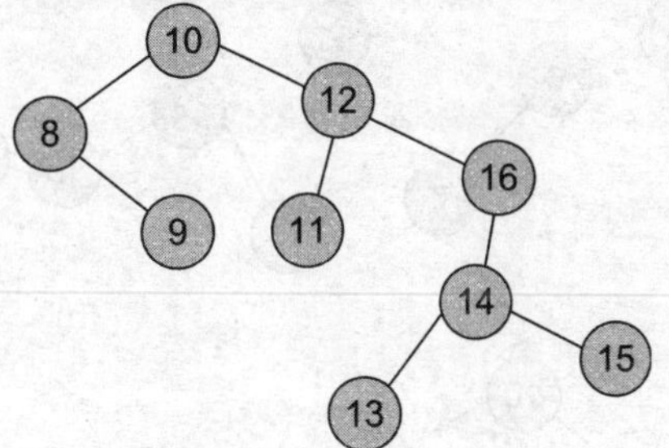

Fig. 7.58 BST after deletion of node with data = 5

Case 2(a): Node not having right subtree If the node to be deleted has a single child link, that is, either right child or left child is `Null` and has only one subtree, the process is still easy. If there is no right subtree, then just link the left subtree of the node to be deleted to its parent and free its memory. If *X* denotes the node to be deleted and *Y* is its parent with *X* as a left child, then we need to set *Y*->Lchild = *X*->Lchild and free the memory. If *X* denotes the node to be deleted and *Y* is its parent with *X* as a right child, then we need to set *Y*->Rchild = *X*->Lchild and free the memory. Let the node to be deleted be with data = 16 and data = 8; the resultant tree is as shown in Figs 7.59(a) and (b), respectively.

Case 2(b): Node not having left subtree If there is no left subtree, then just link the right subtree of the node to be deleted to its parent and free its memory. If *X* denotes the node to be deleted and *Y* is its parent with *X* as a left child, then we need to set *Y*->Lchild = *X*->Rchild and free the memory. If *X* denotes the node to be deleted and *Y* is its parent with *X* as a right child, then we need to set *Y*->Rchild = *X*->Rchild and free the memory. Let the node to be deleted be with data = 5 and data = 12; the resultant tree is as in Figs 7.59(c) and (d), respectively.

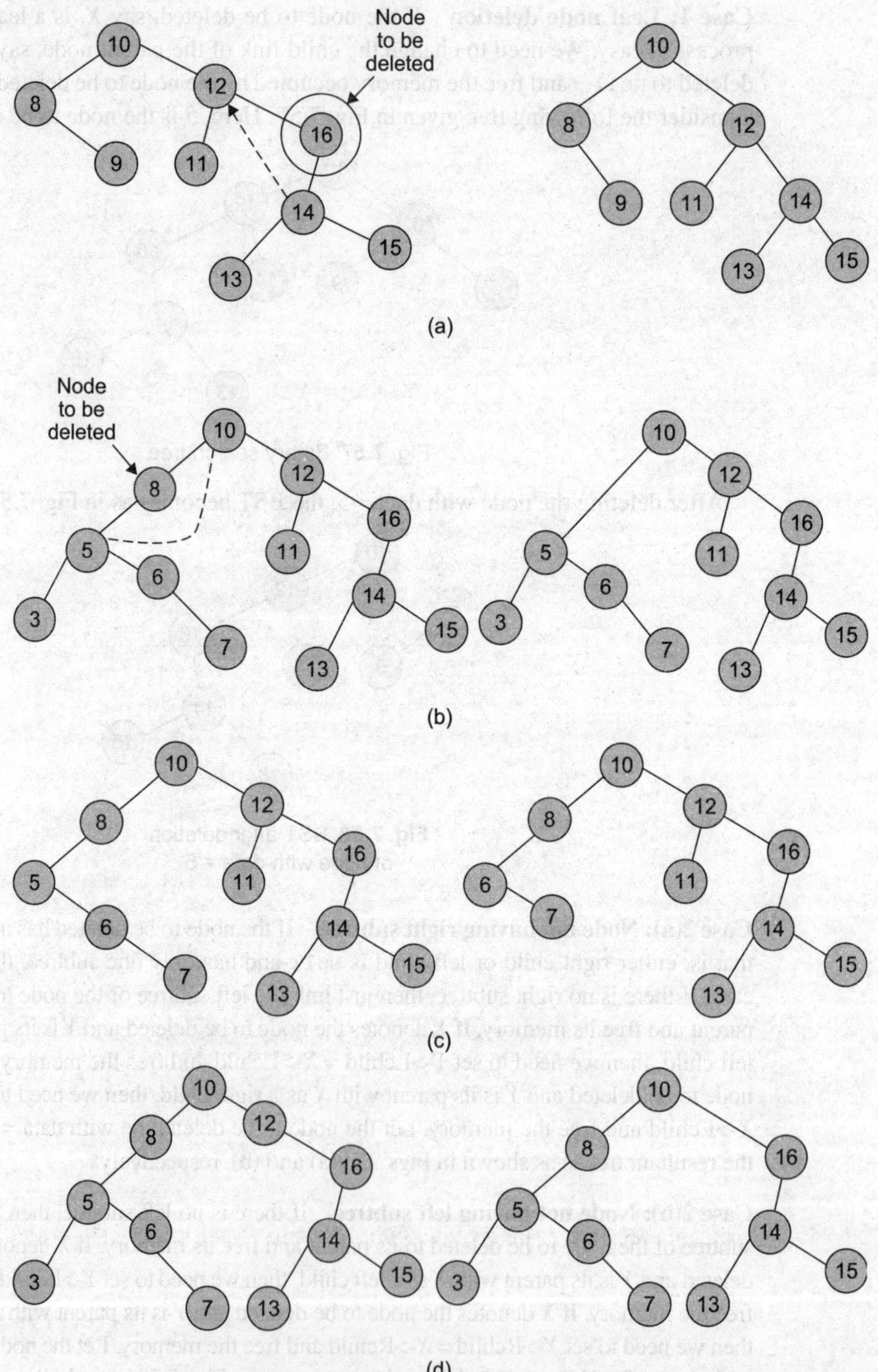

Fig. 7.59 Resultant tree after deletion of node with no left or right subtree (a) Delete 16 (b) Delete 8 (c) Delete 5 (d) Delete 12

Case 3: Node having both subtrees Consider the case when the node to be deleted has both right and left subtrees. This problem is more difficult than the earlier cases. The question is which subtrees should the parent of the deleted node be linked to, what should be done with the other subtrees, and where should the remaining subtrees be linked. One of the solutions is to attach the right subtree in place of the deleted node, and then attach the left subtree onto an appropriate node of the right subtree. This is pictorially shown in Fig. 7.60.

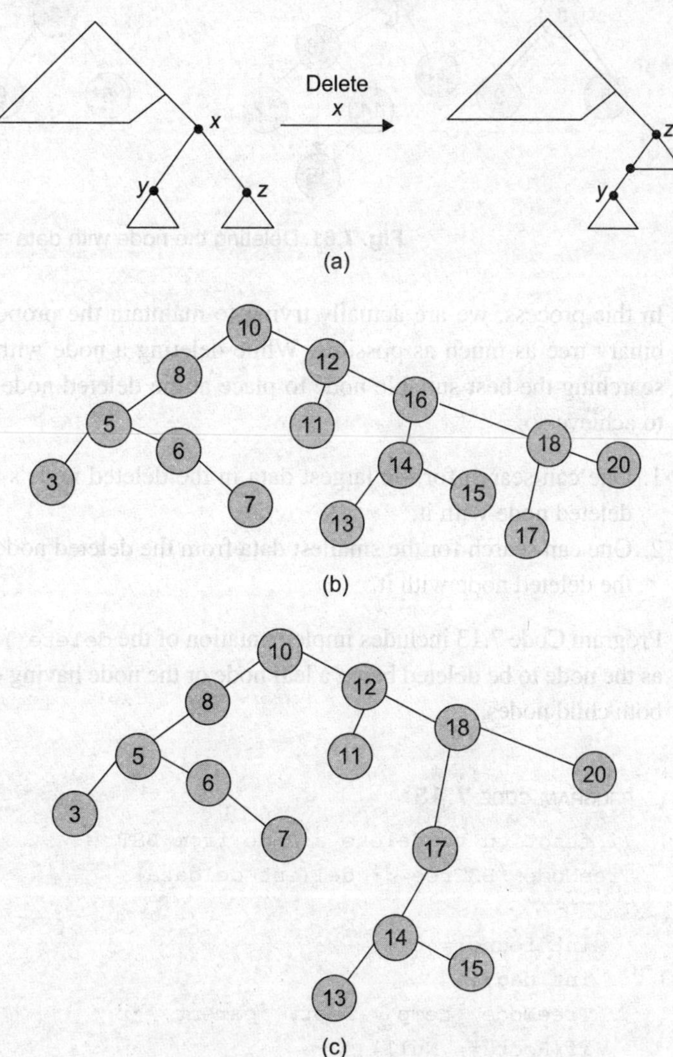

Fig. 7.60 Deleting node with both subtrees (a) Delete *x* (b) Delete 16 (c) Resultant tree after deletion

Another way to delete *X* from *T* is by first deleting the inorder successor of the node *X*, say *Z*, then replace the data content in the node *X* by the data content in the node *Z* (successor of the node *X*). Inorder successor means the node that comes after the node *X* during the inorder traversal of *T*.

Let us consider Fig. 7.61, and let the node to be deleted be the node with data 12.

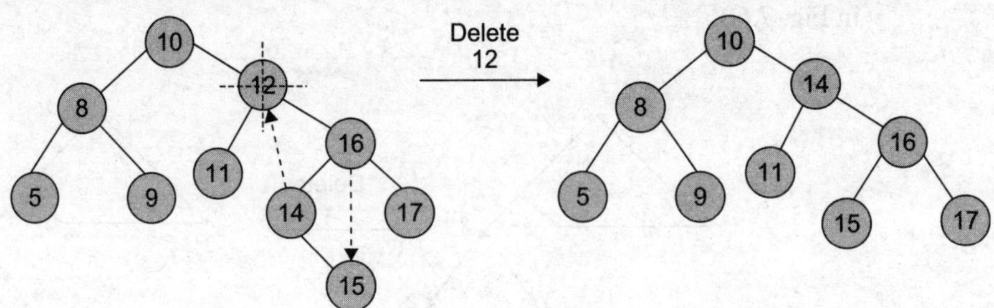

Fig. 7.61 Deleting the node with data = 12

In this process, we are actually trying to maintain the properties and the structure of a binary tree as much as possible. While deleting a node with both subtrees, we attempt searching the best suitable node to place at the deleted node. There are two alternatives to achieve so:

1. One can search for the largest data in the deleted node's left subtree and replace the deleted node with it.
2. One can search for the smallest data from the deleted node's right subtree and replace the deleted node with it.

Program Code 7.13 includes implementation of the `delete()` function with all cases such as the node to be deleted being a leaf node or the node having one child or the node having both child nodes.

PROGRAM CODE 7.13

```
// function to delete a node from BST
TreeNode *BSTree :: del(int deldata)
{
    int found = 0;
    int flag;
    TreeNode *temp = Root, *parent, *x;
    if(Root == Null)
    {
        cout << endl << "\t BST is empty";
        return Null;
    }
```

```
else
{
   parent = temp;
   //Search a BST node to be deleted & its parent
   while(temp != Null)
   {
      if(temp->Data == deldata )
         break;      // found
      if(deldata < temp->Data)
      {
         parent = temp;
         temp = temp->Lchild;
      }
      else
      {
         parent = temp;
         temp = temp->Rchild;
      }
   }      // end of search
   if(temp == Null)
      return(Null);
   else
   {
      //case of BST node having right children
      if(temp->Rchild != Null)
      {
         //find leftmost of right BST node
         //cout << "\n Temp is having right child";
         parent = temp;
         x = temp->Rchild;
         while(x->Lchild != Null)
         {
            parent = x;
            x = x->Lchild;
         }
         temp->Data = x->Data;
         temp = x;
      }
      //case of BST node being a leaf Node
     if(temp->Lchild == Null && temp->Rchild == Null)
      {
         //cout << "\n Leaf node";
        if(temp != root)
```

```
            {
               if(parent->lLchild == temp)
                  parent->Rchild = Null;
               else
                  parent->Rchild = Null;
            }
            else
               root = Null;
            delete temp;
            return(root);
         }
         else if(temp->Lchild!=Null&&temp->Rchild ==
         Null)
            //case of BST node having left children
         {
            //cout << "\n only left";
            if(temp != root)
            {
               if(parent->Lchild == temp)
                  parent->Lchild = temp->Lchild;
               else
                  parent->Rchild = temp->Lchild;
            }
            else
               root = temp->Lchild;
            delete temp;
            return(root);
         }
      }
   }
}
```

7.10.4 Binary Tree and Binary Search Tree

We have studied both binary tree and BST. A BST is a special case of the binary tree. The comparison of both yields the following points:

1. Both of them are trees with degree two, that is, each node has utmost two children. This makes the implementation of both easy.
2. The BST is a binary tree with the property that the value in a node is greater than any value in a node's left subtree and less than any value in a node's right subtree.

3. The BST guarantees fast search time provided the tree is relatively balanced, whereas for a binary tree, the search is relatively slow.

Consider the binary tree and BST shown in Fig. 7.62.

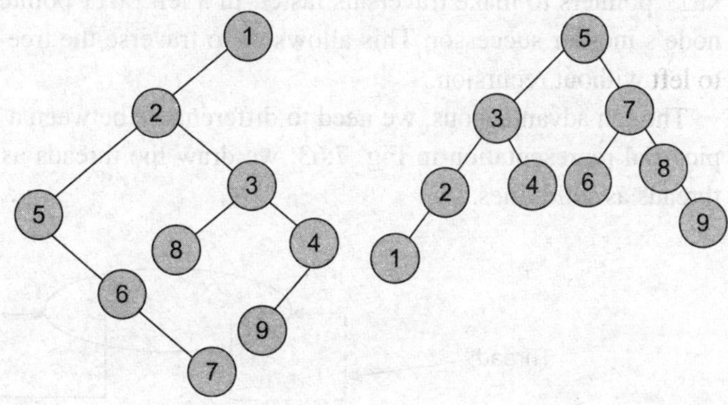

Fig. 7.62 Binary tree and binary search tree

In these trees, if we search for a node with data = 7, the number of searches varies in both trees as we need 5 comparisons for binary tree and 2 comparisons for BST.

Given a binary tree with no duplicates, we can construct a BST from a binary tree. The process is easy; one can traverse the binary tree and construct a BST for it by inserting each node in an initially empty BST.

7.11 THREADED BINARY TREE

We have studied the linked implementation of binary trees and the fundamental operations such as inserting a node, deleting a node, and traversing the tree. There are two key observations—first is that for all leaf nodes and those with one child the Lchild and/or Rchild fields are set to `Null`. The second observation is in the traversal process. The traversal functions use stack to store information about those nodes whose processing has not been finished. In case of non-recursive traversals, user-defined stack is used, and in case of recursive traversals internal stack is used. There is additional time for processing, but additional space for storing the stack is required. This is not a perceptible problem when a tree is of larger size.

To solve this problem, we can modify the node structure to hold information about other nodes in the tree such as parent, sibling, and so on. A.J. Perlis and C. Thornton have suggested replacing all the `Null` links by pointers, called *threads*. A tree with a thread is called a *threaded binary tree* (TBT). Note that both threads and tree pointers are pointers to nodes in the tree. The difference is that the threads are not structural pointers of the tree. They can be removed but still the tree does not change. *Tree pointers* are the pointers that join and hold the tree together. Threads utilize the `Null` pointers' waste space to improve the processing efficiency. One such application is to use these `Null` pointers to make traversals faster. In a left `Null` pointer, we store a pointer to the node's inorder successor. This allows us to traverse the tree both left to right and right to left without recursion.

Though advantageous, we need to differentiate between a thread and a pointer. In the pictorial representation in Fig. 7.63, we draw the threads as dashed lines and the non-threads as solid lines.

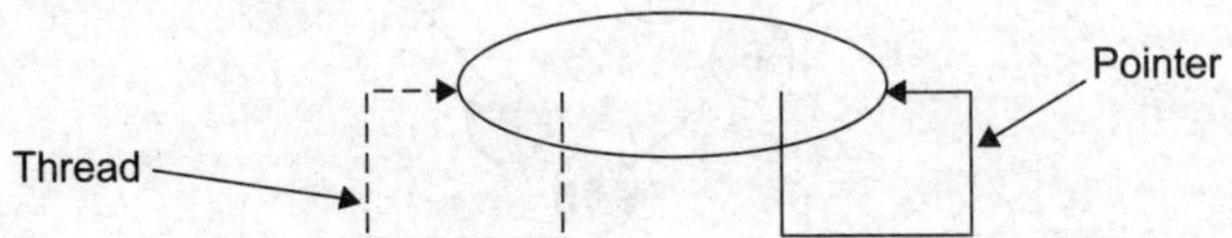

Fig. 7.63 Representation of threads and pointers

However, we need to differentiate between the thread and the pointer in actual implementation, that is, in the memory representation of a tree.

Let us use two additional fields—`Lbit` and `Rbit` to distinguish between a thread and a pointer.

Let us also use a function `IsThread()` that returns `true` if the pointer is a thread, and `false` if it is the conventional pointer to the child in the tree.

`Lbit`(node) = 1 if `Left`(node) is a thread

= 0 if `Left`(node) is a child pointer

`Rbit`(node) = 1 if `Right`(node) is a thread

= 0 if `Right`(node) is a child pointer

```
Class TBTNode
{
   boolean Lbit, Rbit;
   <Datatype> Data;
   TBTNode *Left, *Right;
}; Y
```

Let us consider a tree and also a tree with threads as in Figs 7.64(a) and (b), respectively.

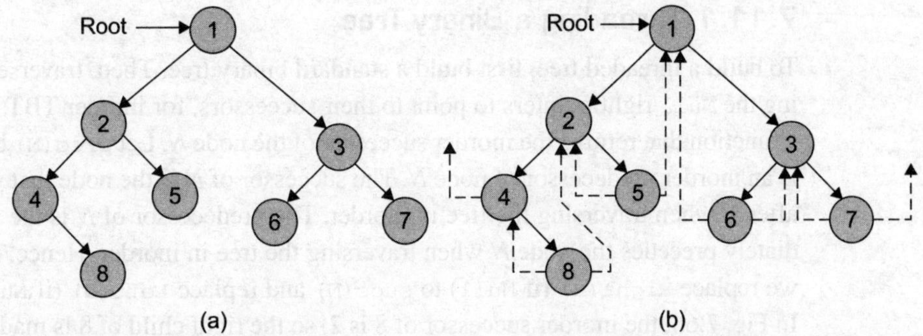

Fig. 7.64 Threaded binary tree (a) Tree (b) Corresponding threaded binary tree

In Fig. 7.64, note that the two threads Left(4) and Right(7) have been left dangling. To avoid such dangling pointers, we use an additional node, a *head node* of all threaded trees. The tree *T* is the left subtree of the head node. An empty tree is represented in Fig. 7.65.

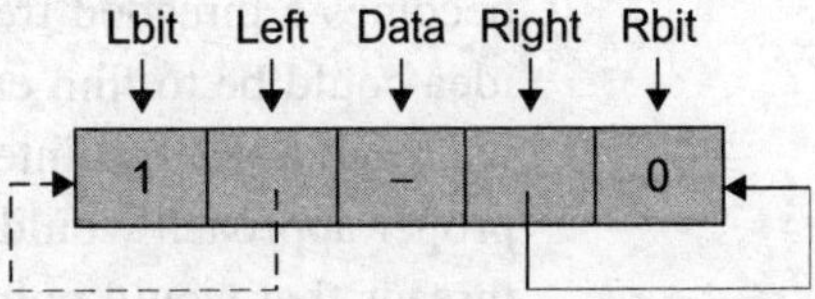

Fig. 7.65 An empty threaded binary tree

The tree in Fig. 7.64 has its TBT drawn. In the TBT as in Fig. 7.65, two threads that are the left thread of a node with data = 4 and the right thread of a node with data = 7 are dangling as they remain unassigned. To avoid this, a head node is added in the tree. The tree in Fig. 7.64 can be redrawn as in Fig. 7.66.

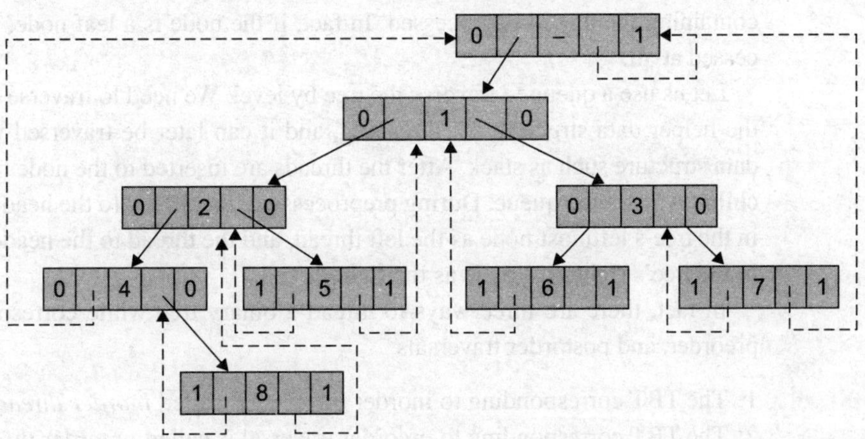

Fig. 7.66 Memory representation of TBT in Fig. 7.64

Here, 1 (true) shows it's a thread and 0 (false) represents that it's not a thread but a pointer to the child subtree.

7.11.1 Threading a Binary Tree

To build a threaded tree, first build a standard binary tree. Then, traverse the tree, changing the `Null` right pointers to point to their successors, for inorder TBT. Let `succ(N)` be a function that returns the inorder successor of the node *N*. Let `pred(N)` be a function that is an inorder predecessor of node *N*. The successor of *N* is the node that would be printed after *N* when traversing the tree in inorder. The predecessor of *N* is the node that immediately precedes the node *N* when traversing the tree in inorder. Hence, for inorder TBT, we replace `Right(N)` (if `Null`) to `succ(N)` and replace `Left(N)` (if `Null`) to `pred(N)`. In Fig. 7.66, the inorder successor of 8 is 2, so the right child of 8 is made a thread which is pointing to 2 and `Rbit` field is made 4.

If we are given a binary tree, it is natural to think how to set threads so that the tree becomes a threaded tree. Threading a binary tree is an interesting problem. The first idea could be to find each `Null` pointer and insert the proper thread. However, when we reach a `Null` pointer, we have no way to determine what the proper thread is. The proper approach would be based on taking any non-leaf (branch) node and setting the threads that would point to it. The successor and predecessor of a node *A* are defined as follows:

1. *successor*—the leftmost node in *A*'s right subtree
2. *predecessor*—the rightmost node in *A*'s left subtree

The algorithm must traverse the tree level-by-level, setting all the threads that should point to each node as it processes the node. Therefore, each thread set before the node containing the thread is processed. In fact, if the node is a leaf node, it need not be processed at all.

Let us use a queue to traverse the tree by level. We need to traverse the tree once using the helper data structure for threading, and it can later be traversed without any helper data structure such as stack. After the threads are inserted to the node being processed, its children go on the queue. During preprocessing, the thread to the header must be inserted in the tree's leftmost node as the left thread, and the thread to the header must be inserted in the tree's rightmost node as the right thread.

In fact, there are three ways to thread a binary tree while corresponding to inorder, preorder, and postorder traversals.

1. The TBT corresponding to inorder traversal is called *inorder threading*.
2. The TBT corresponding to preorder traversal is called *preorder threading*.
3. The TBT corresponding to postorder traversal is called *postorder threading*.

To build a TBT, there is one more method that is popularly used. In this method, the threads are created while building the binary tree. Program Code 7.14 is the C++ code to demonstrate this method.

PROGRAM CODE 7.14

```
// function to create inorder threaded binary search tree
void ThreadedBinaryTree :: create()
{
   Char ans;
   int flag;
   TBTNode *node, *temp;
   Head = new TBTNode;       // create head
   Head->Left = Head;
   Head->Right = Head;
   Head->Rbit = Heat->Lbit = 1;
   // create root for TBST
   Root = new TBTNode;
   cout << "\n Enter data for root";
   cin >> Root->data;
   Root->Left = Head;
   Root->Right = Head;
   // attach root to left of Head
   Head->Left = Root;
   // make thread bit of root 0
   Root->Lbit = Root->Rbit = 0;
   do
   {
      //  create new node for a tree
      node = newTBTNode;
      cout << "\n Enter data";
      cin >> node- data;
      node->Lbit = node->Rbit = 1;
      temp = Root;
      while
      {
         if(node->data < temp->data)
         {
            if(temp->Lbit == 1)
            // check leaf node and attach
            {
               node->Left = temp->Left;
               node->Right = temp;
               // attach node to left of temp
               temp->Lbit = 0;
```

```
                temp->Left = node;
                break;
            }
            else
                temp = temp->Left;
        }
        else
        {
            if(temp->Rbit == 1)       // is thread?
            {
                node->Left = temp;
                node->Right = temp->Right;
                // attaching node to right of temp
                temp->Right = node;
                temp->Rbit = 0;
                break;
            }
            else
                temp = temp->Right;
        }
    }       // end of while
    cout >> "Do you want to add more?";
    cin >> ans;
  }
  while(ans == 'y'||ans == 'Y');
}      // end of create
```

Sample Run

1. Insert root data 50 (Fig. 7.67).

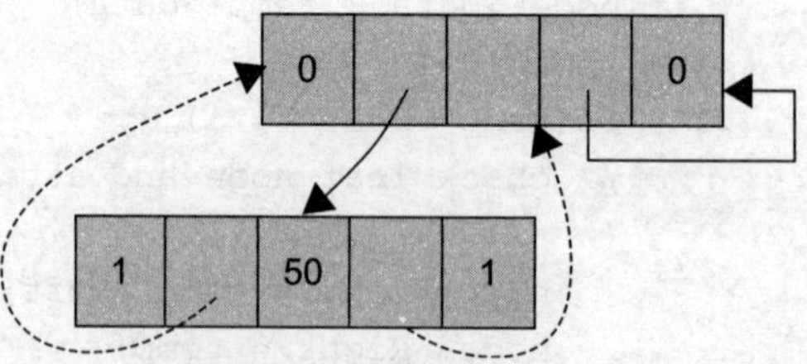

Fig. 7.67 Insert root 50

2. Attach the node with data 30 (Fig. 7.68).

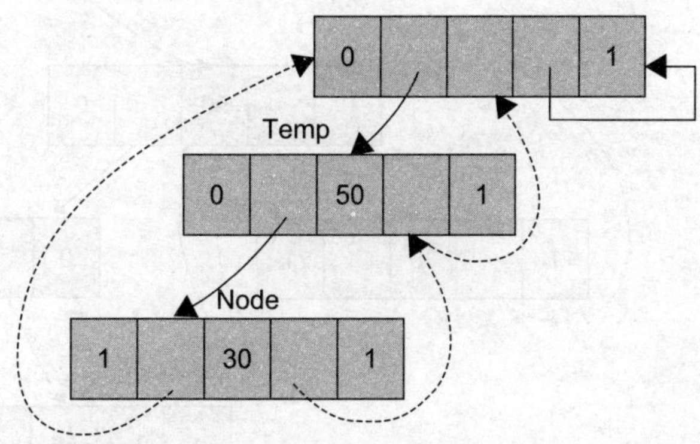

Fig. 7.68 Insert 30

Attach the left of `temp` copy to the left of the `temp` node to make the right child of the node as `temp`.

3. Attach the node with data 60 (Fig. 7.69).

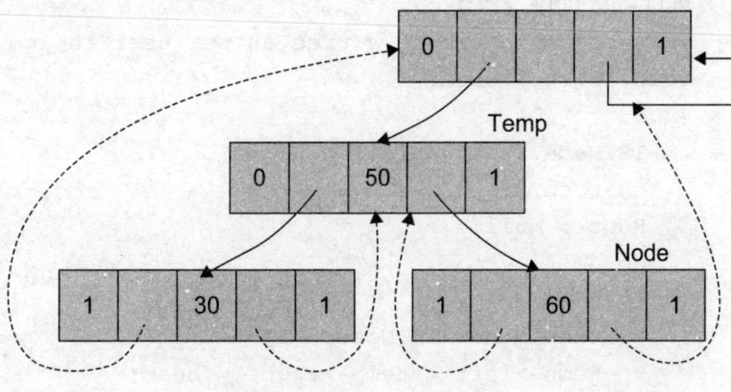

Fig. 7.69 Insert 60

Copy the right of `temp` to the right of the node to make the left of node as `temp`. Attach the node to the right of temp to make `Rbit` 0.

4. Attach the node with data 55 (Fig. 7.70).

   Copy the left of `temp` to the left of node. Make the right of node as `temp`. Then, attach `tnode` to the left of `temp`. Make the `Lbit` of `temp` 0.

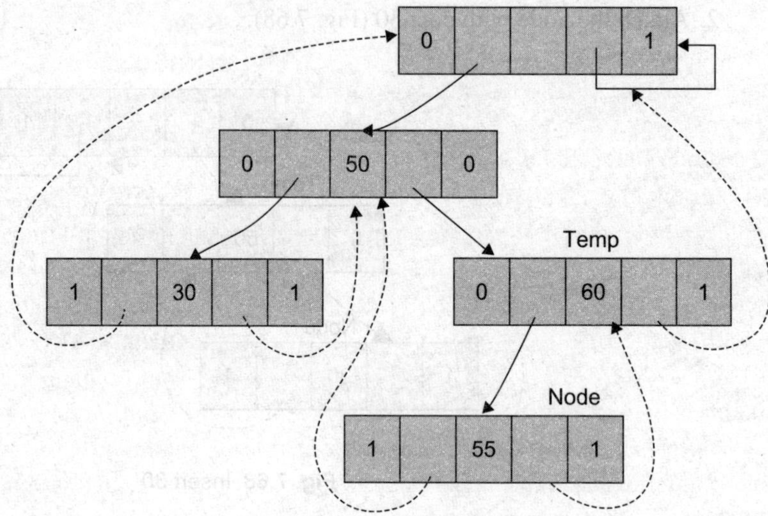

Fig. 7.70 Insert 55

The implementation of function for creating a TBT is given in Program Code 7.15.

PROGRAM CODE 7.15

```
//Function to create a tree as per user choice
void TBTree::create()
{
   TBTNode *temp,*prev;
   char ch,x;
   Root = Null;
   do
   {
      temp = new TBTNode;
      temp->left = temp->right = head;
      temp->lbit = temp->rbit = 0;
      cout << "\nEnter the char data:";
      cin >> temp->data;
      if(Root == Null)
      {
         Root = temp;
         head->left = Root;
         head->lbit = 1;
      }
      else
     {
```

```
         prev = Root;
         while(prev != Null)
         {
            cout << "Left child or Right child of (r/l):
            " << prev->data << " :";
            cin >> x;
            if(x == 'l' || x == 'L')
            {
               if(prev->lbit == 0)
               {
                  temp->left = prev->left;
                  prev->left = temp;
                  prev->lbit = 1;
                  temp->right = prev;
                  break;
               }
               else
                  prev = prev->left;
            }
            else
            {
               if(x == 'r' || x == 'R')
               {
                  if(prev->rbit == 0)
                  {
                     temp->right = prev->right;
                     prev->right = temp;
                     prev->rbit = 1;
                     temp->left = prev;
                     break;
                  }
                  else
                     prev = prev->right;
               }
            }
         }
      }
      cout <<"Do you want to Add more?";
      cin >> ch;
   }
   while(ch == 'y' || ch == 'Y');
}
```

7.11.2 Right-threaded Binary Tree

In a right-threaded binary tree each `Null` right link is replaced by a special link to the successor of that node under inorder traversal, called a *right thread*. The right thread will help us to traverse freely in inorder since we need to only follow either an ordinary link or a thread to find the next node to visit. When we replace each `Null` left link by a special link to the predecessor of the node (left thread) under inorder traversal, the result is fully a TBT.

7.11.3 Inorder Traversal

It can be realized that the inorder traversal in an inorder TBT is very easy. However, the other traversals are a bit difficult. If the preorder or postorder threading of a binary tree is known, then the corresponding traversal can be obtained efficiently.

The code for inorder traversal of a TBT is listed in Program Code 7.16.

PROGRAM CODE 7.16

```
// Traverse a threaded tree in inorder
void TBTree::Inorder()
{
   TBTNode *temp;
   temp = Root;
   int flag = 0;
   if(Root == Null)
   {
      cout << "\nTree not present";
   }
   else
   {
      while(temp != head)
      {
         if(temp->lbit == 1 && flag == 0)
         // go to left till Lbit is 1(till child)
         {
            temp = temp->left;
         }
         else
         {
            cout << temp->data << " ";      // display data
            if(temp->rbit == 1)      // go to right by child
            {
               temp = temp->right;
               flag = 0;
```

```
            }
            else        // go to right by thread
            {
                temp = temp->right;
                flag = 1;
            }
        }
    }
  }
}
```

Note that this traversal does not use stack, whereas for non-threaded binary tree, we require a stack as an intermediate data structure.

The computing time is O(n) for a binary tree with n nodes.

Example of inorder traversal of threaded binary tree Figure 7.71 shows a TBT whose inorder traversal sequence is—Megha, Amit, Arvind, Varsha, Abolee, Hemant, Saurabh.

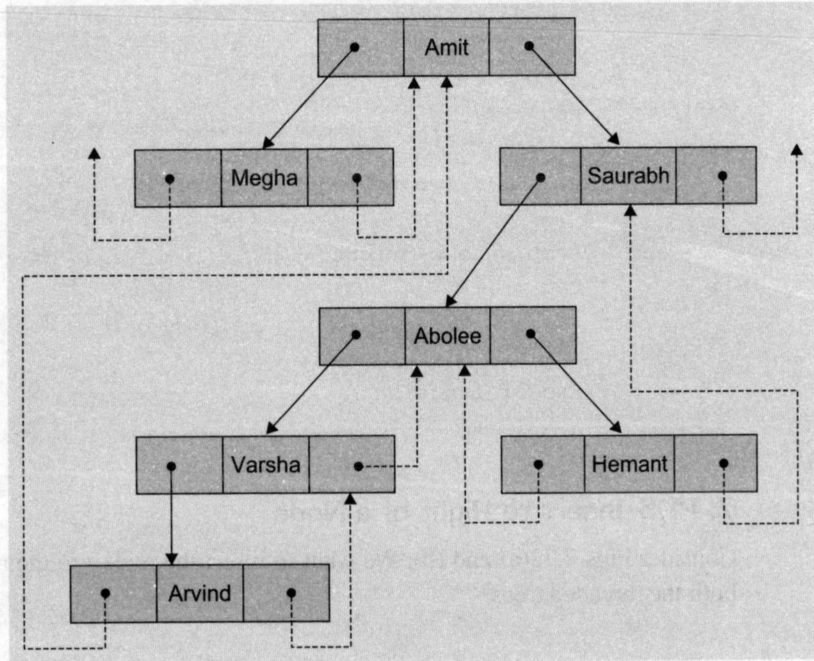

Fig. 7.71 Inorder traversal of a TBT

7.11.4 Preorder Traversal

These threads also simplify the algorithm for preorder and postorder traversals. Program Code 7.17 is the C++ routine for preorder traversal of a TBT.

PROGRAM CODE 7.17

```
// Traverse a threaded tree in preorder
void TBTree :: preorder()
{
   TBTNode *temp;
   int flag = 0;
   temp = Root;
   while(temp != head)
   {
      if(flag == 0) cout << temp->data <<" ";
      if(temp->lbit == 1 && flag == 0)      // go left till
      lbit is 1
      {
         temp = temp->left;
      }
      else if(temp->rbit == 1)      // go to right by child
      {
         temp = temp->right;
         flag = 0;
      }
      else      // go to right by thread
      {
         temp = temp->right;
         flag = 1;
      }
   }
}      //End of function
```

7.11.5 Insert to Right of a Node

Consider Figs 7.72(a) and (b). We want to insert the node *t* to the right of the node *s* in both the threaded trees.

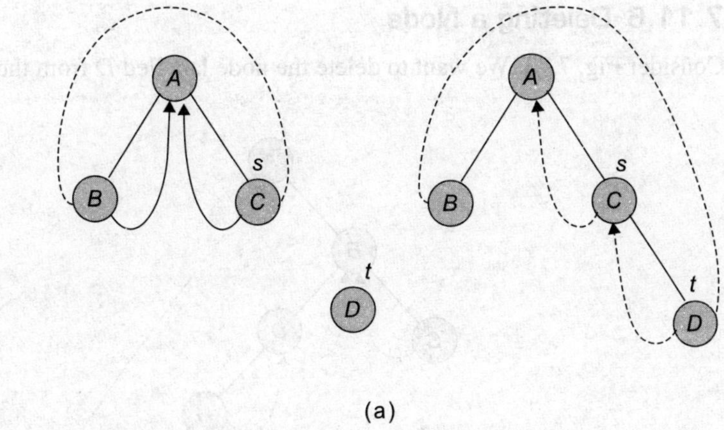

(a)

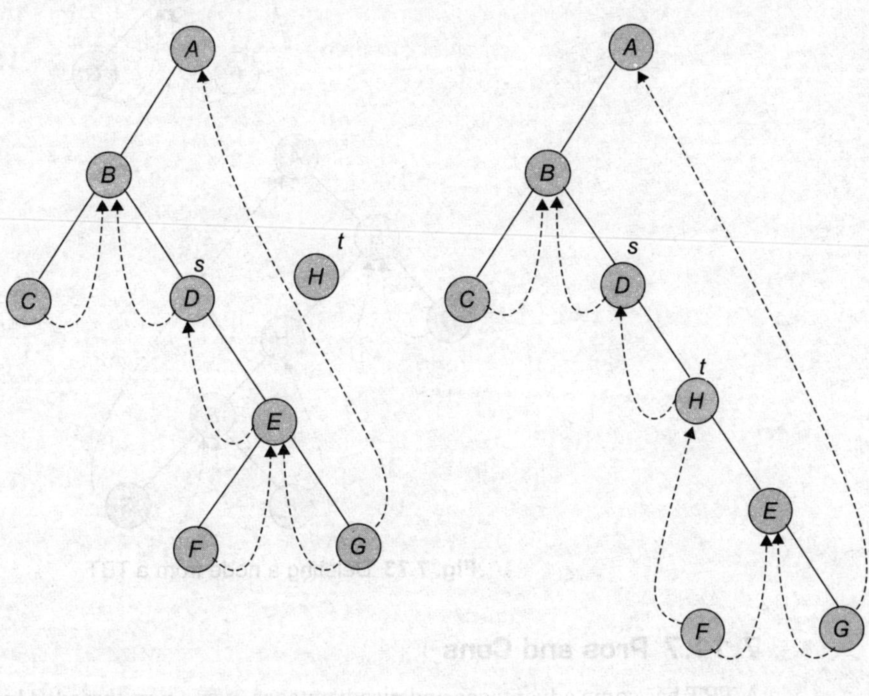

(b)

Fig. 7.72 Inserting nodes in a TBT (a) Inserting node *D* (b) Inserting node *H*

7.11.6 Deleting a Node

Consider Fig. 7.73. We want to delete the node labelled *D* from the TBT.

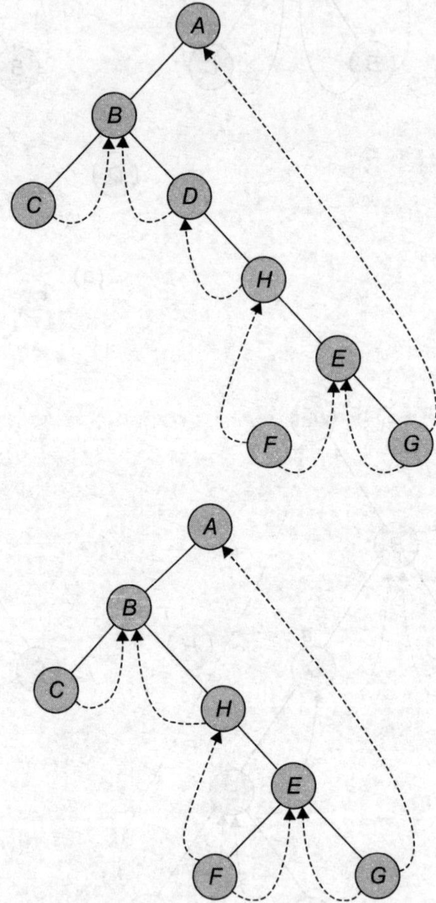

Fig. 7.73 Deleting a node from a TBT

7.11.7 Pros and Cons

A TBT has some advantages and disadvantages over a non-threaded binary tree. They are as follows:

1. The traversal for a TBT is straightforward. No recursion or stack is needed. Once we locate the leftmost node, we loop following the thread to the next node. When we find the null thread, the traversal is complete.

2. At any node, the node's successor and predecessor can be located. In case of non-threaded binary tree, this task is time consuming and difficult. In addition, stack is needed for the same.
3. Threads are usually more upward, whereas links are downward. Thus, in a threaded tree, we can traverse in either direction, and the nodes are in fact circularly linked. Hence, any node can be reached from any other node.
4. Insertions into and deletions from a threaded tree are time consuming as the link and thread are to be manipulated.

7.12 APPLICATIONS OF BINARY TREES

There is a vast set of applications of the binary tree in addition to searching. The applications discussed in this section are gaming, expression tree, Huffman tree for coding, and decision trees.

7.12.1 Expression Tree

A binary tree storing or representing an arithmetic expression is called as *expression tree*. The leaves of an expression tree are *operands*. Operands could be variables or constants. The branch nodes (internal nodes) represent the operators. A binary tree is the most suitable one for arithmetic expressions as it contains either binary or unary operators. The expression tree for expression E, is shown in Fig. 7.74.

$$\text{Let } E = ((A \times B) + (C - D))/(C - E)$$

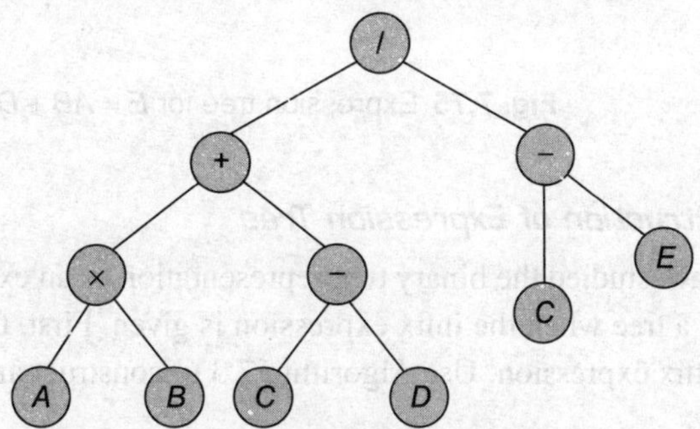

Fig. 7.74 Expression tree for $E = ((A \times B) + (C - D))/(C - E)$

We have studied that the Polish notations are very useful in the compilation process. There is a close relationship between binary trees and expressions in prefix and postfix notations.

In the expression tree as in Fig. 7.74, an infix expression is represented by representing the node as an operator, and the left and right subtrees are the left and right operands of that operator.

If we traverse this tree in preorder, we visit the nodes in the order of: $/ + \times AB - CD - CE$, and this is a prefix form of the infix expression. On the other hand, if we traverse the tree in postorder, the nodes are visited in the following order: $AB \times CD - E - /$, which is a postfix equivalent of the infix notation.

Example 7.7 represents the postfix equivalent of a given infix notation.

EXAMPLE 7.7 Represent $AB + D \times EFAD \times + / + C +$ as an expression tree.

Solution Figure 7.75 represents the given expression in the form of a tree.

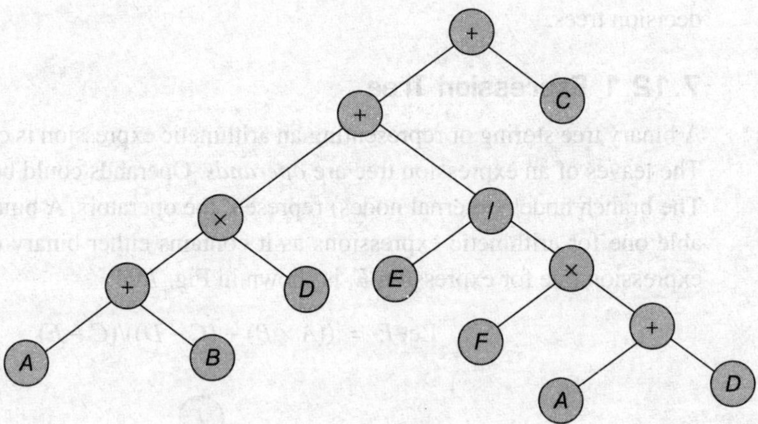

Fig. 7.75 Expression tree for $E = AB + D \times EFAD \times + / + C +$

Construction of Expression Tree

We have studied the binary tree representation of an expression. Let us study how to construct a tree when the infix expression is given. First, the infix expression is converted to a postfix expression. Use Algorithm 7.3 to construct an expression tree.

ALGORITHM 7.3

(Scan the postfix expression from left to right.)

1. Get one token from expression E.
2. Create a node say `curr` for it.

3. If (symbol is operand) then
   (a) push a node `curr` onto a stack.
4. else if (symbol is operator) then
   (a) T_2 = `pop()`
   T_1 = `pop()`
   Here T_1 and T_2 are pointers to left trees and right subtrees of the operator, respectively.
   (b) Attach T_1 to left and T_2 to the right of `curr`.
   (c) Form a tree whose root is the operator and T_1 and T_2 are left and right children, respectively.
   (d) Push the node `curr` having attached left and right subtrees onto a stack.
5. Repeat steps 1–4 till the end of expression.
6. Pop the node curr from the stack, which is a pointer to the root of expression tree.

Example 7.8 shows the steps to construct an expression tree for a given expression, *E*.

EXAMPLE 7.8 Represent $E = (a + b \times c)/d$ as an expression tree.

Solution Let us consider the expression $E = (a + b \times c)/d$

Postfix expression = *abc* ×+ *d*/

The following steps of operations are performed:

1. The operands *a*, *b*, *c* will be pushed onto the stack by forming a one-node tree of each and pushing a pointer to each onto a stack (Fig. 7.76).

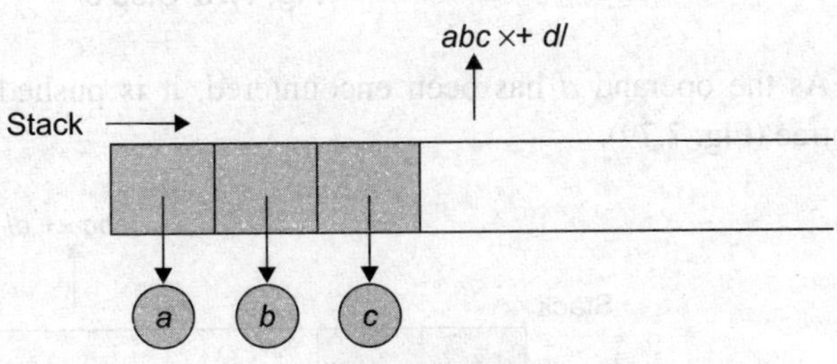

Fig. 7.76 Step 1

2. When the operator × has been encountered, the top two pointers are popped. A tree is formed with × as a root and the two popped pointers as children. The pointer to the root is pushed onto a stack (Fig. 7.77).

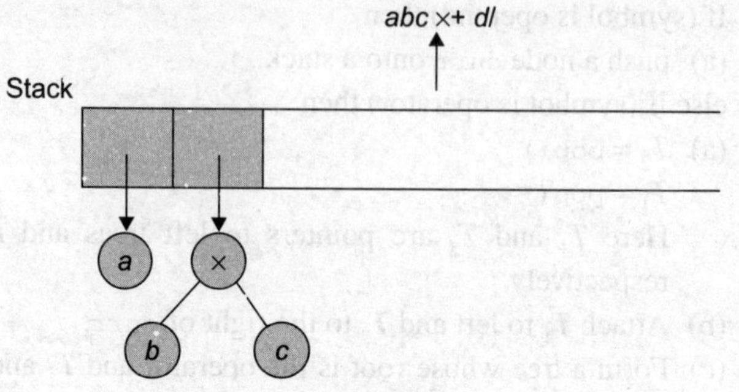

Fig. 7.77 Step 2

3. After the operator + has been encountered, the procedure as in step 2 is executed (Fig. 7.78).

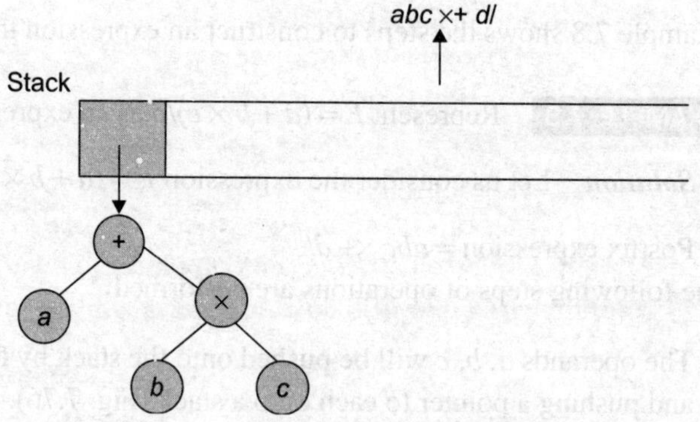

Fig. 7.78 Step 3

4. As the operand *d* has been encountered, it is pushed as a pointer to the one-node tree (Fig. 7.79).

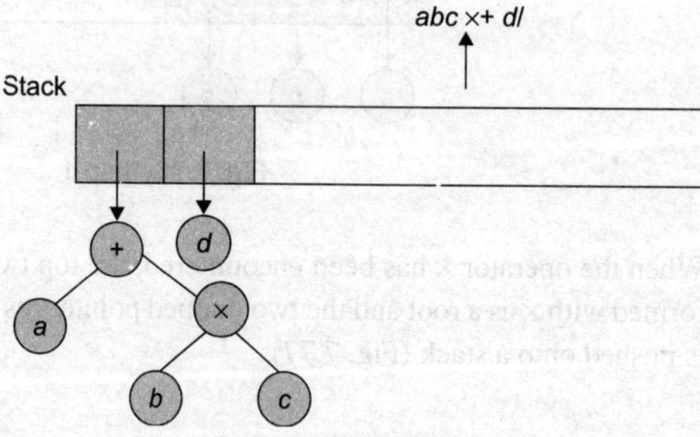

Fig. 7.79 Step 4

5. After the operator has been encountered, it follows the procedure as in step 2 (Fig. 7.80).

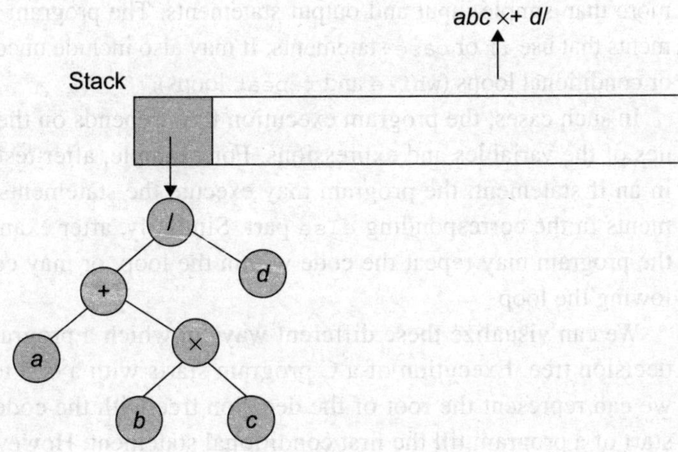

Fig. 7.80 Step 5

6. Pop the stack as the expression has been processed. This returns a pointer to the expression tree's root.

7.12.2 Decision Tree

In practice there are many applications which use trees to store data for rapid retrieval, the most useful application being decision making. These applications, along with a tree as one of the data structures, often oblige some additional structures on the tree. Consider an example tree, a BST. In the BST, the data in a left or right subtree has a particular relationship with the data in the node (such as being greater than or smaller than the data).

We can use trees to arrange the outcomes of various decisions in the required order. We can denote these actions in the form of a tree, called the decision tree.

The *decision tree* is a classifier in the form of a tree where each node is either a branch node or a leaf node. Here the leaf node denotes the value of the target attribute (class) of examples and the branch node is a decision node that denotes some test to be carried out and takes a decision based on a single attribute value, with one branch and subtree for each possible outcome of the test. A decision tree can be used for classification by starting at the root of the tree and moving through it until a leaf node that provides the classification of the instance is reached. The decision tree training is a typical inductive approach to gain the knowledge on classification.

For example, consider the execution of a C program. The initial part of the program contains pre-processor directives followed by global variables and functions including the main function. Initially, the operating systems need to load the code and constants, initialize variables (if any), read the input data, and print the required information. The sequence of these actions depends on the code written. Generally, most programs involve more than simple input and output statements. The program includes conditional statements that use `if` or `case` statements. It may also include unconditional loops (`for` loop) or conditional loops (`while` and `repeat` loops).

In such cases, the program execution flow depends on the results of testing the values of the variables and expressions. For example, after testing a Boolean expression in an if statement, the program may execute the statements following it or the statements in the corresponding `else` part. Similarly, after examining a `while` condition, the program may repeat the code within the loop, or may continue with the code following the loop.

We can visualize these different ways in which a program may execute through a decision tree. Execution of a C program starts with a call to the function `main()`, or we can represent the root of the decision tree with the code that is always run at the start of a program till the first conditional statement. However, at the first conditional statement, the program executes one code segment or another depending upon the value of the condition. In such a situation, the decision tree can be drawn with a child of the root for each code option that the program code follows. For an `if` statement, there are two children of the root—one if the Boolean expression is true where the `then` clause is executed, and another in case the expression is false. For a `case` statement, a different child is drawn for each different case identified by the code, because different paths are followed for each of these situations. Figure 7.81 illustrates all such cases.

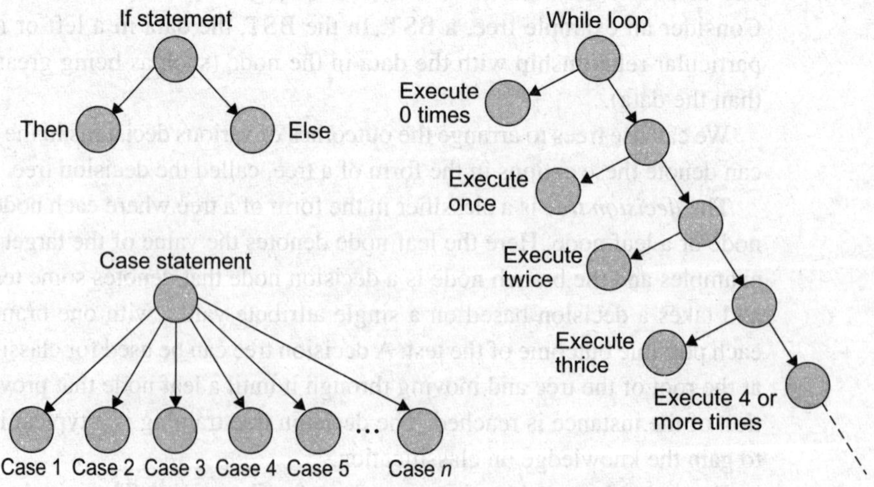

Fig. 7.81 Decision trees for program structures

Figure 7.80 represents pseudo-structures for the Pascal language. In the figure, for a `while` loop, the body of the loop might be executed 0, 1, 2, 3, or more times, after which the program execution continues with the code that follows the `while` statement. Conversely, the execution flow first tests the `exit` condition and then either exits the loop or starts the body of the loop for the first time. If the loop is executed for the first time, then the execution arrives at the `exit` condition a second time and either exits the loop or continues with the loop a second time. The work within the loop continues until the system tests the `exit` condition and determines that the loop should not continue. In tracing the program execution, we add each individual decision into another branch inside a general decision tree.

The example demonstrates the usefulness of the decision trees to demonstrate and test all possible execution paths that might be followed within a program or a piece of code. Decision trees not only provide a mechanism for demonstrating the code execution but they also provide a structure for examining how general algorithms might work. Consider an example of searching an element in a sorted list. We can use a decision tree to demonstrate the working of searching of member in the list. For binary search to be applied on the sorted list, various comparisons are required for deciding which set of elements are to be further searched or whether the search is to be terminated. In a BST, when an element is initially compared with the root, if the search is successful, the process terminates. If the element is lesser than the root, then it is searched in the left subtree, and otherwise in right subtree.

The advantages of decision trees are the following:

1. Decision trees are most suitable for listing all possible decisions from the current state.
2. They are suitable for classification without the need for many computations.

Decision trees are popularly used in expert systems. Although decision trees seem to be very useful, they suffer from a few drawbacks, such as the following:

1. Decision trees are prone to errors in classification problems with more classes
2. They can be computationally expensive for complex problems.

7.12.3 Huffman's Coding

One of the most important applications of the binary tree is in communication. Consider an example of transmitting an English text. We need to represent this text by a sequence of 0s and 1s. To represent the message made of English letters in binary, we represent each alphabet in the binary form, that is, as a sequence of 0s and 1s. Each alphabet must be represented with a unique binary code. We need to assign a code, each of length 5 to each letter in the alphabet as $2^4 < 26 < 2^5$. Now to send a message, we have to simply transmit a long string of 0s and 1s containing the sequences for the letters in the message. At the receiving end, the message received will be divided into sequences of length 5, and the corresponding message is recognized.

Let us consider that a sequence of 1000 letters is to be sent. Now, the total bits to be transmitted will be 1000×5, as we represent each letter with 5 bits. It may happen that among those 1000 letters, the letters a, i, r, e, t, and n appeared maximum number of times in the sequence.

It is observed that the letters in the alphabet are not used with uniform frequencies. For example, the letters e and t are used more frequently than x and z. Hence, we may represent the more frequently used letters with shorter sequences and less frequently used letters with longer sequences so that the overall length of the string will be reduced. In this example, if a, i, r, e, t, and n are assigned say in the sequence of length 2, and let us assume that each one of them appeared 100 times among the sequence of 1000 letters. Now, the length will be reduced by a factor

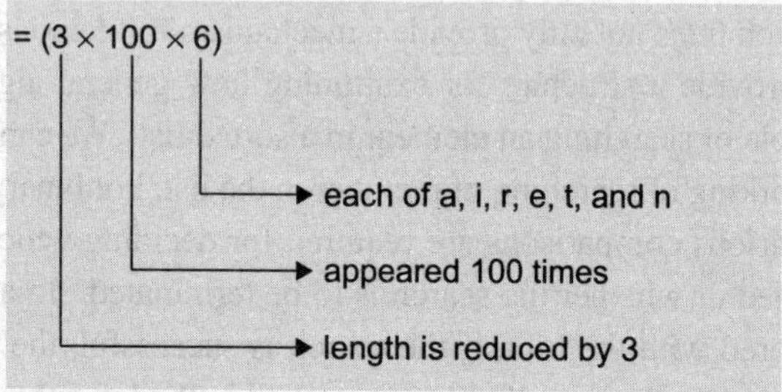

Such a coding is called as *variable length coding*. Even though the variable length coding reduces the overall length of the sequence to be transmitted, an interesting problem arises. When we represent the letters by the sequences of various lengths, there is the question of how one at the receiving end can unambiguously divide a long string of 0s and 1s into the sequences corresponding to the letters. Let us consider an example. Let us use the sequence 00 to represent the letter 'a', 01 to represent letter 'n', and 0001 to represent the letter 't'. Suppose we want to transmit a text of two letters 'an' by transmitting the sequence 0001. Now, at the receiving end, it is difficult to determine whether the transmitted sequence was 'an' or 't'. This is because 00 is a prefix of the code 0001. We must assign variable sequences to the letters such that no code is the prefix of the other.

A set of sequences is said to be a *prefix code* if no sequence in the set is the prefix of another sequence in the set. For example, the set {000, 001, 01, 10, 11} is a prefix code, whereas the set {1, 00, 000, 0001} is not. Hence we must use prefix codes to represent the letters in alphabet. If we represent the letters in the alphabet by the sequences in a prefix code, it will always be possible to divide a received string into sequences representing the letters in a message unambiguously. One of the most useful applications of binary tree is in generating the prefix codes for a given binary tree. We label the two edges incident from each branch node with 0 and 1. To each leaf, assign a code that is a sequence of labels of the edges in the path from the root to that of leaf (Fig. 7.82).

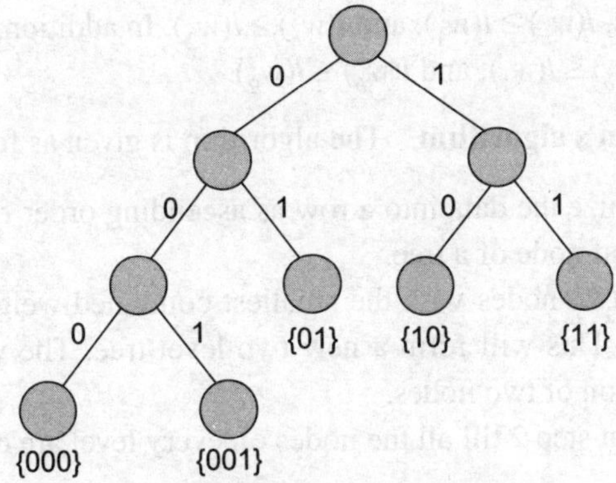

Fig. 7.82 Prefix codes

It is always possible to divide a received sequence of 0s and 1s into the sequences that are in a prefix code. Starting at the root of the binary tree, we shall trace a downward path in the tree according to the bits in the received sequence. At a branch node, we shall follow the edge labelled with 0 if we encounter a 0 in the received sequence, and we shall follow the edge labelled with a 1 if we encounter a 1 in the received sequence. When the downward path reaches a leaf, it shows that the prefix code has been detected. For the next sequence, we should return to the root of the tree. This process clearly assures that the variable length code, which is the prefix code, has no ambiguity.

Now the problem is about constructing a binary tree. Suppose we are given a set of weights $w_1, w_2, ..., w_n$. Let us assume that $w_1 \leq w_2 \leq ... \leq w_n$. A binary tree that has n leaves with weights $w_1, w_2, ..., w_n$ assigned to the leaves is called as binary tree for weight $w_1, w_2, ..., w_n$. Our aim is to assign smaller code to the leaf of higher weights, as the weights here denote the frequency of occurrence. The length of sequence of bits assigned to a leaf node is path length of that node. Hence, we want lesser path length to the leaf nodes with higher weights.

Let the weight of a tree T be denoted by w(T). The weight of a binary tree for weights $w_1, w_2, ..., w_n$ is given by

$$w(\text{T}) = \sum_{i=1}^{n} w_i L(w_i), \text{ where}$$

$$L(w_i) = \text{path length of node of weight } w_i.$$

A binary tree for weights $w_1, w_2, ..., w_n$ is said to be an optimal binary tree if its weight is minimum. Hence, our aim is to construct a tree such that w(T) is minimum.

D.A. Huffman has given a very elegant procedure to construct an optimal binary tree. Suppose we want an optimal tree for the weights w_1, w_2, ..., w_n. Let a be a branch node of largest path length in the tree. Suppose the weights assigned to the sons of a are w_b and w_c. Thus, $l(w_b) \geq l(w_1)$, and $l(w_b) \geq l(w_2)$. In addition, since the tree is optimal, we should have $l(w_b) \leq l(w_1)$, and $l(w_b) \leq l(w_2)$.

Huffman's algorithm The algorithm is given as follows:

1. Organize the data into a row as ascending order frequency weights. Each character is the leaf node of a tree.
2. Find two nodes with the smallest combined weights and join them to form the third node. This will form a new two-level tree. The weight of the new third node is the addition of two nodes.
3. Repeat step 2 till all the nodes on every level are combined to form a single tree.

7.12.4 Game Trees

One of the most exciting applications of trees is in games such as tic-tac-toe, chess, nim, checkers, go, and so on. We shall consider tic-tac-toe as an example for explaining this application of trees.

The game starts with an empty board and each time a player tries for the best move from the given board position. Each player is initially assigned a symbol of either 'X' or 'O'. Depending on the board position the user has to decide how good the position seems to be for a player. For implementation we need to compute a value say, `WinValue`, which of course will have the largest possible value for a winning position, and the smallest value for a losing position. An example of such a `WinValue` computation could be the difference between the number of rows, columns, and diagonals that are left open for one player and those left open for the opponent game partner. Here we can omit the values 9 and –9 as they represent the values for a position that wins and loses, respectively. While computing this value we need not further search for other possible board positions that might result from the current positions, as it just estimates a motionless board position. We can write a function while implementing this game that computes and returns the `WinValue`. Let us name such a function as `ComputeWinValue()`. Considering all the possible positions, it is possible to construct a tree of the possible board positions that may result from each possible move, called a *game tree*.

Now with a given board position, we need to determine the next best move and for that we need to consider all the possible moves and respective resulting positions after the move. For a player the best move is the one that results in a board position with the highest `WinValue`. Careful observation leads to the conclusion that this calculation however, does not always yield the best move. A sample position and the five possible moves that player with symbol X can make from that current position is shown in Fig. 7.83.

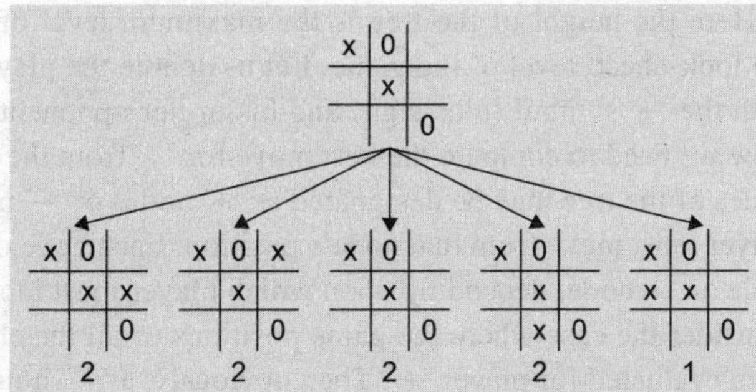

Fig. 7.83 An example game tree and WinValues of each possible move

Now if we compute `WinValue` for the five resulting positions, using the `ComputeWinValue()` function, we get the values as shown in Fig. 7.83. Among them four of the moves result with the same maximum `WinValue`. One can note that the move in the fourth position definitely leads to the victory for the player with the marking symbol X, and the other three moves would lead to the victory of the opponent with the symbol 0.

This shows that the move that yields the smallest `WinValue` is better than the moves that yield a higher `WinValue`. The static `ComputeWinValue()` function, therefore, is not sufficient to guess the result of the game. Hence we need to revise this function. We can have such a function for simple games such as tic-tac-toe, but often, games such as chess are too complex for static functions to determine the best possible move computation.

The best way to predict and play is to look ahead of several moves so as to get a significantly better choice of the next move. Let the variable `LookAhead` be the number of future moves to be taken care of. Considering all the possible positions, it is possible to construct a tree of the possible board positions that may result from each possible move as shown in Fig. 7.84 which shows the game tree for a tic-tac-toe game considering a look-ahead of level of 2.

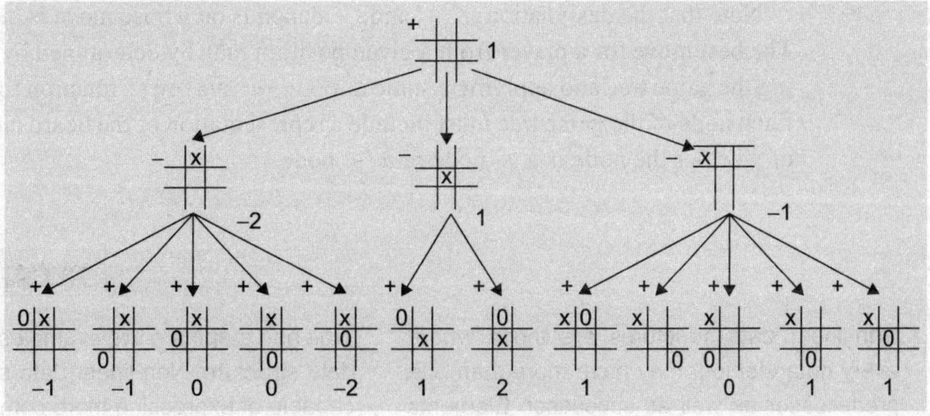

Fig. 7.84 A game tree for tic-tac-toe

Here the height of the tree is the maximum level of the nodes which represents the look-ahead level of the game. Let us denote the player who must begin the game with the '+' symbol (plus sign) and his or her opponent as '–' symbol (minus sign). Now we need to compute the best move for '+' from the root position. The remaining nodes of the tree may be designated as '+' nodes or '–' nodes, depending upon which player must move from that node's position. Each node of Fig. 7.84 is marked as a '+' node or '–' node, depending upon which player must move from that node's position. Consider the case where the game positions of all the child nodes of a '+' node have been evaluated for player '+'. Then obviously, a '+' should select the move that paves the way to the maximum `WinValue`. Thus, the value of a '+' node to player '+' is the maximum of the values of its child nodes. On the other hand, once '+' moves, '–' will choose the move that results in the minimum of the values of its child nodes.

For a player with the symbol 0, Fig. 7.85 shows the best possible moves.

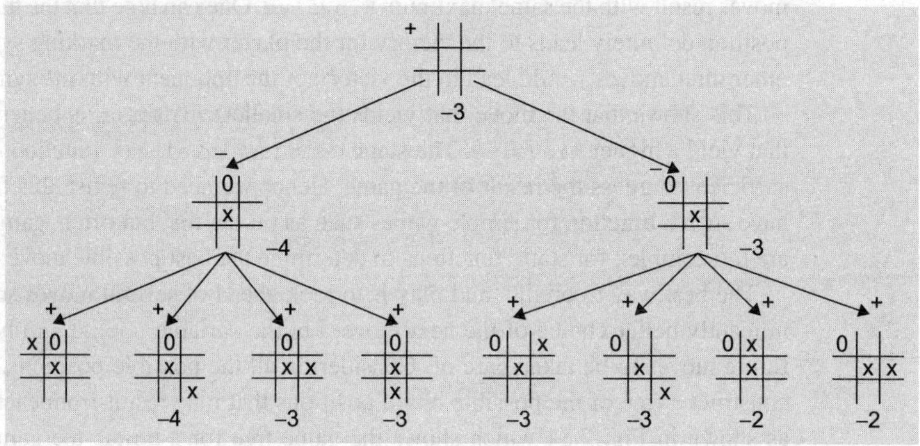

Fig. 7.85 Game tree showing best moves for a player with symbol 0

Note that the designation of '+' and '–' depends on whose move is being calculated. The best move for a player from a given position may by determined by first constructing the game tree and applying a static `ComputeWinValue()` function to the leaf nodes. Each node of the game tree must include a representation of the board and an indication of whether the node is a '+'node or a '–' node.

RECAPITULATION

- Non-linear data structures are those where every data element may have more than one predecessor as well as successor. Elements do not form any particular linear sequence. Tree and graph are two examples of non-linear data structure. Non-linear data structures are capable of expressing more complex relationship than linear data structure.

- Tree, a non-linear data structure, is a mean to maintain and manipulate data in many applications. Wherever the hierarchical relationship among data is to be preserved, tree is used.
- A binary tree is a special form of a tree. It is important and frequently used in various applications of computer science. A binary tree has degree two, and each node has utmost two children. This makes the implementation of tree easier. The implementation of binary tree should represent the hierarchical relationship between the parent node and its left and right children.
- Binary tree has the natural implementation in a linked storage. In a linked organization, we wish that all nodes should be allocated dynamically. Hence, we need each node with data and link fields. Each node of a binary tree has both a left and a right subtree. Each node will have three fields Lchild, Data, and Rchild.
- The operations on a binary tree include insert node, delete node, and traverse tree. Traversal is one of the key operations. Traversal means visiting every node of a binary tree. There are various traversal methods. For a systematic traversal, it is better to visit each node (starting from root) and its both subtrees in the same way.
- Let L represent the left subtree, R represent the right subtree, and D be node data. Three traversals are fundamental: LDR, LRD, and DLR. These are called as *inorder*, *postorder*, and *preorder* traversals because there is a natural correspondence between these traversals producing the infix, postfix, and preorder forms of an arithmetic expressions, respectively. In addition, a traversal where the node is visited before its children are visited is called a *breadth-first traversal*; a walk where the children are visited prior to the parent is called a *depth-first traversal*.
- The binary search tree is a binary tree with the property that the value in a node is greater than any value in a node's left subtree and less than any value in the node's right subtree. This property guarantees fast search time provided the tree is relatively balanced.
- The key applications of tree include the following: expression tree, gaming, Huffman coding, and decision tree.

KEY TERMS

Binary search tree A binary search tree (BST) is a binary tree that is either empty or where every node contains a key and satisfies the following conditions:

1. The key in the left child of a node, if it exists, is less than the key in its parent node.
2. The key in the right child of a node, if it exists, is greater than the key in its parent node.
3. The left and the right subtrees of the node are again BSTs.

Binary tree A binary tree has degree two, each node has atmost two children. A binary tree is either: an empty tree; or consists of a node, called root and two children, left and right, each of which are themselves binary trees.

Breadth- and depth-first traversals A traversal where the node is visited before its children are visited is called a breadth-first traversal; a walk where the children are visited prior to the parent is called a depth-first traversal.

Decision tree Decision tree is a classifier in the form of a tree structure, where each node is either:

a leaf node—indicates the value of the target attribute (class) of examples; or a decision node—specifies some test to be carried out on a single attribute-value, with one branch and sub-tree for each possible outcome of the test.

Expression tree A binary tree storing or representing an arithmetic expression is called as an expression tree. The leaves of an expression tree are operands. Operands could be variables or constants. The branch nodes (internal nodes) represent the operators.

Inorder traversal In this traversal, the left subtree is visited first in inorder, then the root, and finally the right subtree in inorder.

Non-linear data structures Non-linear data structures are used to represent the data containing hierarchical or network relationship between the elements. Trees and graphs are examples of non-linear data structure.

Pre-order traversal In this traversal, the root is visited first, then the left subtree in preorder, and finally the right subtree in preorder.

Threaded binary tree A.J. Perlis and C. Thornton have suggested to replace all the null links in binary tree by pointers, called threads. A tree with thread is called as threaded binary tree.

Tree traversal Traversal of tree means stepping through the nodes of a tree by means of the connections between parents and children; it is also called walking the tree, and the action is called the walk of the tree.

Tree Tree, a non-linear data structure, is a mean to maintain and manipulate data in many applications. Non-linear data structures are capable of expressing more complex relationship than linear data structure. A class of graphs that are acyclic are termed as trees. Trees are useful in describing any structure that involves hierarchy.

EXERCISES

Multiple choice questions

1. Consider the following tree:

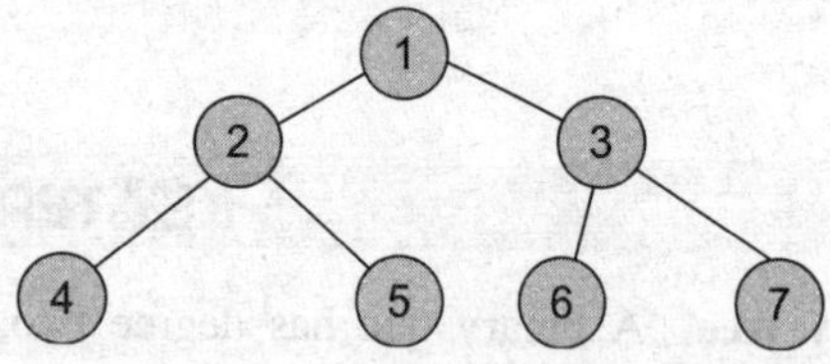

If the postorder traversal gives ($ab - cd +$), then the label of the nodes 1, 2, 3, 4, 5, 6 will be

(a) $+, -, \times, a, b, c, d$
(b) $a, -, b, +, c, \times, d$
(c) $a, b, c, d, -, \times, +$
(d) $-, a, b, +, \times, c, d$

2. A list of integers is read one at a time, and a BST is constructed. Next, the tree is traversed and the integers are printed. Which traversal would print the result in the original order of the input?

(a) Preorder
(b) Postorder
(c) Inorder
(d) None of the above

3. A binary tree T has n leaf nodes. The number of nodes of degree 2 in T is

(a) $\log_2 n$
(b) $n - 1$
(c) n
(d) 2^n

4. Which is the most efficient tree for accessing data from a database?

(a) BST
(b) B-tree
(c) OBST
(d) AVL tree

5. A binary tree where every non-leaf node has non-empty left and right subtrees is called a strictly binary tree. Such a tree with 10 leaves

(a) cannot have more than 19 nodes.

(b) has exactly 19 nodes.
(c) has exactly 17 nodes.
(d) cannot have more than 17 nodes.

6. The depth of a complete binary tree with n nodes is
(a) $\log_2 (n+1) - 1$
(b) $\log_2 n$
(c) $\log_2 (n-1) + 1$
(d) $\log_2 n + 1$

7. Which of the following traversal techniques lists the nodes of a BST in ascending order?
(a) Postorder
(b) Inorder
(c) Preorder
(d) All of a, b, c

8. A binary tree has a height of 5. What is the minimum number of nodes it can have?
(a) 31
(b) 15
(c) 5
(d) 1

9. A binary tree is generated by inserting an inorder as 50, 15, 62, 5, 20, 58, 91, 3, 8, 37, 60, 24. The number of nodes in the left and right subtree, respectively is given by
(a) (4, 7)
(b) (7, 4)
(c) (8, 3)
(d) (3, 8)

10. A BST contains the values 1, 2, 3, 4, 5, 6, 7, 8. The tree is traversed in preorder and the values are printed. The valid output is
(a) 53124786
(b) 53126487
(c) 53241678
(d) 53124768

11. In ________ traversal, the right subtree is processed last.
(a) a preorder
(b) an inorder
(c) a postorder
(d) (a) or (b)

Review questions

1. Consider the binary tree in the following figure.

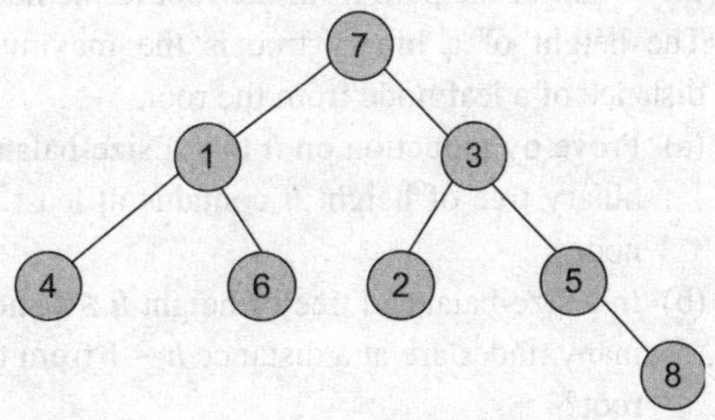

(a) What structure is represented by the binary tree?
(b) Give the different steps for deleting the node with key 5 so that the structure is preserved.
(c) Outline a procedure in pseudo code to delete an arbitrary node from such a binary tree with n nodes that preserves the structure. What is the worst case time complexity of your procedure?

2. Prove by the principal of mathematical induction that for any binary tree where every non-leaf node has 2 descendants, the number of leaves in the tree is one more than the number of non-leaf nodes.
3. A 3-ary tree is a tree where every internal node has exactly 3 children. Use induction to prove that the number of leaves in a 3-ary tree with n internal nodes is $2(n-1)+3$.
4. A rooted tree with 12 nodes has its numbers from 1 to 12 in preorder. When the tree is traversed in postorder, the nodes are visited in following order: 3, 5, 4, 2, 7, 8, 6, 10, 11, 12, 9, 1. Reconstruct the original tree from this information, that is, find the parent of each node. Show the tree diagrammatically.
5. What is the number of binary trees with 3 nodes which when traversed in postorder give the sequence A, B, C? Draw all these binary trees.
6. A size-balanced binary tree is a binary tree where for every node, the difference between the

number of nodes in the left and right subtree is utmost 1. The distance of a node from the root is the length of the path from the root to the node. The height of a binary tree is the maximum distance of a leaf node from the root.

(a) Prove by induction on h that a size-balance binary tree of height h contains at least $2h$ nodes.

(b) In a size-balanced tree of height $h \leq 1$, how many nodes are at a distance $h - 1$ from the root?

7. Let A be an $n \times n$ matrix such that the elements in each row and each column are arranged in ascending order. Draw a decision tree that finds first, second, and third smallest elements in minimum number of comparisons.
8. In a binary tree, a full node is defined to be a node with 2 children. Use induction on the height of a binary tree to prove that the number of full nodes plus one is equal to the number of leaves.
9. (a) Draw a BST (initially empty) that results from inserting the records with the keys

EASYQUESTION

(b) Delete the key Q from the constructed BST.
10. Write a recursive function in C++ that creates a mirror image of a binary tree.
11. What is a BST? Write a recursive C++ function to search for an element in a given BST. Write a non-recursive version of the same.
12. Write a non-recursive C++ function to traverse a binary tree containing integers in preorder.
13. Write a C++ function for insertion of a node into a BST.
14. Write C++ function that traverses a TBT in inorder.
15. Represent a binary tree using pointers and write a function to traverse and point nodes of a tree level-by-level.
16. Represent a binary tree using pointers and write a function to traverse a given tree in inorder.
17. Given the following inorder and postorder sequences of nodes of binary tree, draw the corresponding binary tree. Show the steps.

(a) Inorder : 1 3 5 6 4 2 7

(b) Postorder : 6 5 4 3 7 2 1
18. From the given traversals, construct the binary tree.

(a) Inorder: D B F E A G C L J H K

(b) Postorder: D F E B G L J K H C A
19. Write a pseudocode C++ for non-recursive postorder and inorder traversal for binary tree.
20. List down the steps to convert a general tree to a binary tree. Convert the following general tree to a binary tree.

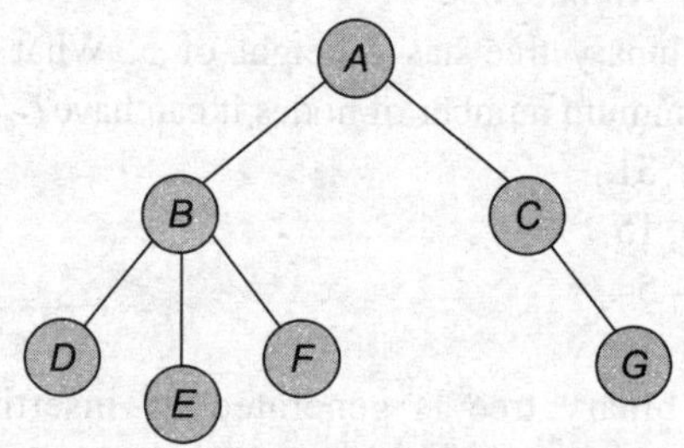

21. Explain the array representation of binary trees using the following figures and state and explain the limitations of this representation.

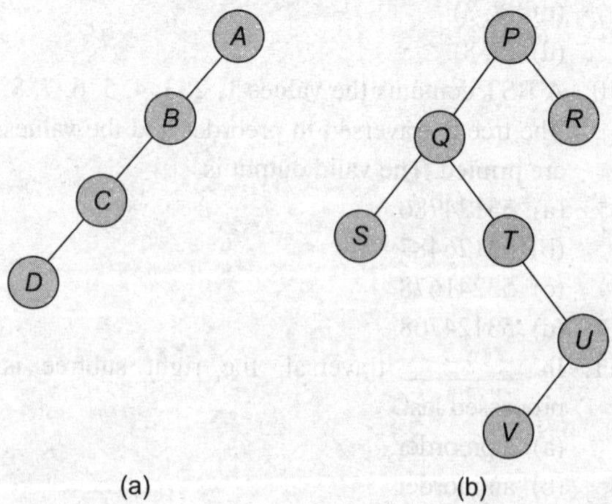

22. Write a pseudocode for deleting a node from a BST. Simulate your algorithm with a BST of 10 nodes and show the deletion process. Especially, show the deletion of the interior nodes and not just the leaf nodes.

23. Write a C ++ function to find the following:
    (a) Height of a given binary tree
    (b) Width (breadth) of a binary tree

Answers to multiple choice questions

1. (a) The postorder traversal yields 4, 5, 2, 6, 7, 3, 1. Comparing with $a, b, -, c, d, \times, +$, we get the labels of nodes 1, 2, 3, 4, 5, 6, 7 as $+, -, \times, a, b, c, d$, respectively.

2. (d) 3. (b) 4. (c) 5. (b) A regular (strictly) binary tree with n leaves must have $(2n - 1)$ nodes. 6. (a) 7. (b) 8. (c) 9. (b) 10. (d) 11. (d)

8 GRAPHS

OBJECTIVES

After completing this chapter, the reader will be able to understand the following:

- Graphs as one of the most important non-linear data structures
- The representation that models various kinds of graphs
- Some useful graph algorithms

In many application areas such as cartography, sociology, chemistry, geography, mathematics, electrical engineering, and computer science, we often need a representation that reflects an arbitrary relationship among the objects. One of the most powerful and natural solutions that models such a relationship is a *graph*. There are many concrete, practical problems such as electrical circuits, Königsberg's bridges, and Instant Insanity that have been simplified and solved using graphs.

Non-linear data structures are used to represent the data containing a network or hierarchical relationship among the elements. Graphs are one of the most important non-linear data structures. In non-linear data structures, every data element may have more than one predecessor as well as successor. Elements do not form any particular linear sequence. We shall study various representations of graphs and important algorithms for processing them in this chapter.

8.1 INTRODUCTION

The seven bridges of Königsberg is an ancient classic problem. It was creatively solved by the great Swiss mathematician Leonhard Euler in 1736, which laid the foundations of graph theory. Another example is Instant Insanity. It is a puzzle consisting of four cubes where each of the four faces of these cubes is painted with one of the four different colours—red, blue, white, or green. The problem is to stack the cubes, one on the top of the other so that whether the cubes are viewed from front, back, left, or right, one sees all the four colours. Since 331,776 different stack combinations are possible, solving it by hand or by the trial-and-error method is impractical. However, the use of graphs makes it possible to discover a solution in a few minutes!

There are many such problems that can be represented and solved using graphs. Finding an abstract mathematical model of the concrete problem can be a difficult task, which may require both skill and experience. Some real-world applications of graphs include communication networking, analysis of electrical circuits, activity network, linguistics, and so on.

8.2 GRAPH ABSTRACT DATA TYPE

Graphs as non-linear data structures represent the relationship among data elements, having more than one predecessor and/or successor. A graph G is a collection of nodes (*vertices*) and arcs joining a pair of the nodes (*edges*). Edges between two vertices represent the relationship between them. For finite graphs, V and E are finite. We can denote the graph as $G = (V, E)$.

Let us define the graph ADT. We need to specify both sets of vertices and edges. Basic operations include creating a graph, inserting and deleting a vertex, inserting and deleting an edge, traversing a graph, and a few others.

A graph is a set of vertices and edges $\{V, E\}$ and can be declared as follows:

```
graph
    create()→Graph
    insert_vertex(Graph, v)→Graph
    delete_vertex(Graph, v)→Graph
    insert_edge(Graph, u, v)→Graph
    delete_edge(Graph, u, v)→Graph
    is_empty(Graph)→Boolean;
end graph
```

These are the primitive operations that are needed for storing and processing a graph.

Create

The create operation provides the appropriate framework for the processing of graphs. The `create()` function is used to create an empty graph. An empty graph has both V and E as null sets. The empty graph has the total number of vertices and edges as zero. However, while implementing, we should have V as a non-empty set and E as an empty set as the mathematical notation normally requires the set of vertices to be non-empty.

Insert Vertex

The insert vertex operation inserts a new vertex into a graph and returns the modified graph. When the vertex is added, it is isolated as it is not connected to any of the vertices in the graph through an edge. If the added vertex is related with one (or more) vertices in the graph, then the respective edge(s) are to be inserted.

Figure 8.1(a) shows a graph $G(V, E)$, where $V = \{a, b, c\}$ and $E = \{(a, b), (a, c), (b, c)\}$, and the resultant graph after inserting the node d. The resultant graph G is shown in Fig. 8.1(b). It shows the inserted vertex with resultant $V = \{a, b, c, d\}$. We can show the adjacency relation with other vertices by adding the edge. So now, E would be $E = \{(a, b), (a, c), (b, c), (b, d)\}$ as shown in Fig. 8.1(c).

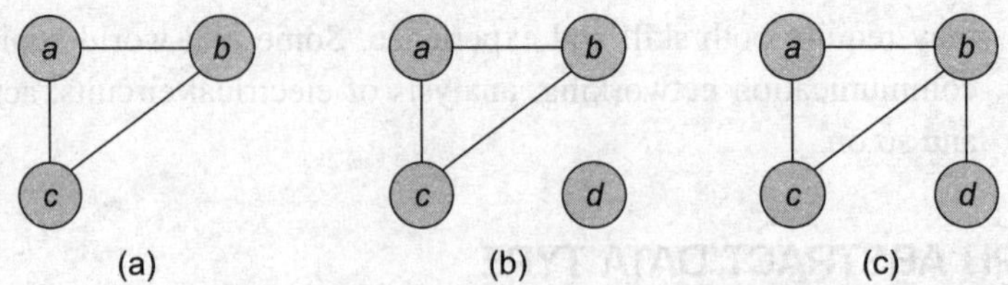

Fig. 8.1 Inserting a vertex in a graph (a) Graph *G* (b) After inserting vertex *d* (c) After adding an edge

Delete Vertex

The delete vertex operation deletes a vertex and all the incident edges on that vertex and returns the modified graph.

Figure 8.2(a) shows a graph $G(V, E)$ where $V = \{a, b, c, d\}$ and $E = \{(a, b), (a, c), (b, c), (b, d)\}$, and the resultant graph after deleting the node c is shown in Fig. 8.2(b) with $V = \{a, b, d\}$ and $E = \{(a, b), (b, d)\}$.

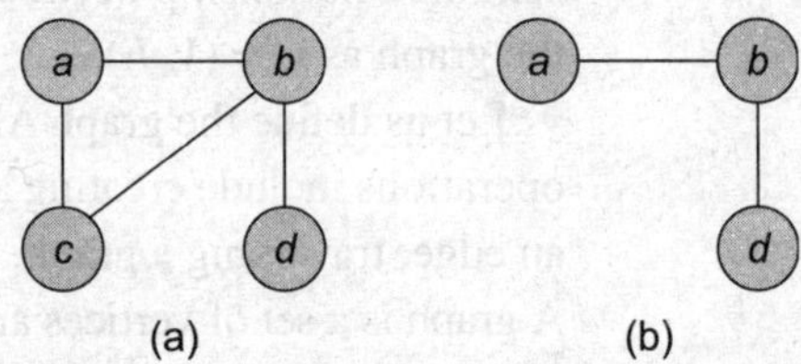

Fig. 8.2 Deleting a vertex from a graph (a) Graph *G* (b) Graph after deleting vertex *c*

Insert Edge

The insert edge operation adds an edge incident between two vertices. In an undirected graph, for adding an edge, the two vertices u and v are to be specified, and for a directed graph along with vertices, the start vertex and the end vertex should be known.

Figure 8.3(a) shows a graph $G(V, E)$ where $V = \{a, b, c, d\}$ and $E = \{(a, b), (a, c), (b, c), (b, d)\}$ and the resultant graph after inserting the edge (c, d) is shown in Fig. 8.3(b) with $V = \{a, b, c, d\}$ and $E = \{(a, b), (a, c), (b, c), (b, d), (c, d)\}$.

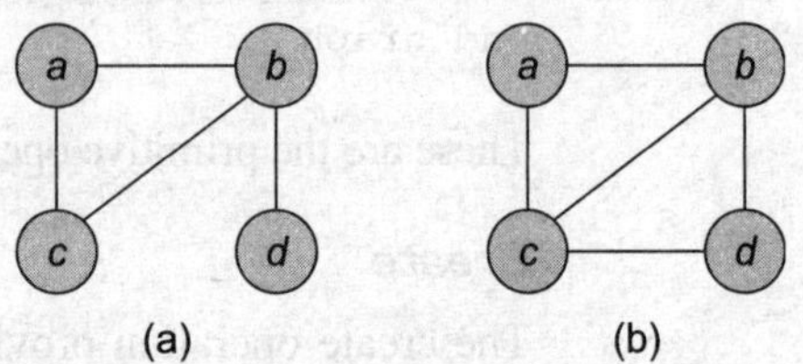

Fig. 8.3 Inserting an edge in a graph (a) Graph *G* (b) After inserting edge (*c*, *d*)

Delete Edge

The delete edge operation removes one edge from the graph. Let the graph G be $G(V, E)$. Now, deleting the edge (u, v) from G deletes the edge incident between vertices u and v and keeps the incident vertices u, v.

Figure 8.4(a) shows a graph $G(V, E)$, where $V = \{a, b, c, d\}$ and $E = \{(a, b), (a, c), (b, c), (b, d)\}$. The resultant graph after deleting the edge (b, d) is shown in Fig. 8.4(b) with $V = \{a, b, c, d\}$ and $E = \{(a, b), (a, c), (b, c)\}$.

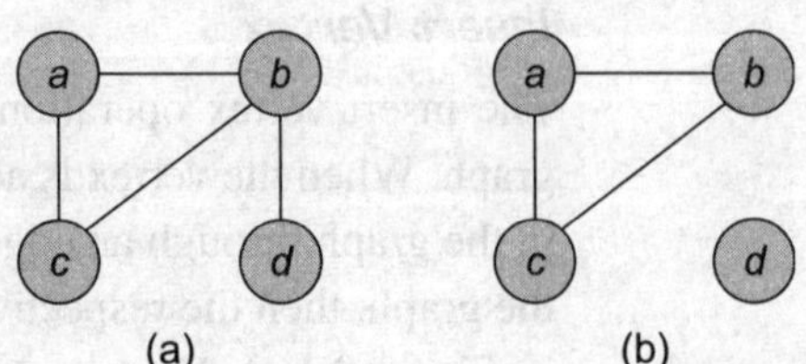

Fig. 8.4 Deleting edge in graph (a) Graph *G* (b) Graph after deleting the edge (*b*, *d*)

Is_empty

The is_empty operation checks whether the graph is empty and returns true if empty else returns false. An empty graph is one where the set V is a null set.

These are the basic operations on graphs, and a few more include getting the set of adjacent nodes of a vertex or an edge and traversing a graph. Checking the adjacency between vertices means verifying the relationship between them, and the relationship is maintained using a suitable data structure.

Graph traversal is also known as searching through a graph. It means systematically passing through the edges and visiting the vertices of the graph. A graph search algorithm can help in listing all vertices, checking connectivity, and discovering the structure of a graph. We shall discuss traversals in Section 8.4.

8.3 REPRESENTATION OF GRAPHS

We need to store two sets V and E to represent a graph. Here V is a set of vertices and E is a set of incident edges. These two sets basically represent the vertices and adjacency relationship among them. There are two standard representations of a graph given as follows:

1. Adjacency matrix (sequential representation) and
2. Adjacency list (linked representation)

Using these two representations, graphs can be realized using the adjacency matrix, adjacency list, or adjacency multilist. Let us study each of them.

8.3.1 Adjacency Matrix

Adjacency matrix is a square, two-dimensional array with one row and one column for each vertex in the graph. An entry in row i and column j is 1 if there is an edge incident between vertex i and vertex j, and is 0 otherwise. If a graph is a weighted graph, then the entry 1 is replaced with the weight. It is one of the most common and simple representations of the edges of a graph; programs can access this information very efficiently.

For a graph $G = (V, E)$, suppose $V = \{1, 2, \ldots, n\}$. The adjacency matrix for G is a two-dimensional $n \times n$ Boolean matrix $\mathbf{A}$ and can be represented as

$\mathbf{A}[i][j] =$ {1 if there exists an edge <*i*, *j*>
0 if edge <*i*, *j*> does not exist}

The adjacency matrix $\mathbf{A}$ has a natural implementation as in the following:

$\mathbf{A}[i][j]$ is 1 (or true) if and only if vertex i is adjacent to vertex j. If the graph is undirected, then

$$\mathbf{A}[i][j] = \mathbf{A}[j][i] = 1$$

If the graph is directed, we interpret 1 stored at $\mathbf{A}[i][j]$, indicating that the edge from i to j exists and not indicating whether or not the edge from j to i exists in the graph.

The graphs G_1, G_2, and G_3 of Fig. 8.5 are represented using the adjacency matrix in Fig. 8.6, among which G_2 is a directed graph.

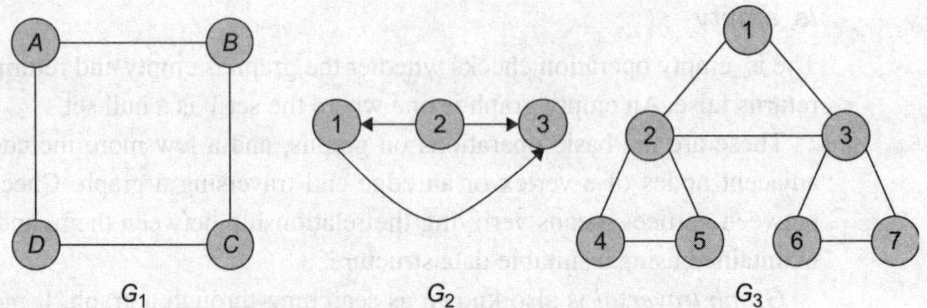

Fig. 8.5 Graphs G_1, G_2, and G_3

G_1

	A	*B*	*C*	*D*
A	0	1	0	1
B	1	0	1	0
C	0	1	0	1
D	1	0	1	0

G_2

	1	2	3
1	0	0	1
2	1	0	1
3	0	0	0

G_3

	1	2	3	4	5	6	7
1	0	1	1	0	0	0	0
2	1	0	1	1	1	0	0
3	1	1	0	0	0	1	1
4	0	1	0	0	1	0	0
5	0	1	0	1	0	0	0
6	0	0	1	0	0	0	1
7	0	0	1	0	0	1	0

Fig. 8.6 Adjacency matrix for G_1, G_2, and G_3 of Fig. 8.5

For a weighted graph, the matrix ***A*** is represented as

$$A[i][j] = \{\text{weight} \quad \text{if the edge } <i, j> \text{ exists}$$
$$0 \quad \text{if there exists no edge } <i, j>\}$$

Here, weight is the label associated with the edge of the graph. For example, Figs 8.7(a) and (b) show the weighted graph and its associated adjacency matrix.

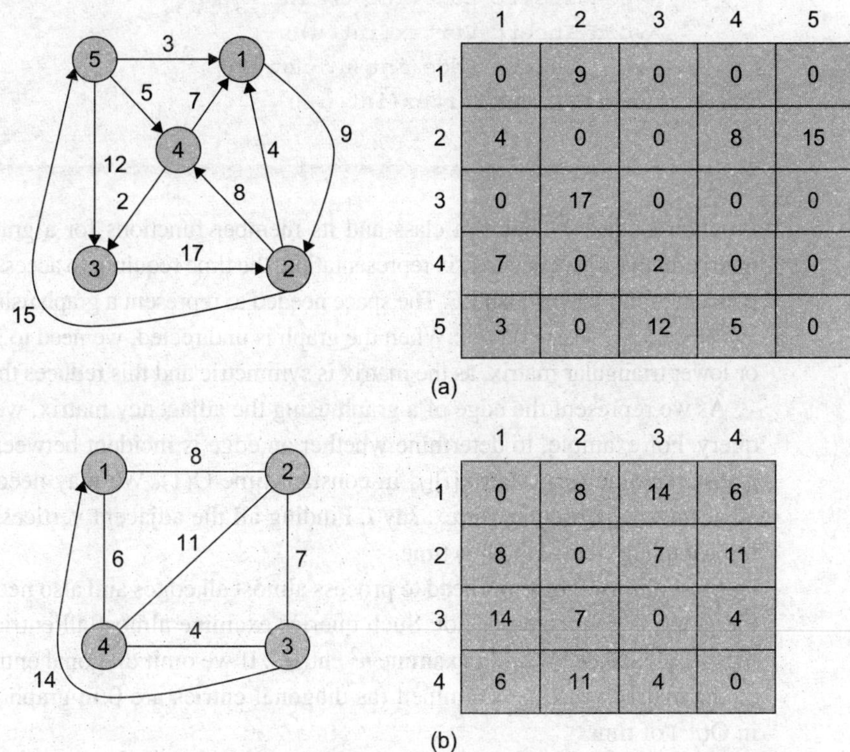

	1	2	3	4	5
1	0	9	0	0	0
2	4	0	0	8	15
3	0	17	0	0	0
4	7	0	2	0	0
5	3	0	12	5	0

	1	2	3	4
1	0	8	14	6
2	8	0	7	11
3	14	7	0	4
4	6	11	4	0

Fig. 8.7 Adjacency matrix (a) Directed weight graph and its adjacency matrix (b) Undirected weight graph and its adjacency matrix

We can note that the adjacency matrix for an undirected graph is symmetric whereas the adjacency matrix for a directed graph need not be symmetric.

Program Code 8.1 shows the class defined for graph implementation using an adjacency matrix with some basic functions.

PROGRAM CODE 8.1

```
class Graph
{
   private:
      int Adj_Matrix[Max_Vertex];      // Adjacency matrix
      int Vertex;      // Number of vertices
      int Edge;     // Number of edges
   public:
```

```
        Graph();      // Constructor
        bool IsEmpty();
        void Insert_Edge(int u, int v);
        void Insert_Vertex(int u);
        void Delete_Edge(int u, int v);
        void Delete_Vertex(int u);
};
```

Program Code 8.1 depicts a class and its member functions for a graph as an adjacency matrix. In the adjacency matrix representation, the time required to access an element is independent of the size of *V* and *E*. The space needed to represent a graph using adjacency matrix is n^2 locations, where $|V| = n$. When the graph is undirected, we need to store only the upper or lower triangular matrix, as the matrix is symmetric and this reduces the space required.

As we represent the edge of a graph using the adjacency matrix, we can place an edge query. For example, to determine whether an edge is incident between the vertices *i* and *j*, just examine Adj_Matrix[*i*][*j*] in constant time O(1). We may need to get all vertices adjacent to a particular vertex, say *i*. Finding all the adjacent vertices requires searching the complete i^{th} row in O(*n*) time.

Most of the algorithms need to process almost all edges and also need to check whether the graph is connected or not. Such queries examine almost all entries in the adjacency matrix. Hence, we need to examine n^2 entries. If we omit diagonal entries, $(n^2 - n)$ entries of the matrix are to be examined (as diagonal entries are 0 in graph without self loops) in $O(n^2)$ of time.

When the graph is sparse, most of the vertices have a few neighbours, that is, a few vertices adjacent to them. Consider the graph in Fig. 8.7. In the adjacency matrix of the graph, very few entries are non-zero. When we need a list of adjacent vertices of a particular vertex, say *i*, we need to transverse the complete i^{th} row though there are very few non-zero entries. Instead, if we keep one list per vertex and list only the vertices adjacent to it, a rapid retrieval in time $O(e + n)$ is possible when we need to process almost all edges. Here *e* is the number of edges in the graph, and the graph is sparse, that is, $e << (n^2/2)$. Such a structure that has a list for each vertex containing all its adjacent vertices is called as *adjacency list*. Let us learn more about adjacency list.

8.3.2 Adjacency List

In this representation, the *n* rows of the adjacency list are represented as *n*-linked lists, one list per vertex of the graph. The adjacency list for a vertex *i* is a list of all vertices adjacent to it. One way of achieving this is to go for an array of pointers, one per vertex. For example, we can represent the graph *G* by an array `Head`, where `Head[i]` is a pointer to the adjacency list of vertex *i*. For list, each node of the list has at least two fields: vertex and link. The vertex field contains the vertex id, and the link field stores a pointer to the next node that stores another vertex adjacent to *i*. Figure 8.8(b) shows an adjacency list representation for a directed graph in Fig. 8.8(a).

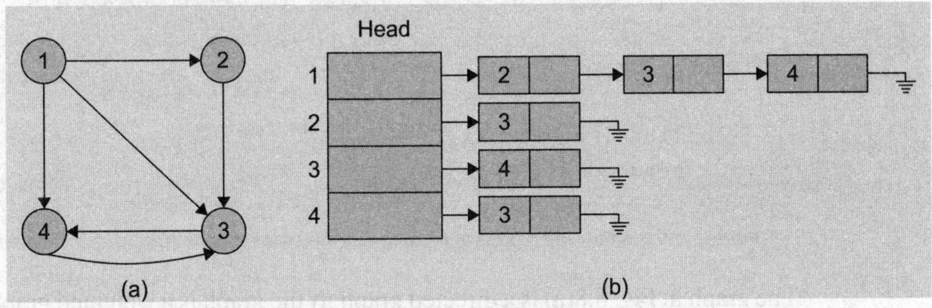

Fig. 8.8 Adjacency list representation (a) Graph G_1 (b) Adjacency list for G_1

Program Code 8.2 lists the class for the node required for adjacency list representation of the graph.

PROGRAM CODE 8.2

```
// Class for the node of the weighted graph
#define max 10
class GraphNode
{
   public:
      int vertex;
      int weight;
      // optional for weight associated with edge
      GraphNode* next;
      GraphNode()
      {
         vertex = 0;
         weight = 0;
         // optional for weight associated with edge
         next = null;
      }
};
class Graph   // class for storing graph as adjacency list
{
   GraphNode* headnodes[max];
   // headnodes list for connected vertices.
   int n;
   int visited[max];
```

```
    public:
        Graph();
        // Constructor to initialize all headnodes to null.
};
Graph :: Graph()
{
    for(int i = 0;i<max;i++)
        headnodes[i] = null;
}
```

The graph in Fig. 8.8(a) is a directed graph. If the graph is a weighted graph, a weight field can be added in the node structure of the list. Figures 8.9(a) and (b) show the adjacency list representation of a weighted directed graph.

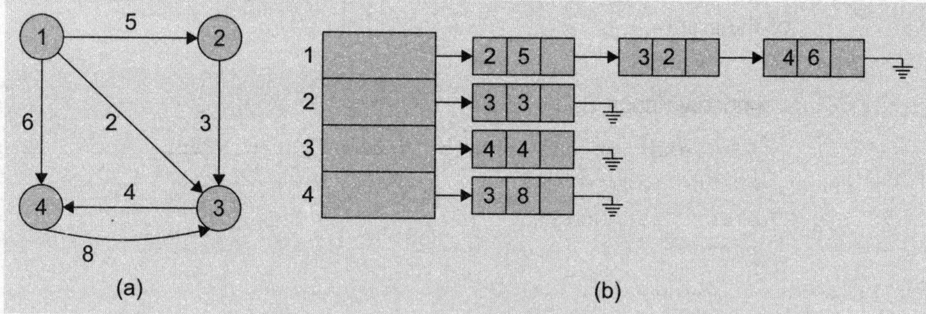

Fig. 8.9 Adjacency list of weighted graph (a) Weighted graph G_2 (b) Adjacency list of G_2

Here, each node has three fields—the first one showing an adjacent node, second showing the weight associated with an edge, and the third showing the link to the next node.

The adjacency list representation of a directed graph requires the storage proportional to the sum of the number of vertices plus the number of edges. It is often used when the number of edges is much lesser, that is, $e << n^2/2$. In case of an undirected graph, with n vertices and e edges, this representation requires $2e$ list nodes. Both directed and undirected graphs require n head nodes per node.

As we represent the edge between the vertices using the adjacency list, we can place an edge query. For example, to determine whether an edge is incident between the vertices i and j, verify by searching the complete list of m nodes adjacent to vertex i in O(m) time and if $m < n$. In worst case, the search time is O(n) when the vertex i has all the remaining $n - 1$ vertices adjacent to it, whereas in adjacency matrix representation, the search time is O(1).

Finding the degree of any vertex, that is, counting the total number of vertices adjacent to it, in an undirected graph may be determined by counting the number of nodes in its adjacency list in O(n) time. In addition, when all the edges are to be processed, the total edges of G may be processed in time O($n + e$).

In case of a directed graph, the outgoing degree of any vertex i may be determined by counting the number of nodes on its adjacency list. For computing an incoming degree of vertex i, we have to traverse the adjacency lists of each of the other vertices to confirm whether it is incident on i. In other words, we will have to search for the vertex i in the adjacency lists of all other vertices. This is a tedious task; hence, it is better to keep another set of lists in addition to the adjacency list called *inverse adjacency lists*. The inverse adjacency list for a vertex i is a list of all vertices j to which i is adjacent to. Inverse adjacency list can be used to compute the incoming degree of a vertex. We shall learn about inverse adjacency list in Section 8.3.4.

Program Code 8.3 depicts the implementation of storing a graph as an adjacency list.

PROGRAM CODE 8.3

```
// Class for the node of the graph class GraphNode
{
   public:
      int vertex;      // The adjacent node
      GraphNode* next;
      GraphNode()
      {
         vertex = 0;
         next = null;
      }
};

// class for storing graph as adjacency list
class Graph
{
   // List of headnodes containing list of connected
   // vertices
   GraphNode* headnodes[max];
   int n;
   int visited[max];
   public:
      Graph();     // Constructor to initialize all
      headnodes to null
      void create();     // To create graph
      // To initialize the visited array to false
      void initialize_visited();
      void BFS(int v);     // Breadth-first search
```

```
        void DFS(int v);      // Depth-First Search
        int examine_n() const {return n;}
        // Return value of n.
};
Graph :: Graph()
{
    for(int i = 0; i < max; i++)
        headnodes[i] = null;
}
// Function to create a graph

void Graph :: create()
{
// Method to create a Graph represented by adjacency
list
    GraphNode *curr,*prev;
    int n1, i, j, vertex, done = false;
    cout << endl << "Enter the no. of vertices :- ";
    cin >> n;
    for(i = 0; i < n; i++)
    {
        if(!(headnodes[i] = new GraphNode))      // Allocate
        memory for new node
        {
            cout << endl << "Insufficient memory";
            exit(0);
        }
        headnodes[i]->vertex = i + 1;
        cout << endl << "Enter the no. of vertices
        connected to" << (i+1) << ":";
        cin >> n1;
        prev = headnodes[i];
        for(j = 0; j < n1; j++)
        {
            if(!(curr = new GraphNode))
            {
                cout << endl << "Insufficient memory.";
                exit(0);
            }
            done = false;
            do
            {
```

```
                    cout << endl << "Enter vertex no. of
                    connected vertex :";
                    cin >> vertex;
                    if(vertex > n && vertex < 1)
                    {
                        cout << endl << "Vertex out of range";
                        cout << endl << "Valid range :- 1 - " << n;
                    }
                    else
                    {
                        curr->vertex = vertex;
                        prev->next = curr;
                        prev = curr;                    // Next node
                        done = true;
                    }
                }
                while(!done);
            }
            if(n1 == 0)
                prev->next = null;
        }
        return;
    }
```

8.3.3 Adjacency Multilist

In the adjacency list representation of an undirected graph, each edge (v_i, v_j) is represented by two entries, one on the list of v_i and the other on the list of v_j. For the graph G_1 in Fig. 8.9, the edge connecting the vertices 1 and 2 is represented twice, in the lists of vertices 1 and 2. In applications such as minimum spanning tree computation, if we process any edge once, then it has to be marked as a processed one. To avoid processing of that edge again, we need to find the other entries for that particular edge and mark it as processed. This adds to time complexity, which should be avoided. This can be achieved if the adjacency list is maintained as multilists such that the nodes are shared among several lists. For each edge, there will be exactly one node, but this node will be in two lists, that is, the adjacency lists for each of the two nodes it is incident on. The node structure of such a list can be represented as follows:

Visited tag	V_1	V_2	Link1 for V_1	Link2 for V_2

Here, the visited tag is a one bit mark field that indicates whether or not the edge has been examined. This tag would be set accordingly when the edge is processed. We can note that the storage requirements for this are the same as that of the normal adjacency lists except the tag field. Figure 8.10 shows the adjacency multilists for the graph G_1.

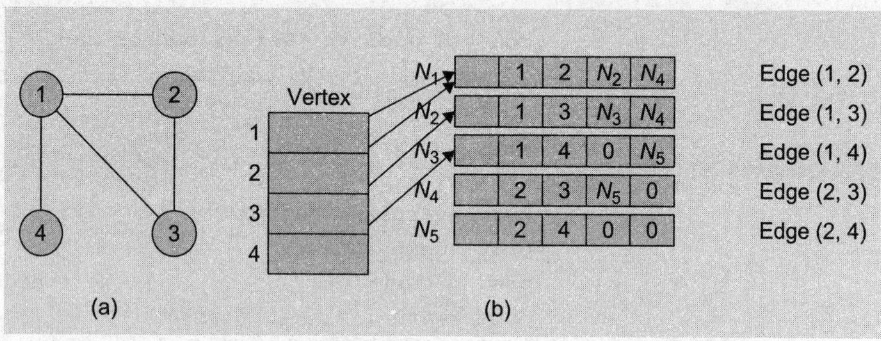

Fig. 8.10 Adjacency multilist (a) Graph G_1 (b) Adjacency multilist for G_1

For Fig. 8.10, the lists are as follows:

Vertex 1: $N_1 \to N_2 \to N_3$
Vertex 2: $N_1 \to N_4 \to N_5$
Vertex 3: $N_2 \to N_5$
Vertex 4: $N_3 \to N_5$

Sometimes, the edges of a graph have weights assigned when the graph is a weighted graph. This weight information can be represented using an adjacency matrix or can also be shown by including an additional field in the node.

8.3.4 Inverse Adjacency List

An *inverse adjacency list* is a set of lists that contains one list for each vertex. Each list contains a node per vertex adjacent to the vertex it represents. Figure 8.11(b) represents the inverse adjacency list for the graph G_2 in Fig. 8.11(a).

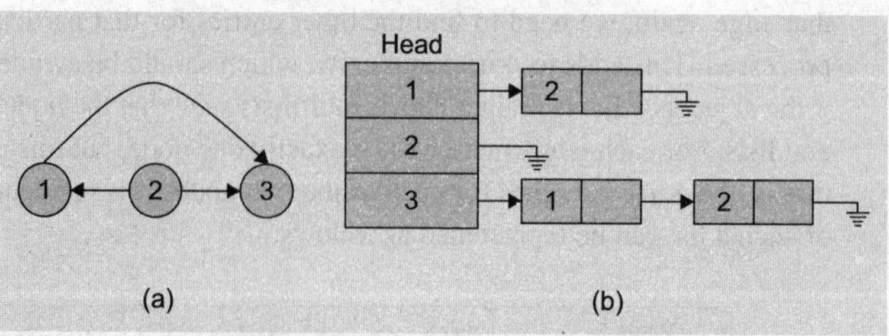

Fig. 8.11 Inverse adjacency list (a) Graph G_2
(b) Inverse adjacency list of G_2

8.3.5 Comparison of Sequential and Linked Representations

Adjacency matrix representation always requires an $n \times n$ matrix with n vertices, regardless of the number of edges. It needs more memory asymptotically. If the graph is sparse, many of the entries are null. However, since it provides direct access, it is suitable for many applications.

Linked representation (adjacency list) of a graph has an advantage of space complexity when a graph is sparse but does not provide direct access. The probable disadvantage of adjacency list is that it does not allow direct access, and hence, we cannot quickly determine whether an edge between any two vertices is incident or not.

When a graph is sparse, the number of edges $|E|$ is much lesser than V_2. The adjacency list representation is usually preferred as it provides a compact way to represent them. For dense graphs, adjacency matrix representation may be preferred since $|E|$ is closer to V_2 and when we also want fast access to information such as whether the edge between any two vertices is incident or not, the weight associated to each edge, and so on.

Though the list representation is asymptotically as efficient as a matrix representation, the simplicity of the matrix is preferred when the graph is small. In addition, for a weighted graph, an additional field is needed in the graph node, whereas for matrix representation, the same matrix can be used. Considering all these aspects, the matrix representation of a graph is more powerful than all the other forms.

8.4 GRAPH TRAVERSAL

To solve many problems modelled with graphs, we need to visit all the vertices and edges in a systematic fashion called *graph traversal*. We shall study two types—*depth-first traversal* and *breadth-first traversal*. Traversal of a graph is commonly used to search a vertex or an edge through the graph; hence, it is also called a *search technique*. Consequently, depth-first and breadth-first traversals are popularly known as *depth-first search* (DFS) and *breadth-first search* (BFS), respectively.

8.4.1 Depth-first Search

In DFS, as the name indicates, from the currently visited vertex in the graph, we keep searching deeper whenever possible. All the vertices are visited by processing a vertex and its descendents before processing its adjacent vertices. This procedure can be written either recursively or non-recursively. For recursive code, the internal stack would be used, and for non-recursive code, we would use a stack.

Depth-first search works by selecting one vertex, say v of G as a start vertex; v is marked as visited. Then, each unvisited vertex adjacent to v is searched using the DFS recursively. Once all the vertices that can be reached from v have been visited, the search for v is complete. If some vertices remain unvisited, we select an unvisited vertex as a new start vertex and then repeat the process until all the vertices of G are marked as visited.

For non-recursive implementation, whenever we reach a node, we shall push it (vertex or node address) onto the stack. We would then pop the vertex, process it, and push all its adjacent vertices onto the stack. Suppose we have a directed graph *G* where all the vertices are initially marked as unvisited. In a graph, we can reach any vertex more than once through different paths. Hence, to assure that each vertex is visited once, we mark each as visited whenever it is processed. Let us use an array say `visited` for the same. Initially, all vertices are marked unvisited. Marking `visited[i]` to 0 indicates that the vertex `i` is unvisited. Whenever we push the vertex say `j` onto the stack, we mark it visited by setting its `visited[j]` to 1.

The recursive algorithm for DFS can be outlined as in Algorithm 8.1.

Algorithm 8.1 shows the recursive working of DFS of a graph.

ALGORITHM 8.1

```
1. for v = 1 to n do
     visited[v] = 0                {unvisited}
2. i = 1    {Let us start at vertex 1)
3. DepthFirstSearch(i)
   begin
      visited[i] = 1
      for each vertex j adjacent to i do
        if(visited[j] = 0)  then
           DepthFirstSearch(j)
         end
4. stop
```

When we need to show its equivalent non-recursive code, we need to use a stack. Non-recursive DFS can be implemented by using a stack for pushing all unvisited vertices adjacent to the one being visited and popping the stack to find the next unvisited vertex.

Consider the graph in Fig. 8.12(a) and its adjacency list in Fig. 8.12(b).

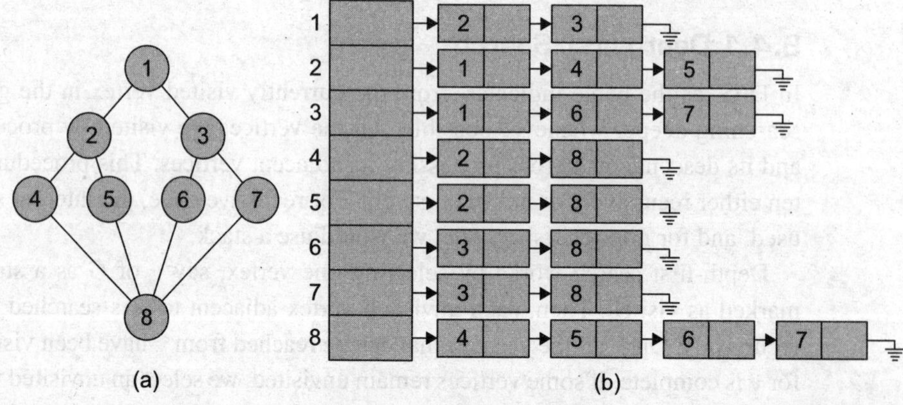

Fig. 8.12 Sample graph for traversal (a) Graph *G* (b) Adjacency list representation of *G*

Let us initiate a traversal from the vertex 1. The order of traversal will be 1, 2, 4, 8, 5, 6, 3, 7. Another possible traversal could be 1, 3, 7, 8, 6, 5, 2, 4. O($n + e$) time is required by the DFS for adjacency list representation and O(n^2) for adjacency matrix representation. Program Code 8.4 is the implementation of the DFS traversal in C++ where the graph is stored as an adjacency matrix.

PROGRAM CODE 8.4

```
// Depth-first search using adjacency matrix
void Graph :: DepthFirstSearch(int i)
{
   int k;
   for(k = 0; k < Vertex; k++)
   visited[k] = 0;
   visited[i] = 1;
   for(k = 0; k < Vertex; k++)
   {
      if(Adj_Matrix[i, k] && !visited[k])
      {
         cout << i + 1;
         void DepthFirstSearch(i);
      }
   }
}

// Function for Depth-first search using adjacency list
void Graph :: DFS(int v)
{
   GraphNode *curr;
   int w;
   curr = headnodes[v];
   cout << "\t" << curr->vertex;
   visited[v] = true;
   curr = curr ->next;
   while(curr != null)
   // For each vertex adjacent to v
   {
      if(!visited[w = (curr->vertex - 1)])
         DFS(w);
      curr = curr->next;
   }
   return;
}
```

Depth-first search for an undirected graph works in a similar way as for a directed graph as shown in Algorithm 8.2. The start vertex `i` is marked visited. Next, an unvisited vertex `j` adjacent to `i` is selected and a DFS from `j` is initiated. When a vertex `k` is reached such that all its adjacent vertices have been visited, the search returns to the last vertex visited which has an unvisited vertex `j` adjacent to it and then initializes the DFS from `j`. The search terminates when no unvisited vertex can be reached from any of the visited vertices. If the graph *G* is represented by its adjacency lists, the adjacent vertices `j` from `i` can be easily searched by following the chain of links through the list of vertex `i`.

ALGORITHM 8.2

```
1. Let us start search at vertex j
2. Push j onto stack
3. Mark all vertices as unvisited
   for i = 1 to n do
      visited[i] = 0
4. while(not empty (stack)) do
   begin
      v = pop(stack)
      if(not visited(v))
      begin
         visited[v] = 1
         push all adjacent vertices of v onto stack
      end
   end
5. stop
```

Let us now consider the graph in Fig. 8.13.

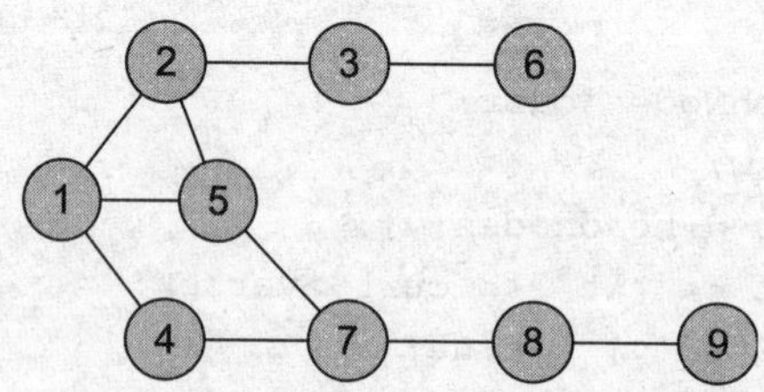

Fig. 8.13 Sample graph

Let us traverse the graph using a non-recursive algorithm that uses stack. Let 1 be the start vertex. Note that the stack is empty initially.

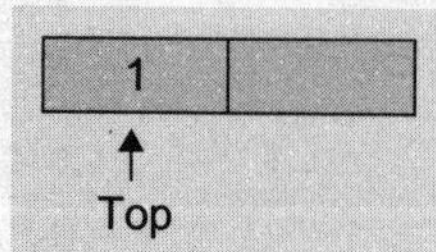

1. Initially, V = set of visited vertices = ϕ. Push 1 onto the stack.
2. As the stack is not empty, `vertex = pop();` we get 1. As 1 is not visited, mark it as visited.

Now $V = \{1\}$. Push all the adjacent vertices of 1 onto the stack.
Since the stack is not empty, `vertex = pop();` we get 2.

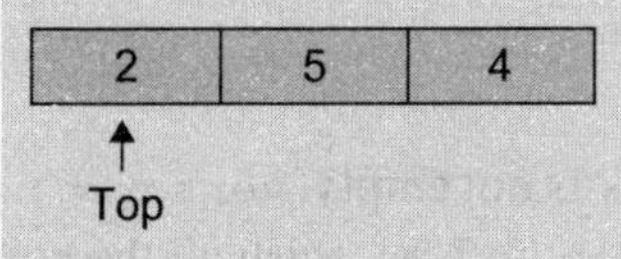

3. As 2 is not visited, mark it as visited, and now $V = \{1, 2\}$. Then, push all the adjacent vertices of 2.

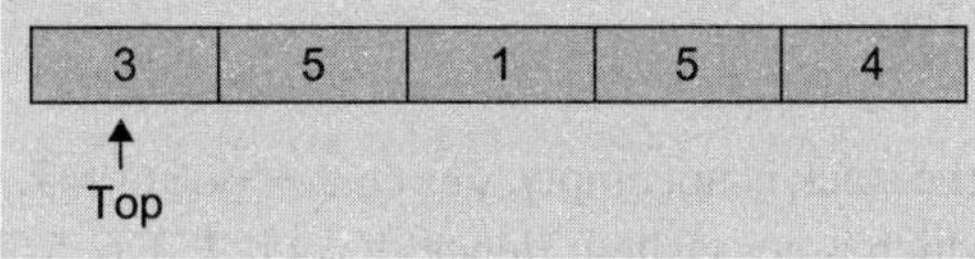

4. Since the stack is not empty, `vertex = pop();` we get 3. As 3 is not visited, mark it as visited. Now $V = \{1, 2, 3\}$. We then push all the adjacent vertices of 3 onto the stack.

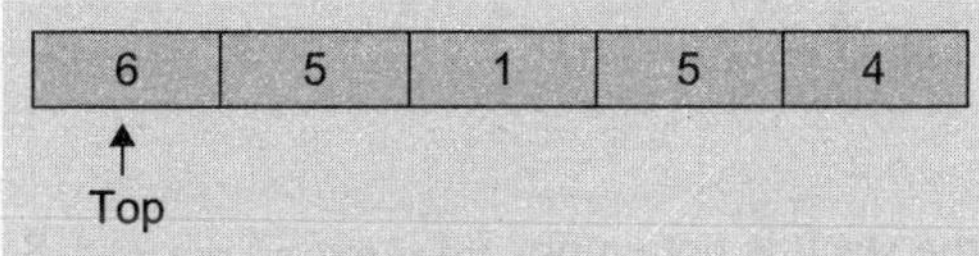

5. Since the stack is not empty, `vertex = pop();` we get 6. As 6 is not visited, mark it as visited. Now $V = \{1, 2, 3, 6\}$. We then push all the adjacent vertices of 6 onto the stack.

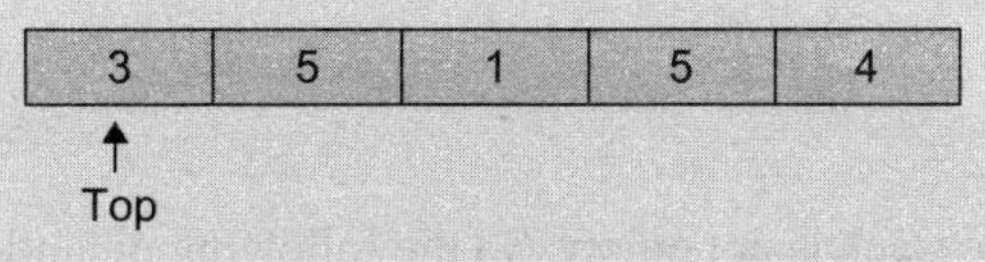

6. Since the stack is not empty, `vertex = pop();` we get 3. As 3 is visited, pop again `vertex = pop();` we then get 5. As 5 is not visited, mark it as visited. Now $V = \{1, 2, 3, 6, 5\}$. Push all the adjacent vertices onto the stack.

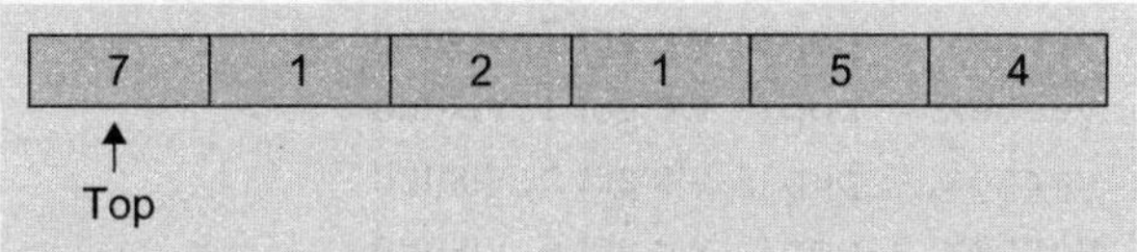

7. As the stack is not empty, `vertex = pop();` we get 7, which is not visited. Hence, $V = \{1, 2, 3, 6, 5, 7\}$; we now push all the adjacent vertices of 7 onto the stack.

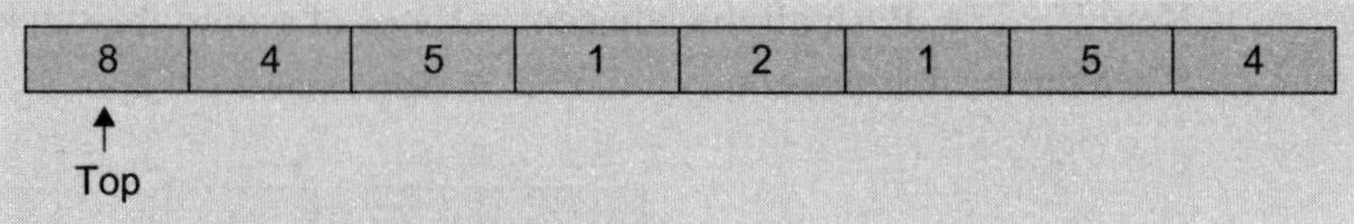

8. As the stack is not empty, `vertex = pop();` we get 8, which is not visited. Hence, $V = \{1, 2, 3, 6, 5, 7, 8\}$. Push all the adjacent vertices of 8 onto the stack.

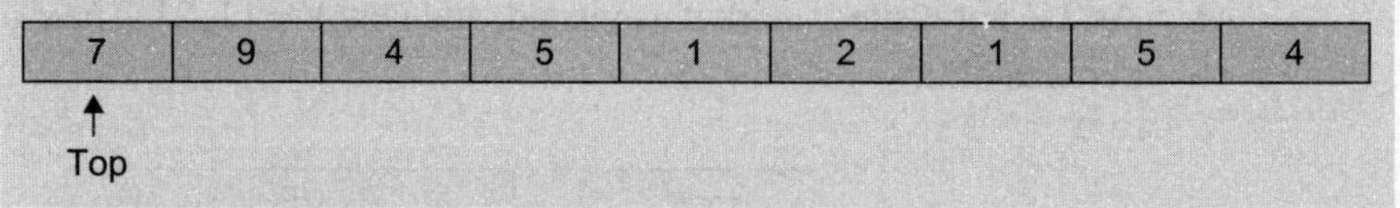

9. As the stack is not empty, `vertex = pop()` = 7, which is visited; `vertex = pop()` = 9, which is not visited. Hence, $V = \{1, 2, 3, 6, 5, 7, 8, 9\}$. Push all the adjacent vertices of 9 onto the stack.

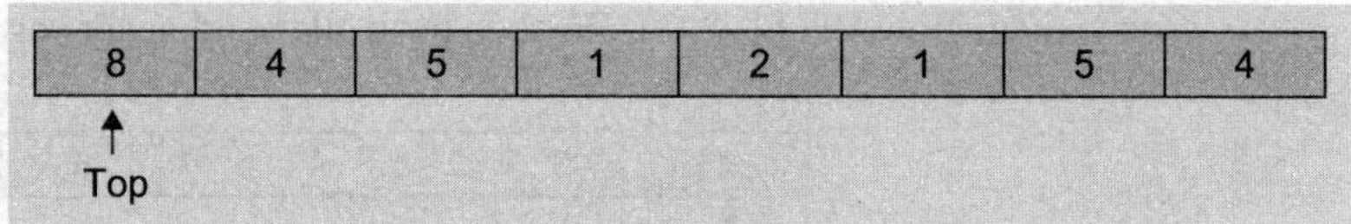

10. As the stack is not empty, `vertex = pop()` = 8, which is visited; so again `vertex = pop()` = 4, which is not visited. Hence, $V = \{1, 2, 3, 6, 5, 7, 8, 9, 4\}$. Push all the adjacent vertices of 4 onto the stack.

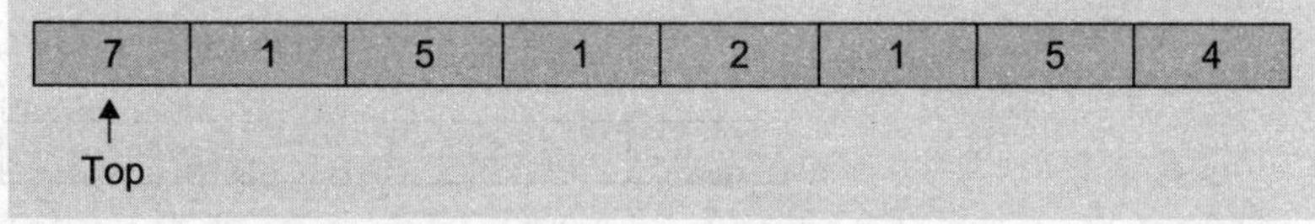

11. The stack is not empty. So the following operations yield:

    `vertex = pop()` we get 7, visited
    `vertex = pop()` we get 1, visited
    `vertex = pop()` we get 5, visited
    `vertex = pop()` we get 1, visited
    `vertex = pop()` we get 2, visited
    `vertex = pop()` we get 1, visited
    `vertex = pop()` we get 5, visited
    `vertex = pop()` we get 4, visited

12. The stack is now empty, Hence, we stop.

The set $V = \{1, 2, 3, 6, 5, 7, 8, 9, 4\}$ represents the order in which they are visited. Hence, the DFS of the graph (Fig. 8.13) gives the sequence as 1, 2, 3, 6, 5, 7, 8, 9, and 4. This is shown in Fig. 8.14.

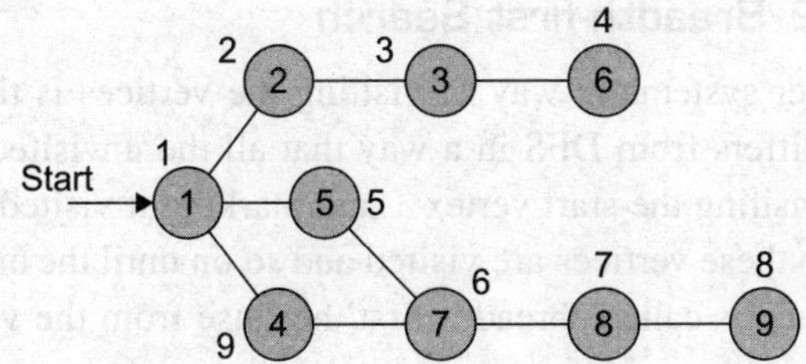

Fig. 8.14 Depth-first traversal for graph in Fig. 8.13

The label at each of the vertices in Fig. 8.14 is the sequence of visit of the traversal. The DFS of the graph is roughly analogous to the preorder traversal of an ordered tree. To find the vertices adjacent to the current vertex, we use a data structure that stores the graph to be traversed. This could be one of the suitable data structures used for graphs, such as adjacency matrix or adjacency list. The sequence in which they are pushed onto the stack and then popped depends on the graph's storage. Hence, the same graph with two different adjacency lists may generate two sequences for DFS, specially, when the graph is an undirected one. A sample graph is given in Fig. 8.15.

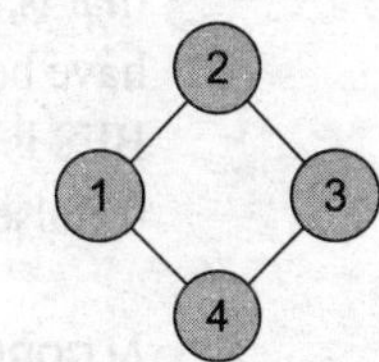

Fig. 8.15 Sample graph

If the adjacency list is as in Fig. 8.16, then the DFS gives the sequences as the following: 1, 2, 3, 4, where the start vertex is 1.

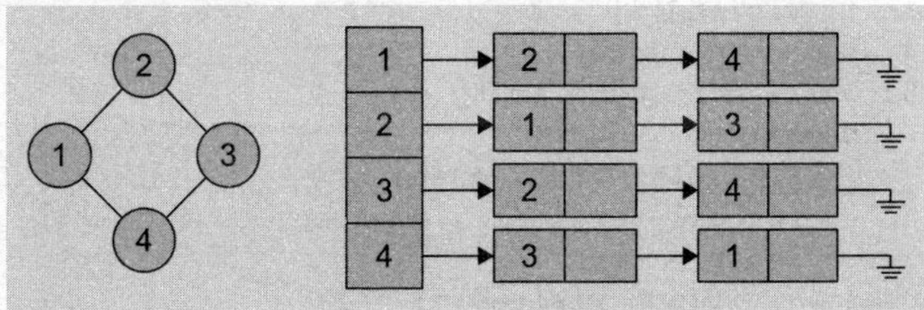

Fig. 8.16 Sample graph *G* and its adjacency list representation

If the adjacency list for the same graph is as in Fig. 8.17, then the DFS sequence will be 1, 4, 3, 2 where the start vertex is 1 and 4, 1, 2, 3 where the start vertex is 4.

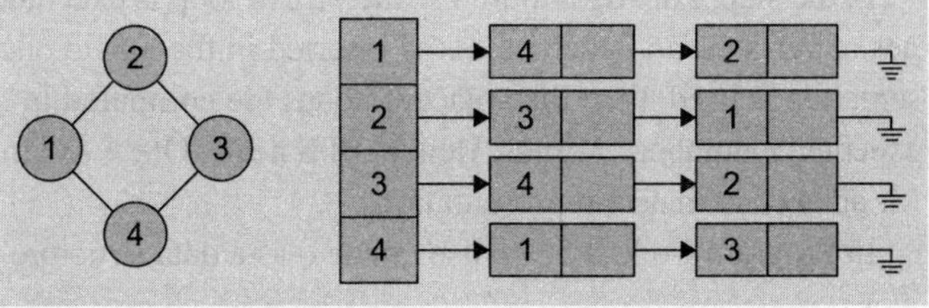

Fig. 8.17 Alternate adjacency list representation of sample graph *G*

8.4.2 Breadth-first Search

Another systematic way of visiting the vertices is the breadth-first search (BFS). The BFS differs from DFS in a way that all the unvisited vertices adjacent to `i` are visited after visiting the start vertex `i` and marking it visited. Next, the unvisited vertices adjacent to these vertices are visited and so on until the entire graph has been traversed. The approach is called 'breadth-first' because from the vertex `i` that we visit, we search as broadly as possible by next visiting all the vertices adjacent to `i`. For example, the BFS of the graph of Fig. 8.13 results in visiting the nodes in the following order: 1, 2, 3, 4, 5, 6, 7, and 8.

This search algorithm uses a queue to store the vertices of each level of the graph as and when they are visited. These vertices are then taken out from the queue in sequence, that is, first in first out (FIFO), and their adjacent vertices are visited until all the vertices have been visited. The algorithm terminates when the queue is empty. The working of the BFS is given in Algorithm 8.3. The algorithm initializes the Boolean array `visited[]` to 0 (false), that is, marks each vertex as unvisited.

ALGORITHM 8.3

```
Breadth-first search (vertex j)
1. Let us start search at vertex j
2. Mark all vertices as unvisited
     for i = 1 to n do
        visited[i] = 0
3. Mark j as visited
     visited[j] = 1
4. Add j in queue
5. while not queue empty do
   begin
     i = delete from queue
     for all vertices j adjacent to i do
     begin
        if(not visited[j] = 1)
          Add j in queue
          visited[j] = 1
        end
     end
6. stop
```

In the step 5 of Algorithm 8.3, the `while` loop is executed n times. Here, n is the number of vertices, and each vertex is inserted in the queue once. If the adjacency list representation is used, then the adjacent nodes are computed in the `for` loop. The `for` loop is executed e number of times. Hence, BFS needs $O(n + e)$ time for adjacency list and $O(n^2)$ for adjacency matrix representation.

In Program Code 8.5, we use queue `Q` as a data structure for traversal.

PROGRAM CODE 8.5

```
// Breadth-first traversal using adjacency matrix
void Graph :: BreadthFirstSearch(int i)
{
   int k, visited[max];
   queue Q;
   for(k = 1; k <= n; k++)
     visited[k] = 0;
   visited[i] = 1;
   Q.Add(i);
   while(!Q.IsEmpty())
   {
     j = Q.Delete();
     for(k = 1; k <= n; k++)
     {
        if(Adj_Matrix [j,k] && !visited[k])
        {
           Q.Add(k);
           visited[k] = 1;
        }
     }
   }
}
// Function for breadth-first search
void Graph :: BFS(int v)
{
   Queue q;
   GraphNode* curr;
   visited[v] = true;
   cout << "\t" << headnodes[v]->vertex;
   q.addq(headnodes[v]);
   while(!q.emptyq())
   {
     curr = q.deleteq();
     curr = curr->next;
     while(curr != null)
     {
        if(!visited[curr->vertex - 1])
        {
           q.addq(headnodes[curr->vertex - 1]);
           cout << "\t" << curr->vertex;
```

```
            visited[curr->vertex - 1] = true;
         }
         curr = curr->next;
      }
   }
   return;
}
```

Here, `add()` and `delete()` are the member functions for adding and deleting the elements from the queue, respectively. Let us consider Fig. 8.13, the graph, again for BFS. Let us traverse the graph using a non-recursive algorithm that uses a queue. Let 1 be the start vertex. Initially, the queue is empty, and the initial set of visited vertices, $V = \phi$.

1. Add 1 to the queue. Mark 1 as visited. $V = \{1\}$.

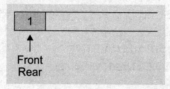

2. As the queue is not empty, `vertex = delete()` from queue, and we get 1.
   Add all the un-visited adjacent vertices of 1 to the queue. In addition, mark them as visited.
   Now, $V = \{1, 2, 5, 4\}$.

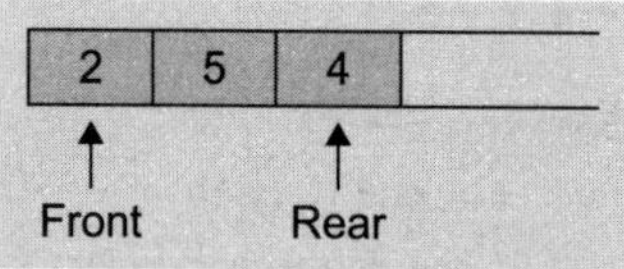

3. As the queue is not empty, `vertex = delete()` and we get 2.
   Add all the adjacent, un-visited vertices of 2 to the queue and mark them as visited.
   Now $V = \{1, 2, 5, 4, 3\}$.

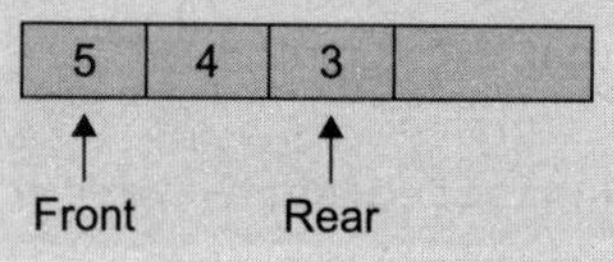

4. As the queue is not empty, `vertex = delete()` from queue, and we get 5.
   Now, add all the adjacent, un-visited vertices adjacent to 5 to the queue and mark them as visited.

Now, $V = \{1, 2, 5, 4, 3, 7\}$.

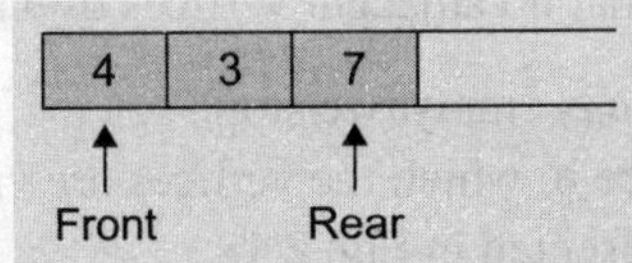

5. As the queue is not empty, `vertex = delete()` from queue, and we get 4.
Now, add all the adjacent, not visited vertices adjacent to 4 to the queue. The vertices 1 and 7 are adjacent to 4 and hence are already visited. Now the next element we get from the queue is 3.
Now, we add all the un-visited vertices adjacent to 3 to the queue, making $V = \{1, 2, 5, 4, 3, 7, 6\}$.

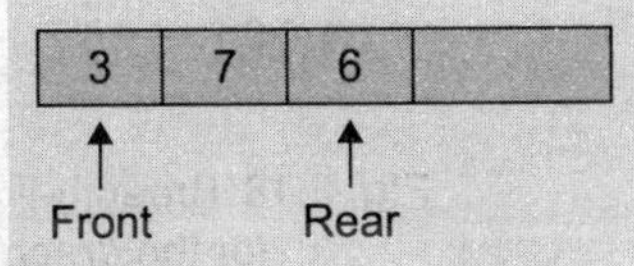

6. As the queue is not empty, `vertex = delete()` and we get 7.
Add all the adjacent, un- visited vertices of 7 to the queue and mark them as visited.
Now, $V = \{1, 2, 5, 4, 3, 7, 6, 8\}$.

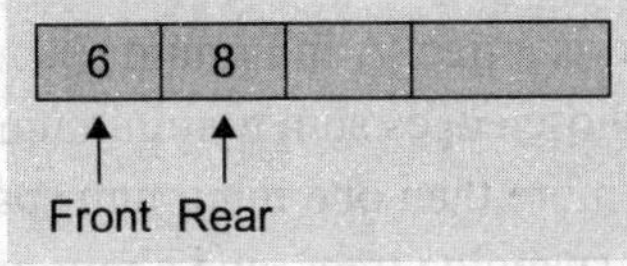

7. As the queue is not empty, `vertex = delete()`, and we get 6.
Then, add all the un-visited adjacent vertices of 6 to the queue and mark them as visited.
Now $V = \{1, 2, 5, 4, 3, 7, 6, 8\}$.

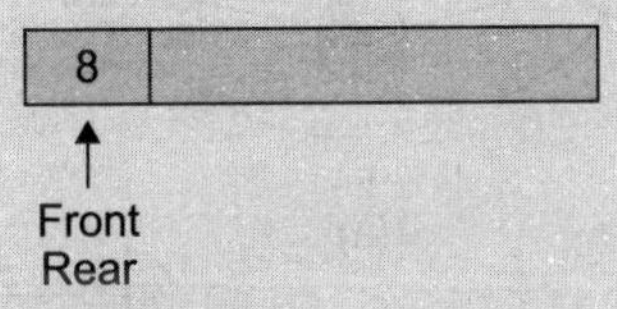

8. As queue is not empty, `vertex = delete()` and we get 8.
Add its adjacent un-visited vertices to the queue and mark them as visited.
$V = \{1, 2, 5, 4, 3, 7, 6, 8, 9\}$.

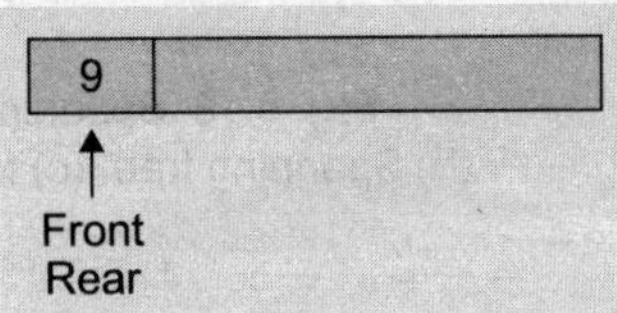

9. As the queue is not empty, `vertex = delete() =`9.
   Here, note that no adjacent vertices of 9 are un-visited.
10. As the queue is empty, we stop.
   The sequence in which the vertices are visited by the BFS is 1, 2, 5, 4, 3, 7, 6, 8, 9
   This is represented in Fig. 8.18.

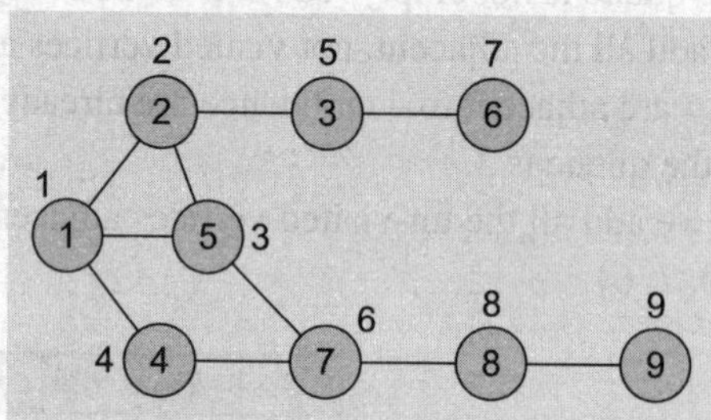

Fig. 8.18 Breadth-first search sequence for the graph in Fig. 8.13

8.5 SPANNING TREE

A tree is a connected graph with no cycles. A spanning tree is a sub-graph of *G* that has all vertices of *G* and is a tree. A minimum spanning tree of a weighted graph *G* is the spanning tree of *G* whose edges sum to minimum weight.

There can be more than one minimum spanning tree for a graph. Figure 8.19 shows a graph, one of its spanning trees, and a minimum spanning tree.

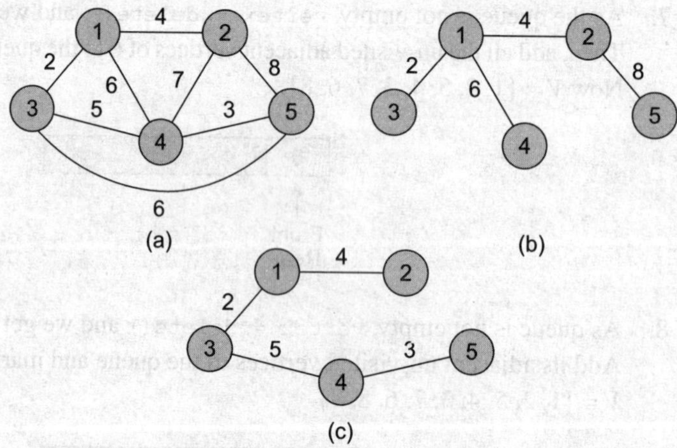

Fig. 8.19 Spanning trees (a) Graph (b) Spanning tree (c) Minimum spanning tree

Minimum spanning trees are useful in many applications such as finding the least amount of wire needed to connect a group of computers, houses, or cities. A minimum spanning tree minimizes the total length over all possible spanning trees.

We want to compute a minimum spanning tree efficiently. In theory, we could enumerate all the spanning trees of a weighted graph and simply choose the tree of least weight. However, if the graph is a complicated one, this is not an easy and efficient way to get it. In this section, we shall study the two most efficient ways discovered in the 1950s by J.B. Kruskal and R.C. Prim. Both the algorithms are greedy algorithms which produce a minimum spanning tree by adding an edge at each stage making the best choice of the next edge. These two popular methods used to compute the minimum spanning tree of a graph are

1. Prim's algorithm
2. Kruskal's algorithm

Before discussing these algorithms, let us learn about connected components.

8.5.1 Connected Components

An undirected graph is *connected* if there is at least one path between every pair of vertices in the graph. A *connected component* of a graph is a *maximal connected* sub-graph, that is, every vertex in a connected component is *reachable* from the vertices in the component.

Fig. 8.20 Sample graph G_1 with one connected component

Consider the graph G_1 in Fig. 8.20. In this undirected graph, there is only one connected component, the graph G_1 itself.

If we delete the edges e_4 and e_5 from the graph G_1, we get a graph G_2 with two connected components: $(\{V_1, V_2, V_3\}, \{E_1, E_2, E_3\})$ and $(\{V_4\}, \emptyset)$. This is represented in Fig. 8.21.

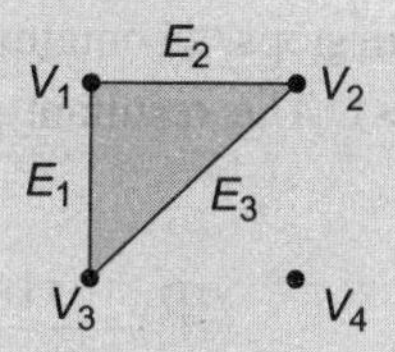

Fig. 8.21 Graph G_2 with two connected components

8.5.2 Prim's Algorithm

All vertices of any connected graph are included in a minimum cost spanning tree of a graph G. Prim's algorithm starts from one vertex and grows the rest of the tree by adding one vertex at a time, by adding the associated edges. This algorithm builds a tree by iteratively adding edges until a minimal spanning tree is obtained, that is, when all nodes are added. At each iteration, a next minimum weight edge is added that adds a new vertex to the tree, if adding that edge does not form a cycle.

Let `G = (V, E)` be the original graph. Let `T` be a spanning tree. `T = (A, B)`, where `A` and `B` are empty sets initially. Let us select an arbitrary vertex `i` from `V` and add it to set `A`. Now `A = {i}`. At each step, Prim's algorithm looks for the shortest possible edge `<u, v>` such that `u` ∈ `A` and `v` ∈ `V − A`. It then adds `v` to `A` making `A = A ∪ {v}` and adds the edge `<u, v>` to `B`. In this way, the edges in `B` at any instant form a minimum spanning tree for the vertices in `A`. We continue thus as long as `A ≠ V`. To illustrate the algorithm, let us consider the graph in Fig. 8.22.

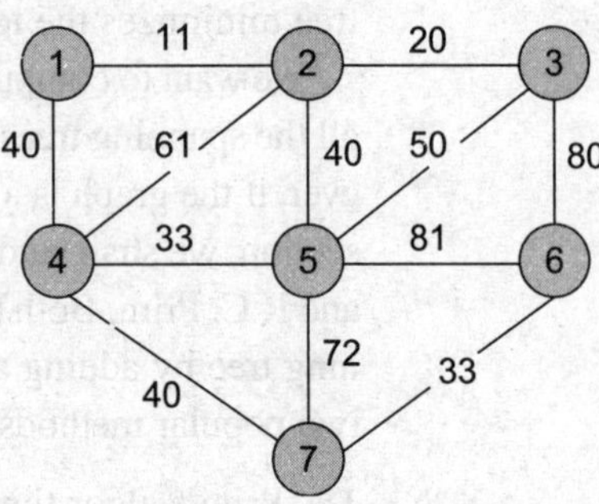

Fig. 8.22 A weighted graph

Let us select node 1 as the starting node. Table 8.1 shows the edge of a minimum weight selected and the set of vertices `A`.

Table 8.1 Construction of spanning tree for graph in Fig. 8.22

Step no.	Edge <*u*, *v*>	Set A
Initial	–	{1}
1	<1, 2>	{1, 2}
2	<2, 3>	{1, 2, 3}
3	<1, 4>	{1, 2, 3, 4}
4	<4, 5>	{1, 2, 3, 4, 5}
5	<4, 7>	{1, 2, 3, 4, 5, 7}
6	<7, 6>	{1, 2, 3, 4, 5, 7, 6}

When the algorithm stops, `B` contains the chosen edges `B = {<1,2>, <2,3>, <1,4>, <4,5>,<4,7>,<7,6>}`. The resultant spanning tree is drawn in Fig. 8.23, which is of weight 177.

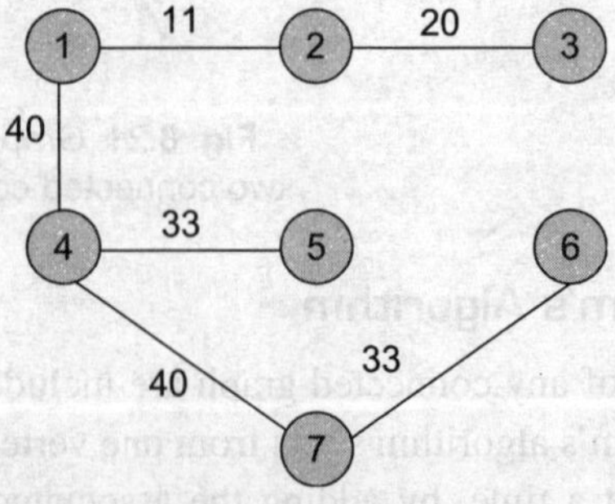

Fig. 8.23 Minimum spanning tree for graph in Fig. 8.22

Algorithm 8.4 is an informal statement of the algorithm. Here, `G` is a graph and `T` is a spanning tree to be computed.

ALGORITHM 8.4

```
1. Let G = {V, E} and T = {A, B}
        A = ϕ and B = ϕ
2. Let i ∈ V, i is a start vertex
3. A = A ∪ {i}
4. while A ≠ V do
   begin
   find edge <u,v> ∈ E of minimum length
        such that u ∈ A and v ∈ V - A
        A = A ∪ {v} and
        B = B ∪ {<u,v>}
   end
5. stop
```

To obtain a simple implementation in any programming language say C++, suppose that the vertices of `G` are numbered from 1 to n so that `V` = {1, 2, …, n}. Let the matrix M give the length of each edge and `L[i][j] = ∞` if the edge `<i,j> ∉ E`, that is, edge `<i,j>` does not exist. Let us use two arrays—`Nearest[]` and `Min_Dist[]`. Let `T = {A, B}` be the minimum spanning tree where initially `A` and `B` are empty. For each vertex `i ∈ V − A`, the array `Nearest[i]` gives the vertex in `A` that is nearest to `i`. Similarly, for each vertex `i ∈ V − A`, the array `Min_Dist[i]` gives the distance from `i` to this nearest vertex. For a `vertex i ∈ A`, we set `Min_Dist[i] = −1`. In this way, we can find out whether a vertex is in `A` or not. The set `A` arbitrarily initializes to {1}.

Consider the graph in Fig. 8.24.

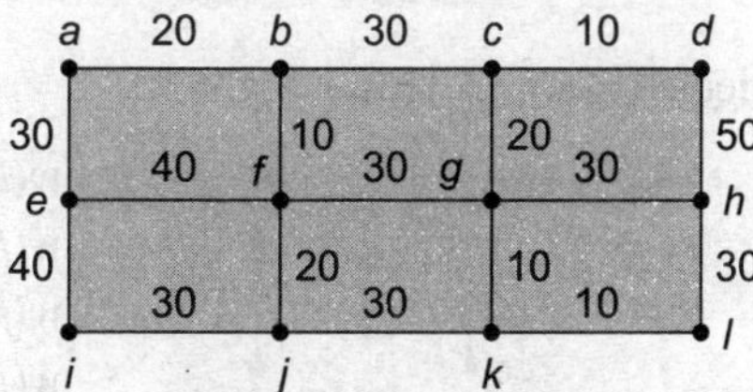

Fig. 8.24 Sample graph

Using Prim's algorithm, we get a spanning tree for this graph in the following steps:

1. Let f be the start vertex.
   Among vertices e, b, g, and j, the vertex b is the nearest one with edge <f, b> and weight 10.

   b — f (10)

   $w(f, e) = 40$
   $w(f, b) = 10 \leftarrow$ min
   $w(f, g) = 30$
   $w(f, j) = 20$

2. Among the vertices adjacent to *b* and *f*, the vertex *a* is the nearest one with edge <*b*, *a*> and weight 20.

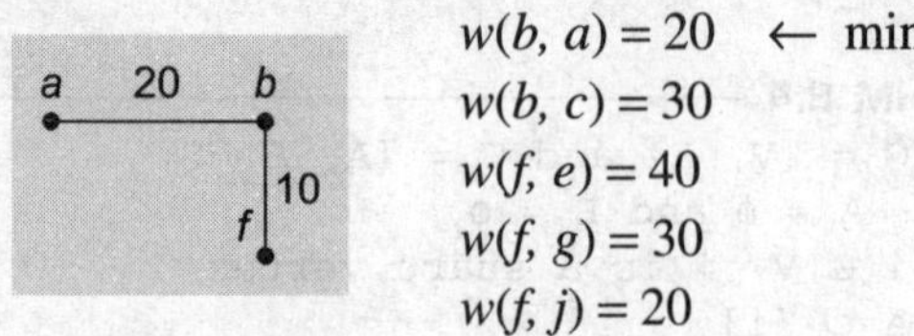

$w(b, a) = 20 \leftarrow \text{min}$
$w(b, c) = 30$
$w(f, e) = 40$
$w(f, g) = 30$
$w(f, j) = 20$

3. Similarly, the nearest vertex adjacent to one of *a*, *b*, and *f* is *j* with the edge <*f*, *j*> and weight 20.

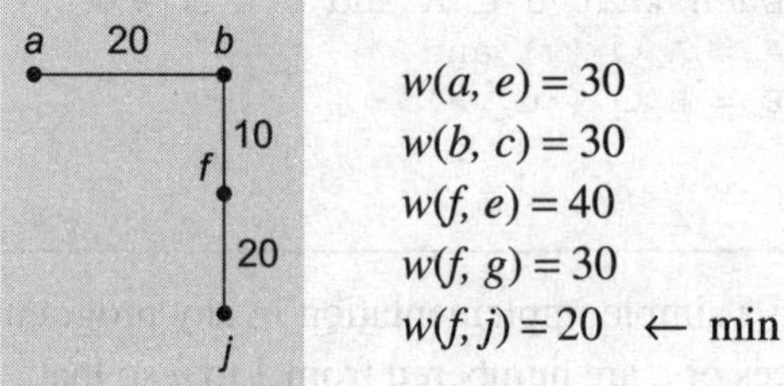

$w(a, e) = 30$
$w(b, c) = 30$
$w(f, e) = 40$
$w(f, g) = 30$
$w(f, j) = 20 \leftarrow \text{min}$

4. Similarly, the next edge added is <*a*, *e*> with weight 30.

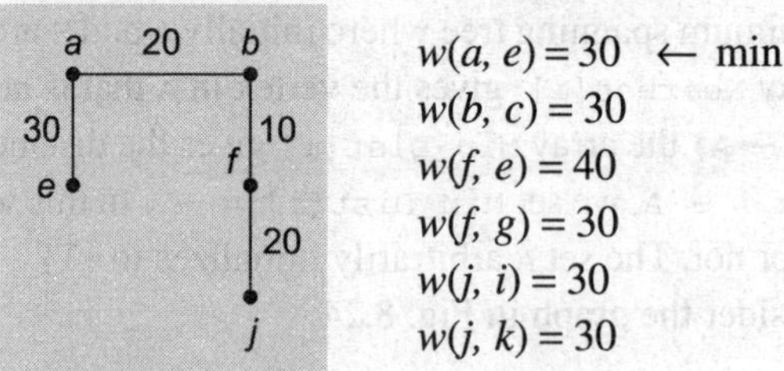

$w(a, e) = 30 \leftarrow \text{min}$
$w(b, c) = 30$
$w(f, e) = 40$
$w(f, g) = 30$
$w(j, i) = 30$
$w(j, k) = 30$

5. Edge selected = <*j*, *i*> with weight 30.

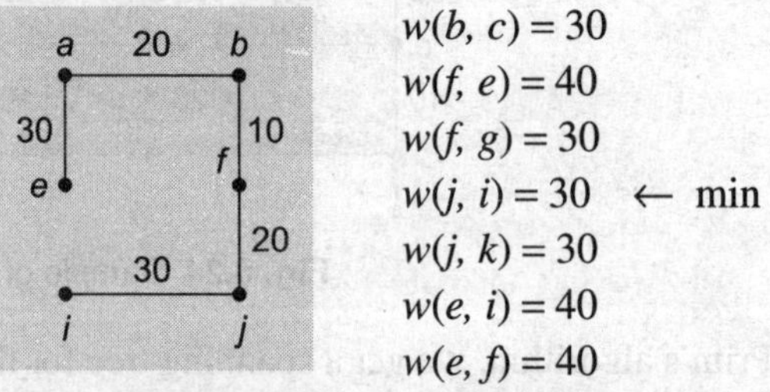

$w(b, c) = 30$
$w(f, e) = 40$
$w(f, g) = 30$
$w(j, i) = 30 \leftarrow \text{min}$
$w(j, k) = 30$
$w(e, i) = 40$
$w(e, f) = 40$

6. Edge selected = <*f*, *g*> with weight 30.

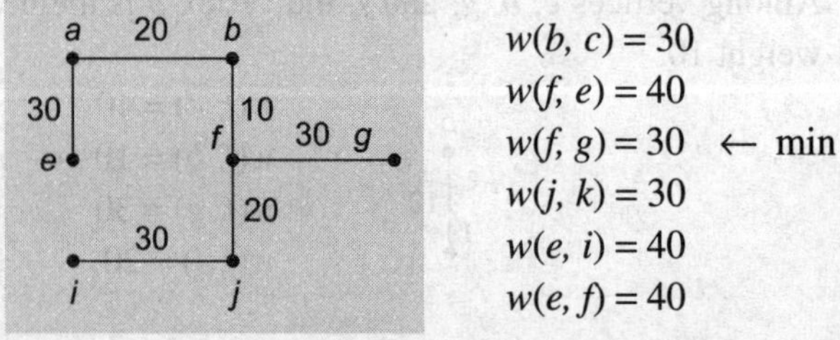

$w(b, c) = 30$
$w(f, e) = 40$
$w(f, g) = 30 \leftarrow \text{min}$
$w(j, k) = 30$
$w(e, i) = 40$
$w(e, f) = 40$

7. Edge selected = <*g*, *k*> with weight 10.

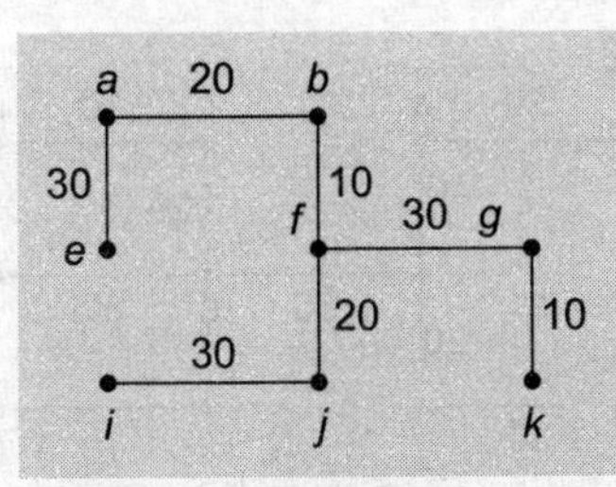

$w(b, c) = 30$
$w(f, e) = 40$
$w(j, k) = 30$
$w(e, i) = 40$
$w(e, f) = 40$
$w(g, c) = 20$
$w(g, k) = 10$ ← min
$w(g, h) = 30$

8. Edge selected = <*k*, *l*> with weight 10.

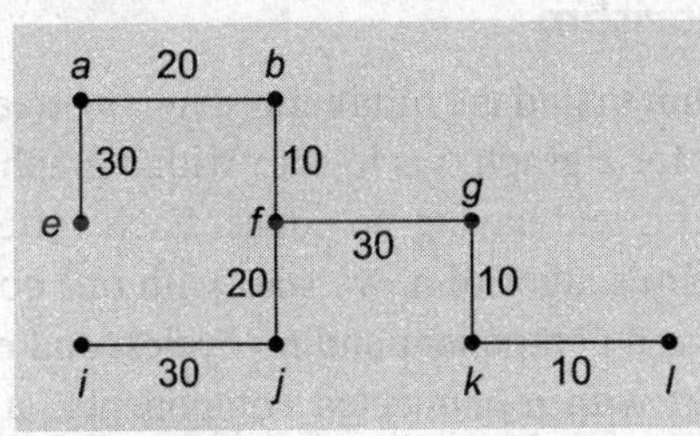

$w(b, c) = 30$
$w(f, e) = 40$
$w(j, k) = 30$
$w(e, i) = 40$
$w(e, f) = 40$
$w(g, c) = 20$
$w(g, h) = 30$
$w(k, l) = 10$ ← min

9. Edge selected = <*g*, *c*> with weight 20.

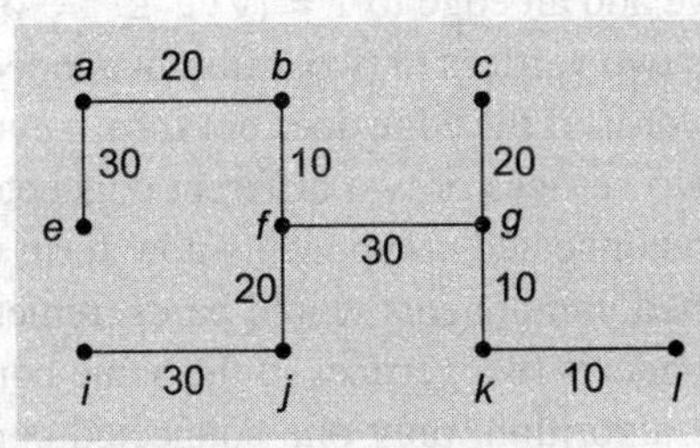

$w(b, c) = 30$
$w(f, e) = 40$
$w(j, k) = 30$
$w(e, i) = 40$
$w(e, f) = 40$
$w(g, c) = 20$ ← min
$w(g, h) = 30$
$w(l, h) = 30$

10. Edge selected = <*c*, *d*> with weight 10.

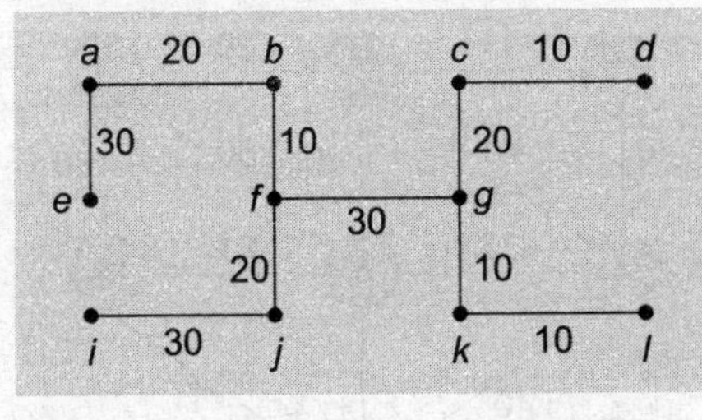

$w(b, c) = 30$
$w(f, e) = 40$
$w(j, k) = 30$
$w(e, i) = 40$
$w(e, f) = 40$
$w(g, h) = 30$
$w(l, h) = 30$
$w(c, d) = 10$ ← min

11. Finally the edge selected = <*g*, *k*> with weight 30.

As all the vertices are added, the algorithm ends. The resultant spanning tree is shown in Fig. 8.25 with a total weight of 220.

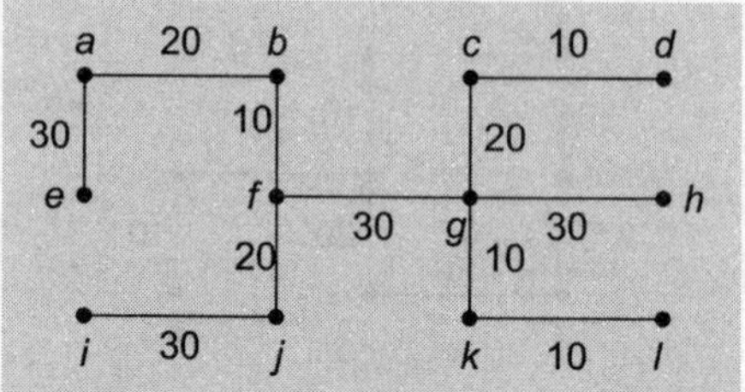

Fig. 8.25 Minimum cost spanning tree for the graph in Fig. 8.24

8.5.3 Kruskal's Algorithm

We studied Prim's algorithm to find the minimum spanning tree. Another way to construct a minimum spanning tree for a graph `G` is to start with a graph `T = (V', E' = ∅)` consisting of the `n` vertices of `G` and having no edges. Each vertex is therefore a connected component in itself. In Prim's algorithm, we start with one connected component, add a vertex to have one connected component and no cycles, and end up with one connected component. Here, we start with `n` connected components; at each step, the number of connected components would reduce by one and end up with one connected component. Here, `n` indicates the total number of vertices in a graph.

We start with all vertices; each vertex is therefore a connected component in itself. As the algorithm progresses, we add an edge to `T = (V', E' = ∅)` by examining the edges from `E`. If the edge connects two vertices in two different connected components, then we add the edge to `T`. In other words, if the edge does not form a cycle in `T`, only then an edge is added. If an edge joins two vertices of two different connected components, we add it to `T`. Consequently, the two connected components now form only one component, and the total number of connected components would be decremented by one. If it forms a cycle, that is, if the edge connects two vertices in the same component, then we discard the edge. At the end of the algorithm, only one connected component remains, so `T` is then a minimum spanning tree for all the vertices of `G`. To build a bigger component, we examine the edges of `G` in the increasing order of their associated weights.

To illustrate the method, consider the graph in Fig. 8.26.

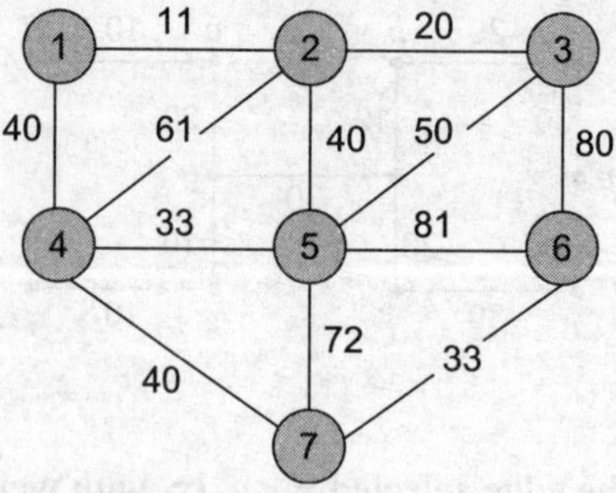

Fig. 8.26 Sample graph

Let us arrange the edges in an increasing order of their weights: <1, 2>, <2, 3>, <4, 5>, <6, 7>, <1, 4>, <2, 5>, <4, 7>, <3, 5>, <2, 4>, <3, 6>, <5, 7>, and <5, 6> with weights 11, 20, 33, 33, 40, 40, 40, 50, 61, 80, 72, and 81, respectively. Selection and addition of edges in a step-by-step manner is shown in Table 8.2.

Table 8.2 Construction of spanning tree for graph in Fig. 8.26

Step no.	Edge considered	Action	Connected component
Initial	–	–	{1} {2} {3} {4} {5} {6} {7}
1	<1, 2>	Add	{1, 2} {3} {4} {5} {6} {7}
2	<2, 3>	Add	{1,2,3} {4} {5} {6} {7}
3	<4, 5>	Add	{1,2,3} {4,5} {6} {7}
4	<6, 7>	Add	{1,2,3} {4,5} {6,7}
5	<1, 4>	Add	{1,2,3,4,5} {6,7}
6	<2, 5>	Rejected	{1,2,3,4,5} {6,7}
7	<4, 7>	Add	{1,2,3,4,5,6,7}

When the algorithm stops, T contains the chosen edges <1, 2>, <2, 3>, <4, 5>, <6, 7>, <1, 4>, and <4, 7>. This minimum spanning tree has the weight as 177 and is drawn in Fig. 8.22. Algorithm 8.5 states these steps in brief.

ALGORITHM 8.5

```
1. Let G = {V, E} and T = {A, B}
2. A = V and B = ϕ, |A| = n and |B| = 0
3. while(|B| < n - 1) do
   begin
     find edge <u,v> of minimum length and add to B
     only if addition of edge <u,v> does not complete a cycle in T
   end
4. stop
```

The graph T initially consists of the vertices of G but no edges. At each iteration, we add an edge <u, v> to T having minimum weight that does not complete a cycle in T. When T gets (n – 1) edges, the algorithm stops. To implement the algorithm, we have to handle a certain number of sets that include vertices of each connected component. Two operations have to be carried out:

1. `Member(x)` tells us which connected component the vertex x is a member of.
2. `Merge(u, v)` is to merge two connected components u and v.

Let us rewrite Algorithm 8.5 by elaborating these steps in Algorithm 8.6.

ALGORITHM 8.6

```
1. Sort E in increasing order of weights
2. Let G = (V, E) and T = (A, B), A = V and E = Null set
   And let n = length (V)
```

```
3. Initialize n sets, each containing a different element of v
4. while(|B| < n - 1) do
   begin
       e = <u,v> the shortest edge not yet considered
       U = Member(u)
       V = Member(v)
       if(U ≠ V)
       {
           Merge(U,V)
           Union(B,u,v)
       }
   end
5. T is the minimum spanning tree
6. stop
```

In step 4 of Algorithm 8.6, when the edge `<u,v>` with minimum weight is to be added in an existing tree, the function `Member()` checks for `u` and `v` for the connected component they belong to. If they are members of two different connected components, the edge is added as it would not form a cycle. If they belong to the same connected component, then adding the edge forms a cycle.

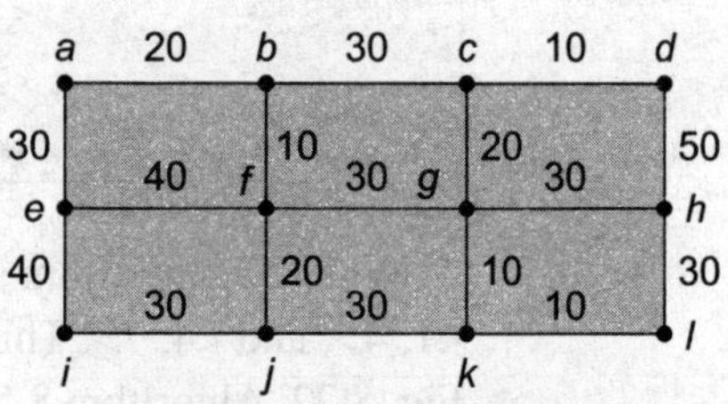

Fig. 8.27 Sample graph for Prim's spanning tree computation

Consider the graph as in Fig. 8.27

Let us use Kruskal's algorithm.

Step 1: The edge with minimum weight is selected edge = <*c, d*>.

Weight of the selected edge = 10.

As the addition of edge to the existing tree does not form a cycle, an edge is added.

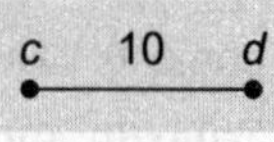

Step 2: Selected edge <*k, l*> with weight 10.

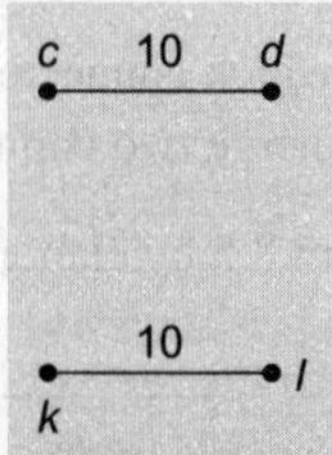

Step 3: Selected edge <*b, f*> with weight 10.

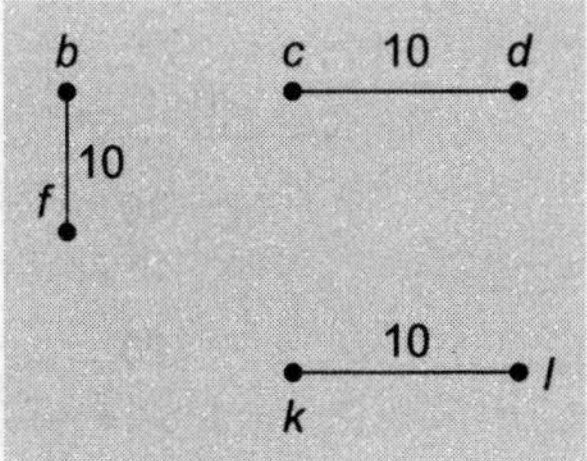

Step 4: Selected edge <*g, k*> with weight 20.

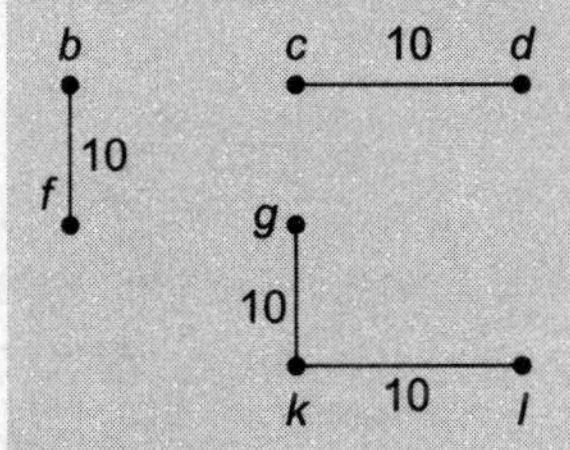

Step 5: Selected edge <*a, b*> weight 20.

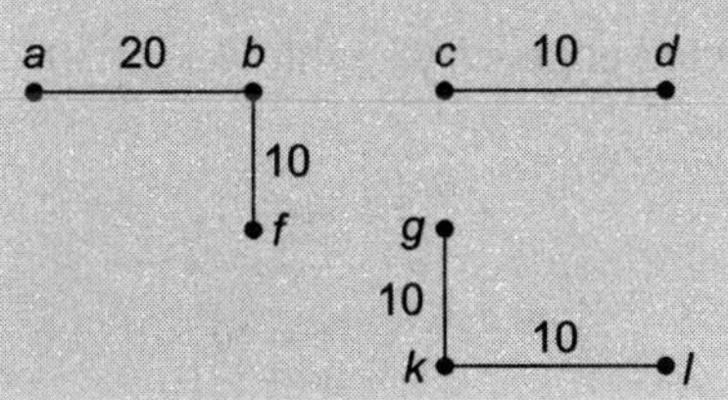

Step 6: Selected edge <*f, j*> with weight 20.

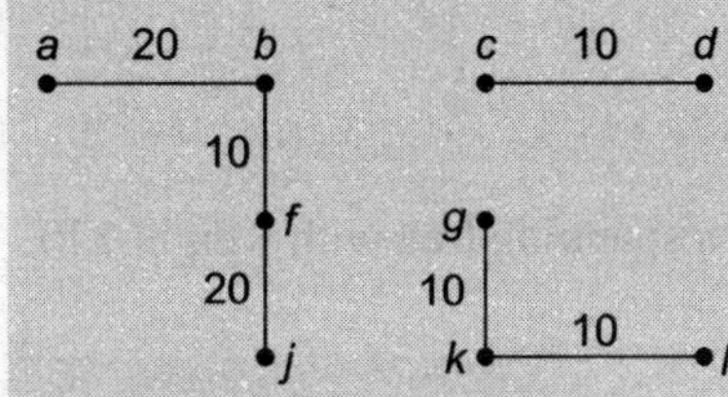

Step 7: Selected edge <*c, g*> with weight 30.

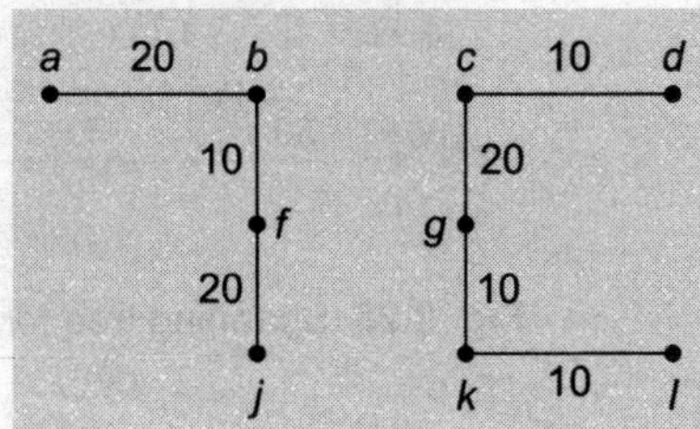

Step 8: Selected edge <*j, k*> with weight 30.

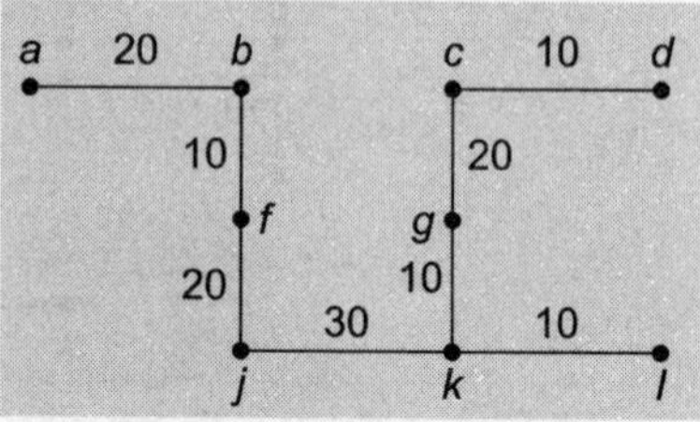

Step 9: Selected edge <*g, h*> with weight 30.

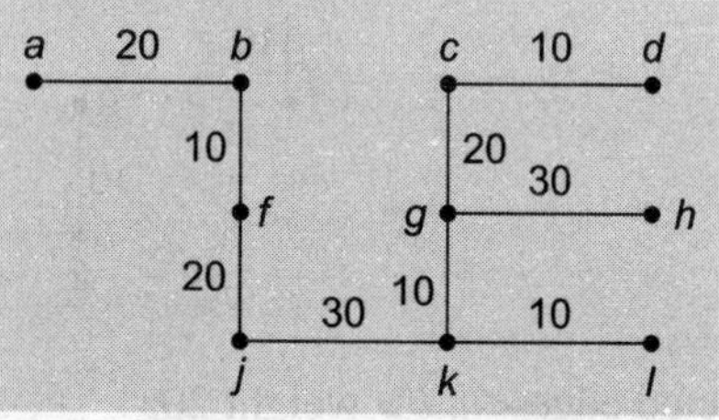

Step 10: Selected edge <*i, j*> with weight 30.

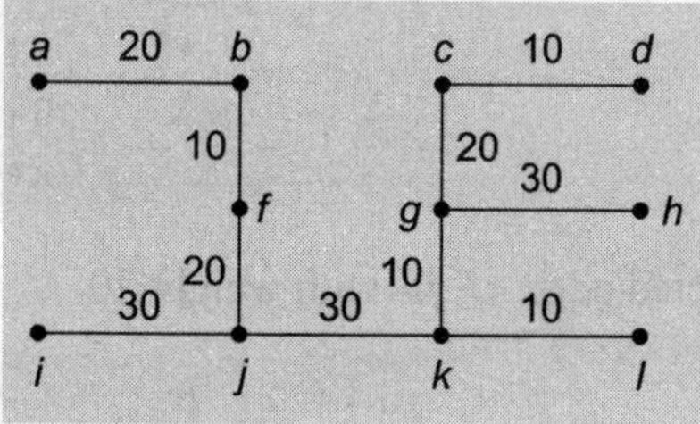

Figure 8.28 is a spanning tree with weight 220.

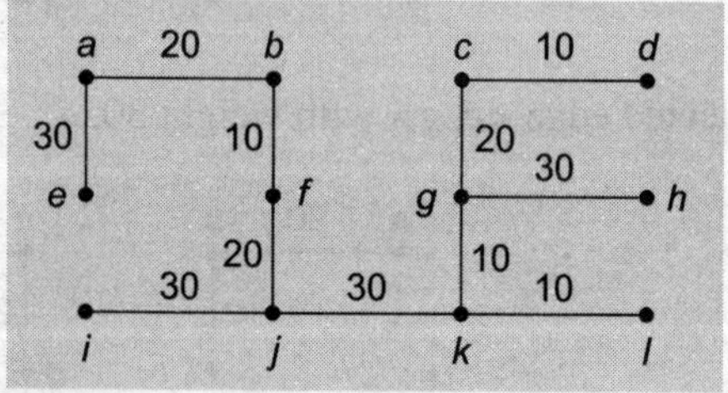

Fig. 8.28 Spanning tree for graph in Fig. 8.27

8.5.4 Biconnected Components

Depth-first search traversal of a graph, one of the most important techniques used for solving a variety of problems is described in Section 8.4.1. DFS can be used to find the connected components of an undirected graph. There are a few non-trivial graph algorithmic problems to be considered.

Consider a graph modelling a communication network problem. We expect the network to be robust under failures of any of the nodes. Even if a node fails, the remaining network should still remain connected. A graph is said to be biconnected if this condition is satisfied.

Often, we need to test whether a given undirected graph is biconnected or not. A biconnected component is a maximal biconnected sub-graph of the graph $G = (V, E)$. Edges and non-separation vertices belong to exactly one component, whereas separation vertices belong to at least two. Biconnected components contain no separation vertices or edges. A separation vertex or edge is one whose removal disconnects G. Between any two vertices, there exists at least two disjoint paths, and G has a simple cycle containing them. Any connected graph can be decomposed into a tree of biconnected components called the *block tree* of the graph. The blocks are attached to each other at shared vertices called *cut vertices* or *articulation points*. Specifically, a cut vertex is any vertex, which, when removed increases the number of connected components. In Fig. 8.29, the separation edge e_1 is between A and B, and the separation vertex is E.

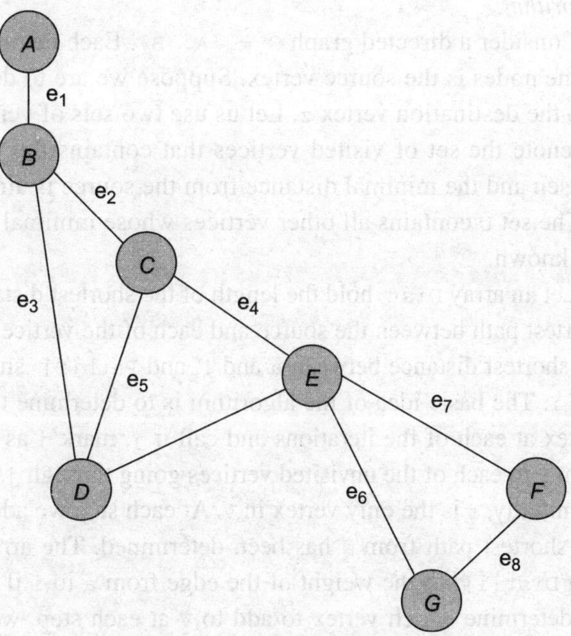

Fig. 8.29 Sample graph with biconnected components

8.5.5 Disjoint Set Operations

In minimum spanning tree computation algorithms, we have used two important set operations. Similar to those, there are many algorithms in which a disjoint-set data structure is used. This data structure keeps track of a set of elements partitioned into a number of disjoint subsets. A union–find algorithm is one that performs two useful operations (i.e., find and union) on such a data structure.

Find This is a membership check of the element. It determines the set in which a particular element is located and is also useful for determining whether two elements are in the same set or not.

Union This operation combines or merges two sets into a single set.

These two operations are supported by a disjoint-set data structure. Hence, it is also called as a *union–find data structure* or *merge–find set*.

8.6 SHORTEST PATH ALGORITHM

A *weighted graph* is a graph where the values are assigned to the edges and the length of a path is the sum of the weight of the edges in the path. We let `w(i, j)` denote the weight of edge `(i, j)`. In a weighted graph, we often need to find the shortest path. The shortest path between two given vertices is the path having minimum length. This problem can be solved by one of the greedy algorithms, by Edger W. Dijkstra, often called as *Dijkstra's algorithm*.

Consider a directed graph `G = {A, B}`. Each edge has a non-negative length. One of the nodes is the source vertex. Suppose we are to determine the shortest path from `a` to the destination vertex `z`. Let us use two sets of vertices, visited and unvisited. Let `V` denote the set of visited vertices that contains the vertices that have already been chosen and the minimal distance from the source is already known for every vertex in `V`. The set `U` contains all other vertices whose minimal distance from the source is not yet known.

Let an array `Dist` hold the length of the shortest distance and the array `Path` hold the shortest path between the source and each of the vertices. At each step, `Dist[i]` shows the shortest distance between `a` and `i`, and `Path[i]` shows the shortest path between `a` and `i`. The basic idea of the algorithm is to determine the minimum cost from `i` to one vertex at each of the iterations and call it `j`, mark `j` as visited, and recalculate the cost from `i` to each of the unvisited vertices going through `j`.

Initially, `a` is the only vertex in `V`. At each step we add to `V`, another vertex, for which the shortest path from `a` has been determined. The array `Dist[]` is initialized by setting `Dist[i]` to the weight of the edge from `a` to `i` if it exists and to ∞ if it does not. To determine which vertex to add to `V` at each step, we apply the criteria of choosing the vertex `j` with the smallest distance recorded in `Dist` such that `j` is not the visited one. When we add `j` to `V` (set of visited vertices), we must update the entries of `Dist` by checking, for each vertex `k` that is not in `V`, whether a path through `j` and then directly to `k` is shorter than the previously recorded distance of `k`. That is, we replace `Dist[k]` by `Dist[j]` + weight of the edge from `j` to `k` if the value of the latter quantity is lesser. Here, `j` is the currently selected vertex. Let `k` be a vertex whose distance is updated. If the distance is updated, then the path is also updated. Then, `path[k]` becomes the path of `j` followed by `k`.

In brief,

```
if Dist[k] > (Dist[j] + weight<j,k>) then
    Dist[k] = Dist[j] + w<j,k>
and
    Path[k] = Path[j] U{k}
```

Algorithm 8.7 is for computing the shortest path from the source vertex to the destination vertex.

ALGORITHM 8.7

```
1. Let G = (A, B) where A = set of vertices
2. Initially, let V = {a} and U = V - {a}
3. Let U be the unvisited and V be the visited vertices
4. Let Dist[t] = w[(a, t)] for every vertex a ∈ A
5. Select the vertex in U that has the smallest value Dist[x]. Let
   x denote this vertex.
6. If x is the vertex we wish to reach from a, goto 9. If not, let
   V = V - {x} and U = U - {x}
7. For every vertex t in A, compute Dist[t] with respect to V as,
       Dist[t] = min{Dist[t], Dist[t] + w (x,t)}
8. Repeat steps 5, 6, and 7
9. Stop
```

Let us consider the graph in Fig. 8.30, and let us compute the shortest path between a and all other vertices using this algorithm.

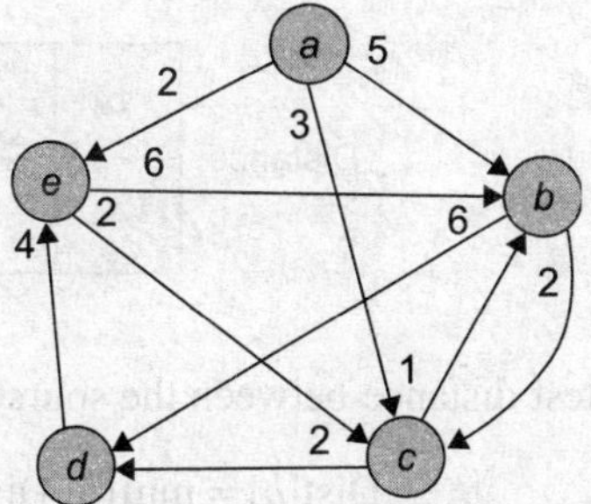

Fig. 8.30 Directed weighted graph

1. Initial step
   The set $V = \{a\}$, where a is the source vertex
   and $U = \{b, c, d, e\}$ is the set of unvisited vertices.
   Dist[ ] = {–, 5, 3, ∞, 2}. This array can also be written as

	b	c	d	e
Distance	5	3	∞	2

This Dist[ ] array represents the current shortest distance between a and other vertices.
   Path = {Ø, *ab*, *ac*, Ø, *ac*}

2. Now, the distance to vertex e is the shortest, so e is added to set V.
   We get, $V = \{a, e\}$; let us update Dist array now.

	b	c	d	e
Distance	5	3	6	2

The weight of the edge between the current selected vertex e and d is 4 and the distance from a to e is 2; hence the distance between a and d becomes 6 as it is less than ∞. Hence, the path is also updated for vertex d by the path of current selected vertex, that is, the path of e.

Path = {Ø, *ab*, *ac*, *aed*, *ae*}

3. Now the distance to vertex c among the unvisited vertices is the shortest. Hence, c is current selected vertex which gets to V.
   Therefore $V = \{a, e, c\}$. Let us update Dist array now.

	b	c	d	e
Distance	4	3	5	2

Here, the shortest distance between the source a to b and d are updated as,

$$\begin{aligned} \text{Dist}[b] &= \min\{5, \text{Dist}[c] + w(c, b)\} \\ &= \min\{5, 3 + 1\} \\ &= 4 \end{aligned}$$

and

$$\begin{aligned}\text{Dist}[d] &= \min\{6, \text{Dist}[c] + w(c, d)\}\\ &= \min\{6, 3 + 2\}\\ &= 5\end{aligned}$$

As the shortest distance of b and d are updated, their respective paths are also updated as in the following expression:

$$\text{Path} = \{\emptyset, acb, ac, acd, ae\}$$

The path vector can also be shown as follows:

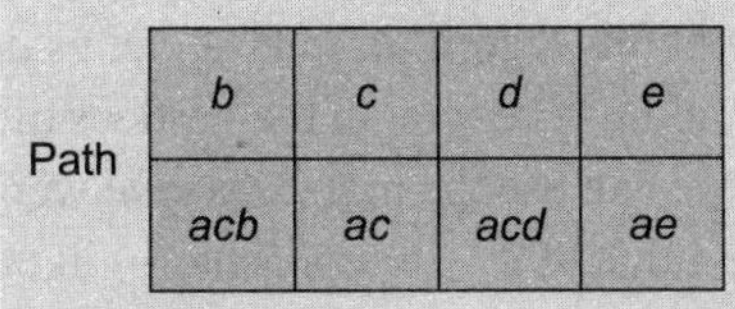

Path	b	c	d	e
	acb	ac	acd	ae

4. Now b is the vertex that has the shortest distance and is unvisited.

Hence, $V = \{a, e, c, b\}$

Distance	b	c	d	e
	4	3	5	2

Here, none of the shortest distances is updated. Hence, the path also remains unchanged.

Path	b	c	d	e
	acb	ac	acd	ae

5. Now d is the next selected vertex, and the final distance and path vectors are the same as stated. Hence, the shortest distances between a and $\{b, c, d, e\}$ are $\{4, 3, 5, 2\}$, respectively. In addition, the shortest path between a and $\{b, c, d, e\}$ are $\{acb, ac, acd, ae\}$, respectively.

In the final two steps, adding the vertices b and d to V yield the paths and distances as shown in Fig. 8.31.

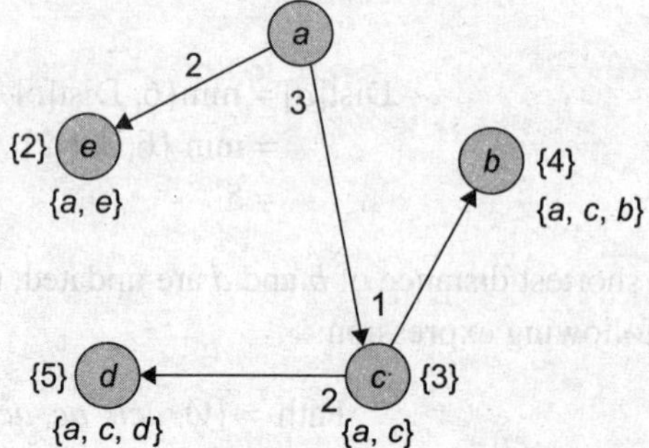

Fig. 8.31 Shortest paths and distances

To implement this algorithm in C++, let us use an adjacency matrix implementation as it facilitates random access to all the vertices of a graph. Moreover, by storing the weights in the matrix, we can use the matrix to give weights as well as adjacencies. We shall place a special large value 9999 (to represent ∞) in positions for which the corresponding edge does not exist (Program Code 8.6).

PROGRAM CODE 8.6

```
// Shortest distance using Dijkstra's algorithm

#include<iostream.h>
#include<conio.h>
#define infinite 999
class graph
{
   int Graph[20][20];
   // Adjacency Matrix int No_of_Vertices;
   public:
      void Accept();
      void Display();
      int Calc_Shortest_Dist();
};

void graph :: Accept()
{
   int i,j;
   cout << "Enter no of vertex";
   cin >> No_of_Vertices;
   for(i = 1; i<= No_of_Vertices; i++)
  {
      for(j = 1; j<= No_of_Vertices; j++)
     {
```

```
            Graph[i][j] = infinite;
         }
      }
      for(i = 1; i<= No_of_Vertices; i++)
      {
         for(j = i + 1; j<= No_of_Vertices; j++)
         {
            cout << "\n Please enter weight from
            "<<i<<"to"<<j<<":";
            cin>> Graph[i][j];
            Graph[j][i] = Graph[i][j];
         }
      }
}

void graph :: Display()
{
     int i,j;
     cout << "Graphs Adjacency Matrix is\n";
     for(i = 1; i<= No_of_Vertices; i++)
     {
         for(j = 1; j<= No_of_Vertices; j++)
         {
            cout << "\t"<< Graph [i][j];
         }
         cout << "\n";
      }
}

int graph :: Calc_Shortest_Dist()
{
    int cost, curr, src, cost1 = 0, desti, start, new1,
    i, k = 1, temp;
    int  visited[20], dist[20];
    cout << "\nEnter the source";
    cin >> src;
    cout << "\nEnter the destination";
    cin >> desti;
    for(i = 0; i<= No_of_Vertices; i++)
    {
       visited[i] = 0;
       dist[i] = infinite;
    }
```

```
    visited[src] = 1;
    dist[src] = 0;
    curr = src;
    cout << "\nPath is"<<src;
    while(curr != desti)
    {
       cost = infinite;
       start = dist[curr];
       for(i = 1; i<= No_of_Vertices; i++)
       {
          if(visited[i] == 0)
          {
             new1 = start + Graph[curr][i];
             if(new1 < dist[i])
                 dist[i] = new1;
                 if(dist[i]<cost)
                 {
                    cost = dist[i];
                    temp = i;
                 }
             }
          }
          curr = temp;
          visited[curr] = 1;
          cout << "\nCurr node is"<<curr;
          // cost1 = cost1 + cost;
    }
return cost1;
}

void main()
{
   clrscr();
   graph G;
   int Shortest_Distance;
   G.Accept();
   G.Display();
   Shortest_Distance = G. Calc_Shortest_Dist();
   cout << "\ndistance is"<< Shortest_Distance;
   getch();
}
```

RECAPITULATION

- Graphs are one of the most important non-linear data structures. A graph is a representation of relation. Vertices represent elements and edges represent relationships. In other words, a graph is a collection of nodes (vertices) and arcs joining pairs of the nodes (edges). The edges between two vertices represent the relationship between them.
- Graphs are classified as directed and undirected graphs. In an undirected graph, an edge is a set of two vertices where order does not make any relevance, whereas in a directed graph, an edge is an ordered pair.
- Graphs are implemented using an array or a linked list representation. An adjacency list is a data structure for representing a graph by keeping a list of the neighbour vertices for each vertex. An adjacency matrix is a data structure for representing a graph as a Boolean matrix where 0 means no edge and 1 corresponds to an edge.
- There are two standard graph traversals—depth-first and breadth-first.
- A minimum spanning tree is a tree, containing all the vertices of a graph, where the total weight of the edges is minimum. The two popularly used algorithms to compute minimum spanning tree are Prim's and Kruskal's algorithms.
- A biconnected component is a maximal subgraph. A component of biconnected graph is useful in modelling a robust communication network.
- A disjoint set is a type of data structure that keeps track of a set of elements partitioned into a number of disjoint subsets. Operations such as union and find are performed on it for respectively merging two sets into one and determining the location of a given set.
- Dijkstra's algorithm is another common algorithm for graphs to find the shortest path between two vertices of a graph.

KEY TERMS

Adjacency list In an adjacency list, the *n* rows of the adjacency list are represented as *n*-linked lists, one list per vertex of the graph. We can represent *G* by an array Head, where Head[*i*] is a pointer to the adjacency list of vertex *i*. Each node of the list has at least two fields: vertex and link. The vertex field contains the vertex id, and link field stores the pointer to the next node storing another vertex adjacent to *i*.

Adjacency matrix The graphs represented using a sequential representation using matrices is called an adjacency matrix.

Adjacency multilist Multilists are lists where nodes may be shared among several other lists. For each edge, instead of two, there will be exactly one node, but this node will be in two lists, that is, the adjacency lists for each of the two nodes it is incident on.

Biconnected component A biconnected component is a maximal biconnected sub-graph of graph $G = (V, E)$ containing no separation vertices or edges.

Breadth-first search (BFS) In BFS, all the unvisited vertices adjacent to *i* are visited after visiting the start vertex *i* and marking it visited. Next, the unvisited vertices adjacent to these vertices are visited and so on until the entire graph has been traversed.

Connected component An undirected graph is connected if there is at least one path between every pair of vertices in the graph. A connected component of a graph is a maximal connected sub-graph, that is, every vertex in a connected component is reachable from the vertices in the component.

Depth-first search (DFS) DFS differs from BFS. It starts at the vertex *v* of *G* as a start vertex and *v* is marked as visited. Then, each unvisited vertex adjacent to *v* is searched using the DFS recursively. Once all the vertices that can be reached from *v* have been visited, the search of *v* is complete. If some vertices remain unvisited, we select an unvisited vertex as a new start vertex and then repeat the process until all the vertices of *G* are marked visited.

Disjoint set This is a type of data structure that keeps track of a set of elements partitioned into a number of disjoint subsets.

Graph traversal Visiting all the vertices and edges in a systematic fashion is called as a graph traversal. The two most common traversals are depth-first traversal and breadth-first traversal.

Graph A graph *G* is a discrete structure consisting of nodes (vertices) and the lines joining the nodes (edges). For finite graphs, *V* and *E* are finite. We can write a graph as $G = (V, E)$.

Inverse adjacency list Inverse adjacency lists is a set of lists that contain one list for vertex. Each list contains a node per vertex adjacent to the vertex it represents.

Spanning tree A tree is a connected graph with no cycles. A spanning tree is a sub-graph of *G* that has all vertices of *G* and is a tree. A minimum spanning tree of a weighted graph *G* is the spanning tree of *G* whose edges sum to minimum weight.

EXERCISES

Multiple choice questions

1. Consider an undirected unweighted graph *G*. Let a breadth-first traversal be done starting from a node *r*. Let the distance $d(r, u)$ and $d(r, v)$ be the lengths of the shortest paths from *r* to *u* and *v*, respectively, in *G*. If *u* is visited before *v* during the breadth-first traversal, which of the following statements is correct?
   (a) $d(r, u) < d(r, v)$
   (b) $d(r, u) > d(r, v)$
   (c) $d(r, u) \leq d(r, v)$
   (d) None of these
2. Kruskal's algorithm for finding a minimum spanning tree of a weighted graph *G* with *n* vertices and *m* edges has the time complexity of
   (a) $O(n^2)$
   (b) $O(m, n)$
   (c) $O(m + n)$
   (d) $(m \log n)$
   (e) $O(m^2)$
3. Consider a simple connected graph *G* with *n* vertices and *n* edges ($n > 2$). Then, which of the following statements is true?
   (a) *G* has no cycles
   (b) The graph obtained by removing any edge from G is not connected
   (c) *G* has at least one cycle
   (d) The graph obtained by removing any two edges from G is not connected
   (e) None of the above
4. Which of the following statements is false?
   (a) Optimal binary search tree construction can be performed efficiently using dynamic programming.
   (b) BFS cannot be used to find the component of a graph.
   (c) The prefix and postfix walks over a binary tree cannot be uniquely constructed.
   (d) DFS can be used to find the connected components of a graph.

5. The number of distinct simple graphs with upto 3 nodes is
   (a) 15
   (b) 10
   (c) 7
   (d) 9
6. Let G be a graph with 100 vertices numbered 1 to 100. Two vertices i and j are adjacent iff $|i - j| = 8$ or $|i - j| = 12$. The number of connected components in G is
   (a) 8
   (b) 4
   (c) 12
   (d) 25
7. The number of articulation points of the following graph is
   (a) 0
   (b) 1
   (c) 2
   (d) 3
8. Let G be an undirected graph. Consider a DFS of G, and let T be the resulting DFS tree. Let u be a vertex in G and let v be the first new (unvisited) vertex. After using u in the traversal, which of the following statements is always true?
   (a) $\{u, v\}$ must be an edge in G, and u is a descendent of u in T.
   (b) $\{u, v\}$ must be an edge in G, and v is a descendent of u in T.
   (c) If $\{u, v\}$ is not an edge in G, then u is a leaf in T.
   (d) If $\{u, v\}$ is not an edge in G, then u and v must have the same parent in T.
9. Which is the most appropriate matching for the following pairs?

X: depth-first search	1: heap
Y: breadth-first search	2: queue
Z: sorting	3: stack

   (a) *X*–1, *Y*–2, *Z*–3
   (b) *X*–3, *Y*–1, *Z*–2
   (c) *X*–3, *Y*–2, *Z*–1
   (d) *X*–2, *Y*–3, *Z*–1
10. Let G be an undirected connected graph with distinct edge weights. Let e_{max} be the edge with maximum weight and e_{min} be the edge with minimum weight. Which of the following statements is false?
   (a) Every minimum spanning tree of G must contain e_{min}
   (b) If e_{max} is a minimum spanning tree, then its removal must disconnect G
   (c) No minimum spanning tree contains e_{max}
   (d) G has a unique minimum spanning tree

Review questions

1. Give the adjacency list representation for the following graph.

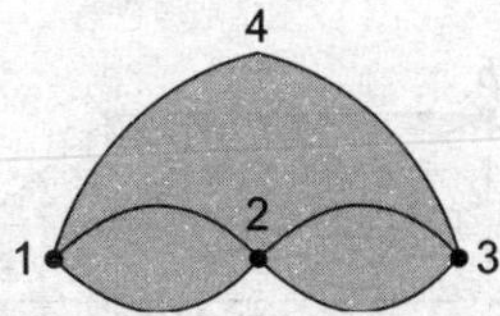

2. Suggest a suitable node structure for a weighted graph's adjacency list representation. Give the adjacency list for the following weighted graph using the suggested node structure.

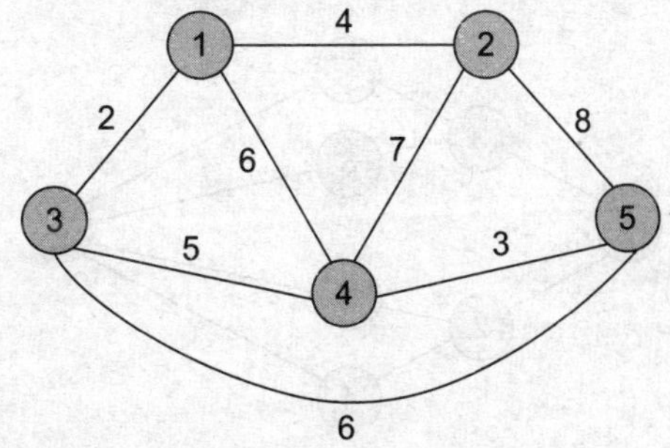

3. Draw a graph for the following adjacency list.

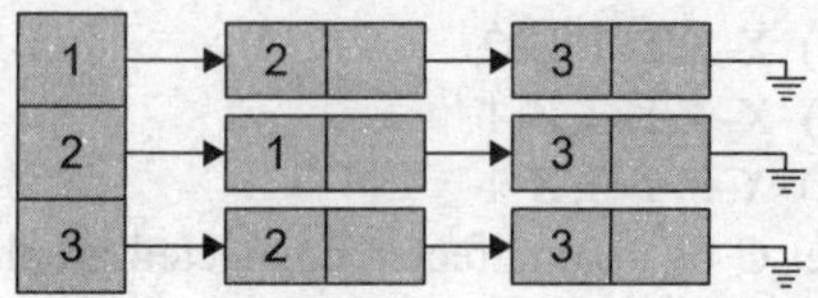

4. Compute the shortest path and the distance between the vertices *a* and *z* in the following graph.

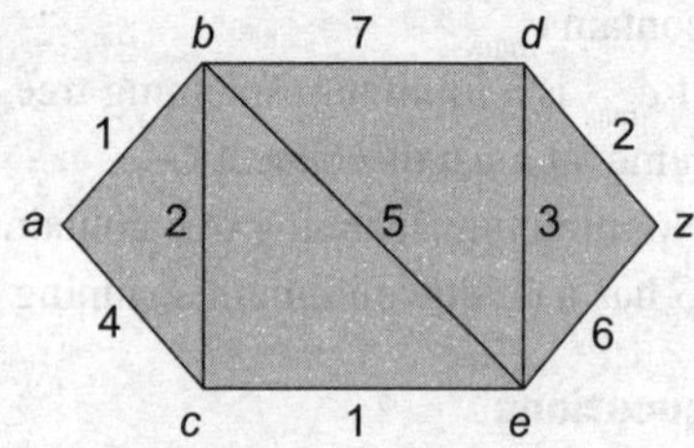

5. For the following graph, compute the shortest path and distance between the vertices *a* and *h*.

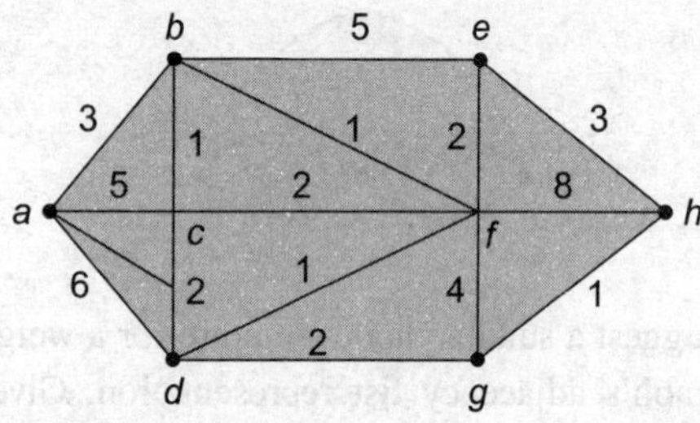

6. For the following graph, give the result of depth-first and breadth-first traversals.

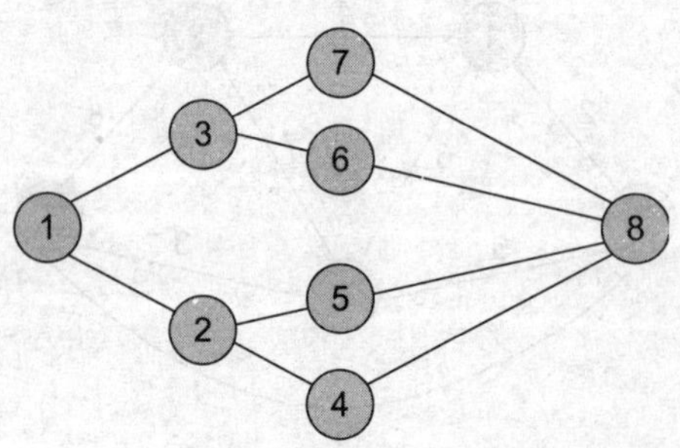

7. Consider the following specification of a graph *G*:

   $V(G) = \{1, 2, 3, 4)$
   $E(G) = \{(1, 2), (1, 3), (3, 3), (3, 4), (4, 1)\}$

   (a) Draw a picture of the undirected graph.
   (b) Draw its adjacency matrix.
8. Write a non-recursive pseudo algorithm for the DFS of a graph.
9. Construct a minimum spanning tree (step-by-step) from the following graph using Kruskal's algorithm.

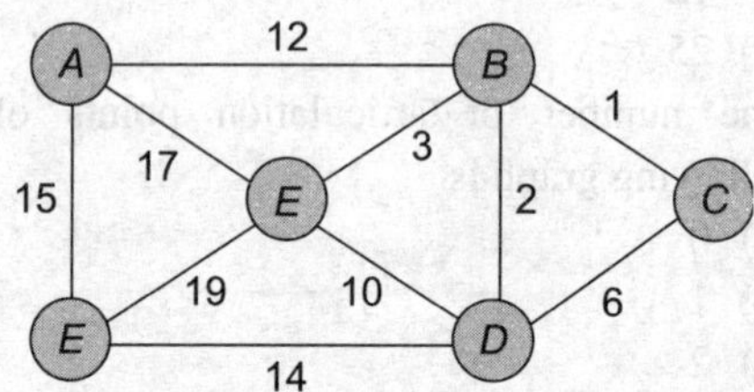

10. Construct an adjacency matrix and adjacency list for the graph in question 9.
11. Construct a minimum spanning tree using Prim's algorithm for the graph in question 9.
12. Write pseudo C++ algorithms for the following:
    (a) BFS
    (b) DFS
    (c) Kruskal's algorithm
    (d) Prim's algorithm
    (e) Dijkstra's algorithm
13. Show that all vertices in an undirected finite graph cannot have distinct degrees if the graph has at least two vertices.
14. A complete, undirected, weighted graph *G* is given on the vertex set $\{0, 1, \ldots, n-1\}$ for any fixed *n*. Draw the minimum spanning tree of *G* if
    (a) the weight of the edge (u, v) is $|u - v|$
    (b) the weight of the edge (u, v) is $u + v$

15. For the graph in the following figure:

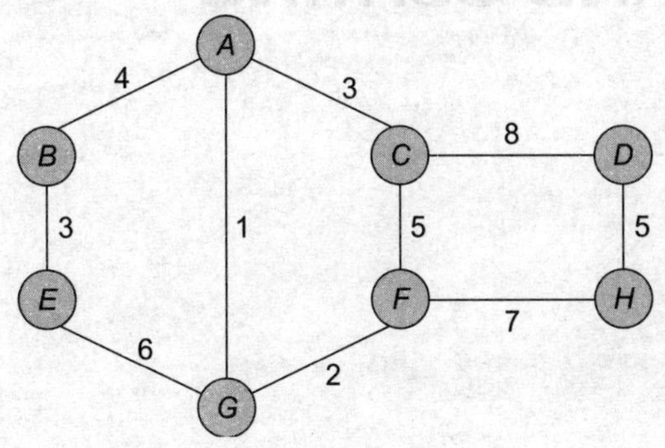

(a) Give the depth-first traversal.
(b) Give the breadth-first traversal.
(c) Draw three spanning trees.
(d) Give the adjacency matrix representation.
(e) Give the adjacency list representation.
(f) Find minimum spanning tree.
(g) Find the shortest path and distance between *A* and all other vertices.

16. Explain the terms connected components, biconnected components, block tree, and cut vertex.

17 Describe the disjoint set operations union and find. Write algorithms for these operations.

Answers to multiple choice questions

1. (c) 2. (c) 3. (c) 4. (b) 5. (a) 6. (a) 7. (d) 8. (b) 9. (c) 10. (c)

9 SEARCHING AND SORTING

OBJECTIVES

After completing this chapter, the reader will be able to understand the following:

- Basic search and sort algorithms
- Algorithms with respect to time and space complexity
- Appropriate algorithms suitable for practical applications

One of the most common and time consuming tasks in computer science is the retrieval of target information from huge data, which needs searching. Searching is the process of finding the location of the target among a list of objects. The two basic search techniques are the following:

1. Sequential search
2. Binary search

There are certain ways of organizing data, which make the search process more efficient. If the data is kept in a proper order, it is much easier to search. Sorting is a process of organizing data in a certain order to help retrieve it more efficiently.

In this chapter, we shall study searching and sorting methods. We shall also analyse the algorithms in terms of time complexity.

9.1 SEARCHING

The process of locating target data is known as *searching*. Consider a situation where you are trying to get the phone number of your friend from a telephone directory. The telephone directory can be thought of as a table or a file, which is a collection of records. Each record has one or more fields such as name, address, and telephone number. The fields, which are used to distinguish records, are known as *keys*. While searching, we are asked to find the record which contains information along with the target key. When we think of a telephone directory, the search is usually by name. However, when we try to locate the record corresponding to a given telephone number, the key will be the telephone number.

If given an address and the person's name and telephone number need to be located, the person's address will be the key.

If the key is unique and if it determines a record uniquely, it is called a *primary key*. For example, telephone number is a primary key. As any field of a record may serve as the key for a particular application, keys may not always be unique. For example, if we use 'name' as the key for a telephone directory, there may be one or more persons with the same name. In addition, sorted organization of a directory makes searching easier and faster.

We may use one of the two linear data structures, arrays and linked lists, for storing the data. Search techniques may vary according to data organization. The data may be stored on a secondary storage or permanent storage area. If the search is applied on the table that resides at the secondary storage (hard disk), it is called as *external searching*, whereas searching of a table that is in primary storage (main memory) is called as *internal searching* which is faster than external searching.

A searching algorithm accepts two arguments as parameters—a target value to be searched and the list to be searched. The search algorithm searches a target value in the list until the target key is found or can conclude that it is not found.

One of the most popular applications of search algorithms is adding a record in the collection of records. While adding, the record is searched by key and if not present, it is inserted in the collection. Such a technique of searching the record and inserting it if not found is known as *search and insert algorithm.*

9.2 SEARCH TECHNIQUES

Depending on the way data is scanned for searching a particular record, the search techniques are categorized as follows:

1. Sequential search
2. Binary search
3. Fibonacci search
4. Index sequential search
5. Hashed search

The performance of a searching algorithm can be computed by counting the number of comparisons to find a given value. We shall study these algorithms with respect to arrays. For sequential search, the same concept applies for searching data in linked lists as well as files.

9.2.1 Sequential Search

The easiest search technique is a sequential search. This is a technique that must be used when records are stored without any consideration given to order, or when the storage medium lacks any type of direct access facility. For example, magnetic tape and linked list are sequential storage media where the data may or may not be ordered. There are two ways for storing the collection of records namely, sequential and non-sequential. For the time being, let us assume that we have a sequential file *F*, and we wish to retrieve a record with a certain key value *k*. If *F* has *n* records with the key value k_i such as $i = 1$ to *n*, then one way to carry out the retrieval is by examining the key values in the order of their arrangement until the correct record is located. Such a search is known as *sequential search* since the records are examined sequentially from the first till the last.

Hence, a sequential search begins with the first available record and proceeds to the next available record repeatedly until we find the target key or conclude that it is not found. Sequential search is also called as *linear search*.

Algorithm 9.1 depicts the steps involved in sequential search.

ALGORITHM 9.1

```
1. Set i = 0, flag = 0
2. Compare key[i] and target
   if(key[i] = target)
      Set flag = 1, location = i and goto step 5
3. Move to next data element
   i = i + 1
4. if(i < n) goto step 2
5. if(flag = 1) then
      return i as position of target located
   else
      report as 'Target not found'
6. stop
```

Figure 9.1 shows a sample sequential unordered data and traces the search for the target data of 89.

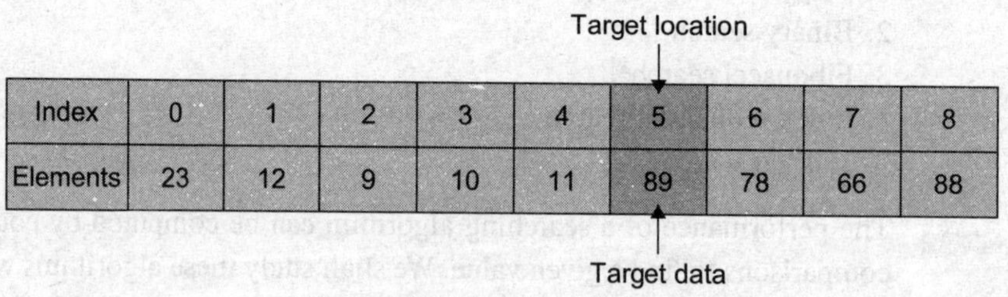

Fig. 9.1 Sequential search for target data of 89

Initially, $i = 0$ and the target element 89 is to be searched. At each pass, the target 89 is compared with the element at the ith location till it is found or the index *i* exceeds the size. At $i = 5$, the search is successful.

Algorithm 9.1 for sequential search is implemented in C++ as shown in Program Code 9.1.

PROGRAM CODE 9.1

```
int SeqSearch (int A[max], int key, int n)
{
   int i,  flag = 0, position;
   for(i = 0; i < n; i++)
   {
      if(key == A[i])
      {
         position = i;
         flag = 1;
         break;
      }
   }
   if(flag == 1)        // if found return position
      return(position);
   else       // return -1 if not found
      return(-1);
}
```

The function `SeqSearch()` is defined with three parameters—the element to be searched, the array `A` where the element is to be searched, and the total number of elements in the array. The function `SeqSearch()` returns the location of the element if found or returns –1 if the element is not found.

Let us compute the amount of time the sequential search needs to search for a target data. For this, we must compute the number of times the comparisons of keys is done. In general, for any search algorithm, the computational complexity is computed by considering the number of comparisons made.

The number of comparisons depends on where the target data is stored in the search list. If the target data is placed at the first location, we get it in just one comparison. Two comparisons are needed if the target data is in the second location. Similarly, i comparisons are required if the target data is at the ith location and n comparisons, if it is at the nth location. As the total number of comparisons depends on the position of the target data, let us compute the average complexity of the algorithm. Average complexity is the sum of number of comparisons for each position of the target data divided by n and is given as follows:

$$\begin{aligned}\text{Average number of comparisons} &= (1 + 2 + 3 + \ldots + n)/n \\ &= (\Sigma n)/n \\ &= ((n(n+1))/2) \times 1/n \\ &= (n+1)/2\end{aligned}$$

Hence, the average number of comparisons done by the sequential search method in the case of a successful search is $(n + 1)/2$. An unsuccessful search is given by n comparisons. The number of comparisons is n and the complexity is denoted as $O(n)$.

The worst case complexity is n, which means that the target data element is at the nth location and hence requires n comparisons. The best case complexity is 1, as the target data element is at the first location and requires only a single comparison. Sequential search is suitable when the data is stored in an unordered manner and also when there is no way to directly access the data elements. For example, to search the data record stored on a magnetic tape, it has to be searched sequentially from the first location till the nth location. The linear list implemented using a linked list cannot access any i^{th} element directly except $(i = 1)$. We need to search through the whole list to retrieve a target data. Hence, sequential search is used if the data is unsorted and if the storage does not provide direct access to the data.

Pros and Cons of Sequential Search

The following lists detail the pros and cons of sequential searching:

Pros

1. A simple and easy method
2. Efficient for small lists
3. Suitable for unsorted data
4. Suitable for storage structures which do not support direct access to data, for example, magnetic tape, linked list, etc.
5. Best case is one comparison, worst case is n comparisons, and average case is $(n + 1)/2$ comparisons
6. Time complexity is in the order of n denoted as $O(n)$.

Cons

1. Highly inefficient for large data
2. In the case of ordered data other search techniques such as binary search are found more suitable.

Variations of Sequential Search

The time complexity of sequential search is $O(n)$; this amounts to one comparison in the best case, n comparisons in the worst case, and $(n + 1)/2$ comparisons in the average case. The algorithm starts at the first location and the search continues till the last element. We can make a few changes leading to a few variations in the sequential search algorithm. There are three such variations:

1. Sentinel search
2. Probability search
3. Ordered list search

Sentinel search We note that in steps 2–4 of Algorithm 9.1, there are two comparisons—one for the element (key) to be searched and the other for the end of the array. The algorithm ends either when the target is found or when the last element is compared. The algorithm can be modified to eliminate the end of list test by placing the target at the end of list as just one additional entry. This additional entry at the end of the list is called as a *sentinel*. Now, we need not test for the end of list condition within the loop and merely check after the loop completes whether we found the actual target or the sentinel. This modification avoids one comparison within the loop that varies *n* times. The only care to be taken is not to consider the sentinel entry as a data member.

Algorithm 9.2 depicts the steps involved in sentinel search.

ALGORITHM 9.2

```
1. Set i = 0
2. list[n] = target {add sentinel}
3. Compare key[i] and target
   if(key[i] = target)
     Set location = i and goto step 6
4. Move to next data element
   i = i + 1
5. goto step 3
6. if(location < n) then
     return location as position of target
7. else
     report as 'Target not found' and return -1
8. stop
```

Algorithm 9.2 is implemented in C++ as in Program Code 9.2.

PROGRAM CODE 9.2

```
int SeqSearch_sentinel (int A[max], int key, int n)
{
    int i, position;
    A[n] = key;       // place target at end of the list
    while(key != A[i])
    {
       i = i + 1;
    }
    //if found at sentinel then return position
    if(i < n)
       return(i);
    else        // return -1 if not found
       return(-1);
}
```

Probability search In probability search, the elements that are more probable are placed at the beginning of the array and those that are less probable are placed at the end of the array.

Ordered list search When elements are ordered, binary search (discussed in Section 9.2.2) is preferred. However, when data is ordered and is of smaller size, sequential search with a small change is preferred to binary search. In addition, when the data is ordered but stored in a data structure such as a linked list, modified sequential search is preferred. While searching an ordered list, we need not continue the search till the end of list to know that the target element is not in the list. While searching in an ascending ordered list, whenever an element that is greater than or equal to the target is encountered, the search stops. We can also add a sentinel to avoid the end of list test.

9.2.2 Binary Search

As discussed, sequential search is not suitable for larger lists. It requires *n* comparisons in the worst case. We have a better method when the data is sorted. Let us consider a typical game played by kids. You are asked to guess the number thought of by your friend in the range of 1 to 100. You are to guess by asking him a minimum number of questions. Of course, you are not allowed to ask him the number itself. The easiest approach is to start asking him, 'Is it 1?' In case the answer is 'No', then ask, 'Is it 2?' Continue this process in the ascending order of integers till you get the answer as 'Yes'.

What if the number your friend has in mind is 99? Obviously, this approach is not an efficient one. The solution to this problem is to ask him a question, 'Is it 50?' If no, another question to be asked is, 'is it greater than 50?' If the answer is 'Yes', then the range to be searched is 51 to 100, which is half of the previous range. If the answer is 'No', the range is 1 to 49, which is again half of the original. You may continue doing so till you guess the number. Surely, the second approach reduces the total number of questions asked on an average.

This method is called *binary search*, as we have divided the list to be searched every time into two lists and the search is done in only one of the lists. Consider that the list is sorted in ascending order. In binary search algorithm, to search for a particular element, it is first compared with the element at the middle position, and if it is found, the search is successful, else if the middle position value is greater than the target, the search will continue in the first half of the list; otherwise, the target will be searched in the second half of the list. The same process is repeated for one of the halves of the list till the list is reduced to size one.

Algorithm 9.3 depicts the logic behind this type of search.

ALGORITHM 9.3

```
1. Let n be size of the list
   Let target be the element to be searched
   Let flag = 0, low = 0, high = n-1
2. if low ≤ high, then
      middle = (low + high)/2
```

```
   else goto step (5)
3. if(key[middle] = target)
      Position = middle, flag = 1
   Goto step (5)
   else if(key[middle] > target) then
      high = middle - 1
   else
      low = middle + 1
4. Goto step(2)
5. if flag = 1
      report as target element found at location 'position'
   else
      report that element is not found in the list
6. stop
```

The effectiveness of the binary search algorithm lies in its continual halving of the list to be searched. For an ordered list of 50,000 keys, the worst case efficiency is a mere 16 accesses. One may note that the dramatic increase in efficiency is noticed as the list gets larger. We can check with a calculator as to how many times 50,000 must be halved to be reduced to 1. The same list that would have necessitated an average wait of two minutes using a sequential search will give a virtually instantaneous response when the binary search is used. In more precise algebraic terms, the halving method yields a worst case search efficiency of $\log_2 n$.

A non-recursive code in C++ that demonstrates the implementation of Algorithm 9.3 is given in Program Code 9.3 and a recursive code for the same is given in Program Code 9.4.

PROGRAM CODE 9.3

```
int Binary_Search_non_recursive(int A[], int n, int key)
{
   int low = 0,high = n-1,mid;
   while(low <= high)
   {  //iterate while first <= last
      mid = (low + high)/2;      //calculate
      mid = (first + last)/2)
      if(A[mid] == key)        //found
         return mid;      // return position (mid)
      else if(key<A[mid])
         //not found; look in upper half of list
         high = mid - 1;
      else
         low = mid + 1;      //look in lower half
   }
   return -1;       //return "not found"
}
```

Although this is a more direct implementation it uses needless stack space, and is much slower on most systems. In addition, this form of recursion is called *tail recursion*, which is the most wasteful form of recursion. Recursion is a powerful tool, which must be used with care. A recursive function is said to be tail recursive if there are no pending operations to be performed on return from a recursive call. Tail recursion is also used to return the value of the last recursive call as the value of the function. It is advantageous as the amount of information which must be stored during computation is independent of the number of recursive calls.

Program Code 9.4 is the recursive code in C++ that demonstrates the implementation of Algorithm 9.3 of binary search.

PROGRAM CODE 9.4

```
// Function binary search (recursive)
int Binary_Search(int A[],int low,int high,int key)
{
    int mid;
    if(low <= high)
    {
        mid = (low + high)/2;
        if(A[mid] == key)
            return mid;
        else if(key < A[mid])
            return Binary_Search(A, low, mid - 1, key);
        else
            return Binary_Search(A,mid + 1,high, key);
    }
    return -1;
}
```

Time Complexity Analysis

Time complexity of binary search is O(log(n)) as it halves the list size in each step. It is a large improvement over linear search; for a list with 10 million entries, linear search will need 10 million key comparisons in the worst case, whereas binary search will need just about 24 comparisons.

The time complexity can be written as a recurrence relation as

$$\mathrm{T}(n) = \begin{cases} \mathrm{T}(1), & n = 1 \\ \mathrm{T}(n/2) + c, & n > 1 \end{cases}$$

The most popular and easiest way to solve a recurrence relation is to repeatedly make substitutions for each occurrence of the function T on the right-hand side until all such occurrences disappear.

$$\begin{aligned}
\text{Therefore, } T(n) = T(n/2) + c &= T(n/2^2) + 2c \quad \text{(after 2}^{\text{nd}}\text{ substitution)}\\
&= T(n/3^3) + 3c \quad \text{(after 3}^{\text{rd}}\text{ substitution)}\\
&\vdots\\
&= T(n/2^i) + ic \quad \text{(after } i^{\text{th}}\text{ substitution)}\\
&\vdots\\
&= T(2^k/2^k) + kc \quad \text{(after } k \text{ steps)}\\
&= T(1)\\
\text{where } 2^k = n,\ k &= \log_2 n\\
T(n) &= O(\log_2 n)
\end{aligned}$$

Although binary search is good, it can again be slightly improved using Fibonacci search.

Pros and Cons of Binary Search

The following are the pros and cons of a binary search:

Pros

1. Suitable for sorted data
2. Efficient for large lists
3. Suitable for storage structures that support direct access to data
4. Time complexity is $O(\log_2(n))$

Cons

1. Not applicable for unsorted data
2. Not suitable for storage structures that do not support direct access to data, for example, magnetic tape and linked list
3. Inefficient for small lists

9.2.3 Fibonacci Search

We all know about Fibonacci numbers. It has many diverse applications from estimation of the number of cells in successive reproductions to the number of leaves on branches. The Fibonacci series has 0 and 1 as the first two terms, and each successive term is the sum of the previous two terms. Fibonacci numbers are 0, 1, 1, 2, 3, 5, 8, 13, 21, 34, ... with $F_n = F_{n-1} + F_{n-2}$ for $n \geq 2$ where, $F_0 = 0$ and $F_1 = 1$.

Fibonacci search modifies the binary search algorithm slightly. Instead of halving the index for a search, a Fibonacci number is subtracted from it. The Fibonacci number to be subtracted decreases as the size of the list decreases.

Fibonacci search starts searching for the target by comparing it with the element at the F_kth location. Here, $F_k \geq n$ and $F_{k-1} < n$. The Fibonacci search works like the binary search but with a few modifications. In binary search, we have low, high, and mid positions for the sub-list. Here, we have mid = $n - F_{k-1} + 1$, $F_1 = F_{k-2}$, and $F_2 = F_{k-3}$. The target to be searched is compared with `A[mid]`. `mid` is computed as follows:

Case 1 if equal the search terminates;

Case 2 if the target is greater and F_1 is 1, then the search terminates with an unsuccessful search; else the search continues at the right of the list with new values of low, high, and mid as

$$\text{mid} = \text{mid} + F_2,\ F_1 = F_{k-4},\ \text{and } F_2 = F_{k-5}$$

Case 3 if the target is smaller and F_2 is 0, then the search terminates with an unsuccessful search; else the search continues at the left of the list with new values of low, high, and mid as

$$\text{mid} = \text{mid} - F_2,\ F_1 = F_{k-3} \text{ and } F_2 = F_{k-4}$$

The search continues by either searching at the left of mid or at the right of mid in the list. Algorithm 9.4 explains the working of this search technique.

ALGORITHM 9.4

1. Set k = m
2. if k = 0, finish and display message "not found" and goto 6
3. if item = A[F_{k-1}], print "found" and goto 6
4. if(item < A[F_{k-1}]), discard entries from positions F_{k-1} + 1 to n, set k = k - 1, and goto 2
5. if item > A[F_{k-1}], discard entries from positions 1 to F_{k-1}, renumber remaining entries from 1 to F_{k-2}, set k = k - 2, and goto 2
6. stop

Program Code 9.5 implements Algorithm 9.4.

PROGRAM CODE 9.5

```
// Function to find nth Fibonacci number
int fibo(int n)
{
    if(n == 0 || n == 1)
        return 1;
    else
        return(fibo(n - 1) + fibo(n - 2));
}

// Function for Fibonacci search
int Fibonacci_Search(int A[],int n, int key)
{
    int f1, f2, t, mid, j, f;
    j = 1;
    while(fibo(j) <= n)
```

```
    {       //find fibo(j) such that fibo(j) >= n
       j++;
    }
    f = fibo(j);
    f1 = fibo(j - 2);        //find lower Fibonacci numbers
    f2 = fibo(j - 3);
    mid = n - f1 + 1;
    while(key != A[mid])        // if not found
    {
       if(mid < 0||key > A[mid])
       {       //look in lower half
          if(f1 == 1)
             return -1;
          mid = mid + f2;       //decrease Fibonacci numbers
          f1 = f1 - f2;
          f2 = f2 - f1;
       }
       else
       {    //look in upper half
          if(f2 == 0)     //if not found return -1
             return -1;
          mid = mid - f2;      //decrease Fibonacci numbers
          t = f1 - f2;        //this time, decrease more
          f1 = f2;      //for smaller list
          f2 = t;
       }
    }
    return mid;
}
```

Example 9.1 illustrates a Fibonacci search in a given list.

EXAMPLE 9.1 Search for 81 using Fibonacci search in the list {6, 14, 23, 36, 55, 67, 76, 78, 81, 89}, where $n = 10$.

Solution

Step 1: Compute F_k such that $F_k \geq 10$

`fibo(7)` = 13, which is greater than 10. Hence, $k = 7$.

Step 2: Compute the initial values of mid, F_1 and F_2.

Now, F_1 = `fibo(7 - 2)` = `fibo(5)` = 5

F_2 = `fibo(7 - 3)` = `fibo(4)` = 3

`mid` $= 10 - F_1 + 1 = 10 - 5 + 1 = 6$

Step 3: Let us search the target by comparing it at `A[mid]`. Now,

(a) compare `A[mid]`, that is 76, and the number to be searched, that is 78, which are not equal.

(b) 78 > `A[mid]`, and F_1 is not 1; hence, let us compute `mid`, F_1, and F_2.

(c) `mid` = `mid` + $F_2 = 6 + 3 = 9$, and $F_1 = 2$, and $F_2 = 1$.

Step 4: Again, 78 is not equal to `A[9]` and is lesser. Hence, let us search the lower half as

`mid` = `mid` − $F_2 = 9 - 1 = 8$, $F_1 = 1$, and $F_2 = 1$

Step 5: Now, compare 78 and `A[mid]`, which are equal; hence, the search stops.

The search terminates with a successful search by locating the target at the eighth location in the second iteration.

Time Complexity of Fibonacci Search

When we solve a recurrence relation $F_n = F_{n-1} + F_{n-2}$ for Fibonacci numbers, we get the solution as $F_n = (1/\text{sqrt}(5)) \times [((1 + \text{sqrt}(5))/2)^n + ((1 + \text{sqrt}(5))/2)^n]$. For large n, the term $((1 - \text{sqrt}(5))/2)^n$ tends to zero. Hence F_n is bounded by $((1 - \text{sqrt}(5))/2)^n$. Hence, $F_n \le n \times \log[(1 + \text{sqrt}(5))/2]$. The number of comparisons is of the order of n, and the time complexity is O(log(n)).

Hence, the algorithm for Fibonacci search is O(log(n)) algorithm. Consider an example where for a list of 10 numbers, each element of the 10 numbers is to be searched once. For an unsuccessful search, the algorithm needs a total of 13 searches. In case of binary search, the number of comparisons would be 40, and for Fibonacci search, it will be 41. Since this is a small-scale example, binary search will score, but in larger instances, it may be the other way around.

Fibonacci search is more efficient than binary search for large lists. However, it is inefficient in case of small lists.

Pros

1. Faster than binary search for larger lists
2. Suitable for sorted lists

Con

1. Inefficient for smaller lists

9.2.4 Indexed Sequential Search

Indexed sequential search is suitable for sequential files. A sequential file with an associated index is just like an index associated with books. File index is a data structure similar to a list of keys and their location or reference to the location of the record associated with the key.

We discussed the drawbacks associated with searching a record sequentially in a file or a table. An index file can be used to effectively overcome the problem associated with sequential files and to speed up the key search. The simplest indexing structure is the single-level one: a file whose records are pairs (key and a pointer), where the pointer is the position in the data file of the record with the given key. Only a subset of data records, evenly spaced along the data file, is indexed to mark the intervals of data records.

A key search then proceeds as follows: the search key is compared with the index to find the highest index key preceding the search, and a linear search is performed from the current record until the search key is matched or until the record pointed by the next index entry is reached. In spite of the double file access (index + data) needed by this kind of search, the decrease in access time with respect to a sequential file is significant.

Consider the data file as in Table 9.1.

Table 9.1 Data file

Record position	Emp. no.	Name	Occupation
1	100	Saurabh	Developer
2	500	Abolee	Project head
3	300	Shweta	Developer
4	200	Vaishali	Project head
5	400	Santosh	Developer

Its corresponding index file is given in Table 9.2.

Table 9.2 Index file of Table 9.1

Emp. no. (Key)	Record position
100	1
200	4
300	3
400	5
500	2

Searching a record from this index file involves the following issues:

1. The index file is ordered, so the searching can be done using the binary search method.
2. The search is successful if we find the target element in the index.
3. The record position is used to access the details of that record from the data file.

Consider, for example, the case of a simple linear search on a file with 1000 records. With the sequential organization, an average of 500 target element comparisons is necessary (assuming uniformly distributed search target elements among the data). However, using an evenly spaced index with 100 entries, the number of comparisons is reduced to 50 in the index file, and 50 in the data file—a 5:l reduction in the number of operations.

This method can apparently be hierarchically extended. An index is a sequential file in itself, amenable to be indexed in turn by a second level index, thus exploiting the hierarchical decomposition of the searches more to decrease the access time. Obviously, if the layering of indices is pushed too far, a point is reached when the advantages of indexing are hampered by the increased storage costs and by the index access times as well. Consider Program Code 9.6 which illustrates the indexed sequential search.

PROGRAM CODE 9.6

```
void createIndex(int index[],int isize,int A[],int asize)
{
   int i, j;
   for(i = 0, j = 0; i < asize; i+=8, j++)
   {
      index[j] = A[i];
   }
   index[j] = A[asize - 1];
}

int indexSeqSearch(int val, int index[], int isize, int A[],
int asize)
{
   int i = 0, j = 0, pos = 0;
   int high = 0,low = 0;
   if(val > index[isize - 1] && val < index[0])
      return -1;
   while(i < isize)
   {
      if(val == index[i])
      {
         pos = 8 * i;       // here 8 is the step size
         return pos;
      }
      if(val < index[i])
      {
         low = 8 * (i - 1);
         high = 8 * i;
         break;
      }
      else
      {
         low = 8 * i;
         high = 8 * (i + 1);
      }
      i++;
   }
   printf("\n low = %d, high = %d", low, high);
   while(low < high)
   // search in array from index low to high
```

```
    {
        if(val == A[low])
            return low;
        else
            low++;
    }
    return -1;
}

int main()
{
    intA[max]={8,20,26,38,90,105,206,221,229,287,309,312,
    340,367,483,492,502,551,618,641,698,711,764,796};
    int index[(max/8) + 1] = {0};
    int position;
    int key, i, choice;
    int opt = 0, pos = 0;
    cout << "Enter number to be searched : ";
    cin >> key;
    createIndex(&index[0],(max/8) + 1,&A[0], max);
    pos = indexSeqSearch(key, index, (max/8) + 1, A, max);
    if(pos != -1)
    {
        cout << "found at position" << pos;
    }
    else
        cout << "not found";
    return 0;
}
/*********************Output*********************
Enter number to be searched: 20
low = 0, high = 8
20 found at position 1

Enter number to be searched: 711
low = 16, high = 24
711 found at position 21

Enter number to be searched: 200
low = 0, high = 8
200 not found
*************************************************/
```

9.2.5 Hashed Search

A hash table is a data structure that uses a hash function to map keys (e.g., a student ID, book accession number) to their associated values (e.g., student name, telephone number, book details, etc.). Therefore, a hash table implements an associative array. The hash function is used to transform the key into the index of an array element where the corresponding value is to be sought. The data organized using a hash table makes searching very efficient.

Consider the following example. Suppose we want to store six records in a file where the key of each record is a person's name. The key can be hashed by taking the address from the ASCII representations of the first character of the name. Table 9.3 is of size 26, that is, one slot for each letter of the alphabet.

Let us assume the names of the persons are Deepa, Alka, Beena, Govind, Ekta, and Zinat.

Table 9.3 Storing records in a hash table

Index	Symbol
0	Alka
1	Beena
2	
3	Deepa
4	Ekta
5	
6	Govind
⋮	
25	Zinat

Hashing is a method of directly computing the index of the table by using a suitable mathematical function called as *hash function*. The hash function operates on the name to be stored in the symbol table or whose attributes are to be retrieved from the symbol table. If h is a hash function and A is a name, then $h(A)$ gives the index of the table, where A along with its attributes can be stored. If A is already stored in the table, then $h(A)$ gives the index of the table, where it is stored to retrieve the attributes of A from the table.

Therefore, the hash table seems to be the best option for the realization of the symbol table, but there is one problem associated with hashing, that is collision. *Hash collision* occurs when two identifiers are mapped into the same hash value. This happens because a hash function defines mapping from a set of valid identifiers to the set of those integers that are used as indices of the table.

Hash table is widely used in the language translation process. It is referred to as a symbol table when used by an assembler or a compiler. A symbol table is nothing but a set of pairs (name, value), where the value represents the collection of attributes associated with the name.

Therefore, when we implement a hash table, a suitable collision-handling mechanism is to be provided, which will be activated when there is a collision. The computational complexity of all these techniques is proportional to n, where n is the number of data elements. Hence, these search techniques are also called as *quantity-dependent search techniques*.

Searching and sorting are the two very important operations performed most commonly on a large amount of information. We have studied various algorithms to search a record, and we notice that it is much easier to find any information that is organized in some proper order. For example, if we want to find any name in the telephone directory, which contains names in any random order, we perhaps have to go through the whole directory sequentially to find the name. Similarly, consider the trouble we might have to take to search for a book in a library where the books are placed anywhere without any order. We can imagine the ease if these books are assigned a specific position and are shelved in a specific order. In general, sorting is performed in business data-processing applications to retrieve information more efficiently. Let us see more details of sorting and methods associated with it. More details on the hash table are covered in Chapter 11.

9.3 SORTING

One of the fundamental problems in computer science is ordering a list of items. There are plenty of solutions to this problem, commonly known as *sorting algorithms*. Some sorting algorithms are simple and iterative, such as the bubble sort. Others such as the quick sort are extremely complicated but produce lightning-fast results.

Sorting is the operation of arranging the records of a table according to the key value of each record, or it can be defined as the process of converting an unordered set of elements to an ordered set.

A table or a filc is an ordered sequence of records $r[1]$, $r[2]$, …, $r[n]$, each containing a key $k[1]$, $k[2]$, … , $k[n]$. This key is usually one of the fields of the entire record. The table is said to be sorted on the key if $i < j$ implies that $k[i]$ precedes $k[j]$ in some ordering on the keys.

9.3.1 Types of Sorting

Sorting algorithms are divided into two categories: internal and external sorts.

If all the records to be sorted are kept internally in the main memory, they can be sorted using an internal sort. However, if there are a large number of records to be sorted, they must be kept in external files on auxiliary storage. They have to be sorted using external sort.

Internal Sorting

Any sort algorithm that uses main memory exclusively during the sorting is called as an *internal sort algorithm*. This assumes high-speed and random access to all data members. All the methods described in this chapter assume that all the data is stored in high-speed main memory of the computer and are therefore internal sorting techniques, except for merge sort. Internal sorting is faster than external sorting. The various internal sorting techniques are the following:

1. Bubble sort
2. Insertion sort
3. Selection sort
4. Quick sort
5. Heap sort
6. Shell sort
7. Bucket sort
8. Radix sort
9. File sort
10. Merge sort

External Sorting

Any sort algorithm that uses external memory, such as tape or disk, during the sorting is called as an *external sort algorithm*. *Merge sort* uses external memory. Do note that the other algorithms may read the initial values from a magnetic tape or write sorted values to a disk, but this is not using external memory during the sort.

Most of the methods to be described involve the movement of records within the table. For example, consider Fig. 9.2(a) where a table of four records is shown. Figure 9.2(b) shows a sorted table, which results when the table of Fig. 9.2(a) is sorted in an increasing order on the numeric key.

(a)

	Key	Other fields
#1	13	Shalu
#2	10	Gilda
#3	20	Raj
#4	5	Usha

(b)

Key	Other fields
5	Usha
10	Gilda
13	Shalu
20	Raj

Fig. 9.2 Movement of records within tables (a) Before sorting (b) After sorting

In this case, the actual records are moved from one place to another in the table.

In certain applications, the records can be quite long, and it is very expensive to move the actual data. One way to reduce record movement is to use an auxiliary table of pointers, each pointing to one record of the table to be sorted. Then, we can move these pointers instead of moving the actual records. For example, consider Fig. 9.3 which contains a table to be sorted and shows sorting using pointers.

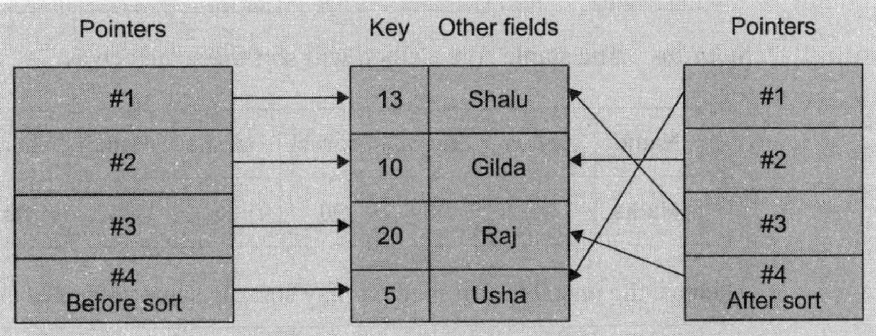

Fig. 9.3 Sorting with pointers

The table at the left is the initial table of pointers. These pointers are adjusted during the sorting process to produce the final table of pointers as on the right of the original table.

We may note the actual records in the table are not moved. While describing the algorithms ahead, we assume that we are moving the actual records, and we will only sort the keys.

9.3.2 General Sort Concepts

Let us now discuss some general terms related to sorting.

Sort Order

Data can be ordered either in ascending or in descending order. The order in which the data is organized, either ascending or descending, is called *sort order*. For example, the percentages of marks obtained by students in the examination are organized in descending order to decide ranks, whereas the names in the telephone directory are organized alphabetically in ascending order.

Sort Stability

A sorting method is said to be stable if at the end of the method, identical elements occur in the same relative order as in the original unsorted set. While sorting, we must take care of the special case—when two or more of the records have the same key, it is important to preserve the order of records in this case of duplicate keys. A sorting algorithm is said to be stable if it preserves the order for all records with duplicate keys; that means, if for all records i and j is such that $k[i]$ is equal to $k[j]$ and if $r[i]$ precedes to $r[j]$ in the unsorted table, then $r[i]$ precedes to $r[j]$ in the sorted table too. Bubble sort, selection sort, and insertion sort are the stable sort methods. Example 9.2 illustrates examples of both stable and unstable sort methods.

EXAMPLE 9.2 Consider the following unsorted sequence of marks to be sorted in descending order. Sort this sequence using the stable and unstable sort methods.

Name	Uma	Saurabh	Sanika	Kasturi	Ashish	Harsha	Lelo
Marks	80	90	93	95	83	90	83

Solution The stable sort method will sort the sequence as

Name	Kasturi	Sanika	**Saurabh**	**Harsha**	**Ashish**	**Lelo**	Uma
Marks	95	93	**90**	**90**	**83**	**83**	80

whereas, the unstable sort method may sort the same sequence as

Name	Kasturi	Sanika	**Harsha**	**Saurabh**	**Lelo**	**Ashish**	Uma
Marks	95	93	**90**	**90**	**83**	**83**	80

Sort Efficiency

Each sorting method may be analysed depending on the amount of time necessary for running the program and the amount of space required for the program. The amount of time for running a program is proportional to the number of key comparisons and the movement of records or the movement of pointers to records.

Sort efficiency is a measure of the relative efficiency of a sort. It is usually an estimate of the number of comparisons and data movement required to sort the data. We will discuss various sorting algorithms in Sections 9.3.3–9.3.12. While analysing our sorting methods, we will concentrate on these aspects of the sorting algorithms. We will start with simple methods such as bubble sort, selection sort, and insertion sort and proceed to more complex and efficient ones such as quick sort, shell sort, and bucket sort.

Passes

During the sorted process, the data is traversed many times. Each traversal of the data is referred to as a *sort pass*. Depending on the algorithm, the sort pass may traverse the whole list or just a section of the list. In addition, the characteristic of a sort pass is the placement of one or more elements in a sorted list.

9.3.3 Bubble Sort

The bubble sort is the oldest and the simplest sort in use. Unfortunately, it is also the slowest. The bubble sort works by comparing each item in the list with the item next to it and swapping them if required. The algorithm repeats this process until it makes a pass all the way through the list without swapping any items (in other words, all items are in the correct order). This causes larger values to 'bubble' to the end of the list while smaller values 'sink' towards the beginning of the list. In brief, the bubble sort derives its name from the fact that the smallest data item bubbles up to the top of the sorted array. Figure 9.4 demonstrates the bubble technique by showing numbers and their moves during each pass.

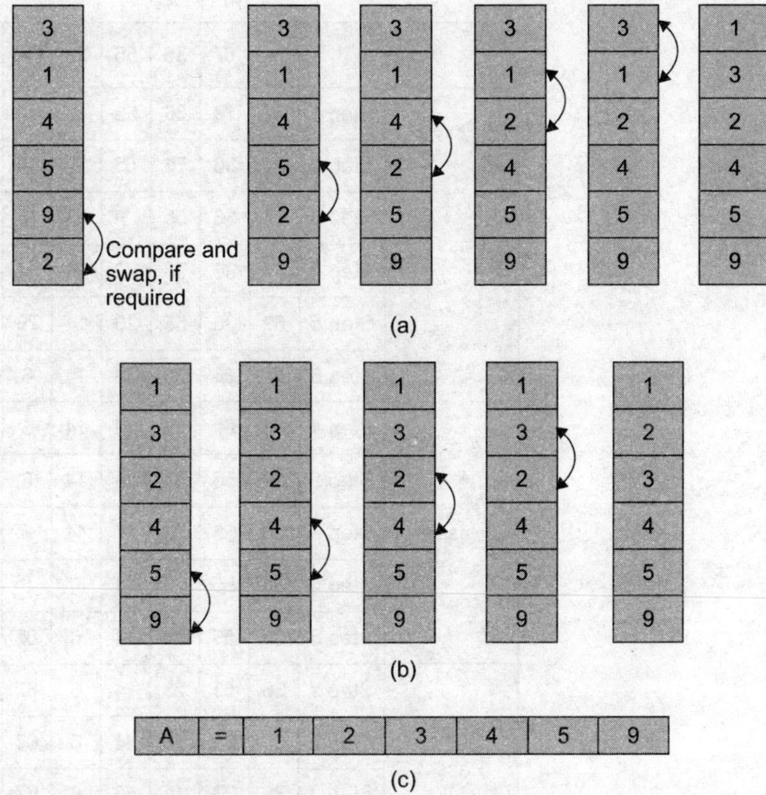

Fig. 9.4 Bubble sort (a) Pass 1 ($i = 1$) (b) Pass 2 ($i = 2$) (c) the resultant sorted array after pass ($n - 1$) ($i = 5$),

Algorithm 9.5 depicts the logic behind bubble sort.

ALGORITHM 9.5

```
1. Let A be the array to be sorted
2. for i = 1 to n - 1
   for j = 0 to n - i
   begin
      if A[j] > A[j+1] then
         Swap A[j] with A[j + 1] as follows
         temp = A[j]
         A[j] = A[j + 1]
         A[j + 1] = temp
      end
   end
3. stop
```

Figure 9.5 illustrates a bubble sort using an array of size 7.

76	**67**	36	55	23	14	06

(a)

Array		**76**	**67**	36	55	23	14	6
Pass 1	Step 1	67	**76**	**36**	55	23	14	6
	Step 2	67	36	**76**	**55**	23	14	6
	Step 3	67	36	55	**76**	**23**	14	6
	Step 4	67	36	55	23	**76**	**14**	6
	Step 5	67	36	55	23	14	**76**	**6**
	Step 6	**67**	**36**	55	23	14	6	**76**
Pass 2	Step 1	36	**67**	**55**	23	14	6	76
	Step 2	36	55	**67**	**23**	14	6	76
	Step 3	36	55	23	**67**	**14**	6	76
	Step 4	36	55	23	14	**67**	**6**	76
	Step 5	**36**	**55**	23	14	6	**67**	**76**
Pass 3	Step 1	36	**55**	**23**	14	6	67	76
	Step 2	36	23	**55**	**14**	6	67	76
	Step 3	36	23	14	**55**	**6**	67	76
	Step 4	**36**	**23**	14	6	**55**	**67**	**76**
Pass 4	Step 1	23	**36**	**14**	6	55	67	76
	Step 2	23	14	**36**	**6**	55	67	76
	Step 3	**23**	**14**	6	**36**	**55**	**67**	**76**
Pass 5	Step 1	14	**23**	**6**	36	55	67	76
	Step 2	**14**	**6**	**23**	**36**	**55**	**67**	**76**
Pass 6	Step 1	6	14	23	36	55	67	76
Final sorted array		**6**	**14**	**23**	**36**	**55**	**67**	**76**

(b)

Fig. 9.5 Example of bubble sorting (a) Initial array (b) Final sorted array with passes

Program Code 9.7 illustrates the bubble sort function.

PROGRAM CODE 9.7

```
// function for bubble sort for array A having n elements
void bubblesort(int A[max], int n)
{
   int i, j,temp;
   for(i = 1; i < n; i++)        // number of passes
   {
      for(j = 0; j < n - i; j++)      // j varies from 0 to
                                      // n - i
      {
         if( A[j] > A[j + 1] )      // compare two successive
                                    // numbers
         {
            temp = A[j];           // swap A[j] with A[j + 1]
            A[j] = A[j + 1];
            A[j + 1] = temp;
         }
      }
   }
}
```

For descending order of sorting, only the comparison condition should be changed in Program Code 9.7.

```
if(A[j] < A[j + 1] )    // change as <
{
   temp = A[j];        // swap A[j] with A[j + 1]
   A[j] = A[j + 1];
   A[j + 1] = temp;
}
```

Analysis of Bubble Sort

The algorithm begins by comparing the top item of the array with the next and swapping them if necessary. After $n - 1$ comparisons, the largest among a total of n items descends to the bottom of the array, that is, to the nth location. The process is then repeated to the remaining $n - 1$ items in the array. For n data items, the method requires $n(n - 1)/2$ comparisons and on an average, almost one-half as many swaps. The bubble sort, therefore, is very inefficient in large sorting jobs.

The analysis of this routine is a bit difficult. If we do not stop iterations when the array is sorted, the analysis is simple.

The number of comparisons made at each of the iterations is as follows:
$(n-1)$ comparisons in the first iteration, $(n-2)$ comparisons in the second iteration, ..., one comparison in the last iteration
This totals up to

$$(n-1) + (n-2) + (n-3) + \ldots + 1 = n(n-1)/2$$

Thus, the total number of comparisons is $n(n-1)/2$, which is $O(n^2)$.
Hence, the time complexity for each of the cases is given by the following:

1. Average case complexity = $O(n^2)$
2. Best case complexity = $O(n^2)$
3. Worst case complexity = $O(n^2)$

9.3.4 Insertion Sort

The insertion sort works just like its name suggests—it inserts each item into its proper place in the final list. The simplest implementation of this requires two list structures: the source list and the list into which the sorted items are inserted.

Let us consider a list $L = \{3, 6, 9, 14\}$. Given this sorted list, we need to insert a new element 5 in it. The commonly used process would involve the following steps:

1. Compare the new element 5 and the last element 14
2. Shift 14 right to get 3, 6, 9, ,14
3. Shift 9 right to get 3, 6, ,9, 14
4. Shift 6 right to get 3, ,6, 9, 14
5. Insert 5 to get 3, 5, 6, 9, 14

These steps could be coded as the following piece of code:

```
// insert t into a[0:i - 1]
int j;
// let X be the element to be inserted
// shift elements from the last member to right by one position
// till you get a smaller one
for(j = i - 1; j >= 0 && X < a[j]; j--)
    a[j + 1] = a[j];
// Insert t at j + 1 location
a[j + 1] = X;
```

These steps when done for each element of the list are to be sorted by considering another list and starting with one element in it. The steps for inserting an element in the sorted list can then be repeatedly used to yield the sorted list. Let us consider the following list of numbers: $L = \{7, 3, 5, 6, 1\}$. The following steps are required to sort this list.

1. Start with 7 and insert 3 => 3, 7
2. Insert 5 => 3, 5, 7

3. Insert 6 => 3, 5, 6, 7
4. Insert 1 => 1, 3, 5, 6, 7

The piece of code needed to do this will look like

```
for(int i = 1; i < n; i++)
{  // insert a[i] into a[0:i - 1]
   // code to insert comes here
}
```

After adding the code for insertion we have already built, the resultant code will be

```
for(int i = 1; i < n; i++)
{    // insert a[i] into a[0:i - 1]
   int t = a[i];
   int j;
   for(j = i - 1; j >= 0 && t < a[j]; j--)
      a[j + 1] = a[j];
   a[j + 1] = t;
}
```

To save memory, most implementations use an in-place sort that works by moving the current item past the already sorted items and repeatedly swapping it with the preceding item until it is in place. The main idea behind the insertion sort is to insert the ith element, in the ith pass, into *A*(1), *A*(2), ..., *A*(*i*), in the right place. Algorithm 9.6 lists the steps for insertion sort.

ALGORITHM 9.6

```
1. Set J = 2, where J is an integer
2. Check if list (J) < list (J - 1): if so interchange them; set J = J -1
   and repeat step (2) until J = 1
3. Set J = 3, 4, 5,. . ., N and keep on executing step (2)
```

The following steps in Example 9.3 essentially define the insertion sort as applied to sorting into ascending order an array list containing *N* elements:

EXAMPLE 9.3 Consider the given unsorted array. Sort this array in ascending order using insertion sort.

	Original unsorted array						
Elements	76	67	36	55	23	14	6
Index	0	1	2	3	4	5	6

Solution Pass 1: Consider the first list is sorted, and insert the second number 67 in the first list.

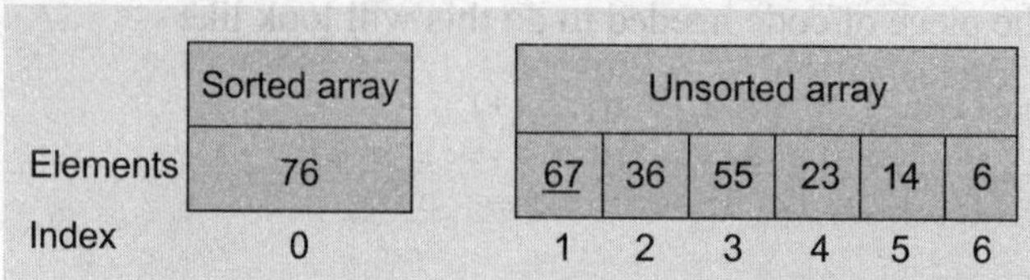

Pass 2: Insert number 36 in the first list.

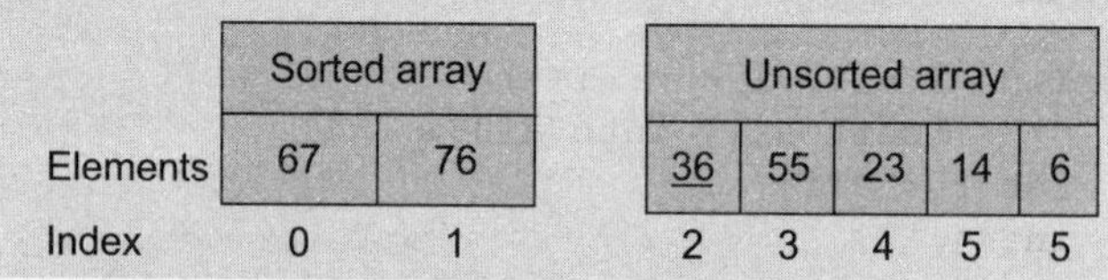

Pass 3: Insert number 55 in the first list.

	Sorted array			Unsorted array			
Elements	36	67	76	<u>55</u>	23	14	6
Index	0	1	2	3	4	5	6

Pass 4: Insert number 23 in the first list.

	Sorted array				Unsorted array		
Elements	36	55	67	76	<u>23</u>	14	6
Index	0	1	2	3	4	5	6

Pass 5: Insert number 14 in the first list.

	Sorted array					Unsorted array	
Elements	23	36	55	67	76	<u>14</u>	6
Index	0	1	2	3	4	5	6

Pass 6: Insert number 6 in the first list.

	Sorted array						Unsorted array
Elements	14	23	36	55	67	76	<u>6</u>
Index	0	1	2	3	4	5	6

The final sorted array is

	Sorted array						
Elements	6	14	23	36	55	67	76
Index	0	1	2	3	4	5	6

Program Code 9.8 defines the `InsertionSort()` function.

PROGRAM CODE 9.8

```
void InsertionSort(int A[], int n)
{
    int i, j, element;
    for(i = 1; i < n; i++)
    {
        element = A[i];
        // insert ith element in 0 to i - 1 array
        j = i;
        while((j > 0) && (A[j - 1] > element))
        //compare if A[j - 1] > element
        {
            A[j] = A[j - 1];        // shift elements
            j = j - 1;
        }
        A[j] = element;         // place element at jth position
    }
}
```

Analysis of Insertion Sort

Although the insertion sort is almost always better than the bubble sort, the time required in both the methods is approximately the same, that is, it is proportional to n^2, where n is the number of data items in the array.

The total number of comparisons is given as follows:

$$(n-1) + (n-2) + \ldots + 1 = (n-1) \times n/2$$

which is $O(n^2)$.

If the data is initially sorted, only one comparison is made on each pass so that the sort time complexity is $O(n)$. The number of interchanges needed in both the methods is on an average $(n^2)/4$, and in the worst case is about $(n^2)/2$.

When the data is already partially ordered, the insertion sort will normally take less time than the bubble sort. The insertion sort is highly efficient if the array is already in an almost sorted order. Example 9.4 provides a pictorial representation of the insertion sort.

EXAMPLE 9.4 Figure 9.6 is an example of insertion sort.

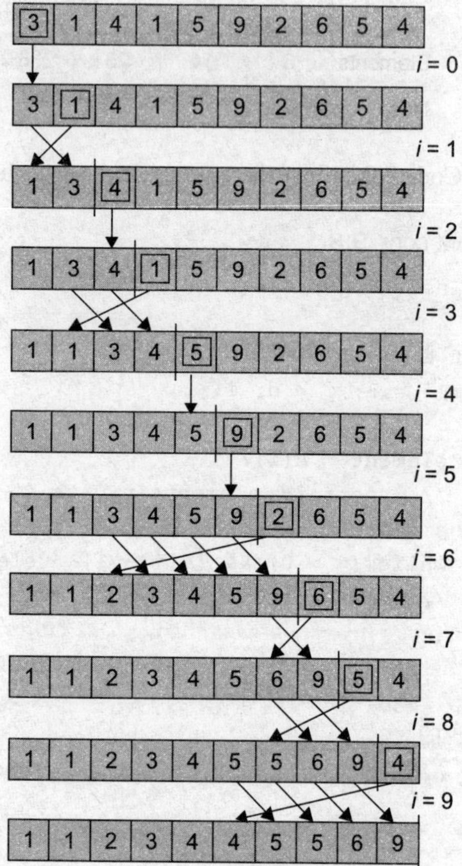

Fig. 9.6 Insertion sorting

9.3.5 Selection Sort

The selection sort algorithms construct the sorted sequence, one element at a time, by adding elements to the sorted sequence *in order*. At each step, the next element to be added to the sorted sequence is selected from the remaining elements.

Because the elements are added to the sorted sequence in order, they are always added at one end. This makes the selection sorting different from the insertion sorting. In insertion sorting, the elements are added to the sorted sequence in an arbitrary order. Therefore, the position in the sorted sequence at which each subsequent element is inserted is arbitrary.

Both selection and insertion sorts sort the arrays *in-place*.

In this method, we sort a set of unsorted elements in two steps. In the first step, find the smallest element in the structure. In the second step, swap the smallest element with the element at the first position. Then, find the next smallest element and swap with the element at the second position. Repeat these steps until all elements get arranged at proper positions.

This is illustrated in Program Code 9.9.

PROGRAM CODE 9.9

```
void SelectionSort(int A[], int n)
{
    int i, j;
    int minpos, temp;
    for(i = 0; i < n - 1; i++)
    {
        minpos = i;
        for(j = i + 1; j < n; j++)
        //find the position of min element as minpos from
        //i + 1 to n - 1
        {
            if(A[j] < A[minpos])
                minpos = j;
        }
        if(minpos != i)
        {
            temp = A[i];
            // swap the ith element and minpos element
            A[i] = A[minpos];
            A[minpos] = temp;
        }
    }
}
```

Look at following array of unsorted integers. The working of selection sort is shown in Table 9.4 with the resultant array after each pass where the updated values of index variable *i* and minpos after each pass are indicated.

	Original unsorted array						
Elements	76	67	36	55	23	14	6
Index	0	1	2	3	4	5	6

Table 9.4 Selection sort

Index	0	1	2	3	4	5	6	*i*	minpos
	76	67	36	55	23	14	6	0	6
Pass 1	6	67	36	55	23	14	76	1	5
Pass 2	6	14	36	55	23	67	76	2	4
Pass 3	6	14	23	55	36	67	76	3	4
Pass 4	6	14	23	36	55	67	76	4	4
Pass 5	6	14	23	36	55	67	76	5	5
Sorted array	6	14	23	36	55	67	76		

The same can be done in reverse order also to arrange the elements. That is, first find the largest element in the structure. In the second step, swap the largest element with the element at the last position. Then, find the next largest element and swap with the element at the last but one position, and so on. Let us have look at one more example on the working of selection sort.

EXAMPLE 9.5 Figure 9.7 shows an unsorted array and the sorting process with the resultant array after each pass.

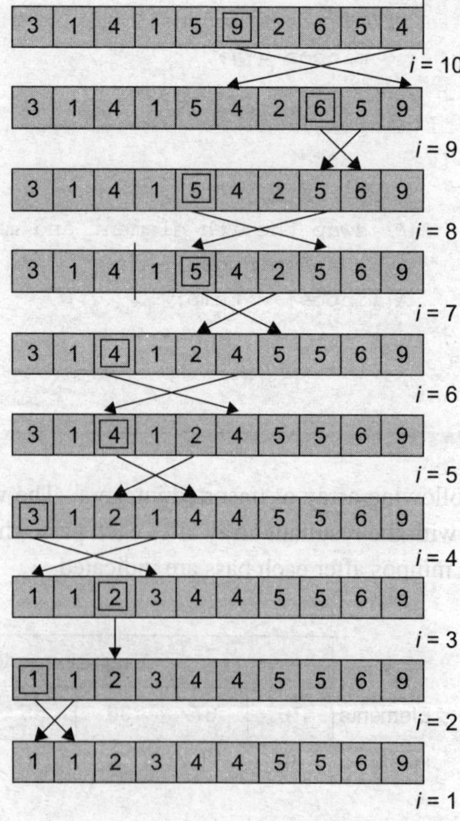

Fig. 9.7 Selection sort sample run

Analysis of Selection Sort

In Program Code 9.9, we can note that there are two loops, one nested within the other. During the first pass, $(n - 1)$ comparisons are made. In the second pass, $(n - 2)$ comparisons are made. In general, for the ith pass, $(n - i)$ comparisons are required.

The total number of comparisons is as follows:

$$(n - 1) + (n - 2) + \ldots + 1 = n(n - 1)/2$$

Therefore, the number of comparisons for the selection sort is proportional to n^2, which means that it is $O(n^2)$. The different cases are as follows:

Average case: $O(n^2)$ Best case: $O(n^2)$ Worst case: $O(n^2)$

The maximum number of interchanges required is $(n - 1)$ as there is utmost one interchange required for each pass. However, the actual number of interchanges depends on the ordering of the original table, because if the smallest key is already at its proper place, the algorithm makes no interchanges.

The selection sort and insertion sort are more efficient than bubble sort. Selection sort is recommended for lists. When records are large, the keys are simple as the selection sort requires lesser swaps than the insertion sort and more comparisons than the insertion sort. If the records are small and the keys are difficult to compare, insertion sort is recommended.

9.3.6 Quick Sort

Quick sort is based on the divide-and-conquer strategy. This sort technique initially selects an element called as *pivot* that is near the middle of the list to be sorted, and then the items on either side are moved so that the elements on one side of pivot are smaller and on the other side are larger. Now, the pivot is at the right position with respect to the sorted sequence. These two steps, selecting the pivot and arranging the elements on either side of pivot, are now applied recursively to both the halves of the list till the list size reduces to one.

Quick sort is thus an in-place, divide-and-conquer-based, massively recursive sort technique. This technique reduces unnecessary swaps and moves the element at a great distance in one move.

To choose the pivot, there are several strategies. The popular way is considering the first element as the pivot.

Thus, the recursive algorithm consists of four steps:

1. If the array size is 1, return immediately.
2. Pick an element in the array to serve as a 'pivot' (usually the left-most element in the list).
3. Partition the array into two parts—one with elements smaller than the pivot and the other with elements larger than the pivot by traversing from both the ends and performing swaps if needed.
4. Recursively repeat the algorithm for both partitions.

Let us consider an example. Let the list of numbers to be sorted be {13, 11, 14, 11, 15, 19, 12, 16, 15, 13, 15, 18, 19}. Now, the first element 13 becomes pivot. We need to place 13 at a proper location so that all elements to its left are smaller and the right are greater.

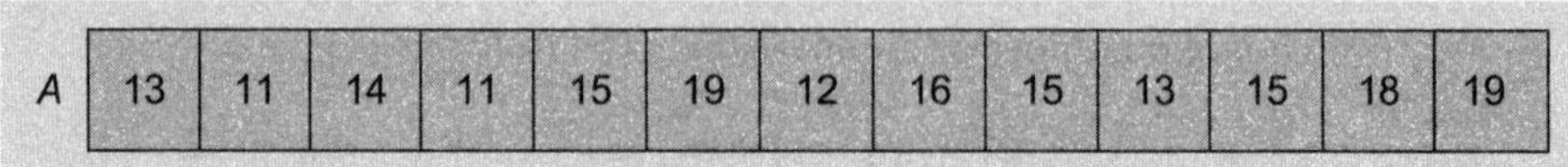

Initially, the array is pivoted about its first element $A[\text{pivot}] = 13$.

0	1	2	3	4	5	6	7	8	9	10	11	12
13	11	14	11	15	19	12	16	15	13	15	18	19

Let us first find the elements larger than the pivot, that is, 13. In addition, let us find the last element not larger than the pivot. These elements are in positions 2 and 9. Let us swap those.

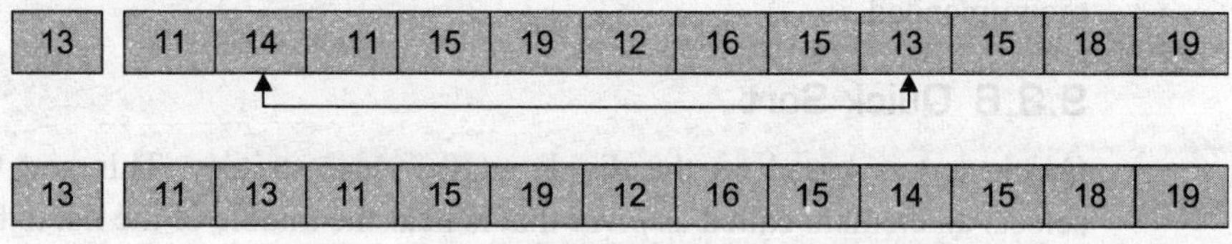

Let us again start scanning from both the directions.

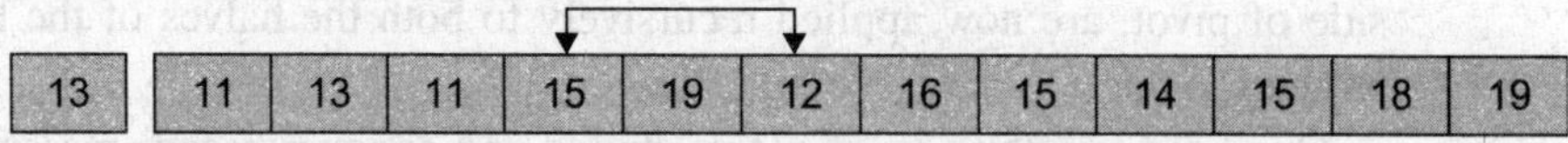

The elements 12 and 15 are to be swapped to get the following sequence:

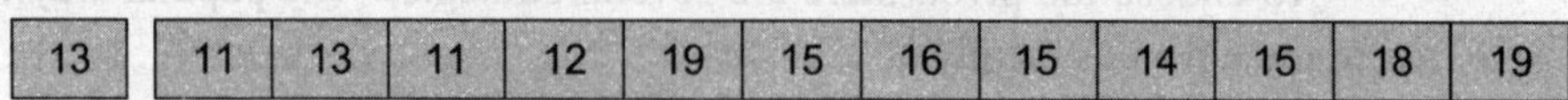

Let us repeat the steps to get the following sequence:

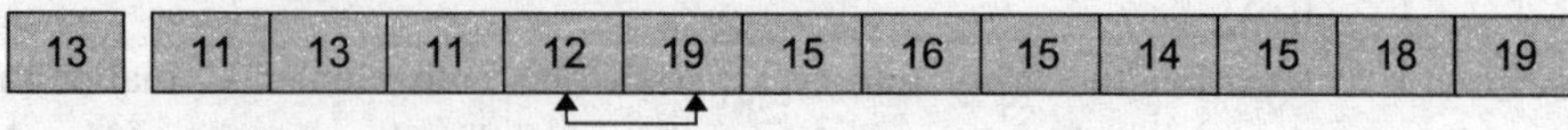

Here, the lower and upper bounds have crossed. So let us now swap the pivot-with element 12.

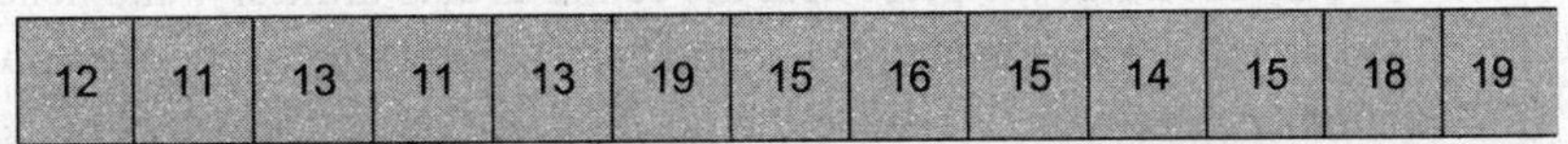

Here, we get two partitions as represented in the following sequence:

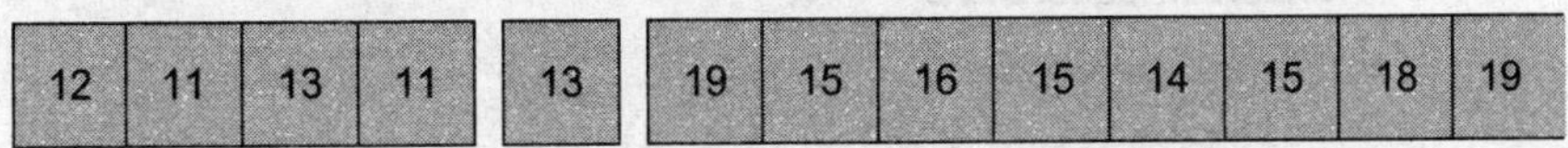

Recursively applying similar steps to each sub-list on the right and left side of the pivot, we get,

This is the final sorted array.

Algorithm 9.7 is written by assuming an array `A` with locations `A[Low]` to `A[High]` to be sorted.

ALGORITHM 9.7

```
Repeat process till low < high
1. Select pivot = A[Low], pivot location P = low
2. i = low and j = high;
3. Increment index i till A[i] >= pivot
4. Decrement index j till A[i] <= pivot
5. Swap A[i] with A[j]
6. Repeat steps 4, 5, 6 till i < j
7. if i < j
      Swap a[P] with a[j]
8. call Quicksort(low, j - 1)
9. call Quicksort(j + 1, high)
10. Stop
```

With the first seven steps of the process, the elements lesser than the key value are placed at the left side and the elements greater than the key value are placed at the right side of the key value.

Choice of Pivot We can choose any entry in the list as the pivot. The choice of the first entry as pivot is popular but often a poor choice. If the list is already sorted, then there will be no element less than the first element selected as pivot, and so one of the sub-lists will be empty.

Hence, we choose a pivot near the centre of the list, in the hope that our choice will position the list in such a manner that about half the elements will come on each side of the pivot.

The choice of the pivot near the centre is also arbitrary, and hence, it is not necessary that it will always divide the list into half. A good way to choose a pivot is to use a random number generator to choose the position of the next pivot in each of the activations of quick sort. Quick sort is illustrated in Program Code 9.10.

PROGRAM CODE 9.10

```
#define max 20
void read(int A[max], int n)
{
   int i;
   for(i = 0; i < n; i++)
      cin >> A[i];
}

void display(int A[max], int n)
{
   int i;
   for(i = 0; i < n; i++)
      cout << A[i];
}

void swap(int *x, int *y)
{
   int temp;
   temp = *x;
   *x = *y;
   *y = temp;
}

void qsort(int A[], int low, int high)
{
   int k;
   if(low < high)
   {
      K = partition(A, low, high);
      qsort(A, low, j - 1);
      qsort(A, j + 1, high);
   }
```

```
}

int partition(int A[],int low, int high)
{
   int pivot, i, j;
   pivot = A[low];
   j = high + 1; i = low;
   do
   {
      i++;
      while(A[i] < pivot && low <= high)
      do
      {
         j++;
      } while(pivot < A[j]);
      if(i < j)
         swap(A[i],A[j]);
   } while(i < j);
   A[low] = A[j];
   A[j] = pivot;
   return j;
}

main()
{
   int A[max], n;
   int i, choice;
   cout << "Enter number of numbers:";
   cin >> n;
   cout << "Enter numbers:";
   read(A, n);
   qsort(A, 0, n - 1);
   cout << "Sorted array is:";
   display(A, n);
}

/*********************Output**********************
 Enter number of numbers: 7
 Enter numbers: 10   5   23   67   20   30   60
 Sorted array is: 5   10   20   23   30   60   67
***************************************************/
```

Analysis of Quick Sort

Now, let us see the efficiency of quick sort. On the first pass, every element in the array is compared to the pivot, so there are n comparisons. The array is then divided into two parts each of size $(n/2)$. We assume that the array is divided into approximately one-half each time. For each of these sub-arrays, $(n/2)$ comparisons are made and four sub-arrays of size $(n/4)$ are formed. So at each level, the number of sub-arrays doubles. It will take $\log_2 n$ divisions if we are dividing the array approximately one-half each time. Therefore, quick sort is $O(n\log_2 n)$ on the average.

If the original array is sorted and array[left] is chosen as a pivot, then order of quick sort turns out to be $O(n^2)$. Therefore, when we choose array[left] as pivot, quick sort works best for files that are completely unsorted and worst for files that are completely sorted. In the case of nearly sorted arrays, choose a random element as a pivot value. The time required to sort the left sub-list and the right sub-lists where we assume that each has the size $n/2$ is as follows:

$$T(n) = c \times n + 2 \times T(n/2)$$

where c is a constant and $T(n/2)$ is the time required to sort the list of size $n/2$.

Similarly, the time required to sort the list of size $n/2$ is equal to the sum of the time required to place the key element at its proper position in the list of size $n/2$ and the time required to sort the left and right sub-lists each assumed to be of size $n/4$, $T(n/2)$. This turns out to be in the following form:

$$T(n/2) = c \times \ n/2 + -2 \times \ T(n/4)$$

where $T(n/4)$ is the time required to sort the list of size $n/4$

$$\therefore \quad T(n/4) = c \times \ n/4 + 2 \times T(n/8)$$

This process continues, and finally we get $T(1) = 1$.

$\therefore \quad T(n) = c \times n + 2(c \times n(n/2) + 2T(n/4))$

$\therefore \quad T(n) = c \times n + c \times n + 4T(n/4)) = 2 \times c \times n + 9T(n/9) = 2 \times c \times n + 9(c \times (n/9) + 2T(n/8))$

$\therefore \quad T(n) = 2 \times c \times n + c \times n + 8T(n/8) = 3 \times c \times n + 8T(n/8)$

$\therefore \quad T(n) = (\log n) \times c \times n + nT(n/n) = (\log n) \times c \times n + nT(1) = n + n \times (\log n) \times c$

$\therefore \quad T(n) \ \alpha \ n\log(n)$

The average complexity of the quick sort algorithm is $O(n\log n)$. However, the worst case time complexity is $O(n^2)$.

9.3.7 Heap Sort

Heap sort is one of the fastest sorting algorithms, which achieves the speed of quick sort and merge sort. The advantages of heap sort are that it does not use recursion, and it is efficient for any data order. There is no worst case scenario in the case of heap sort. We shall discuss heap sort in detail in Chapter 12. Heap sort is a sorting technique that sorts a list of length n with $O(n\log 2(n))$ comparisons and movement of entries, even in the worst case.

Hence, it achieves the worst case bounds better than those of quick sort; and for the list, it is better than merge sort since it needs only a small and constant amount of space apart from the list being sorted. The steps for building a heap sort are as follows:

1. Build the heap tree.
2. Start delete heap operations storing each deleted element at the end of the heap array.

After performing step 2, the order of the elements will be opposite to the order in the heap tree. Hence, if we want the elements to be sorted in ascending order, we need to build the heap tree in descending order—the greatest element will have the highest priority.

Note that we use only one array, treating its parts differently:

1. When building the heap tree, a part of the array will be considered as the heap, and the rest will be the original array.
2. When sorting, a part of the array will be the heap, and the rest will be the sorted array.

Algorithm 9.8 provides the steps followed in sorting data using a heap.

ALGORITHM 9.8

```
1. Build a heap tree with a given set of data
2. Delete root node from heap
   Rebuild the heap after deletion
   Place the deleted node in the output
3. Continue with step 2 until the heap tree is empty
```

Program Code 9.11 illustrates Algorithm 9.8 in C++.

PROGRAM CODE 9.11

```
// reheapup operation is required when a new value is
inserted at the ith location
void reheapdown(int a[], int n, int i)
{
   int temp, j;
   while(2 * i + 1 < n)
   {
      j = 2 * i + 1;      // j index shows the left child of
      the node
      if(j + 1 < n && a[j + 1] > a[j])
      // finding max from left and right child
         j = j + 1;
         if(a[i] > a[j]) break;
         // if root > children then break
```

```
        else
        {
           // swap a[i] with a[j]
           temp = a[i];
           a[i] = a[j];
           a[j] = temp;
           i = j;
        }
     }   // end of while
  }

  Void Heap_Sort (int a[], int n)
  {
     // create heap
     int i, temp;
     for(i = (n - 1)/2; i >= 0; i--)
        reheapdown(a, n, i);
     // delete first value and swap it with last
     while(n > 0)
     {
        //swap first and last element
        temp = a[0];
        a[0] = a[n - 1];
        a[n - 1] = temp;
        n--;      // decrement count
        reheapdown(a, n, 0);
     }
  }

  void main()
  {
     int a[10], n, i;
     cout << "Enter N";
     cin >> n;
     cout << "Enter the elements";
     for(i = 0; i < n; i++)
        cin >> a[i];
     Heap_Sort(a, n);
     cout << "The sorted elements are";
     for(i = 0; i < n; i++)
```

```
        cout << a[i];
    }
/*************** Output *******************************
Enter N: 12
Enter the elements: 44    33    11    55    77    90    40
60    99    22    88    66
The sorted elements are 11    22    33    40    44    55    60    66
77    88    90    99
*****************************************************
```

In each pass of the `while` loop in the function `reheapdown(a,n,0)`, the position i is double; hence, the number of passes cannot exceed $\log(n/i)$. Therefore, the computation time is of the order $O(\log n/i)$.

For building the heap, the `reheapdown` procedure is called $n/2$ times. Hence, the total number of iterations will be as follows:

$$\log(n) + \log(n/2) + \ldots + \log(n/n/2)$$

$$= \sum_{i=1}^{n/2} \log(n/i)$$

$$= n/21\text{og}(n) - \log(n/2)$$

This turns out to be some constant times n.

If we analyse the processing phase, a heap of size i requires $O(\log_2 i)$ comparisons and interchanges even in the worst case.

Therefore, the required number of comparisons and interchanges, on the average, is

$$\sum_{i=2}^{n} \log_2 i + \frac{1}{2}\sum_{i=2}^{n} \log_2 i$$

This is $(n - 1)\log_2 n$. The worst case is quite comparable to the average case, and the number of comparisons and interchanges in this case is given by the following expression:

$$2(n-1)\log_2 n \left(\sum_{i=2}^{n} \log_2 i + \sum_{i=2}^{n} \log_2 i \right)$$

Therefore, heap sort is definitely $O(n\log_2 n)$.

The time complexity analysis of heap sort is as follows:

1. Best case: O(*n*log*n*)
2. Average case: O(*n*log*n*)
3. Worst case: O(*n*log*n*)

9.3.8 Shell sort

The technique used by shell sort (named after its inventor Donald Shell) is interesting. The algorithm is easy to program, and it runs fairly quickly. Its analysis, however, is very difficult. Shell sort is a sorting algorithm, which is an improved version of insertion sort. It makes repetitive use of insertion sort.

In this technique, the elements at a fixed distance are compared. Later, this distance is decremented in the next pass by some value and again the comparisons are made. The fixed distance is called as *gap*. The algorithm begins with the initial gap as *n*/2, where *n* is the total number of elements to be sorted. Later, in the next pass, the gap is modified as *n*/4, *n*/8, and so on till it becomes 1. When gap is 1, it becomes an ordinary insertion sort (Program Code 9.12).

PROGRAM CODE 9.12

```
void shell_sort(int A[], int n)
{
    int temp, gap, i;
    int swapped;
    gap = n/2;
    do
    {
        do
        {
            swapped = 0;
            for(i = 0; i < n - gap; i++)
                if(A[i] > A[i + gap])
                {
                    temp = A[i];
                    A[i] = A[i + gap];
                    A[i + gap] = temp;
                    swapped = 1;
                }
        } while(swapped == 1);
    } while((gap = gap/2) >= 1);
}
```

Figure 9.8 illustrates the sample run using shell sort.

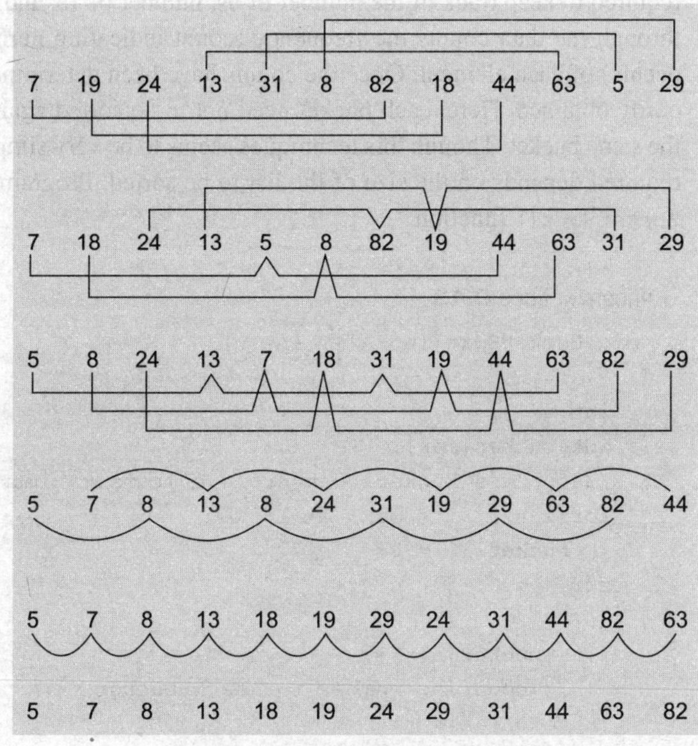

Fig. 9.8 Shell sort sample run

The time complexity of shell sort lies between $O(n\log^2 n)$ and $O(n^{1.5})$.

9.3.9 Bucket Sort

Bucket sort is possibly the simplest distribution sorting algorithm. In bucket sort, initially, a fixed number of buckets are selected. For example, suppose that we are sorting elements from the set of integers in the interval $[0, m - 1]$. The bucket sort uses m buckets or counters. The ith counter/bucket keeps track of the number of occurrences of the ith element of the list. Figure 9.9 illustrates how this is done for $m = 9$.

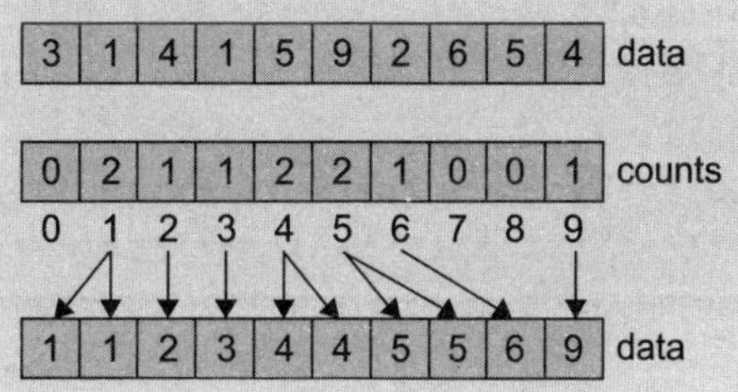

Fig. 9.9 Bucket sort

In Fig. 9.9, the buckets are assumed to be {0, 1, ..., 9}. Therefore, 10 counters are required to keep track of the number of 0s, number of 1s, and so on till 9. A single pass through the data counts the frequency (count indicating number of times the element occurs) of each element. Once the counts have been determined, the sorted sequence is easily obtained. Here, each bucket need not to be sorted again as equal numbers lie in the same bucket. Though this techniques seems to be very simple, the number of buckets required depends on the size of the list to be sorted. Program Code 9.13 illustrates the `BucketSort()` function.

PROGRAM CODE 9.13

```
void BucketSort(int A[], int n)
{
   int i, j;
   int bucket[max];
   //counters/buckets can store numbers maximum 20
   for(i = 0; i < max; i++)
      bucket[i] = 0;
   for(j = 0; j < n; j++)
   {
      ++bucket[A[j]];
      // counting number for each bucket
   }
   for(i = 0, j = 0; i < max; i++)
      for(;bucket[i] > 0; --bucket[i])
      { A[j] = i; j++; }
}
/****************** Output ***************************
 Enter number of numbers: 7
 Enter numbers value < 20: 12 15 07 05 12 09 07
 bucket[12]=1
 bucket[15]=1
 bucket[7]=1
 bucket[5]=1
 bucket[12]=2
 bucket[9]=1
 bucket[7]=2
 Sorted array is 5 7 7 9 12 12 15
************************************************/
```

9.3.10 Radix Sort

Radix sort is a generalization of bucket sort and works in three steps:

1. Distribute all elements into *m* buckets. Here *m* is a suitable integer, for example, to sort decimal numbers with radix 10. We take 10 buckets numbered as 0, 1, 2, …, 9. For sorting strings, we may need 26 buckets, and so on.
2. Sort each bucket individually.
3. Finally, combine all buckets.

To sort each bucket, we may use any of the other sorting techniques or radix sort recursively. To use radix sort recursively, we need more than one pass depending upon the range of numbers to be sorted. For sorting single digit number, we need only one pass, which is discussed in Section 9.3.9. For sorting numbers with two digits mean ranging between 00 and 99, we would need two passes; for the range from 0 to 999, we would need three passes, and so on.

Let us consider a set of two digit number to be sorted. In the first pass, we would distribute numbers in buckets 0 to 9 using the most significant digit (MSD). Now, in the bucket 0, we have all numbers with MSD 0, and all numbers with MSD 1 are in bucket 1, and so on. In the second pass, the numbers in each bucket would be sorted based on the second most significant digit. The buckets are combined to yield a sorted list.

Let us consider a set of numbers to be sorted {07, 10, 99, 02, 80, 14, 25, 63, 88, 33, 11, 72, 68, 39, 21, 50}. Table 9.5 illustrates a sample run for this list using radix sort.

Table 9.5 Sample run for radix sort

Pass 1	
Bucket	**Numbers**
0	02, 07
1	10, 11, 14
2	21, 25
3	39, 33
4	
5	50
6	68, 63
7	72
8	80, 88
9	99

(Continued)

Table 9.5 (Continued)

Pass 2 (only non-empty buckets are shown for distribution based on the second significant digit)		
Bucket	**Numbers**	
	Buckets based on second significant digit	**Numbers**
0	2	02
	7	07
1	0	10
	1	11
	4	14
2	1	21
	5	25
3	3	33
	9	39
4		
5	0	50
6	3	63
	8	68
7	2	72
8	0	80
	8	88
9	9	99

The amount of space needed by a bucket sort depends on how the buckets are stored. If every bucket is to consist of a set of sequential locations (e.g., an array), then each must be allocated enough space to hold the maximum number of elements that might belong in one bucket, and that is *n*. As the number of buckets increases, the speed of the algorithm increases but so does the amount of space used. Linked lists would be better, which would need the space for *n* elements plus links and a list head for each bucket. Program Code 9.14 illustrates this.

PROGRAM CODE 9.14

```
#define max 20
void radixsort(int A[max], int n)
{
   int i, j, temp;
   int bucket[10][15];
   int count[10], digit, k, p, x, nopass, maxval;
   maxval = A[0];
```

```
    for(i = 0; i < n; i++)
        if(maxval < A[i]) maxval = A[i];
    nopass = 0;
    while(maxval != 0)
    {
        maxval = maxval/10;
        nopass++;
    }
    p = 0;
    do
    {
        x = 1;
        for(i = 0; i < 10; i++) count[i] = 0;
        for(i = 0; i < n ; i++)
        {
            digit = (A[i]/x) % 10;
            bucket[digit]*[count[digit]] = A[i];
            // setting up bucket
            count[digit]++;
        }
        k = 0;
        for(i = 0; i < 10; i++)
        {
            if(count[i] != 0)
            {
                for(j = 0; j < count[i]; j++)
                A[k++] = bucket[i][j];
            }
        }
        cout << "Pass" << p;
        display(A, n);
        x = x * 10;
        p++;
    }while(p < nopass);
}
```

9.3.11 File Sort

The sorting algorithms discussed so far use array to hold and process the data to be sorted that resides in memory. Quite often, voluminous files, such as a master file for all the employees in a large corporation, must exist on external storage devices because of their size. These on-line storage devices, such as tapes and disks, carry with them specific software and hardware considerations relating to the access of stored data.

One of the solutions is to bring only portions of large files into the main memory and sort them. The portion of a file that can reside in main memory is a *block*. The sorted block can be sent back to the external storage medium and the next block can be brought in. Finally, the partially sorted blocks must be merged into a completely sorted file.

Because of the nature of secondary storage devices, bringing a block of data items into the main memory takes a longer time than processing it. For instance, it takes time to position the read–write head over the appropriate track of a disk, and more time for the disk to rotate to bring the correct block to the read–write head. An average input/output operation to and from an auxiliary storage device (not bucketing processing in memory) may take as 200 milliseconds. When we design sort algorithms for files on external media, we must consider this time delay.

There are numerous algorithms used to perform sorts external to the computer's main memory. Among the many external sort methods, the polyphase sort is more efficient in terms of speed and utilization of resources. However, it is more complicated, and therefore, in some situations, the other algorithms could be more applicable. In practice, internal sorts are already supplementing these sorting methods. Thus, a number of records from each tape would be read into the main memory and sorted using an internal sort and then output to the tape rather than one record at a time, as was the case initially. Let us study the merge sort method. Merge sort technique is commonly used for external sort and is suitable for internal sort too.

9.3.12 Merge Sort

The most common algorithm used in external sorting is the merge sort. Merging is the process of combining two or more sorted files into the third sorted file. We can use a technique of merging two sorted lists. Divide and conquer is a general algorithm design paradigm that is used for merge sort. Merge sort has three steps to sort an input sequence *S* with *n* elements:

1. Divide—partition *S* into two sequences *S*1 and *S*2 of about *n*/2 elements each
2. Recur—recursively sort *S*1 and *S*2
3. Conquer—merge *S*1 and *S*2 into a sorted sequence

A file (or sub-file) is divided into two files, *f*1 and *f*2. These two files are then compared, one pair of records at a time, and merged. This is done by writing them on two separate new files *M*1 and *M*2. Elements that do not pair off are simply rewritten into the new files. The records in *M*1 and *M*2 are now blocked with two records in each block. The two blocks (i.e., four records), one from *M*1 and one from *M*2, are merged and written onto the original files *f*1 and *f*2. The length of the blocks in each of *f*1 and *f*2 is now increased to four; the merge process is applied again, and the new files are written to *M*1 and *M*2. The process is continued until one of the two files, *f*1 or *f*2, is empty. Merge sort is a divide-and-conquer algorithm. Note that the function `mergesort()` calls itself recursively. Algorithm 9.9 is derived based on the steps discussed.

ALGORITHM 9.9

```
List mergesort(list L, int n)
{
   if(n == 1)
      return(L);
   else
   {
      split L into two halves L1 and L2;
      return(merge(mergesort(L1, n/2), (mergesort(L2, n/2))
   }
}
```

Time Complexity

Let T(n) be the running time of merge sort on an input list of size n. Then,

$$T(n) < C_1 \text{ (if } n = 1\text{), where } C_1 \text{ is a constant and}$$
$$T(n) < 2T(n/2) + C_2 n$$

Here, $2T(n/2)$ is for two recursive calls, and $C_2 n$ is the cost of merging the two sorted lists.

Now, by the substitution method,

$$T(n) = 2T(n/2) + C_2 n$$

If $n = 2^k$ for some k, it can be shown that after k steps

$$T(n) = 2^k T(n/2^k) + C_2 C_2^{\,k}$$

Hence, for $n = 2^k$

$$T(n) = n\log_2 n$$

That is, $T(n) = O(n\log n)$

Let us implement the merge technique for two arrays instead of working on files. Let us write a routine that accepts two sorted arrays, `A` and `B` containing elements $n1$ and $n2$, respectively and merges them into a third array `C` containing $n3$ elements. Here, the array `A` is from `low` to `mid`, array `B` is from `mid + 1` to `high`, and array `C` gives the merging of `A` and `B` This is shown in Program Code 9.15.

PROGRAM CODE 9.15

```
void merge (int A[],int low, int high, int mid)
{
   int i, j, k, C[max];
   i = low;       // index for first part
```

```
    j = mid + 1;       // index for second part
    k = 0;       // index for array C
    while((i <= mid) && (j <= high))
    // merge arrays A & B in array C
    {
       if(A[i] < A[j])
          C[k] = A[i++];
       else
          C[k] = A[j++];
       k++;
    }
    while(i <= mid)
       C[k++] = A[i++];
    while(j <= high)
       C[k++]=A[j++];
    for(i = low, j = 0; i < = high; i++, j++)
     // copy array C contents back to array A
    {
       A[i] = C[j];
    }
}

void MergeSort(int A[], int low, int high)
{
    int mid;
    if(low < high)
    {
       mid = (low + high)/2;
       MergeSort(A, low, mid);
       MergeSort(A, mid + 1, high);
       merge(A, low, high, mid);
    }
}
```

When merge sort is used for files as described in Program Code 9.15, each merge operation requires reading and writing of two files, both of which are on the average about $n/2$ records long. Thus, the total number of blocks read or written in a merge operation is approximately $2n/c$, where c is the number of records in a block. The number of blocks accessed for the whole operation is $O((n(\log_2 n))/c)$, which amounts to $O(\log_2 n)$ passing through the entire original file. This is a considerable improvement over the $O(n)$ passes needed in the preceding algorithms.

9.4 MULTIWAY MERGE AND POLYPHASE MERGE

We have already studied external sorting in Section 9.3.11. It broadly works in the following three steps:

1. Split the data into small sets that fit into main memory.
2. Now sort each of the subsets with a conventional sorting algorithm.
3. Finally merge those so-called runs and get a complete sorted data set.

This merging procedure can obviously be applied to more than two runs at every time and it is called n-way merge or multiway merge. The sophisticated multiway merge algorithms include polyphase merge.

A non-balanced k-way merge that reduces the number of output files needed by reusing the emptied input file or device as one of the output devices is called *polyphase merge*. This is most efficient if the number of output runs in each output file is different. Combining the run creation and run merging calculations together, we find that the overall complexity is $O(n\log_2 n)$. The repeated merging is referred to as polyphase merging. Polyphase merge sorts are ideal for sorting and merging large files. Two pairs of input and output files are opened as file streams. At the end of each iteration, input files are deleted; output files are closed and reopened as input files. The use of file streams makes it possible to sort and merge files that cannot be loaded into the computer's main memory. It is a method of merging, where the keys are kept in more than one backup store or file. Items are merged from the source files to another file. Whenever one of the source files is exhausted, it immediately becomes the destination of the merge operations from the non-exhausted and earlier destination files. When there is only one file left, the process stops.

9.4.1 Comparison of Ordinary Merge Sort and Polyphase Sort

Typically, a merge sort splits items into sorted runs and then recursively merges each run into larger runs. When there is only one run left, it is termed as the sorted result. An ordinary merge sort could use four working files organized as a pair of input files and a pair of output files. At each iteration, two input files are read. The odd-numbered runs of the two input files are merged to the first output file, and the even-numbered runs are merged to the second output file. When the input is exhausted, the new output files are used as the input for the next iteration. The number of runs decreases by a factor of 2 at each iteration. At each iteration, the same level/phase of merge occurs—a file is either completely read or completely written during the iteration.

If the four files were on four separate tape drives, an ordinary merge sort would provide some interesting details. In the first iteration, only one input drive is used and the other input file is empty. In subsequent iterations, each input drive runs at half speed, while one output drive runs at full speed and the second output drive stands idle waiting for the next run. The situation is even worse when six tape drives are used, out of which at least two stand idle. It would be ideal if the idle drives could be put to more use.

Perfect Three-file Polyphase Merge Sort

It is easiest to look at the polyphase merge from its end conditions and working backwards. At the start of each iteration, there are two input files and one output file. At the end of the iteration, one input file is completely consumed and becomes the output file for the next iteration. The current output file will become an input file for the next iteration. The remaining files (just one in the three-file case) are only partially consumed, and their remaining runs are the input for the next iteration.

In the following instance, File 1 is just emptied, and it becomes the new output file. One run is left on each input tape, and merging those runs together will make the sorted file.

```
File 1 (out):                              <1 run> *          (the sorted file)
File 2 (in): ... | <1 run> *      -->   ... <1 run> | *       (consumed)
File 3 (in):     | <1 run> *              <1 run> | *         (consumed)
```

Here,

... denotes the possible runs that have already been read
| marks the read pointer of the file
* marks end of file

In the previous iteration, we read from Files 1 and 2. One run is merged from both files before File 1 goes empty. Notice that File 2 is not completely consumed; it has one run left to match the final merge.

```
File 1 (in): ... | <1 run> *             ... <1 run> | *
File 2 (in):     | <2 run> *      -->       <1 run> | <1 run> *
File 3 (out):                               <1 run> *
```

Stepping back another iteration, two runs are merged from Files 1 and 3 before File 3 goes empty.

```
File 1 (in ):     | <3 run> *             ... <2 run> | <1 run> *
File 2 (out):                     -->         <2 run> *
File 3 (in ): ... | <2 run> *                 <2 run> | *
```

Moving to the previous iteration, three runs are merged from Files 2 and 3 before File 2 goes empty.

```
File 1 (out):                                 <3 run> *
File 2 (in ): ... | <3 run> *     -->     ... <3 run> | *
File 3 (in ):     | <5 run> *                 <3 run> | <2 run> *
```

Moving further back, five runs are merged from Files 1 and 2 before File 1 goes empty.

```
File 1 (in ): ... | <5 run> *             ... <5 run> | *
File 2 (in ):     | <8 run> *     -->         <5 run> | <3 run> *
File 3 (out):                                 <5 run> *
```

The number of runs merged working backwards—1, 2, 3, 5, …,—reveals a Fibonacci sequence. For everything to work out right, the initial file to be sorted must be distributed to the proper input files, and each input file must have the correct number of runs on it. In the example, this would mean that an input file with 13 runs writes 5 runs to File 1 and 8 runs to File 2.

In practice, the input file might not have a Fibonacci number of runs (which would not be known until after the file has been read). The fix is to pad the input files with dummy runs to obtain the required Fibonacci sequence.

For comparison, the ordinary merge sort combines 16 runs in 4 passes using 4 files. The polyphase merge combines 13 runs in 5 passes using only 3 files. Alternatively, a polyphase merge combines 17 runs in 4 passes using 4 files (sequence: 1, 1, 1, 3, 5, 9, 17, 31, 57, ...).

An iteration (or pass) in an ordinary merge sort involves reading and writing the entire file. An iteration in a polyphase sort does not read or write the entire file, so a typical polyphase iteration takes lesser time than a merge sort iteration.

Two-phase, Multiway Merge Sort

The basic idea behind the two-phase, multiway merge sort is simple, and is described as follows:

Phase 1: Repeat the following until all data items have been visited once.

1. Fill a designated region R of main memory with as many data items as it can hold.
2. Sort the data items in R using an internal sort.
3. Write the sorted data items back to new blocks on disk, which yields a sorted 'sub-list' of the original data items.

Phase 2: At the conclusion of the following steps, a sorted file will emerge.

1. Read a block from each of the sub-lists from Phase 1 into a main memory buffer; in addition, set aside an output buffer.
2. Merge the sub-lists into a sorted file by repeating the following steps as often as necessary.
3. Fill the output buffer by repeatedly selecting the smallest (or the largest, depending on the sorting order) remaining data item in the buffers from the sorted sub-lists. If all of the items in a sub-list buffer have been examined, read the next block for that sub-list (if there is no such block, then do not examine the associated buffer anymore).
4. Write the output buffer to disk and reinitialize the buffer for the next output block.

9.5 COMPARISON OF ALL SORTING METHODS

Table 9.6 compares and comments on the sorting methods discussed in this chapter.

Table 9.6 Comparison of sorting techniques

Sorting method	Technique in brief	Best case	Worst case	Memory requirement	Is stable?	Pros	Cons
Bubble sort	Repeatedly stepping through the list to be sorted, comparing each pair of adjacent items and swapping them if they are in the wrong order	O(n^2)	O(n^2)	No extra space needed	Yes	1. A simple and easy method 2. Efficient for small lists $n > 100$	Highly inefficient for large data
Selection sort	Finds the minimum value in the list and then swaps it with the value in the first position, repeats these steps for the remainder of the list (starting at the second position and advancing each time)	O(n^2)	O(n^2)	No extra space needed	No	1. Recommended for small files 2. Good for partially sorted data	Inefficient for large lists
Insertion sort	Every repetition of insertion sort removes an element from the input data, inserts it into the correct position in the already sorted list until no input elements remain. The choice of which element to remove from the input is arbitrary and can be made using almost any choice of algorithm	O(n)	O(n^2)	No extra space needed	Yes	1. Relatively simple and easy to implement 2. Good for almost sorted data	Inefficient for large lists

(Continued)

Table 9.6 (Continued)

Quick sort	Picks an element, called a pivot, from the list. Reorders the list so that all elements with values less than the pivot come before the pivot, whereas all elements with values greater than the pivot come after it (equal values can go either way). After this partitioning, the pivot is in its final position. This is called the partition operation. Recursively sorts the sub-list of the lesser elements and the sub-list of the greater elements.	$O(n\log_2 n)$	$O(n^2)$	No extra space needed	No	1. Extremely fast 2. Inherently recursive	Very complex algorithm
Shell sort	It is a generalization of insertion sort, which exploits the fact that insertion sort works efficiently on input that is already almost sorted. It improves on insertion sort by allowing the comparison and exchange of elements that are far apart. The last step of shell sort is a plain insertion sort, but by then, the array of data is guaranteed to be almost sorted	$O(n^{1.5})$	$O(n\log^2 n)$	No extra space needed	No	1. It is faster than a quick sort for small arrays 2. Its speed and simplicity makes it a good choice in practice	Slower for sufficiently big arrays

(Continued)

Table 9.6 (Continued)

Sorting method	Technique in brief	Best case	Worst case	Memory requirement	Is stable?	Pros	Cons
Radix sort (most significant digit)	Numbers are placed at proper locations by processing individual digits and by comparing individual digits that share the same significant position.	O(*n*)	O(*n*)	Extra space proportional to *n* is needed	Yes	1. Radix sort is very simple and fast 2. In-Place, recursive, and one of the fastest sorting algorithms for numbers or strings of letters	Radix sort can also take more space than other sorting algorithms since in addition to the array that will be sorted, there needs to be a sub-list for each of the possible digits or letters
Merge sort	If the list is of length 0 or 1, then it is already sorted. Otherwise, the algorithm divides the unsorted list into two sub-lists of about half the size Then, it sorts each sub-list recursively by reapplying the merge sort and then merges the two sub-lists back into one sorted list.	$O(n\log_2 n)$	$O(n\log_2 n)$	Extra space proportional to *n* is needed	Yes	1. Good for external file sorting 2.Can be applied to files of any size	1. It requires twice the memory of the heap sort because of the second array used to store the sorted list. 2. It is recursive, which can make it a bad choice for applications that run on machines with limited memory
Heap sort	Heap sort begins by building a heap out of the data set, and then removing the largest item and placing it at the end of the partially sorted array. After removing the largest item, it reconstructs the heap, removes the largest remaining item, and places it in the next open position from the end of the partially sorted array. This is repeated until there are no items left in the heap and the sorted array is full	$O(n\log_2 n)$	$O(n\log_2 n)$	No extra space needed	No	1. Advantageous as it does not use recursion and that heap sort works just as fast for any data order. That is, there is basically no worst case scenario 2. Heaps work well for small tables and the tables where changes are infrequent	Do not work well for most large tables

**n* is the number of data items to be sorted.

RECAPITULATION

- Searching means locating a target element in the list. There are basically two search techniques: sequential (also known as linear search) and binary search. Sequential search is used when the list is not sorted, and binary search is preferred when the list is in sorted order.
- The variations of linear search include sentinel search and probabilistic search. In sentinel search, the check for the end of list is avoided by placing the target at the end of list. The probability search orders the list by placing the most probable elements at the beginning of the list.
- In binary search, the target is first searched at the mid of the list. As the list is sorted (ascending or descending), if the target is not found at the mid, then it is searched either in upper half or in lower half. If the list is in ascending order and if the target is smaller than the element at mid, then it is searched in upper half, else the target is searched in the lower half using binary search.
- The time complexity of linear is O(n), whereas it is O($\log_2 n$) for binary search.
- In case of hashed search, the target key is transformed to address using algorithmic computation. The function used for this transformation is called as hash function. There are different hash functions: modulus, digit extraction, mid_square, folding.
- Sorting means arranging the elements in a particular order. Sorting techniques are broadly classified as internal and external. In internal sorting, during sorting, all the data to be sorted is held in primary storage. In external sorting too, the data to be sorted is held in primary storage, and the data that does not fit in the primary storage is held in secondary storage. Both internal and external sorting methods have their relative efficiencies in different applications.
- If the equal targets maintain their relative input order in the output, then the sorting method is called as the stable sorting method.
- Internal sort techniques are broadly classified as insertion, selection, and exchange. Insertion sorting include insertion sort and shell sort. Selection sorting methods are selection and heap sort. Heap sort is an improved version of selection sort. Bubble sort and quick sort are two exchange sort techniques.
- Quick sort is faster and handles arrays of heterogeneous data fairly efficiently. The shell short is more efficient than the bubble sort, selection sort, and insertion sort.
- Sorting of larger files that cannot fit in main memory is best accomplished by external sorting techniques such as the merge sort.
- Polyphase merge and multiway merge are two sort methods used in the external sorting technique.

KEY TERMS

Binary search In binary search algorithm, to search a particular element, it is first compared with the element at the middle position, and if found, the search is successful. However, if the middle position value is greater than the target, the search will continue in the first half of the list, else the target will be searched in the second half of the list. The same process is repeated for one of the halves of the list till the list reduces to the list of size one.

External sort Any sort algorithm that uses external memory, such as tape or disk, during the sorting is called as external sort algorithm. Merge sort is used in external sorting.

Internal sort Any sort algorithm that uses main memory exclusively during the sorting is called as internal sort algorithm.

Linear search The search begins with the first available record and proceeds to the next available record repeatedly until we find the target key or conclude that it is not found. Such search is known as sequential search and is also called as linear search.

Multiway merge This refers to combining more than two sorted data streams into a single sorted stream.

Passes During the sorting process, the data is traversed many times. Each traversal of the data is referred to as a sort pass.

Polyphase merge This is a non-balanced k-way merge that reduces the number of output files needed by reusing the emptied input file or device as one of the output devices.

Searching The process of locating target data is known as searching.

Sort efficiency Sort efficiency is a measure of the relative efficiency of a sort. It is usually an estimate of the number of comparisons and data movement required to sort the data.

Sort order Data can be ordered either in ascending order or in descending order. The order in which the data is organized, that is, ascending order or descending order, is called as a sort order.

Sort stability A sorting method is said to be stable if at the end of the method, identical elements occur in the same order as in the original unsorted set.

Sorting Sorting is the operation of arranging the records of a table according to the key value of each record, or sorting is a process of converting an unordered set of elements to an ordered set of elements.

EXERCISES

Multiple choice questions

1. The number of swappings needed to sort the numbers 8, 22, 7, 9, 31, 19, 5, 13 in ascending order using bubble sort is
   (a) 11
   (b) 12
   (c) 13
   (d) 14
2. Given two sorted lists of size m and n, respectively, the number of comparisons needed in the worst case by the merge sort algorithm will be
   (a) mn
   (b) $\max(m, n)$
   (c) $\min(m, n)$
   (d) $m + n - 1$
3. The average successful search time taken by binary search on a sorted array of 10 items is
   (a) 2.6
   (b) 2.7
   (c) 2.8
   (d) 2.9
4. Which of the following sorting algorithms has a worst case running time of $O(n^2)$?
   (a) Insertion sort
   (b) Merge sort
   (c) Quick sort
   (d) Bubble sort
5. Choose the correct statements from the following:
   Note: More than one statement could be correct.
   (a) Internal sorting is used if the number of items to be sorted is very large
   (b) External sorting is used if the number of items to be sorted is very large
   (c) External sorting needs auxiliary storage
   (d) Internal sorting needs auxiliary storage
6. A sorting technique that guarantees that records with the same primary key occurs in the same

order in the sorted list as in the original unsorted list is said to be
(a) stable
(b) consistent
(c) external
(d) linear

7. You want to check whether a given set of items is sorted or not. Which of the following sorting methods will be the most efficient if it is already in sorted order?
(a) Bubble sort
(b) Selection sort
(c) Insertion sort
(d) Merge sort

8. The average number of comparisons performed by the merge sort algorithm in merging two sorted lists of length 2 is
(a) 8/3
(b) 8/5
(c) 11/7
(d) 11/6

9. Which of the following sorting methods will be the best if the number of swappings done is the only measure of efficiency?
(a) Bubble sort
(b) Selection sort
(c) Insertion sort
(d) Quick sort

10. As part of maintenance work, you are entrusted with the work of rearranging the library books in a shelf in proper order at the end of each day. The ideal choice will be
(a) Bubble sort
(b) Insertion sort
(c) Selection sort
(d) Heap sort

Review questions

1. A sorted list of integers in ascending order (with no duplication) is available. Write a function that reads a number and searches this number in the list. If the number is not present, the function will add the number at its proper position. Print the scanned list in descending order starting from the position of this number.
2. Write an algorithm for merge sort. Give the time complexity of your algorithm. Show the stepwise execution of the algorithm for the following list of data:
(a) 10, 20, 45, 27, 15, 7, 28, 59, 61, 33
(b) 10, −5, 0, 20, −15, 50, 40, −20, 30
(c) 25, 57, 48, 37, 12, 92, 86, 33
(d) 26, 5, 37, 1, 61, 11, 59, 15, 48, 19
State the time complexity of quick sort for average case and best case.
3. Write a pseudo C++ algorithm for merge sort of integers. Give the number of comparisons required for the best case and the worst case of inputs with examples.
4. Write a pseudo C++ algorithm for quick sort of integers.
5. Discuss with suitable examples any three sorting techniques. Complete them with respect to the computing time giving the best cases and the worst cases of each.
6. Discuss internal and external sorting with suitable examples of each type.
7. Write an algorithm to implement selection sort with suitable example.
8. What is the purpose of searching an algorithm?
9. What are the two major types of searches? How do they differ?
10. Using the selection sort algorithm, manually sort the following list and show your work in each pass: 7, 23, 31, 40, 56, 78, 9, 2.
11. Using the bubble sort algorithm, manually sort the following list and show your work in each pass: 7, 23, 31, 40, 56, 78, 9, 2.
12. A list contains the following elements: 7, 23, 31, 40, 56, 78, 9, 2. Using the binary search algorithm, trace the steps followed to find 88.
13. Trace the series of recursive calls performed by quick sort during the process of sorting the following array: 3, 1, 4, 5, 9, 2, 6, 10, 7, 8.
14. Describe the behaviour of the quick sort algorithm when the input is already sorted. How would this

be different if instead of the first element we selected the mid point as the pivot value?

15. For bubble sort, give the time complexity for average case and best case. Justify your answer.
16. Which of the sorting algorithms has the best performance in terms of storage and time complexity? Justify your answer.
17. Repeated merging is referred to as polyphase merging. Comment.
18. List the situations where polyphase merge is to be used.
19. Elaborate the advantages of multiway merge.

Answers to multiple choice questions

1. (d)
2. (d) Each comparison puts one element in the final stored array. So, in the worst case, $m + n - 1$ comparisons are necessary.
3. (d) For 10 items $i_1, i_2, ..., i_{10}$, to match i_5, the number of comparisons needed is 1; for i_2, it is 2, for i_8 it is 2, for i_1 it is 3, and so on. So, the average is $(1 + (2 + 2) + (3 + 3 + 3 + 3) + (4 + 4 + 4)/10$, i.e., 2.9.
4. (b) 5. (a), (b) 6. (a) 7. (c)
8. (a) Merge sort combines two given sorted lists into one sorted list. For this problem, let the final sorted order be *a*, *b*, *c*, *d*. The 2 lists (of length 2 each) should fall into one of the following three categories:
   (i) *a*, *b* and *c*, *d*
   (ii) *a*, *c* and *b*, *d*
   (iii) *a*, *d* and *b*, *c*
   The number of comparisons needed in each case will be 2, 3, 3. So, average number of comparisons will be $(2 + 3 + 3)/3 = 8/3$
   Here is a better way of solving:
   Let list L_1 have the items *a*, *c* and L_2 have the items *b*, *d*.
   The following tree depicts the different possible cases—*a* and *b* means *a* is compared with *b*. If *a* is smaller, the edge will be labelled *a*. The number within the circle, beside the leaf nodes, is the number of comparisons, needed to reach it.

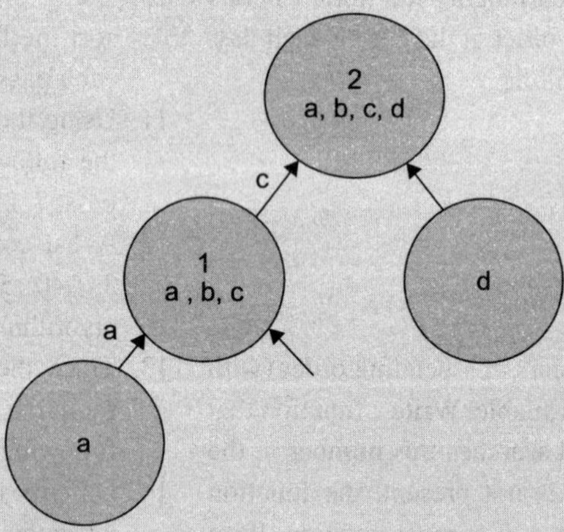

9. (b) 10. (b)

10 SEARCH TREES

OBJECTIVES

After completing this chapter, the reader will be able to understand the following:

- Variations in binary search trees—static and dynamic
- Ways of building trees of each type to ensure that they remain balanced

We have discussed the non-linear data structure, tree, and one of its most popular variations, the search tree, in Chapter 7. The binary search tree (BST) is one of the fundamental data structures extensively used for searching the target in a set of ordered data. BSTs are widely used for retrieving data from databases, look-up tables, and storage dictionaries. It is the most efficient search technique having a time complexity that is logarithmic to the size of the set. There are two cases with respect to BST construction. The first case is a set of keys and the probabilities with which they are searched, which is known in advance. The second is when knowledge about the keys is not available in advance and the keys occur dynamically. These two cases lead to the following two kinds of search trees:

1. *Static BST*—is one that is not allowed to update its structure once it is constructed. In other words, the static BST is an offline algorithm, which is presumably aware of the access sequence beforehand.
2. *Dynamic BST*—is one that changes during the access sequence. We assume that the dynamic BST is an online algorithm, which does not have prior information about the sequence.

In this chapter, we shall study about these two BSTs and the concept of symbol tables.

10.1 SYMBOL TABLE

While compilers and assemblers are scanning a program, each identifier must be examined to determine if it is a keyword. This information concerning the keywords in a programming language is stored in a symbol table. Consider the following C++ statement:

```
int limit;
```

When a compiler processes this statement, it will identify that `int` is a keyword and `limit` is an identifier. However, a question arises as to how a compiler classifies them as a keyword and a user-defined identifier. For identifying `int` as a keyword, the compiler is provided with a table of keywords. For faster search through a list of keywords, the symbol table is used as an efficient data structure.

The symbol table is a kind of a 'keyed table' which stores <key, information> pairs with no additional logical structure.

The operations performed on symbol tables are the following:

1. Inserting the <key, information> pairs into the collection.
2. Removing the <key, information> pairs by specifying the key.
3. Searching for a particular key.
4. Retrieving the information associated with a key.

When a compiler stores information that can be retrieved by some unique key value, it means we are using a keyed table. The field that contains the value by which we want to retrieve the information is the *key field*. When keyed tables are used in a compiler and an assembler, where the key (the symbol) is the programmer's identifier and the information is the location assigned by the assembler to that identifier, the keyed tables are called *symbol tables*.

10.1.1 Representation of Symbol Table

There are two different techniques for implementing a keyed table, namely, the symbol table and the tree table.

Static Tree Tables

When symbols are known in advance and no insertion and deletion is allowed, such a structure is called a *static tree table*. An example of this type of table is a reserved word table in a compiler. This table is searched once for every occurrence of an identifier in a program. If an identifier is not present in the reserved word table, then it is searched for in another table. When we know the keys and their probable frequencies of being searched, we can optimize the search time by building an optimal binary search tree (OBST). The keys have history associated with their use, which is referred to as their *probability of occurrence*. There are four options for searching:

1. Static tree table can be stored as a sorted sequential list and binary search ($O(\log_2 n)$) can be used to search a symbol.
2. Balanced BST can be used to find symbols having equal probabilities.
3. Hash tables, having the search time O(1), can be used to store a symbol table.
4. OBST is used when different symbols are searched with different probabilities.

Dynamic Tree Tables

A dynamic tree table is used when symbols are not known in advance but are inserted as they come and deleted if not required. *Dynamic keyed tables* are those that are built on-the-fly. The keys have no history associated with their use. The dynamically built tree that is a balanced BST is the best choice.

Let us now look into each of these trees in detail.

10.2 OPTIMAL BINARY SEARCH TREE

Before we study OBSTs, let us revise BSTs. A BST is one of the most important data structures in computer science. When arrays are used to store ordered data, we use the very efficient searching technique, that is, binary search. However, its insertion and deletion algorithms are inefficient as they require shifting of data in the array. An alternative is to use a linked list to store ordered data, which although provides efficient insertion and deletion algorithms, its sequential searching algorithm is inefficient. Therefore, a BST is the only data structure left that not only has an efficient searching algorithm but also efficient insertion and deletion algorithms.

A BST can be defined as a key-based tree with the following properties:

1. Every element has a key, and no two elements have the same key (i.e., keys are unique).
2. The keys (if any) in the left subtree are smaller than the key in the root.
3. The keys (if any) in the right subtree are greater than the key in the root.
4. Each subtree in itself is a BST.

A BST has a few problems which are to be overcome. Consider the BST shown in Fig. 10.1.

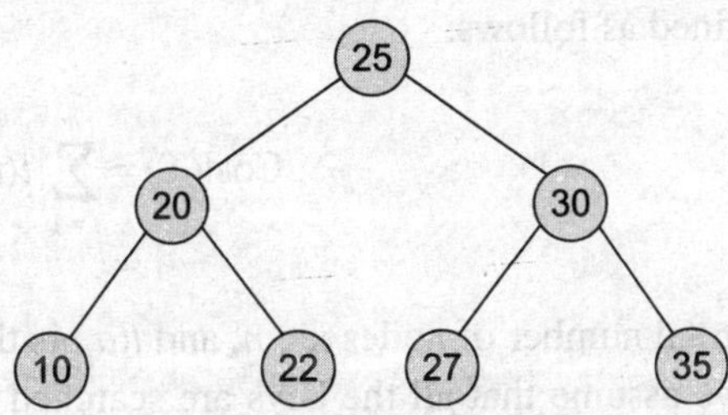

Fig. 10.1 Sample binary search tree

The inorder traversal produces 10, 20, 22, 25, 27, 30, 35. For the same set of keys, depending on their sequence of arrival, the other two search trees can be constructed as in Fig. 10.2.

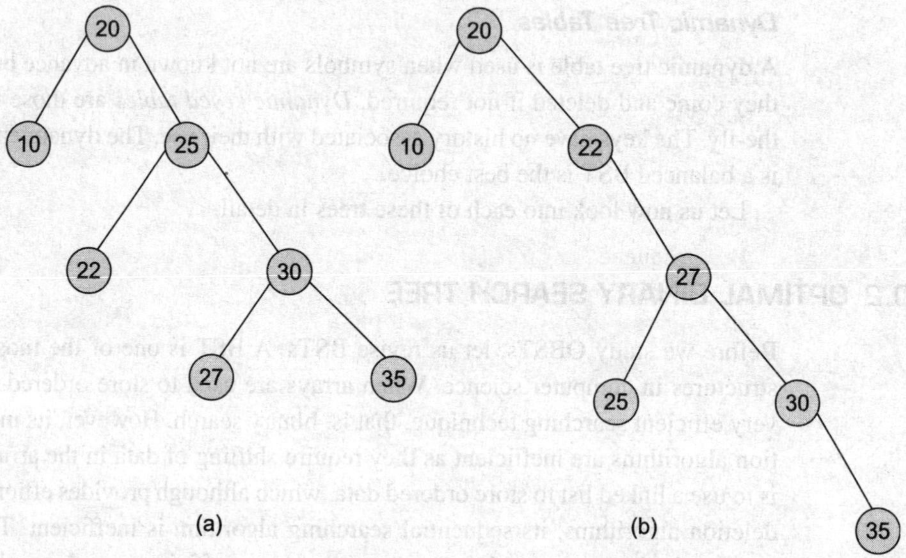

Fig. 10.2 Sample BSTs for keys (25, 10, 35, 27, 35, 20, 22) (a) Sample 1 (b) Sample 2

Note that the left BST in Fig. 10.2(a) requires utmost four comparisons to search the target in the tree, whereas for searching the target in the right tree (Fig. 10.2b), the maximum comparisons needed are five. We can say that the first BST has a better average behaviour than the second.

When the target is at the root (level 0), we need just one comparison; if the target is at level 1, we need two comparisons, and so on. Since the number of comparisons, or in other words iterations, through the search loop determines the cost of search, the cost should be minimum, that is, optimal. Hence, the optimality criteria for a static BST can be stated as minimizing the cost of the BST under a given access sequence. Such a cost can be defined as follows:

$$\text{Cost(T)} = \sum_{i=1}^{n} l(a_i) \qquad (10.1)$$

Here, the total number of nodes are n, and $l(a_i)$ is the length of the ith key, a.

Here, we assume that all the keys are searched with equal probabilities. However, in reality, the keys are searched with different probabilities, and it should be taken care of while constructing the tree so that the keys searched more often should require less time as compared to those searched rarely. This can be achieved by placing the more frequently searched key nodes closer to the root as compared to those that are searched rarely, to reduce the total number of average searches. A node is said to be closer to the root when its path length is lesser than that of the other nodes.

In brief, cost of a tree is computed with respect to its node's probability of search and path length. Hence,

$$\text{Cost(T)} = \sum_{i=1}^{n} W_i \times L_i \tag{10.2}$$

where,

W_i = frequency or probability (also called as weight of the ith node)

L_i = level of a particular node calculated from the root node treated from level 0

Assume that there are four keys $\{P, Q, R, S\}$ that are to be searched with probabilities 0.1, 0.2, 0.4, and 0.3, respectively. There are 14 possible BSTs. A few of them are shown in Fig. 10.3.

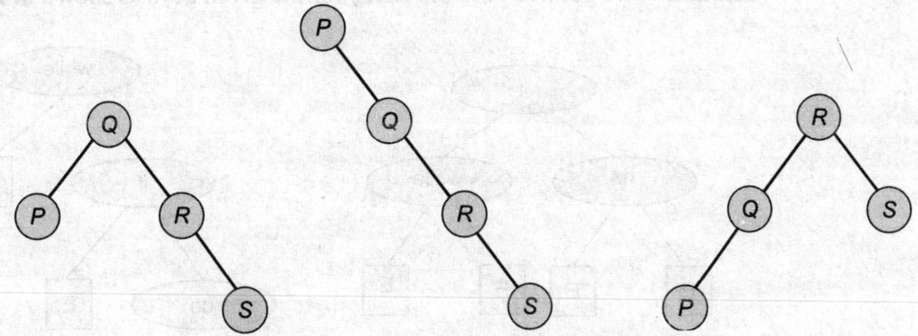

Fig.10.3 Three sample BSTs for keys $\{P, Q, R, S\}$

Now, we need to find out which of these 14 trees is the optimal one. One way to do this is to construct all possible BSTs. However, as the number of keys (n) increases, the total number of search trees also increases. So this approach is unrealistic for a large n. An alternative is to use a general algorithm.

Consider the keys $\{k_1, k_2, \ldots, k_n\}$ such that $k_1 < k_2 < k_3 < \ldots < k_n$. Every successful search for the key k_i has the probability $p(i)$. In addition, every unsuccessful search for the key x has the probability of failure $q(i)$ for $0 \le i \le n$, and $k_i < x < k_{i+1}$. We can add a fictitious node as a child for every leaf node.

For the BSTs in Fig. 10.4, all the keys represent internal nodes; all successful searches will always end at an internal node; all squares denote external nodes, which are fictitious; all unsuccessful searches will end at some external node. If there are n keys, there are $n + 1$ external nodes. So all the keys that are not a part of a BST belong to one of $(n + 1)$ equivalence classes E_i for $0 \le i \le n$. The class E_0 contains all keys $m < k_1$. The class E_1 contains all keys m such that $k_1 < m < k_2$. In general, the class E_i contains all keys m such that $k_i < m < k_{i+1}$. So if an unsuccessful search reaches at the node E_i at level l, it means that $l - 1$ comparisons are already performed. Hence, the cost of such node is $q(i) \times (\text{level}(E_i) - 1)$. Similarly, every successful search that stops at the key k_i at level l has the cost $p(i) \times \text{level}(k_i)$.

Hence, the cost of a BST is given as follows:

$$\sum_{1 \le i \le n} p(i) \times \text{level}(k_i) + \sum_{0 \le i \le n} q(i) \times \text{level}(E_i) - 1 \qquad (10.3)$$

Equation (10.3) defines the cost of a BST in terms of the probabilities of successful and unsuccessful searches and the level of a node. Now, let us define an OBST. We need a BST with an optimal cost. An *OBST* is a BST with the minimum cost. Let us see how to build it by taking Example 10.1.

EXAMPLE 10.1 Given the keys = {while, do, if} and probabilities $p(i) = q(i) = 1/7$ for all i. Compute the cost of all possible BSTs and find the OBST.

Solution We get five possible BSTs for the given keys as shown in Fig. 10.4.

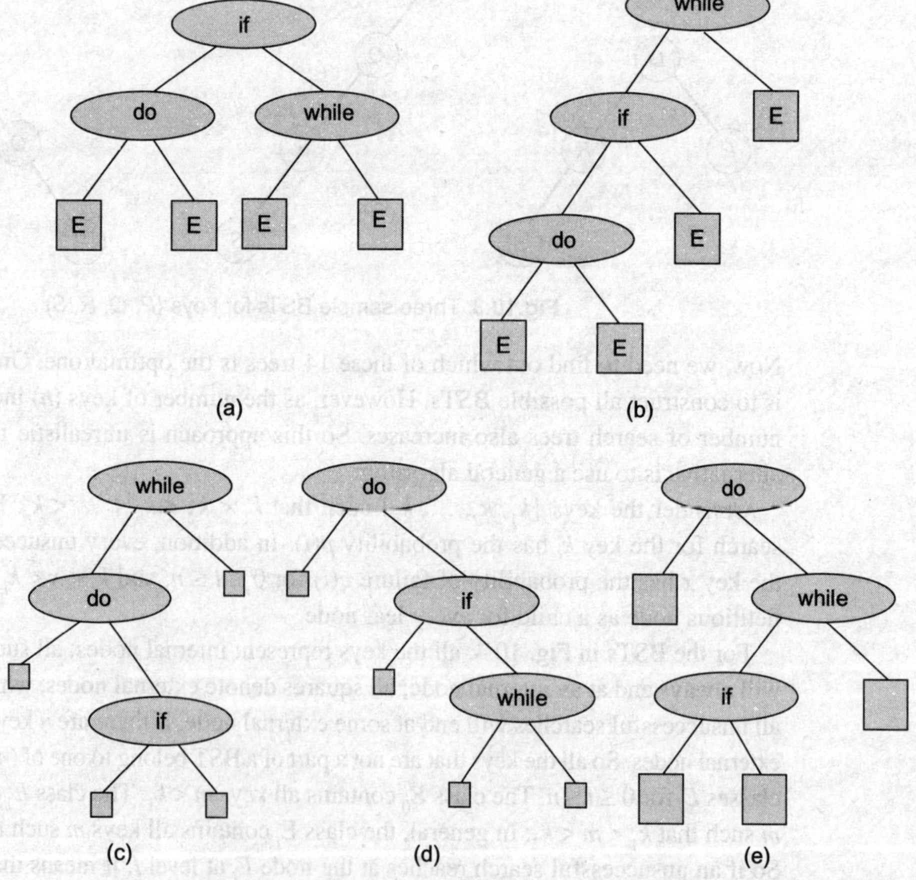

Fig. 10.4 BSTs for the keys {do, while, if} (a) BST1 (b) BST2 (c) BST3 (d) BST 4 (e) BST 5

Let us compute the cost of each BST.
For Fig. 10.4(a),

$$\text{Cost} = \sum_{1\le i\le 3} p(i)\times \text{level}(k_i) + \sum_{0\le i\le 3} q(i)\times \text{level}(E_i) - 1 = \text{A} + \text{B}$$

$$\begin{aligned}\text{A} &= \sum_{1\le i\le 3} p(i)\times \text{level}(k_i) = p_1 \times \text{level}(k_1) + p_2 \times \text{level}(k_2) + p_3 \times \text{level}(k_3)\\ &= 1/7(2+2+1)\\ &= 5/7\end{aligned}$$

$$\begin{aligned}\text{B} &= \sum_{0\le i\le 3} q(i)\times (\text{level}(E_i) - 1) = q_0 \times \text{level}(E_0) - 1 + q_1 \times \text{level}(E_1) - 1\\ &\qquad + q_2 \times \text{level}(E_2) - 1 + q_3 \times \text{level}(E_3) - 1\\ &= 1/7(2+2+2+2)\\ &= 8/7\end{aligned}$$

Therefore, cost = (5/7) + (8/7) = 13/7
For Fig. 10.4(b), total cost = A + B

$$\text{where}\quad \text{A} = \sum_{1\le i\le 3} p(i)\times \text{level}(k_i) = \frac{1}{7}(1+2+3) = 6/7$$

$$\text{B} = \sum_{0\le i\le 3} q(i)\times \text{level}(E_i) = \frac{1}{7}(3+3+2+1) = 9/7$$

Therefore, cost = (6/7) + (9/7) = 15/7

Similarly, for Figs 10.4(c)–(e), the cost of each subtree = 15/7.

The cost of the tree in Fig. 10.4(a) is the least; hence, it is the OBST.

Practically, we cannot use such an approach to find an OBST as we will need to draw all possible BSTs and then find the cost of all BSTs. As the number of keys increases, the number of BSTs also increases. Dynamic programming approach can be used to construct an OBST by considering the probabilities of both successful and unsuccessful searches for the given set of keys.

We construct an OBST step-by-step using the following three formulae:

$$\begin{aligned}&w(i, j) = p(j) + q(j) + w(i, j-1)\\ &c(i, j) = \min_{(i<a\le j)}\{c(i, a-1) + c(a, j)\} + w(i, j)\\ &r(i, j) = a\end{aligned}$$

where,

$w(i, j)$is the weight of node (i, j)

$c(i, j)$is the cost of node (i, j)

$c(i, a-1)$is the cost of left subtree

$c(a, j)$is the cost of right subtree

$r(i, j)$is the root of the tree

The dynamic programming approach can be used to construct an OBST stepwise, where the principal of optimality should hold at each step. Assume that there are n keys $\{k_1, k_2, \ldots, k_n\}$ where $k_1 < k_2 < k_3 < \ldots < k_n$. So at some step, if k_a is the root of a tree, then the resultant tree is as in Fig. 10.5.

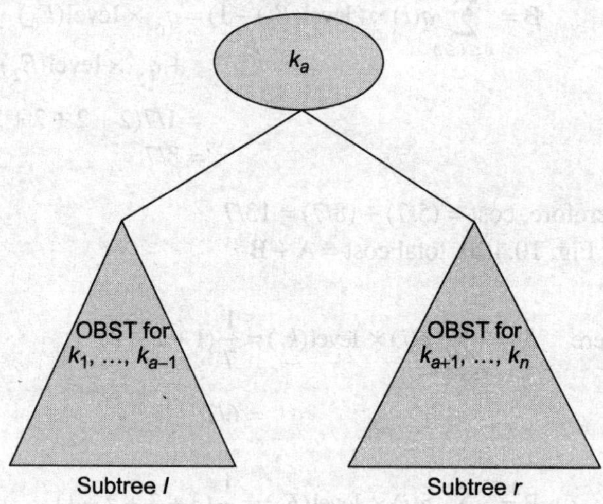

Fig. 10.5 Resultant OBST

Since this is a BST, the left subtree l has keys $k_1, k_2, \ldots, k_{a-1}$, and external nodes $E_0, E_1, \ldots, E_{a-1}$.

Therefore, using Eq. (10.3), the cost of the left subtree l is

$$\text{Cost}(l) = \sum_{1 \le i (a-1)} p(i) \times \text{level}(k_a) + \sum_{0 \le i (a-1)} q(i) \times \text{level}(E_i) - 1 \tag{10.4}$$

Similarly, the cost of right subtree using Eq. (10.3) is

$$\text{Cost}(r) = \sum_{(a+1) \le i \le n} p(i) \times \text{level}(k_a) + \sum_{a \le i \le n} q(i) \times \text{level}(E_i) - 1 \tag{10.5}$$

Therefore, the cost of the tree in Fig. 10.5 is the sum of probability of the node k_a, cost of the left subtree l, cost of the right subtree r, weight of the nodes from 0 to $a - 1$, and weight of the nodes from a to n. In notation, this can be stated as follows:

$$p(a) + \text{cost}(l) + \text{cost}(r) + w(0, a-1) + w(a, n) \tag{10.6}$$

Cost(l) and cost(r) are determined considering their roots at level 1. If cost(l) is minimum and cost(r) is also minimum, then the cost of Eq. (10.5) is also minimum, and thus, we can conclude that the tree in Fig. 10.4(a) is optimal.

Let c(i, j) denote the cost of an OBST t_{ij} having keys k_{i+1}, …, k_j and external nodes E_i, …, E_j. So for the left subtree l of OBST in Fig. 10.5, cost (l) = $c(0, a-1)$ and for its right subtree r, cost(r) = $c(a, n)$.

Hence,

$$p(a) + c(0, a-1) + c(a, n) + w(0, a-1) + w(a, n) \tag{10.7}$$

Equation (10.4) gives the cost of a tree having nodes from k_0 to k_n. In general, we can write an equation that gives the cost for a subtree having nodes from k_i to k_j as

$$p(a) + c(i, a-1) + c(a, j) + w(i, a-1) + w(a, j) \tag{10.8}$$

Obviously, Eq. (10.7) gives the minimum cost only if a is chosen properly. So we have to solve Eq. (10.6) for different values of a and then select the minimum. Hence, we can generalize Eq. (10.7) to get the following equation:

$$c(i,j) = \frac{\min}{i < a \le j}[c(i,a-1) + c(a,j) + w(i,a-1) + p(a) + w(a,j)] \tag{10.9}$$

The steps to find OBST are as follows:

1. We begin by considering all unsuccessful probabilities as initially there are no nodes in the tree. $c(i, i) = 0$, $r(i, i) = 0$, and $w(i, i) = q(i)$ for $0 \le i \le n$, where n is the number of keys.
2. Compute $c(i, j)$ for $j - i = 1$, that is, we are constructing a node of level 1. In addition, compute $w(i, j) = p(j) + q(j) + w(i, j-1)$, and the root $r(i, j)$ is the value of a which minimizes $c(i, j)$.

$$c(i,j) = \frac{\min}{i < a \le j}[c(i,a-1) + c(a,j) + w(i,j)]$$

3. Compute $c(i, j)$ for $j - i = 2$. In addition, compute $w(i, j)$ and $r(i, j)$ as in the previous step.
4. Continue the process till $j - i = n$. Here, w_{on}, c_{on}, and r_{on} denote the weight, cost, and root of OBST, respectively.

5. Finally, we can construct an OBST having the root $r_{on} = a$, which means that the key k_a is the root.

In general, let r_{ij} be any node in an OBST, whose value is a. Then, its left node is $r_{i,a-1}$ and its right node is $r_{a,j}$. It is shown in Fig. 10.6.

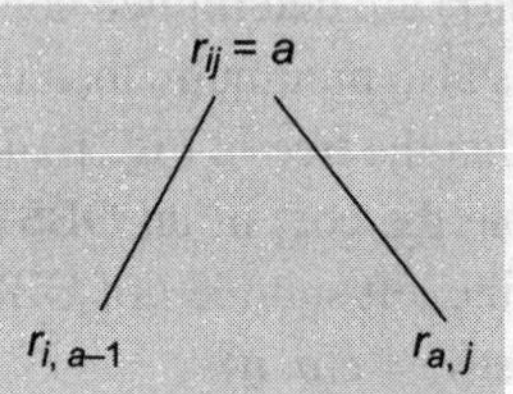

Fig. 10.6 OBST

Using this, we can construct a tree until we get $r_{ij} = 0$ at all the nodes and these are the *external nodes* of a tree.

The initial cost table of the dynamic programming algorithm for constructing an OBST is shown in Fig. 10.7.

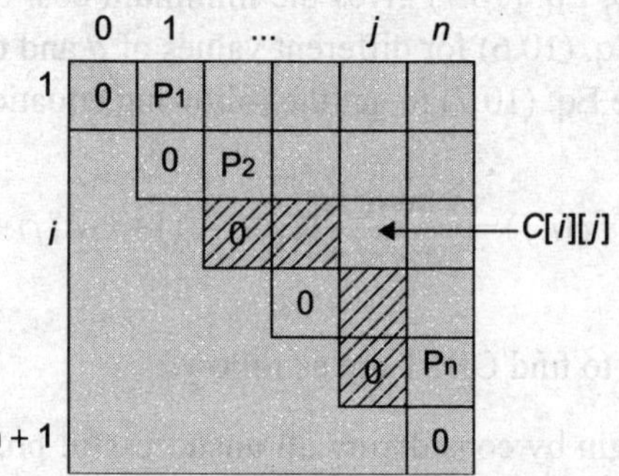

Fig. 10.7 Initial cost table of OBST

The values needed for computing `C[i][j]` are shaded in Fig. 10.7. They are the values in row `i` and to the left of column `j`, and the values in column `j` and the rows below row `i`.

Consider an OBST tree node having the following structure:

```
class leaf
{
   char name[10];
} leaf[max];
```

Program Code 10.1 implements the logic for building an OBST and computing its cost using C++.

PROGRAM CODE 10.1

```
#include<stdio.h>
#define max 20
int i, j, k, n, min, r[max][max];
float p[max], q[max], w[max][max], c[max][max];
void OBST();
void print(int, int);
void print_tab();
main()
{
   cout << "\n Enter no. of leaves in tree:"
   cin >> n;
   cout << "\n Enter leaf label";
   for(i = 1; i <= n; i++)
      cin >> leaf[i].name;
   cout << "\n Enter the probability of successful
   search:";
   for(i = 1; i <= n; i++)
   {
      cout << "p["<<i<<"]";
      cin >> sp[i];
   }
   cout << "\n Enter the probability of unsuccessful
   search: ";
   for(i = 0; i <= n; i++)
   {
      cout << "q["<<i<<"]";
      cin >> q[i];
   }
   cout << "\ninput:\n<<Leaf("<<n<<")";
   for(i = 1; i <= n; i++)
   {
      cout << "leaf["<<i<<"].name";
      cout << "np(1:"<<n<<")";
   }
   for(i = 1; i <= n; i++)
   {
      cout << "p["<<i<<"]";
      cout << "\nq(0:"<<n<<")=";
   }
   for(i = 0; i <= n; i++)
```

```
        cout << "\t<<q[i]";
    OBST();
    print_tab();
    print(0, n);
}

void OBST()
{
    for(i = 0; i < n; i++)
    {
        r[i][i] = c[i][i] = 0; w[i][i] = q[i];
        w[i][i + 1] = p[i + 1] + q[i + 1] + w[i][i];
        c[i][i + 1] = w[i][i + 1];
        r[i][i + 1] = i + 1;
    }
    c[n][n] = 0.0; r[n][n] = 0.0; w[n][n] = q[n];
    for(i = 2; i <= n; i++)
    {
        for(j = 0; j <= n - i; j++)
        {
            w[j][j + i] = w[j][j + i - 1] + p[j + i] + q[j
            + i];
            c[j][j + i] = 999;
            for(k = j + 1; k < j + i; k++)
                if(c[j][j + i] > c[j][k - 1] + c[k][j + i])
                {
                    c[j][j + i] = c[j][k - 1] + c[k][j + i];
                    r[j][j + i] = k;
                }
            c[j][j+i]+=w[j][j+i];
        }
    }
}

void print(int l, int rr)
{
    if(l >= rr) return;
    if(r[l][r[l][rr] - 1] != 0)
        cout <<  "\nleft child of "<<leaf[r[l][rr]].name
```

```
        <<"\t"<<leaf[r[l][r[l][rr] - 1]].name;
    if(r[r[l][rr]][rr] != 0)
        cout << "\nright child of"<< leaf[r[l][rr]].name
        <<"\t" <<leaf[r[r[l][rr]][rr]].name;
    print(l,r[l][rr] - 1);
    print(r[l][rr],rr);
}

void print_tab()
{
    cout << "\noutput:\n";
    cout <<"------------------------------------------
    --------------\n";
    for(i = 0; i <= n; i++)
        cout << "w" << i << i << "=" << w[i][i] << "\n";
    for(i = 0; i <= n; i++)
        cout << "w" << i << i << "=" << c[i][i] << "\n";
    for(i = 0; i <= n; i++)
        cout << "w" << i << i << "=" << r[i][i] << "\n";
    cout << "------------------------------------------
    --------------\n";
    k = 1;
    while(k <= n)
    {
        for(i = 0, j = i + k; i < n, j <= n; i++, j++)
          cout << "w" << i << j << "=" << w[i][j] << "\n";
        for(i = 0, j = i + k; i < n, j <= n; i++, j++)
          cout << "C" << i << j << "=" << c[i][j] << "\n";
        for(i = 0, j = i + k; i < n, j <= n; i++, j++)
          cout << "R" << i << j << "=" << r[i][j] << "\n";
        cout <<"-----------------------------------------
        ----------------\n";
        k++;
            }
     cout << "\nOBST:c[0][n]<<w[0][n]<<leaf[r[0][n]]
     .name"
     cout << \nOBST:c[0][%d] = %0.2f w[0][%d] = %0.2f
     r[0][%d] = %s", n, c[0][n], n, w[0][n], n, leaf[r[0]
     [n]].name);
}
```

Program Code 10.1 is the implementation of the OBST construction through the dynamic approach we just discussed. Let us see its working with Example 10.2.

EXAMPLE 10.2 Find an OBST using a dynamic programming for $n = 4$ and keys $(k_1 < k_2 < k_3 < k_4)$ = (do, if, int, while) given that $p(1:4) = (3, 3, 1, 1)$ and $q(0:4) = (2, 3, 1, 1, 1)$.

Solution

Step 1: Initially, $c(i, i) = 0$, $r(i, i) = 0$, and $w(i, i) = q(i)$ for $0 \le i \le 4$.
Hence, $w(0, 0) = 2$, $w(1, 1) = 3$, $w(2, 2) = w(3, 3) = w(4, 4) = 1$
This is shown in Table 10.1.

Table 10.1 OBST computation for Example 10.2 after step 1

	0	1	2	3	4	
0	$w_{00} = 2$ $c_{00} = 0$ $r_{00} = 0$	$w_{11} = 3$ $c_{11} = 0$ $r_{11} = 0$	$w_{22} = 1$ $c_{22} = 0$ $r_{22} = 0$	$w_{33} = 1$ $c_{33} = 0$ $r_{33} = 0$	$w_{44} = 1$ $c_{44} = 0$ $r_{44} = 0$	Initial values ←
1						
2						
3						
4						

Step 2: $w(i, j) = p(j) + q(j) + w(i, j - 1)$

$$c(i,j) = \min_{i < a \le j} [c(i,a-1) + c(a,j) + w(i,j)]$$

$r = (i, j)$ = value of a which minimizes $c(i, j)$

Let us compute $c(i, j)$ for $j - i = 1$

$w(0, 1) = p(1) + q(1) + w(0, 0)$
$= 3 + 3 + 2 = 8$
$c(0, 1) = w(0, 1) + \min[c(0, 0) + c(1, 1)]$ for $a = 1$
$= 8 + [0 + 0] = 8$
$r(0, 1) = 1$
$w(1, 2) = p(2) + q(2) + w(1, 1) = 3 + 1 + 3 = 7$
$c(1, 2) = w(1, 2) + \min[c(1, 1) + c(2, 2)] = 7 + [0 + 0] = 7$ for $a = 2$

$r(1, 2) = 2$
$w(2, 3) = p(3) + q(3) + w(2, 2) = 1 + 1 + 1 = 3$
$c(2, 3) = w(2, 3) + \min[c(2, 2) + c(3, 3)] = 3 + [0 + 0] = 3$ for $a = 3$
$r(2, 3) = 3$
$w(3, 4) = p(4) + q(4) + w(3, 3) = 1 + 1 + 1 = 3$
$c(3, 4) = w(3, 4) + \min[c(3, 3) + c(4, 4)] = 3 + [0 + 0] = 3$
$r(3, 4) = 4$

This computation is shown in Table 10.2.

Table 10.2 OBST computation for Example 10.2 after step 2

	0	1	2	3	4
0	$w_{00} = 2$ $c_{00} = 0$ $r_{00} = 0$	$w_{11} = 3$ $c_{11} = 0$ $r_{11} = 0$	$w_{22} = 1$ $c_{22} = 0$ $r_{22} = 0$	$w_{33} = 1$ $c_{33} = 0$ $r_{33} = 0$	$w_{44} = 1$ $c_{44} = 0$ $r_{44} = 0$
1	$w_{01} = 8$ $c_{01} = 8$ $r_{01} = 1$	$w_{12} = 7$ $c_{12} = 7$ $r_{12} = 2$	$w_{23} = 3$ $c_{23} = 3$ $r_{23} = 3$	$w_{34} = 3$ $c_{34} = 3$ $r_{34} = 4$	Here $j - i = 1$, that is, while calculating c_{ij}, a took only one value, that is, j.
2					
3					
4					

Step 3: Compute $c(i, j)$ for $j - i = 2$

$$w(0, 2) = p(2) + q(2) + w(0, 1) = 3 + 1 + 8 = 12$$

$$c(0, 2) = w(0, 2) + \min[c(0, 0) + c(1, 2) \text{ for } a = 1,\ c(0, 1) + c(2, 2) \text{ for } a = 2] = 12 + \min[0 + 7, 8 + 0] = 12 + 7 = 19$$

$r(0, 2) = 1$

$$w(1, 3) = \mathrm{p}(3) + \mathrm{q}(3) + \mathrm{w}(1, 2) = 1 + 1 + 7 = 9$$

$$c(1, 3) = w(1, 3) + \min[c(1, 1) + c(2, 3) \text{ for } a = 2,\ c(1, 2) + c(3, 3) \text{ for } a = 3] = 9 + \min[0 + 3, 7 + 0] = 9 + 3 = 12$$

$r(1, 3) = 2$

$w(2, 4) = p(4) + q(4) + w(2, 3) = 1 + 1 + 3 = 5$

$c(2, 4) = w(2, 4) + \min[c(2, 2) + c(3, 4) \text{ for } a = 3\ ,\ c(2, 3) + c(4, 4)]$
$\text{for } a = 4$
$= 5 + \min[0 + 3, 3 + 0]$
$= 5 + 3 = 8$
$r(2, 4) = 3$

Table 10.3 shows this computation.

Table 10.3 OBST computation for Example 10.2 after step 3

	0	1	2	3	4
0	$w_{00} = 2$ $c_{00} = 0$ $r_{00} = 0$	$w_{11} = 3$ $c_{11} = 0$ $r_{11} = 0$	$w_{22} = 1$ $c_{22} = 0$ $r_{22} = 0$	$w_{33} = 1$ $c_{33} = 0$ $r_{33} = 0$	$w_{44} = 1$ $c_{44} = 0$ $r_{44} = 0$
1	$w_{01} = 8$ $c_{01} = 8$ $r_{01} = 1$	$w_{12} = 7$ $c_{12} = 7$ $r_{12} = 2$	$w_{23} = 3$ $c_{23} = 3$ $r_{23} = 3$	$w_{34} = 3$ $c_{34} = 3$ $r_{34} = 4$	
2	$w_{02} = 12$ $c_{02} = 19$ $r_{02} = 1$	$w_{13} = 9$ $c_{13} = 12$ $r_{13} = 2$	$w_{24} = 5$ $c_{24} = 8$ $r_{24} = 3$	Here, $j - i = 2$, that is, while calculating c_{ij}, a took two values.	
3					
4					

Step 4: Compute $c(i, j)$ for $j - i = 3$

$w(0, 3) = p(3) + q(3) + w(0, 2) = 1 + 1 + 12 = 14$
$c(0, 3) = w(0, 3) + \min[c(0, 0) + c(1, 3) \quad \text{for } a = 1, c(0, 1) +$
$c(2, 3) \quad \text{for } a = 2, c(0, 2) + c(3, 4) \quad \text{for } a = 3]$
$= 14 + \min[0 + 12, 8 + 3, 19 + 3]$
$= 14 + \min[12, 11, 22]$
$= 14 + 11 = 25$
$r(0, 3) = 2$
$w(1, 4) = p(4) + q(4) + w(1, 3) = 1 + 1 + 9 = 11$
$c(1, 4) = w(1, 4) + \min[c(1, 1) + c(2, 4) \quad \text{for } a = 2, c(1, 2) +$
$c(3, 4) \quad \text{for } a = 3, c(1, 3) + c(4, 4) \quad \text{for } a = 4]$
$= 11 + \min[0 + 8, 7 + 3, 12 + 0]$
$= 11 + \min[8, 10, 12]$
$= 11 + 8 = 19$
$r(1, 4) = 2$

This computation is shown in Table 10.4.

Table 10.4 OBST computation for Example 10.2 after step 4

	0	1	2	3	4
0	$w_{00} = 2$ $c_{00} = 0$ $r_{00} = 0$	$w_{11} = 3$ $c_{11} = 0$ $r_{11} = 0$	$w_{22} = 1$ $c_{22} = 0$ $r_{22} = 0$	$w_{33} = 1$ $c_{33} = 0$ $r_{33} = 0$	$w_{44} = 1$ $c_{44} = 0$ $r_{44} = 0$
1	$w_{01} = 8$ $c_{01} = 8$ $r_{01} = 1$	$w_{12} = 7$ $c_{12} = 7$ $r_{12} = 2$	$w_{23} = 3$ $c_{23} = 3$ $r_{23} = 3$	$w_{34} = 3$ $c_{34} = 3$ $r_{34} = 4$	
2	$w_{02} = 12$ $c_{02} = 19$ $r_{02} = 1$	$w_{13} = 9$ $c_{13} = 12$ $r_{13} = 2$	$w_{24} = 5$ $c_{24} = 8$ $r_{24} = 3$		
3	$w_{03} = 14$ $c_{03} = 25$ $r_{03} = 2$	$w_{14} = 11$ $c_{14} = 19$ $r_{14} = 2$	Here $j - i = 3$, that is, while calculating c_{ij}, *a* took three values.		
4					

Step 5: Compute $c(i, j)$ for $j - i = 4$

$$w(0, 4) = p(4) + q(4) + w(0, 3) = 1 + 1 + 14 = 16$$

$$\begin{aligned} c(0, 4) &= w(0, 4) + \min[c(0, 0) + c(1, 4) \quad \text{for } a = 1,\ c(0, 1) + c(2, 4) \quad \text{for } a = 2, \\ &\qquad c(0, 2) + c(3, 4) \quad \text{for } a = 3,\ c(0, 3) + c(4, 4) \quad \text{for } a = 4] \\ &= 16 + \min[0 + 19, 8 + 8, 19 + 3, 25 + 0] \\ &= 16 + \min[19, 16, 22, 25] \\ &= 16 + 16 = 32 \end{aligned}$$

$$r(0, 4) = 2$$

All these computations are shown in Table 10.5.

Table 10.5 OBST computation for Example 10.2 after step 5

	0	1	2	3	4
0	$w_{00} = 2$ $c_{00} = 0$ $r_{00} = 0$	$w_{11} = 3$ $c_{11} = 0$ $r_{11} = 0$	$w_{22} = 1$ $c_{22} = 0$ $r_{22} = 0$	$w_{33} = 1$ $c_{33} = 0$ $r_{33} = 0$	$w_{44} = 1$ $c_{44} = 0$ $r_{44} = 0$
1	$w_{01} = 8$ $c_{01} = 8$ $r_{01} = 1$	$w_{12} = 7$ $c_{12} = 7$ $r_{12} = 2$	$w_{23} = 3$ $c_{23} = 3$ $r_{23} = 3$	$w_{34} = 3$ $c_{34} = 3$ $r_{34} = 4$	
2	$w_{02} = 12$ $c_{02} = 19$ $r_{02} = 1$	$w_{13} = 9$ $c_{13} = 12$ $r_{13} = 2$	$w_{24} = 5$ $c_{24} = 8$ $r_{24} = 3$		
3	$w_{03} = 14$ $c_{03} = 25$ $r_{03} = 2$	$w_{14} = 11$ $c_{14} = 19$ $r_{14} = 2$			
4	$w_{04} = 16$ $c_{04} = 32$ $r_{04} = 2$				

In the last step, we obtained $w_{04} = 16$, $c_{04} = 32$, $r_{04} = 2$, which denote that for the given keys = (do, if, int, while), an OBST has weight 16, cost 32, and root k_2 = if.

In Table 10.5, row i and column j shows the result of $w(j, i+j)$, $c(j, i+j)$, and $r(j, i+j)$, respectively. The calculation proceeds row-by-row.

The r values are shown in Fig. 10.8.

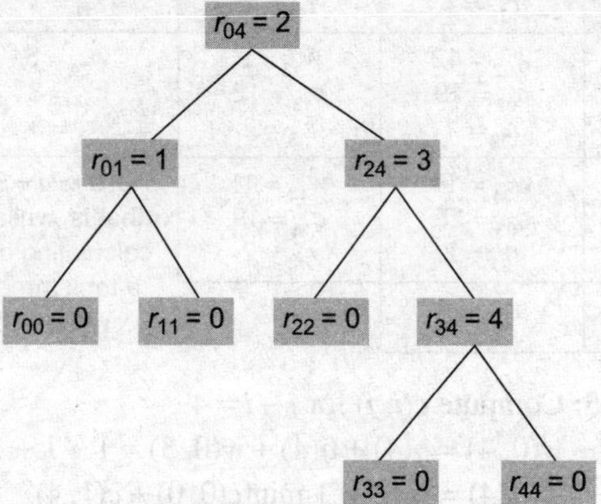

Fig. 10.8 Tree and *r* values

Let us construct an OBST as shown in Fig. 10.9 from the calculations based on these r values.

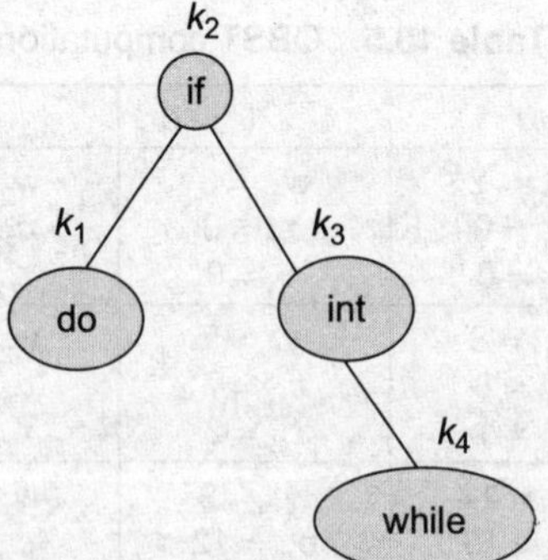

Fig. 10.9 OBST for Example 10.2

Let us now see another example of OBST construction through dynamic approach in Example 10.3.

EXAMPLE 10.3 Find an OBST using the dynamic programming approach for $n = 4$, keys = (count, float, if, while). Compute $w(i, j)$, $r(i, j)$, and $c(i, j)$ for $0 \le i \le j \le 4$ given that $p(1) = 1/20$, $p(2) = 1/5$, $p(3) = 1/10$, $p(4) = 1/20$, $q(0) = 1/5$, $7(1) = 1/10$, $q(2) = 1/5$, $q(3) = 1/20$, and $q(4) = 1/20$. Using $r(i, j)$, construct an OBST.

Solution

$$p(1:4) = \frac{1}{20}, \frac{1}{5}, \frac{1}{10}, \frac{1}{20} = (0.05, 0.2, 0.1, 0.05)$$

$$q(0:4) = \frac{1}{5}, \frac{1}{10}, \frac{1}{5}, \frac{1}{20}, \frac{1}{20} = (0.2, 0.1, 0.2, 0.05, 0.05)$$

Step 1: $c(i, i) = 0$, $r(i, i) = 0$, and $w(i, i) = q(i)$ for $0 \le i \le 4$

Hence, $w_{00} = 0.2$, $w_{11} = 0.1$, $w_{22} = 0.2$, $w_{33} = 0.05$, $w_{44} = 0.05$.

Step 2: $w(i, j) = q(j) + p(j) + w(i, j - 1)$

$$c(i, j) = \frac{\min[c(i, a-1) + c(a, j) + w(i, j)]}{i < a \le j}$$

$r(i, j)$ = value of a which minimizes $c(i, j)$

Compute $c(i, j)$ for $j - i = 1$.

$w(0, 1) = p(1) + q(1) + w(0, 0)$
$= 0.05 + 0.1 + 0.2 = 0.35$

$c(0, 1) = w(0, 1) + \min[c(0, 0) + c(1, 1)]$
$= 0.35 + [0 + 0] = 0.35$

$r(0, 1) = 1$

$w(1, 2) = p(2) + q(2) + w(1, 1) = 0.2 + 0.2 + 0.1 = 0.5$

$c(1, 2) = w(1, 2) + \min[c(1, 1) + c(2, 2)] = 0.5 + [0 + 0] = 0.5$

$r(1, 2) = 2$

$w(2, 3) = p(3) + q(3) + w(2, 2) = 0.1 + 0.05 + 0.2 = 0.35$

$c(2, 3) = w(2, 3) + \min[c(2, 2) + c(3, 3)] = 0.35 + [0 + 0] = 0.35$

$r(2, 3) = 3$

$w(3, 4) = p(4) + q(4) + w(3, 3) = 0.05 + 0.05 + 0.05 = 0.15$

$c(3, 4) = w(3, 4) + \min[c(3, 3) + c(4, 4)] = 0.15 + [0 + 0] = 0.15$

$r(3, 4) = 4$

Step 3: Compute $c(i, j)$ for $j - i = 2$.

$w(0, 2) = p(2) + q(2) + w(0, 1)$
$= 0.2 + 0.2 + 0.35 = 0.75$

$c(0, 2) = w(0, 2) + \min[c(0, 0) + c(1, 2), c(0, 1) + c(2, 2)]$
$= 0.75 + \min[0 + 0.5, 0.35 + 0]$
$= 0.75 + 0.35 = 1.10$
$r(0, 2) = 2$
$w(1, 3) = p(3) + q(3) + w(1, 2) = 0.1 + 0.05 + 0.5 = 0.65$
$c(1, 3) = w(1, 3) + \min[c(1, 1) + c(2, 3), c(1, 2) + c(3, 3)]$
$= 0.65 + \min[0 + 0.35, 0.5 + 0]$
$= 0.65 + 0.35 = 1.00$
$r(1, 3) = 2$
$w(2, 4) = p(4) + q(4) + w(2, 3) = 0.05 + 0.05 + 0.35 = 0.45$
$c(2, 4) = w(2, 4) + \min[c(2, 2) + c(3, 4), c(2, 3) + c(4, 4)]$
$= 0.45 + \min[0 + 0.15, 0.35 + 0]$
$= 0.45 + 0.15 = 0.60$
$r(2, 4) = 3$

Step 4: Compute $c(i, j)$ for $j - i = 3$.
$w(0, 3) = p(3) + q(3) + w(0, 2)$
$= 0.1 + 0.05 + 0.75 = 0.90$
$c(0, 3) = w(0, 3) + \min[c(0, 0) + c(1, 3), c(0, 1) + c(2, 3), c(0, 2) + c(3, 3)]$
$= 0.9 + \min[0 + 1, 0.35 + 0.35, 1.1 + 0]$
$= 0.9 + 0.7 = 1.6$
$r(0, 3) = 2$
$w(1, 4) = p(4) + q(4) + w(1, 3) = 0.05 + 0.05 + 0.65 = 0.75$
$c(1, 4) = w(1, 4) + \min[c(1,1) + c(2, 4), c(1, 2) + c(3, 4), c(1, 3) + c(4, 4)]$
$= 0.75 + \min[0 + 0.6, 0.5 + 0.15, 1 + 0]$
$= 0.75 + \min[0.6, 0.65, 1]$
$= 0.75 + 0.6 = 1.35$
$r(1, 4) = 2$

Step 5: Compute $c(i, j)$ for $j - i = 4$.
$w(0, 4) = p(4) + q(4) + w(0, 3) = 0.05 + 0.05 + 0.9 = 1.00$
$c(0, 4) = w(0, 4) + \min[c(0, 0) + c(1, 4), c(0, 1) + c(2, 4), c(0, 2) + c(3, 4),$
$c(0, 3) + c(4, 4)]$
$= 1 + \min[0 + 1.35, 0.35 + 0.6, 1.1 + 0.15, 1.6 + 0]$
$= 1 + \min[1.35, 0.95, 1.25, 1.6]$
$= 1 + 0.95 = 1.95$
$r(0, 4) = 2$

Hence, for the keys (k_1, k_2, k_3, k_4) = (count, float, if, while), an OBST has weight $w_{04} = 1$, cost $c_{04} = 1.95$ and root $r_{04} = 2$.

These calculations can be written in the table form as in Table 10.6.

Table 10.6 OBST computations for Example 10.3

	0	1	2	3	4
0	$w_{00} = 0.2$ $c_{00} = 0$ $r_{00} = 0$	$w_{11} = 0.1$ $c_{11} = 0$ $r_{11} = 0$	$w_{22} = 0.2$ $c_{22} = 0$ $r_{22} = 0$	$w_{33} = 0.05$ $c_{33} = 0$ $r_{33} = 0$	$w_{44} = 0.05$ $c_{44} = 0$ $r_{44} = 0$
1	$w_{01} = 0.35$ $c_{01} = 0.35$ $r_{01} = 1$	$w_{12} = 0.5$ $c_{12} = 0.5$ $r_{12} = 2$	$w_{23} = 0.35$ $c_{23} = 0.35$ $r_{23} = 3$	$w_{34} = 0.15$ $c_{34} = 0.15$ $r_{34} = 4$	
2	$w_{02} = 0.75$ $c_{02} = 1.1$ $r_{02} = 2$	$w_{13} = 0.65$ $c_{13} = 1$ $r_{13} = 2$	$w_{24} = 0.45$ $c_{24} = 0.6$ $r_{24} = 3$		
3	$w_{03} = 0.9$ $c_{03} = 1.6$ $r_{03} = 2$	$w_{14} = 0.75$ $c_{14} = 1.35$ $r_{14} = 2$			
4	$w_{04} = 1$ $c_{04} = 1.95$ $r_{04} = 2$				

Figure 10.10 shows the calculated r values.

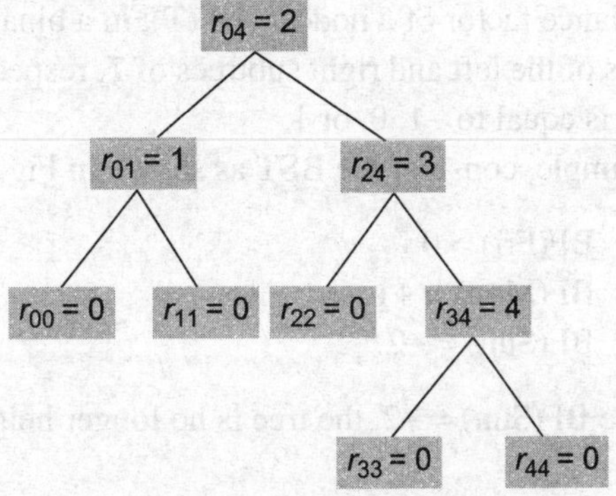

Fig. 10.10 Keys and r value

Figure 10.11 is the OBST obtained for Example 10.3 based on these r values.

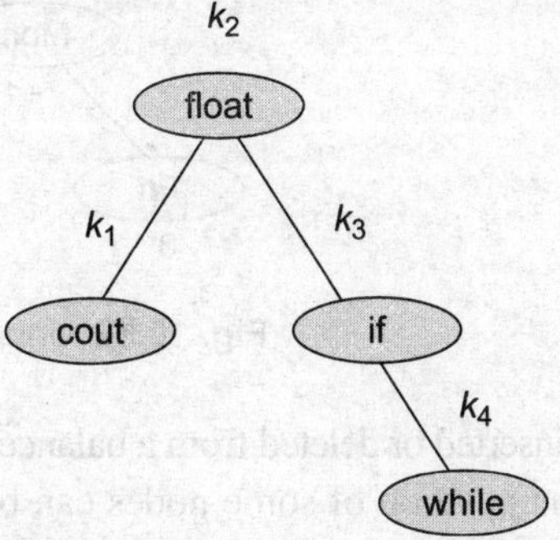

Fig. 10.11 OBST for Example 10.3

10.3 AVL TREE (HEIGHT-BALANCED TREE)

In many applications, insertions and deletions occur frequently with no predictable order. Sometimes, it is important to optimize the search times by keeping the tree balanced at all times. The resulting BST is called AVL tree. It was described by two Russian mathematicians G. M. Adelson-Velskii and E. M. Landis in 1962.

An *AVL tree* is a BST where the heights of the left and right subtrees of the root differ by utmost 1 and the left and right subtrees are again AVL trees. The formal definition is as follows:

Definition: An empty tree is height-balanced, if T is a non-empty binary tree with T_L and T_R as its left and right subtrees, respectively, with the following properties:

1. T_L and T_R are height-balanced.
2. $-1 \leq |h_L - h_R| \leq 1$, where h_L and h_R are the heights of T_L and T_R, respectively.

In an AVL tree with n nodes, the searches, insertions, and deletions can all be achieved in time O(log n), even in the worst case. To keep the tree height-balanced, we have to find out the balance factor of each node in the tree after every insertion or deletion.

The balance factor of a node T, BF(T), in a binary tree is $h_L - h_R$, where h_L and h_R are the heights of the left and right subtrees of T, respectively. For any node T in an AVL tree, the BF(T) is equal to −1, 0, or 1.

For example, consider the BST as shown in Fig. 10.12.

BF(Fri) = 0
BF(Mon) = +1
BF(Sun) = +2

Because BF(Sun) = +2, the tree is no longer height-balanced, and it should be restructured.

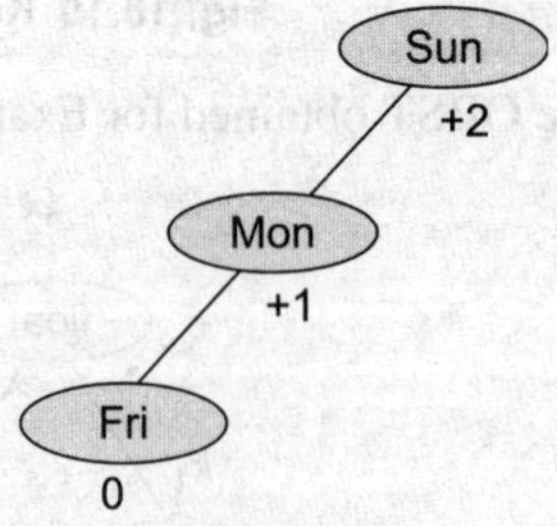

Fig. 10.12 Unbalanced BST

If a node is inserted or deleted from a balanced tree, then it may become unbalanced. So to rebalance it, the position of some nodes can be changed in proper sequence. This can be achieved by performing rotations of nodes. For example, consider the BST as in Fig. 10.13.

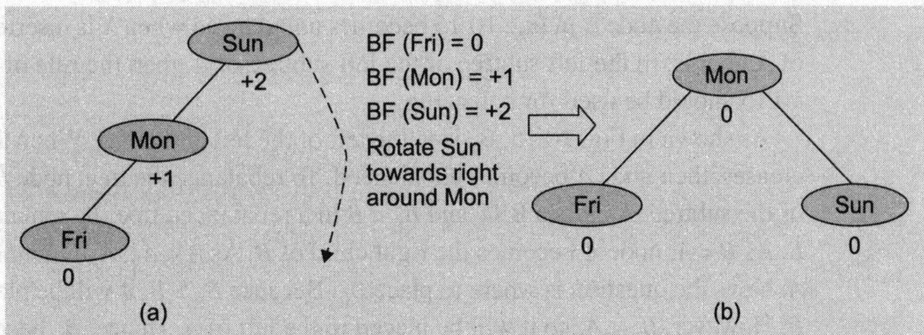

Fig. 10.13 Balancing a tree by rotating towards right (a) Unbalanced tree (b) Balanced tree

Similarly, the rotation can be performed towards left as shown in Fig. 10.14.

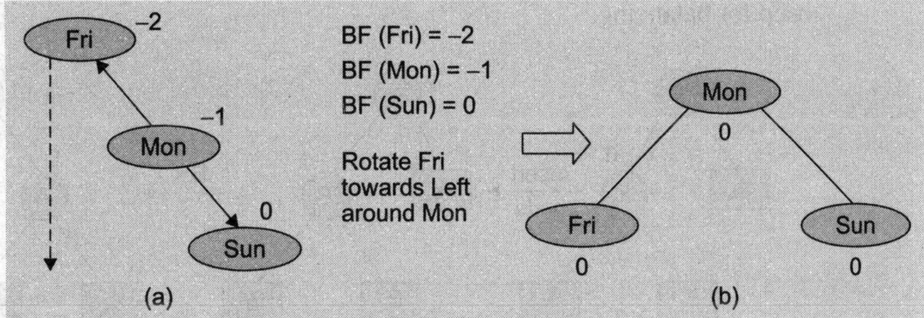

Fig. 10.14 Balancing a tree by rotating towards left (a) Unbalanced tree (b) Balanced tree

Let X be an inserted node and A be an unbalanced node after insertion whose BF = ±2. It depends on the scenario whether a rotation should be performed towards left or right. An unbalanced tree is balanced using one of the following four ways: (a) Left of left (LL) (b) Right of right (RR) (c) Left of right (LR) (d) Right of left (RL).

Case 1: LL (Left of Left) Consider the BST in Fig. 10.15. Note that the nodes drawn as squares represent subtrees.

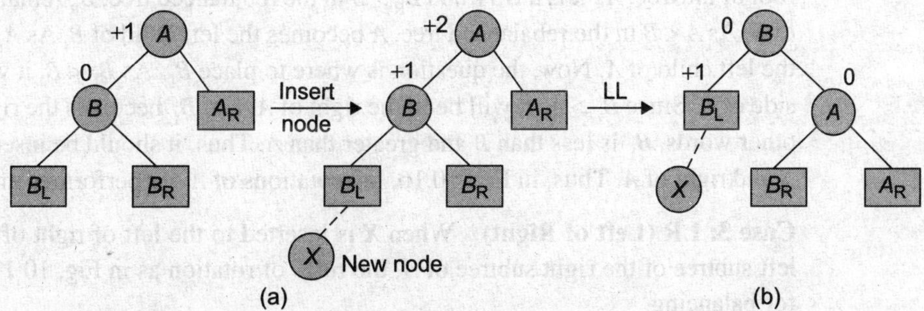

Fig. 10.15 Case LL for unbalanced tree due to insertion at left of left of a node (a) Unbalanced tree due to increase in height of B_L (b) Balanced tree

Suppose the node *A* in Fig. 10.15 becomes unbalanced when *X* is inserted to the left of left of *A*, that is, in the left subtree of the left subtree of *A*, then the rule of rotation as in Fig. 10.15 should be used for balancing.

As shown in Fig. 10.15, B_L is to the left of the left child of *A*. When the height of B_L increases, then node *A* becomes unbalanced. To rebalance the tree, node *B* becomes the root of the subtree. As it is a BST and $B_L < B$ in a rebalanced tree, B_L remains the left child of *B*. As $B < A$, node *A* becomes the right child of *B*. As $A < A_R$, A_R remains the right child of *A*. Now, the question is where to place B_R. Because $B_R > B$, it will be placed to the right of *B*. However, $B_R < A$, so it will be placed to the left of *A*. Hence, B_R becomes the left child of *A*. Thus, in Fig.10.15, right rotation of *A* is performed around the node *B*.

Case 2: RR (Right of Right) When *X* is inserted to the right of right of *A*, that is, in the right subtree of the right subtree of *A*, the rule of rotation as in Fig. 10.16 should be used for balancing.

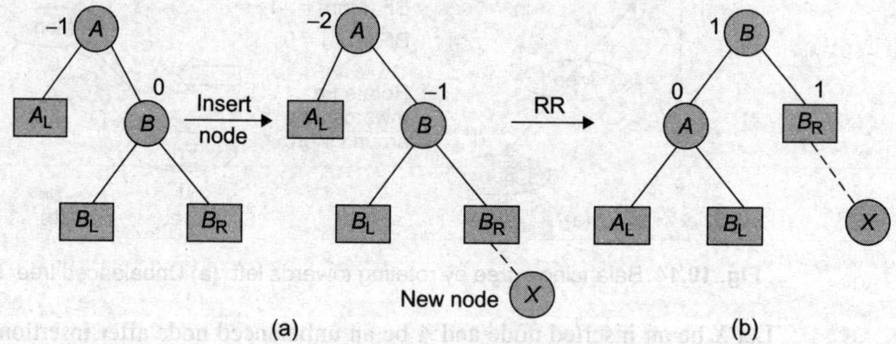

Fig. 10.16 Case RR for unbalanced tree due to insertion at right of right of a node (a) Unbalanced tree due to increase in height of B_R (b) Balanced tree

As shown in Fig. 10.16, B_R is to the right of the right child of *A*. When the height of B_R increases, then node *A* becomes unbalanced. To rebalance the tree, node *B* is made the root of the tree. As it is a BST and $B_R > B$ in the rebalanced tree, B_R remains the right child of *B*. As $A < B$ in the rebalanced tree, *A* becomes the left child of *B*. As $A_L < A$, A_L remains the left child of *A*. Now, the question is where to place B_L. As $B_L < B$, it will be on the left side of *B*. Since $B_L >$ A, it will be to the right of *A*, and B_L becomes the right child of *A*. In other words, B_L is less than *B* and greater than *A*. Thus, it should be inserted in the left of *B* and right of *A*. Thus, in Fig. 10.16, left rotations of *A* are performed around *B*.

Case 3: LR (Left of Right) When *X* is inserted to the left of right of *A*, that is, in the left subtree of the right subtree of *A*, the rules of rotation as in Fig. 10.17 should be used for balancing.

In Fig. 10.17, the case LR is depicted using three different scenarios. Scenario 1 depicts a simplified tree where *A* has no right child, *B* has no left child, and *C* has no

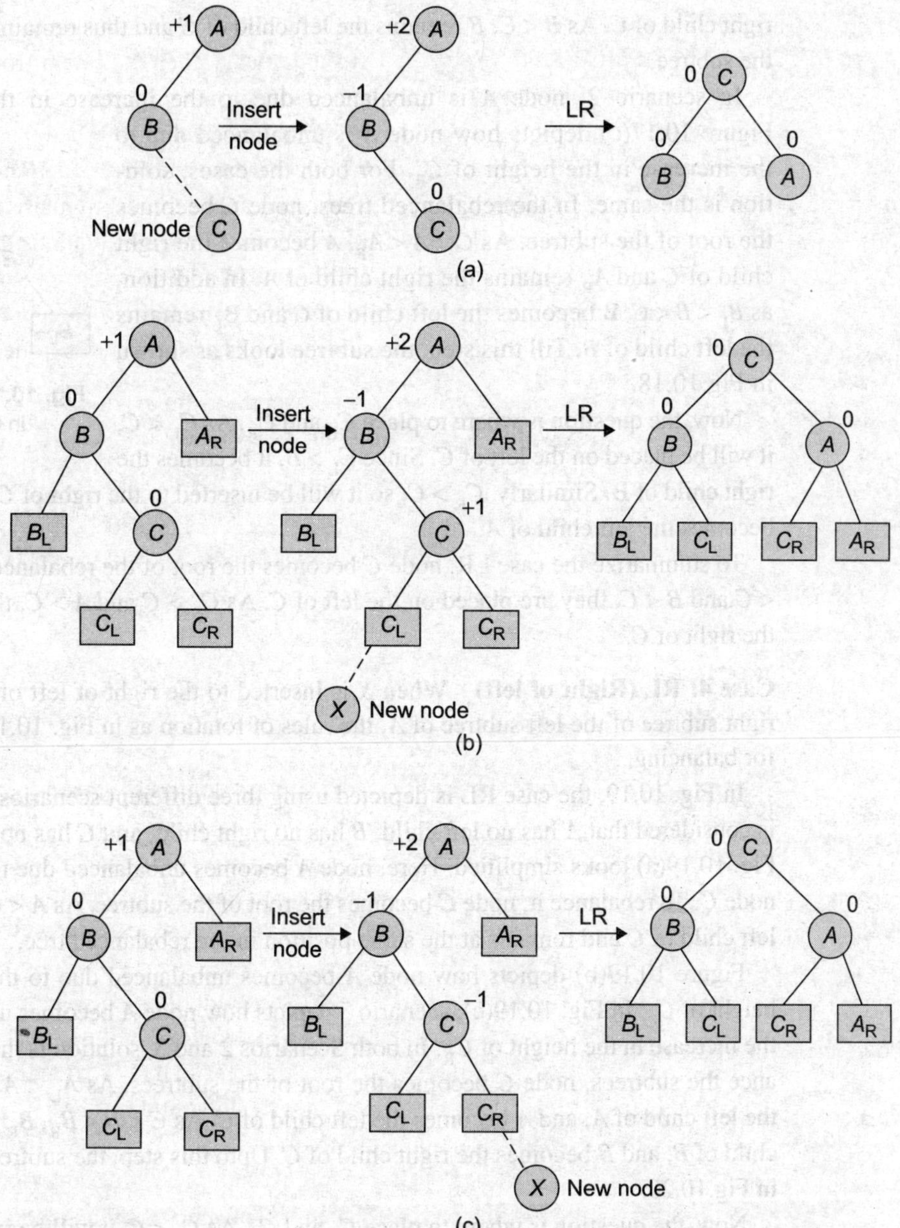

Fig. 10.17 Case LR for unbalanced tree due to insertion in left of right of a node (a) LR rotation (b) Scenario 2—LR rotation after insertion of new node (c) Scenario 3

children. Node A is unbalanced due to the insertion of C to the right of the left child of A. To rebalance the tree. C becomes the root of the subtree. As $C < A$, A becomes the right child of C. As $B < C$, B remains the left child of C and thus remains at its position in the subtree.

In scenario 2, node A is unbalanced due to the increase in the height of C_L. Figure 10.17(c) depicts how node A is unbalanced due to the increase in the height of C_R. For both the cases, solution is the same. In the rebalanced trees, node C becomes the root of the subtree. As $C < A < A_R$, A becomes the right child of C and A_R remains the right child of A. In addition, as $B_L < B < C$, B becomes the left child of C and B_L remains the left child of B. Till this step, the subtree looks as shown in Fig.10.18.

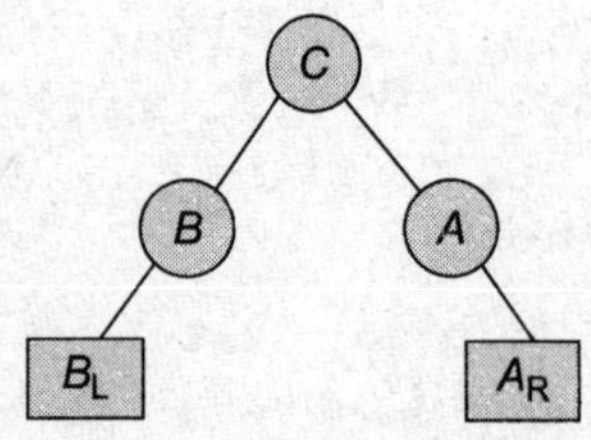

Fig. 10.18 Partial subtree in the LR case

Now, the question is where to place C_L and C_R. As $C_L < C$, it will be placed on the left of C. Since $C_L > B$, it becomes the right child of B. Similarly, $C_R > C$, so it will be inserted to the right of C. Since $C_R < A$, it becomes the left child of A.

To summarize the case LR, node C becomes the root of the rebalanced subtree. As $C_L < C$ and $B < C$, they are placed on the left of C. As $C_R > C$ and $A > C$, they are placed on the right of C.

Case 4: RL (Right of left) When X is inserted to the right of left of A, that is, in the right subtree of the left subtree of A, the rules of rotation as in Fig. 10.19 should be used for balancing.

In Fig. 10.19, the case RL is depicted using three different scenarios. In scenario 1, it is considered that A has no left child, B has no right child, and C has no children. Hence, Fig. 10.19(a) looks simplified. Here, node A becomes unbalanced due to the insertion of node C. To rebalance it, node C becomes the root of the subtree. As $A < C$, A becomes the left child of C and remains at the same position in the rebalanced tree.

Figure 10.19(b) depicts how node A becomes unbalanced due to the increase in the height of C_L. In Fig. 10.19(c), scenario 3 depicts how node A becomes unbalanced due to the increase in the height of C_R. In both Scenarios 2 and 3, solution is the same. To rebalance the subtrees, node C becomes the root of the subtrees. As $A_L < A < C$, A_L remains the left child of A, and A becomes the left child of C. As $C < B < B_R$, B_R remains the right child of B, and B becomes the right child of C. Upto this step, the subtree looks as shown in Fig.10.20.

Now, the question is where to place C_L and C_R. As $C_L < C$, it will be inserted to the left side of C. As $C_L > A$, it becomes the right child of A. Similarly, as $C_R > C$, C_R becomes the right child of C. However, $C_R < B$; hence, it becomes the left child of B.

To summarize the case RL, node C becomes the root of the rebalanced subtree. As $A < C$ and $C_L < C$, they are placed on the left of C. In addition, $B > C$ and $C_R > C$; hence, they are placed to the right of C.

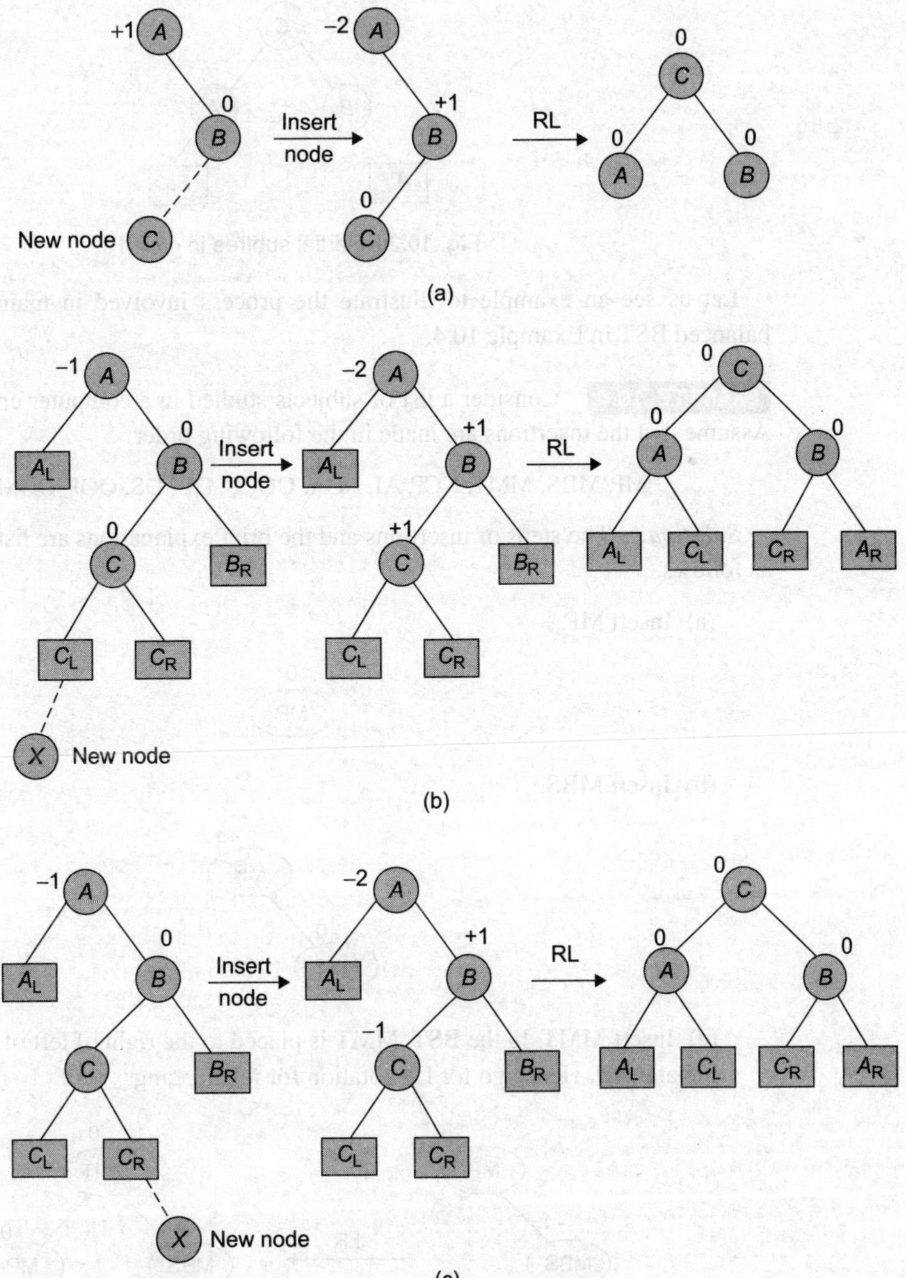

Fig.10.19 Case RL for unbalancing due to insertion in right of left of a node (a) Scenario 1 (b) Scenario 2 (c) Scenario 3

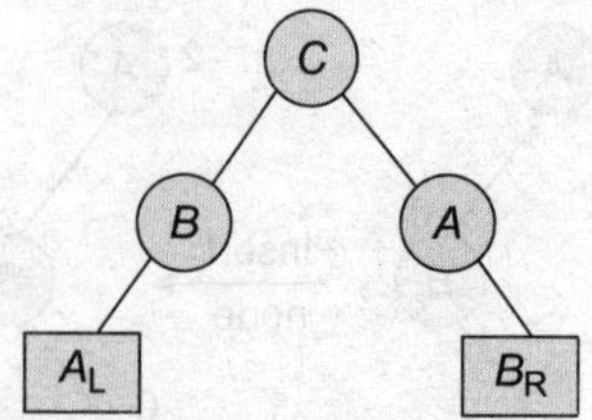

Fig. 10.20 Partial subtree in case RL

Let us see an example to illustrate the process involved in maintaining a height-balanced BST in Example 10.4.

EXAMPLE 10.4 Consider a list of subjects studied in a computer engineering course. Assume that the insertions are made in the following order:

MP, MBS, MMT, NCP, AI, ACA, OOCS, DC, DS, OOP, OOMD

Solution: The steps of insertions and the brief explanations are listed and illustrated as follows.

(a) Insert MP.

(b) Insert MBS.

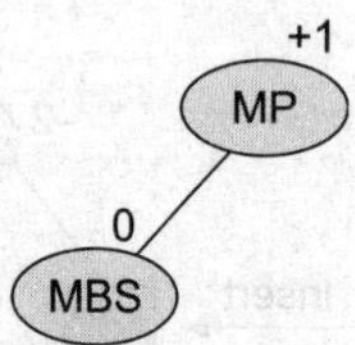

(c) Insert MMT. In the BST, MMT is placed to the right of left of MP, and MP is unbalanced. Hence go for LR rotation for rebalancing.

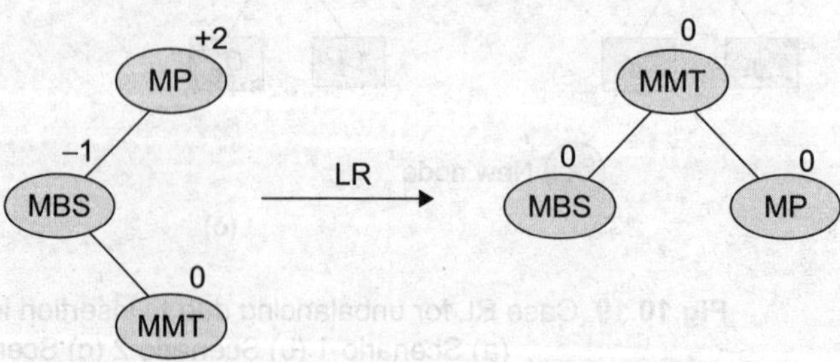

(d) Insert NCP.

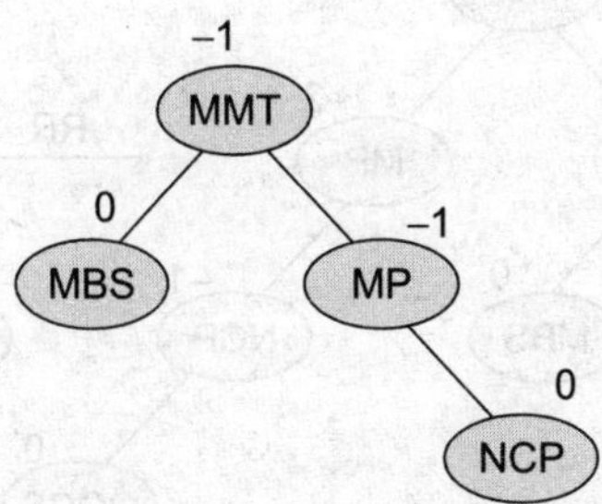

(e) Insert AI.

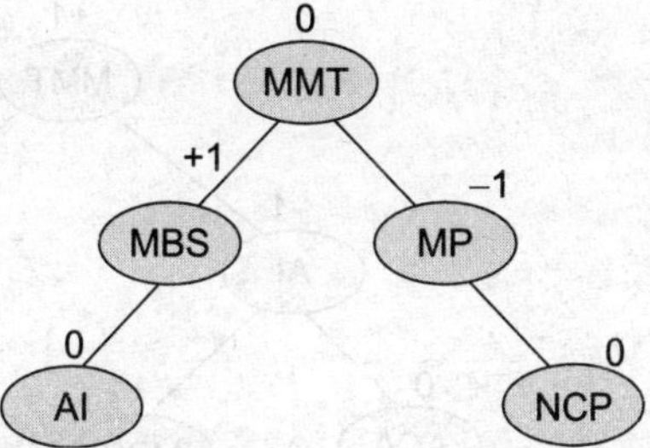

(f) Insert ACA. ACA is placed to the left of left of MBS, and MBS is unbalanced. Hence use LL rotation to rebalance it.

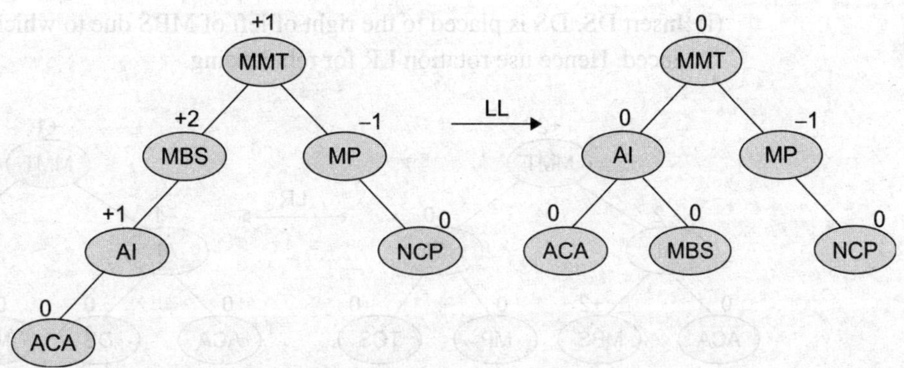

(g) Insert OOCS. OOCS is placed to the right of right of MP and now MP is unbalanced. Hence use RR rotation for rebalancing.

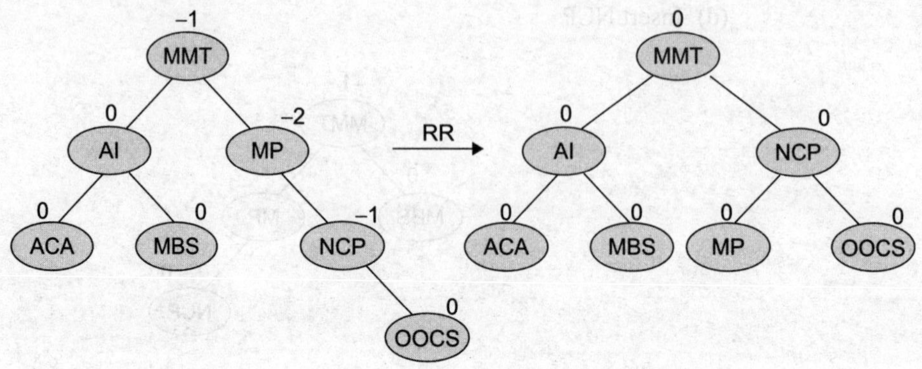

(h) Insert DC.

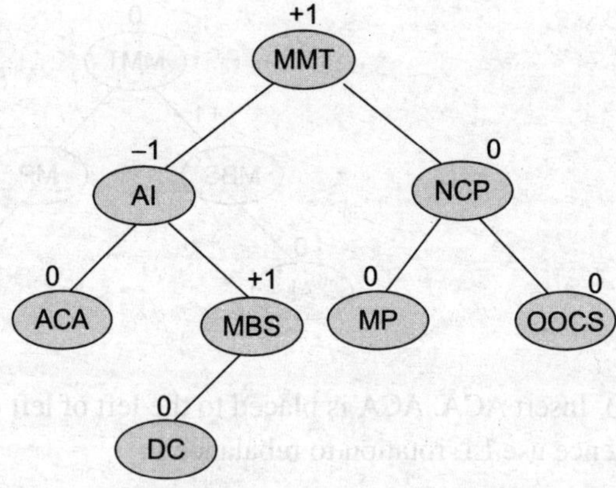

(i) Insert DS. DS is placed to the right of left of MBS due to which MBS is unbalanced. Hence use rotation LR for rebalancing.

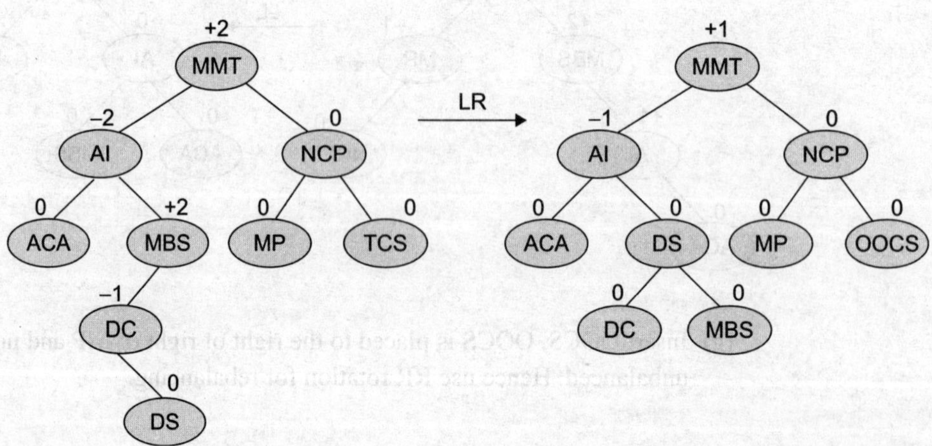

(j) Insert OOP.

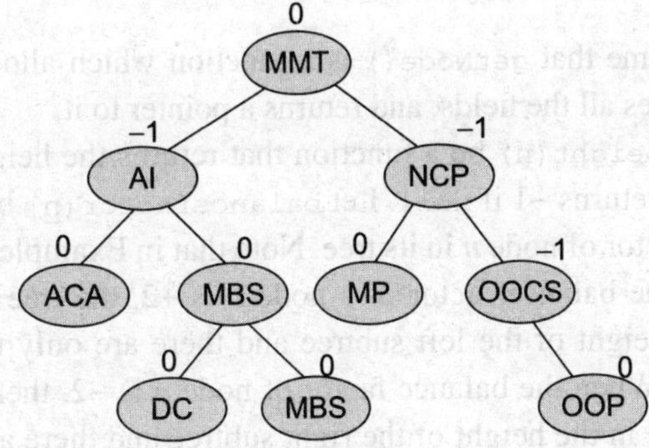

(k) Insert OOMD. OOMD is placed to the left of right of OOCS because of which OOCS is unbalanced. Hence use RL rotation for rebalancing.

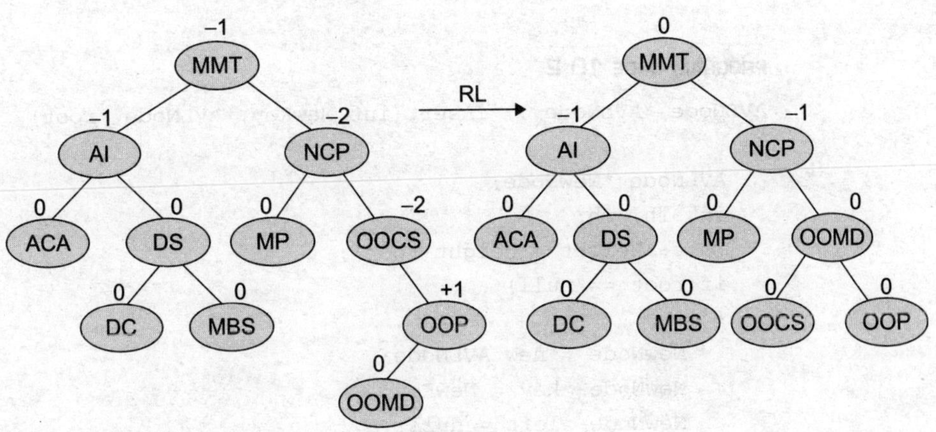

10.3.1 Implementation of AVL Technique

Example 10.4 demonstrates the working procedure to balance a BST. Let us write an algorithm for it. In general, a node in a tree stores data of and pointers to the left and right children. In an AVL tree, each node stores these three fields. To simplify the work, we can store the height of its subtree in each node. Hence, we will define each AVL tree node having as four fields.

Consider an AVL tree node that has the following structure:

```
class AVLNode
{
   KeyType key;
```

```
    AVLNode *Left, *Right;
    int height;
};
```

Assume that `getNode()` is a function which allocates memory for a new `AVLNode`, initializes all the fields, and returns a pointer to it.

Let `height(n)` be a function that returns the height of the subtree with root *n*, otherwise returns –1 if `null`. Let `balancefactor(n)` be a function which returns the balance factor of node *n* in its tree. Note that in Example 10.3 we considered the following: when the balance factor of a node *n* is +2, the tree is unbalanced due to the increase in the height of the left subtree and there are only two possibilities, either go for LL or LR. When the balance factor of node *n* is –2, then the tree is unbalanced due to the increase in the height of the right subtree and there are only two possibilities, either go for RR or RL.

Let us write a function `insert()` which will insert a given key in the AVL tree at its proper position, and rebalance the tree if needed using one of the four rotations: `LL`, `RR`, `LR`, `RL`. This is illustrated in Program Code 10.2.

PROGRAM CODE 10.2

```
AVLNode *AVLNode :: insert(int NewKey, AVLNode *root)
{
    AVLNode *NewNode;
    int lh, rh;
    root->height = height(root);
    if(root == null)
    {
        NewNode = new AVLNode;
        NewNode->key = NewKey;
        NewNode->left = null;
        NewNode->right = null;
        root = NewNode;
    }
    else
    {
        if(NewKey < root->key)
        {
            root->left = insert(NewKey,root->left);
            if(balancefactor(root) == 2)
            {
                // Tree is unbalanced due to increase
```

```
            // in height of left subtree
            if(NewKey < root->left->key)
            {
               cout << "\n LL rotation \n";
               root = LL(root);
            }
            else
            {
               cout << "\n LR rotation \n";
               root = LR(root);
            }
         }
      }
      else if(NewKey > root->key)
      {
         root->right = insert(NewKey, root->right);
         if(balancefactor(root) == -2)
         {
            // Tree is unbalanced due to increase
            // in height of right subtree
            if(NewKey > root->right->key)
            {
               cout << "\n RR rotation \n";
               root = RR(root);
            }
            else
            {
               cout << "\n RL rotation \n";
               root = RL(root);
            }
         }
      }
      else
         cout << "Duplicate key";
   }
   // After insertion, modify field height of the root
   root->height = height(root);
   return root;
}
```

We now know the four rules of rotation. Let us write a code for Case 1: LL. Consider the scenario as in Fig. 10.21 where Program Code 10.3 simulates its operations.

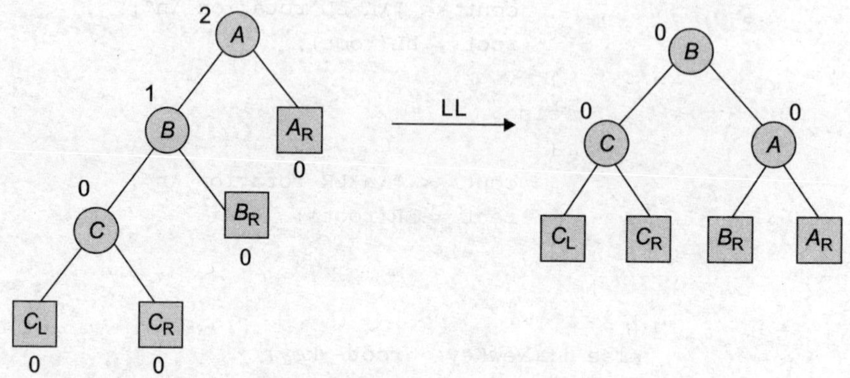

Fig. 10.21 Scenario for case LL

PROGRAM CODE 10.3

```
// rotation: Left
AVLNode *AVLNode :: Left(AVLNode *A)
//function is called with unbalanced node as a parameter
{
   AVLNode *B;
   B = A->right;
   A->right = B->left;
   B->left = A;
   A->height = height(A);
   B->height = height(B);
   return B;      // Set new root to B
}

// Rotation : Right
AVLNode *AVLNode::Right(AVLNode *A)
{
   AVLNode *B;
   B = A->left;
   A->left = B->right;
   B->right = A;
   A->height = height(A);
   B->height = height(B);
```

```
    return B;       // Set new root to B
}
// Case 1 of rotation : LL
AVLNode *AVLNode :: LL(AVLNode *root)
{
    root = Right(root);
    return root;
}

// Case 2 of rotation : RR
AVLNode *AVLNode :: RR(AVLNode *root)
{
    root = Left(root);
    return root;
}
```

Similarly, the function `RR()` can be written for Case 2. Program Code 10.3 shows the simulation of RR. Now, consider Case 3: LR (Fig. 10.22a) and Case 4: RL (Fig. 10.22b).

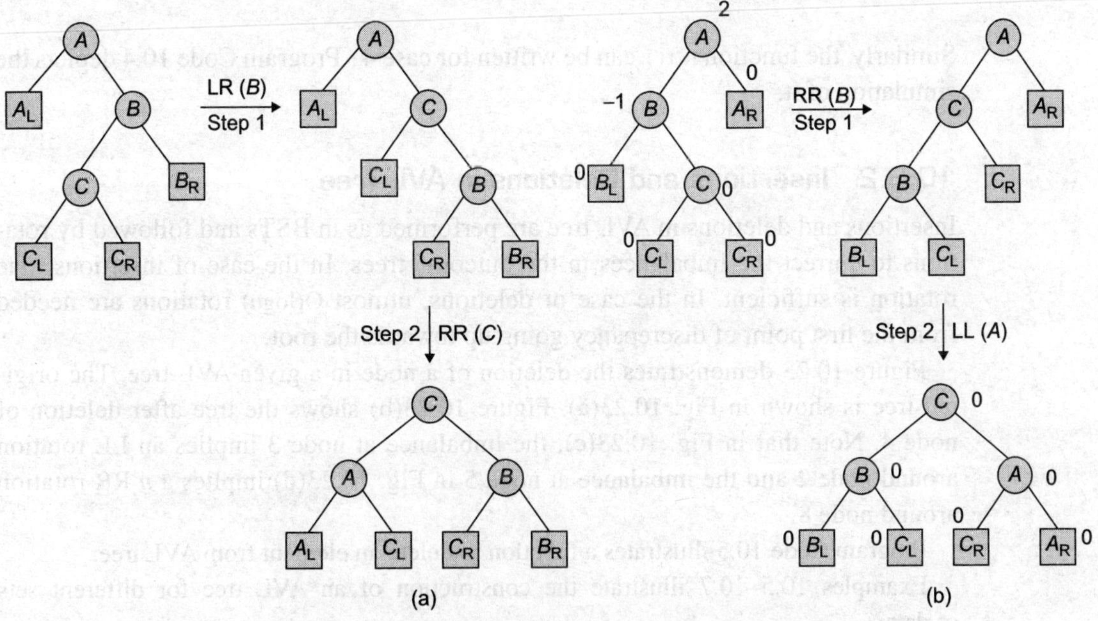

Fig. 10.22 Scenario for case (a) LR (b) RL

We can use the functions LL() and RR() to write the LR() and RL() functions as in Program Code 10.4.

PROGRAM CODE 10.4

```
// Case 3 of rotation:LR
AVLNode *AVLNode :: LR(AVLNode *root)
{
   root->left = Left(root->left);
   root = Right(root);
   return root;
}

//* Case 4 of rotation : RL
AVLNode *AVLnode :: RL(AVLNode *root)
{
   root->right = Right(root->right);
   root = Left(root);
   return root;
}
```

Similarly, the function RL() can be written for case 4. Program Code 10.4 depicts the simulation of it.

10.3.2 Insertions and Deletions in AVL Tree

Insertions and deletions in AVL tree are performed as in BSTs and followed by rotations to correct the imbalances in the outcome trees. In the case of insertions, one rotation is sufficient. In the case of deletions, utmost O(log*n*) rotations are needed from the first point of discrepancy going up towards the root.

Figure 10.23 demonstrates the deletion of a node in a given AVL tree. The original tree is shown in Fig. 10.23(a). Figure 10.23(b) shows the tree after deletion of node 4. Note that in Fig. 10.23(c), the imbalance at node 3 implies an LL rotation around node 2 and the imbalance at node 5 in Fig. 10.23(d) implies a *n* RR rotation around node 8.

Program Code 10.5 illustrates a function to delete an element from AVL tree.

Examples 10.5–10.7 illustrate the construction of an AVL tree for different sets of data.

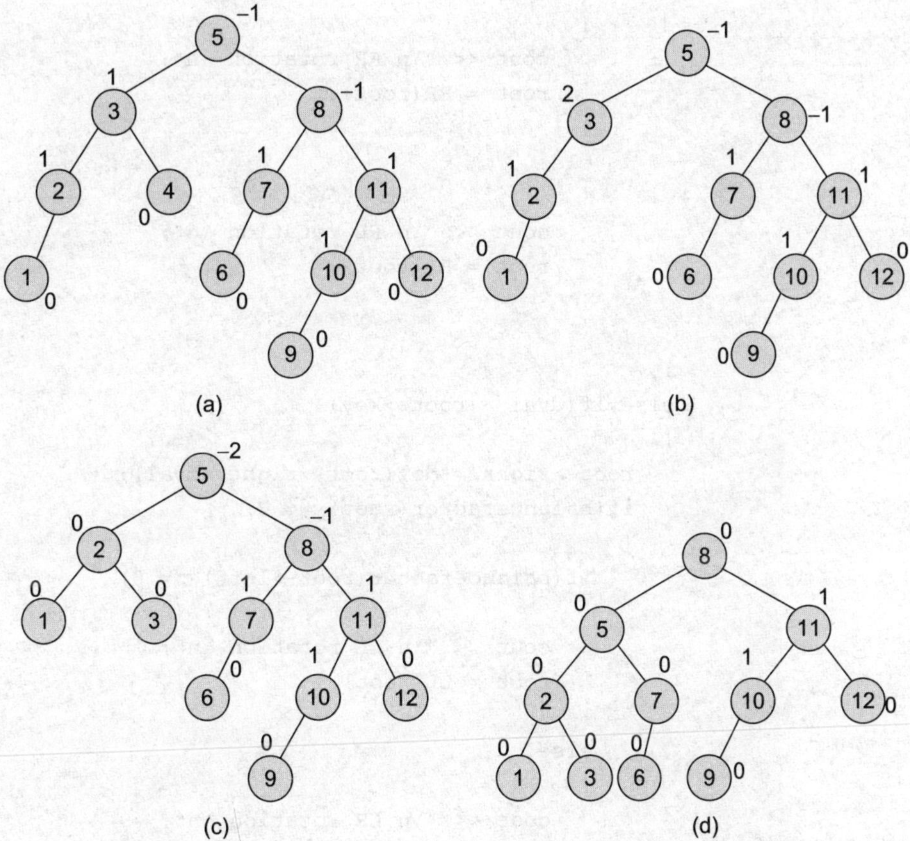

Fig. 10.23 Deletion of a node in AVL tree (a) Original tree (b) After deletion of 4 (*c*) LL rotation around node 2 (d) RR rotation around node 8

PROGRAM CODE 10.5

```
//Function to delete an element from AVL tree
AVLNode *AVLNode :: del(AVLNode *root,int dval)
{
   AVLNode *temp;
   if (root != null)
   {
      if (dval < root->key)
      {
         root->left = del(root->left,dval);
         if(balancefactor(root) == -2)
         {
            if(balancefactor(root->right) <= 0)
```

```
            {
               cout << "\n RR rotation \n";
               root = RR(root);
            }
            else
            {
               cout << "\n RL rotation \n";
               root = RL(root);
            }
         }
      }
      else if(dval > root->key)
      {
         root->right = del(root->right, dval);
         if(balancefactor(root) == 2)
         {
            if(balancefactor(root->left) >= 0)
            {
               cout << "\n LL rotation \n";
               root = LL(root);
            }
            else
            {
               cout << "\n LR rotation \n";
               root = LR(root);
            }
         }
      }
      else
      {
         if(root->right == null)      // No right tree
            return(root->left);
         else
         {
            // find leftmost of right
            temp = root->right;
            while(temp->left != null)
               temp = temp->left;
            root->key = temp->key;
            temp->right = del(root->right, temp->key);
            if(balancefactor(root) == 2)
            {
               if(balancefactor(root->left) >= 0)
```

```
                root = LL(root);
            else
                root = LR(root);
        }
    }
  }
}
else
    return null;
// Update height of root node
root->height = height(root);
return(root);
}
```

EXAMPLE 10.5 Construct an AVL tree for the following data:

30, 31, 32, 23, 22, 28, 24, 29, 26, 27, 34, 36

Solution Let us solve and show the balance factor and the type of rotation performed (if any) at each insertion. Table 10.7 demonstrates the same through the steps stated here.

Table 10.7 Construction of AVL tree for Example 10.5

Data inserted	AVL tree after insertion of BF	Rotation performed	Rebalanced AVL tree
30		→	No balancing required
31	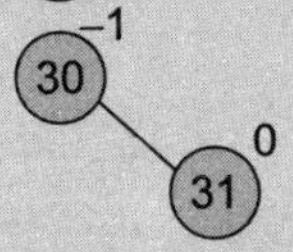	→	No balancing required
32	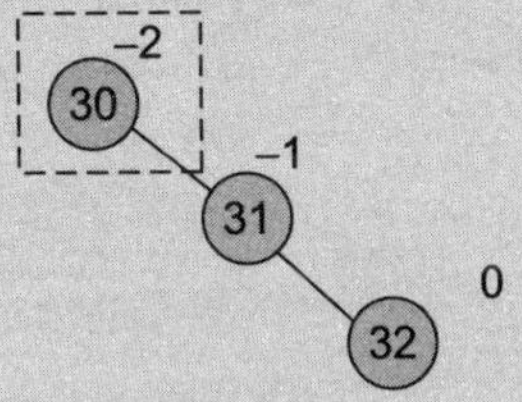	RR →	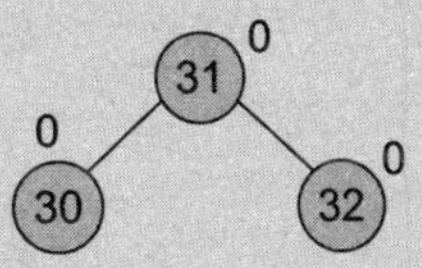
23	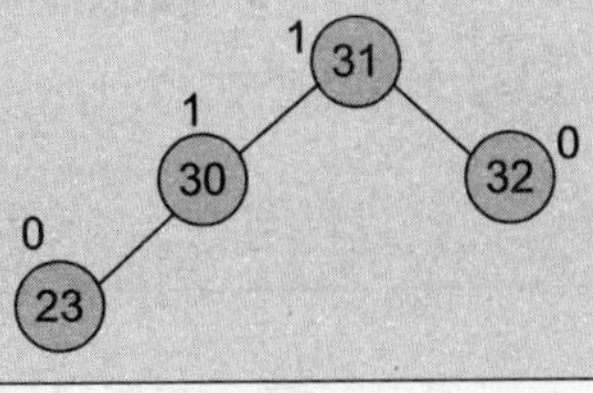	→	No balancing required

(Continued)

Table 10.7 (Continued)

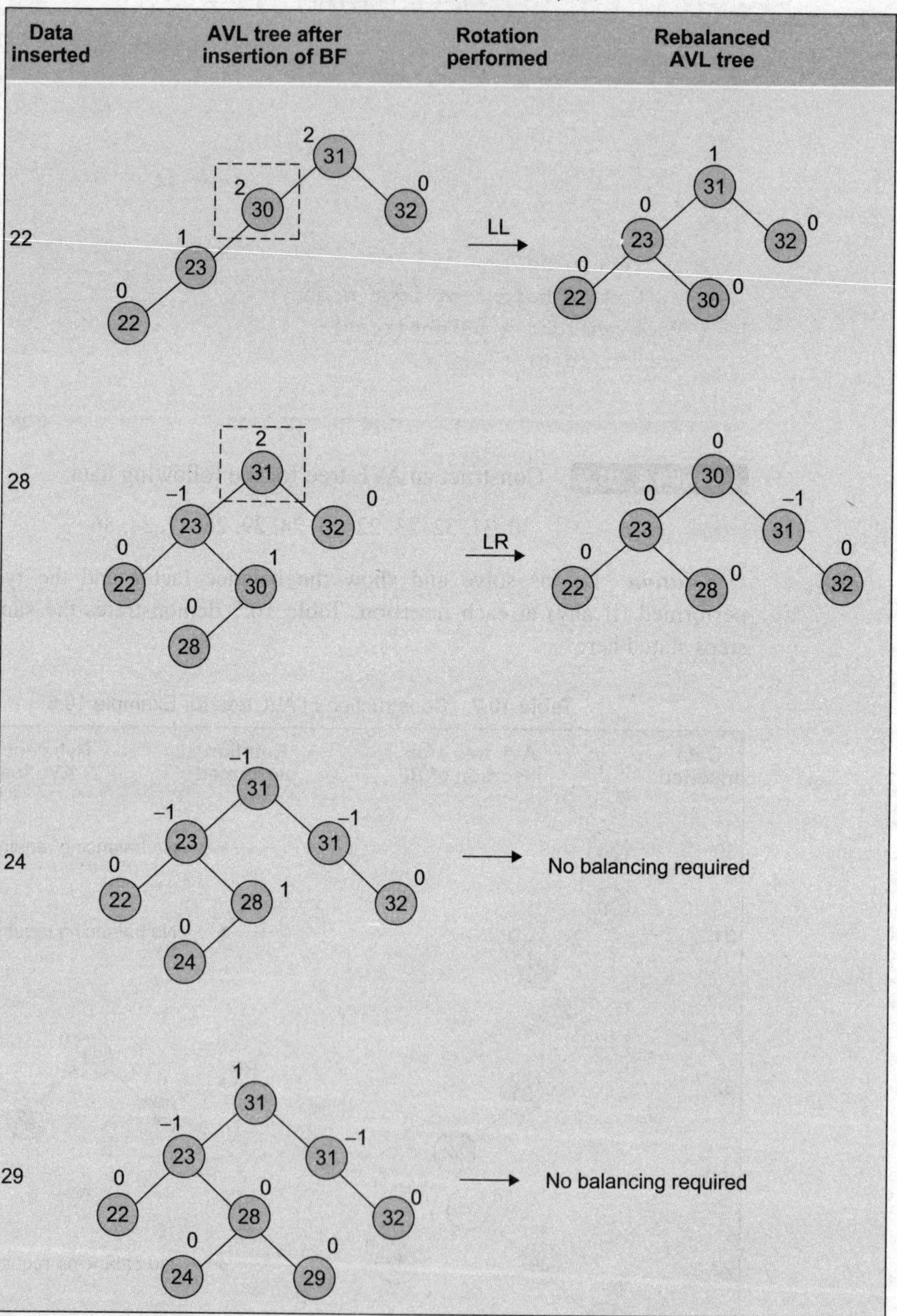

(Continued)

Table 10.7 (Continued)

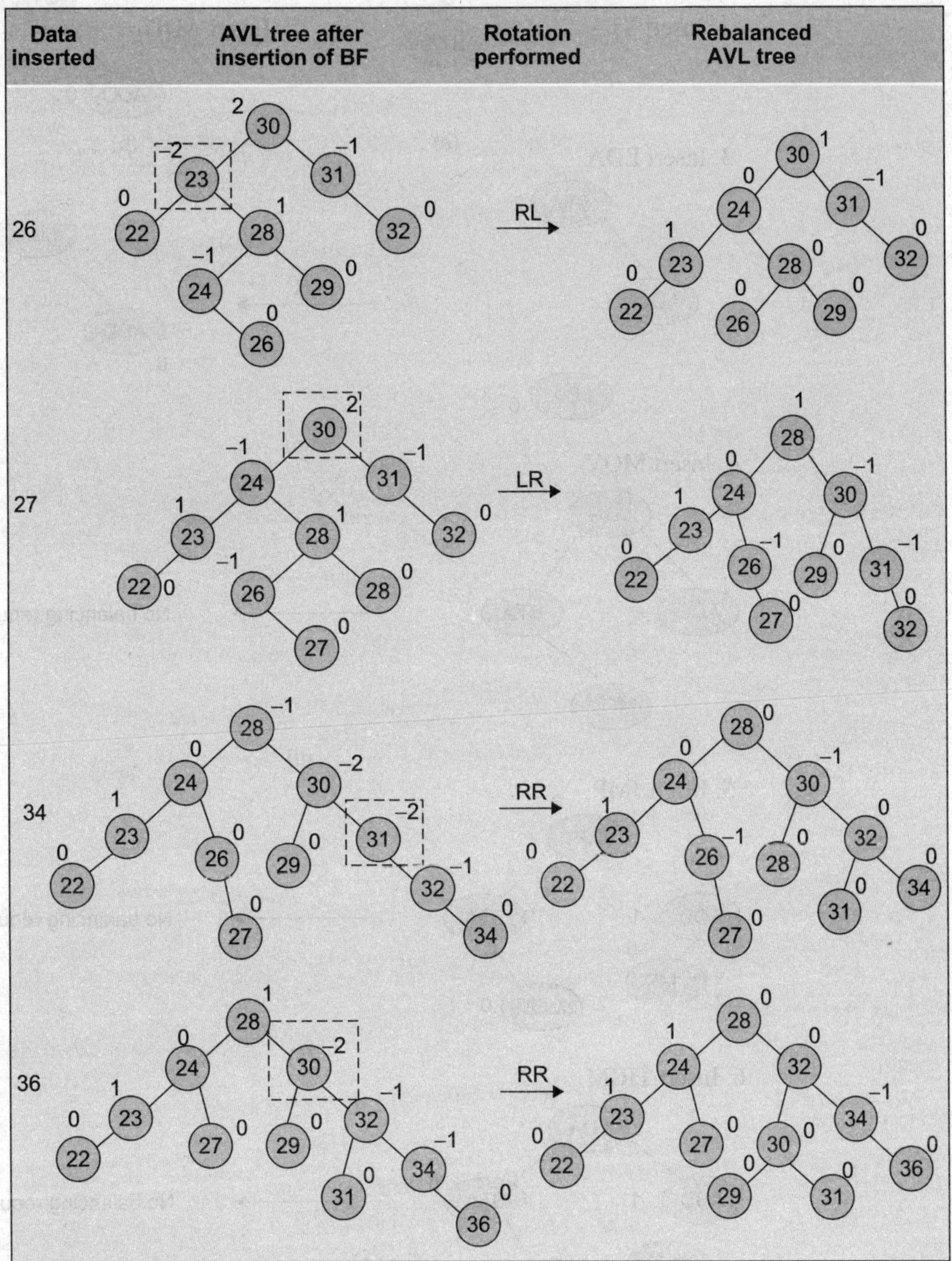

EXAMPLE 10.6 Construct an AVL tree for the following data:

STA, ADD, LDA, MOV, JMP, TRIM, XCHG, MVI, DIV, NOP, IN, JNZ

Solution Figure 10.24 demonstrates the steps involved to construct the AVL tree for the given sequence.

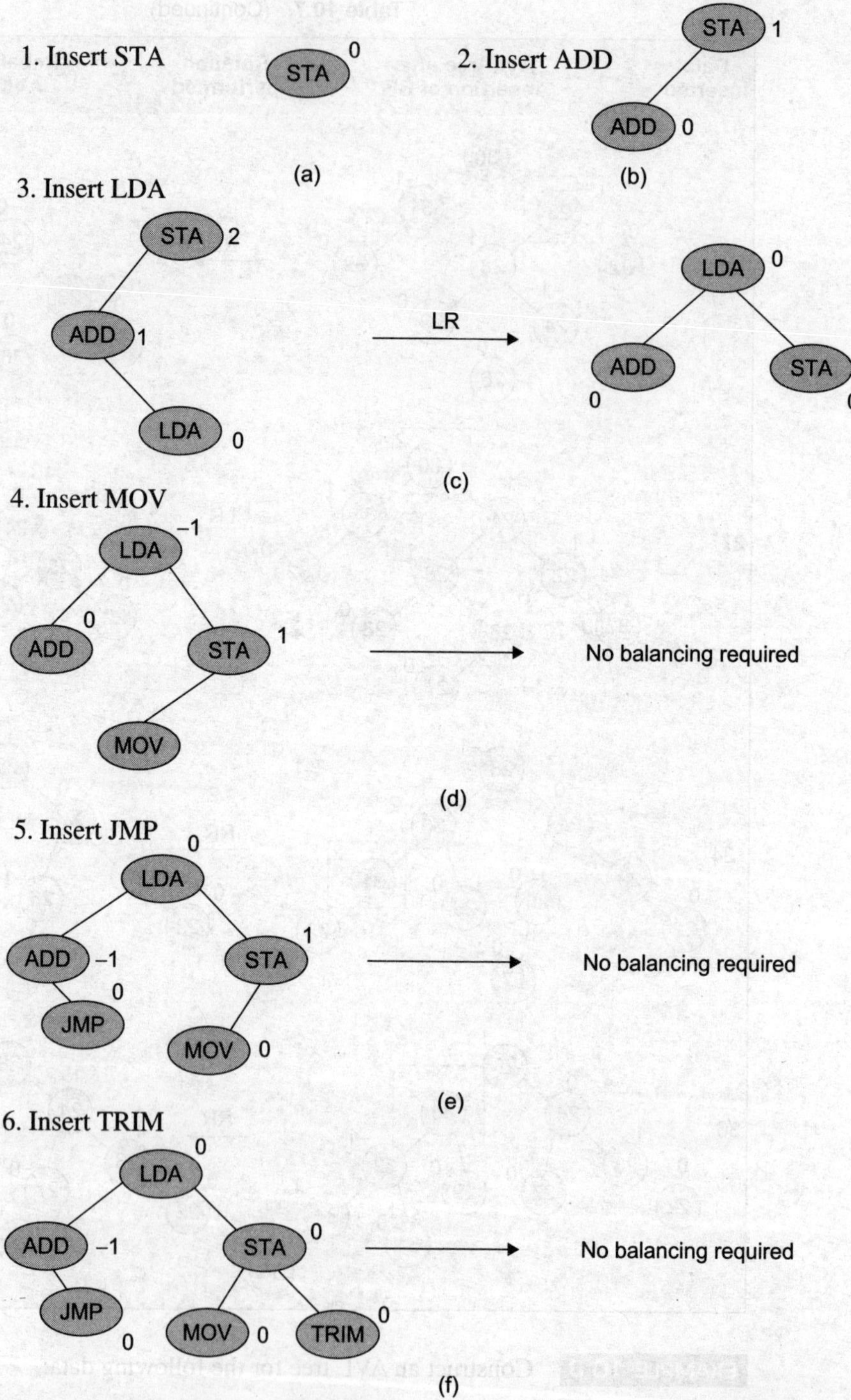

Fig.10.24 Construction of AVL tree for Example 10.6 (a) Key = STA (b) Key = ADD (c) Key = LDA (d) Key = MOV (e) Key = JMP (f) Key = TRIM

(Continued)

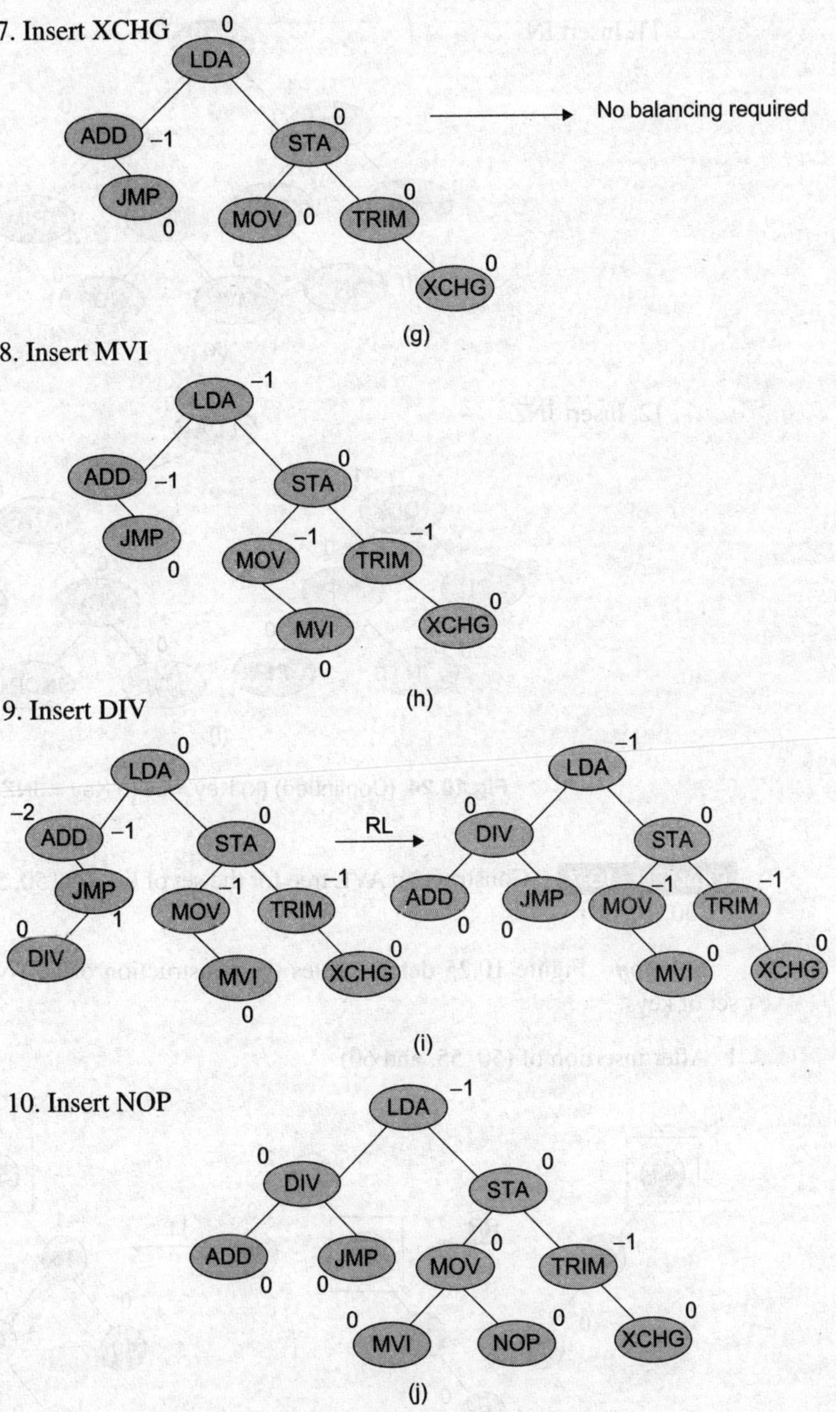

Fig.10.24 (Continued) (g) Key = XCHG (h) Key = MVI (i) Key = DIV (j) Key = NOP

(Continued)

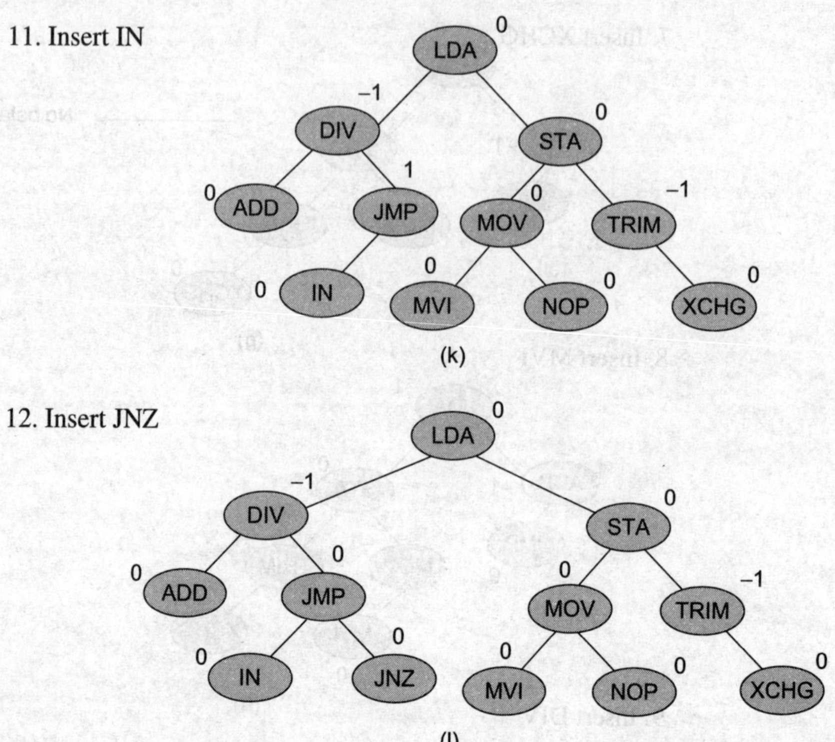

Fig.10.24 (Continued) (k) Key = IN (l) Key = JNZ

EXAMPLE 10.7 Construct an AVL tree for the set of keys = {50, 55, 60, 15, 10, 40, 20, 45, 30, 70, 80}.

Solution Figure 10.25 demonstrates the construction of an AVL tree for the given set of keys.

1. After insertion of (50, 55, and 60):

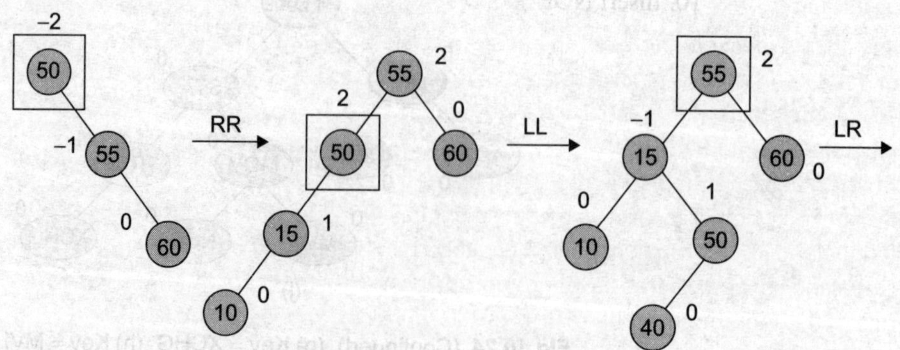

2. After insertion of (15, 10, 40, 20, 45, and 30):

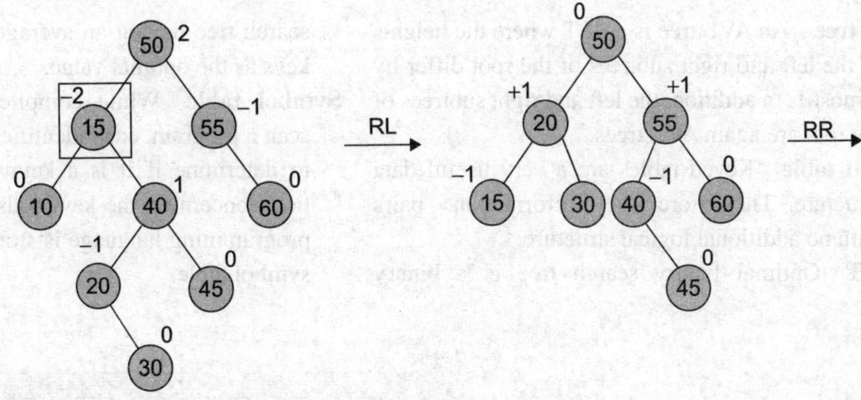

3. After insertion of 70 and 80:

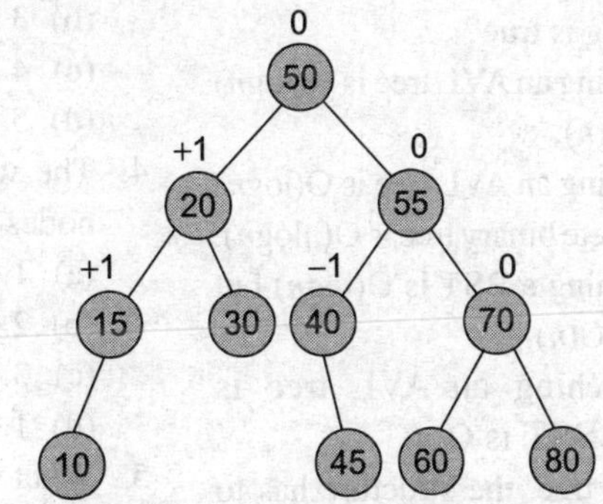

Fig.10.25 Construction of AVL tree for Example 10.7

RECAPITULATION

- Search trees are of great importance in an algorithm design.
- It is always desirable to keep the search time of each node in a tree minimal.
- OBST maintains the optimal average search time of all the nodes.
- In an AVL tree, after insertion of each node, it is checked whether the tree is balanced or not. If unbalanced, it is rebalanced immediately.
- Rebalancing of AVL tree is performed using one of the four rotations: LL, RR, LR, RL.
- AVL trees work by ensuring that all nodes of the left and right subtrees differ in height by utmost 1, which ensures that a tree cannot get too deep.
- Compilers use hash tables to keep track of the declared variables in a source code called as a symbol table.
- Unbalancing of an AVL tree due to insertion is removed in a single rotation. However, unbalancing due to the deletion may require multiple steps for balancing.

KEY TERMS

AVL tree An AVL tree is a BST where the heights of the left and right subtrees of the root differ by utmost 1. In addition, the left and right subtrees of the root are again AVL trees.

Keyed table Keyed tables are a very useful data structure. They store <key, information> pairs with no additional logical structure.

OBST Optimal binary search tree is a binary search tree having an average search time of all keys as the optimal value.

Symbol table While compilers and assemblers scan a program, each identifier must be examined to determine if it is a keyword. This information concerning the keywords and identifier in a programming language is stored in a table called symbol table.

EXERCISES

Multiple choice questions

1. Which of the following is true?
   (a) The cost of searching an AVL tree is O(log*n*) but that of a BST is O(*n*).
   (b) The cost of searching an AVL tree is O(log*n*) but that of a complete binary tree is O(*n*log*n*).
   (c) The cost of searching a BST is O(log*n*) but that of an AVL tree is O(*n*).
   (d) The cost of searching an AVL tree is O(log*n*) but that of a BST is O(*n*)
2. In the following AVL tree, the structure has to be balanced, so we have to rotate it

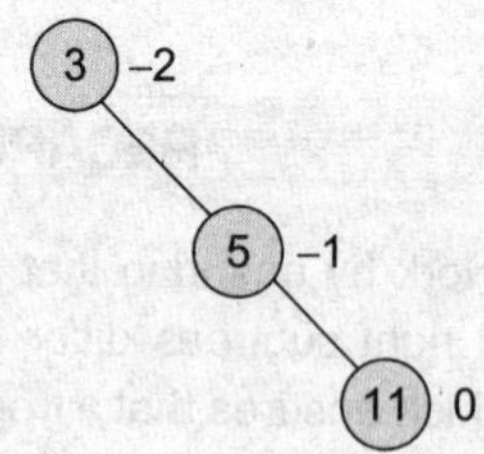

   (a) clockwise
   (b) counter clockwise
   (c) in both the directions
   (d) none of the above
3. What is the maximum height of an AVL tree with seven nodes?
   Note: Assume that the height of a tree with a single node is 0.
   (a) 2
   (b) 3
   (c) 4
   (d) 5
4. The worst case height of an AVL tree with *n* nodes is
   (a) $1.44\log(n+2)$
   (b) $2.44\log(n+2)$
   (c) $3.44\log(n+2)$
   (d) $1.44\log(n+2)$
5. What will be the time complexity for inserting a node into an AVL tree?
   (a) O(*n*)
   (b) O(log*n*)
   (c) *n*
   (d) n^2
6. Which of the following properties of OBST is true?
   (a) The left subtree of a node contains only the nodes with keys less than the node's key.
   (b) The right subtree of a node contains only the nodes with keys greater than the node's key.
   (c) Both the left and right subtrees must also be BSTs.
   (d) All of the above
7. To find the cost of the given OBST,

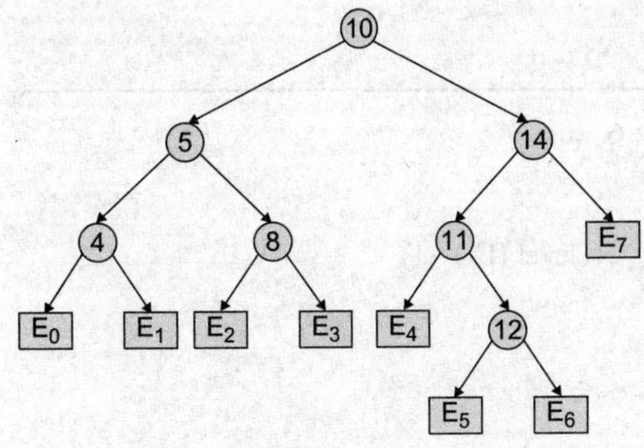

we have to consider

(a) successful search of internal nodes.
(b) unsuccessful search of internal nodes.
(c) successful search of internal nodes and unsuccessful search of external nodes.
(d) unsuccessful search of external nodes.

8. What is the time complexity of an OBST?
   (a) $O(n^3)$
   (b) $O(n\log n)$
   (c) $O(\log n)$
   (d) $O(n^2)$
9. The OBST is an example of
   (a) static symbol table
   (b) dynamic symbol table
   (c) all of the above
   (d) none of the above
10. Compute the total cost of the given OBST, if the probability of successful search is ($p1$, $p2$, $p3$) = (1/7, 1/7, 1/7) and the probability of unsuccessful search is ($q0$, $q1$, $q2$, $q3$) = (1/7, 1/7, 1/7, 1/7)

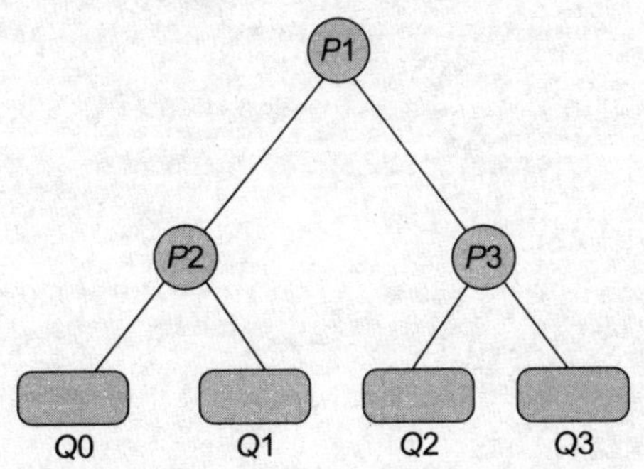

   (a) 2
   (b) 15/7
   (c) 16/7
   (d) 12/7

Review questions

1. A size-balanced binary tree in which for every node, the difference between the number of nodes in the left and right subtree is utmost 1. The distance of a node from the root is the length of path from the root to the node. The height of a binary tree is the maximum distance of a leaf node from the root.
   (a) Prove by using induction on h that a size-balanced binary tree of height h contains at least 2^n nodes.
   (b) In a fixed-balanced binary tree of height $h \leq 1$, how many nodes are at distance $h - 1$ from the root?
2. (a) In a binary tree, a full node is defined to be a node with two children. Use induction on the height of the binary tree to prove that the number of full nodes plus one is equal to the number of leaves.
   (b) Draw the min-heap that results from the insertion of the following elements in order into an initially empty min-heap: 7, 6, 5, 4, 2, 3, 1. Show the result after the deletion of the root of this heap.
3. Consider the following array and draw the heap that this array represents.

90	80	40	50	60	10	20	30

4. What is OBST? Derive the various equations to calculate the cost and weight of each node in OBST. Write the pseudo-C++ code for the OBST algorithm.
5. Insert the following numbers in an AVL tree and show at each stage the required transformations:
   50, 60, 108, 8, 0, 48, 32, 40
   Show the BF of each node throughout the process.
6. Compare OBST with AVL tree.
7. Give one example for each of the four types of rotations possible in an AVL tree.

Answers to multiple choice questions

1. (a) 2. (b) 3. (b) 4. (a) 5. (b) 6. (d)
7. (c) The expected cost of an optimal BST is

$$\sum_{n=1}^{n} P_i \times \text{level}(a_i) + \sum_{n=0}^{n} Q_i \times (\text{level}(E_i) - 1)$$

where,

Internal node: successful search, P*i*

External node: unsuccessful search, Q*i*

8. (a) Construction of OBST

```
for i = 0 to n do
    w_{i,i} = qi
    c_{i,i} = 0
    r_{i,i} = 0
for length = 1 to n do
    for i = 0 to n - length do
        j = i + length
        w_{i,j} = w_{i,j-1} + p_j + q_j
        m = value of k (with i < k ≤ j) which minimizes (c_{i,k-1} + c_{k,j})
        c_{i,j} = w_{i,j} + c_{i,m-1} + c_{m,j}
        r_{i,j} = m
        Leftson(r_{i,j}) = r_{i,m-1}
        Rightson(r_{i,j}) = r_{m,j}
```

The time complexity of this algorithm is $O(n^3)$.

9. (a) 10. (b) The formula to find the cost of OBST is as follows:

$$\sum_{n=1}^{n} P_i \times \text{level}(a_i) + \sum_{n=0}^{n} Q_i \times (\text{level}(E_i) - 1)$$

Hence, cost(tree) = [(1/7 × 1) + (2 × 1/7 + 2 × 1/7)] + [1/7 × (3 – 1) + 1/7 × (3 – 1) + 1/7 × (3 – 1) + 1/7 × (3 – 1)]

= 5/7 + 8/7

= 13/7

11 HASHING

OBJECTIVES

After completing this chapter, the reader will be able to understand the following:

- Use of hashing techniques that support very fast retrieval via a key
- Factors that affect the performance of hashing
- Collision resolution strategies

One of the most frequent and prolonged tasks in computer science is searching for a particular data record from a large amount of data. The expectation is to retrieve data within average constant time. Searching is the process of finding the location of the target among the list of objects using a key. *Key* is a field or combination of more than one field within the data record. It is used to uniquely identify the record and also to manage its access and usage.

We have discussed search techniques in Chapter 9. In both sequential and binary searches as well as in Fibonacci search, we need to perform many operations to locate the target data. The operations include computing the search index, comparing the target with the record at that index, and modifying the index again if not found. In an ideal situation, we expect the target to be searched in one or fewer attempts. One way to achieve this is that we should know (or should be able to obtain) the address of the record where it is stored. *Hashing* is a method of directly computing the address of the record with the help of a key by using a suitable mathematical function called the *hash function*. A *hash table* is an array-based structure used to store <key, information> pairs. In this chapter, we will learn about hashing, hash functions, and other related aspects.

11.1 INTRODUCTION

For many applications, we want to retrieve the target in one access or in constant average time. Hashing is finding an address where the data is to be stored or to locate using a key with the help of an arithmetic function. One of the applications this finds use in is language translators, such as assemblers and compilers. The compiler keeps all the variables used in a program in a symbol table, where the key is an arbitrary character string that corresponds to the identifiers in the language. The operations performed on a symbol table are those of dictionary operations. A hash table is an effective data structure for implementing it. There are many such applications. Let us consider an array implementation for better understanding. The concept can be easily extended to other structures such as files.

Consider an example of an institute that has many departments in it. There is a central library and a departmental library for each department. Suppose we want to make a table of books for the departmental library using their unique identification number, say Accession No (Acc_No) as a key. A set of departmental library books is a subset of central library books, and the set of central library books is large enough. As the data is large enough, the range of Acc_No is 0000001 to 9999999; with 10^7 (may be minus one as we may omit 0000000) possible values. Let us assume that the departmental library has 20,000 books. Let us use an array for storing the book records and call it as Array_Book[]. As these books are from the central library, their Acc_No population is greater than the size of the storage area.

One way to access the book using one attempt is to store a book with Acc_No at (Acc_No)th location of Array_Book[] and for that we need an array of size 1,000,000. Instead of taking an array of size 1,000,000, we can use array of size just 20,000 and use the function $f(x)$ to map the numbers in the domain [0, …, 9,999,999] to the range [0, …, 19,999]. Figure 11.1 represents such mapping.

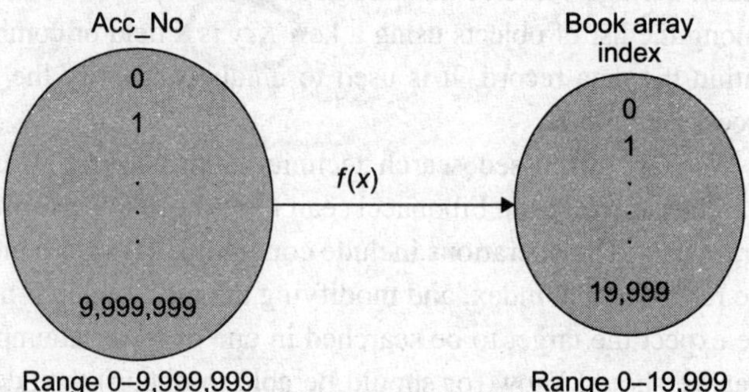

Fig. 11.1 Hash function

The function $f(x)$ will take Acc_No and return the indices where the book record is to be stored in the array and is called the *hash function*. Now each departmental book's address, which is an index in the table named Array_book, is calculated while storing as well as retrieving it. This concept of hashing is shown in Fig. 11.2.

Hash functions transform a key into an address. Hashing is a technique used for storing and retrieving information associated with it that makes use of the individual characters or digits in the key itself.

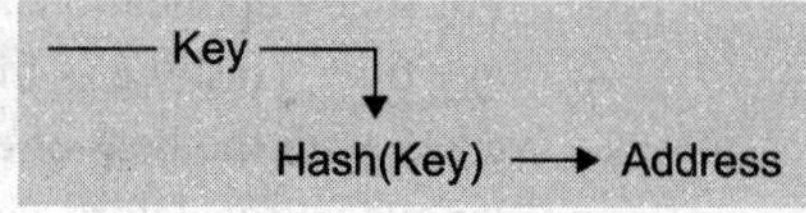

Fig. 11.2 Hashing concept

The resulting address is used as the basis for storing and retrieving records and this address is called the *home address* of the record. For an array to store a record in a hash table, the hash function is applied to the key of the record being stored, returning an index within the range of the hash table. The item is then stored in the table at that index position. To retrieve an item from a hash table, the same scheme that was used to store the record is followed.

Hashing is similar to indexing as it involves associating a key with a relative record address. However, it differs from indexing in the following two important ways:

1. With hashing, the address generated appears to be random—there is no obvious connection between the key and the location of the corresponding record, even though the key is used to determine the location of the record. For this reason, hashing is sometimes referred to as *randomizing*.
2. With hashing, two different keys may be transformed to the same address, so two records may be sent to the same place in a file. When this occurs, it is called a *collision* and some means must be found to deal with it. The two or more records that result in the same home address are known as *synonyms*.

11.2 KEY TERMS AND ISSUES

A problem arises, however, when the hash function returns the same value when applied to two different keys. To handle the situation, where two records need to be hashed to the same address we can implement a table structure, so as to have a room for two or more members at the same index positions. However, what happens if a third key hashes to the same index value? Before discussing such issues let us see some terms associated with hashing and the hash table:

Hash table Hash table is an array [0 to Max – 1] of size Max.

Hash function Hash function is one that maps a key in the range [0 to Max – 1], the result of which is used as an index (or address) in the hash table for storing and retrieving records. One more way to define a hash function is as the function that transforms a key into an address. The address generated by a hashing function is called the *home address*. All home addresses refer to a particular area of the memory called the *prime area.*

Bucket A bucket is an index position in a hash table that can store more than one record. Tables 11.1 and 11.2 show a bucket of size 1 and size 2, respectively. When the same index is mapped

Table 11.1 Table with bucket size 1

Index	Bucket of size 1
0	Alka
1	Bindu
2	
3	Deven
4	Ekta
5	
6	Govind
⋮	⋮
13	Monika
⋮	⋮
18	Sharmila
⋮	⋮
25	Zinat

with two keys, both the records are stored in the same bucket. The assumption is that the buckets are equal in size.

Consider the following example. Suppose we want to store 5 records with the key of each record as the person's name. The key can be hashed by taking the address from the ASCII representations of the first characters of the name. The table is of size 26, i.e., one bucket for each alphabet with size 2 (Table 11.2a) or size 3 (Table 11.2b).

Table 11.2(a) Table with bucket size 2

Index	Bucket of size 2	
0	Alka	Abhay
1	Bindu	Babali
2		
3	Deepa	Deven
4	Ekta	Esha
5		
6	Govind	Gopal
⋮	⋮	⋮
13	Monika	Meera
⋮	⋮	⋮
18	Sharmila	Sindhu
⋮	⋮	⋮
25	Zinat	Ziya

Table 11.2(b) Table with bucket size 3

Index	Bucket of size 3		
0	Alka	Abhay	Asmita
1	Bindu	Babali	Bhanu
2			
3	Deepa	Deven	Deepak
4	Ekta	Esha	Eshwar
5			
6	Govind	Gopal	Gautam
⋮	⋮	⋮	⋮
13	Monika	Meera	Manisha
⋮	⋮	⋮	⋮
18	Sharmila	Sindhu	Shilpi
⋮	⋮	⋮	⋮
25	Zinat	Ziya	Zeba

Probe Each action of address calculation and check for success is called as a *probe.*

Collision The result of two keys hashing into the same address is called collision.

Synonym Keys that hash to the same address are called synonyms.

Overflow The result of many keys hashing to a single address and lack of room in the bucket is known as an overflow. Collision and overflow are synonymous when the bucket is of size 1.

Open or external hashing When we allow records to be stored in potentially unlimited space, it is called as *open* or *external hashing*.

Closed or internal hashing When we use fixed space for storage eventually limiting the number of records to be stored, it is called as *closed* or *internal hashing*.

Hash function Hash function is an arithmetic function that transforms a key into an address which is used for storing and retrieving a record.

Perfect hash function The hash function that transforms different keys into different addresses is called a *perfect hash function*. The worth of a hash function depends on how well it avoids collision.

Load density The maximum storage capacity, that is, the maximum number of records that can be accommodated, is called as *loading density*.

Full table A full table is one in which all locations are occupied. Owing to the characteristics of hash functions, there are always empty locations, rather a hash function should not allow the table to get filled in more than 75%.

Load factor Load factor is the number of records stored in a table divided by the maximum capacity of the table, expressed in terms of percentage.

Rehashing Rehashing is with respect to closed hashing. When we try to store the record with Key1 at the bucket position Hash(Key1) and find that it already holds a record, it is collision situation. To handle collision, we use a strategy to choose a sequence of alternative locations Hash1(Key1), Hash2(Key1), and so on within the bucket table so as to place the record with Key1. This is known as *rehashing*.

Issues in hashing In case of collision, there are two main issues to be considered:

1. We need a good hashing function that minimizes the number of collisions.
2. We want an efficient collision resolution strategy so as to store or locate synonyms.

Let us learn about these two issues and techniques to resolve them in Sections 11.3 and 11.4, respectively.

11.3 HASH FUNCTIONS

To store a record in a hash table, a hash function is applied to the key of the record being stored, returning an index within the range of the hash table. The record is stored at that index position, if it is empty. With direct addressing, a record with key K is stored in slot K. With hashing, this record is stored at the location Hash(K), where Hash(K) is the function. The hash function Hash(K) is used to compute the slot for the key K. Let us discuss some issues regarding the design of good hash functions and also study the schemes for their creation.

11.3.1 Good Hash Function

The average performance of hashing depends on how the hash function distributes the set of keys among the slots. An assumption is that any given record is equally likely to hash into any of the slots, independent of whether any other record has been already hashed to it or not. This assumption is known as *simple uniform hashing*. A good hash function is one which satisfies this assumption.

If the probability that a key 'Key' occurs in our collection is P(Key), and for M slots in our hash table, a uniform hashing function, Hash(Key), should ensure that for $0 \leq \text{Key} \leq M - 1$, Σ P(Key) = 1, are all equiprobable with probability $1/M$. The hash function should ensure that they are hashed to different locations.

Sometimes, this is easy to ensure. For example, if the keys are randomly distributed in [0 ... r], with 0 to $M - 1$ locations then, Hash(Key) = floor(($M \times$ Key)/r) will provide uniform hashing.

Features of a Good Hashing Function

1. Addresses generated from the key are uniformly and randomly distributed.
2. Small variations in the value of the key will cause large variations in the record addresses to distribute records (with similar keys) evenly.
3. The hashing function must minimize the occurrence of collision.

There are many methods of implementing hash functions, let us discuss a few of them.

11.3.2 Division Method

One of the required features of the hash function is that the resultant index must be within the table index range. One simple choice for a hash function is to use the modulus division indicated as MOD (the operator % in C/C++). The function MOD returns the remainder when the first parameter is divided by the second parameter. The result is negative only if the first parameter is negative and the parameters must be integers. The function returns an integer. If any parameter is NULL, the result is NULL.

$$\text{Hash(Key)} = \text{Key} \% M$$

Key is divided by some number M, and the remainder is used as the hash address. This function gives the bucket addresses in the range of 0 through ($M - 1$), so the hash table should at least be of size M. The choice of M is critical. While using this method, we usually avoid certain values of M. Binary keys of length in powers of two are usually avoided. A good choice of M is that it should be a prime number greater than 20.

11.3.3 Multiplication Method

Another hash function that has been widely used in many applications is the multiplication method. The multiplication method works as follows:

1. Multiply the key 'Key' by a constant A in the range $0 < A < 1$ and extract the fractional part of Key $\times A$.
2. Then multiply this value by M and take the floor of the result.

$$\text{Hash(Key)} = \lfloor M \times ((\text{Key} \times A) \text{ MOD } 1)\rfloor,$$

where Key $\times A$ MOD 1 is the fractional part of Key $\times A$,
that is, Key $\times A - \lfloor \text{Key} \times A \rfloor$ and one of the commonly used values of A = (sqrt(5) – 1/2 = 0.6180339887).

An advantage of the multiplication method is that the value of M is not critical. We typically choose it $M = 2^p$ for some integer p, since we can then easily implement the function in any programming language as:

1. Choose $M = 2^p$.
2. Multiply the ω bits of Key by floor ($A \times 2\omega$) to obtain a 2ω bit product.
3. Extract the p most significant bits of the lower half of this product as address.

Note that we have used the function *floor*; *floor* and *ceil* are the commonly used math functions available in the library of almost all programming languages. These functions map a real number to the largest preceding or the smallest following integer, respectively. More precisely, floor(x) = $\lfloor x \rfloor$ is the largest integer not greater than x and ceil(x) = $\lceil x \rceil$ is the smallest integer not less than x.

11.3.4 Extraction Method

When a portion of the key is used for address calculation, the technique is called as the *extraction method.* In digit extraction, a few digits are selected, extracted from the key and are used as the address. For example, if the book accession number is of six digits and we require an address of 3 digits, then we can select the odd number digits—first, third, and fifth—which can be used as the address for the hash table.

For example, Table 11.3 shows the keys with their respective hashed addresses using digit extraction.

Table 11.3 Keys and addresses using digit extraction

Key	Hashed address
345678	357
234137	243
952671	927

Another way is to extract the first two and the last one or two digits. For example, for key 345678, the address is 3478 if the first two and the last two digits are extracted or 348 if the first two and the last digit are extracted.

If the portion of the key is carefully selected, it can be sufficient for hashing, provided the remaining portion distinguishes the keys in an insufficient way.

11.3.5 Mid-square Hashing

Mid-square hashing suggests to take the square of the key and extract the middle digits of the squared key as the address. The difficulty is when the key is large. As the entire key participates in the address calculation, if the key is large, then it is very difficult to store its square as it should not exceed the storage limit. So mid-square is used when the key size is less than or equal to 4 digits. For example, Table 11.4 shows the keys with their hashed addresses. If the key is a string, it has to be preprocessed to produce a number.

Table 11.4 Keys and addresses using mid-square

Key	Square	Hashed address
2341	5480281	802
1671	2792241	922

The difficulty of storing the squares of larger numbers can be overcome if we use fewer digits of the key (instead of the whole key) for squaring. If the key is large, we can select a portion of the key and square it. For example, Table 11.5 gives the keys and the squares of the first three digits with their hashed addresses.

Table 11.5 Keys and addresses using squares of fewer digits

Key	Square	Hashed address
234137	$234 \times 234 = 54756$	475
567187	$567 \times 567 = 321489$	148

11.3.6 Folding Technique

In this technique, the key is subdivided into subparts that are combined or folded and then combined to form the address. For a key with digits, we can subdivide the digits into three parts, add them up, and use the result as an address. Here the size of the subparts of the key is the same as that of the address.

There are two types of folding methods:

1. *Fold shift*—Key value is divided into several parts of the size of the address. Left, right, and middle parts are added.
2. *Fold boundary*—Key value is divided into parts of the size of the address. Left and right parts are folded on the fixed boundary between them and the centre part.

For example, if the key is 987654321, it is understood as

Left 987 Centre 654 Right 321

For fold shift, the sum is $987 + 654 + 321 = 1962$. Now discard digit 1 and the address is 962. For fold boundary, sum of the reverse of the parts is $789 + 456 + 123 = 1368$. Discard digit 1 and the address is 368.

11.3.7 Rotation

When the keys are serial, they vary only in the last digit and this leads to the creation of synonyms. Rotating the key would minimize this problem. This method is used along with other methods. Here, the key is rotated right by one digit and then folding technique is used to avoid synonyms. For example, let the key be 120605, when it is rotated we get 512060. Then the address is calculated using any other hash function.

11.3.8 Universal Hashing

Sometimes wrong operations are performed deliberately, such as choosing *N* keys all of which hash to the same slot, yielding an average retrieval time of O(*n*). Any fixed hash function is helpless to this sort of worst-case behaviour. The only effective way to improve the situation is to choose the hash function randomly in a way that is independent of the keys that are actually going to be stored. This approach is called *universal hashing* and yields good performance on the average, no matter what keys are chosen.

The main idea behind universal hashing is to select the hash function at random at run-time from a carefully designed set of functions. Because of randomization, the algorithm can behave differently on each execution; even for the same input. This approach guarantees good average case performance, no matter what keys are provided as input.

11.4 COLLISION RESOLUTION STRATEGIES

No hash function is perfect. If Hash(Key1) = Hash(Key2), then Key1 and Key2 are synonyms and if bucket size is 1, we say that collision has occurred. As a consequence, we have to store the record Key2 at some other location. A search is made for a bucket in which a record is stored containing Key2, using one of the several collision resolution strategies. The collision resolution strategies are as follows:

1. Open addressing
   (a) Linear probing
   (b) Quadratic probing
   (c) Double hashing
   (d) Key offset
2. Separate chaining (or linked list)
3. Bucket hashing (defers collision but does not prevent it)

The most important factors to be taken care of to avoid collision are the table size and choice of the hash function. As we know, no hash function is perfect and we have a limitation on the table size too. Let us learn a few techniques to resolve this collision.

11.4.1 Open Addressing

In open addressing, when collision occurs, it is resolved by finding an available empty location other than the home address. If Hash(Key) is not empty, the positions are probed in the following sequence until an empty location is found. When we reach the end of table, the search is wrapped around to start and the search continues till the current collision location.

$$N(Hash(Key) + C(1)), N(Hash(Key) + C(2)), \ldots, N(Hash(Key) + C(i)), \ldots \quad (11.1)$$

Here N is the normalizing function, Hash(Key) is the hashing function, and $C(i)$ is the collision resolution (or probing) function with the ith probe. The normalizing function is required when the resulting index is out of range. A commonly used normalization function is MOD.

Closed hash tables use open addressing. In open addressing, all records are stored in the hash table itself also said to be resolving in the prime area which contains all home addresses. In case of chaining, the collisions are resolved by storing them at a separate area known as the *overflow area.*

In open addressing, when collision occurs, the table is searched for empty locations to store synonyms. Each table entry either contains a record or is empty. While searching for a record, we systematically examine table slots until the desired record is found or it is clear that the record is not in the table.

While open addressing, to store the record, we successively examine, or probe, the hash table until we find an empty slot. Three techniques are commonly used to compute the probe sequences required for open addressing—linear probing, quadratic probing, and rehashing.

Linear Probing

A hash table in which a collision is resolved by placing the item in the next empty place following the occupied place is called *linear probing*. This strategy looks for the next free location until it is found. The function that we can use for probing linearly from the next location is as follows:

$$(\text{Hash}(x) + \text{C}(i)) \text{ MOD Max} \qquad (11.2)$$

As C(i) = i for linear probing in Eq. (11.1), the function becomes

$$(\text{Hash}(x) + i) \text{ MOD Max}$$

Initially i = 1, if the location is not empty then it becomes 2, 3, 4, …, and so on till an empty location is found. We simply add one to the current address when collision occurs or till we find an empty location within the hash table limits. Alternatively, we can also add 2, subtract 2, or add 4, etc. Here Max is the table size or the nearest prime number greater than the table size. The use of MOD wraps the linear probing to the table start, if it reaches the end.

Let Max be 100, consider Table 11.6.

Let Key1 be 1044, now it hashes to location 44 and let us save it at that location. Now let Key2 be 3544 that also maps to address 44 and collision occurs as the table location 44 is already occupied. Here 1044 and 3544 are synonyms. Now the locations HashTable[45], HashTable[46], and so on are to be examined until a free location is found. The location 45 is found empty and the key 3544 is stored there.

Table 11.6 Keys and Address

Index	Key
0	
1	
2	⋮
⋮	
44	1044
⋮	3544
98	
99	⋮

Linear probing is easy to implement and the synonyms are stored nearer to the home address resulting in faster searches. When many synonyms are clustered around the home address, it is known as primary clustering. High degree of clustering increases the number of probes for locating data, increasing the average search time. Although linear probing is easy to implement, it tends to form clusters of synonyms, resulting in secondary clustering. The secondary clustering occurs when data is widely distributed in the hash table and have formed clusters throughout the table.

Linear probing can be done using the following:

1. *With replacement*—If the slot is already occupied by the key there are two possibilities, that is, either it is the home address (collision) or the location is occupied by some key. If the key's actual address is different, then the new key having the address at that slot is placed at that position and the key with the other address is placed in the next empty position.
For example, in hash table of size 100, suppose Key1 = 127 is stored at address 25 and a new Key2 = 1325 is to be stored. Address for Key2 (1325 MOD 100) is 25. Now as the location 25 is occupied by Key1, the with replacement strategy places Key2 at location 25 and searches for an empty location for Key1 = 127.
2. *Without replacement*—When some data is to be stored in the hash table, if the slot is already occupied by the key, then another empty location is searched for a new record. There are two possibilities when the location is occupied—it is either its home address or not. In both the cases, the without replacement strategy searches for empty positions for the key that is to be stored.

Example 11.1 provides a better insight into linear probing.

EXAMPLE 11.1 Store the following data into a hash table of size 10 and bucket size 1. Use linear probing for collision resolution.

12, 01, 04, 03, 07, 08, 10, 02, 05, 14

Assume buckets from 0 to 9 and bucket size = 1 using hashing function key % 10.

Solution Let us use both techniques with and without replacement, as follows:

Linear probing with replacement For linear probing with replacement, when collision occurs, if the location is occupied by a record whose home address is not that location, it is replaced and the current record is stored there. Table 11.7 demonstrates all the operations.

Table 11.7 MOD as hash function and linear probing with replacement

Bucket	Initially empty	Insert 12	Insert 01	Insert 04	Insert 03	Insert 07	Insert 08	Insert 10	Insert 02	Insert 05	Insert 14
0								10	10	10	10
1			01	01	01	01	01	01	01	01	01
2		12	12	12	12	12	12	12	12	12	12
3					03	03	03	03	03	03	03
4				04	04	04	04	04	04	04	04
5									02	05	05
6										02	02
7						07	07	07	07	07	07
8							08	08	08	08	08
9											14

Here when key 02 is to be stored, it is hashed to address 2. However, that location is already occupied by 12. As 2 is the home address of 12, it resides there itself, and we linearly probe for the next empty location for key 02 to be stored. The location 5 is found empty and 02 is stored there.

When key 05 is to be stored, it maps to location 5 and is filled with key 02. Location 5 is not the home address of 02 and hence it is replaced. Key 05 is stored at location 5 and we again probe for the next empty location for 02 and store it at location 6.

Linear probing without replacement For linear probing without replacement when collision occurs, if the location is occupied, the next empty location is linearly probed for synonyms. Table 11.8 shows linear probing without replacement.

Table 11.8 MOD as hash function and linear probing without replacement

Bucket	Initially empty	Insert 12	Insert 01	Insert 04	Insert 03	Insert 07	Insert 08	Insert 10	Insert 02	Insert 05	Insert 14
0								10	10	10	10
1			01	01	01	01	01	01	01	01	01
2		12	12	12	12	12	12	12	12	12	12
3					03	03	03	03	03	03	03
4				04	04	04	04	04	04	04	04
5									02	02	02
6										05	05
7						07	07	07	07	07	07
8							08	08	08	08	08
9											14

Program Code 11.1 defines a function for inserting a record using linear probing without replacement.

PROGRAM CODE 11.1

```
//hash function to get position
int hash(int key)
{
   return(key % MAX);
}

//function for inserting a record using linear probe
int linear_prob(int Hashtable[], int key)
{
   int pos, i;
   pos = Hash(Key);
   if(Hashtable[pos] == 0)       // empty slot
```

```
    {
        Hashtable[pos] = key;
        return pos;
    }
    else      // slot is not empty
    {
        for(i = pos + 1; i % MAX != pos; i++)
        {
            if(Hashtable[i] == 0)
            {
                Hashtable[i] = key;
                return i;
            }
        }
    }
    // Table overflow
    return -1;
}
```

Quadratic Probing

In quadratic probing, we add the offset as the square of the collision probe number. In quadratic probing, the empty location is searched by using the following formula:

$$(\text{Hash(Key)} + i^2) \text{ MOD Max where } i \text{ lies between 1 and (Max} - 1)/2 \quad (11.3)$$

Here if Max is a prime number of the form (4 × integer + 3), quadratic probing covers all the buckets in the table.

Quadratic probing works much better than linear probing, but to make full use of the hash table, there are constraints on the values of *i* and Max so that the address lies within the table boundaries. In addition, if two keys have the same initial probe position, then their sequences are the same. Similar to linear probing, the initial probe determines the entire sequence and hence maximum distinct probe sequences are used. As the offset added is not 1, quadratic probing slows down the growth of primary clusters.

Program Code 11.2 depicts this logic.

PROGRAM CODE 11.2

```
//hash function to get position
int hash(int key)
{
    return(key % MAX);
}
```

```
//function for inserting record using linear probe
int quadratic_prob(int Hashtable[], int key)
{
    int pos, i;
    pos = hash(key);
    for(i = 0; i % MAX != pos; i++)
    {
        pos = (pos + i * i ) % MAX;
        if(Hashtable[pos] key == 0) // empty slot
        {
            Hashtable[pos] = key;
            return pos;
        }
    }       // Table overflow
    return -1;
}
```

Let us see Examples 11.2 and 11.3, which use linear probing and quadratic probing, respectively.

EXAMPLE 11.2 Suppose Max = 8 and keys *A*, *B*, *C*, *D* have hash values Hash(*A*) = 3, Hash(*B*) = 0, Hash(*C*) = 4, and Hash(*D*) = 3. Use linear probing for collision resolution.

Solution Linear probing is the simplest strategy where Hash(Key) = Hash((Key + *i*) MOD Max).

Suppose we wish to insert *D* and find that bucket 3 has been filled already, then we would try buckets 4, 5, 6, 7, 0, 1, and 2 in sequence. We find bucket 5 empty and we store *D*.

0	*B*
1	
2	
3	*A*
4	*C*
5	*D*
6	
7	

EXAMPLE 11.3 Consider the keys 22, 17, 32, 16, 5, and 24. Let Max = 7. Let us use quadratic probing to handle synonyms.

Solution Let the hash functions be (Key MOD Max); for quadratic probing (Hash(Key) ± i^2) MOD Max.

After storing 22, 17, 32, 5, and 7, the table looks as shown in the left column of Table 11.9.

Table 11.9 Keys and quadratic probing

Index	Key		Index	Key
0			0	24
1	22		1	22
2	16	insert 24 →	2	16
3	17		3	17
4	32		4	32
5	5		5	5
6			6	

We can see that while inserting 24, the address we get is

$$\text{Hash}(24) = 24 \text{ MOD } 7$$
$$= 3$$

It is also noted that the location 3 is already occupied.
We may now go for the quadratic function as

$$[\text{Hash}(24) - (1)^2 \text{ MOD } 7]$$
$$= (24 \text{ MOD } 7) + 1 \text{ MOD } 7$$
$$= (3 + 1) \text{ MOD } 7 = 4 \text{ which is not occupied.}$$

$$\text{Hence, Hash}(24) + (2)^2 \text{ MOD } 7$$
$$= (3 + 4) \text{ MOD } 7 = 0$$

which is empty, so store 24 there.

Double Hashing

Double hashing uses two hash functions, one for accessing the home address of a Key and the other for resolving the conflict. The sequence for probing is generated as follows:

$$(\text{Hash1(Key)}), (\text{Hash1(Key)} + i \times \text{Hash2(Key)}), \ldots.\ i = 1, 2, 3, 4, \ldots$$

and the resultant address is modulo Max. Example 11.4 illustrates the double hashing concept.

EXAMPLE 11.4 Let the hash function be Key % 10, Max = 10, and the keys be 12, 01, 18, 56, 79, 49. Perform double hashing.

Solution Table 11.10 demonstrates all insertions and collision handling using double hashing.

Table 11.10 Double hashing

	Initially empty	Insert 12	Insert 01	Insert 18	Insert 56	Insert 79	Insert 49
0							
1			01	01	01	01	01
2		12	12	12	12	12	12
3							
4							
5							49
6					56	56	56
7							
8				18	18	18	18
9						79	79

While inserting 49, the hashed location 9 is found occupied by key 79, so let us use Hash2(Key) = R – (Key MOD R), where R is a small prime number, even smaller than the table size. Let us use $R = 7$.

To insert 49, using Hash1(Key) = 49 % 10, we get 9 which is already occupied, so we use Hash2 as follows:

$$\text{Hash2}(49) = 7 - (49 \% 7) = 7 - 0 = 7$$

Hence by double hashing,

$$\begin{aligned}\text{Hash}(49) &= [\text{Hash1}(49) + \text{Hash2}(49)] \% 10\\ &= (9 + 7) \% 10\\ &= 6 \text{ and location 6 is not empty, so let us recompute again.}\end{aligned}$$

$$\begin{aligned}\text{Hash}(49) &= [\text{Hash1}(49) + 2 \times \text{Hash2}(49)] \% 10\\ &= 9 + 2 \times 7\\ &= 25 \% 10\\ &= 5 \text{ and is empty, so store key 49 there.}\end{aligned}$$

Example 11.5 illustrates the various types of open addressing.

EXAMPLE 11.5 Given the input {4371, 1323, 6173, 4199, 4344, 9699, 1889} and hash function as Key % 10, show the results for the following:

1. Open addressing using linear probing
2. Open addressing using quadratic probing
3. Open addressing using double hashing h2(x) = 7 – (x MOD 7)

Solution The results are as follows:

1. Open addressing using linear probing

These keys are inserted using linear probing as shown in Table 11.11

Table 11.11 Inserting keys using linear probing

	Initially empty	Insert 4371	Insert 1323	Insert 6173	Insert 4199	Insert 4344	Insert 9699	Insert 1889
0							9699	9699
1		4371	4371	4371	4371	4371	4371	4371
2								1889
3			1323	1323	1323	1323	1323	1323
4				6173	6173	6173	6173	6173
5						4344	4344	4344
6								
7								
8								
9					4199	4199	4199	4199

Using linear probing, while inserting 9699 and 1889, as the hashed locations are not empty, the keys are stored at the next empty locations probed in circular at positions 0 and 2, respectively.

2. Open addressing using quadratic probing

Let us insert these keys using quadratic probing now as shown in Table 11.12.

Table 11.12 Inserting keys using quadratic probing

	Initially empty	Insert 4371	Insert 1323	Insert 6173	Insert 4199	Insert 4344	Insert 9699	Insert 1889
0							9699	9699
1		4371	4371	4371	4371	4371	4371	4371
2								
3			1323	1323	1323	1323	1323	1323
4				6173	6173	6173	6173	6173
5						4344	4344	4344
6								
7								
8								1889
9					4199	4199	4199	4199

For 6173, the hashed address 6173 % 10 gives 3 and it is not empty, hence using quadratic probing we get the address as follows: Hash(6173) = $(6173 + 1^2)$ % 10 = 4 and as it is empty, the key 6173 is stored there. Now while inserting 4344, the location 4 is not empty and hence quadratic probing generates the address as Hash(4344 + 1^2) % 10 = 5 and as is empty 4344 is stored. For key 9699, the address is Hash(9699 + 1^2) % 10 = 0 and is empty so store it there. While inserting 1889, the address Hash(1889 + 1^2) % 10 = 0 is not empty so probe again. The address Hash(1889 + 2^2) % 10 = 3 is not empty so probe again. The address Hash(1889 + 3^2) % 10 = 8 is empty so store 1889 at location 8.

3. Open addressing using double hash function

Table 11.13 shows the status of the hash table after inserting each key using open addressing using double hashing

Table 11.13 Open addressing using double hash

	Initially empty	Insert 4371	Insert 1323	Insert 6173	Insert 4199	Insert 4344	Insert 9699	Insert 1889
0								1889
1		4371	4371	4371	4371	4371	4371	4371
2							9699	9699
3			1323	1323	1323	1323	1323	1323
4				6173	6173	6173	6173	6173
5								
6								
7						4344	4344	4344
8								
9					4199	4199	4199	4199

While inserting 6173, the address is Hash1(6173) = 6173 % 10 = 3 and 3 is not empty. Let us use double hashing. Hence the address is as follows:

$$\begin{aligned} \text{Hash}(6173) &= [\text{Hash1}(6173) + \text{Hash2}(6173)] \ \% \ 10 \\ &= 3 + (R - 6173 \ \% \ R) \ (\text{let } R \text{ be } 7) \\ &= 3 + (7 - 6) = 4 \end{aligned}$$

Since 4 is empty, we store 6173 at location 4.

Now let us store 4344. The address 4344 % 10 = 4 and as location 4 is not empty, we use double hashing and we get Hash(4344) = 7. Now for 9699 double hashing generates address 2 and as it is empty, we store it there. For key 1889, double hashing generates address 0 and as it is empty, we store 1889 at location 0.

Rehashing

If the table gets full, insertion using open addressing with quadratic probing might fail or it might take too much time. The solution for this problem is to build another table that is about twice as big and scan down the entire original hash table, compute the new hash value for each record, and insert them in a new table.

For example, if initially, the table is of size 7 and the hash function is key % 7 then, this would be as shown in Table 11.14.

As the table is more than 70% full, a new table is created (Table 11.15) and the values are inserted in the new table. The size of the new table is 17, that is next prime of double of 7 that is 14. Rehashing is very expensive, as its running time is O(N).

Table 11.14 Table of size 7

	Insert 7, 15, 13, 74, 73
0	7
1	15
2	
3	73
4	74
5	
6	13

Table 11.15 New table of size 17 when Table 11.14 is 70% full

0	
1	
2	
3	
4	
5	73
6	74
7	7
8	
9	
10	
11	
12	
13	13
14	
15	15
16	

11.4.2 Chaining

We have discussed three techniques that are used to compute probe sequences (to relocate synonyms) namely, linear probing, quadratic probing, and rehashing. Of course, we can store the linked lists inside the hash table, in the unused hash table slots. The technique used to handle synonyms is chaining; it chains together all the records that hash to the same address. Instead of relocating synonyms, a linked list of synonyms is created whose head is the home address of synonyms. In Chapter 6, we have discussed implementing a linked list within an array. However, we need to handle pointers to form a chain of synonyms. The extra memory is needed for storing pointers.

In Fig. 11.3, a hash table with Max = 10, both keys 322 and 262 probe to address 2. A chain, a linked list, stores all items at a particular home address (home address is an address within the hash table itself).

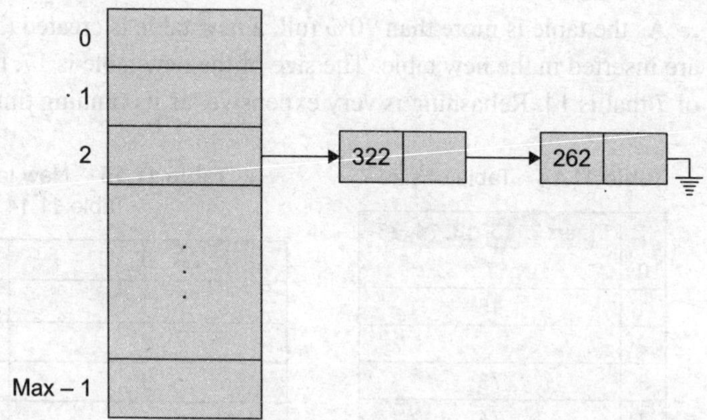

Fig. 11.3 An example of chaining

Let us compare rehashing and chaining (Table 11.16).

Table 11.16 Comparison of chaining and rehashing

Chaining	Rehashing
Unlimited number of synonyms can be handled.	A limited but good number of synonyms are taken care of.
Additional cost to be paid is an overhead of multiple linked lists.	The table size is doubled but no additional fields of links are to be maintained.
Sequential search through the chain takes more time.	Searching is faster when compared to chaining.

Program Code 11.3 illustrates chaining.

PROGRAM CODE 11.3

```
#define MAX 10
class node
{
   public:
      int key;
      struct node *next;
};

Node *hashtable[max];
```

```
void int()
{
   int i;
   for(i = 0; i < n; i++)
   {
      Hashtable[i] = null;
   }
}

int hash(int key)
{
   return(key % 10);
}

void insert(int k)
{
   int pos;
   Node *Curr, *Temp;
   Curr = new node;
   Curr->key = k;
   Curr->next = null;
   pos = hash(Curr->key);
   if(Hashtable[pos] == null)
      Hashtable[pos] = Curr;
   else
   {
      // goto last node and attach
      Temp = Hashtable[pos];
      while(Temp->next != null)
         Temp = Temp->next;
         // attach
         Temp->next = Curr;
   }
}

void display()
{
   Node *Curr;
   for(i = 0; i < 10; i++)
   {
      Curr = Hashtable[i];
```

```
        while(curr != null)
        {
            cout << curr->key << "\t";
            Curr = Curr->next;
        }
    }
}

void search(int x)
{
    Node *Curr;
    pos = hash(x);
    Curr = Hashtable[pos];
    while(curr != null && Curr->key != x)
    {
        cout << curr->key << "\t";
        Curr = Curr->next;
    }
    if(Curr == null)
        cout << "\n Not Found";
    else
        cout << "\n  Key Found";
}
```

11.5 HASH TABLE OVERFLOW

Even if a hashing algorithm (function) is very good, it is likely that collisions will occur. The identifiers that have hashed into the same bucket, as discussed earlier, are called synonyms.

An *overflow* is said to occur when a new identifier is mapped or hashed into a full bucket. When the bucket size is one, a collision and an overflow occur simultaneously. Therefore, any hashing program must incorporate some method for dealing with records that cannot fit into their home addresses. There are a number of techniques for handling overflow of records.

11.5.1 Open Addressing for Overflow Handling

We shall study two ways to handle overflows—open addressing and chaining. In open addressing, we assume that the hash table is an array. When a new identifier is hashed into a full bucket, we need to find another bucket for this identifier. The simplest solution is to find the closest unfilled bucket through linear probing or linear open addressing.

When linear open addressing is used to handle overflows, a hash table search for an identifier I proceeds as follows:

1. Compute Hash(I)
2. Examine identifiers position
   Table[Hash(I)], Table[Hash(I) + 1], …, Table[Hash[I] + i], in order until:
   (a) If Table[Hash(I) + j] = I then
       In this case I is found.
   (b) If Table[Hash(I) + j] is NULL, then I is not in the table.
   (c) If we return to the start position Hash(I), then the table is full and I is not in the table.

One of the problems with linear open addressing is that it tends to create clusters of identifiers. Moreover, these clusters tend to merge as more identifiers are entered, leading to big clusters. An alternative method to retard the growth of clusters is to use a series of hash functions $h_1, h_2, \ldots, h_m$. This method is called as rehashing. Buckets $h_i(x)$, $1 \le i \le m$ are examined in that order.

11.5.2 Overflow Handling by Chaining

Linear probing and its variations are inefficient as the search for an identifier involves comparison with identifiers that have different hash values. Consider the following hash table shown in Fig. 11.4.

0	1	2	3	4	5	6	7	8	9	10	11		25
A	A_2	A_1	D	A_3	A_4	G_A	G	Z_A	E		L	...	Z

Fig. 11.4 Chaining

In the above hash table of 25 buckets, one slot per bucket, searching for the identifier Z_A involves comparisons with the buckets Table[0] to Table[7], even though none of the identifiers in these buckets had a collision with Table[25] and so cannot possibly be Z_A. Many of the comparisons can be saved if we maintain lists of identifiers, one list per bucket, each list containing all the synonyms for that bucket. If this is done, a search involves computing the hash address Hash(I) and examining only those identifiers in the list for Hash(I). Since the sizes of these lists are not known in advance, the best way to maintain them is as linked chains. In each slot, additional space is required for a link. Each chain has a head node. The head node, however, usually is much smaller than the other nodes, since it has to retain only a link. As the list is accessed at random, the head nodes should be sequential. We assume that they are numbered 0 to $n - 1$, if hash function Hash() has range 0 to $n - 1$.

For hash table in Fig. 11.4 can be represented as hash table in Fig. 11.5 using the hash chains.

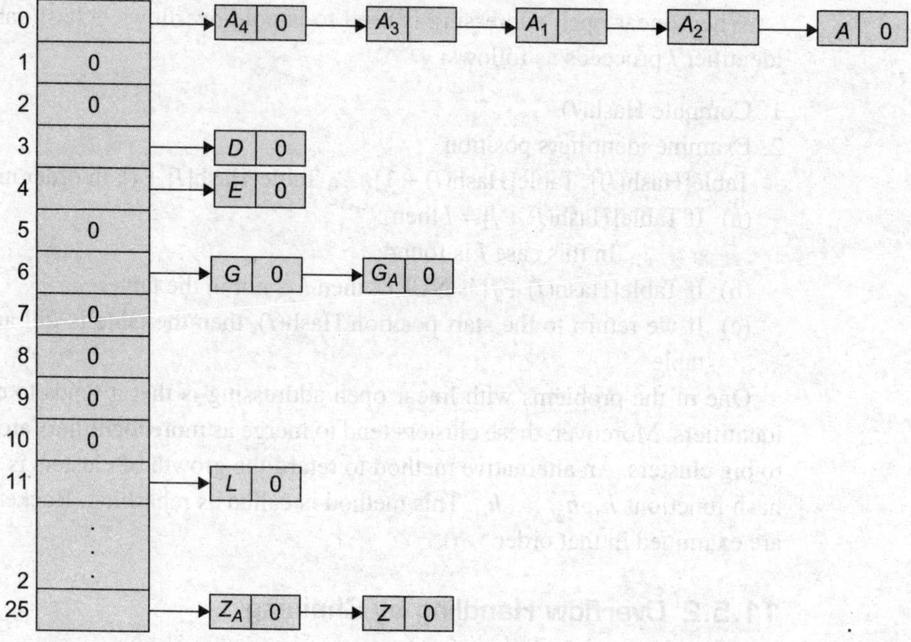

Fig. 11.5 Hash chains

To insert a new identifier, *I*, into a chain, we must first verify that it is not currently in chain. Then, if not present, *I* is inserted at any position in the chain.

11.6 EXTENDIBLE HASHING

If linear probing or separate chaining is used for collision handling, then in case of collision, several blocks are required to be examined to search a key and when table is full, then expensive rehash should be used. For fast searching and less disk access, extendible hashing is used. It is a type of hash system, which treats a hash as a bit string, and uses a trie for bucket lookup.

For example, assume that the hash function Hash(Key) returns a binary number.

The first *i* bits of each string will be used as indices to figure out where they will go in the hash table. Additionally, *i* is the smallest number such that the first *i* bits of all keys are different.

The keys to be used are as follows:

1. *h*(key1) = 100101
2. *h*(key2) = 011110
3. *h*(key3) = 110110

Let us assume that for this particular example, the bucket size is 1. The first two keys to be inserted, key1 and key2, can be distinguished by the most significant bit, and would be inserted into the table as follows:

Directory
0 → Bucket *A* for key2
1 → Bucket *B* for key1

When key3 is hashed to the table, it would not be enough to distinguish all three keys by one bit (because key3 and key1 have 1 as their leftmost bit). Also, because the bucket size is one, the table would overflow. Because comparing the first two most significant bits would give each key a unique location, the directory size is doubled as follows:

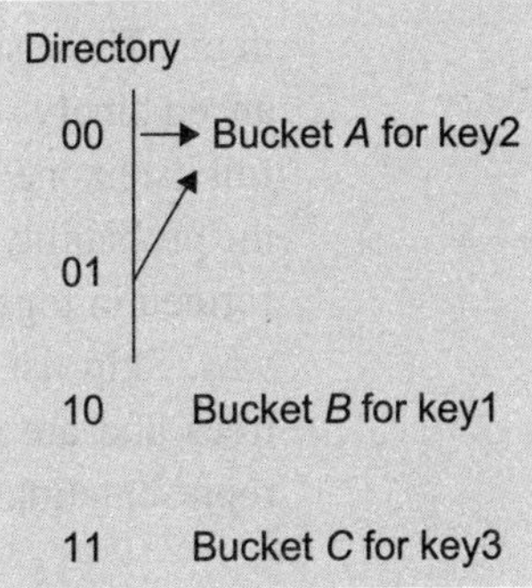

And so now key1 and key3 have unique locations being distinguished by the first two leftmost bits. Since key2 is in the top half of the table, both 00 and 01 point to it because there is no other key that begins with a 0 to compare.

The root of the tree contains four pointers determined by the leading two bits of data. Each leaf has upto 4 records. *D* will be represented by the number of bits used by the root, which is known as a directory.

11.7 DICTIONARY

A set is an unordered collection of distinct elements. Each element has a field called *key* that is usually unique. The requirement of uniqueness is sometimes circumvented and is known as a *multiset* or a *bag*. Multiset is a set whose members are not necessarily distinct. The most common operations performed on a set or multiset are searching, inserting, and deleting elements from a group. A dictionary is a data structure for efficiently implementing these operations. The simplest way to implement a dictionary is through the use of arrays. Arrays are efficient for searching an element, whereas insertion and deletion cannot be easily performed. The proficient implementation has to balance the efficiency of searching with the other two operations. Other sophisticated ways to implement a dictionary is using hashing and balanced search trees.

A typical dictionary includes the following operations:

1. Empty—checks whether the dictionary is empty or not
2. Size—determines the dictionary size
3. Insert—inserts a pair into the dictionary
4. Search—searches the pair with a specified key
5. Delete—deletes the pair with a specified key

11.8 SKIP LIST

A balanced tree is one of the most popular data structures used for searching. One of the variants of balanced trees is the skip list. The skip list is a probabilistic data structure that has become the method of choice for many search-based applications instead of balanced trees.

A skip list stores the sorted data in the form of a linked list. These items are stored as a hierarchy of linked lists where each list links increasingly sparse subsequences of the items. These supplementary lists result in an item search that is as efficient as that of balanced binary search trees. Since each link of the sparser lists skips over many items of the full list in one step, the list is called *skip list*. These forward links are added on the basis of the probability of the element search. Hence, insert, search, and delete operations are performed in logarithmic expected time. The links may also be added in a non-probabilistic way. Skip list algorithms have the same asymptotic expected time bounds as balanced trees and are simpler, faster, and use less space. Figure 11.6 shows the diagrammatic representation of a skip list.

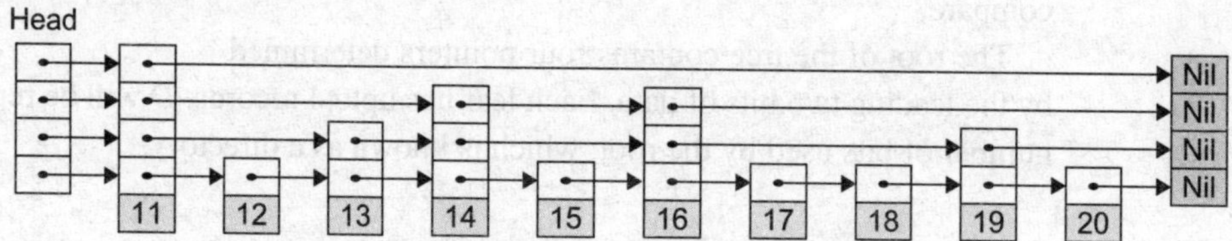

Fig. 11.6 Diagrammatic representation of a skip list

11.9 COMPARISON OF HASHING AND SKIP LISTS

The following is a list of similarities and differences between hashing and skip lists:

- The hash table is a simple array of items; hashing algorithms calculate an index from the data item's key and use this index to place the data into the array. A hash table is an alternative method for representing a dictionary. It is a popular data structure which is simple and easy to implement.
- The skip list is a linked list augmented with layers of pointers for quickly jumping over a large numbers of elements and then descending to the next layer. This process continues down to the bottom layer, which is the actual list. Skip lists are interesting data structures which are powerful and flexible.
- Skip lists are one way of implementing a dictionary abstract data type, which stores a set of items and allows us to add, remove, and search for items. Though hash tables are more popular, skip lists improve the performance of insert and delete operations.
- The expected performance of search and delete operations on skip lists is O(log$n$); however, the worst-case performance is $\Theta(n)$. The hash table is used in many applications. In ideal situations, the hash table search, insert, or delete takes $\Theta(1)$.

- There are many issues associated with hash tables such as the choice of the hash function, overflow handling, and the size (i.e., number of buckets) of the hash table.

RECAPITULATION

- Many applications need a dynamic set of operations that supports only insert, member search, and delete. A keyed table is an effective data structure for implementing them.
- Hashing is an excellent technique for implementing keyed tables. A hash table is an array-based structure used to store <key, information> pairs.
- Hash tables are used to implement insertions and searches in constant average time. To store an item in a hash table, a hash function is applied to the key of the item being stored, returning an index within the range of the hash table.
- Hashing is a technique that is used for storing and retrieving information associated with and that makes use of the individual characters or digits in the key itself.
- A problem arises, however, when the hash function returns the same value when applied to two different keys called collision. However, there are various collision resolution techniques to overcome these problems.
- Dictionary and skip lists are types of data structures used for storing data in the form of an array and linked list, respectively. However, skip list is more efficient and thus the preferred option for performing search operations on a given data set as it is simpler, faster, and uses less space when compared to other techniques.

KEY TERMS

Bucket An index position in hash table that stores a fixed number of buckets.

Collision The result of two keys hashing into the same bucket (index positions).

Dictionary A dictionary is a type of data structure that can efficiently implement operations such as searching, inserting, and deleting elements on a set or multiset from a group.

Hash function To store an item in a hash table, a hash function is applied to the key of the item being stored, returning an index within the range of the hash table.

Hashing Hashing is a technique that is used for storing and retrieving information associated with and that makes use of the individual characters or digits in the key itself. Hashing is an excellent technique for implementing keyed tables.

Hash table A hash table is an array-based structure used to store <key, information> pairs. In other words, we can say that the hash table is a table for storing key and related information.

Overflow When more than one key has the same index and if there is no space in bucket, we say that overflow has occurred.

Skip list A skip list is one of the variants of balanced trees, which is used most efficiently for searching operations.

Synonym Keys that hash to the same bucket are called synonyms.

EXERCISES

Multiple choice questions

1. A hash table with 10 buckets with one slot per bucket is depicted. The symbols S_1 to S_7 are initially entered using a hashing function with linear probing. The maximum number of comparisons needed in searching an item that is not present is
(a) 4
(b) 5
(c) 6
(d) 3
2. A hash function *f* defined as *f*(key) = key MOD 7, with linear probing, is used to insert the keys 37, 38, 72, 48, 98, 11, 56 into a table indexed from 0 to 6. 11 will be stored in the location
(a) 3
(b) 4
(c) 5
(d) 6
3. A text is made up of characters a, b, c, d, e each with probability 0.12, 0.4, 0.15, 0.08, and 0.25, respectively. The optimal coding will give the average length of
(a) 2.15
(b) 3.01
(c) 2.3
(d) 1.78
4. The average search time of hashing, with linear probing will be less if the load factor
(a) is much less than one
(b) equals one
(c) is far greater than one
(d) none of the above
5. A hash table can store a maximum of 10 records. Currently, there are records in locations 1, 3, 4, 7, 8, 9, 10. The probability of a new record going into location 2, with hash function resolving collision by linear probing is
(a) 0.1
(b) 0.6
(c) 0.2
(d) 0.5
6. A hash table has space for 100 records. What is the probability of collision before the table is 10% full?
(a) 0.45
(b) 0.5
(c) 0.3
(d) 0.34

Review questions

1. What is hashing? What is a hashing function? Give at least two examples of a hashing function. Discuss about the characteristics of a good hashing function. How is synonym resolution done during hashing?
2. What are the advantages and disadvantages of the following synonym resolution methods?
(a) Overflow file
(b) Open addressing methods
3. Define:
(a) Key
(b) Hash function
(c) Synonym
4. Write an algorithm for chaining with replacement used as a technique for synonym resolution.
5. Discuss MOD as a hash function.
6. Describe the overflow handling techniques in a hash table.
7. Using the modulo-division method and linear probing, store the following keys in an array with 19 records. How many collisions occurred? What is the density of the list after all the keys have been inserted?

224562	137456	214562
140145	214575	162145
144467	199645	234534

8. Repeat review question 7 using a linked list method for collision. Compare these results with the results obtained in the previous question.

9. Explain the term dictionary. List the suitable data structures for implementation of dictionaries.
10. In what way is a skip list a more suitable data structure for implementing dictionaries?
11. Compare skip lists and hashing.

Answers to multiple choice questions

1. (b) It will be one more than the size of the biggest cluster (which is 4 here). This is because assume a search key hashing onto bin 8. By linear probing, the next location for searching is bin 9, then 0, and then 1. If all these resulted in a mess, we try at bin 2 and stop as it is vacant. Of course, this logic will not work if deletion is performed before search.

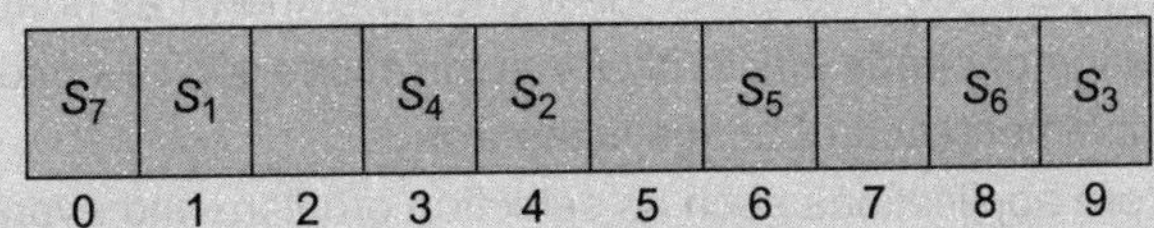

2. (c)
3. (a) Using Huffman code, a is 1111, b is 0, c is 110, d is 1110, e is 10.

$$\text{Average code length} = (4 \times 0.12) + (1 \times 0.4) + (3 \times 0.15) + (4 \times 0.08) + (2 \times 0.25) = 2.15$$

4. (a) Load factor is the ratio of the number records that are currently present and the total number of records that can be present. If the load factor is less, free space will be more. Hence, the probability of collision is less. So the search time will be less.
5. (b) If the new record hashes onto one of the six locations 7, 8, 9, 10, 1 or 2, the location will receive a new record. The probability is 6/10 as 10 is the total possible number of locations.
6. (a)

12 HEAPS

OBJECTIVES

After completing this chapter, the reader will be able to understand the following:

- A specialized tree-based data structure known as heap
- Usage of heaps efficiently for applications such as priority queues
- Implementation of heaps using arrays
- More applications such as selection problem and event simulation

We have studied binary search trees (BSTs) in Chapter 7. In practice, BSTs are rarely used to sort data. In case there is a fixed amount of data and sorting does not need to take place until all the data is collected, the data can be placed in an array and sorted using the quicksort algorithm. On the other hand, when the data must be simultaneously inserted and sorted, there is a data structure which, in practice works more efficiently than BSTs, known as *heaps*.

12.1 BASIC CONCEPTS

A *heap* is a binary tree having the following properties:

1. It is a *complete binary tree*, that is, each level of the tree is completely filled, except the bottom level, where it is filled from left to right.
2. It satisfies the heap-order property, that is, the key value of each node is greater than or equal to the key value of its children, or the key value of each node is lesser than or equal to the key value of its children.

All the binary trees of Fig. 12.1 are heaps, whereas the binary trees of Fig. 12.2 are not.

The second condition is violated in Fig. 12.2(a) as the content of the child node 80 is greater than its parent node 70. The first condition is violated in Fig. 12.2(b) as at level 2, 30 has a right child but no left child, that is, at this level, it should be filled from left to right.

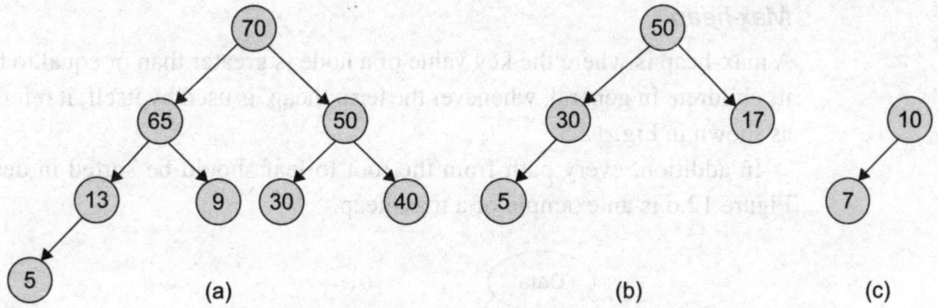

Fig. 12.1 Sample heaps (a) Heap with height three (b) Heap with height two (c) Heap with height one

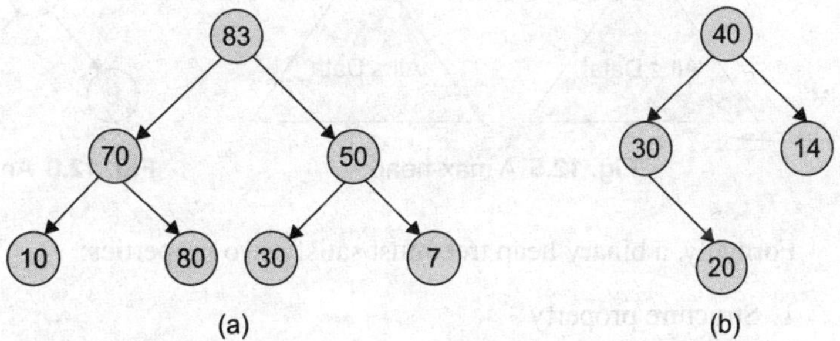

Fig. 12.2 Binary trees but not heaps (a) Sample 1 (b) Sample 2

12.1.1 Min-heap and Max-heap

In this section we discuss two types of heaps, the min-heap and the max-heap.

Min-heap

The structure shown in Fig. 12.3 is called *min-heap*.

In min-heap, the key value of each node is lesser than or equal to the key value of its children. In addition, every path from root to leaf should be sorted in ascending order. Figure 12.4 is an example of a min-heap.

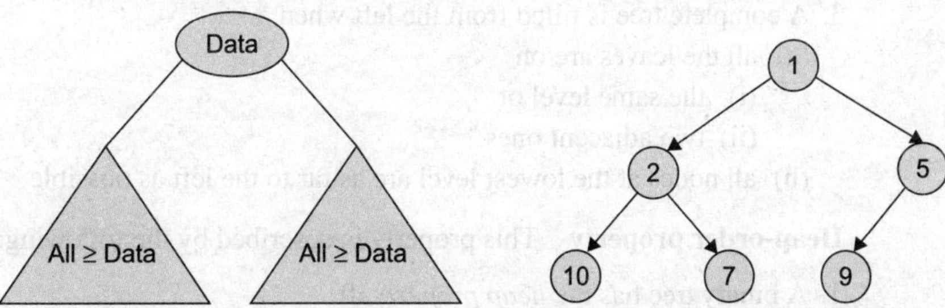

Fig. 12.3 Structure of min-heap **Fig. 12.4** An example of a min-heap

Max-heap

A max-heap is where the key value of a node is greater than or equal to the key value of its children. In general, whenever the term 'heap' is used by itself, it refers to a max-heap as shown in Fig. 12.5.

In addition, every path from the root to leaf should be sorted in descending order. Figure 12.6 is an example of a max-heap.

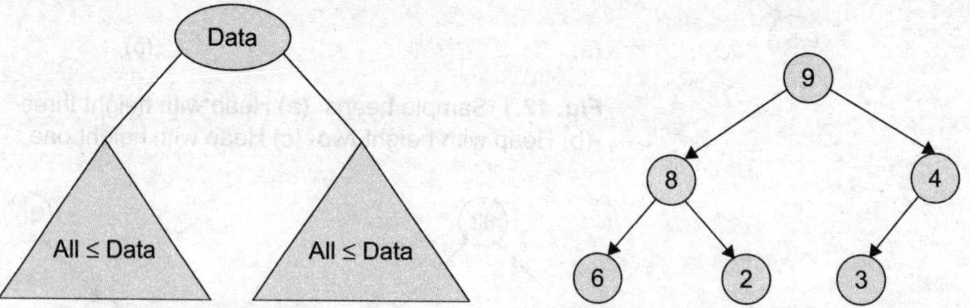

Fig. 12.5 A max-heap

Fig. 12.6 An example of a max-heap

Formally, a binary heap tree must satisfy two properties:

1. Structure property
2. Heap-order property

Let us discuss these properties in detail.

Structure property This property is described by the following list:

1. A binary tree is *complete* if it is of height h and has $2^{h+1} - 1$ nodes.
2. A binary tree of height h is complete iff
   (a) it is empty, or
   (b) its left subtree is complete of height $h - 1$ and its right subtree is completely full of height $h - 2$, or
   (c) its left subtree is completely full of height $h - 1$ and its right subtree is complete of height $h - 1$.
3. A complete tree is filled from the left when
   (a) all the leaves are on
      (i) the same level or
      (ii) two adjacent ones
   (b) all nodes at the lowest level are as far to the left as possible

Heap-order property This property is described by the following:

1. A binary tree has the *heap property* iff
   (a) it is empty or
   (b) the key in the root is larger than either children and both subtrees have the heap property

12.2 IMPLEMENTATION OF HEAP

To implement heaps using array is an easy task. We simply number the nodes in the heap from top to bottom, number the nodes on each level from left to right, and store the ith node in the ith location of the array. The root of the tree is stored at index 0, its left child at index 1, its right child at index 2, and so on.

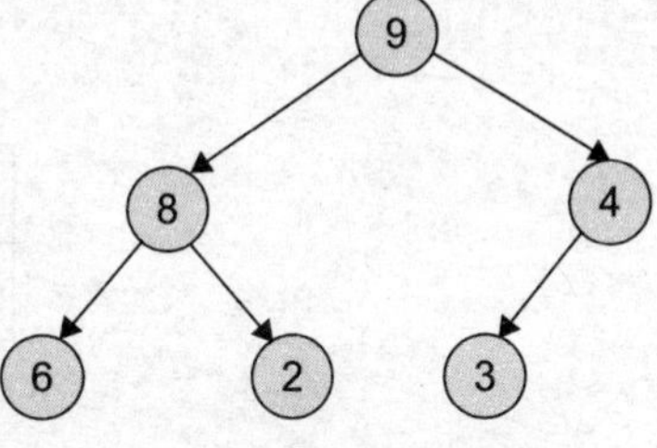

Fig. 12.7 Sample heap

For example, consider Fig 12.7.

Figure 12.8 shows the corresponding array representation of the heap.

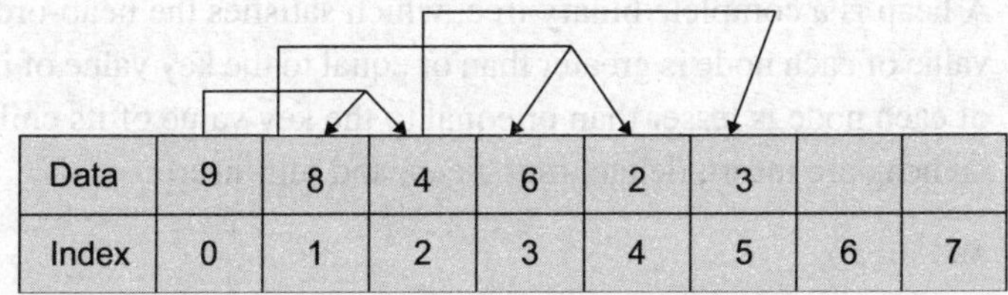

Data	9	8	4	6	2	3		
Index	0	1	2	3	4	5	6	7

Fig 12.8 Array representation of heap in Fig. 12.7

In this array,

1. parent of the node at index i is at index $(i - 1)/2$
2. left child of the node at index i is at index $2 \times i + 1$
3. right child of the node at index i is at index $2 \times i + 2$

For example, in Fig. 12.8,

1. the node having value 8 is at the 1st location.
2. Its parent is at 0/2, that is, at the 0th location (value is 9).
3. Its left child is at $2 \times 1 + 1$, that is, at the 3rd location (value is 6).
4. Its right child is at $2 \times 1 + 2$, that is, at the 4th location (value is 2).

Let us consider the heap tree in Fig. 12.9 in its logical form.

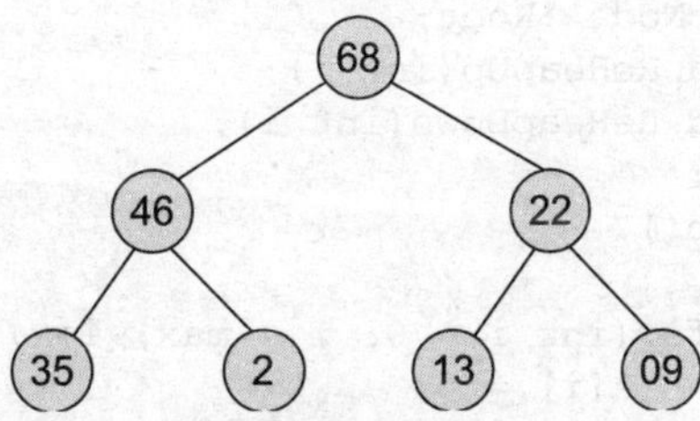

Fig. 12.9 A heap tree

The physical representation of the heap tree of Fig. 12.9 is shown in Fig. 12.10. We represent the tree using an array as in Fig. 12.10 using the rules stated.

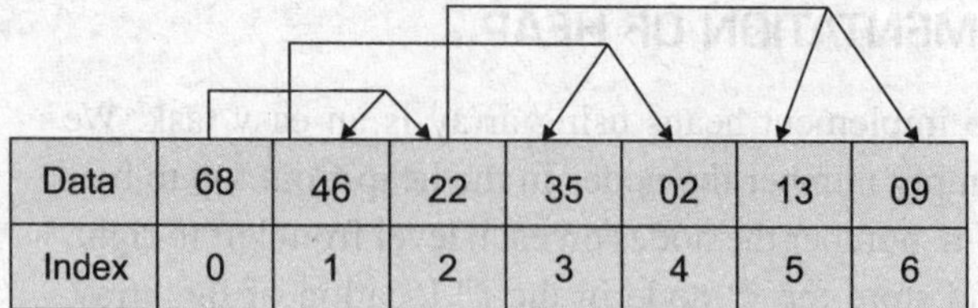

Data	68	46	22	35	02	13	09
Index	0	1	2	3	4	5	6

Fig. 12.10 Representation of heap in Fig. 12.9 as array

12.3 HEAP AS ABSTRACT DATA TYPE

A heap is a complete binary tree, which satisfies the heap-order property, that is, the key value of each node is greater than or equal to the key value of its children (or the key value of each node is lesser than or equal to the key value of its children). The basic operations on heap are insert, delete, max-heap, and min-heap.

```
ADT Heap
1.Create()→Heap
2.Insert(Heap, Data)→Heap
3.DeleteMaxVal(Heap)→Heap
4.ReHeapDown(Heap, Child)→Heap
5.ReHeapUp(Heap, Root)→Heap
End
```

The C++ class declaration for this ADT is as follows:

```
class HeapNode
{
   int A[max];
   int n;      //No. of elements heap contains
};

class Heap
{
   private:
      HeapNode *Root;
      void ReHeapUp(int i);
      void ReHeapDown(int i);
   public:
      Heap();
      {
         for(int i = 0; i < max; i++)
            A[i] = 0;
      }
   void Create();
   void Insert(int i);
   void DeleteMaxVal();
};
```

12.3.1 Operations on Heaps

The basic operations on heaps are listed as follows:

1. `Create`—creates an empty heap to which the root points
2. `Insert`—inserts an element into the heap
3. `Delete`—deletes max (or min) element from the heap
4. `ReheapUp`—rebuilds the heap when we use the insert() function
5. `ReheapDown`—rebuilds the heap when we use the delete() function

A heap is generally not traversed, searched, or printed. To implement the insert and delete operations, we need two other operations: reheapUp and reheapDown. The advanced operations include merge, which merges two heaps.

ReheapUp

If we have a nearly complete binary tree with n elements, the first $n - 1$ elements satisfy the order property of heaps, but the last element does not. That is, the structure would be a heap if the last element was not there. The reheapUp operation repairs the structure so that it is a heap by lifting the last element up the tree until that element reaches a proper position in the tree. This restructuring can be graphically viewed in Fig. 12.11.

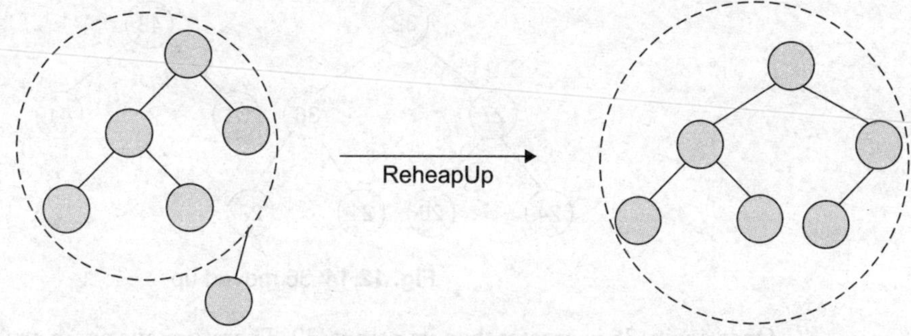

Fig. 12.11 ReheapUp operation

We can note that in Fig. 12.11 the last node in the heap was out of order. After the reheap, it is in its correct location, and the heap has been extended by one node.

As a heap is a complete or nearly complete tree, the node must be placed in the last leaf level at the first leftmost empty position as in Fig. 12.11. If the new node's key is larger than its parent, it is lifted up the tree by exchanging the child and parent keys and the data. The data eventually moves to the correct position in the heap by repeatedly exchanging child–parent keys and data. In brief, reheapUp repairs a broken heap by lifting the last element up the tree until it reaches the correct location in the heap.

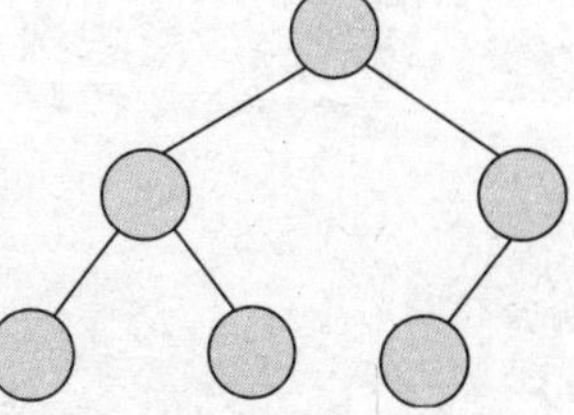

Fig. 12.12 General heap structure

Figure 12.12 shows a general heap structure. Let us consider an example.

Figure 12.13 shows a tree which is not a heap after adding 36.

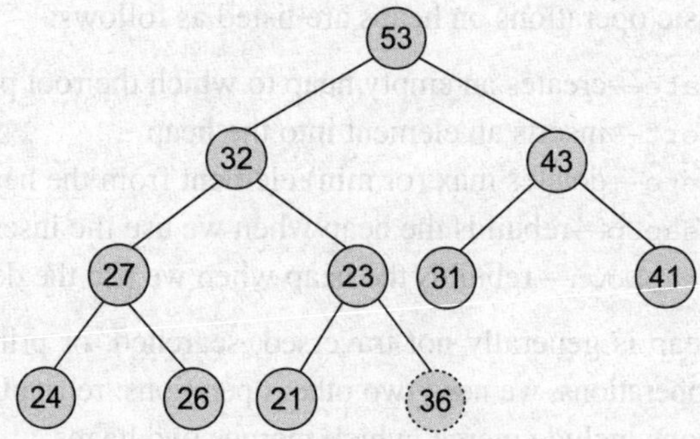

Fig. 12.13 A tree, not a heap

Here, 36 is greater than its parent, 23; hence, it is an invalid heap. We therefore exchange 36 and 23 and call reheapUp to test its current position in the heap. We obtain the tree as shown in Fig. 12.14.

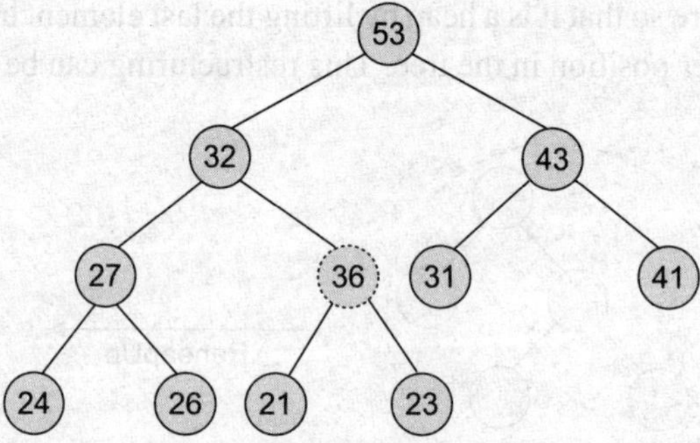

Fig. 12.14 36 moved up

Once again, 36 is greater than its parent, 32. Therefore, we again exchange the data and find that when reheapUp is called, the node is placed at the correct position, and hence, the operation stops. We get the heap as shown in Fig. 12.15.

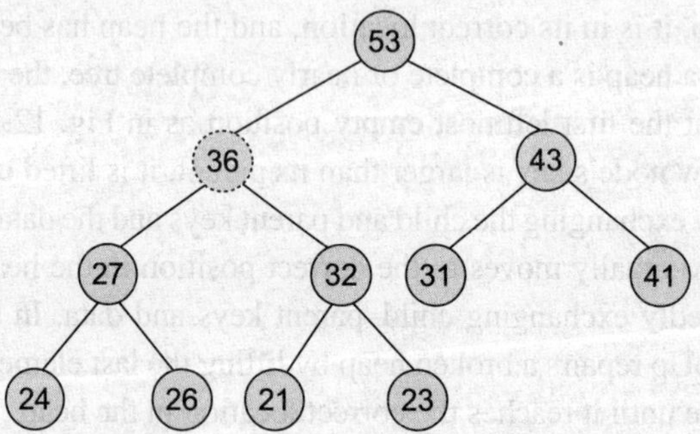

Fig. 12.15 A heap after 36 is moved up

Let us see this process through a C++ code given in Program Code 12.1.

PROGRAM CODE 12.1

```
// ReheapUp operation is required when a new value is
// inserted at the ith location
void Heap :: ReHeapUp(int i)
{
   int temp;
   while(i > 0 and a[i] > a[(i - 1)/2])
   {
     // swap a[i] with its parent, i.e., [(i - 1)/2]th element
     temp = a[i]; A[i] = a[(i - 1)/2]; A[(i - 1)/2] = temp;
     i = i/2;
   }
}
// Following is the function code for inserting a number
// into heap.
void Heap :: Insert(int x)
{
   // new element x is inserted at last position of an array
   a[n] = x;
   // reheap operation is called after inserting new value
   ReHeapUp(n);
}
```

ReheapDown

When we have a nearly complete binary tree that satisfies the heap-order property except in the root position, we need the reheapDown operation. Such situations occur when the root is deleted from the tree, leaving two disjointed heaps. To correct such situations, we move the data in the last tree node to the root. Obviously, such actions disturb the tree's heap properties. To restore the heap, we need an operation that will sink the root down until the heap ordering property is satisfied and thus the operation reheapDown comes into action. Figure 12.16 shows a reheapDown operation.

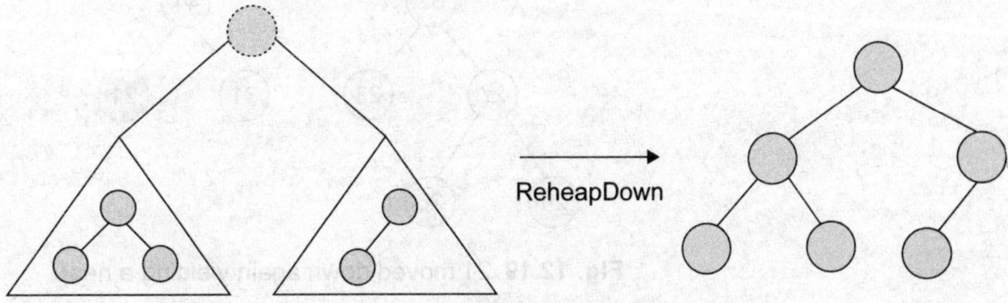

Fig. 12.16 ReheapDown

Let us consider a broken heap as in Fig. 12.17.

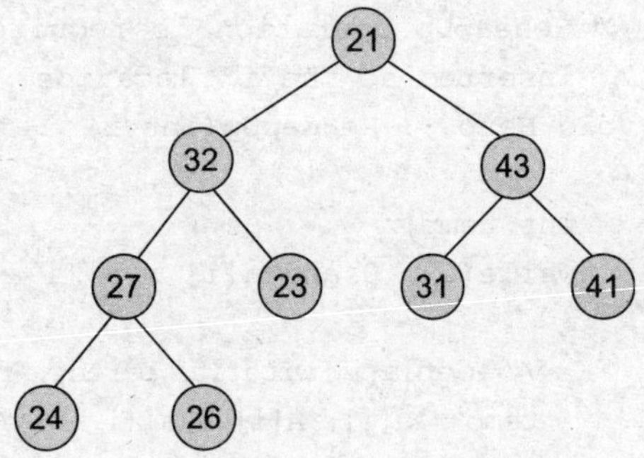

Fig. 12.17 Original tree, not a heap

Here, the root 21 is smaller than its subtrees. We examine them and select the larger of the two to exchange it with the root, which is now 43.

Having made the exchange, as in Fig. 12.18, we check whether 21 is smaller than its keys.

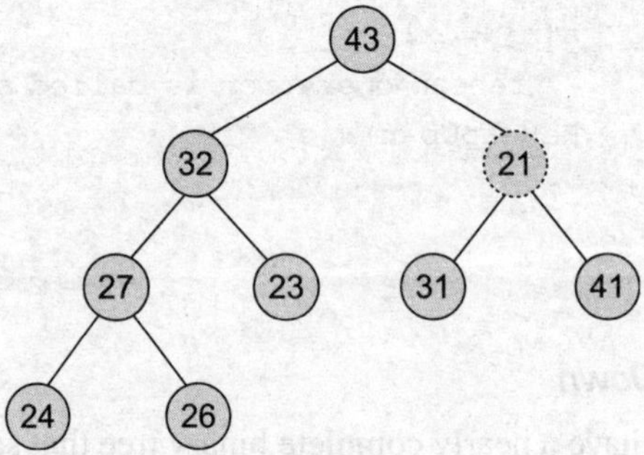

Fig. 12.18 Root 21 moved down to the right

Once again, we exchange 21 with the larger subtree 41 and get the tree as in Fig. 12.19.

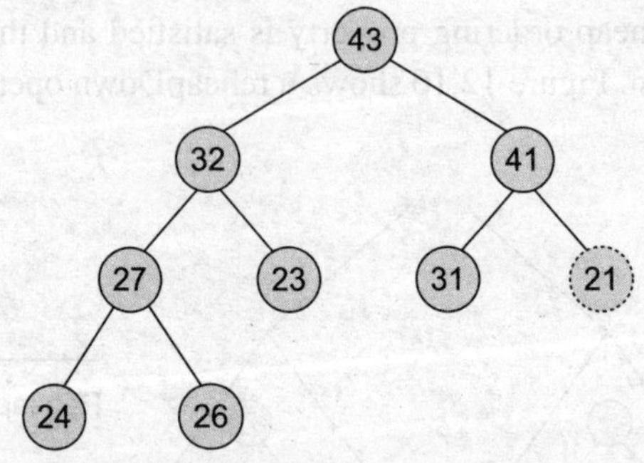

Fig. 12.19 21 moved down again yielding a heap

From Fig. 12.19, we can see that we have reached a leaf and can stop now.

Let us see how this can be implemented using C++ in Program Code 12.2.

PROGRAM CODE 12.2

```
// ReheapDown operation is required when deleting an
// element from top location
void Heap :: ReHeapDown(int i)
{
   int temp;
   while(2 * i < n)
   {
      j = 2 * i + 1;
      // j index shows the left child of the node
      if(j + 1 < n && a[j + 1] > a[j])
      // finding max from left and right child
         j = j + 1;
      if(a[i] > a[j]) break;
      // if root > children then break
      else
      {
         // swap a[i] with a[j]
         temp = a[i];
         a[i] = a[j];
         a[j] = temp;
         i = j;
      }
   }     // end of while
}
// Following is the code for function for deleting
// maximum value from heap.
void Heap :: Delete_MaxVal()
{
   int temp;
   // swap 0th element with last value of an array
   temp = a[0];
   a[0] = a[n - 1];
   a[n - 1] = temp;
   // reheapdown operation is called to delete max
   value from first location
   ReHeapDown(0);
}
```

Insert

A node can be inserted in a heap which has already been built, if there is an empty location in the array. To insert a node, we need to search the first empty leaf in the array. We find it immediately after the last node in the tree. To insert a node, we move the new data to the first empty leaf and perform reheapUp. Let us consider the heap already built as in Fig. 12.20.

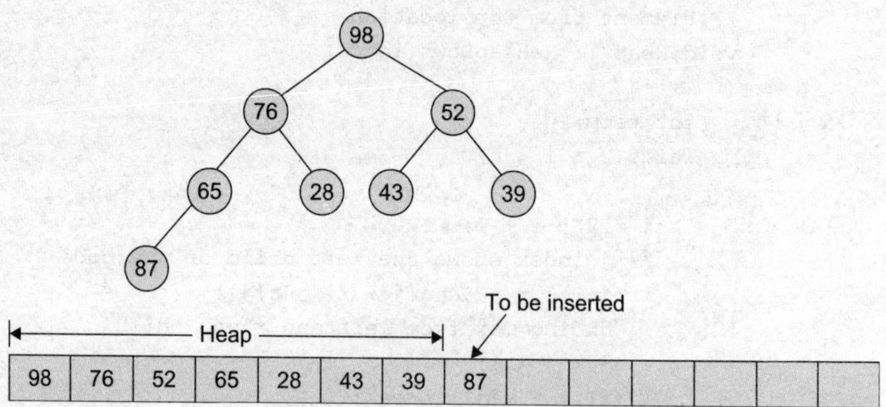

Fig. 12.20 Sample heap

The heap in Fig. 12.20 has seven elements in it. Let us consider that the element 87 is to be inserted. Initially, 87 is stored at the last empty location as the first empty leaf of the heap. Thus, we heapify it to store the element in the proper position. The resultant heap is shown in Fig. 12.21.

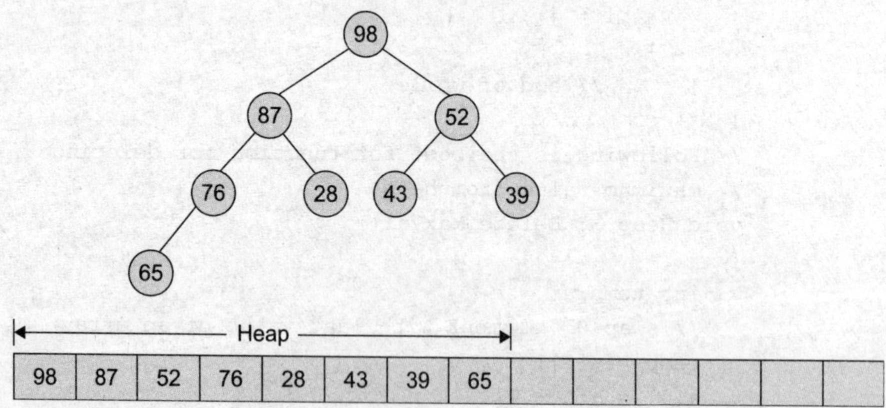

Fig. 12.21 Heap after insertion of 87

Delete

While removing a node from a heap, the most common and meaningful logic is to delete the root. The heap is thus left without a root. To reconstruct the heap, we move the data in the last heap node to the root and perform reheapDown. Let us consider the heap tree as shown in Fig. 12.22. The data at the top of the heap is returned by the delete operation.

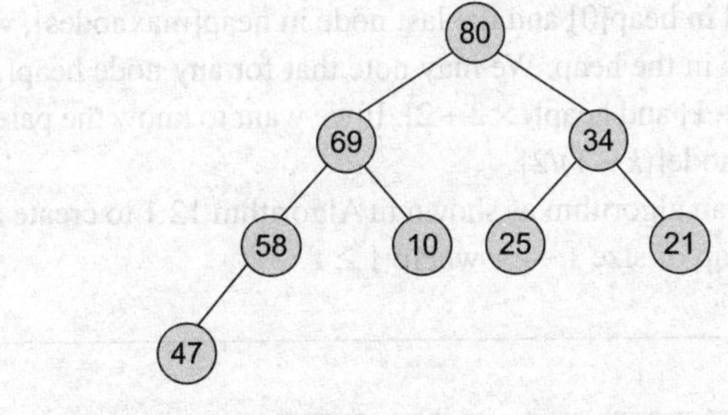

Fig. 12.22 Sample heap

When the delete operation is performed for the heap in Fig. 12.22, it returns the element 80 at the root. In the delete operation, 47 (the last node value) is placed at the root value. Now, reheapDown is performed again to reconstruct a heap. The reconstructed heap is shown in Fig. 12.23.

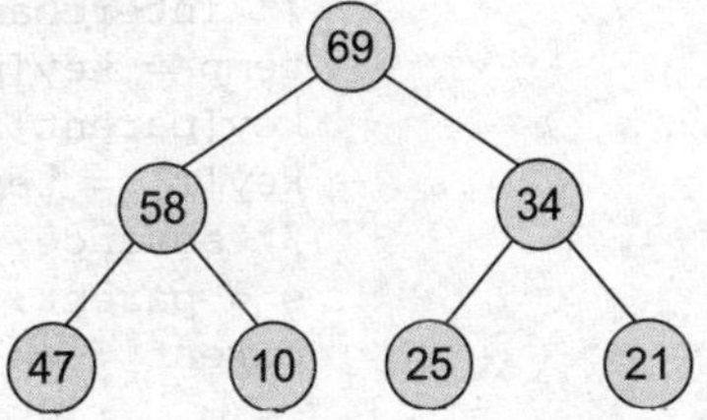

Fig. 12.23 Reconstructed heap after deletion of 80

Creating a Heap

The unsorted keys are taken sequentially one at a time and added into a heap. The size of the heap grows with the addition of each key. The ith key (k_i) is added into an existing heap of size $i - 1$ and a heap of size i is obtained. Initially, the node is placed in the heap of size $i - 1$ in such a way that an almost complete constraint is satisfied. The value of k_i is then compared with its parent's key value. If k_i is greater, the contents of the newly added node and that of the parent's node are exchanged. This process continues until either k_i is at the root node or the parent's key value is not less than k_i. The final tree is a heap of size i.

Let us assume that the heap is housed in an array where the relationships of the tree are not physically represented by link fields. Instead, they are implicit in the way we store them in the array. We store the binary tree in the array level-by-level, left to right. For example, Fig. 12.24 shows a binary tree.

Figure 12.25 shows its corresponding representation as an array.

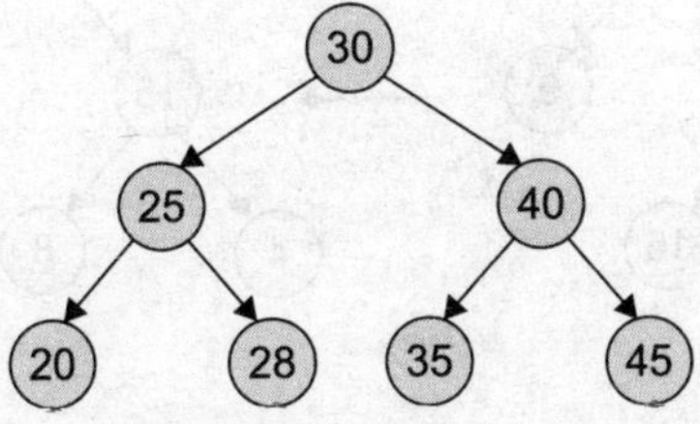

Fig. 12.24 Binary tree

Index	Value
[0]	30
[1]	25
[2]	40
[3]	20
[4]	28
[5]	35
[6]	45

Fig. 12.25 Array representation of Fig. 12.24

The root is stored in heap[0] and the last node in heap[maxnodes], where maxnodes is the number of nodes in the heap. We may note that for any node heap[i], its two children reside in heap[$i \times 2 + 1$] and heap[$i \times 2 + 2$]. If we want to know the parent of any node[k], we can get it at the node[(k – 1)/2].

Now, let us write an algorithm as shown in Algorithm 12.1 to create a heap of size `i` by adding a key to a heap of size `i - 1` where `i` ≥ `1`.

ALGORITHM 12.1

```
s = i;
/* find the parent node of i in the array */
parent = (s - 1)/2;
key[s] = newkey;
while(s >= 0 && key[parent] <= key[s])
{
   /* interchange parent and child */
   temp = key[parent];
   key[parent] = key [s];
   key[s] = temp;
   /* advance one level up in the tree */
   s = parent;
   parent = (s - 1)/2;
}
```

This algorithm is called for each addition of a new key to the heap.

For example, consider the following unsorted list of keys.

8, 20, 9, 4, 15, 10, 7, 22, 3, 12

Figures 12.26(a)–(j) show the building of a heap using this list of keys.

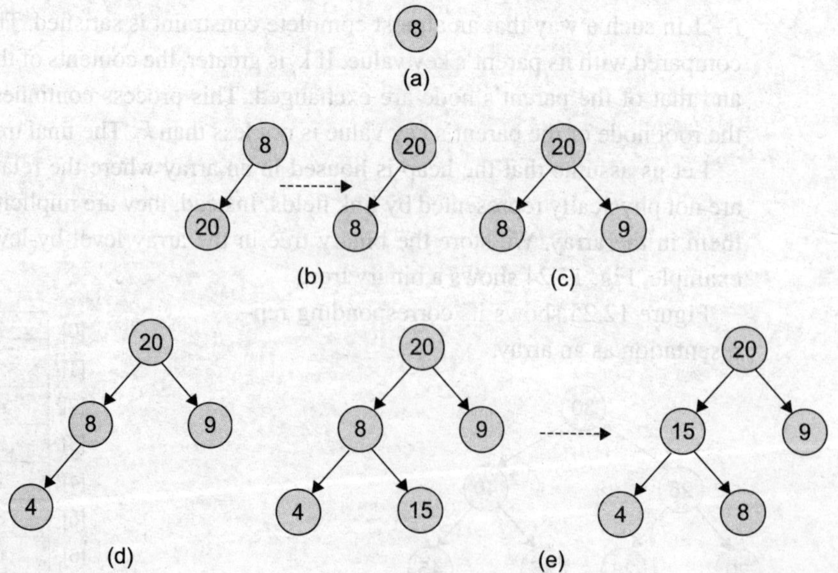

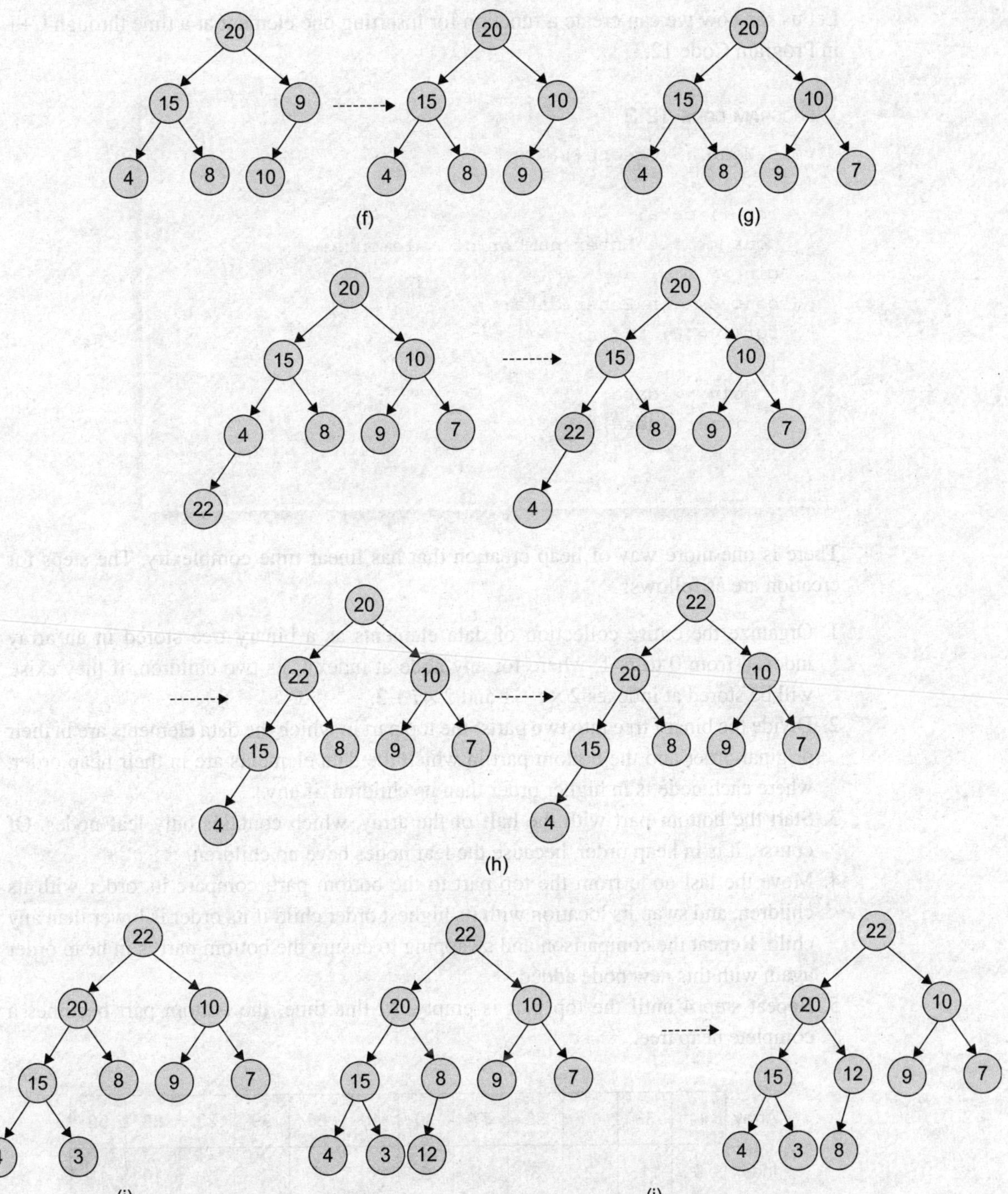

Fig. 12.26 Building a heap (a) Heap size 1 (b) Heap size 2 (c) Heap size 3 (d) Heap size 4 (e) Heap size 5 (f) Heap size 6 (g) Heap size 7 (h) Heap size 8 (i) Heap size 9 (j) Heap size 10

Let us see how we can create a function for inserting one element at a time through C++ in Program Code 12.3.

PROGRAM CODE 12.3

```
void Heap :: Create()
{
    int i, data;
    cout << "\n Enter number of  elements: ";
    cin >> n;
    cout << "\n Enter data:";
    for(i = 0; i < n; i++)
    {
        cin >> data;
        insert(data);
    }
}
```

There is one more way of heap creation that has linear time complexity. The steps for creation are as follows:

1. Organize the entire collection of data elements as a binary tree stored in an array indexed from 0 to n–1, where for any node at index i, its two children, if they exist, will be stored at indexes $2 \times i + 1$ and $2 \times i + 2$.
2. Divide the binary tree into two parts: the top part in which the data elements are in their original order and the bottom part in which the data elements are in their heap order, where each node is in higher order than its children, if any.
3. Start the bottom part with the half of the array, which contains only leaf nodes. Of course, it is in heap order, because the leaf nodes have no children.
4. Move the last node from the top part to the bottom part, compare its order with its children, and swap its location with its highest order child if its order is lower than any child. Repeat the comparison and swapping to ensure the bottom part is in heap order again with this new node added.
5. Repeat step 4 until the top part is empty. At this time, the bottom part becomes a complete heap tree.

Array	44	33	11	55	77	90	40	60	99	22	88	66
Index	0	1	2	3	4	5	6	7	8	9	10	11

The steps to build the heap are shown in Fig. 12.27.

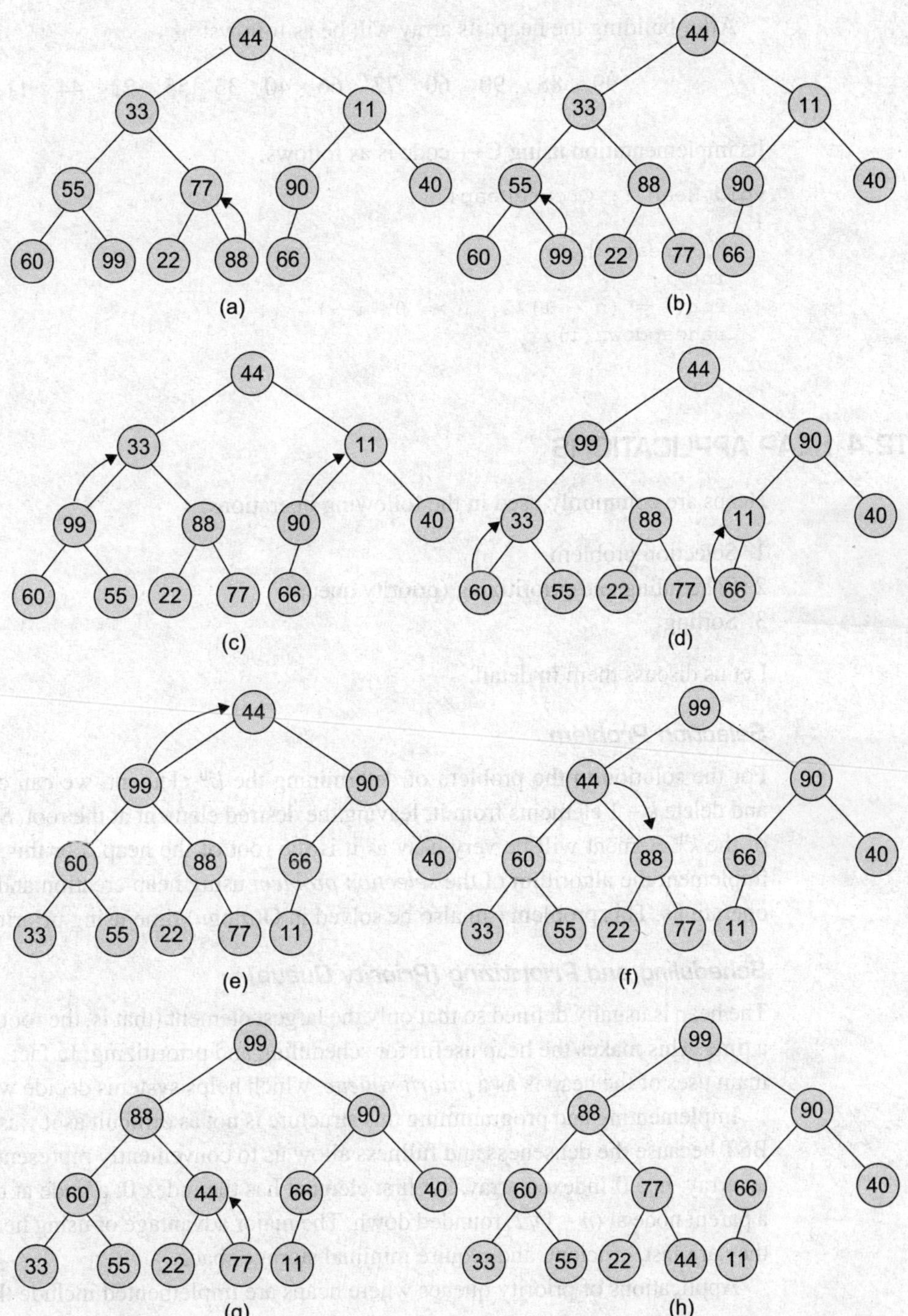

Fig. 12.27 Steps to build a heap for the array (44, 33, 11, 55, 77, 90, 40, 60, 99, 22, 88, 66)

After building the heap, its array will be as follows:

99 88 90 60 77 66 40 33 55 22 44 11

Its implementation using C++ code is as follows:

```
void Heap :: CreateHeap()
{
   // create heap
   int i;
   for(i = (n - 1)/2; i >= 0; i--)
   reheapdown(i);
}
```

12.4 HEAP APPLICATIONS

Heaps are commonly used in the following operations:

1. Selection problem
2. Scheduling and prioritizing (priority queue)
3. Sorting

Let us discuss them in detail.

Selection Problem

For the solution to the problem of determining the kth element, we can create the heap and delete $k - 1$ elements from it, leaving the desired element at the root. So the selection of the kth element will be very easy as it is the root of the heap. For this, we can easily implement the algorithm of the *selection problem* using heap creation and heap deletion operations. This problem can also solved in $O(n\log n)$ time using priority queues.

Scheduling and Prioritizing (Priority Queue)

The heap is usually defined so that only the largest element (that is, the root) is removed at a time. This makes the heap useful for scheduling and prioritizing. In fact, one of the two main uses of the heap is as a *priority queue*, which helps systems decide what to do next.

Implementing and programming this structure is not as difficult as it was with a normal BST because the denseness and fullness allow us to conveniently represent the heap with an array. In a 0-indexed array, the first element has the index 0; a node at the index n has a parent node at $(n - 1)/2$, rounded down. The major advantage of using heaps here is that they are fast, efficient, and require minimal storage space.

Applications of priority queues where heaps are implemented include the following:

1. CPU scheduling
2. I/O scheduling
3. Process scheduling

Sorting

Other than as a priority queue, the heap has one other important usage, heap sort. *Heap sort* is one of the fastest sorting algorithms, achieving speed as that of the quicksort and merge sort algorithms. The advantages of heap sort are that it does not use recursion, and it is efficient for any data order. There is no worst-case scenario in the case of heap sort. Let us discuss heap sort in detail.

12.5 HEAP SORT

The steps for building heap sort are as follows:

1. Build the heap tree.
2. Start deleteHeap operations, storing each deleted element at the end of the heap array.

After performing step 2, the order of the elements will be opposite to that in the heap tree. Hence, if we want the elements to be sorted in ascending order, we need to build the heap tree in descending order—the greatest element will have the highest priority. Note that we use only one array, treating its parts differently.

1. When building the heap tree, a part of the array will be considered as the heap, and the remaining part will be the original array.
2. When sorting, a part of the array will be the heap, and the remaining part will be the sorted array.

Consider the array 13, 17, 11, 6, 15, 8 as an example for heap sort. Using this example, let us illustrate both the steps for heap sort.

Build heap tree The given array is represented as a tree, complete, but not ordered.

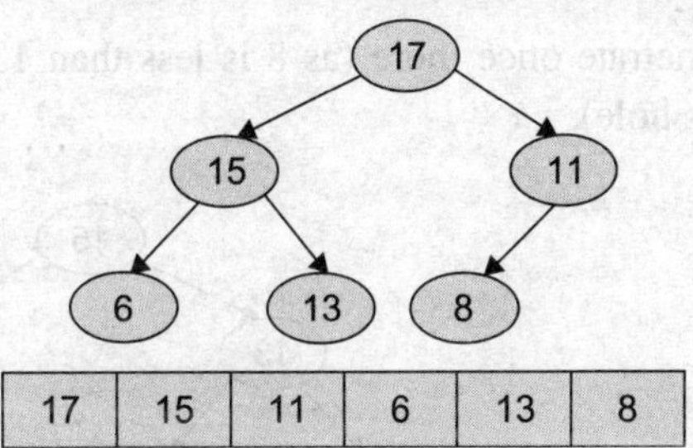

The following steps illustrate sorting by performing the deleteHeap operation till the heap is empty.

Delete top element 17 The following steps illustrate the deletion of element 17.

Step 1: Store 17 in a temporary place. A hole is created at the top as shown in the following figure.

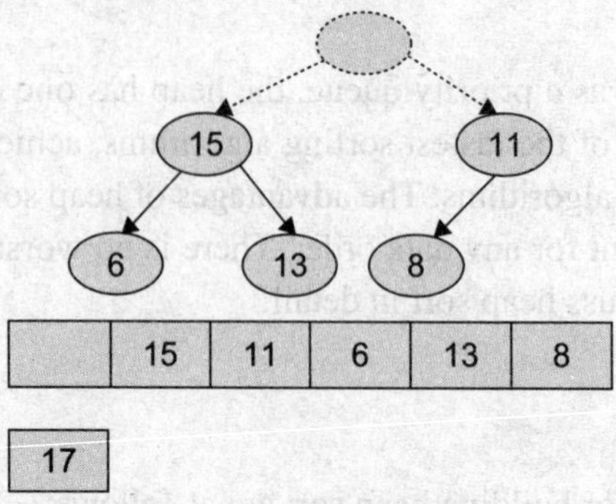

Step 2: Swap 17 with the last element of the heap. As 8 will be adjusted in the heap, its cell will no longer be a part of the heap. Instead, it becomes a cell from the sorted array.

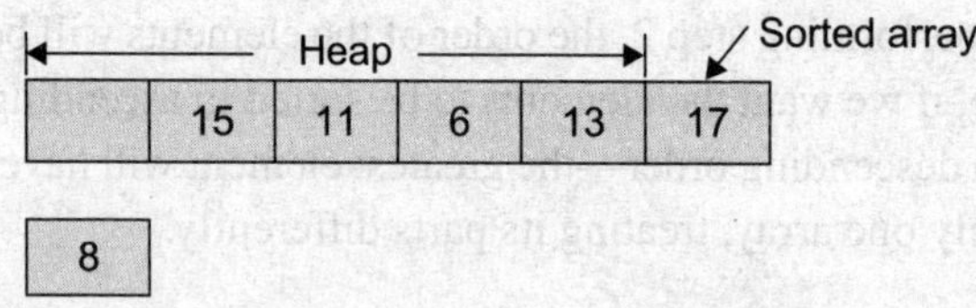

Step 3: Penetrate down the hole (8 is less than 15, so it cannot be inserted in the previous hole).

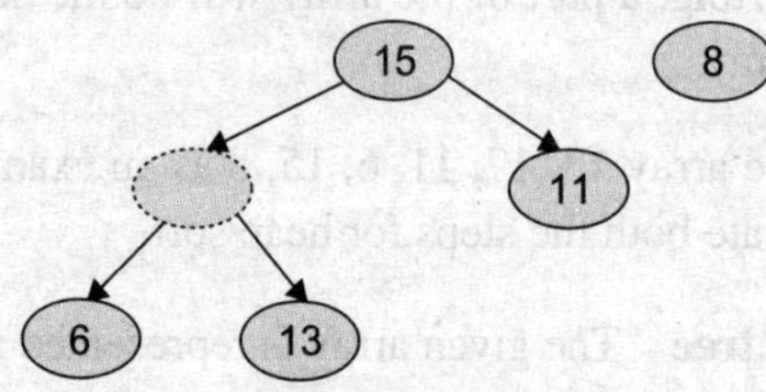

Step 4: Penetrate once more (as 8 is less than 13, here also it cannot be inserted in the previous hole).

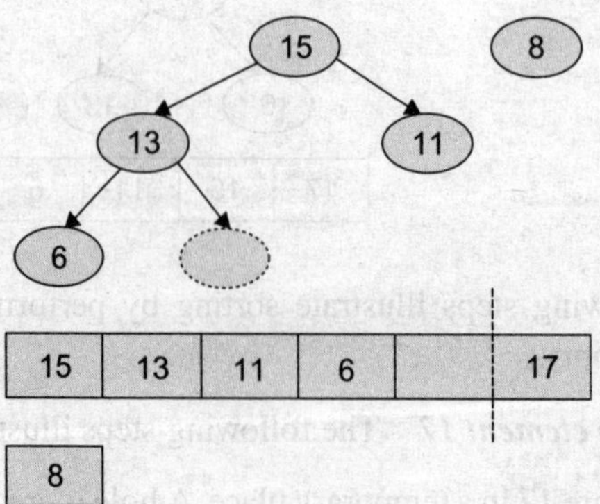

Now, 8 can be inserted in the hole.

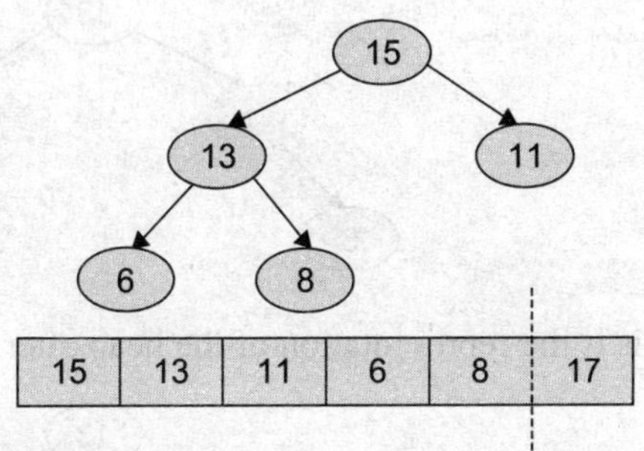

Delete top element 15 The following steps illustrate the deletion of the top element, 15.

Step 1: Store 15 in a temporary place. A hole is created at the top.

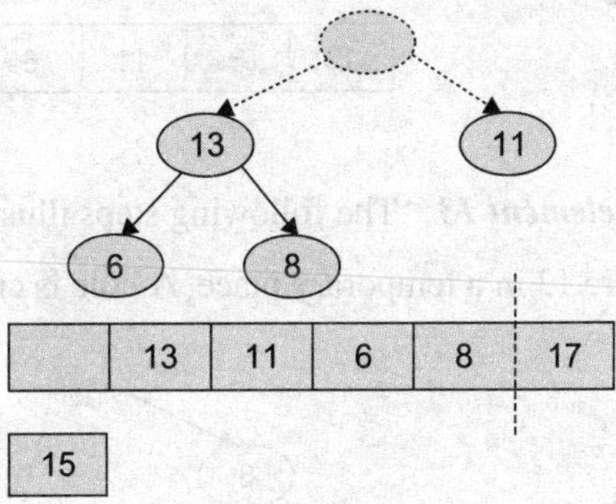

Step 2: Swap 15 with the last element of the heap. As 8 will be adjusted in the heap, its cell will no longer be a part of the heap. Instead, it becomes a cell from the sorted array.

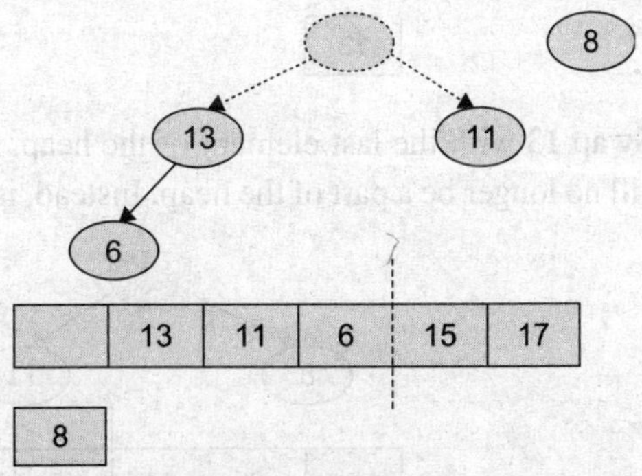

Step 3: Penetrate down the hole, as 8 is less than 13.

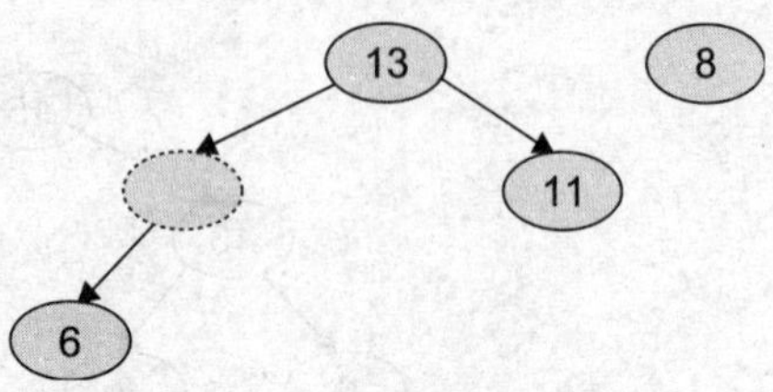

Step 4: This is the representation of the heap after the penetration.

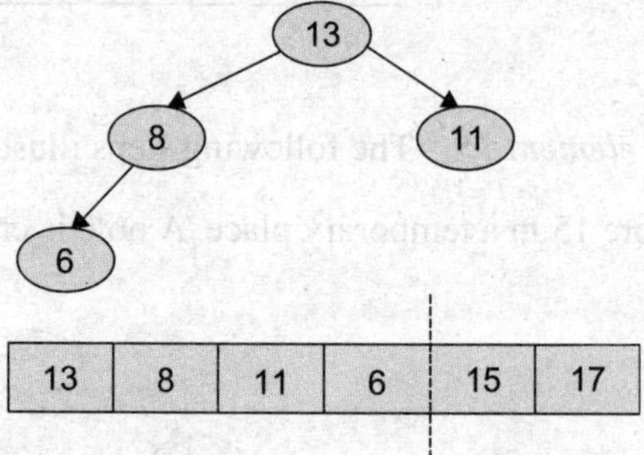

Delete top element 13 The following steps illustrate the deletion of element 13.

Step 1: Store 13 in a temporary place. A hole is created at the top.

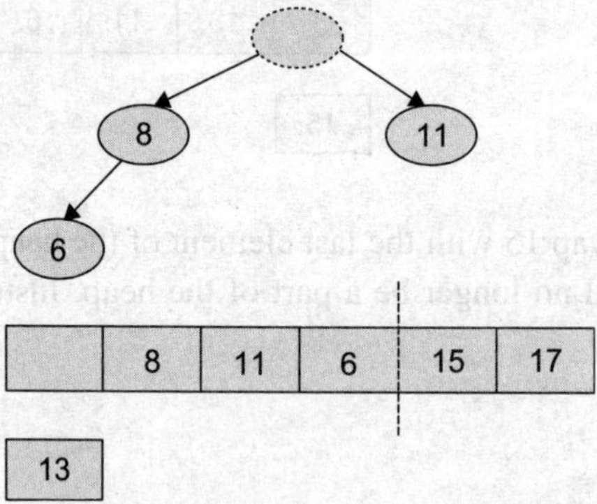

Step 2: Swap 13 with the last element of the heap. As 6 will be adjusted in the heap, its cell will no longer be a part of the heap. Instead, it becomes a cell from the sorted array.

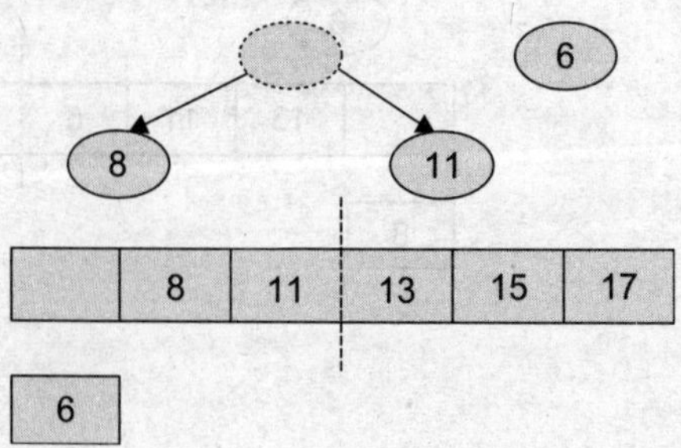

Step 3: Penetrate down the hole, as 6 is less than 11.

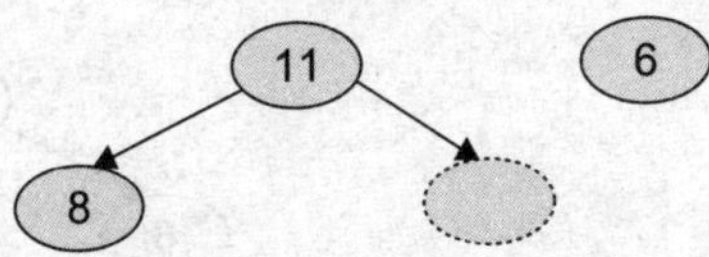

Step 4: The heap looks like this after the penetration.

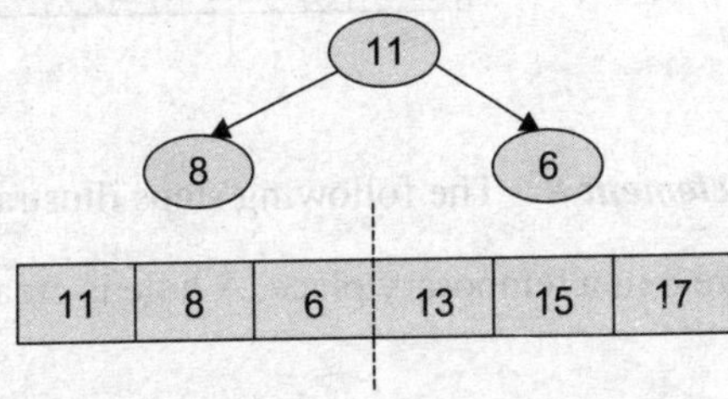

Delete top element 11 The following steps illustrate the deletion of the top element 11.

Step 1: Store 11 in a temporary place. A hole is created at the top.

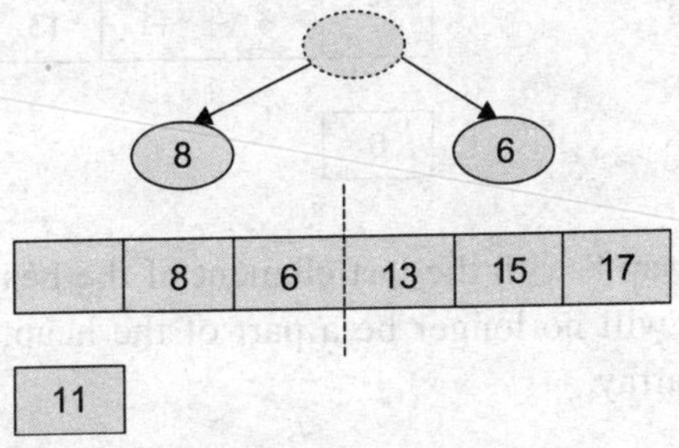

Step 2: Swap 11 with the last element of the heap. As 6 will be adjusted in the heap, its cell will no longer be a part of the heap. Instead, it becomes a cell from the sorted array.

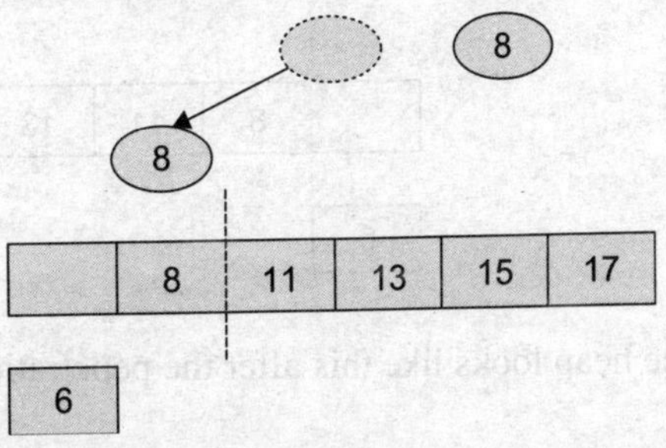

Step 3: Penetrate down the hole, as 6 is less than 8.

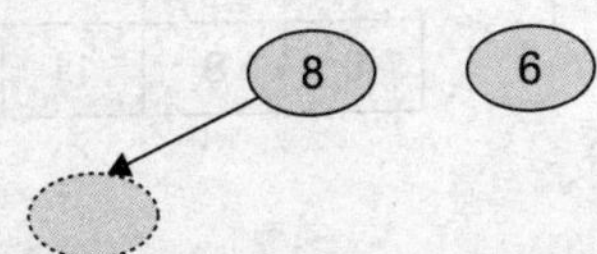

Step 4: The heap looks like this after the penetration.

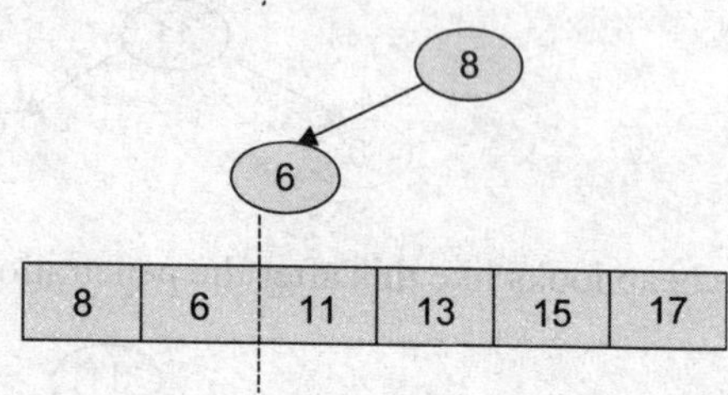

Delete top element 8 The following steps illustrate the deletion of the top element 8.

Step 1: Store 8 in a temporary place. A hole is created at the top.

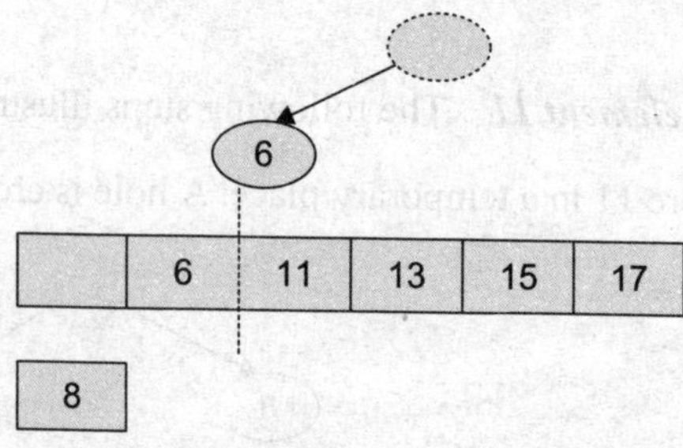

Step 2: Swap 8 with the last element of the heap. As 6 will be adjusted in the heap, its cell will no longer be a part of the heap. Instead, it becomes a cell from the sorted array.

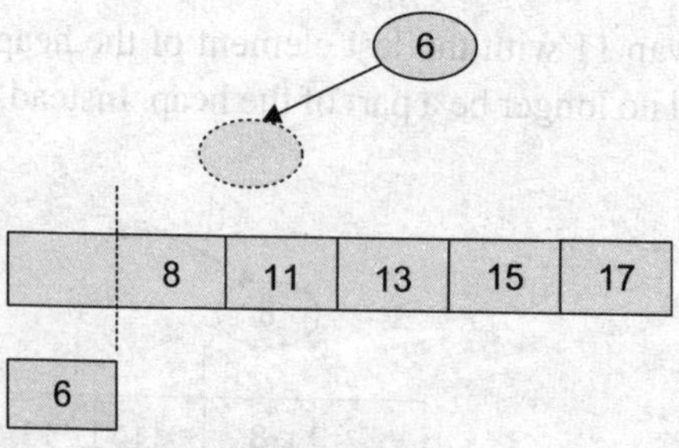

Step 3: The heap looks like this after the penetration.

Delete top element 6 The following steps illustrate the deletion of the top element 6.

Step 1: Store 6 in a temporary place. A hole is created at the top.

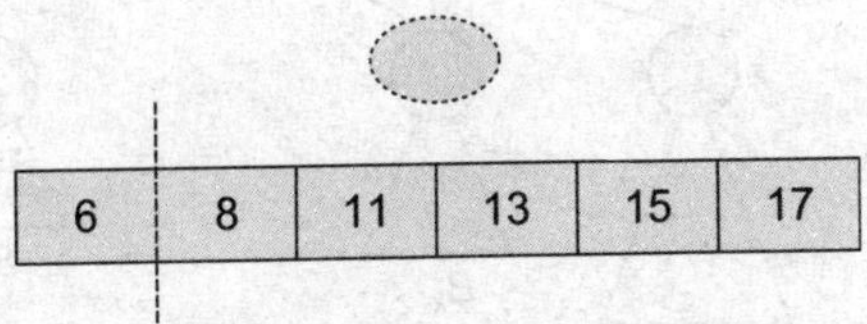

Empty heap Now, the heap is empty, so we stop and finally get the sorted array.

6	8	11	13	15	17

12.6 BINOMIAL TREES AND HEAPS

A binomial heap is a collection of binomial trees. We shall discuss binomial trees and heaps in more detail in Sections 12.6.1 and 12.6.2.

12.6.1 Binomial Trees

A *binomial tree* is an ordered tree defined recursively. Figure 12.28 shows the binomial trees.

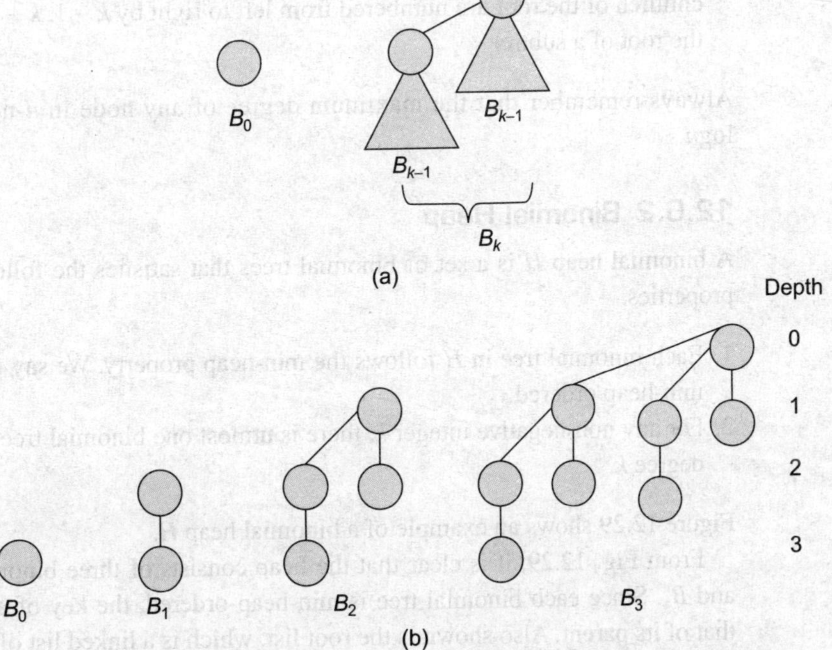

Fig. 12.28 Binomial trees (a) Recursive definition of the binomial tree B_k (b) Binomial tree B_0 through B_3

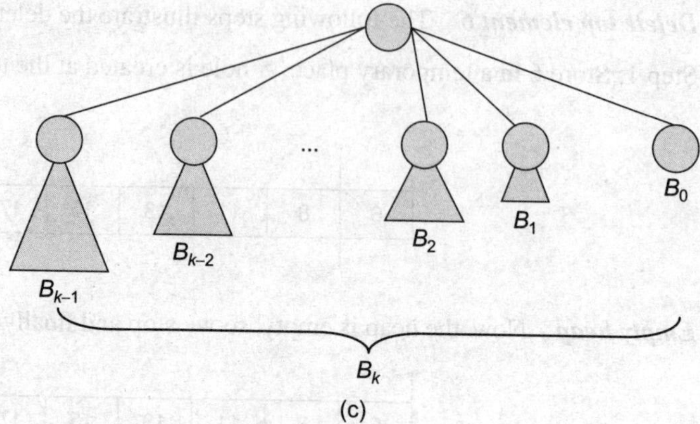

Fig. 12.28 Binomial trees (c) Another way of looking at the binomial tree B_k

As shown in Fig. 12.28(a), the binomial tree B_0 consists of a single node. For the binomial tree B_k,

1. there are 2^k nodes
2. the height of the tree is k
3. there are exactly $\binom{k}{i}$ nodes at depth i for $i = 0, 1, \ldots, k$
4. the root has degree k, which is greater than that of any other node; moreover, if the children of the root are numbered from left to right by $k - 1, k - 2, \ldots, 0$, the child i is the root of a subtree

Always remember that the maximum degree of any node in n-node binomial tree is $\log n$.

12.6.2 Binomial Heap

A binomial heap H is a set of binomial trees that satisfies the following binomial heap properties.

1. Each binomial tree in H follows the min-heap property. We say that each such tree is min-heap ordered.
2. For any non-negative integer k, there is utmost one binomial tree in H whose root has degree k.

Figure 12.29 shows an example of a binomial heap H.

From Fig. 12.29, it is clear that the heap consists of three binomial trees B_0, B_1, B_2, and B_3. Since each binomial tree is min-heap-ordered, the key of any node is less than that of its parent. Also shown is the root list, which is a linked list of roots in the order of increasing degree.

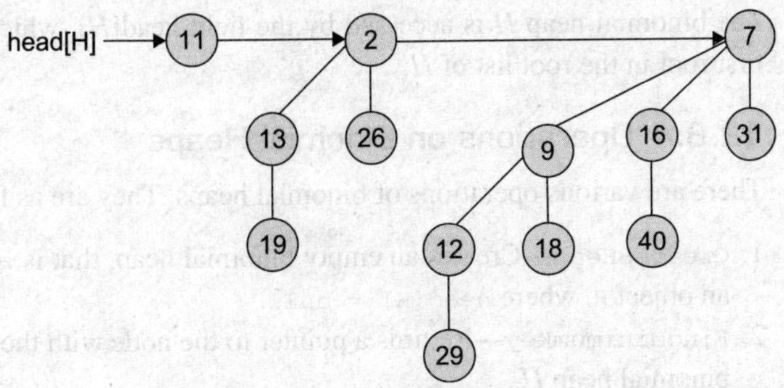

Fig. 12.29 A binomial heap with 13 nodes

12.6.3 Representation of Binomial Heap

The node of a binomial heap can be represented by five tuples as shown in Fig. 12.30.

Parent Points to the parent node

Key Key value, that is, data

Degree Degree of each node, that is, the number of children it has

Child Points to any of its child node (mostly pointing to its leftmost child)

Siblings Points to a sibling node, that is, used to maintain the singly-circular lists of siblings

Parent	
Key	
Degree	
Child	Sibling

Fig. 12.30 Representation of a node of binomial heap

As shown in Fig. 12.31, the roots of the binomial trees are organized in a linked list, which we refer to as root list.

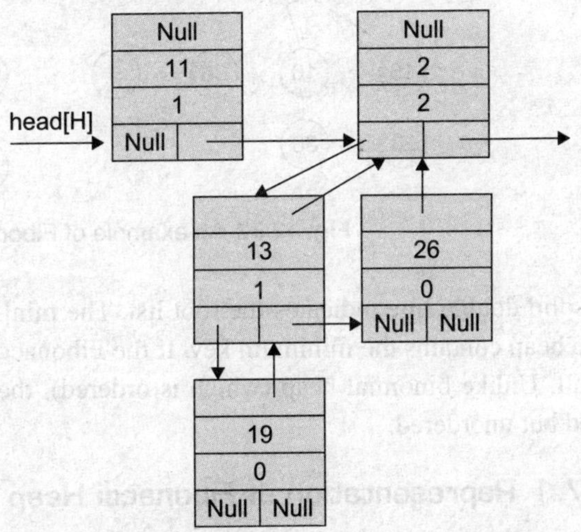

Fig. 12.31 Representation of binomial heap of Fig. 12.29 using five-tuple node

The binomial heap H is accessed by the field head[H], which is simply a pointer to the first root in the root list of H.

12.6.4 Operations on Binomial Heaps

There are various operations of binomial heaps. They are as follows:

1. `CreateBHeap`—Creates an empty binomial heap, that is, simply allocates and returns an object `H`, where `head[H] = null`.
2. `FindMinimumKey`—Returns a pointer to the node with the minimum key in an n-node binomial heap H.
3. `UnitingTwoBHeap`—Takes the union of the two binomial heaps.
4. `InsertNode`—Inserts a node into binomial heap H.
5. `ExtractMinimumKeyNode`—Extracts the node with the minimum key from a binomial heap H and returns the pointer to the extracted node.
6. `DecreaseKey`—Decreases the key of a node in a binomial heap H to a new value k.
7. `DeleteKey`—Deletes the specified key from binomial heap H.

12.7 FIBONACCI HEAP

Similar to the binomial heap, Fibonacci heap is a collection of min-heap-ordered trees. The trees in a Fibonacci are not constrained to be binomial trees. Figure 12.32 shows an example of the Fibonacci heap consisting of 5 min-heap-ordered trees and 15 nodes.

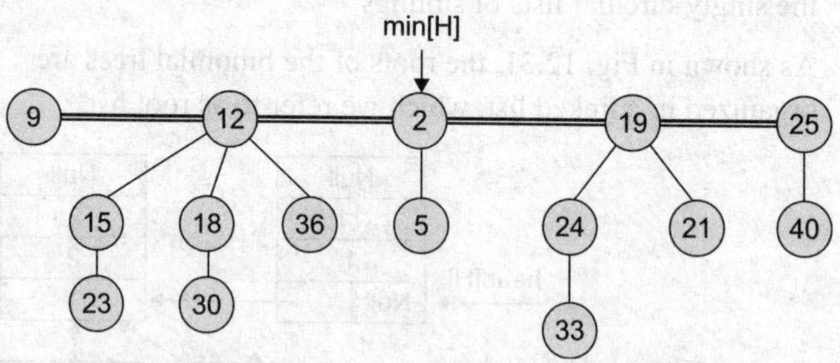

Fig. 12.32 An example of Fibonacci heap

The solid double line indicates the root list. The min[H] pointing to the minimum node of the heap contains the minimum key. If the Fibonacci heap is empty, then min[H] will be null. Unlike binomial heap (which is ordered), the trees within Fibonacci heaps are rooted but unordered.

12.7.1 Representation of Fibonacci Heap

Fibonacci heap can be represented using the Fibonacci heap nodes. The representation of such a node is shown in Fig. 12.33.

The node of a Fibonacci heap can be represented by seven tuples.

Parent Points to the parent node

Key Key value, that is, data

Degree Degree of each node, that is, the number of children it has

Child Points to any of its child node (mostly pointing to its leftmost child)

Mark The Boolean-valued field indicates whether the node has lost a child since the last time the node was made the child of another node. The newly created nodes are unmarked (i.e., the default value is false)

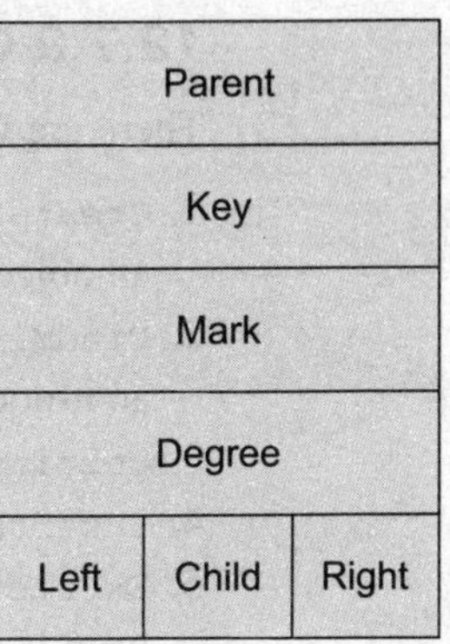

Fig. 12.33 Representation of a node of Fibonacci heap

Left Points to the left sibling node, that is, used to maintain the doubly circular lists of siblings

Right Points to the right sibling node, that is, used to maintain the doubly circular lists of siblings

The roots of all the trees in Fibonacci heap are linked together using left and right pointers into circular doubly-linked list called *root list* of the Fibonacci heap (Fig. 12.34).

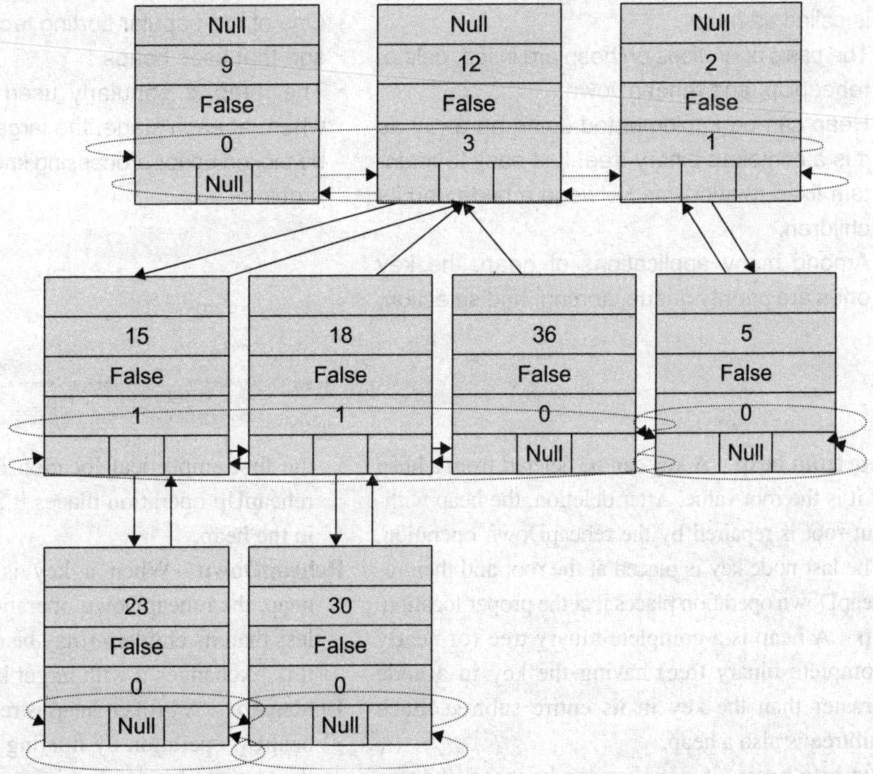

Fig. 12.34 Representation of binomial heap of Fig. 12.32 using seven-tuple node

12.7.2 Operations on Fibonacci Heaps

There are various operations of binomial heaps. They are as follows:

1. `CreateFHeap`—Creates an empty Fibonacci Heap, that is, simply allocates and returns an object `H`, where `min[H]=null`
2. `FindMinimumKey`—Returns `min[H]`, a pointer to the node with the minimum key in an *n*-node Fibonacci heap H
3. `UnitingTwoFHeap`—Takes the union of the two Fibonacci heaps
4. `InsertNode`—Inserts a node into Fibonacci heap H
5. `ExtractMinimumKeyNode`—Extracts the node with minimum key from Fibonacci heap H and returns the pointer to the extracted node
6. `DecreaseKey`—Decreases the key of a node in a Fibonacci heap H to a new value *k*.
7. `DeleteKey`—Deletes the specified key from Fibonacci heap H.

RECAPITULATION

- A complete or nearly complete binary tree where each node is greater or equal to its children with each subtree satisfying this property is called as *heap*.
- The basic operations on heap are insert, delete, reheapUp, and reheapDown.
- Heap can be implemented using an array as it is a complete binary tree. It is easy to maintain fixed relationship between a node and its children.
- Among many applications of heap, the key ones are priority queue, sorting, and selection.
- Priority queue is implemented using heap by maintaining its relationship of element with other members in a list.
- One of the popular sorting techniques is heap sort that uses heaps.
- The heap is popularly used in applications where at each stage, the largest element is to be picked up for processing known as *selection problem*.

KEY TERMS

Delete from heap A key can be deleted from a heap if it is the root value. After deletion, the heap without root is repaired by the reheapDown operation. The last node key is placed at the root and then reheapDown operation places it at the proper location.

Heap A heap is a complete binary tree (or nearly complete binary tree) having the key in a node greater than the key in its entire subtree. Each subtree is also a heap.

Insert into heap A new key can be inserted into a heap. Initially, a new key is inserted by locating the first empty leaf location in an array, and the reheapUp operation places it in a proper location in the heap.

ReheapDown When a key is pushed down the heap, the reheapDown operation ensures that it is less than its children (may be one or more), and if it is, exchanges it with larger key.

ReheapUp A broken heap is repaired using the reheapUp operation by floating the last element up the tree until it reaches its correct location in the heap.

EXERCISES

Multiple choice questions

1. For the given array representation of a heap, which of these represents a min-heap?
   (i) 0 2 4 7 5 5 6
   (ii) 5 7 8 6 9 9 10
   (a) (i) only
   (b) (ii) only
   (c) Both (i) and (ii)
   (d) None
2. What will be the array representation of a max-heap with the following insertions?
   40, 80, 35, 90, 45, 50, 70
   (a) 90 80 70 40 45 35 50
   (b) 90 80 70 45 40 50 35
   (c) 90 70 80 40 45 35 50
   (d) 90 70 80 45 40 50 35
3. If 100 is added to the heap 40, 80, 35, 90, 45, 50, 70, what will be the new array representation?
   (a) 90 80 70 40 45 35 50 100
   (b) 100 90 70 80 45 35 50 40
   (c) 100 90 80 70 40 45 35 50
   (d) 100 80 90 70 40 45 35 50
4. What is the minimum and maximum number of elements in a heap of size *h*?
   (a) $2(h-1), (2h+1)-1$
   (b) $2h, (2h+1)-1$
   (c) $2(h-1), (2h)-1$
   (d) $(2h)-1, (2h+1)-1$
5. What feature of heaps allows them to be efficiently implemented using a partially filled array?
   (a) Heaps are binary search trees.
   (b) Heaps are complete binary trees.
   (c) Heaps are full binary trees.
   (d) Heaps contain only integer data.
6. What will be the number of elements in the left subtree and right subtree of the heap if the following elements are inserted in the order: 45, 26, 84, 63, 27, 94, 47?
   (a) (3, 3)
   (b) (2, 4)
   (c) (4, 3)
   (d) (4, 2)
7. For the following heap, what will be the corresponding array representation?

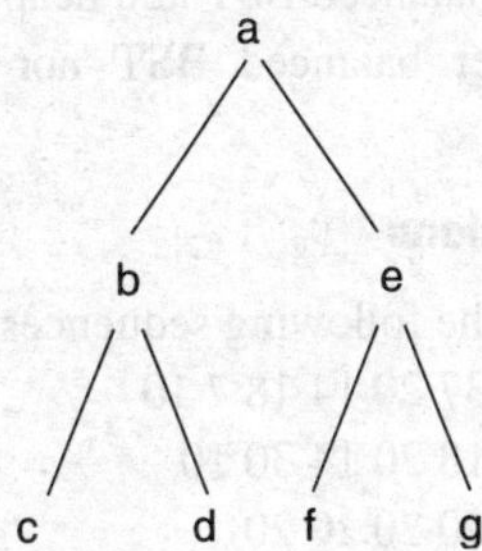

   (a) a b e c d f g
   (b) a b e c f d g
   (c) a b e d f c g
   (d) a b e c d f g

(Hint: Perform breadth-first traversal.)

8. A priority queue is implemented as a max-heap. Initially, it has five elements. The level order traversal of the heap is given here.
   10, 8, 5, 3, 2
   The two new elements 1 and 7 are inserted in the heap in that order. A level order traversal of the heap after the insertion of the elements is:
   (a) 10, 8, 7, 5, 3, 2, 1
   (b) 10, 8, 7, 2, 3, 1, 5
   (c) 10, 8, 7, 1, 2, 3, 5
   (d) 10, 8, 7, 3, 2, 1, 5
9. In a heap with *n* elements with the smallest element at the root, the 7th smallest element can be found in time
   (a) _(*n*log*n*)
   (b) (*n*)
   (c) _(log*n*)
   (d) _(1)
10. A data structure is required for storing a set of integers such that each of the following operations can be done in (log*n*) time, where *n* is the number of elements in the set.
    (i) Deletion of the smallest element

(ii) Insertion of an element if it is not already present in the set

Which of the following data structures can be used for this purpose?

(a) A heap can be used but not a balanced BST.
(b) A balanced BST can be used but not a heap.
(c) Both balanced BST and heap can be used.
(d) Neither balanced BST nor heap can be used.

Review questions

1. Which of the following sequences are heaps?
   (a) 42 35 37 20 14 18 7 10
   (b) 42 35 18 20 14 30 10
   (c) 20 20 20 20 20 20
2. Show which item would be deleted from the following heaps after calling the delete algorithm thrice:
   50 30 40 20 10 25 35 10 5
3. Show the resulting heap after 33, 22, and 8 are added to the following heap:
   50 30 40 20 10 25 35 10 5
4. Show the step-by-step creation of a binary heap for the given keys:
   11, 19, 17, 5, 80, 14, 1, 10, 23, 34, 22
5. Write a function to insert a node in binary heap. Give an example.
   (a) Show the array implementation of heap
   (b) Apply the deletion operation to the heap. Repair the heap after deletion
   (c) Insert 38 into the following heap. Repair the heap after insertion

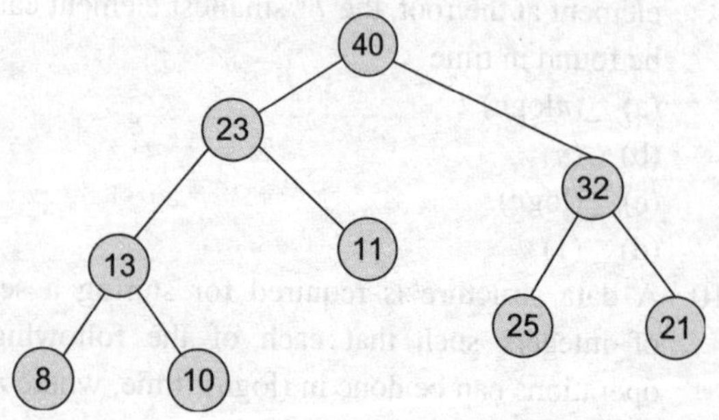

   (d) Using the delete operation, delete root 40 and replace with the last value 10 at the root and reheapDown for the following tree.

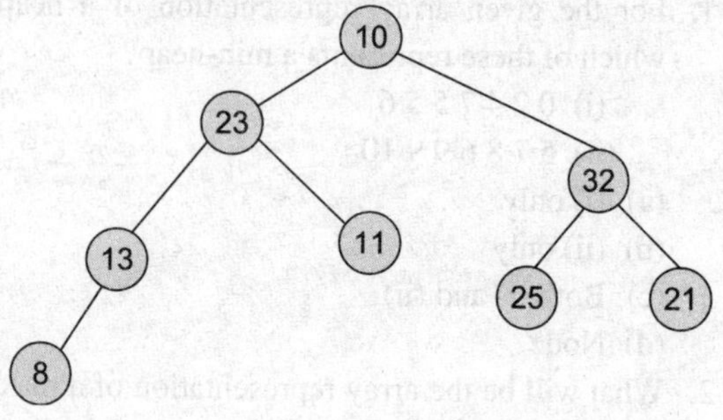

   (e) Insert 38 into the following heap. Repair the heap after insertion.

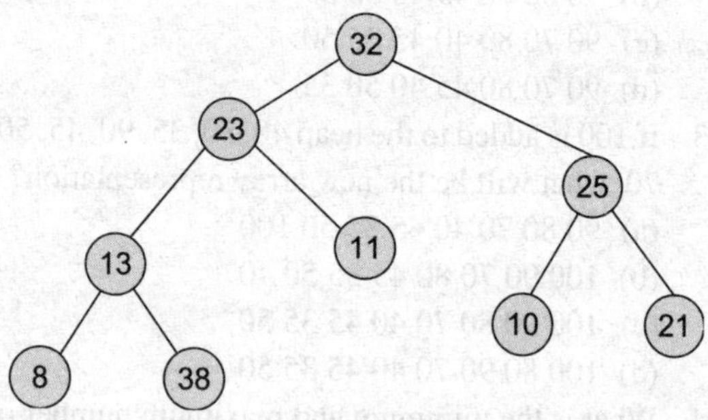

6. Define max-heap. Write a pseudo C++ code for the following operations on max-heap. Mention time complexity of each operation.
   (a) Insertion of an element in max-heap
   (b) Deletion of max element from max-heap
7. Write an algorithm to take *n* elements and do the following operations:
   (a) Insert them into the heap one by one.
   (b) Build a heap in linear time.
8. Write a pseudo C++ code to convert a given complete binary tree into a min-heap. Analyse your algorithm for computation time.
9. Show the result of inserting 10, 12, 1, 14, 6, 5, 8, 15, 3, 9, 7, 4, 11, 13, 2, one element at a time, into an initially empty binary heap.

10. After creating the heap for question 9, delete the element 8 from the heap. How do you repair the heap?
11. Write a C++ code to implement binomial heap and its operations.
12. Write a C++ code to implement Fibonacci heap and its operations.
13. Compare binomial heap and Fibonacci heap.
14. Create a priority queue using the following data. The first number is a priority and the letter is the data: 3-A 5-B 3-C 2-D 1-E 2-F 3-G 2-H 2-I 2-J
15. Show the contents of the priority queue 11, 19, 17, 5, 80, 14, 1, 10, 23, 34, 22 after deleting the items from the queue.
16. Show the contents of the priority queue 11, 19, 17, 5, 80, 14, 1, 10, 23, 34, 22 after deleting three elements from it.
17. Write a pseudo C++ code for reheapUp to build a minimum heap.
18. Write a pseudo C++ code for reheapDown to create a minimum heap.

Answers to multiple choice questions

1. (a) 2. (a) 3. (b)

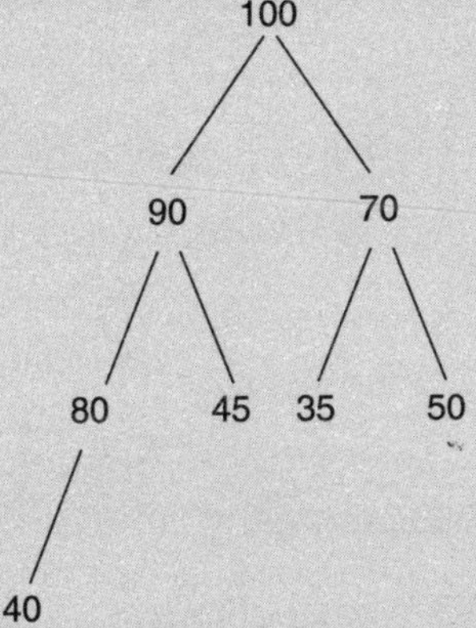

4. (c) Given: Minimum number of nodes with height $n(h) = 1$

Number of nodes upto height $n(h_i - 1) = (2h - 1) - 1$

Thus, the min. number of nodes at height = Sum of preceding two equations

$$= (2h - 1) - 1 + 1 = 2h - 1$$

The maximum number of nodes at height = $2h - 1$.

Thus, the option is 3.

5. (d) By definition. To make a guess, a bridge in real life connects two parts. Hence, its removal should separate them.
6. (a) The final heap will be

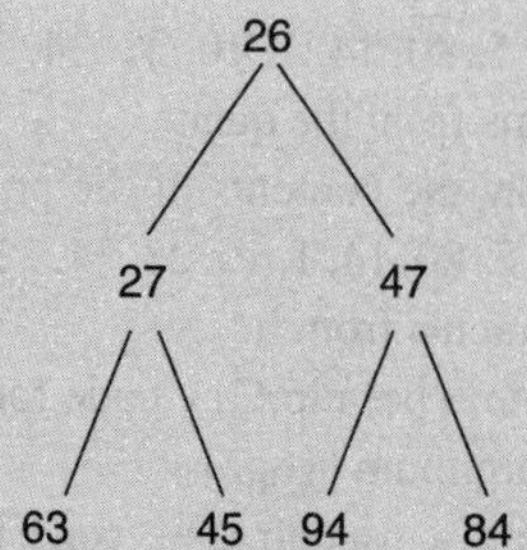

One need not even construct the tree. The simplest way is that there are seven nodes, that is, six nodes for left and right subtree. For a heap, it's quite obvious that the division has to be 3–3, as a heap is a complete binary tree.

7. (d) 8. (d) 9. (d)

With large *n*, the number of comparisons required for finding the 7th smallest element becomes irrelevant of the height (log*n*) of the heap. It can be found out in constant time. Hence, the answer is option (d).

10. (c)

13 INDEXING AND MULTIWAY TREES

OBJECTIVES

After completing this chapter, the reader will be able to understand the following:

- Indexing techniques
- B-trees which prove invaluable for problems of external information retrieval
- A class of trees called tries, which share some properties of table lookup
- Important uses of trees in many search techniques

An important area in computer science is information retrieval. An information retrieval application, a database, which may contain a wide variety of data structures, is maintained on an online basis using large random access files. These files are searched for requested information based on index items generated from a user query. One of the problems associated with information retrieval systems and especially automated library systems is creating a good indexing scheme. We shall learn about indexing schemes in this chapter.

13.1 INTRODUCTION

A *file* is a collection of records, each record having one or more fields. The fields used to distinguish among the records are known as *keys*. *File organization* describes the way in which records are stored in a file. File organization is concerned with representing data records on an external storage media. The choice of such a representation depends on the environment where the file is to operate, for example, real-time, batched, simple query, one key, or multiple keys. When there is only one key, the records may be stored on this key and stored sequentially either on a tape or a disk. This results in a sequentially ordered file. This organization is good for files operating in batched retrieval and update modes when the number of transactions batched is large enough to make the processing cost effective. When the number of keys is more than one or when real time responses are needed, a sequential organization is not adequate. In a general situation, several indices may have to be maintained. In these cases, the file organization breaks down into two more aspects:

Directory for the collection of indices

File organization for the physical organization of records

Many alternative file organizations exist, each suitable in a particular situation. File organization is the way records are organized on a physical storage. One such organization is *sequential* (ordered and unordered). In this general framework, processing a query or updating a request would proceed in two steps:

1. The indices would be interrogated to determine the parts of the physical file to be searched.
2. These parts of the physical file will be searched.

Depending upon the kinds of indices maintained, the second stage may involve only the accessing of records satisfying the query or may involve retrieving non-relevant records too.

Let us study about indexing and the different indexing schemes.

13.2 INDEXING

One of the most popular indices is a book index. An index of a book is a table containing a list of topics (keys) and page numbers where the topic can be found (reference fields).

An index, whether it is a book or a data file index (in computer memory), is based on the basic concepts such as keys and reference fields. The index to a book provides a way to find a topic quickly. Imagine a book that does not have a good index. Then, we have only one solution, that is, to scan the whole book sequentially for finding a particular topic. In general, indexing is a way of finding things quickly.

To search some topics in a book is a problem which cannot be solved by methods we have studied in Chapter 9, searching and sorting. Rearranging all the words in the book in alphabetical order certainly would make finding any particular term easier, but would obviously have disastrous effects on the meaning of the book. Even though this book example, where the words in the book are referred to as pinned records, is absurd, it clearly underscores the power and importance of the index as a conceptual tool. Indexing works on indirect addressing. An index lets us impose order on a file without rearranging the file.

One more example where indexing is used is a library. To locate a book by a specific author, title, or subject, we can take the card catalog. The card catalog is actually a set of three indices, each using a different key field and all of them using the same catalog number as a reference field. Another use of indexing is to provide multiple access paths to a file. The advantage of indexing is that it gives keyed access to variable length records.

13.2.1 Indexing Techniques

A directory is a collection of indices. It may contain one index for every key or only one index for some of the keys. If an index contains an entry for every record, then it is called a *dense index*. If an index contains an entry for only some of the records, then it is *non-dense index*. In some cases, all the indices may be integrated into one large index.

The index is a collection of pairs of the form (key value, address). For example, consider the sample data for employee file as in Table 13.1.

Table 13.1 Employee records

Record	Emp. no.	Name	Occupation	Disk address
A	100	Saurabh	Developer	P1
B	500	Abolee	Project head	P2
C	300	Anagha	Developer	P3
D	200	Abhijeet	Project head	P4
E	400	Devnarayanan	Developer	P5

Suppose P1, P2, P3, P4, P5 are the disk addresses where these records are stored. Let 'Emp. no.' be the key. Then, the index will have the entries (100, P1), (500, P2), (300, P3), (200, P4), and (400, P5). This is a dense index because the key is distinct for all records and there is an entry for each record. If we keep 'Occupation' as the key, then the index will be (Developer, q1), (Project Head), q2), where q1 is a disk address that stores the list of addresses of all developers, that is, P1, P3, and P5, and q2 is a disk address that stores the list of addresses of all project heads, that is, P2 and P4. This is also a dense index.

Index can also be maintained as the key value—address1, address2, ..., address*n*. However, if the number of records associated with each key varies, then it results in variable size nodes and complex storage management.

Different operations on the index are searching a key, modifying some entry in the index, inserting a new entry, and deleting an entry from the index. An index is too large and has to be maintained on the external storage. Let us see some indexing techniques.

Cylinder-surface Indexing

This is the simplest type of index organization. It is useful only for the primary key index of a sequentially ordered file. In a sequentially ordered file, the physical sequence of records is ordered by the key, called the *primary key*. The employee file in Table 13.1 is not sequentially ordered if 'Emp. no.' is a primary key because that field is not sorted. The sequentially ordered file can be stored on a tape or a disk. Disk memory has many surfaces, each surface having tracks. A cylinder *j* consists of track *j* on all the surfaces. So, the sequential interpretation of disk memory can be done in the following way. First, all tracks on cylinder 1 are accessed, then cylinder 2, and so on. So the read/write heads are moved one cylinder at a time. This is shown in Fig. 13.1.

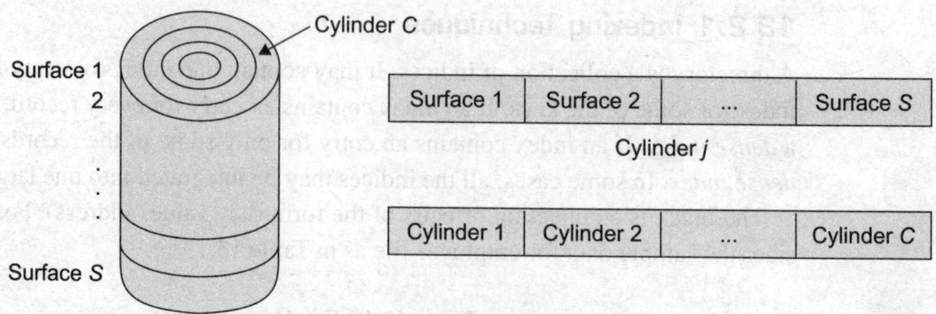

Fig. 13.1 Cylinder-surface indexing

The cylinder-surface index consists of a cylinder index and several surface indices. If the file requires 1 through C cylinders, then there are C entries in the cylinder index. There is one entry corresponding to the largest key value in each cylinder. For each cylinder, there is a surface index. If the disk has S usable surfaces, then each surface index has S entries. The total number of surface index entries is $C \times S$. For example, consider Table 13.2.

Table 13.2 Employee records cylinder-surface indexing

Emp. no.	Emp. name	Cylinder	Surface
1	Abolee	1	1
2	Anand	1	1
3	Amit	1	2
4	Amol	1	2
5	Rohit	2	1
6	Santosh	2	1
7	Saurabh	2	2
8	Shila	2	2

Let there be two surfaces and two records stored per track. The file is organized sequentially on the field 'Emp. name'. The corresponding cylinder index is given in Table 13.3.

Table 13.3 Cylinder index for Table 13.2

Cylinder	Highest key value
1	Amol
2	Shila

The surface index for cylinder 1 is the surface highest key value: Anand, Amol.

The surface index for cylinder 2 is the surface highest key value: Santosh, Shila.

A search for a record with a particular key value K is done in the following way. First, the key cylinder index is read into memory. In general, it has a few hundred entries, so it fits in one track. The cylinder index is searched to determine the required cylinder number, and then, for this cylinder, its surface index is read into memory and searched for the track. Then, this track is read in and searched for the key. For example, if we search for a record with the key 'Rohit', then the cylinder index tells that the record is either on cylinder 2 or not in the file. If the surface index of cylinder 2 is searched, then it shows that the record is either on surface 1 or not in the file. So in the second track t2, 1 is read and searched for. The desired record is found on this track. So the total number of disk accesses to get a record is three—one for the cylinder index, one for the surface index, and one for the track of records. If the track sizes are very large, then a sector index is maintained. If several disks are used to store a file, then a disk index is also maintained.

This method of maintaining a file and index is referred to as indexed sequential access method (ISAM). It is the simplest file organization for single key files but not useful for multiple key files.

Hashed Indexing

The operations related to hashed indices are the same as those for hash tables. This has been discussed in detail in Chapter 11.

13.3 TYPES OF SEARCH TREES

We have studied BSTs (binary search trees), AVL trees, optimal binary search trees, and heaps in Chapter 7. These were binary trees with outgoing degree two. For large data, these trees grow to a great height. To avoid these problems, we retain the properties of BSTs and increase the outgoing degree more than two. In a BST, the node maintains two links for its left and right child, whereas in a multiway search tree, each node can maintain more than two links for its more than two subtrees. Such search trees have vast applications such as dictionary, spell checks, and external file indices.

13.3.1 Multiway Search Tree

Binary search trees generalize directly to multiway search trees. A multiway search tree is a tree of order m, where each node has utmost m children. Here m is an integer. If $k \le m$ is the number of children, then the node contains exactly $k - 1$ keys, which partition all the keys in the subtrees into k subsets. If some of these subsets are empty, then the corresponding children in the tree are empty. Figure 13.2 shows a 5-way search tree.

We always want to construct a multiway search tree that will minimize file accesses. So the height of the tree should be as small as possible, for example, B-tree and B+ tree.

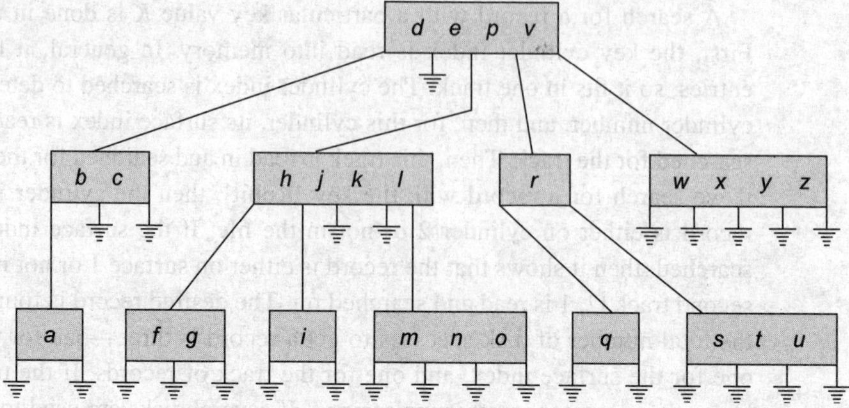

Fig. 13.2 5-way search tree

13.3.2 B-tree

When we want to locate and retrieve records stored in a disk file, the time required for a single access is thousand times greater for external retrieval than for internal information retrieval.

Our goal in external searching is to minimize the number of disk access since each access takes so long compared to internal computation. Multiway trees are especially appropriate for external searching.

A B-tree is a balanced multiway tree. A node of the tree contains many records or keys of records and pointers to children.

To reduce disk access, the following points are applicable:

1. Height is kept minimum.
2. All leaves are kept at the same level.
3. All nodes other than leaves must have at least minimum number of children.

B-tree Definition

A B-tree of order *m* is a multiway tree with the following properties:

1. The number of keys in each internal node is one less than the number of its non-empty children, and these keys partition the keys in the children in the fashion of the search tree.
2. All leaves are on the same level.
3. All internal nodes except the root have utmost *m* non-empty children and at least $\lceil m/2 \rceil$ non-empty children.
4. The root is either a leaf node, or it has from two to *m* children.
5. A leaf node contains no more than $m - 1$ keys.

Its node structure is given in Fig. 13.3.

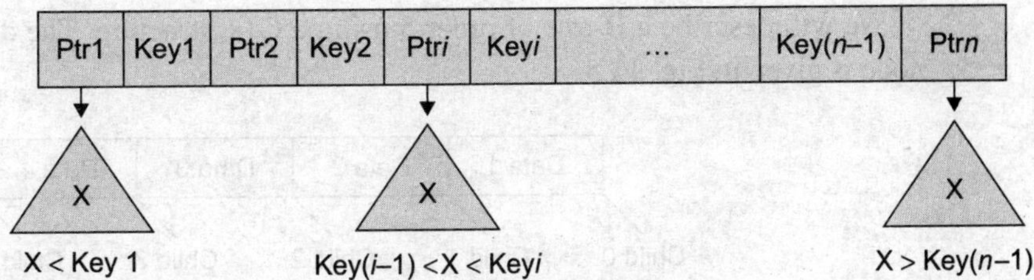

Fig. 13.3 Node structure for B-tree

The B-tree of order 5 for Fig. 13.3 shown in Fig. 13.4.

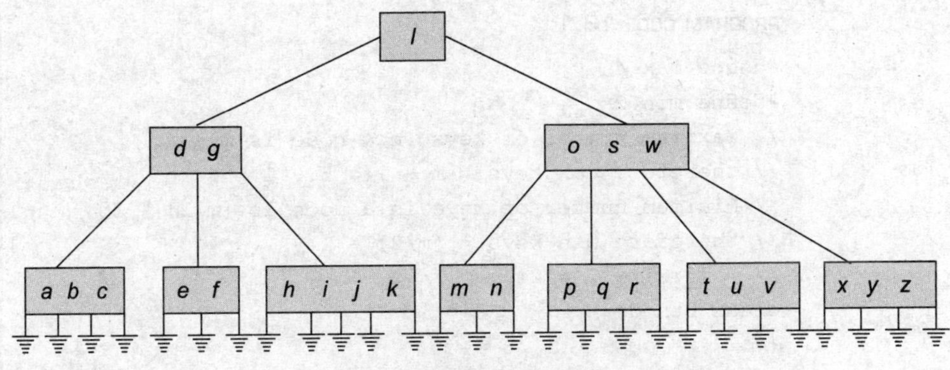

Fig. 13.4 B-tree of order 5

The maximum number of items in a B-tree of order m and height h is shown in Table 13.4.

Table 13.4 B-tree of order m and height h

Level	Number of keys
Root	$m - 1$
Level 1	$m(m - 1)$
Level 2	$m^2(m - 1)$
⋮	
Level h	$m^h(m - 1)$

So, the total number of items is

$$(1 + m + m^2 + m^3 + \dots + m^h)(m - 1) = [(m^{h+1} - 1)/\ (m - 1)]\ (m - 1) = m^{h+1} - 1 \qquad (13.1)$$

When $m = 5$ and $h = 2$, Eq. (13.1) gives $5^3 - 1 = 124$.

We will describe a B-tree of order 5 using a C++ structure. The declaration of B-tree node is given in Fig. 13.5.

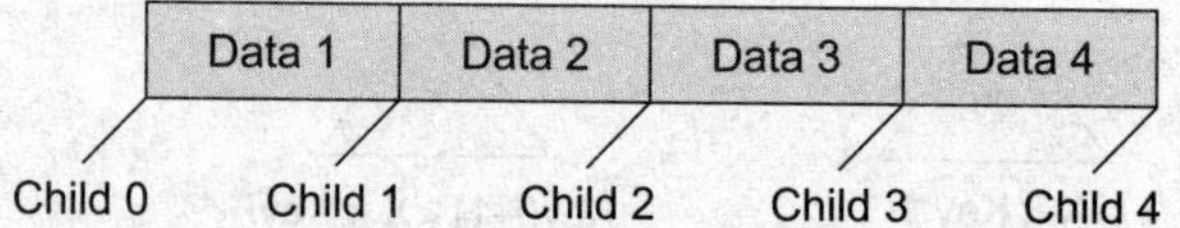

Fig. 13.5 Node structure of 5-way B-tree

Let us see how this can be implemented using the C++ code as in Program Code 13.1.

PROGRAM CODE 13.1

```
#define max 4
#define min 2
// Maximum number of keys in a node is m - 1,
// therefore max_keys = m - 1 = 5 - 1 = 4
// Minimum number of keys in a node is [m/2] - 1,
// therefore min_keys = [m/2] - 1
// = [5/2] - 1 = 2
class btnode
{
   public:
      int count;
      int data[max + 1];
      btnode *child[max + 1];
};

class btree
{
   int push_down(int, btnode*, int*, btnode**);
   void pushin(int, btnode*, btnode*, int);
   void split_node(int, btnode*, btnode*, int, int*,
   btnode**);
   void del_node(int, btnode*);
   void remove_key(btnode*, int);
   void successor(btnode*, int);
   void restore(btnode*, int);
   void move_right(btnode*, int);
   void move_left(btnode*, int);
   void combine_nodes(btnode*, int);
  int search_node(int, btnode*, int*);
```

```
    btnode*search(int, btnode*, int*);
    public:
        btnode* root;
        void display();
        btnode* del(int, btnode*);
        void pre_rec(btnode*);
        btnode* insert(int, btnode*);
};
```

Reasons for using B-trees B-trees are widely used for the following reasons:

1. The cost of each disk transfer is high when the searching tables are held on disk and do not depend much on the amount of data transferred, especially if the consecutive items are transferred. Consider a condition of the B-tree of order 101. We can transfer each node in one disk read operation.
2. A B-tree of order 101 and height 3 can hold $101^4 - 1$ items (approximately 100 million), and any item can be accessed with three disk reads (assuming we hold the root in memory).
3. When a balanced tree is required and if we take $m = 3$, we get a '2–3 tree', where the non-leaf nodes have two or three children (i.e., one or two keys).
4. B-trees are always balanced (since the leaves are all at the same level), so 2-3 trees make a good type of balanced tree.

Operations on B-tree

The following are the operations performed on a B-tree.

Searching a node The function `search_node()` determines if the new key is in the current node and if not, finds which of the children should be searched for. This is described in Program Code 13.2.

PROGRAM CODE 13.2

```
/* Search_node() searches a new key in the current node.
If found returns its position in the current node, else
returns child which should be searched next */
int btree :: search_node(int newkey, btnode *curr, int
*pos)
{
    if(newkey < curr->data[1])
    {
        *pos = 0;
        return 0;
    }
```

```
    else
    {
       *pos = curr->count;
       while((newkey < curr->data[*pos]) && (*pos > 1))
          (*pos)--;
       if(newkey == curr->data[*pos])
          return 1;
       else
          return 0;
    }
}
```

Searching a B-tree In Program Code 13.3, the `search()` function traverses the B-tree.

PROGRAM CODE 13.3

```
btnode * btree :: search(int newkey, btnode *root, int
*pos)
{
    if(!root)
    {
       return null;
    }
    else if(search_node(newkey, root, pos))
       return root;
    else
       return search(newkey, root->child[*pos], pos);
}
```

If a new key is present in it, then it returns the pointer to the node and the position of the new key in it; otherwise, it returns `null`.

Inserting a key into a B-tree Binary search trees grow at their leaves, but the B-trees grow at the root. The general method of insertion is as follows:

1. First, the new key is searched in the tree. If the new key is not found, then the search terminates at a leaf.
2. Attempt to insert the new key into a leaf.
3. If the leaf node is not full, then the new key is added to it and the insertion is finished.
4. If the leaf node is full, then it splits into two nodes on the same level, except that the median key is sent up the tree to be inserted into the parent node.

5. If this would result in the parent becoming too big, split the parent into two, promoting the middle key.
6. This strategy might have to be repeated all the way to the top.
7. If necessary, the root is split into two and the middle key is promoted to a new root, making the tree one level higher.

Let us see one example to build a B-tree of order 5 for the following data: 78, 21, 14, 11, 97, 85, 74, 63, 45, 42, 57, 20, 16, 19, 52, 30, 21. This is illustrated in Figs 13.6(a)–(g). First the numbers 78, 21, 14, and 11 are inserted. The tree looks as in Fig. 13.6(a) post insertion. Then 97 is inserted, an overflow occurs at 21, and the tree is split as in Fig. 13.6(b). The numbers 85, 74, and 63 are inserted and again the tree is split as shown in Fig. 13.6(c). Figure 13.6(d) shows the split tree after insertion of 45, 42, and 57; Fig. 13.6(e) shows the split tree after insertion of 20, 16, and 19. Finally 52, 30, and 21 are inserted as shown in Fig. 13.6(f) and the final tree after split is shown in Fig. 13.6(g). The overflow in each step is depicted by encircling the number.

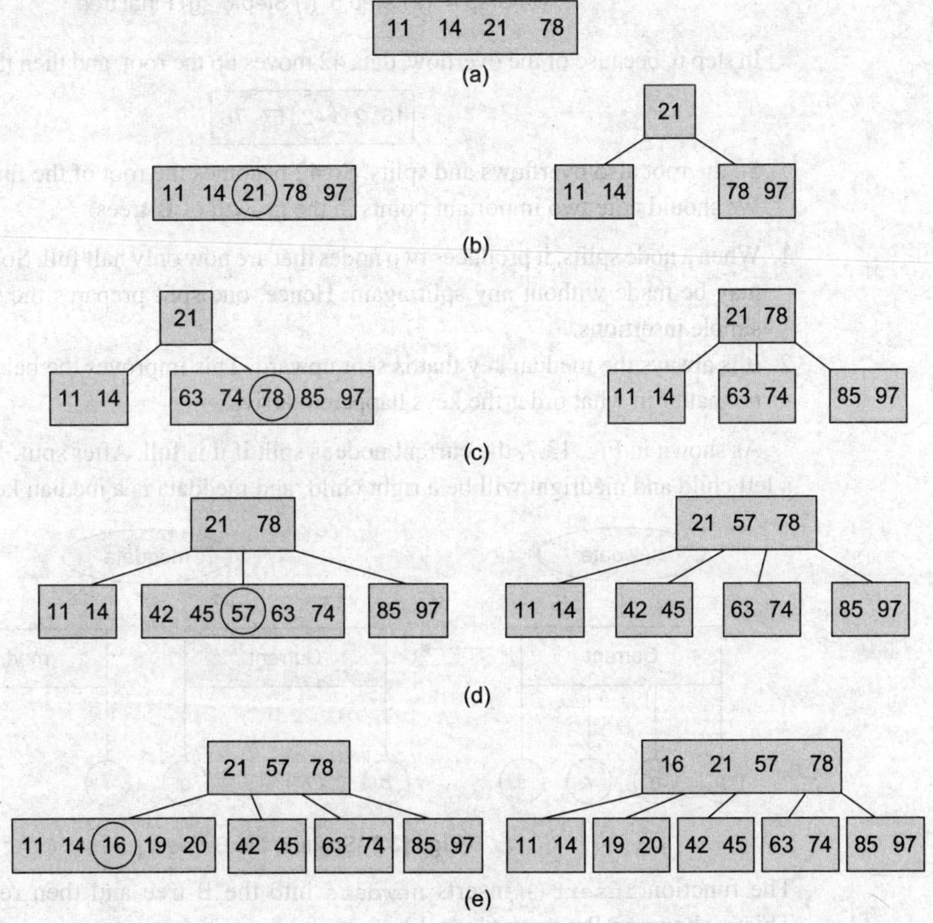

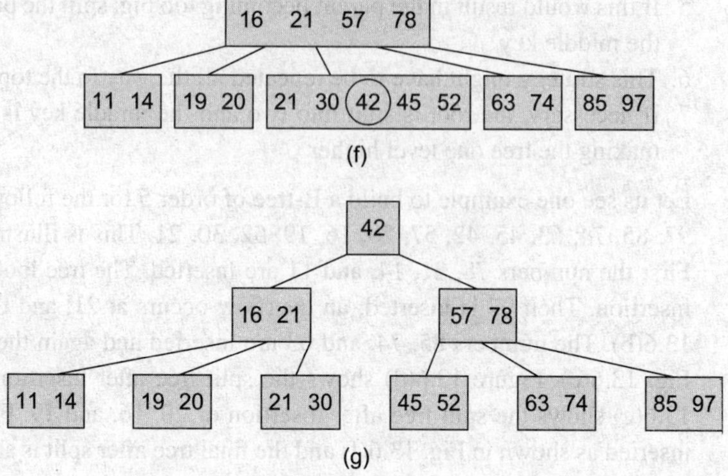

Fig. 13.6 Building a B-tree (a) Step 1 (b) Step 2 (c) Step 3 (d) Step 4 (e) Step 5 (f) Step 6 (g) Final tree

In step 6, because of the overflow, data 42 moves up the root, and then the root becomes

16 21 (42) 57 78

So the root also overflows and splits. So 42 becomes the root of the final B-tree.

We should note two important points in the growth of B-trees.

1. When a node splits, it produces two nodes that are now only half full. So, later insertions may be made without any split again. Hence, one split prepares the way for several simple insertions.
2. It is always the median key that is sent upward. This improves the balance of the tree, no matter in what order the keys happen to arrive.

As shown in Fig. 13.7, the current node is split if it is full. After split, 'current' will be a left child and medright will be a right child, and meddata is a median key.

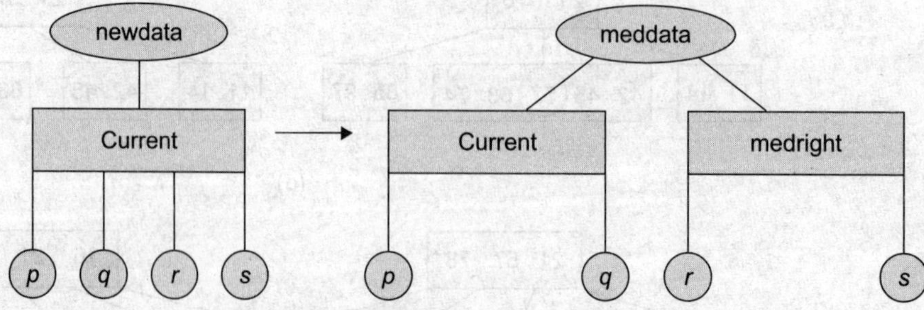

Fig. 13.7 Splitting the B-tree

The function `insert()` inserts `newdata` into the B-tree and then returns the root. This is shown in Program Code 13.4.

PROGRAM CODE 13.4

```
/* Function to insert newdata in B-tree */
btnode *btree :: insert(int newdata, btnode *root)
{
   int meddata;
   btnode *medright, *newroot;
   if(push_down(newdata, root, &meddata, &medright))
   {
      /* Tree if growing */
      newroot = new btnode;
      newroot->count = 1;
      newroot->data[1] = meddata;
      newroot->child[0] = root;
      newroot->child[1] = medright;
      return newroot;
   }
   return root;
}
```

In Program Code 13.5, `push_down()` recursively moves down the B-tree searching for new data. `newdata` is inserted into the subtree to which the node 'current' points. If `true` is returned, then the height of the subtree is increased and `meddata` should be reinserted higher in the tree, with subtree `medright` on its right.

PROGRAM CODE 13.5

```
Int btree :: push_down(int newdata, btnode *curr, int
*meddata, btnode **medright)
{
   int pos;
   if(curr == null)
   {
      /* cannot insert into empty subtree, so terminate */
      *meddata = newdata;
      *medright = null;
      return 1;
   }
  else
   {
      /* Search the current node */
     if(search_node(newdata, curr, &pos))
```

```
            cout << "\n\nError Duplicate Keys Cannot Be
            Inserted!!";
        if(push_down(newdata, curr->child[pos], meddata,
        medright))
        {
            if(curr->count < max)
            {
                /* Reinsert median key */
                pushin(*meddata, *medright, curr, pos);
                return 0;
            }
            else
            {
                /* Split node */
                split_node(*meddata, *medright, curr, pos,
                meddata, medright);
                return 1;
            }
        }
        return 0;
    }
}
```

In Program Code 13.6, `pushin()` inserts the key `meddata` and its right-hand pointer `medright` into the node `*curr` at index `pos`.

PROGRAM CODE 13.6

```
void btree :: pushin(int meddata, btnode *medright,
btnode *curr, int pos)
{
   int p;
   for(p = curr->count; p > pos; p--)
   {
      /* Shift all the keys and child pointers to the
      right */
      curr->data[p + 1] = curr->data[p];
      curr->child[p + 1] = curr->child[p];
   }
   curr->data[pos + 1] = meddata;
   curr->child[pos + 1] = medright;
   curr->count++;
}
```

Splitting a full node The `split_node()` function splits a full node `*curr` with data `meddata`, and child pointer `medright` at index `pos` into nodes `*curr` and `*newright` and leaves the median key in the new median. The C++ code for splitting node is provided in Program Code 13.7.

PROGRAM CODE 13.7

```
void btree :: split_node(int meddata, btnode *medright,
btnode *curr, int pos, int *newmedian, btnode **newright)
{
   int p, median;
   if(pos <= min)
      median = min;
   else
      median = min + 1;
   /* Create a new node and put it on the right */
   *newright = new btnode;
   for(p = median + 1; p <= max; p++)
   {
      /* Move half the keys */
      (*newright)->data[p - median] = curr->data[p];
      (*newright)->child[p - median] = curr->child[p];
   }
   (*newright)->count = max - median;
   curr->count = median;
   if(pos <= min)
   {
      pushin(meddata, medright, curr, pos);
   }
   else
   {
     pushin(meddata, medright, *newright, pos - median);
   }
   *newmedian = curr->data[curr->count];
   (*newright)->child[0] = curr->child[curr->count];
   curr->count--;
}
```

Deleting from a B-tree During insertion, the key always goes *into* a leaf. For deletion, if we wish to remove *from* a leaf, there are three possible ways mentioned as follows:

1. If the key is already in a leaf node and removing it does not cause that leaf node to have too few keys, then simply remove the key to be deleted.

2. If the key is *not* in a leaf, then it is guaranteed (by the nature of a B-tree) that its predecessor or successor will be in a leaf—in this case, we can delete the key and promote the predecessor or successor key to the non-leaf deleted key's position.
3. If these two conditions lead to a leaf node containing less than the minimum number of keys, then we have to look at the siblings immediately adjacent to the leaf in questions listed as follows:
   (a) If one of them has more than the minimum number of keys, then we can promote one of its keys to the parent and take the parent key into our lacking leaf.
   (b) If neither of them has more than the minimum number of keys, then the lacking leaf and one of its neighbours can be combined with their shared parent (the opposite of promoting a key), and the new leaf will have the correct number of keys; if this step leaves the parent with very few keys, then we repeat the process up to the root itself, if required.

If the leaf contains more than the minimum number of entries, then the data can be deleted with no further action.

Consider the example as in Figs 13.8(a) and (b).

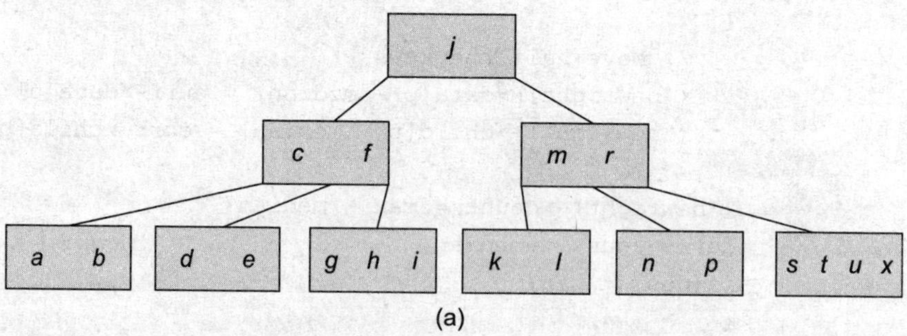

(a)

Now, delete *h*.

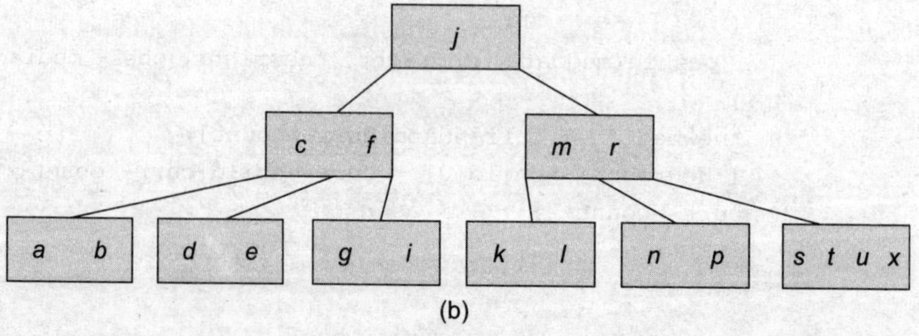

(b)

Fig. 13.8 Sample tree (a) Before deleting *h* (b) After deleting *h*

If the node contains the minimum number of entries, then look at the two leaves that are immediately adjacent to each other and are children of the same node. If one of these has more than the minimum number of entries, then one of them can be moved into the parent node, and the entry from the parent can be moved into the leaf where the deletion occurs.

Figure 13.9 shows the B-tree when the leaf node *r* is deleted from Fig. 13.8(b).

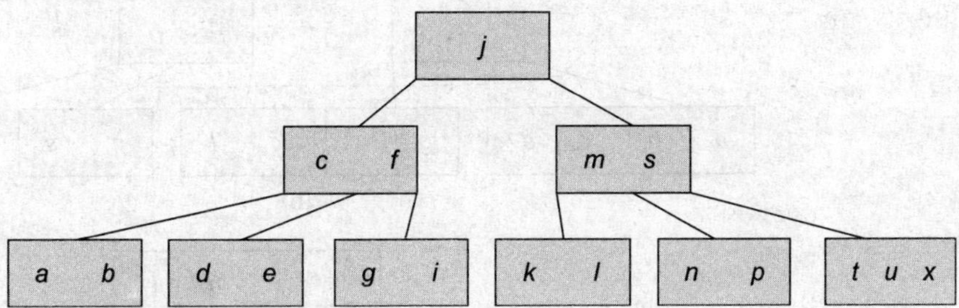

Fig. 13.9 Tree after *r* is deleted and *s* is moved to parent

Figure 13.10 shows the tree after deletion of *p*.

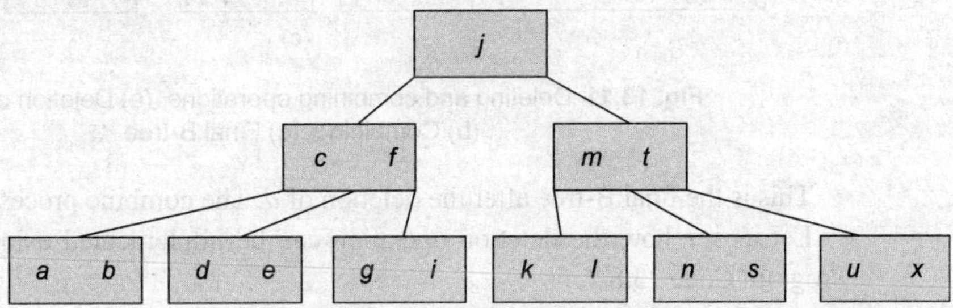

Fig. 13.10 Tree after *p* is deleted, *s* is moved down, and *t* is moved up to the parent

If the adjacent leaf has only the minimum number of entries, then the two leaves and the median entry from the parent can be combined as one new leaf, which will contain no more than the maximum number of entries allowed.

The process is repeated if required.

From the B-tree in Fig. 13.10, the leaf node *d* is deleted. The process of deleting and combining is shown in Figs 13.11(a)–(c).

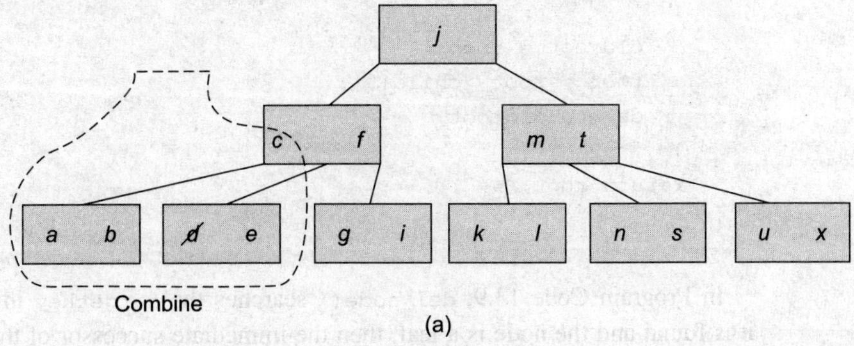

(a)

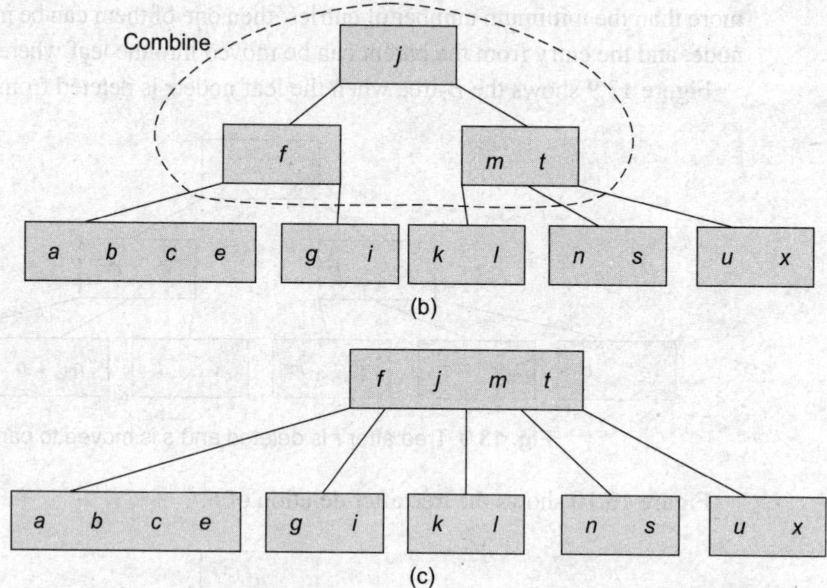

Fig. 13.11 Deleting and combining operations (a) Deletion of node *d* (b) Combining (c) Final B-tree

This is the final B-tree after the deletion of *d*. The combine process is repeated twice.

Let us see how the deletion operation can be implemented using C++ as shown in Program Code 13.8.

PROGRAM CODE 13.8

```
// DeleteBtree() deletes targetkey from the B-tree and
// returns the root
btnode *btree :: del(int key, btnode *root)
{
   btnode *oldroot;
   del_node(key, root);
   if(root->count == 0)
   {
      oldroot = root;
      root = root->child[0];
      delete oldroot;
   }
   return root;
}
```

In Program Code 13.9, `del_node()` searches the `targetkey` in the `curr` node. If it is found and the node is a leaf, then the immediate successor of the key is found and is placed in the current node, and the successor is deleted. After deletion, the function checks to see if enough entries remain in the appropriate node, and if not, move entries as required.

PROGRAM CODE 13.9

```
void btree :: del_node(int key, btnode *curr)
{
   int pos;
   if(!curr)
   {
      cout << "\n\n Target Not Found";
      return ;
   }
   else
   {
      if(search_node(key, curr, &pos))
      {
         if(curr->child[pos - 1])
         {
            /* targetkey found, replace data [pos] by
            it successor */
            successor(curr, pos);
            del_node(curr->data[pos], curr->child[pos]);
         }
         else
            remove_key(curr,pos); /* removes key from
            pos of *current */
      }
      else       /* Target key not found in the current
                 node, search a subtree */
         del_node(key, curr->child[pos]);
      if(curr->child[pos])
      {
          if(curr->child[pos]->count < min)
             restore(curr, pos);
      }
   }
}
```

The `remove_key()` function removes the target key from `pos` in the `curr` node and shifts the remaining keys one position ahead. The implementation of this operation is as in Program Code 13.10.

PROGRAM CODE 13.10

```
void btree :: remove_key (btnode *curr, int pos)
{
   int p;
   for(p = pos + 1; p <= curr->count; p++)
   {
      curr->data[p - 1] = curr->data[p];
      curr->child[p - 1] = curr->child[p];
   }
   curr->count--;
}

void btree :: successor (btnode *curr, int pos)
{
   btnode *leaf;
   leaf = curr->child[pos];
   while(leaf->child[0])
      leaf = leaf->child[0];
   curr->data[pos] = leaf->data[1];
}
```

The function `restore()` restores the minimum number of entries. It first searches the sibling on the left to take an entry and uses the right sibling only when there are no entries to spare in the left one. The working is shown in Program Code 13.11 using the function `restore()`.

PROGRAM CODE 13.11

```
void btree :: restore (btnode *curr, int pos)
{
   if(pos == 0)       /* leftmost key */
   {
      if(curr->child[1]->count > min)
         move_left(curr, 1);
      else
         combine_nodes(curr, 1);
   }
   else if(pos == curr->count)
   {
      if(curr->child[pos - 1]->count > min)
         move_right(curr, pos);
      else
         combine_nodes(curr, pos);
```

```
        /* Remaining cases */
    }
    else if(curr->child[pos - 1]->count > min)
        move_right(curr, pos);
    else if(curr->child[pos + 1]->count > min)
        move_left(curr, pos + 1);
    else
        combine_nodes(curr, pos);
}
```

Figure 13.12 shows the working of the `move_right()` function.

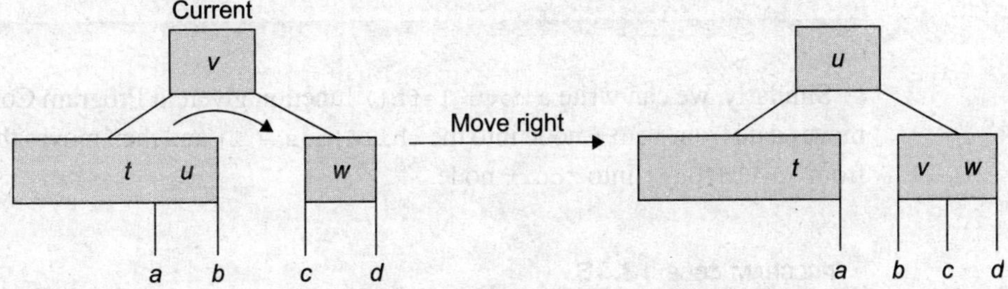

Fig. 13.12 Move right function

The `move_right()` function as given in Program Code 13.12, moves data from `*curr` node into the `child[pos]` and then moves the rightmost data from `child[pos - 1]` into the current node.

PROGRAM CODE 13.12

```
void btree :: move_right (btnode *curr, int pos)
{
    int p;
    btnode *temp;
    /* Set temp to right node of current */
    Temp = curr->child[pos];
    for(p = temp->count; p > 0; p--)
    {
        /* Shift all keys in the right node one position
        ahead */
        temp->data[p + 1] = temp->data[p];
        temp->child[p + 1] = temp->child[p];
    }
```

```
    temp->child[1] = temp->child[0];
    /* Increase count of right node */
    temp->count++;
    /* Move data from current to first place of right
    node */
    temp->data[1] = curr->data[pos];
    temp = curr->child[pos - 1];
    /* Move last data from left node into current */
    curr->data[pos] = temp->data[temp->count];
    curr->child[pos]->child[0] = temp->child[temp->count];
    /* Decrease count of left node */
    temp->count--;
}
```

Similarly, we can write a `move_left()` function given in Program Code 13.13, which moves data from `*curr` node into the `child[pos - 1]` and then moves the leftmost entry from `child[pos]` into `*curr` node.

PROGRAM CODE 13.13

```
void btree :: move_left (btnode *curr, int pos)
{
    int p;
    btnode *temp;
    temp = curr->child[pos - 1];
    /* Increase count of right node */
    /* Move data from current into last place of left
    node and increase its count */
    temp->count++;
    temp->data[temp->count] = curr->data[pos];
    temp->child[temp->count] = curr->child[pos]->child[0];
    /* Set temp to right node of current */
    temp = current→child[pos];
    /* Move data from first place of right node
    into last place of current and decrease count of
    right node */
   curr->data[pos] = temp->data[1];
    temp->child[0] = temp->child[1];
    temp->count--;
    /* Shift all keys in right node one position left */
   for(p = 1; p <= temp->count; p++)
```

```
    {
        temp->data[p] = temp->data[p + 1];
        temp->child[p] = temp->child[p + 1];
    }
}
```

Figure 13.13 illustrates the combining of nodes.

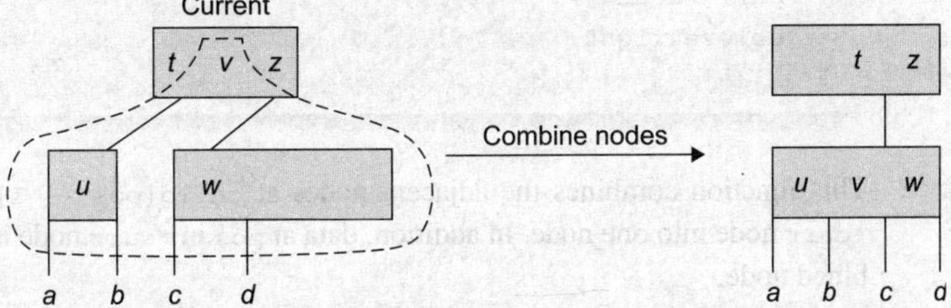

Fig. 13.13 Combining nodes

Program Code 13.14 elaborates the working of the function `combine_nodes()`.

PROGRAM CODE 13.14

```
void btree :: combine_nodes(btnode *curr, int pos)
{
    int p;
    btnode*left, *right;
    left = curr->child[pos - 1];
    right = curr->child[pos];
    /* Move data from current into left node and
    increase count of left, decrease count of current
    */
    left->count++;
    left->data[left->count] = curr->data[pos];
    left->child[left->count] = right->child[0];
    /* Copy all data and child pointers from right node
    into left node */
    for(p = 1; p <= right->count; p++)
   {
       left->count++;
       left->data[left->count] = right->data[p];
       left->child[left->count] = right->child[p];
    }
```

```
    /* Delete the data from current which is moved into
left node and shift the remaining data one position
left */
    for(p = pos; p < curr->count; p++)
    {
        curr->data[p] = curr->data[p + 1];
        curr->child[p] = curr->child[p + 1];
    }
    curr->count--;
    delete right;
}
```

This function combines the adjacent nodes at `child[pos - 1]` and `child[pos]` of `*curr` node into one node. In addition, data at `pos` in `*curr` node is moved into the combined node.

B-tree as Abstract Data Type

We have studied the implementation of various functions for a B-tree. The B-tree as an ADT is defined in Program Code 13.15.

PROGRAM CODE 13.15

```
/*****Implementation of B-tree*****/
#include<iostream.h>
#include<conio.h>
#include<stdio.h>
#include<process.h>
#define max 4
#define min 2
class btnode;
class qnode
{
    public:
        btnode* data;
        qnode* next;
        qnode(btnode* t){data = t; next = null;}
};

class queue
{
    qnode* front;
    qnode* rear;
```

```
    public:
       queue(){front = null; rear = null;}
       void add(btnode* t);
       btnode* remove();
       int isempty(){if(front == null)return 1;else
       return 0;}
};

void queue :: add(btnode* t)
{
   if(front == null)
      front = rear = new qnode(t);
   else
      rear = rear->next = new qnode(t);
}

btnode* queue :: remove()
{
   btnode* t;
   if(isempty())
      return 0;
   qnode* x = front;
   t = front->data;
   front = x->next;
   delete x;
   return t;
}

class btnode
{
   public:
      int count;
      int data[max + 1];
      btnode *child[max + 1];
};

class btree
{
   int push_down(int, btnode*, int*, btnode**);
   void pushin(int, btnode*, btnode*, int);
   void split_node(int, btnode*, btnode*, int, int*,
   btnode**);
   void del_node(int, btnode*);
```

```
    void remove_key(btnode*, int);
    void successor(btnode*, int);
    void restore(btnode*, int);
    void move_right(btnode*, int);
    void move_left(btnode*, int);
    void combine_nodes(btnode*, int);
    int search_node(int, btnode*, int*);
    btnode*search(int, btnode*, int*);
    public:
        btnode* root;
        void display();
        btnode* del(int, btnode*);
        void pre_rec(btnode*);
        btnode* insert(int, btnode*);
};

void btree :: display()
{
    queue q;
    btnode* m;
    m = root;
    while(m)
    {
        for(int i = 0; i < m->count; i++)
            cout << m->data[i] << "    ";
        for(i = 0; i < 5; i++)
        {
            if(m->child[i])
                q.add(m->child[i]);
        }
        m = q.remove();
        cout << "\n";
    }
}

void btree :: pre_rec(btnode *n)
{
    int i;
    if(n != null)
    {
        cout << endl << endl;
        for(i = 1; i <= n->count; i++)
```

```
        {
           cout << "\t" << n->data[i];
        }
        for(i = 0; i < n->count; i = i + 2)
        {
           pre_rec(n->child[i]);
           pre_rec(n->child[i + 1]);
        }
        if(n->count%2 == 0)
        {
           pre_rec(n->child[n->count]);
        }
     }
}

btnode * btree :: del(int key, btnode *root)
{
   btnode *oldroot;
   del_node(key, root);
   if(root->count == 0)
   {
      oldroot = root;
      root = root->child[0];
      delete oldroot;
   }
   return root;
}

void btree :: del_node(int key, btnode *curr)
{
   int pos;
   if(!curr)
   {
      cout << "\n\n Target Not Found";
      return;
   }
   else
   {
      if(search_node(key, curr, &pos))
         if(curr->child[pos - 1])
         {
            successor(curr, pos);
```

```
            del_node(curr->data[pos], curr->child[pos]);
        }
        else
        {
            remove_key(curr, pos);
        }
        else
            del_node(key, curr->child[pos]);
        if(curr->child[pos])
        {
            if(curr->child[pos]->count < min)
                restore(curr, pos);
        }
    }
}

void btree :: remove_key (btnode *curr, int pos)
{
    int p;
    for(p = pos + 1; p <= curr->count; p++)
    {
        curr->data[p - 1] = curr->data[p];
        curr->child[p - 1] = curr->child[p];
    }
    curr->count--;
}

void btree :: successor (btnode *curr, int pos)
{
    btnode *leaf;
    leaf = curr->child[pos];
    while(leaf->child[0])
        leaf = leaf->child[0];
        curr->data[pos] = leaf->data[1];
}

void btree :: restore (btnode *curr, int pos)
{
    if(pos == 0)
        if(curr->child[1]->count > min)
            move_left(curr, 1);
        else
```

```
            combine_nodes(curr, 1);
        else if(pos == curr->count)
            if(curr->child[pos - 1]->count > min)
            {
                move_right(curr, pos);
            }
            else
            {
                combine_nodes(curr, pos);
            }
            else if(curr->child[pos - 1]->count > min)
                move_right(curr, pos);
            else if(curr->child[pos + 1]->count > min)
                move_left(curr, pos + 1);
            else
                combine_nodes(curr, pos);
}

void btree :: move_right (btnode *curr, int pos)
{
    int p;
    btnode *temp;
    temp = curr->child[pos];
    for(p = temp->count; p > 0; p--)
    {
        temp->data[p + 1] = temp->data[p];
        temp->child[p + 1] = temp->child[p];
    }
    temp->child[1] = temp->child[0];
    temp->count++;
    temp->data[1] = curr->data[pos];
    temp = curr->child[pos - 1];
    curr->data[pos] = temp->data[temp->count];
    curr->child[pos]->child[0] = temp->child[temp-
    >count];
    temp->count--;
}

void btree :: move_left (btnode *curr, int pos)
{
    int p;
    btnode *temp;
```

```
    temp = curr->child[pos - 1];
    temp->count++;
    temp->data[temp->count] = curr->data[pos];
    temp->child[temp->count] = curr->child[pos]-
    >child[0];
    temp = curr->child[pos];
    curr->data[pos] = temp->data[1];
    temp->child[0] = temp->child[1];
    temp->count--;
    for(p = 1; p <= temp->count; p++)
    {
       temp->data[p] = temp->data[p + 1];
       temp->child[p] = temp->child[p + 1];
    }
}

void btree :: combine_nodes (btnode *curr, int pos)
{
    int p;
    btnode*left, *right;
    left = curr->child[pos - 1];
    right = curr->child[pos];
    left->count++;
    left->data[left->count] = curr->data[pos];
    left->child[left->count] = right->child[0];
    for(p = 1; p <= right->count; p++)
    {
       left->count++;
       left->data[left->count] = right->data[p];
       left->child[left->count] = right->child[p];
    }
    for(p = pos; p < curr->count; p++)
    {
       curr->data[p] = curr->data[p + 1];
       curr->child[p] = curr->child[p + 1];
    }
    curr->count--;
    delete right;
}

int btree :: search_node(int newkey, btnode *curr,
int *pos)
```

```
{
   if(newkey < curr->data[1])
   {
      *pos = 0;
      return 0;
   }
   else
   {
      *pos = curr->count;
      while((newkey < curr->data[*pos]) && (*pos > 1))
         (*pos)--;
      if(newkey == curr->data[*pos])
         return 1;
      else
         return 0;
   }
}

btnode * btree :: search(int newkey, btnode *root, int
*pos)
{
   if(!root)
   {
      return null;
   }
   else if(search_node(newkey, root, pos))
      return root;
   else
      return search(newkey, root->child[*pos], pos);
}

btnode *btree :: insert(int newdata, btnode *root)
{
   int meddata;
   btnode *medright, *newroot;
   if(push_down(newdata, root, &meddata, &medright))
   {
      newroot = new btnode;
      newroot->count = 1;
      newroot->data[1] = meddata;
      newroot->child[0] = root;
      newroot->child[1] = medright;
```

```
        return newroot;
    }
    return root;
}

int btree :: push_down(int newdata, btnode *curr, int
*meddata, btnode **medright)
{
    int pos;
    if(curr == null)
    {
        *meddata = newdata;
        *medright = null;
        return 1;
    }
    else
    {
        if(search_node(newdata, curr, &pos))
            cout << "\n\nError Duplicate Keys Cannot Be
            Inserted!!";
        if(push_down(newdata, curr->child[pos], meddata,
        medright))
            if(curr->count < max)
            {
                pushin(*meddata, *medright, curr, pos);
                return 0;
            }
            else
            {
                split_node(*meddata, *medright, curr, pos,
                meddata, medright);
                return 1;
            }
            return 0;
    }
}

void btree :: pushin(int meddata, btnode *medright,
btnode *curr, int pos)
{
    int p;
    for(p = curr->count; p > pos; p--)
```

```
    {
        curr->data[p + 1] = curr->data[p];
        curr->child[p + 1] = curr->child[p];
    }
    curr->data[pos + 1] = meddata;
    curr->child[pos + 1] = medright;
    curr->count++;
}

void btree :: split_node(int meddata, btnode *medright,
btnode *curr, int pos, int *newmedian, btnode *newright)
{
    int p, median;
    if(pos <= min)
    {
        median = min;
    }
    else
    {
        median = min + 1;
    }
    *newright = new btnode;
    for(p = median + 1; p <= max; p++)
    {
        (*newright)->data[p - median] = curr->data[p];
        (*newright)->child[p - median] = curr->child[p];
    }
    (*newright)->count = max - median;
    curr->count = median;
    if(pos <= min)
    {
        pushin(meddata, medright, curr, pos);
    }
    else
    {
        pushin(meddata, medright, *newright, pos - median);
    }
    *newmedian = curr->data[curr->count];
    (*newright)->child[0] = curr->child[curr->count];
    curr->count--;
}
```

```
void main()
{
   int ch, c, n;
   char ans;
   btree b;
   b.root = null;
   clrscr();
   do
   {
      cout << "\n\t\t>>>>>>>B-tree operations main
      menu<<<<<<<<<<<<"
      <<"\n\n 1. Insert a key"
      <<"\n\n 2. Display the B-tree"
      <<"\n\n 3. Delete a key"
      <<"\n\n 4. Exit"
      <<"\n\n Enter choice:";
      ch = getche();
      ch = ch - '0';
      switch(ch)
      {
      case 1:
      do
      {
         cout << "\n\n\n\n Enter data:";
         cin >> n;
         b.root = b.insert(n, b.root);
        cout << "\n\n Do you want to insert more keys?";
         ans = getche();
         if(ans == 'n' || ans == 'N')
         break;
      }while(1);
      getch();
      break;
      case 2:
         b.pre_rec(b.root);
         getch();
      break;
      case 3:
         cout << "\n\n Enter key to be deleted: ";
         cin >> n;
         b.root = b.del(n, b.root);
         getch();
```

```
      break;
     case 4:
         exit(0);
         default:
         cout << "\n\tYou Have Entered An Invalid
         Choice!!!!!!!";
         getch();
      break;
   }
   }while(1);
}

/*********************** OUTPUT ***********************
 >>>>>>>B-tree operations main menu<<<<<<<<<<<
1. Insert a key
2. Display the B-tree
3. Delete a key
4. Exit
Enter choice: 1
Enter data:10
Do you want to insert more keys? y
Enter data: 20
Do you want to insert more keys?  y
Enter data: 30
Do you want to insert more keys? n
>>>>>>>B-tree operations main menu<<<<<<<<<<<
1. Insert a key
2. Display the B-tree
3. Delete a key
4. Exit
Enter choice: 2
   10   20   30
>>>>>>>B-tree operations main menu<<<<<<<<<<<
1. Insert a key
2. Display the B-tree
3. Delete a key
4. Exit
Enter choice: 1
Enter data: 40
Do you want to insert more keys? y
Enter data: 50
```

```
Do you want to insert more keys? n
>>>>>>>B-tree operations main menu<<<<<<<<<<<
1. Insert a key
2. Display the B-tree
3. Delete a key
4. Exit
Enter choice: 2
   30   10   20   40   50
>>>>>>>B-tree operations main menu<<<<<<<<<<<
1. Insert a key
2. Display the B-tree
3. Delete a key
4. Exit
Enter choice: 3
Enter key to be deleted: 10
>>>>>>>B-tree operations main menu<<<<<<<<<<<
1. Insert a key
2. Display the B-tree
3. Delete a key
4. Exit
Enter choice: 2
   20   30   40   50
```

13.3.3 B+ Tree

B+ trees are internal data structures. That is, the nodes contain whatever information is associated with the key as well as the key values. A variant of B-trees is often used as an *index tree*. A B+ tree combines the features of ISAM and B-trees as follows:

1. In an index tree, the pointers in the internal nodes point to other index nodes.
2. The pointers in the leaf nodes are not *nil*, but rather point to where the information associated with each key is stored on disk.
3. Each key must appear in a leaf node.
4. B-trees whose keys are only in the internal nodes of the tree and whose pointers in the leaf nodes print to where the related information is stored externally are called B+ trees.
5. Leaves are connected to form a linked list of keys in sequential order.
6. It has two parts—the index part consists of interior nodes and the sequence set consists of leaf nodes.
7. B+ trees are used to store index sequential file organization; the key values in the sequence set are the key values of record collections.

B+ Tree Structure

The structure of a B+ tree can be understood from the following points:

1. A B+ tree is in the form of a balanced tree where every path from the root of the tree to a leaf of the tree is of the same length.
2. Each non-leaf node (internal node) in the tree has between $\lceil n/2 \rceil$ and n children, where n is fixed.
3. The pointer (Ptr) can point to either a file record or a bucket of pointers so as to point to a file record.
4. Searching time is less in B+ trees but has some problem of wasted space.

Nodes of B+ Tree

A typical node structure of a B+ tree is shown in Fig. 13.14 with the nodes having the following characteristics:

1. Internal node of a B+ tree with $q-1$ search values.
2. Leaf node of a B+ tree with $q-1$ search values and $q-1$ data pointers.

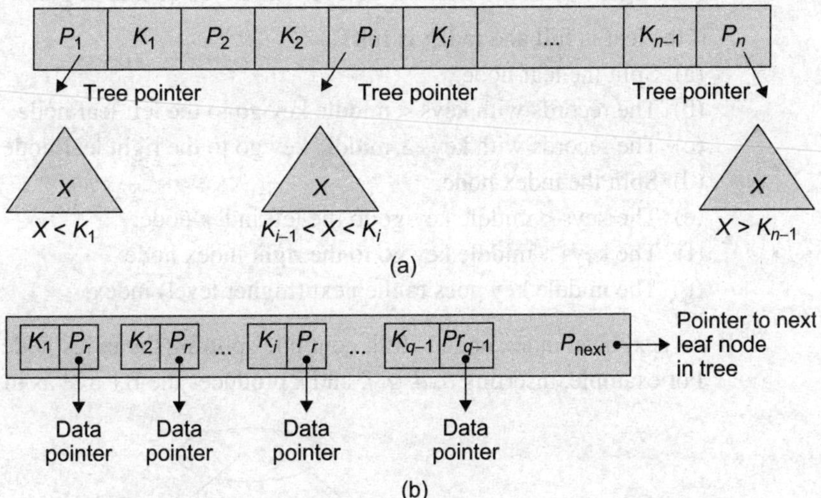

Fig. 13.14 Nodes of a B+ tree (a) Internal node of a B+ tree with $q-1$ search values (b) Leaf node of a B+ tree with $q-1$ search values and $q-1$ data pointers

Non-leaf nodes form a multi-level sparse index on the leaf nodes.

1. Each leaf can hold up to $n-1$ values and must contain at least $\lceil (n-1)/2 \rceil$ values.
2. Non-leaf node pointers point to tree nodes (leaf nodes). Non-leaf nodes can hold up to n pointers and must hold at least $\lceil n/2 \rceil$ pointers.

This seemingly minor change has some major effects on the algorithms. For example, the leaf nodes and the internal nodes are treated differently when they split. When a leaf node splits, a copy of the middle key is moved up to be a separator at the next level. When an internal (index) node splits, the key itself is moved up to act as a separator.

Inserting nodes into a B+ tree The key value determines a record's placement in a B+ tree. The leaf nodes are maintained in sequential order and a doubly linked list (not shown) connects each leaf page with its sibling page(s). This doubly linked list speeds the data movement as the pages grow and contract.

We must consider three scenarios when we add a record to a B+ tree. Each scenario causes a different action.

1. If the leaf is not full and index (internal) is not full
   (a) Place the record in sorted position in the appropriate leaf node.
2. If the leaf is full and index is not full
   (a) Split the leaf node.
   (b) Place the middle key in the index node in sorted order.
   (c) Left leaf node contains records with keys below the middle key.
   (d) Right leaf node contains records with keys equal to or greater than the middle key.
3. If the leaf is full and index is full
   (a) Split the leaf node.
   (b) The records with keys < middle key go to the left leaf node.
   (c) The records with keys ≥ middle key go to the right leaf node.
   (d) Split the index node.
   (e) The keys < middle key go to the left index node.
   (f) The keys > middle key go to the right index node.
   (g) The middle key goes to the next (higher level) index.

If the next level index node is full, continue splitting the index node.

For example, inserting *a, d, g, f,* and *k* produces the B+ tree as in Fig. 13.15.

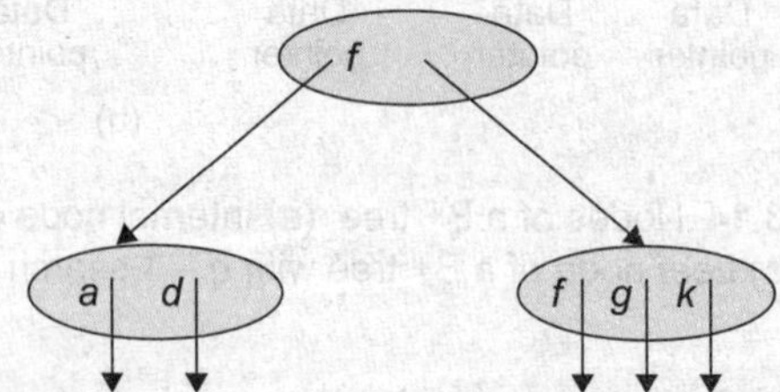

Fig. 13.15 Representation of insert operation

The arrow from the leaf nodes point to where the information associated with the key can be found.

Deleting nodes from a B+ tree The delete algorithm for B+ trees is listed as follows:

1. Leaf node not having keys < minimum keys and internal or index nodes not below the fill factor.

   Delete the record from the leaf page. Arrange keys in ascending order to fill `void`. If the key of the deleted record appears in the index page, use the next key to replace it.

2. Leaf node having keys < minimum keys and internal or index nodes not below the fill factor.

   Combine the leaf page and its sibling. Change the index page to reflect the change.

3. Leaf node having keys < minimum keys and internal or index nodes below the fill factor.
   (a) Combine the leaf page and its sibling.
   (b) Adjust the index page to reflect the change.
   (c) Combine the index page with its sibling.

Continue combining index pages until you reach a page with the correct fill factor or you reach the root page.

Another change is that the keys are deleted only from the leaf nodes. If a key to be deleted is also a part of the indexing structure (that is, appears in an internal node), it can remain in the index, for example, deleting *f* and *j* from the tree in Fig. 13.16 gives the B+ tree as in Fig. 13.17.

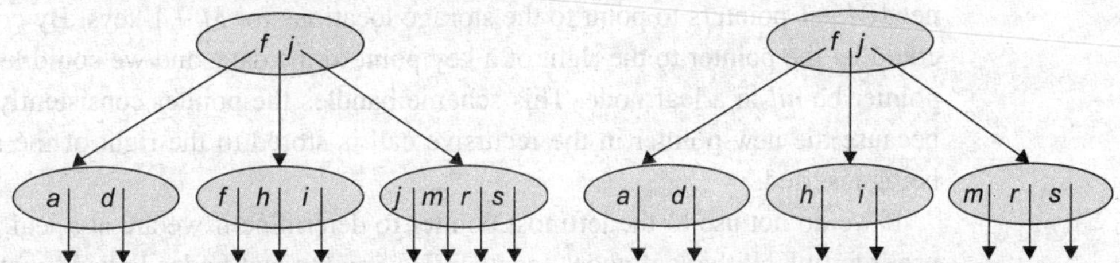

Fig. 13.16 Sample B+ tree

Fig. 13.17 Resultant tree after deletion of *f* and *i* from Fig. 13.16

The index says that all keys less than *f* are in the left subtree and those greater than or equal to *f* are in the right subtree. Likewise, all keys less than *j* are in the right subtree, all keys less than *j* are in the left subtree, and those greater than or equal to *g* are in the right subtree. This is still true.

Borrowing and coalescing are also slightly different because the old separator key can be discarded.

For example, deleting *g* from the B+ tree as in Fig. 13.18 leaves the leftmost node one key short.

Figure 13.19 is the result of borrowing *h*.

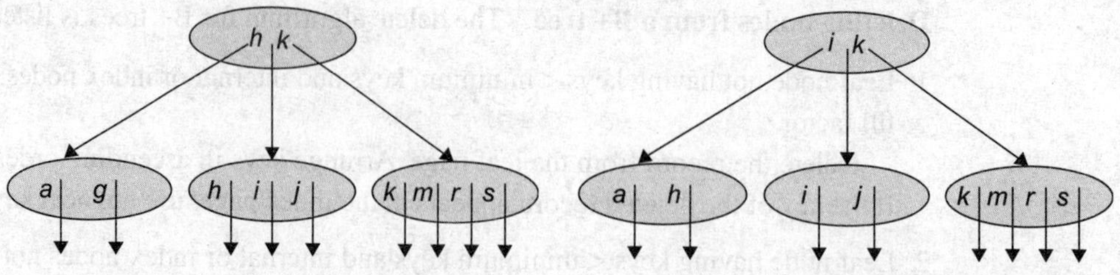

Fig. 13.18 Sample tree for deletion of *g*

Fig. 13.19 Resultant tree after borrowing *h* from Fig. 13.18

Notice the difference in the B-tree. We rotated keys from one sibling to parent to other sibling. Here, the borrowed key goes directly into the sibling node and a copy of the new leftmost node becomes the separator in the parent. If we borrow from the left, however, a copy of the borrowed key becomes the separator.

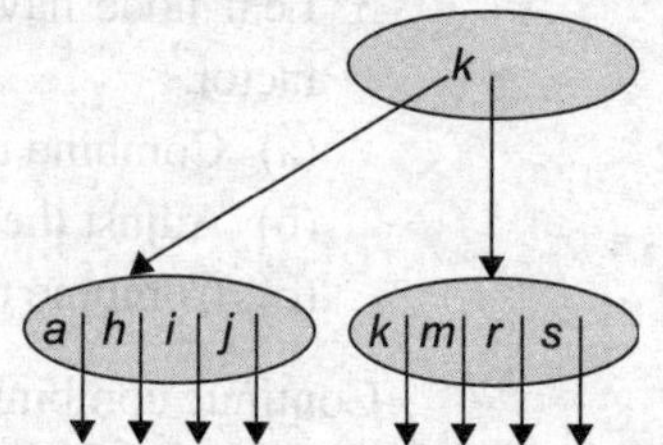

Fig. 13.20 Resultant tree after coalescing the keys *h*, *i*, and *j* into the leftmost node of Fig. 13.19

If we coalesce, the keys *h*, *i*, and *j* go into the leftmost node. This is shown in Fig. 13.20.

Since the pointers in the leaf nodes are not nil, we must have another way to recognize a leaf node. One way is to have a field in each node to mark the node as either an internal node or a leaf node. Another way is to continue using the leftmost child pointer as the flag because we need $M - 1$ pointers to point to the storage locations for $M - 1$ keys. By convention, we could let the pointer to the right of a key point to the data, and we could let the leftmost pointer be *nil* in a leaf node. This scheme handles the pointer consistently on insertion because the new pointer in the recursive call is stored to the right of the separator key being inserted.

If we do not use to the leftmost pointer to determine if we are at a leaf node, we can use it to link all the leaf nodes together. Having the leaf nodes linked together allows us to process the items in the file in order as well as access the items randomly via the index.

Advantages of B+ Trees over Indexed Sequential Access Method

The B+ tree is a dynamic index structure that adjusts gracefully to insertions and deletions It has the following advantages:

1. It is a balanced tree.
2. The leaf pages are not allocated sequentially. They are linked together through pointers (a doubly linked list).

13.3.4 Trie Tree

Instead of searching a tree using the entire key, we can consider the key to be a sequence of characters (letters or digits, for example), and use these characters to determine a multiway branch at each step. If we consider alphabetic keys, then we make a lexical

26-ary tree. At the first level, take a branch according to the first letter; at the second level of a tree, take a branch according to the second letter, and so on. If we consider the keys made up of three letters p, q, r, of maximum size 3, then the lexical tree will be 3-ary tree of level 3; nodes at first level having 3 pointers and 3 nodes at second level having 3 pointers each. So we get a total of 3 × 3 pointers at the second level and 3 × 3 × 3 pointers at the third level. Finally, we store the actual key at a leaf.

The largest word determines the height of the lexical tree. So the drawback of the lexical tree is that after a few levels, it becomes very large. One solution is to prune from the tree all the branches that do not lead to any key. The resulting tree is called a *trie* (short for reTRIEvaL and pronounced 'try').

Consider a trie describing the words made only from the letters p, q, and r. The pruned branch can be shown as a null pointer marked with a cross in the node. Along with the branches to the next level of the trie, each node contains a data pointer to a key. Figure 13.21 shows a trie tree.

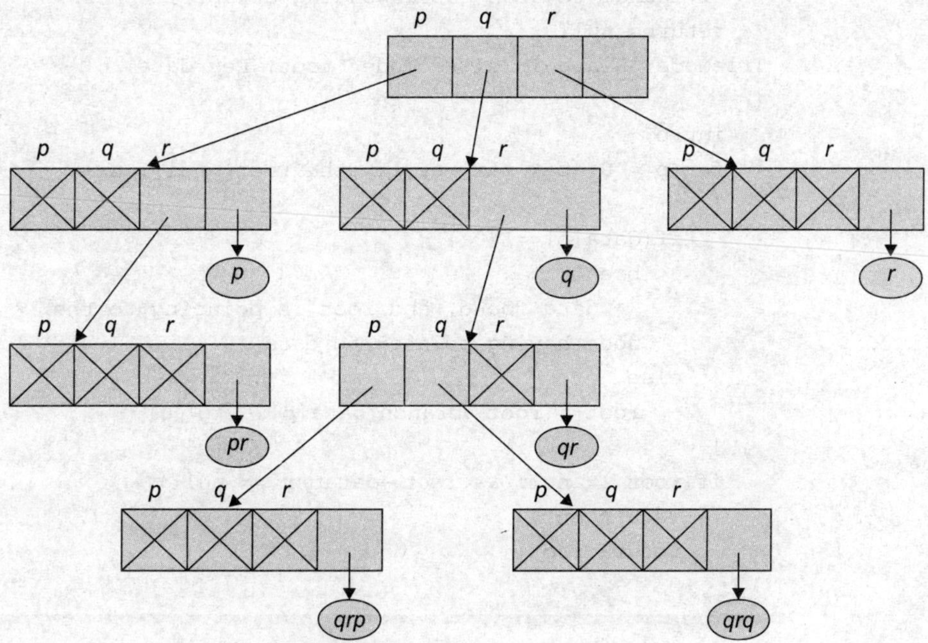

Fig. 13.21 Example of a trie tree

So the number of steps needed to search a trie is proportional to the number of characters in a key.

Declaration for Trie Tree

In each node of a trie tree, we have pointers to the next level and a pointer to the data. Program Code 13.16 is implementation of trie tree and the various operations that can be performed on it.

PROGRAM CODE 13.16

```
#define maxchar 3 /* Key is formed using 3 letters p,
q, r only */
#define max_key_length 5
class trieNode
{
  public:
     TrieNode *branch[maxchar];
     TrieData *dataptr;
};

typedef char key[max_key_length];
// SearchTrie() searches for the data starting from
// the root.
// If found, returns corresponding dataptr, otherwise
// returns null
TrieNode *SearchTrie(TrieNode *root, Key data)
{
   int p;
   for(p = 0; p < max_key_length&&root!=null; p++)
   {
      if(data[p]=='\0')
         break;
         /* data found, and root is pointing to the
         node having pointer to data */
      else
         root = root→branch[data[p] - 'p'];
   }
   if(root != null && root→dataptr == null)
      return null;
      return root;
}
```

13.3.5 Splay Tree

Of the many other variations on balanced binary trees, perhaps the most intriguing are the *splay trees*, introduced by Sleator and Tarjan, which are self-adjusting.

Splay trees are a form of BSTs. A splay tree maintains a balance without any explicit balance condition such as colour. Instead, 'splay operations', which involve rotations, are performed within the tree every time an access is made. The amortized cost of each operation on an n-node tree is $O(\log_2 n)$. One application of splay trees simplifies dynamic trees.

In an *amortized analysis*, the time required to perform a sequence of data structure operations is averaged over all the operations performed. Amortized analysis can be used to show that the average cost of an operation is small, if one averages over a sequence of operations, even though a single operation might be expensive. Amortized analysis differs from the average case analysis where the probability is not involved; an amortized analysis guarantees the average performance of each operation in the worst case.

Let us consider Example 13.1 to understand how indexing and search trees help in implementing practical applications efficiently.

EXAMPLE 13.1 Consider a hospital management system maintaining patient records. A patient who is currently in the hospital is said to be an active record, being consulted and updated continuously by attending physicians and nurses. When the patient leaves the hospital, the records become passive but still needed occasionally by the patient's physician or others. If, later, the patient is readmitted to the hospital, then the record becomes active again. The process of making such records active should be done faster.

Solution If we use a BST or even an AVL tree, then the records of the newly admitted patient's records will go to a leaf position, far from the root, and the access will be slower. Instead, we want to keep the records that are newly inserted or frequently accessed very near to the root, while the inactive records are kept far off, that is, in the leaf positions. However, we do not want to rebuild the tree into the desired shape. Instead, we need to make a tree a *self-adjusting data* structure that automatically changes its shape to bring the records closer to the root as they are used frequently, allowing inactive records to drift slowly down towards the leaves. Such trees are called as *splay trees*.

Splay trees are BSTs that achieve our goals by being self-adjusting in the following way: every time we access a node of the tree, whether for insertion or retrieval, we perform radical survey on the tree, lifting the newly accessed node all the way up so that it becomes the root of the modified tree. Other nodes are pushed out of the way as necessary to make space for this new root and not spacing them too far from the top position. Inactive nodes, on the other hand, will slowly be pushed farther and farther from the root.

13.3.6 Red-black Tree

A BST of height h can implement any of the basic dynamic set of operations in $O(h)$ time. Here, the operations are fast and the height of the search tree is small, but if its height is more, the performance may be no better than the linked list. *Red-black trees* are one of many search-tree schemes that are *balanced*. In order to guarantee that basic dynamic set operations, take $O(\log_2 n)$ time in the worst case.

Definition: A *red–black tree* is a BST with one extra bit of storage per node: its *colour*, which can either be red or black. Red–black trees were invented by R. Bayer under the same name 'symmetric binary B-trees'. Guibas and Sedgewick studied their properties at length and introduced the red/black colour convention.

The tree is balanced by constraining the way nodes can be coloured on any path from the root to a leaf; red-black tree ensures that no such path is more than twice as long as any other.

Properties of red–black trees Red–black trees have all the characteristics of BSTs. In addition, red-black trees have the following properties. In other words, a BST is a red-black tree if it satisfies the following properties.

Each node of a tree contains these fields: colour, key, left, right, parent (and an optional field rank). If a child or the parent of a node does not exist, the corresponding pointer field of the node contains the value null.

1. Every node is either red or black.

2. All the external nodes (leaf nodes) are black.
3. The rank in a tree goes from zero upto the maximum rank which occurs at the root. The rank of two consecutive nodes differs by utmost 1. Each leaf node has a rank 0.
4. If a node is red, then both its children are black. In other words, consecutive red nodes are disallowed. This means every red node is followed by a black node; on the other hand, a black node may be followed by a black or a red node. This implies that utmost 50% of the nodes on any path from external node to root are red.
5. The number of black nodes on any path from but not including the node x to leaf is called as *black height* of the node x, denoted as bh(x).

   Every simple path from the root to a leaf contains the same number of black nodes. In addition, every simple path from a node to a descendent leaf contains the same number of black nodes.
6. If a black node has a rank r, then its parent has the rank $r + 1$.

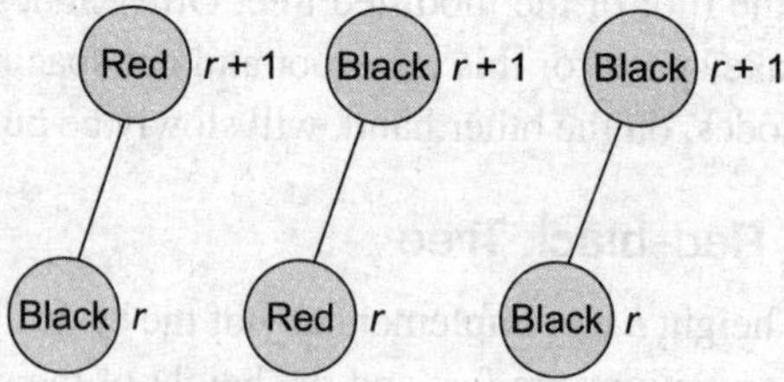

7. If a red node has a rank r, then its parent will have the rank r as well.

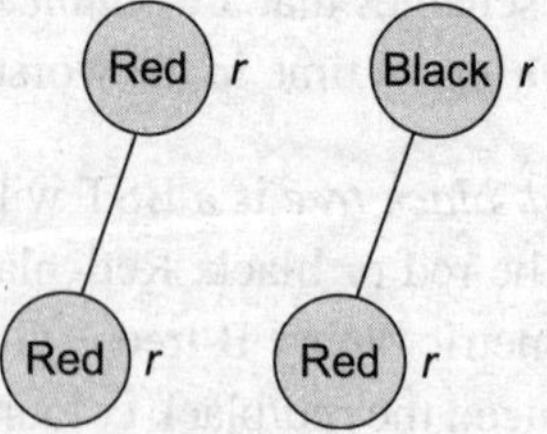

Example of a red–black tree Figure 13.22 is an example of a red–black tree with five levels. We have set ranks starting at the bottom.

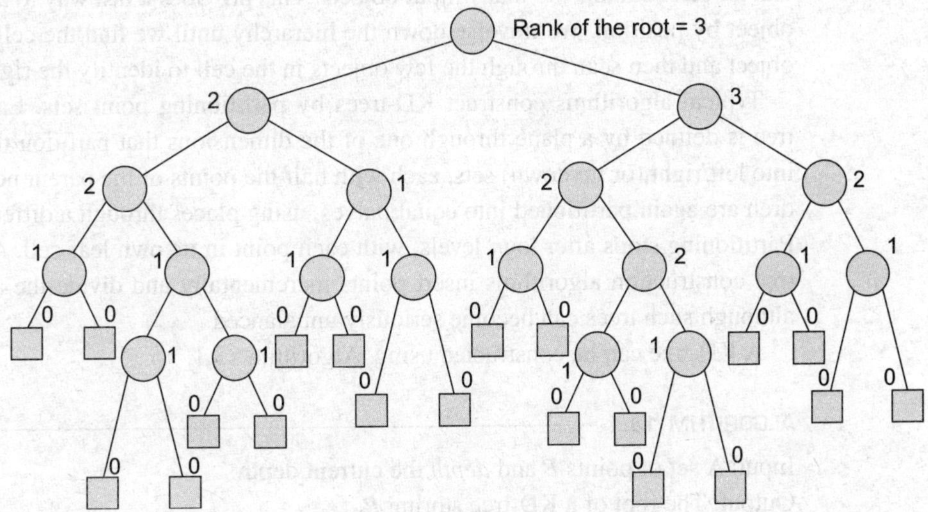

Fig. 13.22 Red–black tree

13.3.7 *K*-dimensional Tree

A *K*-dimensional tree (KD-tree) is a data structure used in computer science during orthogonal range searching, for instance, to find the set of points that fall into a given rectangle in a plane. Given a KD-tree of the points in question, it is possible to find the resulting points in O(sqrt(n) + k) time, where n is the number of points and k is the number of resultant points.

An example of KD-tree is shown in Fig. 13.23.

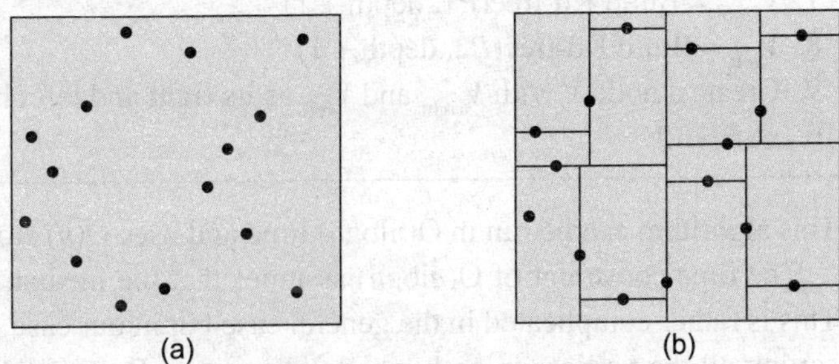

Fig. 13.23 KD-trees (a) Input (b) Output

Input description Let there be a set S of n points in k-dimensions.

Problem Construct a tree which partitions the space by half-planes such that each point is contained in its own region.

Although many different flavours of KD-trees have been devised, their purpose is always to hierarchically decompose space into a relatively small number of cells such that no cell contains too many input objects. This provides a fast way to access any input object by position. We traverse down the hierarchy until we find the cell containing the object and then scan through the few objects in the cell to identify the right one.

Typical algorithms construct KD-trees by partitioning point sets. Each node in the tree is defined by a plane through one of the dimensions that partition the set of points into left/right (or up/down) sets, each with half the points of the parent node. These children are again partitioned into equal halves, using places through a different dimension. Partitioning stops after log*n* levels, with each point in its own leaf cell. Alternative KD-tree construction algorithms insert points incrementally and divide the appropriate cell although such trees can become seriously unbalanced.

A KD-tree can be constructed using Algorithm 13.1.

ALGORITHM 13.1

Input: A set of points *P* and *depth* the current depth
Output: The root of a KD-tree storing *P*

1. `if` *P* contains only one point `then`
2. `return` a leaf storing this point
3. `else if` depth is seven `then`
4. Split *P* into two subsets with a vertical line 1 through the median *x*-coordinate of the points in *P*. Let *P*1 be the set of points to the left and *P*2 be the set of points to the right. The points exactly on the line belong to *P*1
5. `else`
6. Split *P* into two subsets with a horizontal line 1 through the median *y*-coordinate of the points in *P*. Let *P*1 be the set of points above 1 and *P*2 be the points below 1. The points exactly on the line belong to *P*1
7. V_{right} = Build Kd-tree(*P*1, depth + 1)
8. V_{left} = Build Kd-tree(*P*2, depth + 1)
9. Create a node *V* with V_{right} and V_{left} as its right and left children, respectively
10. `return` *V*

This algorithm can be run in O(*n*log*n*) time and uses O(*n*) storage.

The time constraint of O(*n*log*n*) assumes that the median can be found in O(*n*) time. This is rather complicated in the general case but in our case can be made simply by pre-sorting all the vertices in both *x* and *y* directions. Sorting takes O(*n*log*n*) time and does therefore not worsen the time complexity of the overall algorithm.

13.3.8 AA Tree

We studied BSTs. A BST of *n* nodes is said to be balanced if the height is O(log*n*). A balanced tree supports efficient operations since most operations only have to traverse or on two root-to-leaf paths. There are many implementations of balanced BSTs, including AVL trees, red–black trees, and AA trees. An AA tree is another alternative to AVL trees. An *AA tree* is a balanced BST with the following properties:

1. Every node is coloured either red or black.
2. The root is black.
3. If a node is red, both of its children are black.
4. Every path from a node to a null reference has the same number of black nodes.
5. Left children may not be red.

Figure 13.24 is an example of an AA tree.

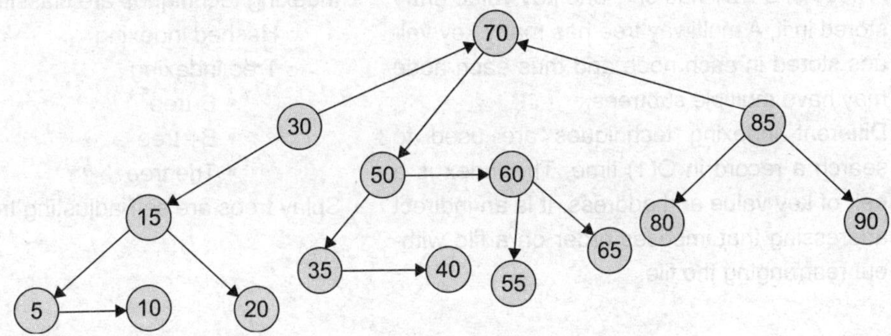

Fig. 13.24 AA tree

Advantages of AA Trees

AA trees are more advantageous as they simplify the algorithms. The following list explains the advantages:

1. They eliminate half the reconstructing cases.
2. They simplify deletion by removing an annoying case.
   (a) If an internal node has only one child, that child must be a red child.
   (b) We can always replace a node with the smallest child in the right subtree; it will either be a leaf node or have a red child.
3. An AA tree, which is a balanced BST, supports efficient operations, since most operations only have to traverse one or two root-to-leaf paths.

Representing Balance Information in AA Tree

In each node of AA tree, we store a *level*. The *level* is defined by the following rules:

1. If a node is a leaf, its level is one.
2. If a node is red, its level is the level of its parent.
3. If a node is black, its level is one less than the level of its parent.

Here, the *level* is the number of left links to a null reference.

Links in an AA tree A horizontal link is a connection between a node and a child with equal levels. The properties of such horizontal links are as follows:

1. Horizontal links are right references.
2. There cannot be two consecutives horizontal links.
3. Nodes at level two or higher must have two children.
4. If a node has no right horizontal link, its two children are at the same level.

RECAPITULATION

- A node of a BST has only one key value entry stored in it. A multiway tree has many key values stored in each node and thus each node may have multiple subtrees.
- Different indexing techniques are used to search a record in O(1) time. The index is a pair of key value and address. It is an indirect addressing that imposes order on a file without rearranging the file.
- Indexing techniques are classified as
  - o Hashed indexing
  - o Tree indexing
    - B-tree
    - B+ tree
    - Trie tree
- Splay trees are self-adjusting trees.

KEY TERMS

File organization A file is a collection of records, each record having one or more fields. The fields are used to distinguish among the records using keys. File organization is all about the way in which the records are stored in a file in an external storage media.

Index The index is a collection of pairs of the form (key value, address). It is an indirect addressing that imposes order on a file without rearranging it.

KD-tree A KD-tree is a data structure used in computer science during orthogonal range searching, for instance to find the set of points that fall into a given rectangle in a plane.

Multiway search tree In multiway search tree, there are 0 to m subtrees for each node, the node having k subtrees $(k \leq m)$ with k pointers and $k - 1$ value entries. The key values in the first subtree are all less than the key in the first entry; the key value in the other subtrees are all greater than or equal to the key in their parent entry.

Red–black tree A red-black tree is a BST with one extra bit of storage per node: its colour, which can either be red or black.

EXERCISES

Multiple choice questions

1. Which of the following remarks about the trie tree are false?

   Hint: More than one choice can be correct.

   (a) It is efficient in dealing with strings of variable length.

   (b) It is efficient if there are few number of data items.

(c) The number of disk accesses cannot exceed the length of the particular string that is searched.
(d) It can handle insertions and deletions, dynamically and efficiently.

2. Which of the following remarks about the trie tree are true?
(a) It is an *m*-ary tree.
(b) It is a search tree of order *m*.
(c) Successful searches should terminate in leaf nodes.
(d) Unsuccessful searches may terminate at any level of tree structure.

3. Indexing consists of
(a) a list of keys
(b) pointers to the master file
(c) both (a) and (b)
(d) none of the above

4. An indexing operation
(a) sorts a file using a single key
(b) sorts a file using two keys
(c) establishes an index for a file
(d) both (b) and (c)

5. Which of the following is an implementation of balanced BSTs?
(a) AVL tree
(b) Red-black tree
(c) AA tree
(d) All of the above

6. B+ trees are preferred to binary trees in databases because
(a) disk capacities are greater than memory capacities
(b) disk access is much slower than memory access
(c) disk data transfer rates are much less than memory data transfer rates
(d) disks are more reliable than memory

Review questions

1. What is a B-tree? Draw the tree B-tree of order 3 created by inserting data arriving in the following sequence:

   82, 14, 7, 8, 12, 9, 23, 5, 6, 16, 19, 20, 78

2. Why do we need index file? Compare the linear and tree index organization. What are static and dynamic indices?
3. Explain the steps to build a B-tree of order 5 for the following data:

   78, 21, 14, 11, 97, 85, 74, 63, 45, 42, 57, 20, 16, 19, 52, 30, 21

4. Draw diagrams to show the different stages during the building of a B+ tree for the keys arriving in the following sequence: A, Z, B, Y, C, X, D, W, E, V, F, M, R.
5. In each case of question 4, show the balance factors of all nodes and name the type of rotation used for balancing.
6. What are the advantages of the variations of balanced binary tree—splay tree, KD tree, and red–black tree?
7. Compare B-tree and B+ tree.
8. Write a C++ code for the following functions:
   (a) Searching in a B-tree
   (b) Traversing a trie and print in lexical order
   (c) Counting the nodes in a B-tree
   (d) Inserting and deleting in a B-tree

Answers to multiple choice questions

1. (a), (c), (d) 2. (a), (c), (d) 3. (c) 4. (c) 5. (a) 6. (b)

14 FILES

OBJECTIVES

After completing this chapter, the reader will be able to understand the following:

- The purpose of standard data organization methods
- Various file organizations such as sequential, indexed sequential, and direct access, and their application-specific suitability
- The advantages and disadvantages of file organizations

14.1 INTRODUCTION

The prime role of computers is problem solving and data processing. In any computer application, the basic entity is data. Data can be either simple or it may have multiple attributes. One needs to select the appropriate data structure based on the nature of the application and data.

Data can have one or more attributes (fields). For example, an entity *Number_of_Students* can only be of the integer data type, whereas an entity *Student* may have multiple attributes or fields such as *Roll_No*, *Name*, *DOB*, *City*, and *Sex* to describe it. Each field of *Student* can be of a different data type. In such situations, we need a structure that will accommodate an aggregation of dissimilar data types that represents one occurrence of such a complex entity. This object is called a *record*.

Records that hold information about similar items of data are usually grouped together into a *file*. A file is a collection of records where each record consists of one or more fields.

For example, a file *Student* can have one or more records with fields such as *Roll_No*, *Name*, *DOB*, *City*, and *Sex*. Table 14.1 indicates the fields and their associated data type for this record.

Table 14.1 Student record

Field	Roll_No	Name	DOB	City	Sex
Datatype	Integer	Array of characters	Array of characters	Array of characters	Character

We have studied the representation of and operations on various data structures such as arrays, stacks, queues, linked lists, trees, and graphs. The storage representations and data manipulations described are applied only to data entities, which reside in the main memory. In many situations, all information that is to be processed does not reside in the main memory. There are two reasons for this. First, there are some large programs and data, which cannot fit conveniently into the main memory. Secondly, it is often desirable or necessary to store information from one run of a program to the next run. Let us consider a student's information system. We need the data to be preserved even after the execution of the program is over. Therefore, large volumes of data and archival data are commonly stored in external memory as special data holding entities—*files*.

Each record contains attributes to describe one entity. Generally, all records for one entity type are usually of the same form. Mostly, each of them has the same fields in the same quantity, order, and length. Such records are known as *fixed length records.* Structures in C/C++ support this type of record.

Records that are not necessarily of the same length are known as *variable length records.* C/C++ unions support this type of record. Variable length records are less common than fixed length records, as they are more difficult to handle. They tend to complicate the storage schemes and are sometimes impractical for some structures. When variable records are used, we need to maintain more information about each record.

Magnetic tapes, floppy disks, and hard disks are a few examples of secondary storage devices. When data is organized in a file data structure, the data is *non-volatile*, which means that the data will reside on storage after data processing is over.

14.2 EXTERNAL STORAGE DEVICES

For persistent storage, large volumes of data and archival data are commonly stored in external memory as special data holding entities, namely files. Before we learn about file organization and operations on files, let us discuss the storage devices, which hold the files.

The external storage devices are those on which information or data can be stored and from which it can be retrieved. The data resides on these devices as a non-volatile memory. The storage and retrieval operations are known as writing and reading, respectively. Capacity of external storage devices is larger than that of the main memory and is also slower and less expensive per bit of information stored when compared to the main memory.

External storage devices are mainly used for the following:

1. Overlay or backup of programs during execution
2. Storage of programs for future use
3. Storage of information in files

We shall mainly concentrate on the third use, discuss the most common external storage devices in the order of their uses, and study magnetic tapes, drums, and disk drives.

14.2.1 Magnetic Tape

A tape is made up of a plastic material coated with a ferrite substance that is easily magnetized. The physical appearance of the tape is similar to the tape used for sound recording. Computer tapes are wider with several thousand feet of tape wound on one reel, where information is encoded on the tape, character by character. A number of channels or tracks run along the length of the tape, one channel being required for each bit position in the binary coded representation of a character. Information is read or written on the tape through the use of a magnetic tape drive.

A limitation of magnetic tape devices is that records must be processed in the order in which they reside on the tape. Therefore, accessing a record requires the scanning of all records that precede it. This form of access is called *sequential access*. The magnetic tape is probably the cheapest form of external bulk storage. A reel of tape can be easily placed on and removed from a tape drive, and hence it can be used for off-line storage and data.

14.2.2 Magnetic Drum

A magnetic drum is a metal cylinder, from 10 to 36 inches in diameter, which has an outside surface coated with a magnetic recording material. The cylindrical surface of the drum is divided into a number of parallel bands called tracks. The tracks are further divided into either sectors or blocks, depending on the nature of the drum. The sector or block is the smallest addressable unit. A particular sector or block is directly addressable, that is, to access a sector or block of a drum, it is not necessary to access sectors or blocks 1 to $n - 1$, as in the case of a sequential tape. Hence, a drum is called as a *direct access* storage device.

The addressable units (sectors or blocks) on drums are rapidly accessed for data transfers, and no scanning of extraneous data is required as with a magnetic tape. Also, unlike a magnetic tape, a drum cannot be removed from its shaft or drive. Hence, the maximum storage capacity for a drum device is limited to the capacity of a single drum.

14.2.3 Magnetic Disk

The magnetic disk is a direct access storage device, which has become more widely used than the magnetic drum, mainly because of its lower cost. Disk devices provide relatively low access times and high-speed data transfer. There are two types of disk devices, namely, fixed disks and exchangeable disks. For both types, the disk unit or pack consists of a number of metal platters, which are stacked on top of each other on a spindle. The upper and lower surfaces of each platter are coated with ferromagnetic particles that provide an information storage media.

The surfaces of each platter are divided into concentric bands called tracks. Each track is further divided into sectors (or blocks) that are addressable units. There are read/write heads floating just above or below the surface of the disk while the disk is rotating. An exchangeable disk device has movable read/write heads. The heads are attached to a movable arm to form a comb-like access assembly. When data on a particular track must be accessed, the whole assembly moves to position the read/write heads over the derived track. Although many heads may be in position for a read/write transaction at a given point in time, data transmission can only take place through one head at a time.

14.3 FILE ORGANIZATION

Files contain records which are collection of information arranged in a specific manner. File organization mainly refers to the logical arrangement of data in a file system. In order to be able to retrieve a target record from a file, it is preferred to be arranged in some defined or proper way. It is necessary to organize data records in a particular pattern. The proper arrangement of records within a file is known as *file organization*.

There are various ways in which records in a file can be stored. Files are presented to the application as a stream of bytes and at the end, it contains an EOF (end of file) mark. An attribute or combination of attribute values that are used to uniquely identify records within a file is called as a *key*. Keys are used to arrange and/or to retrieve records to/from a file. Primary key is one of the keys that can be used to identify a unique record in a file. Non-primary keys are called as secondary keys.

14.3.1 Schemes of File Organization

Various schemes for file organization are available. All these schemes decide the way in which records are stored and accessed in a file. Some of the file organizations are as follows:

Sequential file In sequential file, records are stored in the sequential order of their entry. This is the simplest kind of data organization. In sequential files, the records are stored in ascending or descending order of keys. When the records are not arranged in an organized fashion, they are stored as per their sequence of arrival; this organization is known as serial organization.

Direct or random access file Though we search the records using a key, we still need to know the address of the record to retrieve it directly. The file organization that supports such access is called as direct or random file organization. The word 'random' refers to the fact that the records are not usually stored in sequence but randomized to individual storage positions. So to get the address of the record using a key, there must be some relationship between the key and the address. With direct access file, the address for record storage and retrieval is computed by using a 'hashing' algorithm. As we retrieve the record directly with the help of the key and the hash function, without considering the position of the record in the file, the organization is known as direct access file organization.

Indexed sequential file Records are stored sequentially but the index file is prepared for accessing the record directly. An index file contains records ordered by a record key. The record key uniquely identifies the record and determines the sequence in which it is accessed with respect to other records.

Multi-indexed file In a multi-indexed file, the data file is associated with one or more logically separated index files. Inverted files and multilist files are examples of multi-indexed files.

14.3.2 Factors Affecting File Organization

File organization describes a way in which the records are stored in a file. The objective of file organization is to provide predefined and efficient means for the record storage, retrieval, and update.

The update process includes changes in some of the existing fields of records, addition of new records, or deletion of some existing records. The retrieval of data is done by specifying values for some or all the keys. A query is a combination of key values formed for retrieval of a specific record. Some factors affect file organization and similarly, file organization affects the design of algorithms as it deals with the records in the file.

The factors that mainly affect file organization are the following:

Storage device The way data is arranged in a file depends on the storage device. The magnetic tape is suitable for sequential organization. Direct access devices such as hard disks are suitable for random access file organization.

Type of query Depending on the type of query, file organization will be affected. In a simple query, values for the single key are specified. In a range query, range for the keys is specified. Accordingly, the file organization needs to be changed.

Number of keys The file may or may not have a key. Each key may have one or more fields. Accessing the desired record is made easy with the keys.

Mode of retrieval/update of record The mode of retrieval or update may be real-time or batched. In real-time retrieval, the response time for any query should be minimum. In a railway reservation system, the availability of a particular train should be retrieved in minimum time, whereas in a payroll system all records are processed in a batch.

14.3.3 Factors Involved in Selecting File Organization

Choosing a specific file organization depends on the nature of data and the algorithm used in the application. The overall combination should achieve good performance. The following are the criteria used to choose file organization:

Speed Rapid access to a single record or a collection of records

Operations Convenience of update, that is, addition, modification, or deletion of records

Capacity Efficiency of storage

Size Volume of transaction

Integrity Redundancy, being the method of ensuring data integrity

Security Special backup and recovery processes must exist to prevent exposure to the risks of loss of accuracy

A file should be organized in such a way that the records are always available for processing with no delay. This should be done in line with the activity and volatility of the information.

14.4 FILES USING C++

File handling is an important part of programming. Most of the applications have their own features to save data to the secondary storage and read from it again. File I/O classes in C++ simplify such file read/write operations.

14.4.1 File I/O Classes

The I/O system of C++ contains a set of classes that define the file handling methods. They are ifstream, ofstream, and fstream. These classes are included in the 'fstream.h' header file.

ifstream This class provides input operations.

ofstream This class provides output operations.

fstream This class provides both input and output operations.

14.4.2 Primitive Functions

There are several ways of reading (or writing) the text from (or to) a file, however, all of them share a common approach as follows.

1. Open the file
2. Read (or write) the data
3. Close the file

Opening a file Creating a file stream object to manage the stream using the ofstream, ifstream, or fstream classes is done using the following commands. The file name can be initialized while creating an object.

1. To create an object `ofile` and open a file with name `student.dat` for output only
```
ofstream ofile("student.dat");
```
2. To create an object `ifile` and open a file with name `sports.dat` for input only
```
ifstream ifile("sports.dat");
```
3. To create an object `file1` and open a file with name `employee.dat` for input and output
```
fstream file1("employee.dat");
```

4. To open a file using `open()`

```
ofstream.ofile;    // create an object ofile
ofile.open("sports");      // open file "sports" for output
fstream file;      // create object file of fstream class
file.open(filename, mode);
```

The file mode parameters are given in Table 14.2.

Table 14.2 File mode paratmeters

Mode	Meaning
ios::app	Append to the end of file
ios::ate	Go to the end of file on opening
ios::binary	Binary file
ios::in	Open file for reading
ios::nocreate	Open fails if file does not exist
ios::out	Open file for writing

For example,

```
file.open("data", ios::out |
ios::binary);
// Binary file with name data
is opened in output mode,
i.e., for writing only
```

Reading a character from a file A single character is read from a stream using the `get()` function.

```
file.get(ch);      // read one character from the file and store it to ch
```

Writing a character to a file The `put()` function writes a character to a stream.

```
file.put(ch);       // write the character of ch to the file
```

Reading binary data from a file The `read()` function is used to read binary data from a file.

```
file.read((char *) &V, sizeof(V));       // Reads value in variable V
                                         // from file
```

Consider the following code:

```
class item_rec
{
   int id;
   char itemname[20];
};
item_rec item;    // object item
file.read((char *) &item, sizeof(item));      // Reads item record from
                                              // file
```

Writing binary data to a file The `write()` function is used to write binary data to a file.

```
file.write((char *) &V, sizeof(V));      // Writes value of V in file
file.write((char *) &item, sizeof(item));     // Writes item record
                                              // to file
```

Manipulating file pointers The `seekg()` function moves the `input(get)` pointer to a specific position.

```
seekg(offset, reference);
```

Here `offset` is the number of bytes and `reference` may be one of the following:

1. `ios::beg`—from the start of the file
2. `ios::end`—from the end of the file
3. `ios::cur`—from the current position of the file
4. `seekp()`—moves the `output(put)` pointer to a specific position
5. `tellg()`—gives the current position of the `get` position
6. `tellp()`—gives the current position of the `put` position

Checking end of file The `eof()` function is used to check the EOF.

```
if(file.eof())
cout << "\n EOF";
```

or we can check `eof` using the following statement:

```
if(!file)
cout << "\n EOF";
```

Closing a file To close a file, we can use the `close()` function as follows:

```
file.close();
ifile.close();
```

File handling in C++ is demonstrated using Program Code 14.1.

PROGRAM CODE 14.1

```
//Sample program in C++ for file handling
#include<iostream.h>
#include<stdio.h>
#include<stdlib.h>
#include<fstream.h>
#include <string.h>
// class for storing passenger record
class passenger
{
   char f_name[15], l_name[15];
   int age;
  public:
      void get_data();
      void put_data();
};

// Function for getting passenger data
void passenger :: get_data()
{
   cout << endl << "Enter First name: ";
```

```
    cin >> f_name;
    cout << endl << "Enter Last name: ";
    cin >> l_name;
    cout << endl << "Age: ";
    cin >> age;
}

// Function for displaying passenger data
void passenger :: put_data()
{
    cout << endl << " \t" << f_name << "\t" << l_name
    << "\t" << age;
}

class PassengerFile
{
    private:
        char fname[12];
    public:
        void getfilename()
        {
            cout << "\n Enter filename : " ;
            cin >> fname;
        }
        void create();
        void displayall();
};

void PassengerFile :: create()
{
    fstream file;
    int n, i;
    file.open(fname, ios::out | ios::binary);
    cout << "\nHow many records do you want to enter?";
    cin >> n;
    for(i = 0; i < n; i++)
    {
        p.get_data();
        file.write((char*) &p, sizeof(p));
        flushall();
    }
    file.close();
}
```

```
void PassengerFile :: displayall()
{
    passenger p;        // object for passenger
    fstream file;
    file.open(fname, ios::in);
    if(file.bad())
        cout<<"\nOpening error...";
    else
    {
        cout << "\nid   Fname   Lname  Age \n";
        while(!file.eof())
        {
            file.read((char*) &p, sizeof(p));
            if(!file.eof())
            {
                p.put_data();
            }
        }
        file.close();
    }
}

void main()
{
    Passengerfile pfile;
    pfile.getfilename();
    pfile.create();
    pfile.displayall();
}
```

14.4.3 Binary and Text Files

The file in C++ is either a binary file or a text file. The difference between the two is due to the format in which data is organized within the file. The text file contains plain ASCII characters. It contains text data which is marked by 'end_of_line' at the end of each record. This end of record mark helps to perform operations such as read and write easily. A text file cannot store graphical data. On the other hand, a binary file consists of binary data. It can store text, graphics, and sound data in binary format. Binary files cannot be read directly.

C++ uses the `fopen(file, mode)` statement to open a file and the mode identifies whether you are opening the file to read, write, or append and also whether the file is to be opened in binary or text mode. C++ opens a file by linking it to a stream so we do not have to specify whether the file is to be opened in binary or text mode on the open statement. Instead the method that we use to read and/or write the file determines which mode we are using. If we use '<<' to read from the file and the '>>' operator to write to the file, then the file will be accessed in binary mode.This is illustrated in Program Code 14.2.

PROGRAM CODE 14.2

```
//Implementation of a simple text file in C++
#include <stdio.h>
#include<conio.h>
#include<iostream.h>
#include<fstream.h>
#include<string.h>
#include<process.h>
fstream fp, fp1; // declaration of file objects
//create a file by entering characters and at end enter #
class myfile
{
   char fname[30];
   public:
      myfile(char tname[30])
      {
         strcpy(fname,tname);
      }
      void create();
      void display();
      void display(char*);
      void count();
      void copy(char*);
};
void myfile :: create()
{
   char ch;
   fp.open(fname, ios::out);     /* Open the file in
   write mode */
   cout << "\nEnter the text::\n";
   do
   {
      ch = getchar();       /* read character    */
      /* write character in file */
     if(ch != '#')
```

```
        fp.write((char *)&ch, sizeof(ch));
    }while(ch != '#');
    fp.close();        // close a file
}

// Display a text file
void myfile :: display()
{
    char ch;
    fp.open(fname, ios::in);        /* Open the file in
    read mode */
    while(!fp.eof())
    {
        /* read character from file */
        fp.read((char *)&ch, sizeof(ch));
        cout << ch;        /* display character */
    }
    fp.close();
}

// Display a text file
void myfile :: display(char tname[30])
{
    char ch;
    fp.open(tname,ios::in);        /* Open the file in
    read mode */
    while(!fp.eof())
    {
        /* read character from file */
        fp.read((char*)&ch, sizeof(ch));
        cout << ch;        /* display character */
    }
    fp.close();
}

/* Function to count the number of lines, words, and
characters */
void myfile :: count()
{
    char ch;
    int c = 0, w = 0, line = 0;
    fp.open(fname, ios::in);
```

```
   while(!fp.eof())
   {
      fp.read((char *)&ch, sizeof(ch));
      c++;
      if((ch == ' ' || ch == '\n' || ch == '\t'))
         w++;
      if(ch == '\n')
         line++;
   }
   fp.close();
   printf("\nNo of lines %d \nNo of words %d \nNo of
   chars %d", line, w, c);
}

// Copy source file to destination file
void myfile :: copy(char dfname[30])
{
   char ch;
   fp.open(fname, ios::in);      /* Open source file in
   read mode */
   fp1.open(dfname, ios::out);      /* Open
   destination  file in write mode */
   while(!fp.eof())
   {
      /* read character from source file */
      fp.read((char *)&ch, sizeof(ch));
      /* write character to destination file */
      fp1.write((char *)&ch, sizeof(ch));
   }
   fp.close();
   fp1.close();
}
void main()
{
   int choice;
   myfile fobj("c:\\vst\\stud.dat");
   char fname[30];
   clrscr();
   do
   {
     printf("\n\n Menu");
     printf("\n 1. Create");
     printf("\n 2. Display");
```

```
        printf("\n 3. Count lines, words, characters");
        printf("\n 4. Copy file");
        printf("\n 5. Exit");
        printf("\nEnter your choice");
        scanf("%d", &choice);
        switch(choice)
        {
            case 1: fobj.create();
            break;
            case 2: fobj.display();
            break;
            case 3: fobj.count();
            break;
            case 4:
                char dfname[30];
                cout << "\nEnter the destination filename : ";
                cin >> dfname;
                fobj.copy(dfname);
                fobj.display(dfname);
            break;
            case 5: exit(0);
        }
    }while(choice < 5);
    getch();
}
```

14.5 SEQUENTIAL FILE ORGANIZATION

A sequential file stores records in the order they are entered. The order of the records is fixed. The records are stored and sorted in physical, contiguous blocks. Within each block, the records are in sequence. New records always appear at the end of the file. Therefore, the record found in the first position is the oldest record and the last record in the file is the one most recently added. Records in these files can only be read or written sequentially. Records may be either fixed or variable in length for this file type. This is a significant advantage of sequential files. However the search time associated with sequential files is more because records are accessed sequentially from the beginning of the file. Sequential files are compatible to the magnetic tape storage as shown in the following figure.

Record 1	Record 2	Record 3	Record 4	Record 5	...	...	End

1. Here, if we want to access Record 5, then we have to access records from Record 1 to Record 5 sequentially.
2. If we want to add a record, it is added at the end.

Important data is usually processed in sequential files, the reason being security is easily ensured in sequential files.

14.5.1 Primitive Operations

The set of primitive operations for a sequential file is small. The file pointer or currency pointer is a logical pointer to the current record in a file. Programming languages support explicit command to move file pointer, and a file pointer is also moved implicitly by primitive operations.

Primitive operations are those provided by the basic file system, language, and operating system. The following are the primitive operations of the sequential file organization:

Open This operation opens the file and sets the file pointer to the first record.

Read-next This operation returns the next record to the user. If no record is present, then EOF condition will be set.

Close This operation closes the file and terminates access to the file.

Write-next File pointers are set to next of last record and this record is written to the file.

EOF If EOF condition occurs, this operation returns true, otherwise it returns false.

Search This operation searches for the record with a given key.

Update The current record is written at the same position with updated values.

The number of records in a sequential file is given as (size of file)/(size of a record). The basic file operations are discussed as follows:

Add

Adding a record to the sequential file is a one-operation algorithm. The new record is simply appended to the end of the file. One physical write is required for appending a record in a file. Also many records can be collected in the buffer and a block of records can be written at a time in the file. The following are the steps involved in addition.

1. Add a record.
2. Open a file in append mode.
3. Read a record from user.
4. Write a record to the file.
5. Close the file.

Search

A particular record is searched through the file using a key sequentially by comparing with each record key. The search starts from the first record and continues till the EOF. The following steps are involved in searching:

1. Open a file in read mode.
2. Read the value of the record key of the record to be searched.
3. Read the next record from the file.
4. If record key = value, display record and go to 7.
5. If not EOF, then go to 3.
6. Display 'Record not found'.
7. Close the file.

Delete

There is no reasonable way to delete records from sequential file. Deletion is done in two ways:

1. Logical deletion
2. Physical deletion

Logical deletion When disk files are used, records may be *logically deleted* by just flagging them as having been deleted. This can be done by assigning a specific value to one of the attributes of the record. This method needs one extra field to be maintained with each record. The algorithm also needs to modify and check the flag field during operations.

Another method keeps a record of active and deleted records in a *bit map* file. A bit map is a one-dimensional array in which each bit represents a record in a file. The first bit refers to the first record, and so on. Bit value '1' tells that the record is active and '0' indicates that the record is deleted. So to delete a record, its corresponding bit value in a bit map file is set to zero. However, the map array may be stored in a separate file or in the beginning of the same file, as one or more records. The following steps are involved in logical deletion:

1. Open a file in read + write mode.
2. Read the record key of the record to be deleted.
3. Read the next record from the file.
4. If record key = value
   (a) Change status or deleted flag as 1
   (b) Write record back to the same position
   (c) Go to step 7
5. If not EOF, then go to 3.

6. Display 'Record not found'.
7. Close the file.

Physical deletion (pack or reorganize) For *physical deletion* of records, we need to copy the records to another file, skipping the deleted records, and rename the file. When the number of the logically deleted records is high, then it is advisable to delete them physically which is known as *reorganization of file*. The following steps are involved in physical deletion (pack):

1. Open a file in read mode.
2. Open 'temporary' file in write mode.
3. Read the record key of the record to be deleted.
4. Read the next record from the file.
5. If record key ! = value, write the record to temporary file.
6. If not EOF, then go to 4.
7. Close both the files.
8. Delete the original file.
9. Rename temporary file as original file.
10. Close the file.

Updation (Modification)

A record is updated when one or more fields is changed by modifying the information. The following steps are involved in updation:

1. Open a file in write mode.
2. Read the record key of the record to be modified.
3. Read the new attributes of the record to be modified.
4. If record key = value, modify record and go to 7.
5. If not EOF, then go to 4.
6. Display 'Record not found'.
7. Close the file.

14.5.2 Advantages

The following are the main advantages of sequential file organization:

1. Owing to its simplicity, it can be used with a variety of media, including magnetic tapes and disks.
2. It is compatible with variable length records, while most other file organizations are not.
3. Security is ensured with ease.
4. For a run in which a high proportion of a block is hit, as compared to other file organizations, sequential file is efficient specially when processed in batches.

14.5.3 Drawbacks

The following are some drawbacks of using sequential file organization:

1. Insertion and deletion of records in in-between positions cause huge data movement.
2. Accessing any record requires a pass through all the preceding records, which is time consuming. Therefore, searching a record also takes more time.
3. Needs reorganization of the file from time to time. If too many records are deleted logically, then the file must be reorganized to free the space occupied by unwanted records.

14.6 DIRECT ACCESS FILE ORGANIZATION

Files that have been designed to make direct record retrieval as easy and efficient as possible are known as directly organized files. This is achieved by retrieving a record with a key by getting the address of a record using the key. To achieve this, a suitable algorithm, called as hashing, is used to convert the keys to addresses.

Direct access files are of great use for immediate access to large amounts of information. They are often used in accessing large databases. When a query concerning a particular subject arrives, we compute which block contains the answer and then read that block directly to provide the desired information. A random access file is one in which the records are accessed directly by referring to the address where it is placed in a file.

One way to achieve this is to use the record number or the primary key (unique identification) as an address of record. In this approach, Record_No gives the location of the record in a file. In this respect, the file looks like a one-dimensional array where each element in an array is a record and the subscript is a record number.

If the range of the record number or the primary key is larger than that of the the file size, it is difficult or rather impossible to adopt the aforementioned strategy. This happens in some applications where only some of the records are selected (randomly) out of the many records. For example, out of 1000 students from a university, the data of the 100 computer science students is to be managed. However when they are admitted at a university, they are given a unique ID called an enrollment number, which ranges from 1 to 1000. Hence, we cannot adopt this strategy of inserting the element in position as the enrollment number for direct access.

To achieve direct access by having a file size as total number of records, another technique is used. In this technique, mapping of a larger range is done to a smaller range. To do this, a function is used, which generates a natural address (whose range lies between 1 and file size) from primary key of larger range. This function is known as the *hash function*, for example, MOD (primary key MOD N). A *synonym* is defined as a key, which generates the same address as that generated by a different key. A good hashing function must minimize the creation of synonyms. We have discussed hashing in Chapter 11.

A well-designed direct access file gives a very fast response to random queries than a sequential file. Many applications need both sequential and random access files. Though direct files can be processed sequentially, it would be much higher when sequential file is organized in a proper manner.

14.6.1 Primitive Operations

The primitive operations for the direct access file are as follows:

Open It opens the file and sets the file pointer to the first record.

Read-next It returns the next record to user. If no records are present, then EOF (end of file) condition will be set.

Read-direct It sets the file pointer to a specific position and gets the record for the user. If the slot is empty or out of range, then it gives error.

Write-direct It sets the file pointer to a specific position and writes the record to file at that position. If the slot is out of range, then it gives error.

Update Current record is written at the same position with updated values.

Close This will terminate the access to the file.

EOF If EOF condition occurs, it returns true otherwise it returns false.

We can use the `fseek()` function for direct access. The prototype of `fseek()` is :

```
int fseek(File *fp, long num-bytes, int origin);
```

The `fseek()` function sets the file position indicator. Here `fp` is a file pointer. The `num-bytes` parameter specifies the number of bytes from the origin that will become the new current position and `origin` can be one of the following as shown in Table 14.3.

Table 14.3 File position indicators

Origin	Value	Macro name
Beginning of file	0	seek _set
Current position	1	seek_cur
End of file	2	seek _ end

The `fseek()` function returns 0 when successful, and a non-zero value in case of an error. The implementation of direct access file organization is demonstrated in Program Code 14.3.

PROGRAM CODE 14.3

```
/* Direct access file. Collision handling to be done
by chaining without replacement for employee data as
empcode, empname */
```

```
#include<iostream.h>
#include<string.h>
#include<conio.h>
#include<fstream.h>
#include<process.h>
#include<math.h>
#define max 15
class employee
{
   public:
      char name[max];
      int empid;
      int chain;
      int delflag;
};

class hashfile
{
   fstream hfile;
   public:
      hashfile();
      int hash(int x){return x % 10;}
      void insert();
      void search();
      void display();
};

// function to initialize empty file
hashfile :: hashfile()
{
   int i;
   employee rec2;
   fstream iofile;
   iofile.open("hfile.dat", ios::out | ios::binary);
   strcpy(rec2.name, "\0");
   rec2.chain = -1;
   rec2.delflag = 0;
   for(i = 0; i < 10; i++)
   {
      rec2.empid = 0;
      iofile.write((char*)&rec2, sizeof(rec2));
   }
```

```
    iofile.close();
}

// function to insert a record in hash file
void hashfile :: insert()
{
    int i, flag = 0, pos, cnt = 0;
    long temp, start, size;
    fstream iofile;
    employee insertrec, rec3, trec;
    cout << "Enter name";
    cin >> insertrec.name;
    cout << "Enter no. of empid";
    cin >> insertrec.empid;
    insertrec.chain = -1;
    insertrec.delflag = 0;
    size = sizeof(insertrec);
    pos = hash(insertrec.empid);
    iofile.open("hfile.dat", ios :: in | ios :: out | ios
    :: binary);
    iofile.seekg(0);
    temp = pos * sizeof(insertrec);
    iofile.seekg(temp);
    // move to position given by hash function
    flag = 0;
    iofile.read((char*) &rec3, sizeof(rec3));
    if(rec3.empid == 0)       // slot is empty
   {
        flag = 1;
        temp = pos * sizeof(rec3);
        iofile.seekp(temp);       /* move to position
        given by hash function */
        iofile.write ((char*) &insertrec, sizeof(insertrec));
        return;
    }
    else       // slot is not empty
    {
        if(hash(rec3.empid) == hash(insertrec.empid))
        {
            while(rec3.chain != -1)
            {
                iofile.seekg(rec3.chain * sizeof (rec3));
```

```
            pos = rec3.chain;
            iofile.read((char*) &rec3, sizeof(rec3));
          }
          flag = 2;
        }
        int nextpos = pos;
        trec = rec3;
        while(iofile.read((char*) &rec3, sizeof(rec3)))
        // find next empty position
        {
          if(rec3.empid == 0)      // empty slot
          {
            iofile.seekp((nextpos+1) * sizeof(rec3));
            // move to position given by hash function
            iofile.write((char*) &insertrec,
            sizeof(insertrec));
            if(flag == 2)
            {
              iofile.seekp(pos * sizeof (rec3));
              trec.chain = nextpos + 1;
              iofile.write ((char*) &trec, sizeof(trec));
            }
            flag = 1;
            break;
          }
          nextpos++;
        }
      }
      if(flag != 1)
      {
        cout << "Error this rec was not inserted";
        cout << "The file is full after this index";
        getch();      return;
      }
      getch();
      iofile.close();
}     // end of insert

// function to search a record of hash file
void hashfile :: search()
{
   int pos = 0, t_empid;
```

```
    fstream iofile;
    employee rec1;
    cout << "Enter the empid of the book to be searched";
    cin >> t_empid;
    pos = hash(t_empid);
    // get the position of search record
    iofile.open("hfile.dat", ios::in | ios::binary);
    iofile.seekg(0);
    iofile.seekg(pos*sizeof(rec1));
    while(iofile.read((char *)&rec1, sizeof(rec1)))
    // read record at position
    {
       if(rec1.empid == t_empid)        // found
       {
          cout << "name" << rec1.name << "empid" << rec1.
empid;
          getch();
          iofile.close();
          return;
       }
       else if(hash(rec1.empid) == pos)
       // if record is stored at position
       {
          iofile.seekg(0);
          if(rec1.chain != -1)
             iofile.seekg(rec1.chain*sizeof(rec1));
             // jump at position of chain
       }
    }
    cout << "error no. such rec exist";
    getch();
    iofile.close();
}

void hashfile :: display()
{
    int i = 0;
    employee rec2;
    fstream iofile;
    cout << "\n\nserial\tempid\tname\tchain";
    iofile.open("hfile.dat", ios :: in | ios :: binary);
    while(iofile.read((char *)&rec2, sizeof(rec2)))
```

```
        cout << "\n\n" << i++;
        cout << "\t" << rec2.empid;
        {
        cout << "\t" << rec2.name;
        cout << "\t" << rec2.chain;
        }
    getch();
    iofile.close();
}

void main()
{
    int ch, pos;
    float flag = 1.1;
    hashfile file1;
    // rec.init();
    // clrscr();
    do
    {
        cout << "\n 1.Insert a rec";
        cout << "\n 2.Disp  all rec";
        cout << "\n 3.Search a rec";
        cout << "\n 4.Exit";
        cout << "\n Enter choice";
        cin >> ch;
        switch(ch)
        {
            case 1:
                file1.insert();
            break;
            case 2:
                file1.display();
            break;
            case 3:
                file1.search();
            break;
            case 4:
                exit(0);
        }
    }while(ch != 4);
}
```

14.7 INDEXED SEQUENTIAL FILE ORGANIZATION

Sequential processing of data files makes up a larger proportion of data. However, there is often a need to refer to sequential files just to satisfy the queries. Such a need can be met by processing the whole file sequentially and looking for the records that are to be retrieved. This is very efficient when the file is huge, the query may take long time, which is not affordable for the application. One solution is to improve the speed of retrieving target by using indexed sequential file.

A file that is loaded in key sequence but can be accessed directly by use of one or more indices is known as an indexed sequential file. A sequential data file that is indexed is called as indexed sequential file.

An indexed file contains records ordered by a *record key*. Each record contains a field that contains the record key. The record key uniquely identifies the record and determines the sequence in which it is accessed with respect to the other records. An indexed file can also use *alternate indices*, that is, record keys that let you access the file using a different logical arrangement of the records. For example, you could access the file through the employee department rather than through the employee number.

When indexed files are read or written sequentially, the sequence followed is that of the key values. Index is a data structure that allows particular records in a file to be located more quickly. An index can be sparse (record for only some of the search key values) or dense (index is maintained for each record), e.g., index in a book.

14.7.1 Types of Indices

Indices may be of the following three types:

Primary index It is an index ordered in the same way as the data file, which is sequentially ordered according to a key. The indexing field is equal to this key.

Secondary index This is an index that is defined on a non-ordering field of the data file. In this case, the indexing field need not contain unique values.

Clustering index A data file can associate with utmost one primary index and several secondary indices. In this organization, key searches are improved. The single-level indexing structure is the simplest one where a file, whose records are pairs, contains a key and a pointer. This pointer is the position in the data file of the record with the given key.

A key search is performed as follows: the search key is compared with the index keys to find the highest index key coming in front of the search key, while a linear search is performed from the record that the index key points to, until the search key is matched or until the record pointed to by the next index entry is reached.

Hardware for indexed sequential organization is usually disk-based, rather than tape. Records are physically ordered by primary key and the index gives the physical location of each record. Records can be accessed sequentially or directly, via the index. The index is stored in a file and read into memory at the point when the file is opened. The indices must also be maintained.

14.7.2 Structure of Indexed Sequential File

The file structure is selected according to the physical storage device. The external storage device should have the capability to access directly a record as per the key. Devices like magnetic tape can access all records sequentially. The magnetic drum or disk supports direct access.

In primary area, actual data records are stored. Data records are stored as sequential file. The second area is an index area in which the index is stored and is automatically generated. An index file consists of three areas:

Primary storage area This includes some unused space to allow for additions made in data.

Separate index or indices Each query will reference this index first; it will redirect query to part of data file in which the target record is saved.

Overflow area This is optional separate overflow area.

A number of index levels may be involved in an index sequential file. The lowest level of an index is track index, which is written at track 0, i.e., first track of the cylinder. The track index contains two entries for each prime track of the cylinders for the index sequential file. The normal entry is composed of the address of prime track to which the entry is associated and the highest value of the keys for the records is stored on that track. The track index describes how records are stored on the track of cylinder and the cylinder index indicates how records are distributed over number of cylinders. In index sequential file, records are organized in sequence of key field known as primary key. For fast searching, it is supported by index. Index is a pair of key and address where that record is stored in the main file. Number of records are same as number of blocks of the main file.

14.7.3 Characteristics of Indexed Sequential File

The following are the characterictics of an indexed sequential file:

1. Records are stored sequentially and a separate index file is maintained for accessing the record directly.
2. Records can be accessed randomly in constant time.
3. Magnetic tape is not suitable for indexed sequential storage.
4. Index is the address of physical storage of a record.
5. When very few records are to be accessed, then indexed sequential file is better.
6. This is a faster access method.
7. Additional overhead is that the index is to be maintained
8. Indexed sequential files are popularly used in many applications such as a digital library.

Consider that an employee file is stored as an indexed sequential file. The entries are as shown in Fig. 14.1.

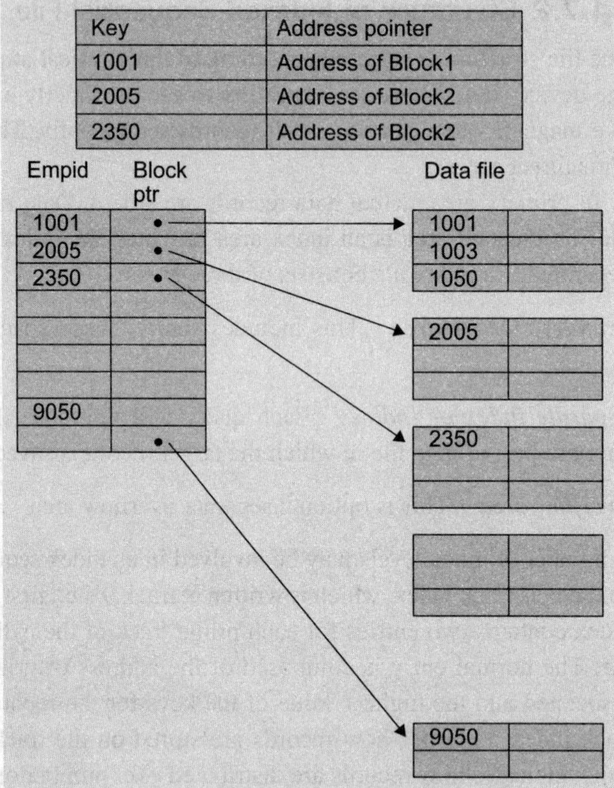

Fig. 14.1 Index sequential file organization

This organization is slower than a sequential file. For a sequential file, retrieval and access time for direct retrieval are greater than the well-designed direct access file. The advantage of such file organization is that it can handle requirements of mixed access application much better than other organizations.

Advantages

1. Accessing any record is more efficient than sequential file organization.
2. Large amount of data can be stored using this type of file organization.

Disadvantage

1. Often more than one index is needed which occupies a large storage area.

Program Code 14.4 demonstrates the implementation of index sequential file.

PROGRAM CODE 14.4

```
//Index sequential file (one to one map index)
#include <stdio.h>
#include <conio.h>
#include<iostream.h>
#include<fstream.h>
/* Item record */
struct itemrec
{
   int itemcode;
   char itemname[20];
   float cost;
};

/* Index record */
struct indexrec
{
   int itemcode;
   int position;
   int flag;
};

/* Display the contents of index file */
void displayindexfile()
{
   fstream indexfile;
   struct indexrec index;
   indexfile.open("index.dat", ios::in);
   cout << "\n Index file is n";
   cout << "\n Itemcode \t Position \t Del Flag";
   while(!indexfile.eof())
   {
      indexfile.read((char*)&index, sizeof(indexrec));
      if(indexfile.eof())
         break;
      if(index.flag == 1)
         cout << endl << index.itemcode <<
         index.position<<index.flag;
      else
         cout << "deleted=";
         cout << endl << index.itemcode <<
         index.position << index.flag;
```

```
    }
}

/* Insert a record */
void insertrecord()
{
    struct itemrec item;
    struct indexrec index;
    stream indexfile, itemfile;
    long position;
    cout << "\n Enter itemcode";
    cin >> item.itemcode;
    cout << "\n Enter itemname";
    cin >> item.itemname;
    cout << "\n Enter cost";
    cin >> item.cost;
    /* Get the position of the new record in item file */
    itemfile.open("item.dat", ios::in);
    itemfile.seekg(seek_end);
    position = itemfile.tellg()/sizeof(item);
    itemfile.close();
    /* Add a record in item file */
    itemfile.open("item.dat", ios::in | ios::out |
    ios::app);
    itemfile.write((char*)&item, sizeof(itemrec));
    itemfile.close();
    /*Add a record in index file */
    indexfile.open("index.dat", ios::in | ios::out |
    ios::app);
    index.itemcode = item.itemcode;
    index.position = position;
    index.flag = 1;
    indexfile.write((char*)&index, sizeof(indexrec));
    indexfile.close();
}

/* Search a record */
void search()
{
    int searchitcode;
    struct itemrec item;
    struct indexrec index;
   fstream indexfile, itemfile;
    long position, found = 0;
```

```
    cout << "\n Enter itemcode to be searched";
    cin >> searchitcode;
    indexfile.open("index.dat", ios::in);
    while(!indexfile.eof())
    {
       indexfile.read((char*)&index, sizeof(indexrec));
       if(index.itemcode == searchitcode && index.flag
       == 1)
       {
          found = 1;
          break;
       }
   }
    if(found == 1)
    {
       itemfile.open("item.dat", ios::in);
       /*Take the position from index file and go to
       that record in item file */
       itemfile.seekg((index.position) * sizeof(item));
       itemfile.read((char*)&item, sizeof(item));
       cout << "\n Item Record is";
       cout << "\nItemcode \t Item name \t Cost";
       cout << item.itemcode << item.itemname <<
       item.cost;
       itemfile.close();
    }
    else
      cout << "\n Record not found";
       indexfile.close();
}

/* Delete a record */
void deleterecord()
{
    int searchitcode;
    struct indexrec index;
    fstream indexfile;
    long position,found = 0, c;
    cout << "\n Enter itemcode to be deleted";
    cin >> searchitcode;
    indexfile.open("index.dat", ios::in | ios::out |
    ios::app);
    c = 0;
    while(!indexfile.eof())
```

```
    {
        indexfile.read((char*)&index, sizeof(indexrec));
        if(index.itemcode == searchitcode && index.flag
        == 1)
        {
            found = 1;
            break;
        }
        c++;
    }
    if(found == 1)
    {
        indexfile.seekg(c * sizeof(index));
        index.flag = 0;        // Make a delete flag 0
        indexfile.write((char*)&index, sizeof(index));
    }
    else
        cout << "\n Record not found";
        indexfile.close();
}

void main()
{
    int choice;
    clrscr();
    do
    {
        cout << "\n 1. Insert \n 2. Search \n 3. Delete a
        record";
        cout << "\n 4. Display Index file \n 5. Exit";
        cout << "\n Enter choice : ";
        cin >> choice;
        switch(choice)
        {
            case 1 : insertrecord();
            break;
            case 2 : search();
            break;
            case 3 : deleterecord();
            break;
            case 4 : displayindexfile();
            break;
        }
```

```
    }
    while(choice < 5);
}
```

14.8 LINKED ORGANIZATION

In linked organization, the physical sequence of records is different from the logical sequence of records. The next logical record is obtained by following a link value from the present record. Records are linked according to increasing primary key, so insertion and deletion is easy. If index is not maintained, then direct searching is difficult and only sequential search is possible.

14.8.1 Multilist Files

To make searching easy, several indexes are maintained as per primary key and secondary keys, one index per key. The record may be present in different lists as per key. Consider the following file of office staff in Table 14.4.

Table 14.4 Staff data

Staff ID	Occupation	Salary	Record
106	Clerk	5000	A
150	Accountant	4000	B
360	Clerk	3000	C
400	Accountant	3500	D
700	Clerk	2000	E

We can maintain indices on the staff ID. We can group staff ID with ranges 101–300, 301–600, 601–900, and so on. Now all the records with staff ID in the same range will be linked together as shown in Fig. 14.2.

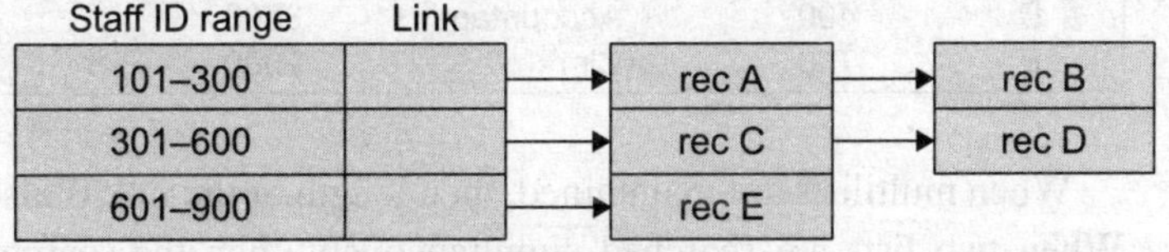

Fig. 14.2 Sample multilist file

Now each record will have values of all the fields as well as link to the next record in the group.

We can have multilist structure for file representation by maintaining different indices on different keys and allow records to be in more than one list. Suppose indices are maintained on occupation and salary fields, then the multilist structure will look as shown in Fig. 14.3.

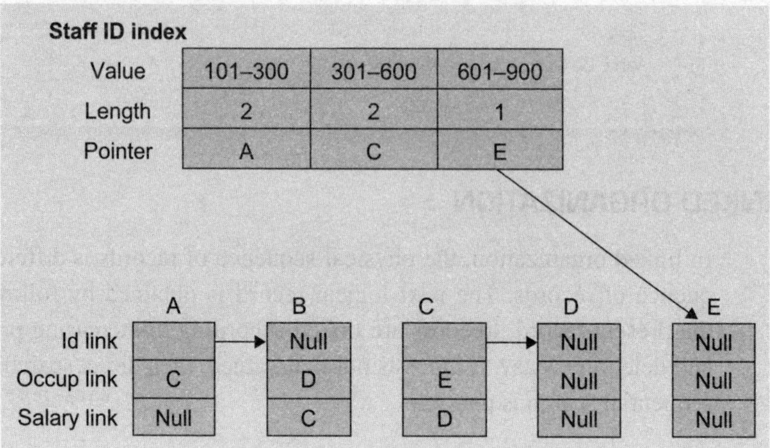

Fig. 14.3 Linked organization

Table 14.5 lists the staff details and links for the following values of occupation and salary:

Occupation index

Value	Clerk	Accountant
Length	3	2
Pointer	A	B

Salary index

Value	<= 2000	<= 4000	<= 6000
Length	1	3	1
Pointer	E	B	A

Table 14.5 Staff data and links

Record	Staff ID	Occupation	Salary	Occupation link	Salary link
A	106	Clerk	5000	C	–
B	150	Accountant	4000	D	C
C	360	Clerk	3000	E	D
D	400	Accountant	3500	–	–
E	700	Clerk	2000	–	–

When multilists are maintained, then length of the link is also maintained in the index. When two lists are searched simultaneously, then the search time can be reduced by searching the smaller list.

The logical order of records in the list may or may not be important according to the application. If salary index is not maintained in increasing order, then insertion can be done at the beginning or at the end of the list, otherwise we have to find a proper position in the link to insert new record. Also because only single link is maintained, deletion is difficult. This problem can be overcome by maintaining double link. But these links require storage. So, if space is of importance, then the alternative is the coral ring structure.

14.8.2 Coral Rings

In this, doubly linked multilist structure is used as shown in Fig.14.4. Each list is circular list with headnode.

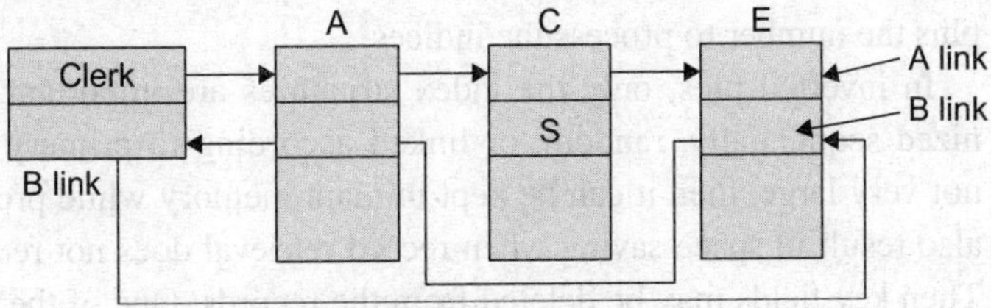

Fig. 14.4 Sample doubly linked list

'A link' field is used to link all records with same key value. 'B link' is used for some records back pointer and for others it is pointer to head node. 'S' is headnode of the list of 'Clerk'. Owing to these back pointers, deletion is easy without going to start. Indexes are maintained as per multilists.

14.8.3 Inverted Files

The concept of the inverted files and multilists is similar. The difference is that, in multilists records with the same key value are linked together and links are kept in each record. But in the inverted files, the link information is kept in the index itself.

For example, consider the same file of office staff used in the link organization. The indices for fully inverted file are shown in Fig. 14.5.

Staff ID index (increasing order)	Occupation index
106	A
150	B
360	C
400	D
700	E

Accountant	B, D
Clerk	A, C, E

Salary index	
2000	E
4000	B, C, D
6000	A

Fig. 14.5 Inverted files

All these are dense indices and contain an entry for each record in the file. But now because links are kept in the indices, index entries become variable length and therefore index maintenance becomes more complex than for multilists.

The inversion process is associated with the information of inverted list. Normally, a record is searched via a primary key. For example, if staff ID is a primary key, then records can be searched using staff ID. But the inverted list provides staff ID and further a particular staff's name and other details can be accessed through index.

In inverted files, the record is accessed in two steps. First, the indices are searched to obtain a list of required records and then second, records are retrieved using these lists. The number of disk accesses required is equal to the number of records being retrieved plus the number to process the indices.

In inverted files, only the index structures are important. The records can be organized sequentially, random, or linked according to primary key. If a list of records is not very large, then it can be kept in main memory while processing. Inverted files may also result in space saving when record retrieval does not require retrieval of key fields. Then key fields may be deleted from the records. One of the major disadvantages of the inverted files is that the item values being inverted generally have to be included in both the inverted list and the master file.

14.8.4 Cellular Partitions

To decrease file search time, the storage media may be divided into cells. A cell may be an entire disk or a cylinder. Lists are localized to lie within a cell. If a cylinder is used as a cell, then all records on the same cylinder may be accessed without moving the read/write heads. We divide multilists organized on several different cylinders into several small lists which are stored on the same cylinder.

For example, consider Table 14.6, an example of a multilist structure with cellular partitioning for student–teacher data.

Table 14.6 Multilist structure with cellular partitioning

	Primary key	Secondary key		
Position	Student ID	Course teacher ID	Link	
1	100	A	o → (position 4)	Cell 1
2	200	B	Null	Cell 1
3	300	C	Null	Cell 1
4	400	A	Null	Cell 1
1	500	D	o → (position 4)	Cell 2
2	600	B	Null	Cell 2
3	700	A	Null	Cell 2
4	800	D	Null	Cell 2
1	900	E	Null	Cell 3
2	1000	C	Null	Cell 3
3	1100	D	Null	Cell 3
4	1200	A	Null	Cell 3

An entry is created in the secondary index whenever the item value occurs one or more times in a cellular partition. The relative secondary index records for the data in Table 14.6 are shown in Table 14.7.

Table 14.7 Teacher's data and secondary index

Course teacher ID	Position	Cell no.	Length of link
A	1	1	2
	3	2	1
	4	3	1
B	2	1	1
	2	2	1
C	3	1	1
	2	3	1
D	1	2	2
	3	3	1
E	1	3	1

The course teacher ID 'A' has entries in each cell, at two positions in cell 1, at one position in cell 2, and at one position in cell 3. Therefore, the entry of 'A' has three rows in the secondary index. The course teacher ID 'E' has entry only in cell 3 at position 1, so in the secondary index, 'E' has only one row.

A multilist structure with cellular partitioning is primarily useful when there are a large number of records residing in a cell. If there are few records in each cell, then the link field can be omitted.

The length field and the relative record position can also be omitted. One such structure is cellular serial structure shown in Table 14.8.

Table 14.8 Cellular serial structure

Course teacher ID	Cell no.
A	1
	2
	3
B	1
	2
C	1
	3
D	2
	3
E	3

One more type of structure is the cellular inverted list which is represented as a binary matrix. Each matrix element is either 0 meaning that the item is absent, or 1 meaning that the item is present in the cellular partition. The structure is shown as in Table 14.9.

Table 14.9 Cellular inverted list

Secondary index item	Cell no.		
A	1	1	1
B	1	1	0
C	1	0	1
D	0	1	1
E	0	0	1

For cellular multilist structures, index entries may have to be updated with the addition or deletion of records or individual secondary index items. Such changes are minimal when cellular serial or cellular inverted lists are used. A major advantage of cellular partitioning is that several read operations can be initiated simultaneously and these operations can be overlapped with the query processing. But the disadvantage is that if there are many records per cell, then access time may be large.

RECAPITULATION

- Data processing is one of the core tasks of computers. Large volumes of data and archival data need to be preserved even after execution of program is over. Such data is commonly stored in the external memory as special data holding entities, files.
- Magnetic tapes, floppy disks, and hard disks are a few examples of secondary storage devices. When we organize data in a file data structure, the data is non-volatile, which means data will reside on storage after data processing is over.
- Files contain records. In order to be able to retrieve a target record from a file, it is preferred to arrange in some defined or proper way. Necessity is to organize data records in a particular pattern. The proper arrangement of records within a file is called as file organization.
- Various schemes for file organization are available such as sequential, direct access, and index sequential organization. All these schemes decide the way in which records are stored and accessed in a file.
- In sequential files, records are stored in ascending or descending order of key and stored as per their sequence of arrival. This type of organization is known as serial organization. When data arises in sorted order, the serial organization becomes sequential organization.
- To get faster access, the records are organized randomly in a file by computing the address using key and hash function. File organization that supports direct access to record by computing its address using key is called as direct or random file organization.
- In index sequential file, the records are stored sequentially. For each record, its corresponding address is saved as index in index file for accessing the record directly.
- C++ supports file operations through library functions.

KEY TERMS

Direct access file organization The file organization that supports direct access to record by computing its address using key is called as direct or random file organization.

File Records that hold information about similar items of data are usually grouped together into a file. A file is a collection of records where each record consists of one or more fields.

File organization File organization refers to the logical arrangement of data in a file system. Various schemes for file organization are available such as sequential, direct access, and index sequential organization.

Index sequential file organization An index file contains records ordered by a record key. The record key uniquely identifies the record and determines the sequence in which it is accessed with respect to other records.

Sequential file organization The simplest kind of data organization, sequential file organization is the one in which records are stored in the sequential order of their entry arising in ascending or descending order of key.

EXERCISES

Multiple choice questions

1. Assume a file of 10,000 records distributed over 100 blocks, i.e., every block has 100 records, also assume that every record is equally likely to be accessed. In trying to locate a particular record, we first examine the index, which is assumed to be within a single block. To locate the block containing the required record, we have to examine each index entry. The number of comparisons required are
   (a) 1000
   (b) 110
   (c) 100
   (d) 101
2. There are five records in a database as follows:

Name	Age	Occupation	Category
Rama	27	CON	A
Abdul	22	ENG	A
Jeniffer	28	DOC	B
Maya	32	SER	D
Dev	24	MUS	C

   There is an index file associated with this and it contains the values 1, 3, 2, 5, and 4. Which one of the fields is the index built from?
   (a) Age
   (b) Name
   (c) Occupation
   (d) Category
3. In the index allocation scheme of a block to a file, the maximum possible size of the file depends on
   (a) the size of the blocks and the size of the address of the blocks.
   (b) the number of blocks used for the index and the size of the blocks.
   (c) the size of the blocks, the number of blocks used for the index, and the size of the address of the blocks.
   (d) None of the above
4. Consider a file of 16,384 records. Each record is 32 bytes long and its key field is of size 6 bytes. The file is ordered on a non-key field, and the file organization is unspanned. The file is stored in a file system with block size of 1024 bytes, and the size of the block pointer is 10 bytes. If the secondary index is built on the key field of the file, and multi-level index scheme is used to store the secondary index, the number of first-level and second-level blocks in the multi-level index are respectively.
   (a) 8 and 0
   (b) 128 and 6
   (c) 256 and 4
   (d) 512 and 5
5. What will happen if you execute the following program?

```
#include "stdio.h"
void main()
{
    unsigned char c;
    file *fp;
    fp = fopen("test.txt", "r");
    while((c = fgetc(fp))!=EOF)
        printf("%c", c);
    fclose(fp);
    getch();
}
```

   Given: //test.txt
   I am reading file handling in cmagical.blogspot.com
   (a) It will print the content of the file text.txt.
   (b) It will enter into an infinite loop.
   (c) It will display nothing.
   (d) Error
6. Which of the following file organization methods is most efficient for a file with a high degree of file activity?
   (a) Sequential
   (b) ISAM
   (c) VSAM
   (d) B-tree index

7. The two basic types of record access methods are
   (a) sequential and random
   (b) sequential and indexed
   (c) direct and immediate
   (d) on-line and real time
8. Which file organization is allowed by a direct access storage device?
   (a) Direct only
   (b) Sequential and direct only
   (c) Indexed and direct only
   (d) Sequential, indexed, and direct
   (e) None of the above
9. Sequential file organization is most appropriate for which of the following applications?
   (a) Grocery store checkout
   (b) Bank checking account
   (c) Payroll
   (d) Airline reservations
   (e) None of the above
10. Which of the following file organization methods is most efficient for a file with a high degree of file activity?
    (a) Sequential
    (b) ISAM
    (c) VSAM
    (d) B-tree
    (e) All of the above
11. One disadvantage of a direct access file is
    (a) the delay in computing the storage address
    (b) duplication of address locations
    (c) unused, but available, storage locations
    (d) all of the above
12. Electronic spreadsheets are most useful in a situation where relatively ________ data must be input but ________ calculations are required.
    (a) little; simple
    (b) large; simple
    (c) large; complex
    (d) little; complex

Review questions

1. A file of employees records, has 'employee no' as a primary key and the 'department code' and the 'designation code' as the secondary keys. Write a procedure to answer the following query—'Which employees from systems department are above designation level 4?'.
2. Compare sequential file organization with direct access file organization. Write a C implementation of primitives for either of the two organizations.
3. Write short notes on:
   (a) Factors affecting the file organization
   (b) Indexed sequential files
   (c) Indexing techniques
4. Compare sequential, indexed sequential, and direct access files.
5. Describe the basic types of file organization each with one example.
6. State the advantages, disadvantages, and primitive operation of sequential files.
7. What are indexed files? Explain with a suitable example. Compare sequential and direct access files.
8. Write notes on:
   (a) Inverted files
   (b) Cellular partition
9. What is a multi-index file? Give suitable examples.

Answers to multiple choice questions

1. (d) 2. (c) 3. (b) 4. (c) 5. (b) 6. (a) 7. (a) 8. (d) 9. (c)
10. (a) 11. (a) 12. (d)

15 STANDARD TEMPLATE LIBRARY

OBJECTIVES

After completing this chapter, the reader will be able to understand the following:

- Abstract data type (ADT) implementation in C++ and the rationale for using them
- How ADTs aid code reuse
- Five components of standard template library (STL)
- How to simplify the task of writing application codes with the use of STL

C++ classes provide information for creating a library of data structures. The STL is a part of the standard C++ class library and can be used as the standard approach for storing and processing data. In this chapter, we shall study the STL and learn how to use it. The C++ class allows for implementation of ADTs with appropriate hiding of implementation details. Let us discuss how to achieve this.

15.1 ABSTRACT DATA TYPE

One of the factors that contribute to the success of a software project is the choices made in the representation of data and algorithms designed to process the data. The proper choice of a data structure can be a key point in the design of many algorithms. Clearly, we need good ways to describe, organize, and process data.

A data type consists of a collection of values together with a set of basic operations defined on these values. A data type is called an ADT if a programmer can use it without having access to and also without knowing the details of how the values and operations are implemented.

Specifying a data structure by the details of its implementation means that if one wants to change the representation later, one has to find every piece of code that manipulates the data and make sure that it corresponds to the new definition. The best way to avoid this problem is to make sure that all the data types we define are ADTs. In addition, every software professional wants a way to specify data which satisfies the following properties:

Abstract Every user should be able to use it without knowing the details of its representation and implementation, thus making the code easier to understand and maintain.

Safe A user should be able to use the data without having access to it. This provides control over the manipulation of data and keeps it safe.

Modifiable Representation of data should be in a way that enables easy modification.

Reusable Data and operations encapsulated together with abstraction make the code reusable. This is the motivation behind using ADTs.

15.1.1 Abstract Data Type and Data Structures

The term *ADT* describes a comprehensive collection of data values and operations. The term *data structure* refers to the study of data and how to represent data objects within a program, that is, the implementation of a structured relationship. The way in which software professionals view data structures has undergone an evolution in the last few years. They implement with the view of abstract properties of classes of data objects in addition to how these data objects might be represented in a program. Depending on the point of view, a data object is characterized by its type (for the user) or by its structure (for the implementer).

The topic of data structures has now been subsumed under the broader topic of ADTs: the study of classes of objects whose logical behaviour is defined by a set of operations.

The traditional model of studying data structures is based on the characteristic of the implementation of the structures. For example, stacks and queues are linear lists with restricted access. These data structures can be represented as last in first out (LIFO) and first in first out (FIFO), respectively. However, a user of these two ADTs does not care about the intricacies of the data structure and restricted access. In fact, the user does not (rather should not) care about what happens when an item is stored either in a stack or a queue; he/she is only interested in what is inserted into or deleted from the stack or the queue. Therefore, it is essential to revise the concept of data structures as an ADT and also learn how to implement them using C++.

15.1.2 Creating Abstract Data Types

To create an ADT, we specify the data by its operation rather than by its implementation, that is, we talk about what the data can do and how it is used, but not the details of the code that implemented it. An ADT's specification describes what data can be stored, that is, its characteristics, and how it can be used, that is, the operations, but not how it is implemented in the program.

An ADT specification may be quite formal, written in a specific language, or may be an informal description in English. Likewise, an implementation could be a program in a particular programming language such as C++ or Pascal or could be a pseudocode description.

15.1.3 Stack Abstract Data Type

Any set of elements of the same data type can be used as a data object for stacks. The meaning of 'same data type' is that all the elements in the stack should be of the same nature having common representational logical properties. A stack of integers, a stack of names of students, a stack of employee records, or a stack of records of processes of the operating system are some examples of data objects for the stack.

The following five functions comprise a functional definition of a stack:

1. `create(S)`—creates an empty stack.
2. `push(i, S)`—inserts the element `i` on the stack `S` and returns the modified stack.
3. `pop(S)`—removes the topmost element from the stack `S` and returns the modified stack.
4. `getTop(S)`—returns the topmost element of the stack `S`.
5. `is_empty(S)`—returns true if `S` is empty otherwise returns false.

When we choose to represent a stack, it must be possible to build these operations. However, before we do this let us formally describe the structure of the stack, as in Algorithm 15.1.

ALGORITHM 15.1

```
ADT stack(element)
 1. Declare create()→stack
 2. push(element, stack)→stack
 3. pop(stack)→stack
 4. getTop(stack)→element
 5. is_empty(stack)→Boolean;
 6. for all S ∈ stack, e ∈ element, Let
 7. is_empty(create) = true
 8. is_empty(push(e, S)) = false
 9. pop(create()) = error
10. pop(push(e,S)) = S
11. getTop(create) =  error
12. getTop(push(e, S)) = e
13. end
14. end stack
```

The five functions with their domains and ranges are declared in lines 1 through 5. Lines 6 through 13 are the set of axioms that describe how the functions are related. Lines 10 and 12 are important because they define the LIFO behaviour of the stack. This definition describes an infinite stack for no upper bound or roof on the number of elements specified. To implement the ADT stack in C++, these operations are often implemented as functions to provide the data abstraction. A program, which uses stacks, would access the stacks only through these functions and would not be concerned about the implementation.

15.2 SURVEY OF PROGRAMMING TECHNIQUES

Let us have a short survey of programming techniques, also known as *programming paradigms*. They are as follows:

1. Unstructured programming
2. Procedural programming
3. Modular programming
4. Object-oriented programming

Unstructured Programming

Usually, people start learning programming by writing small and simple programs consisting of one main program. Here the *main* program stands for a sequence of commands or *statements* that modify data which is global throughout the whole program. We can illustrate this as shown in Fig. 15.1.

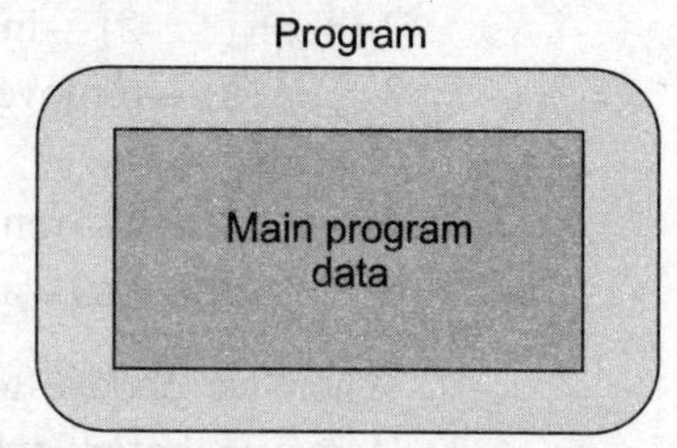

Fig. 15.1 Unstructured programming

As we all know, this programming technique provides tremendous disadvantages once the program becomes sufficiently large. For example, if the same statement sequence is needed at different locations within the program, the sequence must be copied. This has led to the idea of extracting these sequences, naming them, and offering a technique to call and return from these procedures.

Procedural Programming

With procedural programming, we are able to combine returning sequences of statements into one single place. A *procedure call* is used to invoke the procedure. After the sequence is processed, the flow of control proceeds right after the position where the call was made (Fig. 15.2).

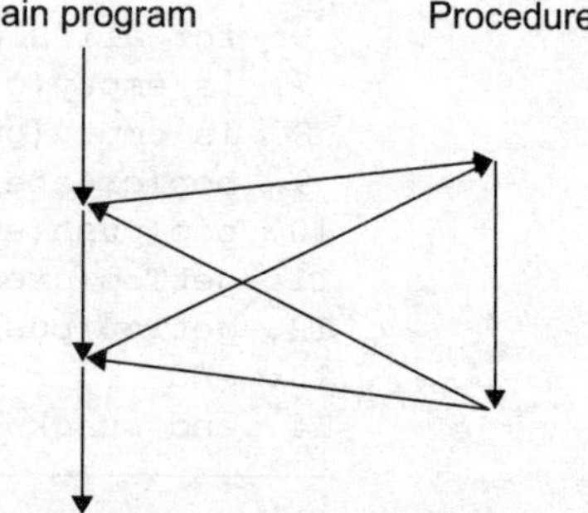

Fig. 15.2 Execution of procedures

With the introduction of *parameters* as well as procedures of procedures (*sub-procedures*), the programs can now be written in a more structured and error-free way. For example, if a procedure is correct, every time it is used, it produces correct results. Consequently, in case of errors, we can narrow our search to those places that are not proven to be correct.

Now, a program can be viewed as a sequence of procedure calls. The main program is responsible to pass data to the individual calls; the data is processed by the procedures, and once the program is finished, the resulting data is presented. Thus, the flow of data can be illustrated as a hierarchical graph, a *tree*,

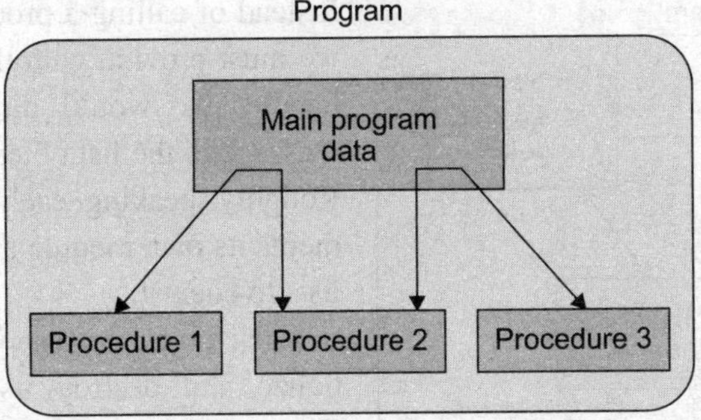

Fig. 15.3 Procedural programming

as shown in Fig. 15.3 for a program with no sub-procedures.

To sum up, we now have a single program that is divided into small pieces called *procedures*. To enable the usage of general procedures or groups of procedures in other programs too, they must be separately available. For that reason, modular programming allows grouping of procedures into modules.

Modular Programming

With modular programming, procedures of a common functionality are grouped together into separate *modules*. A program therefore no longer consists of only one single part. It is now divided into several smaller parts that interact through procedure calls and form the whole program (Fig. 15.4).

The main program coordinates the calls to procedures in separate modules and hands over appropriate data as parameters.

Each module can have its own data. This allows each module to manage an internal *state* which is modified by calls to procedures of this module. However, there is only one state per module, and each module exists utmost once in the whole program.

There are some problems in modular programming such as explicit creation and destruction, decoupled data and operations, and missing type safety.

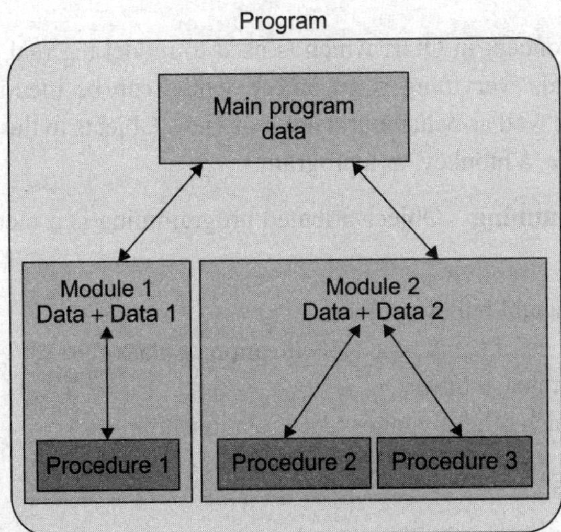

Fig. 15.4 Modular programming

Object-oriented Programming

Object-oriented programming (OOP) solves some of the aforementioned problems. In contrast to the other techniques, we now have a web of interacting objects, each housekeeping its own state (Fig. 15.5).

Consider the multiple lists example. The problem with modular programming is that we must explicitly create and destroy the list handles. Then, we use the procedures of the module to modify each of the handles.

In contrast to this, in object-oriented programming, we would have as many list objects as needed.

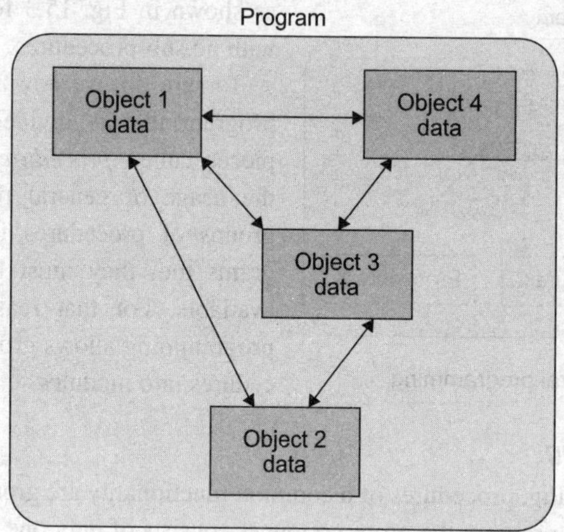

Fig. 15.5 Object-oriented programming

Instead of calling a procedure, which we must provide with the correct list handle, we would directly send a message to the list object in question. Roughly speaking, each object implements its own module allowing many lists to coexist.

Each object is responsible to initialize and destroy itself correctly. Consequently, there is no longer the need to explicitly call a creation or termination procedure. We shall discuss object-oriented design and programming in detail in this section.

Object-oriented Design

Object-oriented design represents a fundamental change from the structured programming design method. Traditional structured programming has used algorithmic decomposition. Algorithmic or functional decomposition views software as a process. It decomposes the software/program into modules that represent steps of the process. These modules are implemented by language constructs such as procedures in Pascal, subroutines in FORTRAN, or functions in C.

Object-oriented decomposition views software as a set of well-defined objects that model entities in the application domain. These objects interact with each other to form a software system. Functional decomposition is addressed after the system has been decomposed into objects.

An object is a basic concept in OOP, which is used to model the real world through objects. In our real world, everything is an object, which can be identified from one another by the physical as well as behavioural point of view. Objects in the real world can be anything, be it an apple, a monkey, or a program.

Object-oriented programming Object-oriented programming is a method of implementation in which

1. objects are the fundamental building blocks;
2. each object is an instance of some type (specification or class);
3. objects can interact with each other;
4. classes are related to each other by inheritance relationship.

Object-oriented language An object-oriented language is the one that

1. supports objects and programs divided into objects,
2. contains objects belonging to a class, and
3. supports inheritance.

Basic Concepts of Object-oriented Programming

We shall discuss some of the basic concepts of OOP.

Objects Objects are the basic runtime entities in an object-oriented system. A programming problem is analysed in terms of objects and the nature of communication between them. Each object contains data and code to manipulate the data.

Classes Object-oriented programming encapsulates data (attributes) and functions (behaviour) into packages called as *classes*. A class is a user-defined data type.

Data abstraction and encapsulation Combining a number of variables and functions into a single package, such as an object of some class, is called as *encapsulation*. *Abstraction* refers to the act of representing essential features without including the details of implementation. Generally, data members are made private and are accessible to only class member functions. This insulation of data from direct access by the program is called *data hiding* or *information hiding*.

Inheritance *Inheritance* is a process by which the objects of one class inherit the properties of another class. Classes in C++ support the concept of hierarchical classification.

Reusability The concept of inheritance provides the feature of reusability by additional features to the existing class without modifying the existing one leads to a new class.

Polymorphism Polymorphism means the ability to take more than one form. Polymorphism is a means by which we can request an object to do something without knowing exactly what kind of object it is, and the object will figure out how to process the request appropriately.

Dynamic binding Binding refers to the linking of a procedure call to the code to be executed in response to the call. Dynamic binding means that the code associated with a given procedure call is not known until the time of call at runtime. This is associated with polymorphism and inheritance.

Message passing An OOP consists of a set of objects that communicate with each other. Message for an object is a request for execution of a procedure and therefore will invoke a function in the receiving object that generates the desired result. Message passing involves specifying the name of the object, the name of the function (message), and the information to be sent.

List Abstract Data Type

We have studied about ADTs. An ADT consists of a data type and operations that manipulate the data. From the application program's perspective, it is also independent of the data structure used to implement it. The user while using the list ADT is not aware of the implementation of how the data is manipulated and what data structure is used. Hence, we could implement the list using either an array or a linked list. Further, linked list can be realized using array or using pointers and dynamic memory management. Thus, if we implement a list using linked list, we could change the implementation from a linked list to an array, and the application program would not need to be changed. To achieve this, in C++, we implement the list ADT using class template, which allows the application programmer to declare the data while allowing the class to control it. The class also encapsulates all the list functions that use it. Let us see linked list implementation of list ADT. Figure 15.6 is the representation of ADT list structure.

The linked list is implemented as the `LinkList` class with its data encapsulated within the class. The data will be declared as private. We do not know what type of application data will be stored in the list. If our linked list class is to be able to store any type of data, we must have some way of letting the user define them while writing the program through the use of templates.

A *class template* is a generic class declaration that allows the user to provide the data structure through parameters that the compiler resolved.

The structure template can be with two items: data and link. The link field is declared with the node structure to be a self-referential pointer to the next node. The data will be mapped to a programmer-declared type when the program is compiled. Let us see the declaration using C++ in Program Code 15.1.

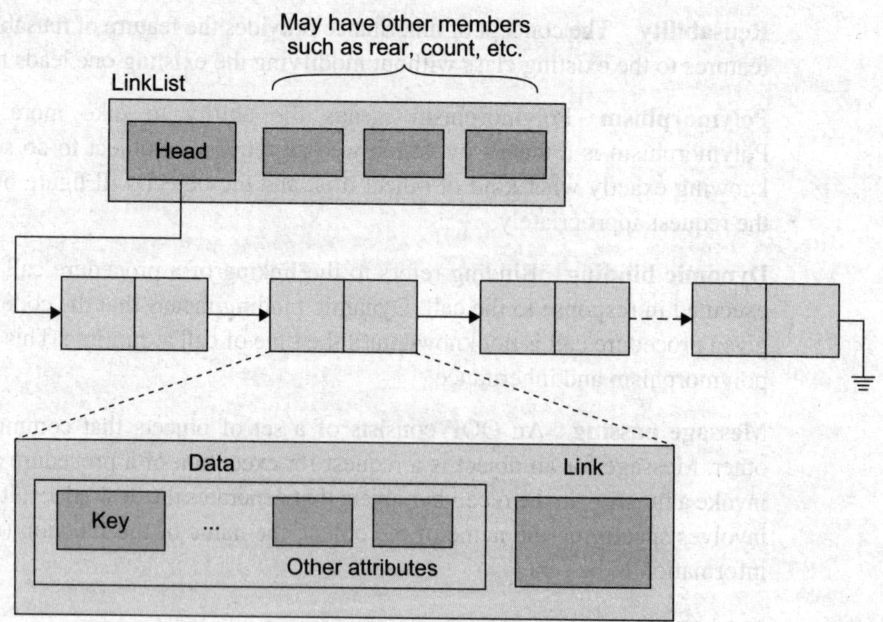

Fig. 15.6 Linked list ADT structure

PROGRAM CODE 15.1

```
//Node template declaration
template <class type>
class Node
```

```
{
    type data;
    Node *link;
};

//Class template
template <class type>
class LinkList
{
    private:
        Node <type>*Head;
    public:
        LinkList(void);
        void Insert(type x);
        void Display();
};
```

We have studied the linked list data structure as a way to store the data in the form of collection of nodes storing data and links to other nodes. Nodes can be located anywhere in the memory, not necessarily in sequential locations. The links are established by storing the addresses of other node(s) (next or previous) in the link field of each node.

Although the linked list can be implemented in a variety of ways, the most flexible implementation is by using pointers. To implement the same in C++, we can view the entire linked list as an object of class `LinkList`. The individual data items or links are represented by the structure of type `Node`.

```
class Node
{
   int data;
   :  }
   :  }      There could be more data members of the class
   :  }
   Node *link;
};
```

Fig. 15.7 Abstract representation of linked list

Abstract representation of a linked list is shown in Fig. 15.7 with respect to the `Node` definition, with two fields in it—data and link.

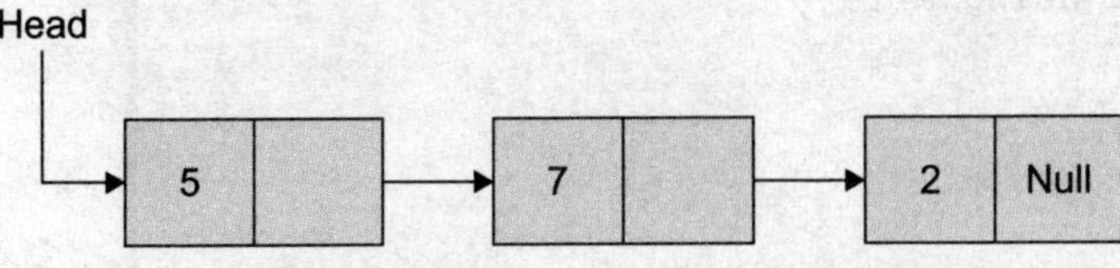

Fig. 15.8 Linked list with header pointer

Each linked list has to have a special external link (or pointer), `Head`. We call it an external link because it is not stored in the list.

We shall now extend the abstract notation to show the external link. Figure 15.8 illustrates the list with the external link, `Head`.

To represent this linked list as shown in Fig. 15.8, we represent the linked list as an object of the `LinkList` class. The definition of the class is shown in Program Code 15.2.

PROGRAM CODE 15.2

```
class SLL       // Singly linked list
{
   private:
     Node *Head;
   public:
      SLL();       // Constructor
      ~SLL();       // Destructor
      void Insert(int x);
      void Display();
       :
       :    More member functions here
       :
};
```

The `LinkList` class has only one member data item, the `Head` pointer to the first node of the list. The `Head` is used to access the list. The member functions including `constructor` and `destructor` are used to process the list. Note that the `Head` is private and all other member functions are public. This is because particular nodes of the list are accessible to outside objects through pointers. Nodes are made inaccessible to outside objects by declaring `Head` private so that the information hiding principle is not really compromised. In Program Code 15.3,

1. array `stk[]` and `top` are private members, which are hidden and cannot be accessed by outside functions;
2. methods `push`, `pop`, `isFull`, `isEmpty` are public, which can be accessed by outside functions;
3. the two main features data abstraction and encapsulation are satisfied in this declaration.

PROGRAM CODE 15.3

```
/*Class of stack using array*/
#define size 20
class stack
{
   int stk[size];
```

```
    int top;
    public:
       stack(){top= -1;}
       // constructor to initialize top
       int isEmpty()
       {
          if(top  ==  -1) return 1;
             return 0;
       }
       int isFull()
       {
          if(top == size - 1) return 1;
             return 0;
       }
       void push(int element)
       {
          if(isFull())
             cout << "\n Stack Full";
          else
          {
             top++;
             stk[top] = element;
          }
       }
       int pop()
       {
          if(isEmpty())
             cout << "\n Stack is empty";
          else
             return(stk[top--]);
       }
};      // end of class stack
```

We can define the objects of the stack as in Program Code 15.4.

PROGRAM CODE 15.4

```
void  main()
{
   stack s, s1, s2;        // defining 3 objects s, s1,
                           s2 of the stack
  // calling functions as
```

```
    s.push(5);          // calling function push and 5 is
                        pushed into stack s
    s.push(8);          // 8 is pushed into stack s
    s1.push(10);          // 10 is pushed into stack s1
}
```

Implementation of Stacks Using Linked List

In Section 15.1.3, we implemented the stack using arrays. However, an array implementation has certain limitations. One of the limitations is that stacks cannot grow or shrink during the execution of a program. This drawback can be overcome by using linked list organization for stacks. A stack implemented using linked list is also called as *linked stack*. This is illustrated in Program Code 15.5.

PROGRAM CODE 15.5

```
/*Class of stack using linked list*/
class node
{
    public:
        int Data;
        node *link;
};

class stack
{
    node * top;         // top is pointer
    public:
        stack(){top = null;}
        // constructor to initialize top
        int isEmpty()
        {
            if(top ==  null) return 1;
                return 0;
        }
        void push(int element)
        {
            node *curr;
            if(isFull())
                cout << "\n Stack Full";
            else
            {
                curr = new node();
```

```
            curr->Data = element;
            curr->link = null;
            if(top == null)
               top = curr;
            else
            {
               curr->next = top;
               top=curr;
               // change top as new node
            }
         }
      }      //end of push
      int pop()
      {
         node *curr; int element;
         if(isEmpty())
            cout << "\n Stack is empty";
         else
         {
            curr = top;
            element = top->Data;
            top = top->next;
            delete(curr);
            return(element);
         }
      }   // end of pop
};    // end of class stack
```

We can define objects of the `stack` class in the same way as the previous stack class in Program Code 15.6.

PROGRAM CODE 15.6

```
void main()
{
   stack s, s1, s2;        // defining 3 objects of stack
                              s, s1, s2
   // calling functions same as previous class
   s.push(5);        // 5 is pushed in stack s
   s.push(8); );          // 8 is pushed in stack s
   s1.push(10); );         // 10 is pushed in stack s1
}
```

In both implementations (using array and linked list), we can see that the implementation may be different and can be hidden. We also see that independent of the implementation, Program Codes 15.4 and 15.6 are the same.

Classes to Produce Abstract Data Types

A *class* is a type that we define, unlike types such as `int` and `char` that are already defined for us. A value for a class type is a set of values of the member variables. Consider the following class:

```
class student_account
{
   private:
   int BackAccountNo;
   :
   :
   public:
   void update();
   double getbalance();
   :
   :
};
```

The programmer who uses this class need not be concerned about how the member functions are implemented.

Creating an Abstract Data Type

In order to define a class so that it is an ADT, we need to separate the specification of how the type is used by a programmer from the details of how the type is implemented. The separation should be so complete that if we change the implementation of the class, any program that uses the class ADT should not need any additional changes. Hence, the following steps must be adhered to:

1. Make all the member variables as private members of the class.
2. Make each of the basic operations for ADT either a public member, or a friend function, or an ordinary function, or an overloaded operator. Group the class definition and the function and operator prototypes together. This group along with comments is called the *interface* for ADT.
3. Fully specify how to use each of these functions or operators in comments given with the class or with the function or operator prototypes.
4. Make the implementation of basic operations unavailable to programmers who use ADT. The implementation consists of the function definitions and overloaded operator definitions; put them in different files.
5. Put all these definitions mentioned in a separate file called as the *implementation file*. This file must contain an *include directive* that names the interface file, say #include 'student.h'. The interface file and implementation file traditionally have the same name but end with different suffixes. The interface file ends with .h and implementation file ends in the same suffix that we use for files that contain C++ code.

6. Compile implementation file separately.
7. If we want to use the ADT in a program, we place the main part of the program, any additional function definitions, and constant declarations in another file called an *application file*. This file, also contains an include directive naming the interface file, as in,
   #include 'student.h'.
8. We must first link the object code produced by compiling the application file and the object code produced by compiling the implementation file. In some systems, linking may be done automatically or semi-automatically.

15.3 STANDARD TEMPLATE LIBRARY

C++ classes provide information for creating a library of data structures. The C++ STL is a collection of containers, adaptors, iterators, functions, and algorithms. The STL is a part of the standard C++ class library and can be used as a standard approach for storing and processing data. The task of writing complex application codes can be made easy with the use of STL. The C++ class allows for the implementation of ADTs with appropriate hiding of implementation details.

Standard template library was developed by Alexander Stepanov and Meng Lee of Hewlett Packard. In past, compiler vendors and many third party developers have offered libraries of container classes to handle the storage and processing of data. However, now, standard C++ includes its own built-in container class library, STL. C++ classes provide an excellent mechanism for creating a library of data structures. STL contains many kinds of entities. The three most important kinds are the following:

1. Containers
2. Algorithms
3. Iterators

The STL allows a programmer to use these classes and functions directly in programs to increase productivity.

15.3.1 Containers

Container is a way to store data whether the data consists of built-in types such as `int` and `float`, or of class objects, that is, `container` classes whose purpose is to contain other objects.

Many times, a programmer uses many objects of a particular class. For example, arrays. Array can be considered as one of the most basic and elementary containers. Arrays are one of the most powerful data structures. Many other data structures use array as a building block. If STL makes such a data structure available, a programmer will be able to use it as a ready-to-use data structure.

The STL makes seven basic kinds of containers available and three more that are desired from the basic kinds. In addition, we can create our own containers based on these basic kinds of containers.

Use of containers is for achieving efficiency. We have learnt and used array as a data structure and its pros and cons. An array could be slow in many situations; and it might be time consuming to switch to other data structure, implement the same, and then use it. Use of STL is less time consuming. STL provides many kinds of containers. The programmer can choose one or a few of them as per the need of the application without knowing the implementation details. Table 15.1 lists some examples of container classes.

Table 15.1 List of container classes

Container class	Description
Vector	Array
List	Doubly linked list
Slist	Singly linked list
Queue	Queue structure, that is, FIFO structure
Stack	Stack structure, that is, LIFO structure
Deque	Combination of stack and queue, having facility for insertion and removal from both ends
Set	Set of unique elements
Map	Store key and data pair

Containers are categorized into two types:

1. Sequence containers
2. Associative containers

Sequence Containers

A *sequence container* stores a set of elements which can be visualized as a line, similar to houses on a street. Each element is related to the other by its position along the line. Each element, except at ends, is preceded by one specific element and followed by a specific element. These containers refer to sequential organization of elements, such as in arrays.

The sequence containers are as follows:

1. Vectors
2. Lists
3. Deques

The containers that are derived from sequence containers are stacks, queues, and priority queues.To instantiate an STL container object, we must include an appropriate header file. We then use the template format with the kind of objects to be stored as the parameters. For example,

```
deque <int> intDeque; and
list<student> SEcomp;
```

Here, `student` is a defined data type. The containers take care of all memory allocations that a user need not specify.

Vectors The array data structure has certain limitations. Owing to its static implementation, it results into poor utilization and runtime difficulties of not exceeding the size. In addition, array size is to be specified at the compile time; that is, in the source code. All these difficulties can be overcome through the vector container provided by STL. The template class describes an object that controls a varying-length sequence of elements of type T.

A vector is a sequence container that supports random access iterators. It is optimized for insertions and deletions at the ends of the collection. Insertions and deletions anywhere else in the collection, such as the beginning or middle, take linear time. Storage management is handled automatically. It supports for any data type and for automatic resizing when adding elements.

Vector reallocation occurs when a member function must grow the controlled sequence beyond its current storage capacity.

Table 15.2 lists the common vector constructors, functions, and operators.

Table 15.2 List of vector constructors, functions, and operators

Function/constructor/operator	Description
vector<T> *v*;	Creates an empty vector of data type T
vector<T> *v*(*n*);	Creates a vector of *n* default values
vector<T> *v*(*n*, *e*);	Creates a vector of *n* copies of *e*
v.~vector<T>();	Destroys all elements and frees memory
i = *v*.size();	Gets the number of elements
I = *v*.capacity();	Maximum number of elements before reallocation
I = *v*.max_size();	Implementation of maximum number of elements
B = *v*.empty();	True, if empty. Same as *v*.size() == 0
v.reserve(*n*);	Sets the capacity to *n* before reallocation
v = *v*1;	Assigns *v*1 to *v*
v[*i*] = *e*;	Assigns the ith element as *e*
v.at(*i*) = *e*;	At the ith position set element *e*
v.front() = *e*;	Same as *v*[0] = *e*
v.back() =*e*;	Same as *v*[*v*.size() – 1] = *e*
v.push_back(*e*);	Adds *e* to the end of *v*. Expands *v* if necessary
v.pop_back();	Removes the last element of *v*
v.clear();	Removes all elements
iter = *v*.assign(*n*, *e*);	Replaces the existing elements with *n* copies of *e*

(Continued)

Table 15.2 (Continued)

Function/constructor/operator	Description
iter = *v*.assign(*beg*, *end*);	Replaces the existing elements with copies from the range beg–end
the iter2 = *v*.insert(*iter*, *e*);	Inserts a copy of *e* at the iter position and returns its position
v.insert(*iter*, *n*, *e*);	Inserts *n* copies of *e* starting at the iter position
v.insert(iter, beg, end);	Inserts all the elements in the range beg–end, starting at iter position
iter2 = *v*.erase(iter);	Removes an element at the iter position and returns position of next element
Iter = *v*.erase(beg, end);	Removes range beg–end and returns position of next element
E = *v*[*i*];	Gets the ith element
E = *v*.at(*i*);	Gets the element at the ith position
E = *v*.front();	Gets the first element
E = *v*.back();	Gets the last element
Iter = *v*.begin();	Returns the iterator to the first element
Iter = *v*.end();	Returns the iterator to after last element
Riter = *v*.rbegin();	Returns the iterator to the first (in reverse order) element
Riter = *v*.rend();	Returns the iterator to after the last (in reverse order) element

Program Code 15.7 shows how an integer vector uses STL and iterators and processes them.

PROGRAM CODE 15.7

```
// Integer vector using STL
#include <vector>
void main()
{
   const int size = 20;
   vector <int> A(size);
   //Define an iterator for template class vector of int
   vector<int> :: iterator start, end, it;
   // Read int values
   int i, n;
   cout << "\n Enter how many numbers";
   cin >> n;
   for(i = 0; i < n; i++)
```

```
        {
            cin >> A[i]);
        }
        start = A.begin();         // location of first element
        end = start + n;          // one past the location last
                                  element of A
        cout << "All Numbers \n";
        for(it = start; it != end; it++)
        // Accessing vector elements using iterator
           cout << (*it) << "\t";
        // To remove element at position 2
        A.remove(2);
    }
```

Doubly ended queue *Deque* is the container, which can be thought of as a combination of a stack and a queue. A stack is a LIFO structure, and a queue is a FIFO structure. A deque combines these approaches so we can insert and delete from either end and hence is called as *doubly ended queue*.

Table 15.3 lists some functions related to deque as follows:

Table 15.3 List of functions for doubly ended queue

Function	Description
at()	Returns a reference to the element at a specified location in the deque
back()	Returns a reference to the last element of the deque
begin()	Returns an iterator addressing the first element in the deque
clear()	Erases all the elements of a deque
Deque()	Constructs a deque of a specific size
Empty()	Tests if a deque is empty
end()	Returns an iterator that addresses the location succeeding the last element in a deque
erase()	Removes an element or a range of elements in a deque from specified positions
front()	Returns a reference to the first element in a deque
insert()	Inserts an element or a number of elements or a range of elements into the deque at a specified position
pop_back()	Deletes the element at the end of the deque
pop_front()	Deletes the element at the beginning of the deque
push_back()	Adds an element to the end of the deque
push_front()	Adds an element to the beginning of the deque
size()	Returns the number of elements in the deque

The implementation of deque of integers using STL is given in Program Code 15.8.

PROGRAM CODE 15.8

```
// Deque of integer data using STL
#include <deque>
#include <iostream>
using namespace std;
void print_contents(deque);
void main()
{
   int choice;
   char ele;
   //create
   deque <char> DQueue;
   do
   {
      cout << "1. Insert at Begin" << endl;
      cout << "2. Insert at End" << endl;
      cout << "3. Delete from Begin" << endl;
      cout << "4. Delete from End" << endl;
      cout << "5. Display" << endl;
      cout << "6. Exit" << endl;
      cout << "Enter your Choice:";
      cin >> choice;
      switch(choice)
      {
         case 1: cout << "You are inserting at the
         beginning of queue" << endl;
         cout << "Enter Element:";
         cin >> ele;
         DQueue.insert(DQueue.begin(), ele);
         //print out the contents
         print_contents(DQueue);
         break;
         case 2 :cout << "You are inserting at end of
         queue" << endl;
         cout << "Enter Element:";
         cin >> ele;
         DQueue.insert(DQueue.end(), ele);
         //print out the contents
        print_contents(DQueue);
        break;
```

```
            case 3:       // erase the begin element
            cout << "Deleting front element:";
            if(!DQueue.empty())
            {
               cout << DQueue.front() << endl;
               DQueue.erase(DQueue.begin());
            }
            //print out the contents
            print_contents(DQueue);
            break;
            case 4:      // erase the End element
            cout << "Deleting rear element:";
            if(!DQueue.empty())
            {
               cout << DQueue.back() << endl;
               DQueue.erase(DQueue.end());
            }
            //print out the contents
            print_contents(DQueue);
            break;
            case 5:      // print out the contents
            print_contents(DQueue);
         }     // end of switch
      }while(choice < 6);
   }

   //function to print the contents of deque
   void print_contents(dqueue DQueue)
   {
      dqueue<char> :: iterator pdeque;
      cout << "The output is:";
      if(!dqueue.empty())
      {
         for(pdeque = dqueue.begin(); pdeque != dqueue.
         end(); pdeque++)
         {
            cout << *pdeque << " ";
         }
         cout << endl;
      }
      else
         cout << "DQ is empty";
   }
```

List One more problem associated with arrays is that the insertion and deletion operations at the middle need a lot of data movement. To solve this problem, the STL provides the *list* container, which is based on the idea of a linked list. A list sequence container provides support for the bidirectional iterators with constant time insert and delete operations anywhere in the list; however, it does not support random access to the elements. Thus, the list is specially designed for sequential access. Storage management is handled automatically.

The list sequence container is an implementation of various operations on the nodes of a linked list. The STL implements a list as a generic doubly linked list (DLL) with pointers to the head and to the tail. An instance of such list that stores integers could be used in a program. The class list can be used in a program only if it is included as #<include> <list>.

A new list is generated with the instruction

```
list <data_type> L1;
```

where data_type can be any data type. If it is user-defined, the type must also include a default constructor which is required for initialization of new nodes. Various member functions such as insert(), empty(), clear(), remove(), reverse(), and many more are included in the list container.

Table 15.4 lists some functions available in STL.

Table 15.4 List of a few functions for list in STL

Method	Description
list()	Creates an empty list
list(size_type *n*)	Creates a list of *n* elements initialized to their default value
T &back(void)	Returns a reference to the last element in the list
T &front(void)	Returns a reference to the first element in the list
void push_back(const T &value)	Inserts a value to the end of the list
void push_front(const T &value)	Inserts a value to the beginning to the list
void pop_back(void)	Deletes the last element of the list
void pop_front(void)	Deletes the first element of the list
void remove(const T &value)	Deletes all elements that match the value. Comparison is performed using the == operator
void reverse(void)	Reverses the order of elements in the list
void sort(void)	Sorts the entries contained in the list using the < operator

Table 15.4 lists the set of commonly used functions for list operations. Program Code 15.9 demonstrates the use for them for creating a list of students using STL.

PROGRAM CODE 15.9

```
// List operations using STL
#include
#include <iostream>
```

```
using namespace std;
class student
{
   private:
      int roll;
      char name[20];
      float marks;
   public:
      void getdata()
      {
         cout << "\n Enter roll, name, marks of student:";
         cin >> roll >> name >> marks;
      }
      void displaydata()
      {
         cout << "\n" << roll << "\t\t" << name <<
         "\t\t" << marks;
      }
      int getroll()
      {
         return roll;
      }
};

void main()
{
   student s;      // object of student
   list <student> student_list;      // list of students
   list <student> :: iterator sptr;
   int choice;
   int ele;
   do
   {
      cout << "\n Menu \n";
      cout << "1. Add" << endl;
      cout << "2. Display" << endl;
     cout << "3. Delete" << endl;
     cout << "4. Insert" << endl;
      cout << "5. Exit";
      cout << "\nEnter your choice:";
      cin >> choice;
      switch(choice)
      {
         case 1:
```

```
        cout << "\n Enter student record:\n";
        s.getdata();
        student_list.push_back(s);
    break;
    case 2:
        cout << "Roll   Name   Marks" << endl;
        if(!student_list.empty())
        {
            for(sptr = student_list.begin(); sptr
            != student_list.end(); sptr++)
              sptr->displaydata();
        }
        else
            cout << "\n List is empty";
    break;
    case 3 :
        int r;
        cout << "\n Enter roll no to be deleted :: ";
        cin >> r;
        if(!student_list.empty())
        {
            for(sptr = student_list.begin();
            sptr != student_list.end(); sptr++)
            {
                if(sptr->getroll() == r)
                {
                    cout << "\n Deleting \n";
                    sptr->displaydata();
                    student_list.erase(sptr);
                    break;
                }
            }
        }
        else
            cout << "\n List is empty";
    break;
    case 4 :
        int br;
        cout << "\n Enter record to be inserted : ";
        s.getdata();
        cout << "\n Enter roll no before which to
        be inserted :: ";
```

```
        cin >> br;
            if(!student_list.empty())
            {
                for(sptr=student_list.begin(); sptr
                != student_list.end(); sptr++)
                {
                    if(sptr->getroll() == br)
                    {
                        cout << "\n Inserting \n";
                        sptr->displaydata();
                        student_list.insert(sptr, s);
                        break;
                    }
                }
            }
            else
                cout << "\n List is empty";
        }
    }while(choice < 5);
}
```

Stack The template class describes an object that controls a varying-length sequence of elements, having the functions `empty()`, `size()`, `top()`, `push()`, and `pop()`. This is illustrated in Program Code 15.10.

PROGRAM CODE 15.10

```
// Stack using STL
#include <stack>
#include <iostream>
using namespace std;
void main()
{
    stack <int> stack1;//
    int choice;
    int ele;
    do
    {
        cout << "1. Push " << endl;
        cout << "2. Pop" << endl;
        cout << "3. Exit" << endl;
```

```
        cout << "Enter your choice : ";
       cin >> choice;
        switch(choice)
        {
           case 1: cout << "Pushg an Element in Stack"
           << endl;
              cout << "Enter Element:";
              cin >> else;
              stack1.push(ele);
           break;
           case 2: cout << "Pop element from stack" <<
           endl;
              if(!stack1.empty())
              {
                 cout << "top returned" << stack1.top()
                 << endl;
                 stack1.pop();
              }
              else
                 cout << "\n Stack is empty";
           break;
        }
     }while(choice < 3);
  }
```

Table 15.5 summarizes the characteristics of STL sequence container including the ordinary C++ array.

Table 15.5 List of containers and their characteristics

Container	Characteristics	Advantages/disadvantages
C++ array (not container)	Fixed size	• Quick random access • Slow insert and delete • Size cannot be changed at runtime
Vector	Relocating, expandable array	• Quick random access • Slow insert/delete in middle • Quick insert/delete at ends
List	Doubly linked list	• Quick insert/delete • Quick access at ends • Slow random access
Deque	Like vector but can be accessed at either ends	• Quick random access • Slow inset or delete in middle • Quick insert or delete at the ends

Associative Containers

An *associative container* is a collection of stored objects that allow fast retrieval using a key. In each container, the key must be unique. There are four standard associative containers classified into two classes:

1. Sets
   (a) Set
   (b) Multiset
2. Maps
   (a) Map
   (b) Multimap list

An associative container is not sequential; instead, it uses keys to access data. The keys, typically numbers or strings, are used automatically by the container to arrange the stored elements in a specific order. It is like an ordinary English dictionary where we access data by searching in alphabetical order. Both the containers, sets and maps, store data in tree structure, which offer fast searching, insertion, and deletion. *Map container* supports unique key and bidirectional iterators. It provides fast retrieval of values of another type based on the keys. A multimap is an associative container that supports duplicate keys and bidirectional iterators.

A *set* is an associative container that supports unique key and bidirectional iterators. Sets are simpler and more commonly used than maps. A set stores a number of items that contain keys. The keys are attributes used to order the items. For example, a set of books might be ordered as per the unique ID number or can be ordered alphabetically on author's name. The desired author's book can be quickly located by searching for a book specified by the author name.

A map stores pairs of objects: a key object and a value object. A map is often used as a container that is somewhat like an array, except that the index used for accessing the element is the key object.

15.3.2 Algorithms

An *algorithm* is a function that processes the items in a container. Algorithms in STL are not member functions or even friends of container classes. They can be used with built-in C++ arrays or with container classes created by us.The header `<algorithm>` defines a collection of functions especially designed to be used on ranges of elements. These algorithms can be divided into six groups:

1. Minimum and maximum algorithms
2. Numeric algorithms
3. Non-mutating sequence algorithms
4. Sorting algorithms
5. Set operations on sorted sequence
6. Heap operation

For example, suppose we create an array of type `int` storing the marks of a student. Then,

```
int marks[6] = {73, 44, 42, 51, 59, 50}
```

We can use STL `sort()` as

```
sort(marks, marks + 6)
```

Here, `marks` and `marks + 6` are the start and end addresses, respectively.

Other example of sorting a vector is as follows:

```
vector<int> m;
// having values 73, 44, 42, 51, 59, 50
sort(m.begin(), m.end());
// Output is 42, 44, 50, 51, 59, 73
sort(v.begin(), v.end(), greater<int>());
// Output is 73, 59, 51, 50, 44, 42
```

For reversing, we can use the reverse algorithm as the following:

```
vector<int> m;
// vector m having values 73, 44, 42, 51, 59, 50
reverse(m.begin(), m.end());
// vector m changed as 50 59, 51, 42, 44, 73
```

Table 15.6 lists some of the functions in `<algorithm>`.

Table 15.6 List of functions with their brief descriptions available in STL

Functions	Description
find()	Find value in range
find_if()	Find element in range
count()	Count appearances of value in range
equal()	Test whether the elements in two ranges are equal
copy()	Copy the range of elements
swap()	Exchange values of two objects
replace()	Replace value in range
fill()	Fill range with value
remove()	Remove value from range
reverse()	Reverse range
sort()	Sort elements in range
partial_sort()	Partially sort elements in range
nth_element()	Sort element in range
binary_search()	Test if value exists in sorted array
merge()	Merge sorted ranges
min()	Return the lesser of two arguments
max()	Return the greater of two arguments
Min_element()	Return the smallest element in range
max_element()	Return the largest element in range

We know that an algorithm processes the items in a container. Algorithms in STL can be used with built-in C++ arrays or with container classes created by us. Program Code 15.11 demonstrates its use for sorting the list of persons.

PROGRAM CODE 15.11

```
// Sort elements in a sequence
#include <iostream>
#include <algorithm>
#include <vector>
#include <string>
using namespace std;
class person
{
   public:
      int id;
      char first_name[20];
      char last_name[20];
      long phone;
};

bool operator < (person &a, person &b)
{
   // function used to select field for sort
   if(strcmp(a.last_name, b.last_name) < 0)
      return(1);
      return(0);
}

void main()
{
   const int vector_size = 20;
   vector<person> Per(vector_size);
   //Define an iterator for template class vector of
   strings
   vector<person> :: iterator start, end, it ;
   // Read person records
   int i, size;
   char ans;
   i = 0;
  cout <<
  do
  {
     cout << "\n Enter person id : ";
```

```
        cin >> Per[i].id;
        cout << "\n Enter person first name : ";
        cin >> Per[i].first_name;
        cout << "\n Enter person last name : ";
        cin >> Per[i].last_name;
        cout << "\n Enter pnone : ";
        cin >> Per[i].phone;
        i++;
        cout << "More? (y/n)";
        cin >> ans;
    }
    while(ans == 'y' || ans == 'Y');
        size = i;
      start = Per.begin();
        // location of first element of Person
        end = Per.end();
        // one past the location last element of Person
        cout << "Before calling partial_sort\n" << endl ;
        // print content of Person
        cout << "\n All records of person \n" ;
        for(it = start; it != start + i; it++)
            cout << (*it).id << " " << (*it).first_name <<
            "\t" << (*it).last_name << "\t" << it->phone
            << endl;
            // sort elements of person on last name
            sort(Per.begin(), Per.begin() + size);
            cout << "After calling sort elements of
            person on last name \n" << endl;
            cout << "\n All records of person \n";
            for(it = start; it != start + i; it++)
                cout << (*it).id << " " << (*it).first_name
                << "\t" << (*it).last_name << "\t" << it-
                >phone << endl;
                cout << endl;
}
```

15.3.3 Iterators

Iterators are pointer-like entities that are used to access individual data items in a container. They work like regular pointers in C++. They can be used to store and retrieve objects in C++. They are often used to move sequentially from element to element, a process called *iterating*, through the container. We can increment iterators with the ++ operator so they point to the next element, and dereference them with the * operator to obtain the value of the element they point to. In the STL, an iterator is represented by the object of an *iterator class.*

STL defines five different iterators:

1. Input
2. Output
3. Forward
4. Bidirectional
5. Random access

Input Iterator

An input iterator can be used only to retrieve a value from the input stream; it cannot be used to store a value. It can only move in the forward direction, retrieving the objects one by one. It cannot go backward and it cannot jump to any arbitrary position. Figure 15.9 elaborates the concept better.

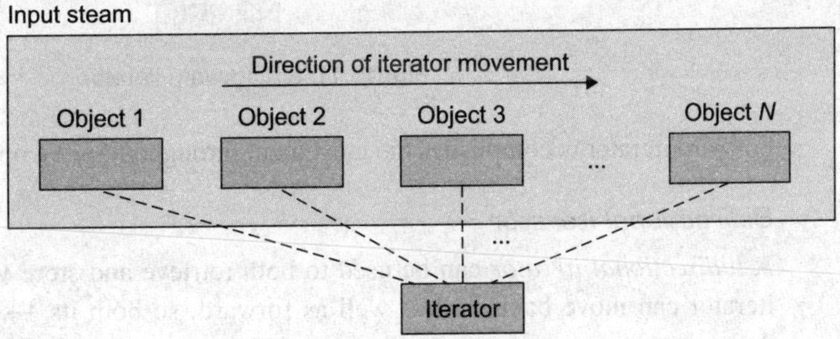

Fig. 15.9 STL input iterator

Output Iterator

An *output iterator* is used only to store a value in an output stream; it cannot be used to retrieve a value. It only moves in the forward direction, storing objects one by one. It cannot go backward and it cannot jump. Figure 15.10 elaborates the concept.

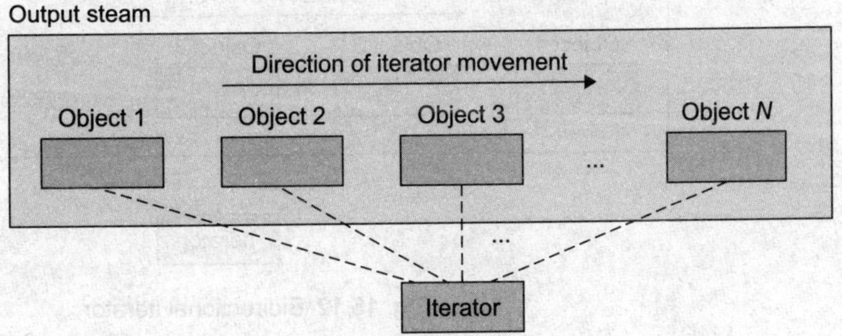

Fig. 15.10 STL output iterator

Forward Iterator

A *forward iterator* can be used to both retrieve and store a value. It can only move in the forward direction, visiting the objects one by one. It cannot go backward and it cannot jump, that is, it cannot be set to an arbitrary location in the middle of the container.

Figure 15.11 describes the forward iterator.

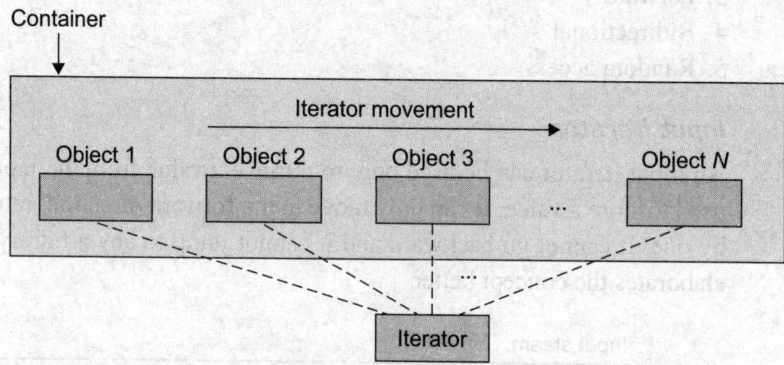

Fig. 15.11 STL forward iterator

Forward iterator accomplishes the movement throughout its ++ operator.

Bidirectional Iterator

A *bidirectional iterator* can be used to both retrieve and store values. A bidirectional iterator can move backward as well as forward, so both its ++ and –– operators are defined.

A bidirectional iterator too cannot be set to an arbitrary location like forward, input, and output iterators. It can move forward or backward, one object at a time. Figure 15.12 describes a bidirectional iterator.

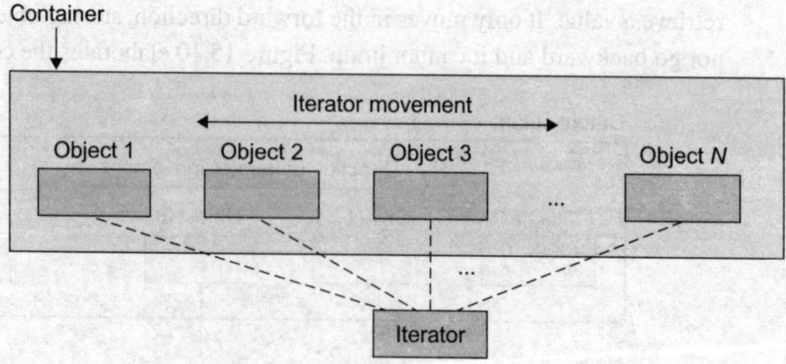

Fig. 15.12 Bidirectional iterator

Random Access Iterator

A *random access iterator*, in addition to moving backward and forward, can jump to an arbitrary location. We can set the iterator to access any location *i*. Like a bidirectional iterator, it can move (rather jump) in both directions.

An input iterator points to an input device (cin or a file) to read sequential data items into a container, and an output iterator points to an output device (count or file) and write elements from a container to the device. While the values of forward, bidirectional, and random access iterators can be stored, the values of input and output iterators cannot be. This makes sense as the first three iterators point to memory locations, while the input and output iterators point to I/O devices for which the stored 'pointer' values have no meaning. Table 15.7 defines the characteristics of these different kinds of iterators.

Table 15.7 Iterator characteristics

Iterator type	Read/write	Iterator can be saved	Direction	Access
Random access	Read and write	Yes	Forward and backward	Random
Bidirectional	Read and write	Yes	Forward and backward	Linear
Forward	Read and write	Yes	Forward only	Linear
Input	Read only	No	Forward only	Linear
Output	Write only	No	Forward only	Linear

We can note that there is a hierarchical relation between the iterators. Every forward iterator is also an input and output iterator. Every bidirectional iterator is also a forward iterator. A random access iterator is also a bidirectional iterator. Figure 15.13 shows this hierarchical relationship among these five iterators.

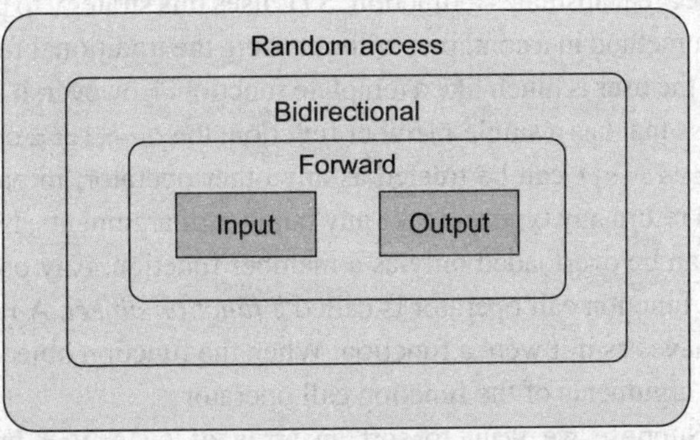

Fig. 15.13 Hierarchical relationship among iterators

Operators Supported by Iterators

Each iterator supports different operators as per its type. Table 15.8 shows the operators supported by each iterator.

Table 15.8 Iterator operators

Iterator	Operator
Input	×, =, ++, ==, !=, →
Output	×, =, ++
Forward	×, =, ++, ==, !=, →
Bidirectional	×, =, ++, ==, !=, →
Random access	+, =, ++, ==, !=, –>, – –, +, –
	<, >, <=, >=, [ ]

Pros and Cons of Standard Template Library

The STL is a robust and versatile system. Errors tend to be caught at compile time rather than at runtime. The different algorithms and containers present a very consistent interface; what works with one container or algorithm will usually work with another when used appropriately.

The sophistication of the STL's template classes places a strain on compilers, and not all of them respond well. It is hard to find errors reported by the compiler. Errors could be reported as being deep in header file when they are actually in the class as user's code. The STL may sometimes generate spurious compiler warnings, which appear to be harmless and can be ignored.

15.3.4 Function Objects

Some algorithms can take an object called a function object as an argument. A function object encapsulates a function. STL uses this strategy to pass a function to an algorithm or to a method in a container without using the traditional function pointer. A function object for the user is much like a template function. However, it is actually an object of a template class that has a single member function, the `overload` operator. In C++, the function call `operator()` can be treated as any other operator; in particular, it can be overloaded. It can return any type and take any number of arguments, but like the `assignment` operator, it can be overloaded only as a member function. Any object that includes a definition of the function call operator is called a *function object*. A function object is an object, but it behaves as if it were a function. When the function object is called, its arguments become the arguments of the function call operator.

Suppose we want to sort an array of `Roll_Nos` into descending order instead of ascending order. Program Code 15.12 shows how to do it using the `greater<>(1)` function object.

PROGRAM CODE 15.12

```
#include<iostream.h>
#include<functional>
#include<algorithm>
int Roll_No[] = {6, 7, 3, 1, 2, 5, 4};
int main()
{
   sort(Roll_No, Roll_No + 7, greater<int>());
   for(int j = 0; j < 7; j++)
      cout << Roll_No[j];
   cout << endl;
   return 0;
}
```

The `sort()` algorithm usually sorts in ascending order, but the use of `greater<>()` function object, the third argument of `sort()`, reverses the sorting order.

We get the output as 7, 6, 5, 4, 3, 2, 1

Besides comparisons, there are function objects for arithmetical and logical operators. User can substitute a user-written function for a function object.

RECAPITULATION

- A data type is said to be an ADT if one can use it without having access to and without knowing the details of its implementation. The ADT concept can be best implemented in an object-oriented fashion.
- STL is a part of standard C++ library, which includes container class that provides an excellent mechanism for storage and processing of data. STL consists of three main components: containers, algorithms, and iterators.
- Containers are of two categories: sequential, associative. Algorithms carry out operations on containers, such as sorting, copying, and searching. Iterators act like pointer to container element and provide connection between algorithm and containers.

KEY TERMS

Algorithm An algorithm is a function for processing the items in a container. Algorithms in STL can be used with built-in C++ arrays or with container classes created by us.

Container Container class contains other objects. Container is a way to store data, whether the data consists of built-in types such as `int` and `float`, or of class objects.

Iterator Iterator is pointer like entity, which is used to access individual data items in a container, and it is used to store and retrieve objects in C++.

Object An object is an entity that performs computations and has a local state. It is also viewed as a combination of data and procedural (behavioural) elements.

Object-oriented programming Object-oriented programming (OOP) is a programming paradigm that encapsulates data (attributes) and functions (behaviour) into package called as classes. Class is a user-defined data type.

Standard template library The C++ STL is a collection of containers, adaptors, iterators, functions, and algorithms. The STL is a part of the standard C++ class library and can be used as a standard approach for storing and processing data.

EXERCISES

Multiple choice questions

1. The acronym STL stands for
   (a) Standard tools library
   (b) Standard template library
   (c) Simple tools library
   (d) Simple template library
2. The C++ language is a collection of
   (a) Containers, functions, and classes
   (b) Containers, functions, iterators, and classes
   (c) Containers, functions, iterators, algorithms, and adaptors
   (d) Containers, functions, iterators, algorithms, and classes
3. The C++ STL containers are categorized into
   (a) associative containers and simple containers
   (b) assembled containers and sequence containers
   (c) associative containers and standard containers
   (d) associative containers and sequence containers
4. For an algorithm in STL, which of the following is true?
   (a) An algorithm is a function that processes the items in a container.
   (b) Algorithms in STL are not member functions or even friends of container classes.
   (c) Algorithms can be used with built-in C++ arrays or with container classes created by us.
   (d) All of the above

Review questions

1. Use the STL algorithm to sort an element list into ascending order and search an element using binary search.
2. Use the STL algorithm 'count' and compute the occurrence of zero in the array of integers.
3. What is a container? What are the types of STL containers?
4. What is an iterator? Define the five different types of iterators.
5. Write the code for using STL containers and STL algorithms for the following:
   (a) To reverse a list
   (b) To convert a decimal to binary form using stack
   (c) Queue operations
6. Using STL, implement polynomial operations using linked list in C++.
7. Write a program to create array of specified size and use the algorithm `fill` to
   (a) initialize it to value –1
   (b) set values of lower half to 99
8. A test for 60 students has been conducted for 50 marks for subject 'Data Structures'. The passing is scoring 40% of total marks that is 20. Write a

program to create an array of specified size for storing marks of 60 students in the class. Use STL algorithm 'count' and compute the total number of failures in the subject.

9. The students' club members (MemberID, name, phone, email) list is to be maintained. The common operations performed include these: add member, search member, delete member, and update the information. Write a program that uses `list` from STL to implement the same. Use iterator.

10. Implement doubly ended queue using STL. Use it for processing members queue of jobs submitted to printer. Make use of deque for stacking the members and process them as LIFO.

Answers to multiple choice questions

1. (b) 2. (c) 3. (d) 4. (d)

16 ALGORITHM ANALYSIS AND DESIGN

OBJECTIVES

After completing this chapter, the reader will be able to understand the following:

- Basic tools needed to develop and analyse algorithms
- Methods to compute the efficiency of algorithms
- Ways to make a wise choice among many solutions for a given problem

The study of algorithms is fundamental to computer science. An algorithm can be defined as a set of steps to solve a particular problem effectively and efficiently. The study of algorithms includes learning tools for algorithm development, various design strategies, and analysis of algorithms.

The intention of this chapter is to present the foundation for these aspects associated with algorithm study.

16.1 INTRODUCTION

We have discussed data structures, programming languages, algorithms, and their analysis in Chapter 1. Software development desires to utilize each of these efficiently. The basic programming style is influenced by typical design approaches called *algorithmic strategies*. An algorithmic strategy (also known as *design technique* or *paradigm*) is a general approach to solving problems algorithmically. This methodology is appropriate for various problems suitable for different areas of computing.

It is true that devising an algorithm is an art that may never be fully automated. We shall study various design techniques that have proven to be useful to devise new algorithms. Dynamic programming is one such technique along with others such as divide-and-conquer, greedy, and backtracking.

More than one technique may be applicable to a specific problem, but it is often the case that an algorithm constructed using a particular approach is clearly superior to equivalent solutions built using alternative techniques. Hence, the choice of the design paradigm is an important feature of algorithm synthesis.

16.1.1 Algorithm Analysis

In computer science, an algorithm is a way to formulate a stepwise solution to a problem. It outlines the initial conditions, processing steps/sequence, and final outcome of the problem. For any specific problem definition, more than one solution approach may exist. In other words, a problem can have multiple algorithms for its solution. If multiple algorithms provide solutions to the same problem, their performance will surely vary over a wide range of performance measuring parameters.

In practice, each algorithm's performance is unique. Each algorithm's way of solving a problem, its prerequisites, and presentation of the final solution is independent. Thus, suitability of each algorithm for problem solving varies from application to application.To measure the performance of each algorithm, we need analysis, and based on the appropriate analysis design, selection of efficient or better algorithms is possible. Hence, the study of algorithms and their analysis plays a vital role in software development.

The performance measuring parameters have been highlighted in Chapter 1. We can evaluate an algorithm's efficiency in terms of its time and space consumption. These parameters are measured in terms of asymptotic complexity bounds of the algorithms. Let us discuss a few fundamental algorithmic strategies in relation with asymptotic complexities in the following sections.

16.1.2 Asymptotic Notations (Ω, θ, O)

More than one solution may exist for a single problem. To identify the best among them, we need to quantify their performances with factors such as time and space complexities. Asymptotic complexity helps us to quantify the performance of the algorithms. Big O, omega (Ω), and theta (θ) are the asymptotic notations used in this algorithmic analysis.

Big O or Oh

Definition The function $f(n) = O(g(n))$ is called '$f(n)$ is the big O of $g(n)$' if and only if there exist positive constants c and N, such that $f(n) \leq c \times g(n)$ for all $n \geq N$.

Big O formally represents the upper bound of the algorithm's time complexity as it suggests the maximum value or upper limit of the time taken by an algorithm to execute.

If an algorithm's time complexity is represented as $O(g(n))$, then it indicates that in all possible data considerations of size n, at any instance, the algorithm would consume $f(n)$ time, which is always less than constant c times $g(n)$.

Let us consider an example of linear search. Linear search will consume maximum time if the element we want to search for, say x, lies either at the last location or is absent. In such situations, linear search will take n comparisons, where n is the data size. So, in the case of linear search, the upper limit for time complexity will be n in the worst possible situation. This is represented as $O(n)$.

Big Omega (Ω)

Definition The function $f(n) = \Omega(g(n))$ is called '$f(n)$ is omega of $g(n)$' if and only if there exist positive constants c and N such that $f(n) \geq c \times g(n)$ for all $n \geq N$.

Big Theta (Θ)

Definition The function $f(n) = \Theta(g(n))$ is called '$f(n)$ is theta of $g(n)$', if and only if there exist positive constants c and N such that $f(n) \leq c \times g(n)$ for $n \geq N$.

Algorithms can be iterative or recursive; can make decisions randomly or approximately; can propagate the decision-making policies in the forward or backward manner. The algorithmic strategies work on all such characteristics and are broadly classified as follows:

1. Divide-and-conquer
2. Greedy method
3. Dynamic programming

The study of algorithm and design strategies

1. makes available templates suitable for solving a set of diverse problems;
2. can be translated into common control and data structures provided by most high-level languages;
3. analyses the temporal and spatial requirements of the algorithms in a precise manner.

16.2 DIVIDE-AND-CONQUER

Divide-and-conquer is one of the most popular algorithmic strategies. It works in two phases. In the first phase, the problem is divided into subproblems of smaller size till each problem can be easily solved. In the latter phase, the solutions to all such subproblems are gathered together to get the final solution. This approach, especially when used recursively, often yields efficient solutions to problems in which the subproblems are smaller versions of the original problem and can be independently solved.

Often, even the subproblems are relatively large, and the divide-and-conquer strategy is reapplied. In addition, the subproblems resulting from a divide-and-conquer design are of the same type as the original problem. For those cases, applying this design again is naturally expressed by a recursive procedure. The process of splitting the input into distinct subsets continues till these smaller subproblems, which are of the same kind, are small enough to be solved without further splitting.

16.2.1 Unique Characteristics and Use

Popularly, the divide-and-conquer strategy is designed keeping in mind a single processor computer. However, it is ideally suited for parallel computations as each subproblem can be solved simultaneously by its own processor. The following are some unique characteristics of the divide-and-conquer method:

1. The divide-and-conquer technique is well suited when a data set can be divided into smaller subsets of data elements and each data set can be independently processed.

2. It is useful in cases where algorithms are inherently recursive.
3. It is not suitable for data elements that are not suitably subdivided and if the subtasks cannot be independently processed.

16.2.2 General Method

With n inputs in hand, the divide-and-conquer strategy recommends splitting the inputs into k distinct subsets, $1 < k \le n$, yielding k subproblems. Each of the k subproblems is to be solved independently, and then by a suitable method these subsolutions should be combined to yield a solution to the whole. To each subproblem, divide-and-conquer is reapplied till the subproblem is small enough to be solved without further subdivision.

For a general method, let the `n` inputs to be processed be stored in a global array `A[1, n]`. Let `D_and_C` be a function that is initially invoked as `D_and_C(1, n)`. `D_and_C(i, j)` solves a problem instance denied by the input `A[i, j]`. The following steps elaborate the general structure of the divide-and-conquer strategy.

1. If the data size n of problem P is fundamental, calculate the result of $P(n)$ and go to step 4.
2. If the data size n of problem P is not fundamental, divide the problem $P(n)$ into equivalent subproblems $P(n_1)$, $P(n_2)$, … $P(n_i)$ such that $i \ge 1$.
3. Apply divide-and-conquer recursively to each individual subproblem $P(n_1)$, $P(n_2)$, …, $P(n_i)$.
4. Combine the results of all subproblems $P(n_1)$, $P(n_2)$,…, $P(n_i)$ to get the final solution of $P(n)$.

Algorithm 16.1 illustrates the divide-and-conquer algorithm.

ALGORITHM 16.1

```
Algorithm Divide_and_Conquer(A, lower, upper)
1. start
2. if small(lower, upper) then
     return Soln(lower, upper)
3. else Divide A into smaller instances say A1, A2, … Ak
4. for i = 1 to k do
     Apply Divide_and_Conquer to Ai
5. return conquer(Divide_and_Conquer(A1)),
     Divide_and_Conquer(A2),
     …
     Divide_and_Conquer(Ak))
6. stop
```

The computing time of `D_and_C` is described by the following recurrance relation:

$$T(n) = \begin{cases} g(n), & \text{if } n \text{ is small} \\ T(n_1) + T(n_2) + \ldots + T(n_k) + f(n), & \text{otherwise} \end{cases}$$

The complexity of many divide-and-conquer algorithms is given by a recurrence of the form

$$T(n) = \begin{cases} T(1) & n = 1 \\ aT(n/b) + f(n) & n > 1 \end{cases}$$

where a and b are known constants. We assume that $T(1)$ is known and n is a power of b (i.e., $n = b^k$).

One of the methods for solving any such recurrence relation is the substitution method. This method repeatedly makes substitutions for each occurrence and the function T in the right hand side (RHS) until all such occurrences disappear.

16.2.3 Binary Search

The binary search algorithm, discussed in Chapter 9, is the best example of the divide-and-conquer strategy. Often, sequential search is not suitable. For larger lists, it requires n comparisons in the worst case. Consider that one wants to search the name of a friend Zeenath sequentially in a list of students. If the list is not sorted alphabetically, the task becomes lengthy. Obviously, linear search through a directory is not an efficient method. Hence, a better method is to use binary search, when the data is sorted.

This method is called *binary search* as we divide the list to be searched into two lists and search in only one of the lists. Consider that the list is sorted in ascending order. In a binary search algorithm, to search a particular element, it is first compared with the element at the middle position; if found, the search is successful. Else, if the middle position value is greater than the target, the search will continue in the first half of the list; otherwise, it will resume in the second half of the list. The same process is repeated for one of the halves of the list till the list reduces to size one.

The effectiveness of the binary search algorithm lies in its continual halving of the list to be searched. For an ordered list of 50,000 keys, the worst case efficiency is a mere 16 accesses. The same file that would have necessitated an average wait of few minutes using a sequential search will permit a virtually instantaneous response when the binary search strategy is used. In more precise algebraic terms, the halving method yields a worst case search efficiency of $\log_2 n$.

Let us discuss binary search as an example of the divide-and-conquer strategy with the help of an example. Let A be an array of size n, where $n = 8$. For the binary search to be effective, the array A must be presorted.

Element to be searched = 24

	low			mid				high
A	**1**	2	3	**4**	5	6	7	**8**
	2	4	6	**8**	10	22	24	**60**

mid = (low + high)/2 = 9/2 ≅ 4

Check if A[mid] <= 24
Since A[4] = 8 which is less than 24, the right half needs to be searched.
Hence now, low = mid = 4; high= 8.

				low		mid		high
A	1	2	3	**4**	5	**6**	7	**8**
	2	4	6	**8**	10	**22**	24	**60**

mid = (low + high)/2 = 12/2 ≅ 6
Check if A[mid] <= 24
Since A[6] = 22 which is less than 24, the right half needs to be searched.
Hence now, low = mid = 6; high = 8.

						low	mid	high
A	1	2	3	4	5	**6**	**7**	**8**
	2	4	6	8	10	**22**	**24**	**60**

mid = (low + high)/2 = 14/2 ≅ 7
Check if A[mid] <= 24
A[7] = 24 which is equal to 24.
Since the required element is found, stop
Binary search is illustrated by Algorithm 16.2.

ALGORITHM 16.2

```
int Binary_Search(int list[], int first, int last, int x)
{
  int mid;
  if(first <= last)
  {
    mid = (first + last)/2;
    if(list[mid] == x)
        return mid;
    else if(x < list[mid])
        return Binary_Search(list, first, mid - 1, x);
    else
        return Binary_Search(list, mid + 1, last, x);
  }
  return -1;
}
```

Although this is a more direct implementation of the earlier description, it uses needless stack space and is much slower in most systems. In addition, this is known as *tail recursion*, which is the most wasteful form of recursion. Recursion is a powerful tool, which must be used with care.

Binary search requires O(log(n)) as it halves the list size in each step. It is a large improvement over linear search; for a list with 10 million entries, linear search will need 10 million key comparisons, whereas binary search will need just about 24.

Time complexity of binary search can be written as a recurrence relation as follows:

$$T(n) = \begin{cases} T(1) & \text{if } n = 1 \\ T(n/2) + \text{c} & \text{if } n > 1 \end{cases}$$

The most popular and easiest way to solve recurrence relation is to repeatedly make substitutions for each occurrence of the function T in the RHS until all such occurrences disappear.

Therefore, $T(n) = T(n/2) + c$

$$= T(n/4) + 2c$$
$$= T(n/8) + 3c$$
$$\vdots$$
$$= T(n/2^k) + kc$$
$$\vdots$$
$$= T(n/n) + kc = T(1) + kc$$

where $2^k = n$; hence, $k = \log_2 n$

$\therefore$ $T(n) = T(1) + c\log_2 n$

$T(n) = O(\log_2 n)$

16.2.4 Merge Sort

Merge sort is another example of the divide-and-conquer strategy. It is the most common technique used in external sorting. Initially, merge sort considers the individual elements. In the next step, it considers a group of two elements and sorts them. At the end of the second step, subarrays of size two are available. In the next step, it considers two subarrays of size two and merges them. It repeats this procedure till all the elements are covered or until one of the two sublists is empty. The same concept of merge sort can be applied to file merging.

Let us discuss the implementation of the merge sort technique for two arrays. Algorithm 16.3 describes the steps to sort two arrays `A` and `B`.

ALGORITHM 16.3

```
Algorithm MergeSort(List L, int n)
begin
if(n = 1)then
   return(L);
else
   begin
   split L into two halves A and B
```

```
        return(Merge(MergeSort(A, n/2), MergeSort(B, n/2)));
        end
end
```

Algorithm 16.4 accepts two sorted arrays A and B containing elements n_1 and n_2, respectively, and merges them into a third array C containing n_3 elements.

ALGORITHM 16.4

```
Algorithm Merge(A, B, C, n1, n2, n3)
begin
i = j = k = 1;
while(i < n1 and j < n2)
   begin
      if(A[i] < B[j])
         begin
            C[k] = A[i]
            i = i + 1
         end
      else
         begin
            C[k] = B[j]
            j = j + 1
         end
         k = k + 1
   end
   while(i <= n1)
      begin
         C[k] = A[i]
         i = i + 1
         k = k + 1
      end
   while(j <= n2)
      begin
         C[k] = B[j]
         k = k + 1; j = j + 1;
      end
end
```

The merge sort algorithm illustrates all the facets of the divide-and-conquer strategy. When the number of elements to be sorted is greater than one, merge sort separates the list into two subinstances, solves each of these recursively, and then combines the two sorted halves to obtain the solution by calling Algorithm Merge.

Let $T = \{13, 11,14, 11, 15, 19, 12, 16, 13, 15, 18, 19\}$

T is split into two halves as follows:

$A = \{13, 11,14, 11, 15, 19\}, B = \{12, 16, 13, 15, 18, 19\}$

A and B are recursively sorted again by calling merge sort for each as follows:

$A = \{11, 11, 13, 14, 15, 19\}$, $B = \{12, 13, 15, 16, 18, 19\}$

Now, a call to merge results in the following T:

$T = \{11, 11, 12, 13, 13, 14, 15, 15, 16, 18, 19, 19\}$

Time complexity of merge sort is O($n$log$n$).

When merge sort is used for files as described here, each merge operation requires reading and writing of two files, both of which are about $n/2$ records long. Thus, the total number of blocks read or written in a merge operation is approximately $2n/c$, where c is the number of records in a segment. The number of segments accessed for the whole operation is $O((n(\log_2 n))/c)$, which amounts to $O(\log_2 n)$ passing through the entire original file.

EXAMPLE 16.1 Suppose we have an external file containing the following data:

f: (2, 6, 3, 1, 4, 31, 23, 8, 11, 19, 21, 37, 14, 57, 28, 45, 30, 9, 35, 12, 13, 18, 5, 89, 77)
Apply merge sort.

Solution We divide the given data into two original files as follows:

f_1: (2, 6, 3, 1, 4, 31, 23, 8, 11, 19, 21, 37)
f_2: (14, 57, 28, 45, 30, 9, 35, 12, 13, 18, 5, 89, 77)

After the first pass of segments of length 1, we have

M_1: ((2, 14), (3, 28), (4, 30), (23, 35), (11, 13), (5, 21))
M_2: ((6, 57), (1, 45), (9, 31), (8, 12), (18, 19), (37, 89), 77)

After the second pass of segments of length 2 we have

f_1: ((2, 6, 14, 57), (4, 9, 30, 31), (11, 13, 18, 19))
f_2: ((1, 3, 28, 25), (8, 12, 23, 35), (5, 21, 37, 89), 77))

After the third pass of segments of length 4 we have

M_1: ((1, 2, 3, 6, 14, 28, 45, 57), (5, 11, 13, 18, 19, 21, 37, 89)
M_2: ((4, 8, 9, 12, 23, 30, 31, 35), 77))

After the fourth pass of segments of length 8 we have

f_1: (1, 2, 3, 4, 6, 8, 9, 12, 14, 23, 28, 30, 31, 35, 45, 57)
f_2: (5, 11, 13, 18, 19, 21, 37, 77, 89)

After the fifth pass of blocks of length 16 we get

M_1: (1, 2, 3, 4, 5, 6, 8, 9, 12, 13, 14, 18, 19, 21, 23, 28, 30, 31, 35, 37, 45, 57, 77, 89)
M_2 is empty.

The algorithm was described beginning with segments of length 1. Substantially larger length segments can be stored in the main memory, so taking conveniently larger segments can enhance the efficiency of the algorithm. For example, if an external file has 100,000 records, and a segment of 1000 such records can be stored in the main memory, then the entire file can be sorted in seven passes. The segments in each pass can be ordered by a suitable sorting method such as the quick sort. The procedure for merge sort usually deals with an external file medium and is therefore system-dependent.

Analysis of Merge Sort

The merge sort algorithm has a property that its time complexity is O($n$log$n$) even in the worst case. If the time for the merging operation is proportional to n, then the computing time for merge sort is described by the following recurrence relation:

$$T(n) = \begin{cases} a, & \text{if } n = 1 \\ 2T(n/2) + cn, & \text{if } n > 1 \end{cases}$$

Here, a and c are constants. When n is a power of 2, $n = 2^i$. We can solve this recurrence by the substitution method as shown here:

$$\begin{aligned} T(n) &= 2T(n/2) + cn = 2[2T(n/4) + cn/2] + cn \\ &= 4T(n/4) + 2cn = 4[2T(n/8) + cn/4] + 2cn \\ &= 8T(n/8) + 3cn = 8[2T(n/16) + cn/8] + 3cn \\ &= 16T(n/16) + 4cn \\ &\quad \cdots \\ &= 2^i\, T(n/2^i) + icn = 2\log_2{}^n \cdot T(n/2\log_2 n) + cn\log_2 n \\ &= nT(1) + cn\log_2 n = an + cn\log_2 n \end{aligned}$$

If $2^i < n \le 2^{i+1}$, then $T(n) \le T(2^{i+1})$.

Therefore, $T(n) = \mathrm{O}(n\log n)$.

Thus, the time complexity for merge sort is O($n$log$n$) even in the worst case. In merge sort, we perform a maximum of n comparisons in each pass. The number of passes is equivalent to the height of a binary tree. So, we can say that the worst case time complexity of a merge sort is O($n\log_2 n$).

16.2.5 Quick Sort

As the name suggests, the quick sort method is the fastest. It is an in-place, divide-and-conquer, massively recursive sort. The algorithm is simple in theory but not so easy to code. The purpose of quick sort is to move a data item in the correct direction just enough for it to reach its final place in the array. The method, therefore, reduces unnecessary swaps and moves an item a great distance in one move. A pivot item near the middle of the array is chosen, and then, items on either side are moved so that the data items on one side of the pivot are smaller than the pivot, whereas those on the other side are larger. The middle (pivot) item is now in its correct position. The procedure is then applied recursively to the two parts of the array, on either side of the pivot, until all the numbers are sorted.

The recursive algorithm consists of four steps:

1. If there is one element in the array to be sorted, return immediately.
2. Pick an element in the array to serve as a 'pivot' point. Usually the leftmost element in the array is used.
3. Split the array into two parts—one with elements smaller than the pivot and the other with elements larger than the pivot.
4. Recursively repeat the algorithm for both halves of the original array.

In quick sort, the given array is divided into two subarrays so that the sorted subarrays need not be merged later. This is accomplished by rearranging the elements in `A[1:n]` such that `A[i] < A[j]` for all `i` between `1` and `m` and all `j` between `m + 1` and `n` for some `m`, $1 \leq m \leq n$. Thus, the elements in `A[1:m]` and `A[m + 1:n]` can be independently sorted. No merge is needed.

The rearrangement of elements is accomplished by picking some element of array `A[]`, say `t = A[5]` and then reordering the other elements so that all elements appearing before `t` in `A[1:n]` are less than or equal to `t`, and those appearing after `t` are greater than or equal to `t`. This rearrangement is called *partitioning*.

Let us assume that `m` represents the first position in a partition in Algorithm 16.5 which describes partitioning.

ALGORITHM 16.5

```
Algorithm Partition(A, m, p)
begin
    v = A[m], i = m, j = p
    do
    begin
        // find first element lesser than pivot
        do i = i + 1 while(A(i) ≤ v);
        // find first element greater than pivot
        do j = j - 1 while(A(j) ≥ v);
        if i < j exchange(A(i), A(j))
    end
    while(i ≤j);
        A(m) = A(j), A(j) = v       // place pivot at its correct
        position
    return(j);
end
```

Algorithm 16.6 is the quick sort algorithm.

ALGORITHM 16.6

```
Algorithm qsort (p, q)
/* p and q are start and end positions of a partition */
begin
    if(p < q) then
      begin
        j = q + 1
```

```
            m = partition (A, p, j)     // pivot has taken its correct
            position
            qsort(p, m - 1)         // sort left partition of pivot
            qsort(m + 1, q)         // sort right partition of pivot
        end
end
```

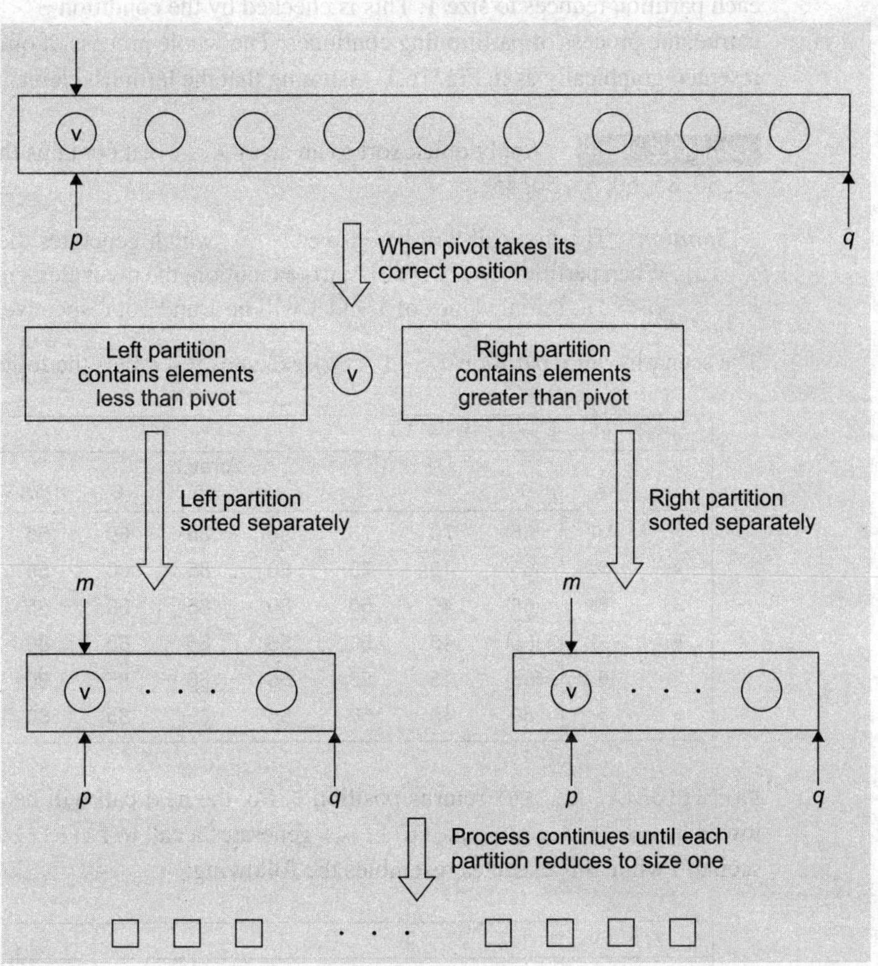

Fig. 16.1 Quick sort

The partition algorithm takes care of partitioning. It takes three arguments. The first argument is an array `A`, which contains all the elements. The second argument `m` and the third argument `p` denote the start and end positions of a partition to be rearranged, respectively. Here, the first element of the partition `A[m]` is being used as the pivot element `v`. Any element can be used as a pivot element, however, in practice, the first element is generally used. The algorithm will rearrange the elements `A[m]`, `A[m + 1]`, ..., `A[p]` such that the pivot element is at position `j`. All the elements from positions `m` to `j - 1` are smaller than the pivot element, that is, `A[u] < A[j]` for all `m ≤ u < j`. All the elements between `j + 1` and `p` are greater than or equal to the pivot element, that is, `A[u] ≥ A[j]` for all `j < u ≤ p`.

The algorithm `qsort` sorts the elements `A[p], ..., A[q]`, which belong to an array `A[n]` in an ascending order. The array `A` is defined as global. The algorithm stops when each partition reduces to size 1. This is checked by the condition `p < q`. If the condition is true, the process of partitioning continues. The whole process of quick sort can be represented graphically as in Fig. 16.1, assuming that the leftmost element is used as a pivot.

EXAMPLE 16.2 Apply quick sort to an array `A[9]` that contains the elements 65, 70, 75, 80, 85, 60, 55, 50, 45.

Solution The first call will be `qsort(1, 9)`, which generates the call partition `(A, 1, 10)`. When partition `(A, 1, 10)` starts execution, the pivot element `v = A[1] = 65, m = 1, p = 10`. Initial values of `i` and `j` will be `1` and `10`, respectively.

The scenario while partition `(A, 1, 10)` executes resembles the following:

v = 65, m = 1, p = 10										
		Array A								
i	j	1	2	3	4	5	6	7	8	9
1	10	(65)	70	75	80	85	60	55	50	45
2	9	(65)	<u>45</u>	75	80	85	60	55	50	<u>70</u>
3	8	(65)	45	<u>50</u>	80	85	60	55	<u>75</u>	70
4	7	(65)	45	50	<u>55</u>	85	60	<u>80</u>	75	70
5	6	(65)	45	50	55	<u>60</u>	<u>85</u>	80	75	70
6	5	60	45	50	55	(65)	85	80	75	70

`Partition(A, 1, 10)` returns position `5`. So, the next call will be `qsort(1, 4)` followed by `qsort(6, 10)`. `qsort(1, 4)` generates a call to `Partition(A, 1, 5)`. The scenario while this executes resembles the following:

v = 60, m = 1, p = 5										
		Array A								
i	j	1	2	3	4	5	6	7	8	9
1	5	(60)	45	50	55	65	85	80	75	70
2	5									
3	5									
4	5									
5	4	55	45	50	(60)					

`Partition(A, 1, 5)` returns position 4. So, the next call will be `qsort(1, 3)`.

Similarly, the process continues until all the partitions reduce to size one.

Analysis of Quicksort

Now, let us discuss the efficiency of quick sort. On the first pass, every element in the array is compared to the pivot, so there are n comparisons. The array is then divided into two parts. (We assume that the array is divided into approximately one half each time). For each of these subarrays, ($n/2$) comparisons are made and four subarrays of size ($n/4$) are formed. So at each level, the number of subarrays doubles. It will take $\log_2 n$ divisions if we are dividing the array approximately one half each time. Therefore, order of quick sort is $O(n\log n)$ on the average.

If the original array is sorted and array[left] is chosen as a pivot, the order of quick sort turns out to be $O(n^2)$. Therefore, when we choose array[left] as pivot, quick sort works best for files that are completely unsorted and worst for files that are completely sorted. In the case of nearly sorted arrays, a random element is chosen as the pivot value.

Let us analyse this again using another method.

When analysing `qsort()`, we count only the number of element comparisons $C(n)$ and make the following assumption:

The n elements to be sorted are distinct and the *i/p* distribution is such that partition element $v = A[m]$ in the call to `Partition (A, m, p)` has an equal probability of being i^{th} smallest element, $1 \le i \le (p - m)$ in $A(m, p - 1)$.

Worst case At level one, only one call to a partition is made with n elements; at level two, utmost two calls are made with elements $(n - 1)$, and so on.

$$C(n) = O(n^2)$$

Average case $C_A(n)$ A partition requires $(n + 1)$ element comparisons on its first call. The partition element has an equal probability of being the ith smallest element in the array.

$$\therefore \quad C_A = (n+1) + \frac{1}{n} \sum_{1 \le k \le n} C_A(k-1) + C_A(n-k)$$

Multiplying by n we get

$$nC_A(n) = n(n+1) + \sum_{1<k<n} C_A(k-1) + C_A(n-k)$$

$$= n(n+1) + C_A(0) + C_A(1) + \ldots + C_A(n-1) + C_A(n-1) + C_A(n-2) + \ldots + C_A(0)$$

$$= n(n+1) + 2\,[C_A(0) + C_A(1) + \ldots + C_A(n-1)] \quad (16.1)$$

Replacing n by $n - 1$ we get

$$(n-1)\, C_A(n-1) = (n-1)\, n + 2\,[C_A(0) + C_A(1) + \ldots + C_A(n-2)] \quad (16.2)$$

Subtracting Eq. (16.2) from Eq. (16.1) we get

$$nC_A(n) - (n-1)\,C_A(n-1) = n(n+1) - n(n-1) + 2C_A(n-1)$$
$$nC_A(n) = n^2 + n - n^2 + n + 2C_A(n-1) + (n-1)\,C_A(n-1)$$
$$= 2n + C_A(n-1)\,(2 + n - 1)$$
$$nC_A(n) = 2n + (n+1)\,C_A(n-1) \tag{16.3}$$
$$\frac{C_A(n)}{n+1} = \frac{2}{(n+1)} + \frac{1}{n}C_A(n-1)$$
$$\frac{C_A(n)}{n+1} = \frac{2n + (n+1)C_A(n-1)}{(n+1)n}$$

Use Eq. (16.3) for $C_A(n-1)$, $C_A(n-2)$, …

$$\frac{C_A(n)}{n+1} = \left[\frac{C_A(n-1)}{n}\right] + \frac{2}{n+1}$$
$$= \left[\frac{nC_A(n-2) + 2n - 2}{n(n-1)}\right] + \frac{2}{n+1}$$
$$= \frac{C_A(n-2)}{n-1} + \frac{2}{n} + \frac{2}{n+1}$$
$$\frac{C_A(n)}{n+1} = \frac{C_A(n-3)}{n-2} + \frac{2}{n-1} + \frac{2}{n} + \frac{2}{n+1} \tag{16.4}$$
$$\frac{C_A(1)}{2} + 2\sum_{3 \le k \le n+1} \frac{1}{k}$$

However, $C_A(0) = C_A(1) = 0$.

$$= 2\sum_{3 \le k \le n+1} \frac{1}{k}$$
$$= 2\sum_{3 \le k \le n+1} \frac{1}{k} \int_1^{n+1} \frac{1}{x}\,\partial x$$
$$= 2(\log_e(n+1) - \log_e 2)$$
$$\therefore \quad \frac{C_A(n)}{n+1} = 2(\log_e(n+1) - \log_e 2)$$
$$= 2(n+1) \times [\log(n+1) - \log_e 2]$$
$$= (2n+2)\log(n+1) - 2n\log_e 2 - 2\log_e 2$$
$$= 2n\log(n+1) + 2\log(n+1) - 2n\log_e 2 - 2\log_e 2$$
$$= O(n\log n)$$

16.2.6 Strassen's Algorithm for Matrix Multiplication

The multiplication of two matrices is one of the most basic operations of linear algebra and scientific computing, and it has provided an important focus in the search for methods to speed up scientific computation.

Let $\boldsymbol{A}$, $\boldsymbol{B}$ be two square matrices used to calculate the matrix product $\boldsymbol{C} = \boldsymbol{A} \times \boldsymbol{B}$.

Conventional matrix multiplication involves the following steps:

```
for(int i = 0; i < m; i++)
  for(int j = 0; j < n; j++)
  {
    C[i][j] = 0.0;
    for(int k = 0; k < p; k++)
      C[i][j] += A[i][k] * B[k][j];
  }
```

The time complexity of the conventional approach is $O(n^3)$. Thus, any speed up in matrix multiplication can improve the performance of a wide variety of numerical algorithms. To calculate the matrix product $\boldsymbol{C} = \boldsymbol{A} \times \boldsymbol{B}$, Strassen's algorithm partitions the data to reduce the number of multiplications performed. This algorithm requires $\boldsymbol{M}$, $\boldsymbol{N}$, and $\boldsymbol{P}$ to be powers of 2 and is described by the following steps:

1. Let us partition $\boldsymbol{A}$, $\boldsymbol{B}$, and $\boldsymbol{C}$ into four equal parts.

If the matrices $\boldsymbol{A}$ and $\boldsymbol{B}$ are not of type $2n \times 2n$, we fill the missing rows and columns with zeros. We partition $\boldsymbol{A}$, $\boldsymbol{B}$, and $\boldsymbol{C}$ into equally sized block matrices as

$$\boldsymbol{A} = \begin{bmatrix} A_{1,1} & A_{1,2} \\ A_{2,1} & A_{2,2} \end{bmatrix}; \quad \boldsymbol{B} = \begin{bmatrix} B_{1,1} & B_{1,2} \\ B_{2,1} & B_{2,2} \end{bmatrix}; \quad \boldsymbol{C} = \begin{bmatrix} C_{1,1} & C_{1,2} \\ C_{2,1} & C_{2,2} \end{bmatrix}$$

2. Generate the intermediate matrices:
   1. $\boldsymbol{M}_1 = (A_{11} + A_{22})(B_{11} + B_{22})$
   2. $\boldsymbol{M}_2 = (A_{21} + A_{22}) B_{11}$
   3. $\boldsymbol{M}_3 = A_{11}(B_{12} - B_{22})$
   4. $\boldsymbol{M}_4 = A_{22}(B_{21} - B_{11})$
   5. $\boldsymbol{M}_5 = (A_{11} + A_{12}) B_{22}$
   6. $\boldsymbol{M}_6 = (A_{21} - A_{11})(B_{11} + B_{12})$
   7. $\boldsymbol{M}_7 = (A_{12} - A_{22})(B_{21} + B_{22})$

These are then used to express $C_{i,j}$ in terms of $\boldsymbol{M}_k$. This eliminates one matrix multiplication and reduces the number of multiplications to seven (one multiplication for each $\boldsymbol{M}_k$) and expresses $C_{i,j}$ as in Step 3.

3. Now, construct the resultant matrix $\boldsymbol{C}$ using the intermediate matrices as follows:

$C_{11} = \boldsymbol{M}_1 + \boldsymbol{M}_4 - \boldsymbol{M}_5 + \boldsymbol{M}_7$
$C_{12} = \boldsymbol{M}_3 + \boldsymbol{M}_5$
$C_{21} = \boldsymbol{M}_2 + \boldsymbol{M}_4$
$C_{22} = \boldsymbol{M}_1 - \boldsymbol{M}_2 + \boldsymbol{M}_3 + \boldsymbol{M}_6$

In brief, we follow the following three steps:

1. Partition ***A*** and ***B*** into quarter matrices.
2. Compute the intermediate matrices:
   (a) If the sizes of the matrices are greater than a threshold value, multiply them recursively using Strassen's algorithm.
   (b) Else, use the traditional matrix multiplication algorithm.
3. Construct ***C*** using the intermediate matrices.

With this construction, we have not yet reduced the number of multiplications. We still need eight multiplications to calculate the $C_{i,j}$ matrices; the same number of multiplications needed while using the standard matrix multiplication. We iterate this division process *n* times until the submatrices degenerate into numbers.

Practical implementations of Strassen's algorithm result in standard methods of matrix multiplication for smaller submatrices, for which those algorithms are more efficient.

Let us compute the time complexity of this algorithm. The standard matrix multiplication takes approximately $2N^3$ (where $N = 2^n$) arithmetic operations (additions and multiplications); the asymptotic complexity is $O(N^3)$. The number of additions and multiplications required in the Strassen's algorithm can be calculated as follows:

Let $f(n)$ be the number of operations for a $2^n \times 2^n$ matrix. Then, by recursive application of the Strassen's algorithm, we see that $T(n) = 7T(n - 1) + 14n$ for some constant that depends on the number of additions performed at each application of the algorithm. Hence, $T(n) = (7 + O(1))n$, that is, the asymptotic complexity for multiplying matrices of size $N = 2^n$ using the Strassen's algorithm is

$$O\left(\left[7+O(1)\right]^n\right) = O\left(N^{\log_2 7+O(1)}\right) \approx O\left(N^{2.807}\right)$$

Note the reduction in the number of arithmetic operations achieved at the additional cost of reduced numerical stability.

16.3 GREEDY METHOD

A greedy method is any algorithm that follows the problem-solving heuristic of making the locally optimal choice at each stage with the hope of finding the optimum solution. For example, applying the greedy strategy to the travelling salesman problem yields the following algorithm: 'At each stage, visit the unvisited city nearest to the current city'. In general, greedy algorithms are used for optimization problems. Often, we look at optimization problems whose performance is exponential. A feasible solution to which the optimization function has the best possible value is called an *optimal solution*.

In greedy method, we attempt to construct an optimal solution in the sequence of choice. At each choice, we make a decision that appears to be the best at that time. A decision made at one choice is not changed at a later choice, so each decision should assure feasibility. A greedy method could, at each choice, increase the total amount of change reflected to a great extent.

A greedy method is optimal for some change systems. To find a solution under normal circumstances, all the combinations are required and such combinations are many; in this case, the greedy algorithm reduces combinatonic explosions.

16.3.1 General Greedy Method

The greedy algorithm suggests that one can devise an algorithm that works in stages, considering one input at a time. At each stage, a decision is made based on whether or not a particular input is an optimal solution.

Any subset of input that satisfies the given constraints is called a *feasible solution.* A feasible solution that maximizes or minimizes a given objective is called an *optimal solution*. There is usually an obvious way to determine a feasible solution but not necessarily an optimal solution.

As mentioned earlier, this method considers one input at a time and based on whether a particular input is an optimal solution, a decision is arrived at each stage. This is done by considering the inputs in an order determined by some selection procedure. If the inclusion of the next input into the partially constructed optimal solution results in an infeasible solution, then this input is not added to the partial solution. Otherwise, it is added. The selection procedure itself is based on optimization measures. We need to find a feasible solution that either maximizes or minimizes a given objective function. The measure may be an objective function.

In Algorithm 16.7, the function selects an input from an array `a[]` and removes it. The selected input value is assigned to `x`. `feasible()` is a Boolean-valued function that determines whether `x` can be included in the solution vector. The function `union()` combines `x` with the solution and updates the objective function. The function `Greedy()` describes the essential way that a greedy algorithm will look like once a particular problem is chosen, and the functions `select()`, `feasible()`, and `union()` are properly implemented.

ALGORITHM 16.7

```
Algorithm Greedy(a, n)
{ a[1:n] contains n inputs }
begin
solution = nil
for i = 1 to n do
  begin
     x = select(a)
     if feasible(solution, x) then
        solution = union(solution, x)
  end
return solution
end
```

Elements of Greedy Strategy

To decide whether a problem can be solved using a greedy strategy, the following elements should be considered:

1. Greedy-choice property
2. Optimal substructure

Greedy-choice property A problem exhibits greedy-choice property if a globally optimal solution can be arrived at by making a locally optimal greedy choice. That is, we make the choice that seems best at that time without considering the results from the subproblems.

When the dynamic programming makes a choice at each step, it considers the solutions to the subproblems. So, it proceeds from smaller subproblems to larger ones in a bottom-up approach. However, when the greedy algorithm makes a choice at each step, it uses the choice that looks best at that time and then solves the problem. So, it never depends on future solutions. Thus, it proceeds in a top-down manner and reduces each problem instance to a smaller one. It is often possible to design an efficient algorithm by making greedy choices quickly. This can be achieved by using the appropriate data structure or by preprocessing the input.

The concept of optimal substructure is explained in Section 16.4.2.

16.3.2 Knapsack Problem

We are given *n* objects and a knapsack or a bag. Each object has a positive weight w_i and a positive profit p_i for $i = 1$ to n. The maximum capacity of the knapsack is M. Our aim is to fill up the knapsack such that the profit is maximized while satisfying the constraint that the knapsack will not carry a total weight more than M. We assume that the objects can be taken in parts, that is, some fraction of total weight x_j. In this case, the object i contributes $x_i w_i$ to the total weight and $x_i p_i$ to the profit.

Hence, our aim is to fill up the knapsack such that

$$\overset{n}{\underset{i=1}{S}} x_i p_i \text{ is } S_{\text{maximum}} \text{ subject to } \overset{n}{\underset{i=1}{S}} x_i w_i \leq M$$

where $0 \leq x \leq 1$

We shall use a greedy algorithm to solve this problem. In terms of control abstraction, a feasible solution is one that satisfies these constraints.

In an optimal solution, $\overset{n}{\underset{i=1}{S}} x_i w_i = M$ and $\overset{n}{\underset{i=1}{S}} x_i p_i$ is maximum.

Since we are working on a greedy algorithm, our strategy will be to select each object in some suitable order, to put as large a fraction as possible of the selected objects, and to stop when the knapsack is full. This is illustrated in Algorithm 16.8.

ALGORITHM 16.8

```
Knapsack-Greedy(w[], p[], M)
begin
weight = 0, profit = 0
while(weight ≤M) do
```

```
    begin
    i = object with highest profit
    if(weight + w[i] ≤ M) then
       begin
       x[i] = 1
       weight = weight + w[i]
       end
    else
       begin
       x[i] = (w - weight)/w[i]
       weight = M
       end
    end
end
```

EXAMPLE 16.3 Find an optimal solution for a knapsack problem with objects $n = 5$, maximum capacity of knapsack $M = 100$, profit $P = \{20, 30, 66, 40, 60\}$, and weight $W = \{10, 20, 30, 40, 50\}$.

Solution

Case 1: Let us choose the objects in decreasing order of profits. We first choose object 3 with weight 30 and then object 5 with weight 50. Now, the total weight = 30 + 50 = 80.

So, we have to fill the knapsack with the partial weight of object 4, which is given by

$$\frac{\text{Maximum allowed weight} - \text{Current weight}}{\text{Weight of object 4}} = \frac{100 - 80}{40} = \frac{20}{40} = \frac{1}{2}$$

So, the total weight of knapsack = 30 + 50 + (40/2) = 100.

Here, we have used whole objects 3 and 5, and half fraction of object 4. So, the total profit = profit of object 5 + profit of object 3 + half the profit of object 4 = 60 + 66 + (40/2) = 146. Hence, the total profit earned is 146 if we select the objects according to profit.

Case 2: Let us choose the objects in the increasing order of weights. So first, we choose object 1 with weight 10, then object 2 with weight 20, followed by object 3 with weight 30, and finally object 4 with weight 40. So, the total weight = 10 + 20 + 30 + 40 = 100. All the objects are used as a whole. Thus, the total profit is equal to the sum of profits of all the objects.

$$\therefore \text{Total profit} = 20 + 30 + 66 + 40 = 156.$$

Hence, the total profit is 156 if we choose the objects according to weight.

Case 3: Let us choose objects in an order such that the object with maximum profit per unit weight is used. The profit/weight ratios of the given objects are calculated as follows:

$$\text{Profit/weight ratios} = \left\{\frac{20}{10}, \frac{30}{20}, \frac{66}{30}, \frac{40}{40}, \frac{60}{50}\right\} = \left\{2, \frac{3}{2}, \frac{22}{10}, 1, \frac{6}{5}\right\}$$

$$= \{2, 1.5, 2.2, 1, 1.2\}$$

Since object 3 gives the maximum profit per unit, it is selected first, and its weight is 30. Then, object 1 with weight 10 is selected. Then, object 2 with weight 20 is selected. Total weight = 30 + 10 + 20 = 60. Now, object 5 with weight 50 is selected partially. So, the fraction of object 5 selected is equal to

$$\frac{\text{Maximum allowed weight} - \text{Current weight}}{\text{Weight of object 5}} = \frac{100-60}{50} = \frac{40}{50} = \frac{4}{5}$$

So, the total weight = 30 + 10 + 20 + 50 × (4/5) = 100. Here, objects 3, 1, 2 are used as a whole and 4/5th of object 5 is used. So, the total profit = 66 + 20 + 30 + 60 × (4/5) = 164.

Hence, the total profit is 164 if we choose objects in the order of profit per unit.

Conclusion If we observe the profits of three cases, Case 3 gives the maximum profit. This case actually uses the knapsack–greedy algorithm. So, the solution obtained is surely optimal.

EXAMPLE 16.4 Find an optimal solution to the knapsack instance with objects $n = 7$, maximum capacity of knapsack $M = 15$, profits $(p_1, p_2, \ldots, p_7) = (10, 5, 15, 7, 6, 18, 3)$, and weights $(w_1, w_2, \ldots, w_7) = (2, 3, 5, 7, 1, 4, 1)$.

Solution Using the knapsack–greedy algorithm, we can directly select the objects such that the object with maximum profit per unit of weight is used.

$$\text{Profit/unit} = \left(\frac{10}{2}, \frac{5}{3}, \frac{15}{5}, \frac{7}{7}, \frac{6}{1}, \frac{18}{4}, \frac{3}{1}\right)$$

$$\doteq (5, 1.67, 3, 1, 6, 4.5, 3)$$

Hence objects 5 and 1 with profits/unit of 6 and 5, respectively, are chosen as a whole. The next object with highest profit/unit ratio is object 6 which is chosen as a fraction.

16.4 DYNAMIC PROGRAMMING

Dynamic programming has evolved into a major paradigm of algorithm design in computer science. However, its name is a mystery to many people. The name was coined in 1957 by Richard Bellman to describe a type of optimum control problem. The name originally described the problem rather than the technique of the solution. This type of programming denotes 'a series of choices', similar to the programming of a radio station. The word dynamic conveys the idea that these choices may depend on the current state rather than being decided ahead of time. A radio show where the listeners phone in their requests might be said to be dynamically programmed in contrast with the usual format where the selections of songs are decided before the show begins. Bellman described a method to solve dynamic programming problems, which has become an inspiration for many computer algorithms. The main feature of this method is that it has replaced an exponential time computation by a polynomial time computation. This continues to be a common feature of dynamic programming algorithms.

In all the algorithms we have studied so far, achieving accuracy was easier than efficiency. In optimization problems, we are interested in finding the solution that maximizes or minimizes the same function. In designing algorithms for an optimization problem, we must design one that gives the best possible solution.

Greedy algorithms, which take the best local decision of each step, occasionally produce a global optimum solution, but we need to prove the same. Dynamic programming is a technique for computing recurrence relations efficiently by sorting partial results. A dynamic programming algorithm stores results, or solutions, to small subproblems. Later it uses these stored solutions instead of recomputing them to solve larger subproblems. Thus, dynamic programming is especially well suited to problems where a recursive algorithm would solve many of the subproblems repeatedly.

We will introduce a characterization of dynamic programming algorithms that provides a unified framework for a wide variety of published algorithms that might seem quite different on the surface. This framework permits a recursive solution to be converted into a dynamic programming algorithm and provides a way to analyse its complexity.

16.4.1 General Method of Dynamic Programming

Dynamic programming is an algorithm design method that can be used when the solution to a problem may be viewed as the result of a sequence of decisions. Similar to the greedy method, for many problems, it is not possible to make stepwise decisions (based only on local information) in such a manner that the sequence of decisions made is optimal. One way to solve such problems is to try out all possible decision sequences. We could enumerate all decision sequences and then choose the best. Dynamic programming often drastically reduces the amount of enumeration by avoiding the enumeration of some decision sequences that cannot possibly be optimal. In dynamic programming, an optimal sequence of decisions is arrived at by making an explicit appeal to the principle of optimality.

The following are the four steps to develop a dynamic programming algorithm:

1. Characterize the structure of an optimal solution.
2. Recursively define the value of an optimal solution.
3. Compute the value of an optimal solution in a bottom-up manner. This can also be done using the recursive method.
4. Construct an optimal solution from the computed information by making use of the computed results.

The generic problem structure is as follows:

$$t_n = \begin{cases} \text{constant value}, & \text{if trivial } (p) \\ \text{combine } f(p_1), f(p_2), \ldots, f(p_n), & \text{otherwise} \end{cases}$$

16.4.2 Elements of Dynamic Programming

A dynamic programming solution has the following three components:

1. Formulate the answer as a recurrence relation or a recursive algorithm.
2. Show that the number of different instances of your recurrence is bounded by a polynomial.
3. Specify an order of evaluation for the recurrence.

To decide whether a problem can be solved using the dynamic programming method, the following three elements of dynamic programming should be considered:

1. Optimal substructure
2. Overlapping subproblems
3. Memorization

Optimal Substructure

A problem exhibits optimal substructure if an optimal solution to the problem contains within it optimal solutions to subproblems. It also means that dynamic programming (and greedy method) might apply. As the optimal solution to the problem is built from the optimal solution to the subproblems, this requirement becomes necessary.

The execution time of a dynamic programming algorithm depends on the product of two factors: the overall number of subproblems and the number of choices we look at for each subproblem.

Dynamic programming uses optimal substructure in a bottom-up manner. It first finds optimal solutions to the subproblems. When the subproblems are solved, then it finds an optimal solution to the problem.

Overlapping Subproblems

When a recursive algorithm revisits the same problem repeatedly, it is said that the optimization problem has overlapping subproblems. This is beneficial for dynamic programming. It solves each subproblem once and stores the answer in a table. This answer can be searched in constant time when required. This is contradictory to the divide-and-conquer strategy where a new problem is generated at each step of recursion.

Memorization

In general, dynamic programming maintains a table for the solutions to all subproblems. However, it uses the control structure similar to the recursive algorithm. In a memorized recursive algorithm, an entry is maintained in a table for the solution to each subproblem. Initially, all entries contain a special value, which indicates that the entry is not yet used. For each subproblem, which is encountered for the first time, its solution is computed and stored in the table. Next time, for that subproblem, its entry is searched and the value is used. This can be implemented using hashing.

16.4.3 Principle of Optimality

The principle of optimality states that an optimal sequence of decisions has the property that whatever the initial state and decision are, the remaining decisions must constitute an optimal decision sequence with regard to the state resulting from the first decision.

Difference between Greedy Method and Dynamic Programming

The essential difference between the greedy method and dynamic programming is that in greedy method only one decision sequence is generated. In dynamic programming, many decision sequences may be generated. However, sequences containing suboptimal subsequences will not be generated if the principle of optimality holds. One may feel that in this method, one has to look at all possible decision sequences to obtain an optimal decision sequence using dynamic programming. This is not the case as, due to the use of the principle of optimality, decision sequences containing subsequences that are sub-optimal are not considered. Although the total number of different decision sequences is exponential, dynamic programming algorithms often have a polynomial complexity. An exponential number of decisions can be generated because if there are d choices for each of the n decisions to be made, then there are d^n possible decision sequences.

Another important feature of the dynamic programming approach is that optimal solutions to subproblems are retained to avoid recomputing their values. The use of these tabulated values makes it natural to recast the recursive equations into an iterative algorithm. Most dynamic programming algorithms are often expressed in this way.

The following are the unique characteristics of dynamic programming:

1. The solution to a problem is viewed as a result of a sequence of decisions.
2. It avoids enumeration of some decision sequences that cannot be possibly optimal.
3. An optimal sequence of decisions is arrived at by making an explicit appeal to the principle of optimality.
4. In contrast to greedy method where only one decision sequence is ever generated, in dynamic programming, many decision sequences may be generated. However, sequences containing suboptimal sequences cannot be optimal and so will not be generated.
5. There are two approaches to dynamic programming. Let $(x_1, x_2, \ldots, x_n)$ be variables.
   (a) Forward approach: Decision x_i is made in terms of optimal decision sequences for $x_1, \ldots, x_n$.
   (b) Backward approach: Decision x_i is made in terms of optimal decision sequences for $x_1, x_2, \ldots, x_{i-1}$.
6. Dynamic programming is a technique for solving problems with overlapping subproblems. Typically, these subproblems arise from a recurrence relating a solution to a given problem with solutions to its smaller subproblems of the same type.
7. Rather than repeatedly solving overlapping subproblems, dynamic programming suggests solving each of the smaller subproblems only once and recording the results in a table, from which we can obtain a solution to the original problem.

8. Applicability of dynamic programming to an optimization problem requires the problem to satisfy the principle of optimality—an optimal solution to any of its instances must be made of optimal solutions to its subinstances.

16.4.4 Limitations of Dynamic Programming

Dynamic programming can be applied to any problem that observes the principle of optimality. This means that partial solutions can be optimally extended with regard to the state after the partial solution instead of the partial solution itself. For example, to decide whether to extend an approximate string matching by a substitution, insertion, or deletion, we need not know the exact sequence of operations performed. In fact, there may be several different edit sequences that achieve a cost of C on the first p characters of pattern P and t characters of string T. Future decisions will be made on the basis of the consequences of previous decisions, and not the actual decisions themselves.

Problems in which the actual operations matter, as opposed to just the cost of the operations, do not satisfy the principle of optimality. Consider a form of edit distance where we are not allowed to use combinations of operations in a particular order.

The biggest limitation in using dynamic programming is the number of partial solutions we must keep track of. For all of the examples discussed here, the partial solutions can be completely described by specifying the stopping places in the input. This is because all the combinatorial objects being worked on (strings, numerical sequences, and polygons) have an implicit order defined upon their elements. This order cannot be scrambled without completely changing the problem. Once the order is fixed, there are relatively a few possible stopping places or states, so we get efficient algorithms. However, if the objects are not firmly ordered, we would have an exponential number of possible partial solutions which require an infeasible amount of memory.

16.4.5 Knapsack Problem

We are given n objects and a knapsack. Object i has a weight w_i and the knapsack has a capacity M. If $x_i = 1$, the object i is placed into the knapsack and a profit $p_i x_i$ is earned. If $x_i = 0$, the object is not added into the knapsack, and hence no profit is earned. The objective is to obtain a filling of the knapsack that minimizes the total profit earned. Since the capacity is M, we require the total weight of all the chosen objects to be almost M. This can be stated formally as follows:

$$\text{Maximize } \underset{1 \le i \le n}{S} p_i x_i \text{ subject to } \underset{1 \le i \le n}{S} w_i x_i \le M \text{ and } x_i = 0 \text{ or } 1, \text{ where } 1 \le i \le n$$

A feasible solution is any set $(x_1, x_2, \ldots, x_n)$ satisfying these equations, and an optimal solution is a feasible solution for which $\Sigma p_i x_i$ is maximum.

Let $y_1, y_2, \ldots, y_n$ be an optimal sequence of 0/1 values for $x_1, x_2, \ldots, x_n$, respectively. If $y_1 = 0$, then $y_2, y_3, \ldots, y_n$ must constitute an optimal sequence for the problem knapsack(2, n, M). If it does not, then $y_1, y_2, \ldots, y_n$ is not an optimal sequence for knapsack(1, n, M).

If $y_1 = 1$, then $y_2, y_3, \ldots, y_n$ must be an optimal sequence for the problem knapsack(2, n, $M - w_1$). If it is not, then there is another 0/1 sequence $z_2, z_3, \ldots, z_n$ such that

$$\underset{2 \le i \le n}{S} w_i z_i \le M - w_1$$

and

$$\underset{2 \le i \le n}{S} P_i z_i > \underset{2 \le i \le n}{S} P_i y_i$$

Hence, $y_1, z_2, z_3, \ldots, z_n$ is a sequence for $\sum w_i x_i$ with a greater value.

In dynamic programming, formulating the optimal sequence for a knapsack problem can be achieved either in forward or backward approach. Let $x_1, x_2, \ldots, x_n$ be the variables for which a sequence of decisions has to be made. In the forward approach, the formulation of decision x_i is made in terms of optimal decision sequences for $x_{i+1}, \ldots, x_n$. In the backward approach, the formulation for decision x_i is made in terms of optimal decision sequences for $x_1, \ldots, x_{i-1}$. In the forward approach, we look ahead on the decision sequence $x_1, x_2, \ldots, x_n$, and in the backward formulation, we look backwards on the decision sequence $x_1, x_2, \ldots, x_n$.

For an integer y such that $0 \le y \le M$, $f_i(y)$ is an ascending function.

$$y_1 < y_2 < \ldots < y_k \text{ such that}$$
$$f_i(y_1) < f_i(y_2) < \ldots < f_i(y_k)$$
$$f_i(y) = -\infty \text{ for } y < y_1$$
$$f_i(y) = f(y_k) \text{ for } y \ge y_k$$

We use the ordered set

$$f_i(y) = S^i = \{(p, w) \mid 1 \le j \le k\}$$

where $p = f_i(y_j)$ and $w = y_j$.

The following steps are used to solve all knapsack problems using dynamic programming forward approach:

1. Initially $S^0 = \{(0, 0)\}$
2. $S_1^i = \{(p, w) \mid (p - p_i), (w - w_i) \in S^i\}$
   That is, to obtain S^{i+1}, we either include x_{i+1} or do not include x_{i+1}.
   (a) If $x_{i+1} = 1$ is not included, then $S_1^i = S^i$.
   (b) If $x_{i+1} = 1$ is included, then the resulting states in S_1^i are obtained by adding (p_{i+1}, w_{i+1}) to each state in S^i.
3. S^{i+1} can be computed by merging and purging the states in S^i and S_1^i together, using the dominance rule—if S^{i+1} contains two pairs (p_a, w_a) and (p_b, w_b), where $p_a \le p_b$ and $w_a \ge w_b$, then (p_a, w_a) is dominated by (p_b, w_b) pair. Hence, the pair (p_a, w_a) is discarded. In this way, dominated tuples get purged. We can also purge all pairs (p, w) with $w > M$ because the knapsack capacity is M.
4. Repeat steps 2 and 3 until S^n is obtained.

5. $f_n(M) = S^n$. Using this, we can find the solution to knapsack(1, *n*, *m*).
6. If the last pair in S^n is (p, w), then
   (a) set $x_n = 0$ if $(p, w) \in S^{n-1}$
   (b) set $x_n = 1$ if $(p, w) \notin S^{n-1}$, and compute $p = p - x_n$ and $w = w - w_n$.
7. Repeat step 6 for $x = n, \ldots, 1$.

Let us solve a few examples based on this concept.

EXAMPLE 16.5 Generate the sets S^i, $0 \le i \le 3$, for the following knapsack instance: $n = 3$, $(w_1, w_2, w_3) = (2, 3, 4)$, $(p_1, p_2, p_3) = (1, 2, 5)$, and $M = 6$. In addition, find an optimal solution.

Solution

$S^0 = \{(0, 0)\}$

S_1^0 is obtained by adding $(p_1, w_1) = (1, 2)$ to each pair of S^0.

$S_1^0 = \{(1, 2)\}$

S^1 is obtained by merging and purging S^0 and S_1^0.

$S^1 = \{(0, 0), (1, 2)\}$

S_1^1 is obtained by adding $(p_2, w_2) = (2, 3)$ to each pair of S^1.

$S_1^1 = \{(2, 3), (3, 5)\}$

S^2 is obtained by merging and purging S^1 and S_1^1.

$S^2 = \{(0, 0), (1, 2), (2, 3), (3, 5)\}$

S_1^2 is obtained by adding $(p_3, w_3) = (5, 4)$ to each pair of S^2.

$S_1^2 = \{(5, 4), (6, 6), \{(7, 7), (8, 9)\}$

S^3 is obtained by merging and purging S^2 and S_1^2.

$S^3 = \{(0, 0), (1, 2), \{(2, 3), (5, 4), (6, 6)\}$

The pair (3, 5) gets purged here by dominance rule. In addition, the pairs (7, 7) and (8, 9) get purged because $w > M$.

The last pair in S^3 is $(p, w) = (6, 6) \notin S^2$; hence, $x_3 = 1$. However, $(p_3, w_3) = (5, 4)$. Hence, $(p, w) = (6 - 5, 6 - 4) = (1, 2)$.

Since $(1, 2) \in S^2$ and $(1, 2) \in S^1$, set $x_2 = 0$.

Since $(1, 2) \notin S^0$; set $x_1 = 1$. Hence, an optimal solution for the given knapsack problem is $(x_1, x_2, x_3) = (1, 0, 1)$.

EXAMPLE 16.6 Generate the sets S^i, $0 \le i \le 4$, for the following knapsack instance: $n = 4$; $(w_1, w_2, w_3, w_4) = (10, 15, 6, 9)$; $(p_1, p_2, p_3, p_4) = (2, 5, 8, 1)$; and $M = 30$.

Solution

$S^0 = \{(0, 0)\}$

By adding $(p_1, w_1) = (2, 10)$ to each pair of S^0 we get

$S_1^0 = \{(2, 10)\}$

By merging and purging S^0 and S_1^0 we get

$S^1 = \{(0, 0), (2, 10)\}$

By adding $(p_2, w_2) = (5, 15)$ to each pair of S^1 we get

$S_1^1 = \{(5, 15), (7, 25)\}$

By merging and purging S^1 and S_1^1 we get

$S^2 = \{(0, 0), (2, 10), \{(5, 15), (7, 25)\}$

By adding $(p_3, w_3) = (8, 6)$ to each pair of S^2 we get

$S_1^2 = \{(8, 6), (10, 16), \{(13, 21), (15, 31)\}$

By merging and purging S^2 and S_1^2 we get

$S^3 = \{(0, 0), (8, 6), \{(10, 16), (13, 21), (15, 31)\}$

The pairs (2, 10), (5, 15), (7, 25) get purged here by the dominance rule.

By adding $(p_4, w_4) = (1, 9)$ to each pair of S^3 we get

$S_1^3 = \{(1, 9), (9, 15), (11, 25), (14, 30), (16, 40)\}$

By merging and purging S^3 and S_1^3 we get

$S^4 = \{(0, 0), (8, 6), (9, 15), (10, 16), (13, 21), (14, 30), (15, 31), (16, 40)\}$

Here, we have to eliminate the pairs (10, 16), (13, 21), and (15, 31). With $M = 30$, searching a Tuple with the value 30, we get (14, 30) in S^4; so, $x_4 = 1$. Similarly, we get $x_3 = 1$, $x_2 = 1$, and since $((5 - 5), (15 - 15)) = (0, 0)$, we get $x_1 = 0$. Thus the optimal solution is $(x_1, x_2, x_3, x_4)(0, 1, 1, 1)$.

EXAMPLE 16.7 Generate the sets S^i and find an optimal solution for the following knapsack instance: $n = 6$, $(p_1, p_2, p_3, p_4, p_5, p_6) = (w_1, w_2, w_3, w_4, w_5, w_6) = (100, 50, 20, 10, 7, 3)$, and $M = 165$.

Solution Here, $p_i = w_i$ for all i; hence, each pair $(p, w) = p$.

$S^0 = \{0\}$	$S^2 = \{0, 50, 100, 150\}$
$S_1^0 = \{100\}$	$S_1^2 = \{20, 70, 120, 170\}$
$S^1 = \{0, 100\}$	$S^3 = \{0, 20, 50, 70, 100, 120, 150\}$
$S_1^1 = \{50, 150\}$	

Here, 170 is purged because $170 > M$.

$S_1^3 = \{10, 30, 60, 80, 110, 130, 160\}$

$S^4 = \{0, 10, 20, 30, 50, 60, 70, 80, 100, 110, 120, 130, 150, 160\}$

$S_1^4 = \{7, 17, 27, 37, 57, 67, 77, 87, 107, 117, 127, 137, 157, 167\}$

$S^5 = \{0, 7, 10, 17, 20, 27, 30, 37, 50, 57, 60, 67, 70, 77, 80, 87, 100, 107, 110, 117, 120, 127, 130, 137, 150, 157, 160\}$

$S_1^5 = \{3, 10, 13, 20, 23, 30, 33, 40, 53, 60, 63, 70, 73, 80, 83, 90, 103, 110, 113, 120, 123, 130, 133, 140, 153, 160, 163\}$

$S^6 = \{0, 3, 7, 10, 13, 17, 20, 23, 27, 33, 37, 40, 50, 53, 57, 60, 63, 67, 70, 73, 77, 80, 83, 87, 90, 100, 103, 107, 110, 113, 117, 120, 123, 127, 130, 133, 137, 140, 150, 153, 157, 160, 163\}$

The value of $F_6(165)$ can be determined from S^6. The last tuple in S^6 is $p = w = 163 \notin S^5$. Hence, $x_6 = 1$. However, $p_6 = w_6 = 3$. Hence, $p - p_6 = 163 - 3 = 160 \in S^5$ and also, $160 \in S^4$. Hence, $x_5 = 0$. Now, $160 \notin S^3$; hence, $x_4 = 1$. However, $p_4 = 10$; hence, $p - p_4 = 160 - 10 = 150 \in S^3$ and also, $150 \in S^2$; hence, $x_3 = 0$.

However, $150 \notin S^1$; hence, $x_2 = 1$.

Here, $p_2 = 50$. Hence, $p - p_2 = 150 - 50 = 100 \in S^1$ and $100 \notin S^0$; hence, $x_1 = 1$.

Hence, the optimal solution is

$$(x_1, x_2, x_3, x_4, x_5, x_6) = (1, 1, 0, 1, 0, 1)$$

Let us write a function `DKnapsack` that takes four input parameters—an array `p[1:n]` for profits, an array `w[1:n]` for weights, number of objects `n`, and maximum capacity of knapsack `M`. This is shown in Algorithm 16.9.

ALGORITHM 16.9

```
Algorithm DKnapsack (p, w, n, M)
begin
S⁰ = {(0, 0)}
for i = 0 to n - 1
begin
   Sᵢ₁ = {(p, w) | for all (x, y) ∈ Sⁱ, compute (p, w) = (x + pᵢ₊₁,
y + wᵢ₊₁)}
   Sⁱ⁺¹ = MergeAndPurge(Sⁱ, Sⁱ₁)
end
Let (pₓ, wₓ) be the last pair in Sⁿ.
(pᵧ, wᵧ) = (p′ + pₙ, w′ + wₙ),
where w′ is the largest w in any pair in Sⁿ such that w + wₙ ≤ M
Trace back for xₙ, xₙ₋₁, …, x₁
if(pₓ > pᵧ) then
   xₙ = 0
else
   xₙ = 1
Trace back for (xₙ₋₁, …, x₁)
end
```

The complexity of the algorithm depends on how S^i and S_1^i are represented.

16.5 PATTERN MATCHING

Pattern matching is the process of finding the presence of a particular string (pattern) in the given string (text). Let us consider an example of string `S` as 'prospect' and the pattern string `P` as 'spe'. Here, the pattern `P` exists in the string `S`, whereas pattern 'spet' does not exist in string `S`. There are plenty of applications where this concept is needed such as searching a name in the phone directory of a mobile or searching for document on the web that includes text of a particular pattern. A few such applications are as follows:

1. Database search
2. Search engine
3. Text editors
4. Intrusion detection
5. Natural language processing
6. Feature detection in digitized images

Starting from a simple approach, there exists a wide number of popular techniques for string pattern search. The most popular are the following:

1. Brute-force approach
2. Boyer–Moore algorithm
3. Knuth–Morris–Pratt algorithm
4. Robin–Karp algorithm
5. Text partitioning algorithm
6. Semi-numerical algorithm

Let us revise a few preliminary concepts related to string pattern search before learning a few of these popular techniques.

String A string is a finite sequence of symbols that are chosen from a set or alphabet (Fig. 16.2). Alphabet is a set of characters or symbols.

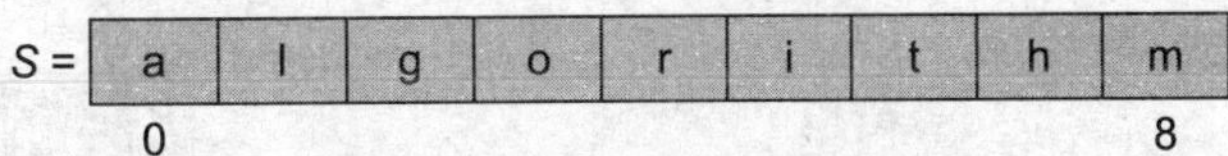

Fig. 16.2 An example string

Substring A substring or subsequence of a string is a subset of the symbols in a string where the order of elements is preserved.

Suffix A suffix of *S* is a substring *S*[*i*, …, *m* – 1], where *i* ranges between 0 and *m* – 1. For example, let us consider string *S* = algorithm.
Possible suffixes of *S* are the following:

Algorithm, lgorithm, gorithm, orithm, rithm, ithm, thm, hm, m

Prefix Prefix is a letter or group of letters attached to the beginning of a word that partly indicates its meaning.

For example, sort *S* as in Fig. 16.3.

S =

a	l	g	o	r	i	t	h	m
0								8

Fig. 16.3 An example string

A prefix of *S* is a substring *S*[0, …, *i*] where *i* ranges between 0 and *m* – 1.

All possible prefixes of `S` are listed as follows:

Algorithm, algorithm, algorit, algori, algor, algo, alg, al, a

16.5.1 Brute-force Approach

This is a simple straightforward approach based on the comparison of a pattern character by character with a string. Let the pattern `P` be a string with length `m` that is to be searched in text `T`, which is a complete string (or paragraph) with length `n`. In the brute-force approach, the first character of the pattern is compared with the first character of the text, and if we succeed, the process is repeated with the second character, and so on. If we come across a mismatch, then we slide the pattern ahead by one character and try again. When we find a match, we return the position of its starting location.

The steps involved in this approach are as follows:

1. Adjust the pattern `P` at the beginning of the text.
2. Start moving from left to right and compare the character of pattern to the corresponding character in text.
3. Continue with step 2 until successful (all characters of the pattern are matched) or unsuccessful (a mismatch is detected).

Let us consider string `T` as follows:

`T[0...n - 1] =`

T =	s	a	n	j	i	v	a	n	i
	0								8

where pattern `P[0...m - 1]` is given by

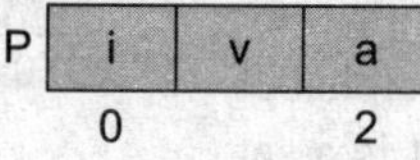

Let us search now.

Attempt 1 Here, the characters do not match. Try again by comparing `P[0]` with `T[1]` onwards. `T[0]` is compared with `P[0]`.

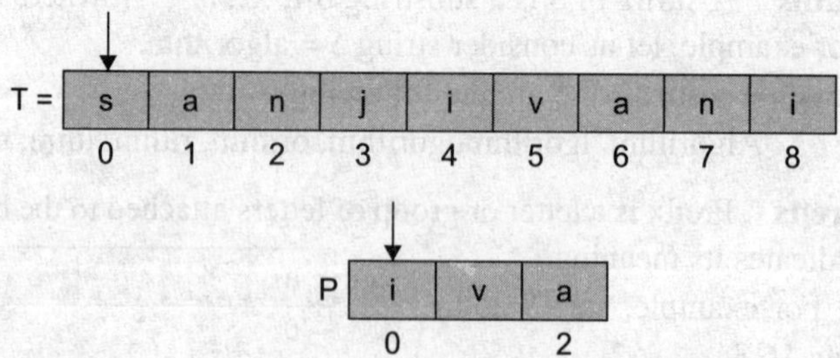

Attempt 2 Let us compare `T[1]` with `P[0]`, where the characters do not match; let us try again by comparing `P[0]` with `T[1]` onwards.

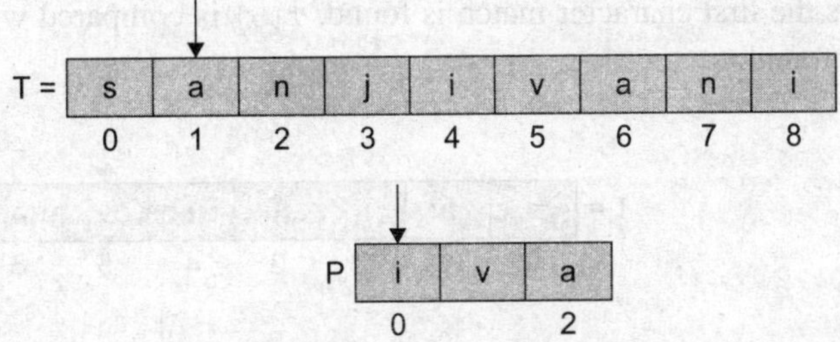

Attempt 3 Let us compare `T[2]` with `P[0]`. Here too, the characters do not match.

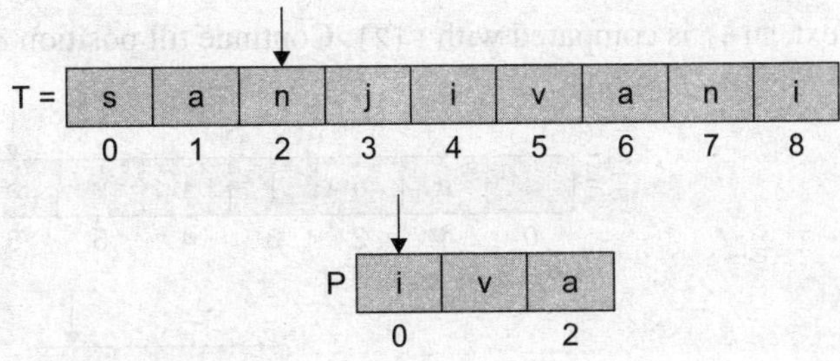

Attempt 4 Now, `T[3]` is compared with `P[0]`.

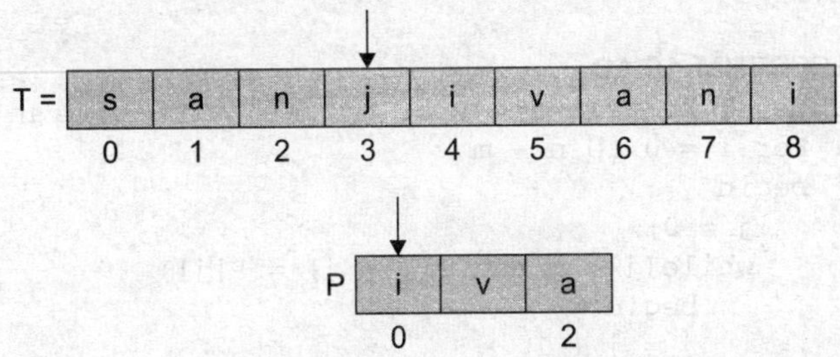

Again, the match is not found.

Attempt 5 Now, let us compare `T[4]` with `P[0]`, and the characters match.

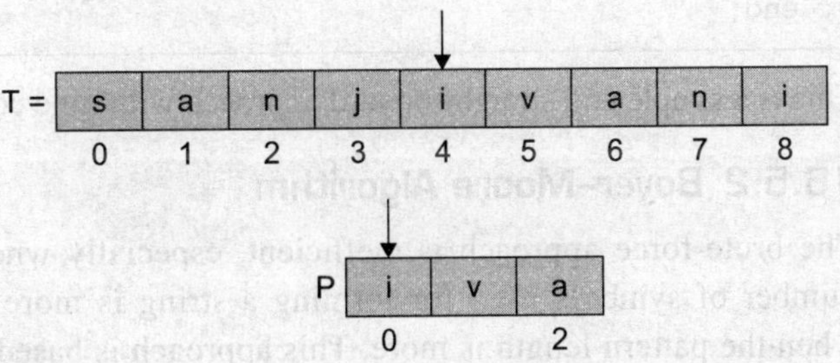

As the first character match is found, `T[5]` is compared with `P[1]`, and here, the match is found.

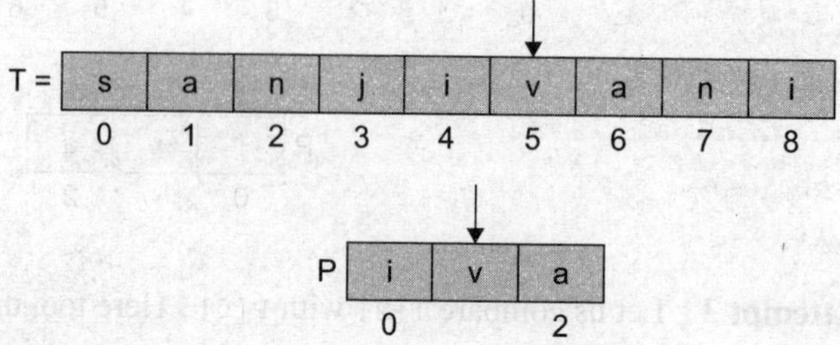

Next, `T[6]` is compared with `P[2]`. Continue till position 8 of the text string.

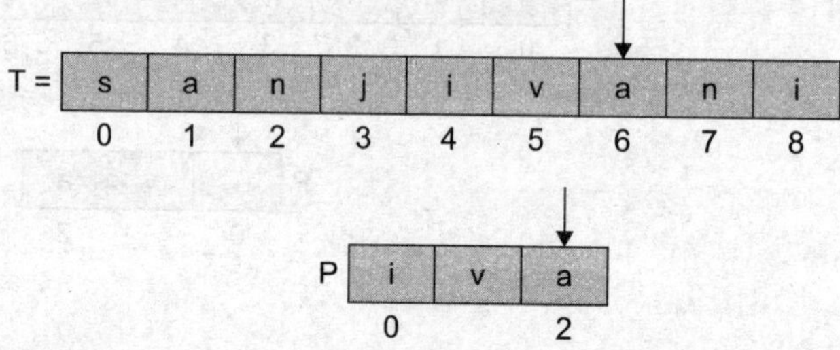

Algorithm 16.10 illustrates this approach.

ALGORITHM 16.10

```
1. Let T be text and P be pattern with size n and m, respectively
2. For i = 0 to n - m
   begin
      j = 0;
      while(j < m and T[i + j] = P[j])
         begin
         j = j + 1
         end
      if(j = m) Print "Match found at position i", goto 4
   end
3. print "No match found"
4. end
```

This is a simple and straightforward approach with time complexity O(*mn*).

16.5.2 Boyer–Moore Algorithm

The brute-force approach is inefficient, especially when the alphabet is large (the number of symbols used for forming a string is more as in natural language) and when the pattern length is more. This approach is based on the logic that it is necessary to examine every character in text to locate a pattern as a substring. To reduce the time complexity of brute-force approach, the researchers Boyer and Moore have developed an efficient pattern matching algorithm. Instead of sliding by one character to the right at a time, in Boyer–Moore approach, the sliding to the right is done in longer steps.

The algorithm scans the character of pattern from right to left beginning with the rightmost character. If the text symbol compared with the rightmost pattern symbol does not occur in the pattern at all, then the pattern can be shifted by `m` positions (where `m` is length of pattern).

In this approach, the key is to use the information learned in failed match attempts to decide what to do next. This is done with the use of pre-computed tables. For text `T` of length `n` and pattern `P` of length `m`, the algorithm checks to see if we have a successful match of `P` at a particular location in `T` and work backwards. So, if we are checking to see if we have a match starting at `T[i]`, we start by checking to see if `P[m - 1]` matches `T[i + m - 1]`, and so on.

The reason for this backwards approach is to make more progress in case the attempted match fails. For example, suppose we are trying to match the pattern `P` = 'Sanj' at position `i` of the input `T` = 'MrsKaleSanjivani'. However, at `T[i + 4]`, we find the character 'r'. The character 'r' does not appear anywhere in 'Sanj', so we can skip ahead and start looking for a match at `T[i + 5]` since we know that 'k' prevents a match from occurring any earlier.

Let us consider an example.

```
T = BEHIND EVERY SUCCESSFUL MAN THERE IS A WOMAN
P = WOMAN
```

Now, the comparison between the `D` and `W` found a mismatch, so shift the pattern by five positions because `D` does not occur in the pattern.

The best case of Boyer–Moore algorithm is attained if at each attempt the first compared text symbol does not occur in the pattern. The algorithm requires $O(n/m)$.

16.5.3 Knuth–Morris–Pratt Algorithm

We have studied two approaches for searching a pattern in a string. The researchers Knuth, Morris, and Pratt proposed a linear time algorithm for the string matching problem. In this approach, a matching time of $O(n)$ is achieved by avoiding comparisons with characters of `T` that have previously been involved in comparison with some element of the pattern `P` to be matched so that backtracking is avoided.

```
BEHINDEVERYSUCCESSFULMANTHEREISAWOMAN
          |    \
        WOMAN
             WOMAN
```

Before we learn the algorithm, let us discuss its components.

Prefix Function π

The prefix function π for a pattern embeds knowledge about how the pattern matches against its shifts. This information is to be used to avoid unnecessary shifts of the pattern `P` to avoid backtracking on the text `T`.

KMP Matcher

The KMP matcher finds the occurrence of the pattern P in text T and returns the number of shifts of P, after which the occurrence is found taking T, P, and prefix function π as inputs.

A pseudocode to compute the prefix function π is shown in Algorithm 16.11.

ALGORITHM 16.11

```
1. start
2. Compute length of pattern m = length[P]
3. Initially, let π[1] =0 and k = 0
4. for i = 2 to m
   while(k > 0 and p[k + 1]!= p[q]) do
      begin
      k = π[k]
   if p[k + 1] = p[i]
      then k = k + 1
      π[i] = k
      end
5. return π
```

Let us consider an example for computing π (Fig. 16.4) for the following pattern P:

P = a b a b a c a

The KMP matcher, with pattern P, text T, and prefix function π as the input finds a match of P in T. The pseudocode in Algorithm 16.12 computes the matching component of KMP algorithm.

ALGORITHM 16.12

```
Algorithm KMP matcher
1. start
2. let n denote length of text T
   Compute n = length[T] and m ← length[P]
3. π = compute prefix function(P)
4. j = 0
5. for i= 1 to n do
   while j > 0 and P[j + 1] != T[i] do
      begin
      j = π[j]
   if P[j + 1] = T[i]
      then j = j + 1
   if j = m
      then print "Pattern occurs with shift i - m"
      j = π[j]
      end
6. stop
```

Initially: m = length[p] = 7
π[1] = 0
k = 0

Step 1: q = 2, k = 0
π[2] = 0

q	1	2	3	4	5	6	7
p	a	b	a	b	a	c	a
π	0	0					

Step 2: q = 3, k = 0
π[3] = 1

q	1	2	3	4	5	6	7
p	a	b	a	b	a	c	a
π	0	0	1				

Step 3: q = 4, k = 1
π[4] = 2

q	1	2	3	4	5	6	7
p	a	b	a	b	a	c	a
π	0	0	1	2			

Step 4: q = 5, k = 2
π[5] = 3

q	1	2	3	4	5	6	7
p	a	b	a	b	a	c	a
π	0	0	1	2	3		

Step 5: q = 6, k =3
π[6] = 1

q	1	2	3	4	5	6	7
p	a	b	a	b	a	c	a
π	0	0	1	2	3	1	

Step 6: q = 7, k = 1
π[7] = 1

q	1	2	3	4	5	6	7
p	a	b	a	b	a	c	a
π	0	0	1	2	3	1	1

After iterating 6 times, the prefix function computation is complete: →

q	1	2	3	4	5	6	7
p	a	b	a	b	a	c	a
π	0	0	1	2	3	1	1

Fig. 16.4 An example for computing π

Note that KMP finds every occurrence of a P in text T, and hence, KMP does not terminate; rather, it searches the remaining part of T for any more occurrences of P.

Let us consider T and pattern P as follows:

Text T =

b	a	c	b	a	b	a	b	a	b	a	c	a	c	a

Pattern P =

a	b	a	b	a	c	a

Let us execute the KMP algorithm to find whether P occurs in the string S or not, and if yes, we find the number of its occurrences.

For P, the prefix function π was computed previously and is as follows:

Q	1	2	3	4	5	6	7
P	a	b	a	b	a	c	a
π	0	0	1	2	3	1	1

Initially, n = size of S = 15

m = size of P = 7

Step 1: i = 1, q = 0

Now, compare P[1] with S[1].

We notice that P[1] does not match with S[1].

So, let us shift P by one position to the right.

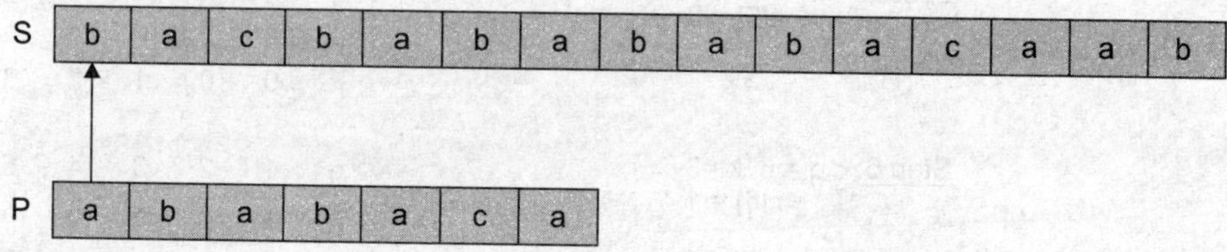

Step 2: Now, i = 2, q = 0

Comparing P[1] with S[2], we see that there is a match; P is not shifted.

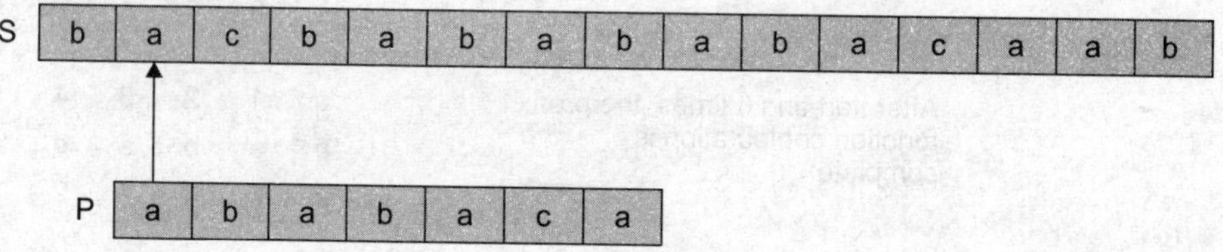

Step 3: Currently, i = 3, q = 1. Comparing P[2] with S[3], we notice that P[2] does not match with S[3].

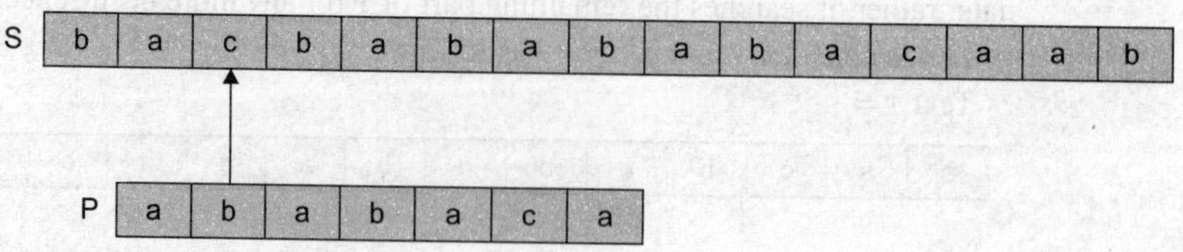

Now, backtrack on P and compare P[1] and S[3].

Step 4: Here, i = 4, q = 0; comparing P[1] with S[4], we notice that P[1] does not match with S[4].

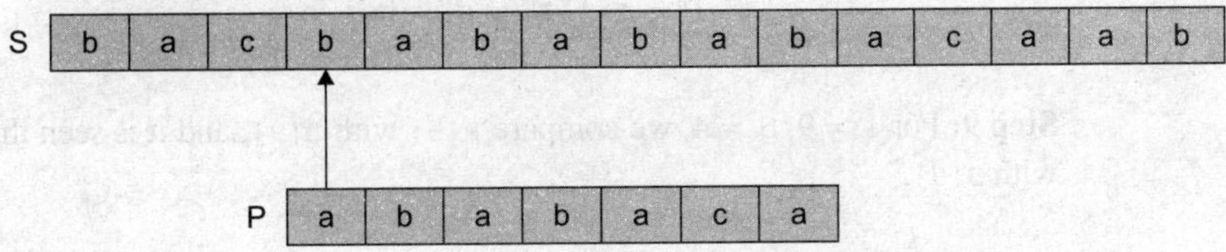

Step 5: Currently, i = 5, q = 0; comparing P[1] with S[5], we notice that P[1] matches with S[5].

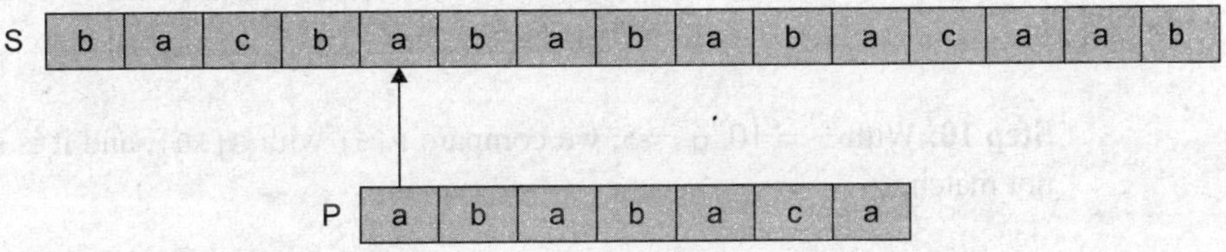

Step 6: For i = 6, q = 1, we compare P[2] with S[6]. We see that P[2] matches with S[6].

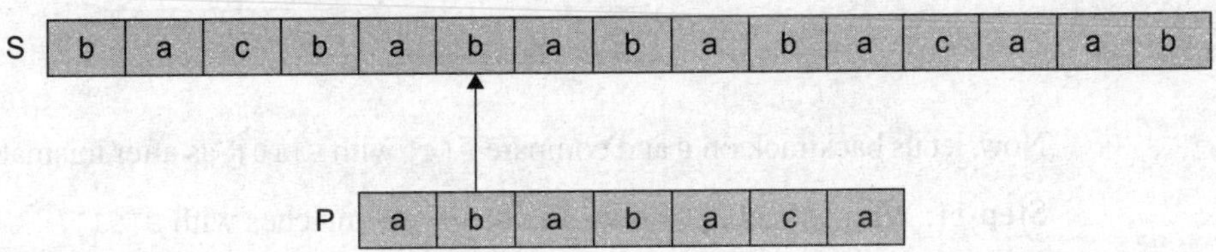

Step 7: For i = 7, q = 2, we compare P[3] with S[7], and we see that P[3] matches with S[7].

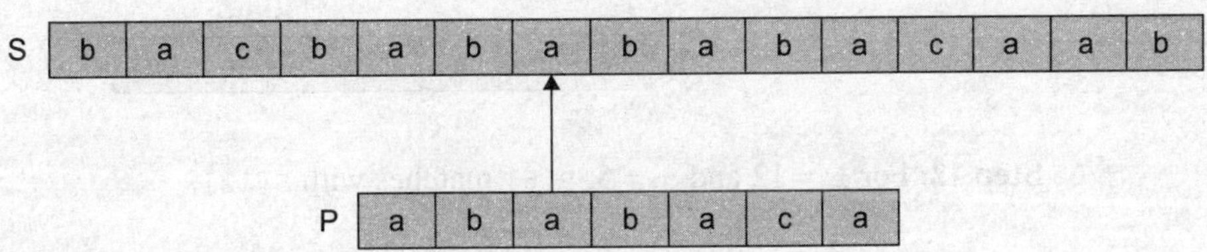

Step 8: With i = 8, q = 3, and when P[4] and S[8] are compared, it results in P[4] matching with S[8].

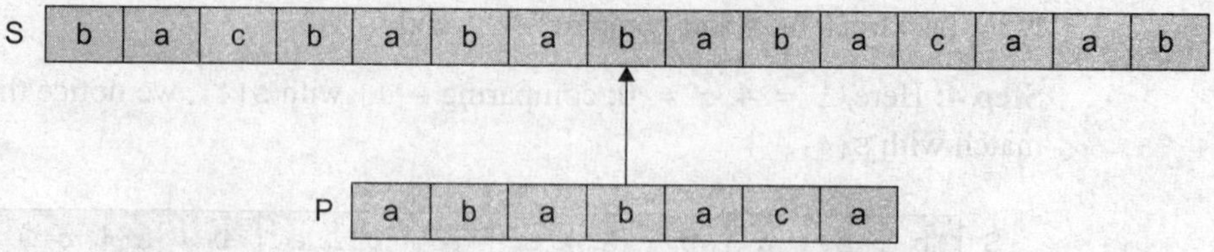

Step 9: For `i` = 9, `q` = 4, we compare `P[5]` with `S[9]`, and it is seen that `P[5]` matches with `S[9]`.

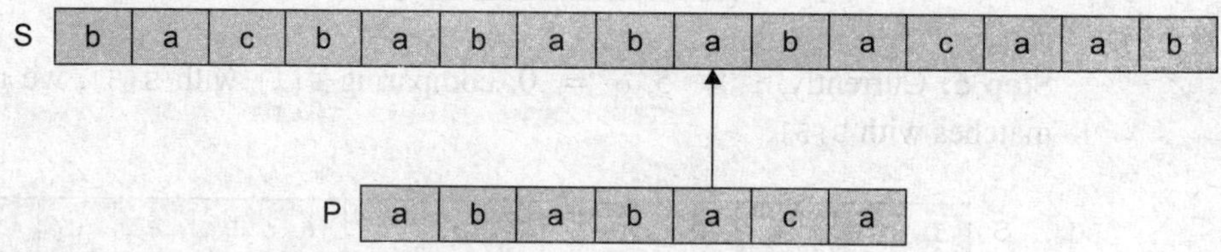

Step 10: With `i` = 10, `q` = 5, we compare `P[6]` with `S[10]`, and it is seen that they do not match.

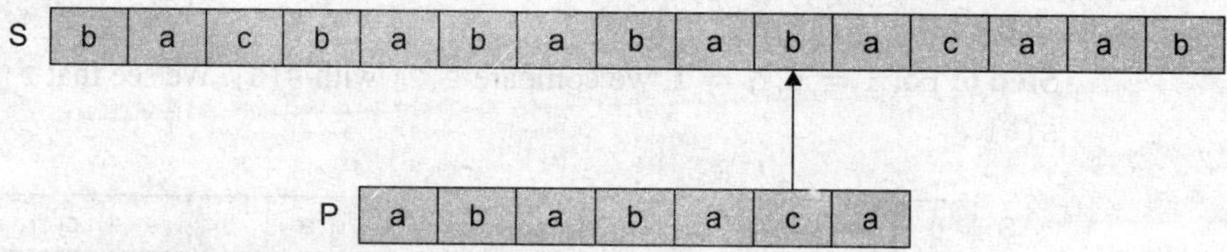

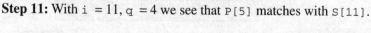

Now, let us backtrack on `P` and compare `P[4]` with `S[10]`, as after mismatch, `q` = π`[5]` = 3.

Step 11: With `i` = 11, `q` = 4 we see that `P[5]` matches with `S[11]`.

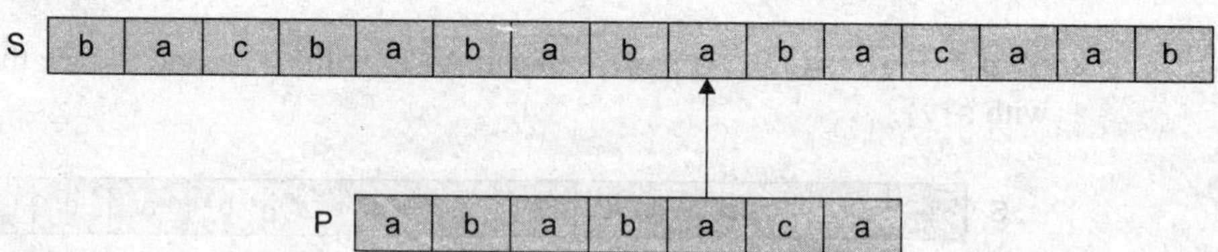

Step 12: For `i` = 12 and `q` = 5, `P[6]` matches with `S[12]`.

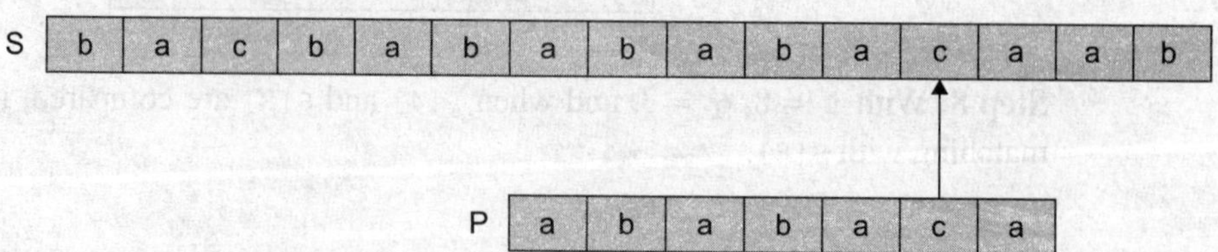

Step 13: With `i` = 13 and `q` = 6, `P[7]` matches with `S[13]`.

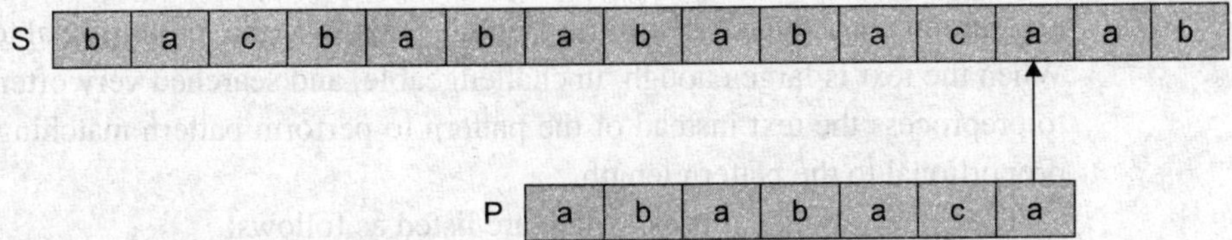

Here, we notice that the pattern `P` has been found in `S`. The total number of shifts that took place for the matches to be found are `i` – `m` = 13 – 7 = 6 shifts.

Let us compute the time complexity of this algorithm. We can see that `compute_prefix_function()`, uses `for` loop from step 4 to step 10 and runs `m` times. Steps 1–3 take constant time. Hence, the running time of `compute_prefix_function()` is $\Theta(m)$. In `KMP matcher`, the `for` loop beginning in step 5 runs `n` times, that is, as long as the length of the string `S`. Since steps 1–4 take constant time, the running time is dominated by this `for` loop. Thus, the running time of the matching function is $\Theta(n)$.

16.6 TRIES

see a book? sell stock!

see a bush! stop!

bid stock! buy book!

stock sell? buy book!

Fig. 16.5 Example text for query search

We have discussed algorithms that efficiently search for patterns in a text. Let us now learn about a compact data structure that represents a set of strings (such as all the words in a text) known as *tries*. A trie is a tree-based data structure for storing strings to make pattern matching faster. A trie helps in pattern matching in time that is proportional to the length of the pattern. Tries can be used to perform prefix query for information retrieval. Prefix query searches for the longest prefix of a given string that matches a prefix of some string in the tries. Figure 16.5 shows an example text used in a query search.

A trie for this text is drawn as in Fig. 16.6.

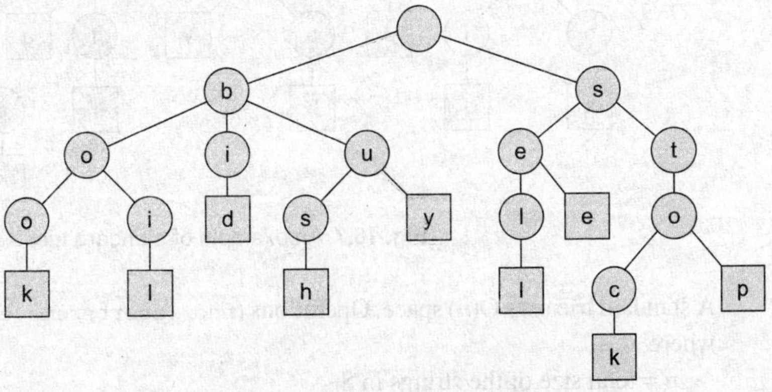

Fig. 16.6 An example trie

It is true that preprocessing the pattern speeds up pattern matching queries. Once preprocessed, the pattern in time is proportional to the pattern length. The Boyer–Moore algorithm then searches an arbitrary English text in a time proportional to the text length. When the text is large enough, unchallengeable, and searched very often, it is suggested to preprocess the text instead of the pattern to perform pattern matching queries in time proportional to the pattern length.

There are variants of tries, which are listed as follows:

1. Standard tries
2. Compressed tries
3. Suffix tries

16.6.1 Standard Tries

We have already seen that a trie is a tree-based data structure for storing strings to make pattern matching faster. For pattern matching to be done in time that is proportional to the length of the pattern, trie has proved to be one of the best solutions. Among variants of tries, the standard trie is the most popular and simplest approach.

The standard trie for a set of strings *S* is an ordered tree such that

1. each node but the root is labelled with a character;
2. the children of a node are alphabetically ordered;
3. the paths from the external nodes to the root yield the strings of *S*.

For example, consider the standard trie in Fig. 16.7 for the set of strings *S* = { bush, boil, bid, book, buy, sell, stock, stop }

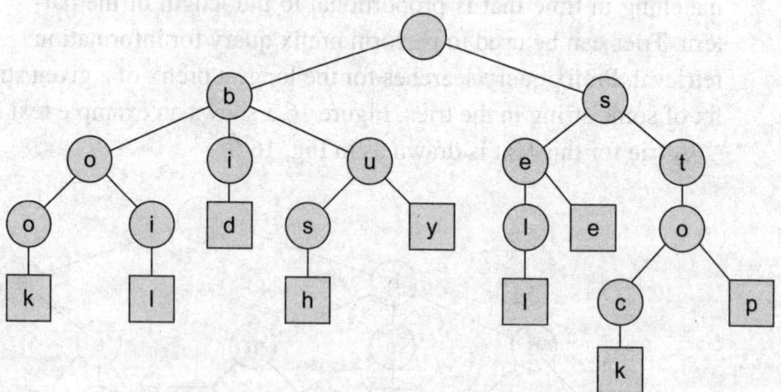

Fig. 16.7 An example of standard trie

A standard trie uses O(*n*) space. Operations (`find`, `insert`, `remove`) each take time O(*dm*), where

n = total size of the strings in S

m = size of the string parameter of the operation
d = alphabet size

Another example is shown in Fig. 16.8.

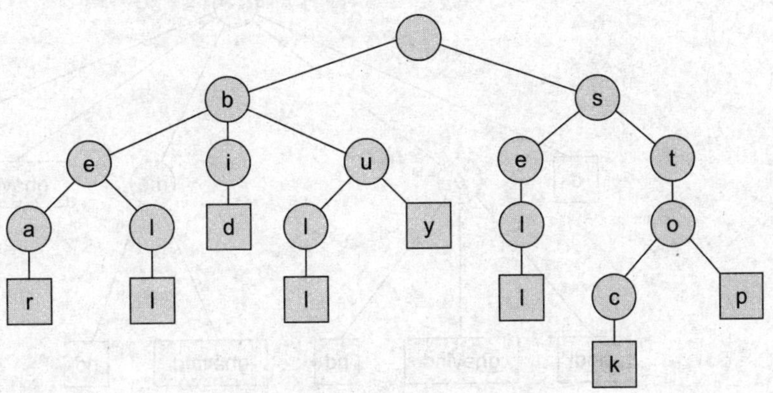

Fig. 16.8 Another example of standard trie

16.6.2 Compressed Tries

Similar to the standard trie, a compressed trie (Fig. 16.9) is a tree-based data structure for storing strings in order to make pattern matching much faster. This is an optimized approach for pattern matching specially suitable for applications where time is a more crucial factor. Following are the unique characteristics of compressed trie:

1. A compressed trie (or *Patricia trie*) has internal nodes of degree at least 2.
2. It is obtained from standard trie by compressing chains of redundant nodes.

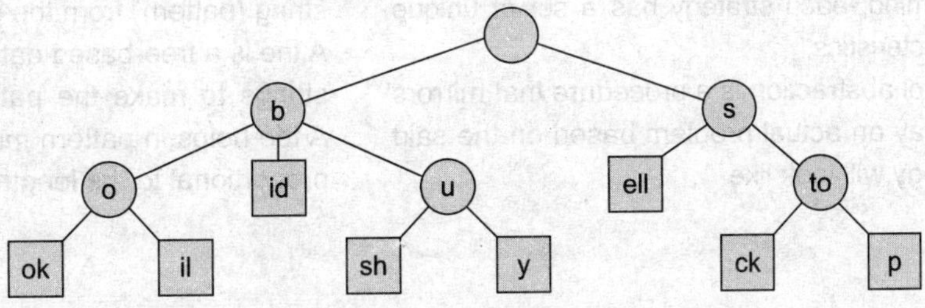

Fig. 16.9 Compressed trie

16.6.3 Suffix Tries

A suffix trie is a compressed trie for all the suffixes of a text. This is a compressed trie, and hence, possesses all features a compressed trie and makes it more powerful for making a search faster as it includes all suffixes of a text. Let us consider an example as in Fig. 16.10.

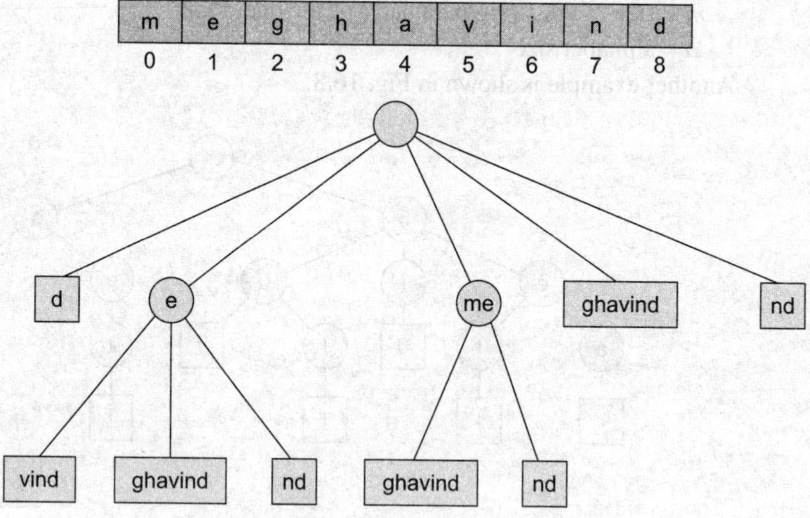

Fig. 16.10 Suffix trie

RECAPITULATION

- Algorithms are used as design tools for solving real world problems.
- Asymptotic notation helps us to define lower and upper bounds of time complexity.
- Commonly used algorithm strategies are divide-and-conquer, greedy method, and dynamic programming; each strategy has a set of unique characteristics.
- Control abstraction is a procedure that mirrors the way an actual problem based on the said strategy will look like.
- Dynamic programming is an algorithm design method that can be used when the solution to a problem may be viewed as the result of a sequence of decisions.
- Pattern matching can be defined as the process of finding the presence of a particular string (pattern) from the given string (text).
- A trie is a tree-based data structure for storing strings to make the pattern matching faster. A trie helps in pattern matching in time that is proportional to the length of the pattern.

KEY TERMS

Asymptotic analysis In computer science, the analysis of algorithms considers the performance of algorithms when applied to very large datasets. Asymptotic complexity helps us quantify the performance measures of an algorithm.

Divide-and-conquer method This method is an algorithm design paradigm in which a problem is broken down into two or more subproblems of the same type, which are then solved independently. These solutions are then combined to provide a solution to the parent problem.

Dynamic programming Dynamic programming is well suited to problems where a recursive algorithm would solve many of the subproblems repeatedly. The dynamic programming algorithm stores results, or solutions, for small subproblems. Later on, it uses these stored solutions instead of recomputing them to solve larger subproblems.

Greedy method Greedy method is defined as an algorithm paradigm that follows the problem-solving heuristic of making the locally optimal choice at each stage with the hope of finding the optimum solution.

Pattern matching It is the process of finding the presence of a particular string (pattern) from a given string (text).

Trie A trie is a tree-based data structure for storing strings to make pattern matching faster. It helps in pattern matching in time that is proportional to the length of pattern. It is useful in performing prefix query for information retrieval.

EXERCISES

Multiple choice questions

1. Which of the following algorithm design techniques is used in quicksort algorithm?
   (a) Dynamic programming
   (b) Backtracking
   (c) Divide-and-conquer
   (d) Greedy
2. Merge sort uses
   (a) triangulization
   (b) quicksort
   (c) n-queens
   (d) heuristics
3. Dynamic programming is based on the principle of
   (a) optimality
   (b) heuristics
   (c) regularity
   (d) none of the above
4. The complexity function of which of the following strategies is generally in the form of a recurrence relation?
   (a) Dynamic
   (b) Divide-and-conquer
   (c) Both (a) and (b)
   (d) None of the above
5. Time complexity of ternary search is
   (a) $\log_3 n$
   (b) $\log_2 3$
   (c) $\log_2 n$
   (d) n^3
6. Time complexity is
   (a) the space required by a program
   (b) an amount of machine time necessary for running a program
   (c) the time required for a programmer to code
   (d) all of the above
7. The worst case complexity is (for instance, of size *n*)
   (a) a function defined by maximum number of steps taken
   (b) a function defined by average number of steps taken
   (c) a function defined by minimum number of steps taken
   (d) all of the above
8. The best case complexity (for instance, of size *n*) is
   (a) a function defined by maximum number of steps taken
   (b) a function defined by average number of steps taken
   (c) a function defined by minimum number of steps taken
   (d) all of the above

Review questions

1. What is an algorithm? Write the essential properties and the performance measures of an algorithm.

2. Explain the characteristics and uses of greedy and dynamic programming algorithmic strategies.
3. What is big O notation? Arrange the following functions by growth value:

   $N, \sqrt{N}, N^2, N\log_2 N, N\log_2^2 N, N^2, N^3, 2^N$

4. Write a C program for binary search and compute its time complexity.
5. Write a C program for ternary search and compute its time complexity.
6. What do you mean by best case, average case, and worst case time complexity? Give suitable examples.
7. Find the frequency count of the following programs:

   (a)
```
for(i = 1; i <= n; i++)
    for(j = 1; j <= i; j++)
        x = x + 1;
```
   (b)
```
i = 1;
while(i <= n)
{
    x = x + 1;
    i = i + 1;
}
```
8. Find the frequency count of the following programs:

   (a)
```
for(i = 1; i <= n; i++)
    for(j = 1; j <= n; j++)
        a = a + 2;
```
   (b)
```
i = 1;
do {
    x = x + 2;
    i++;
} while(i <= n);
```
   (c)
```
for i = 1 to n do
    for j = i + 1 to n do
        for k = j + 1 to n  do
            x = x + 1;
```
   (d)
```
i = 1
do
{
    x++;
    if(i == 10)
        break;
    i++;
} while(i <= n);
```
9. Write the control abstraction for the following algorithm strategies:
   (a) Divide-and-conquer
   (b) Greedy method
   (c) Dynamic programming
10. Compare greedy and dynamic strategies.
11. Give typical applications in which the divide–conquer is the best suitable algorithmic strategy.
12. Describe each of the following with respect to their unique characteristics, control abstraction, and an example:
    (a) Divide-and-conquer
    (b) Dynamic
    (c) Greedy
13. Write a quicksort algorithm. Analyse the same with respect to time complexity.

Answers to multiple choice questions

1. (c) 2. (c) 3. (a) 4. (c) 5. (a) 6. (b) 7. (a) 8. (c)

APPENDIX OVERVIEW OF C++ PROGRAMMING

The most suitable language for the implementation of abstract data types (ADTs) is the object-oriented C++, as it implements them as a class. We have already discussed ADTs in Chapter 1; let us now revise the concept of ADTs.

A.1 ABSTRACT DATA TYPE

A data type consists of a collection of values together with a set of basic operations defined on these values. A data type is called an abstract data type if a programmer can use it without having access to it and without knowing the details of how the values and operations are implemented.

Specifying a data structure by the details of its implementation means that if the programmer wants to change the representation of the data type, he/she will have to find every piece of code that manipulates the data and make sure it corresponds to the new definition. The best way to avoid this problem is to make sure that all data types defined are ADTs.

An ADT expresses an all-inclusive collection of data values and operations. The term *data structure* means the study of data and refers to the representation of data objects within a program, that is, the implementation of a structured relationship.

A software professional's idea of a data structure has undergone an evolution in the last few years. Data structures are implemented based on the abstract properties of the classes of data objects in addition to how these data objects might be represented in a program. Depending on this point of view, a data object is characterized by its type (for the user) or by its structure (for the implementer).

Hence, the study of data structures has now been popularly referred to as the study of ADTs, which covers the study of classes of objects whose logical behaviour is defined by a set of operations.

The traditional model of studying data structures is based on the characteristics of the implementation of structures. For example, consider the example of stacks and queues which are linear lists with restricted access. The properties of stacks and queues can be represented as last in first out (LIFO) and first in first out (FIFO), respectively. However, the user of these two ADTs is not interested about the location where the data is being processed in the data structure or about the restricted access. In fact, the user does not (rather should not) care about what happens when an item is stored in a stack or a queue and is only interested in what is inserted or what is deleted. Thus, it is essential to learn data structures as ADTs.

Let us now discuss how to implement ADTs using C++.

A.2 INTRODUCTION TO C++

To overcome some of the shortcomings of the C language, Bjarne Stroustrup of AT&T Bell Laboratories developed C++ in the early 1980s. Stroustrup designed C++ to be a better version of C. Most of C is a subset of C++, and so most C programs are also C++ programs. Thus, C++ is also known as *C with classes*. However, unlike C, C++ supports the object-oriented programming (OOP) paradigm.

A.2.1 Sample C++ Program

A typical C++ code uses two kinds of files—header files and source files. Header files have a '.h' extension. They allow programmers to separate certain parts of the source code into reusable files. These files commonly contain forward declarations of classes, subroutines, variables, and other identifiers. Declarations of standardized identifiers from more than one source file can be placed in a single header file, and programs can then include these files whenever the header contents are required. One such header file is <iostream.h>, which stands for input/output stream, as used in Program Code A.1. The header file iostream provides basic input and output services for C++ programs. It uses the objects cin, cout, cerr, and clog for sending data to and from the standard streams input, output, error, and log, respectively.

PROGRAM CODE A.1

```
//A sample C++ program
#include<iostream.h>
int main()
{
   float Base, Height, Area;
   cout << "Enter Base:";
   cin >> Base;
   cout << "Enter Height:";
   cin >> Height;
   Area = (Base * Height)/2;
   cout << "Area of Triangle = ";
   cout << Area;
   return;
}

Output:
   Enter Base: 7
   Enter Height: 6
   Area of Triangle = 21
```

In the beginning of this program, a header file `<iostream.h>` is included, which is system-defined. These header files can also be user-defined. Source files are used to store C++ source code. The suffix used is generally '.cpp', which depends on the compiler in use.

A.2.2 C++ Statements and Operators

Syntax and semantics of statements in C++ are similar to that used in C. In addition, C++ operators are identical to operators in C except `new` and `delete` operators. Another difference is that C++ uses the shift left << and the shift right >> operators. However, an important difference is that C++ allows operator overloading, that is, an operator is allowed to have different functionalities depending on the type of operands.

A.2.3 Comments in C++

A programmer is often very clear about the objective and outcome of the code during the coding phase. However, when someone else tries to understand or modify the code, or even when the programmer returns to the program after a long period of time, it could be quite confusing and unclear. A comment is a text, used to annotate a code for future reference, that the compiler ignores but is useful for programmers. In C++, a programmer can use the following two types of comments:

1. Block comment—used to include multiple lines as a comment

   /* block of statements
   ...
   */

2. Line comment—used for single line comments

   // Comment line here

A.2.4 Input/Output in C++

To perform I/O in C++, we have to include the system-defined header file `iostream.h`. The keyword `cout` is used to output data to the standard output device is separated from each entity being printed by the << operator. The entries being output are printed from left to right on the standard output device. The shift left operator << is overloaded in C++. It is also called *output operator* or *insertion operator*. It can be used to display data of any type. Program Code A.2 illustrates the use of iostream in C++.

PROGRAM CODE A.2

```
// A C++ program explaining—I/O stream
#include<iostream.h>
main()
{
    int a = 110;
    float b = 0.11;
```

```
    char MyName[];
    cout << "a:" << a << endl;
    cout << "b:" << b << endl;
    cout << "Your name please:";
    cin << MyName;
    cout << "Welcome dear" << MyName << "to the world
of C++!";
}

Output:
    a: 110
    b: 0.11
    Your name please: Saurabh
    Welcome dear Saurabh to the world of C++!
```

The keyword `cin` is used for input in C++. The operator >> is used to separate the variables being input or output. A whitespace is used to separate items corresponding to different variables on the standard input device. The shift right operator >> is overloaded by C++ for this purpose. It is also called *input operator* or *extraction operator*. Program Code A.3 uses `cin` and `cout` for accepting two integers from the user and then displaying the sum of the two input numbers.

PROGRAM CODE A.3

```
//A sample C++ program for illustrating cin and cout
#include<iostream.h>
main()
{
    int a, b;
    cout << "Enter values of a & b:";
    cin >> a >> b;
    cout << a << " +" << b << "=" << a + b;
}


Output:
    Enter values of a & b: 5 6
    5 + 6 = 11
```

An advantage of I/O in C++ is that it is format-free, that is, the programmer is not required to use formatting symbols to specify the type and order of items being input or output. Similar to other C++ operators, I/O operators can also be overloaded.

A.3 FUNCTIONS IN C++

There are two kinds of functions in C++, namely regular functions and member functions. Member functions those that are associated with a specif ic C++ class. Both types of functions are similar in all features excluding their scope.

A function consists of a function name, a list of arguments (input), a return type (output), and a body (code that implements a function). In Program Code A.4, `Max` is the function name, `float a` and `float b` are the list of arguments, where float is the return type, and the statements between { and } form the body of the function. Similarly, `Square()` is a function with `int a` as argument and int as the return type. Here, `SayHello()` is another function that has no argument, and it does not return any value, so its return type is void.

PROGRAM CODE A.4

```
// A sample C++ program—function
void SayHello()
{
   cout << "Hello, welcome to the world of C with
   classes";
}
int Square(int a)
{
   return a * a;
}
float max(float a, float b)
{
   if(a > b)
      return a;
   else
      return b;
}
void main()
{
   int x, y, z;
   SayHello();
   cout << endl;
  cout << "Enter number";
   cin >> x;
   cout << "Square of" << x << "is =" << Square(x);
   cout << "\nEnter two integers";
   cin >> y >> z;
   cout << "Maximum between" << y << "and" << z <<
   "is" << max(y, z);
}
```

```
Output:
Hello, welcome to the world of C with classes
Enter number 5
Square of 5 is 25
Enter two integers 9 4
Maximum between 9 and 4 is 9
```

All functions in C++ return a value. If a function is not meant to return anything, we use void to denote its return type. A value is returned from a function by using the `return` statement. The `return` statement must return a value that is of the same type as the function's return type or should be converted to the desired type. The function terminates when a return statement is encountered. A function is invoked by supplying the actual arguments. Some examples are as follows:

A call to function `max(55.23,76.89)` returns `76.89`.
A call to function `Square(5)` returns `25`.
A call to function `SayHello` displays the message `"Hello, welcome to the world of C with classes"`.

A.3.1 Inline Function

An inline function is declared by adding the keyword inline to the function definition as in Program Code A.5. Function `PrintLine()` is an inline function, whereas function `PrintLine1()` is not.

PROGRAM CODE A.5

```
// A sample C++ program—inline function
inline void PrintLine()
{
    cout << "----------";
    cout << endl;
}
void PrintLine1(int n, char ch)
{
    for(i = 1; i <= n; i++)
        cout << ch;
    cout << endl;
}
// calling function
void main()
{
```

```
    PrintLine();
    PrintLine1(10, '$');
}

Output:
----------
$$$$$$$$$$
```

The inline keyword instructs the compiler that any calls to the inline function `Print-line()` must be replaced by the body of the called function. This eliminates the overhead from performing a function call and copying arguments when the program is executing. When a member function is defined within a class definition as in Program Code A.6, it is automatically made inline.

The objective of the `inline` and `const` keywords is to avoid the use of preprocessor directives such as `#define`. This preprocessor directive has been traditionally used to perform macro substitution. A macro is similar to a function except for the difference that functions are called whereas macros are substituted. Excessive use of preprocessor directives makes it hard to use programming tools such as debuggers and profilers (used for debugging) efficiently.

The use of an inline function is beneficial for shorter code. However, as inline function calls are replaced by function definitions, this expansion results in larger code in case of lengthy functions. The compiler may ignore the demand to make a function inline in some cases when a function is recursive or it contains static variables or loop, switch, or goto statements.

PROGRAM CODE A.6

```
// A sample C++ program—inline function
#include<iostream.h>
class ABC
{
    int a, b, c;
    public:
        void GetData()
        {
            cin << a << b << c;
        }
};
void ABC :: ShowData()
{
    cout << a << "\t" << b << "\t" << c;
}
```

Here, `ShowData()` is a member function whose code is written outside the class definition. The function `GetData()` is defined inside the class definition, and hence is considered as an inline function. If the user wishes to define a function outside the class and still wants to make it an inline function, it can be done by explicitly instructing the compiler to do so, as shown in Program Code A.7.

PROGRAM CODE A.7

```
// A sample C++ program with inline function outside
class
#include<iostream.h>
class ABC
{
   int a, b, c;
   public:
      void GetData()
      {
         cin << a << b << c;
      }
};

inline void ABC :: ShowData()
{
   cout << a << "\t" << b << "\t" << c;
}
```

We have discussed that an inline function call is replaced by its code, similar to macro expansion. However, there is one major difference between an inline function and a macro. Let us consider the code in Program Code A.8.

PROGRAM CODE A.8

```
// A sample C++ program with—macro and inline function
#include<iostream.h>
#define Square1(x) x * x
inline int Square2(int x)
{
   return x * x;
}
int main()
{
   cout << "\n Using macro" << Square1(5 + 5);
```

```
    cout << "\n Using inline function" << Square2(5 + 5);
}

Output:
    Using macro 30
    Using inline function 100
```

If we observe the output of the code, we see that the expected output is correctly provided by the inline function and not by the macro. This difference makes inline functions far superior to macros.

A.4 C++ CLASS AND ABSTRACT DATA TYPE

Classes in C++ are a natural evolution of the C notation `struct`. C++ also has the concept of structures. The only difference between a structure and a class in C++ is that, by default, the members of a class are private, whereas the members of a structure are public. Object-oriented programming encapsulates data (attributes) and functions (behaviour) into packages called classes.

A.4.1 Class

A class is a user-defined data type whose variables are objects. It is created using the keyword `class`. A class is similar to a blue print. Based on a blue print, a builder can build one or more houses. Similarly, based on a class, a programmer can create one or more objects. One class can be reused many times to make many objects of the same class. Classes enable the programmer to model objects that have certain attributes (data members) and behaviour (operations). A sample class definition is given in Program Code A.9.

PROGRAM CODE A.9

```
// A sample C++ class definition
class Time
{
    private:
        int Hour;
        int Minute;
        int Second;
    public:
        Time();
        void SetTime(int, int, int);
        void DisplayTime();
};
```

A class specification has two parts—class declaration and definition of class member functions. The class declaration describes the type and scope of its members. The general form of class declaration is as follows:

```
class class_name
{
   private data members & member functions access_specifier:
   data members & member functions access_specifier:
   data members & member functions
   .
   .
   .
}object_list;
```

Here, `object list` is optional. The access specifier can be public, private, or protected. By default, the access specifier is private. Private data and functions can be accessed only by other member functions of the same class, whereas public data and functions are accessible by other parts of the program. The protected access specifier is needed only when a class is inherited. A class declaration combines data and code together in a single package. This binding of code and data, called *encapsulation*, keeps both safe from outside interference and misuse.

Variables that are elements of a class are called *data members* or *member variables* while functions that are declared within a class are called *member functions*. Member functions can access all elements of the class of which they are a part. Data hiding is achieved by making the data members private.

Note that the member functions listed in class `Time` in Program Code A.9 are function prototypes. A class definition generally contains only the prototypes of its member functions. The definitions for the member functions can be defined elsewhere.

When a member function is defined outside the class declaration, then the definition must include the class name because there may be two or more classes that have member functions with the same name. The definition of a member function is similar to the conventional function definition with a few differences.

Scope Resolution Operator (::)

The (::) operator is called the *scope resolution operator*, and it serves a purpose similar to that of the dot operator. Both the dot operator and the scope resolution operator are used to indicate which function is a member of which class. However, the scope resolution operator is used with a class name, whereas the dot operator is used with an object, that is, with a class variable. The scope resolution operator is denoted by two colons with no space between them. The class name preceding the scope resolution operator is often called *type qualifier* because it specifies (qualifies) the function name to one particular type.

```
Return type class_name :: functionname (parameter list)
{
   function body statemen
}
```

PROGRAM CODE A.10

```
/* A sample C++ program with member function definition
outside the class */
class Time
{
    int Hour;
    int Minute;
    int Second;
    Time();
    void SetTime(int, int, int);
    void DisplayTime();
};
void Time :: SetTime()
{
    cin >> Hour;
    cin >> Minute;
    cin >> Second;
}
void Time :: DisplayTime()
{
    cout << Hour << ":" << Minute << ":" << Second;
}
```

In Program Code A.10, the member function `SetTime()` is defined. Note that here the data members `Hour`, `Minute`, and `Second` are used without providing the object and the dot operator. The definition of `SetTime()` will apply to all objects of type `Time`, but at this point, since the names of the objects are not known, they are not given.

Let us consider following piece of code:

The member function is called as

```
Time Now;
Now.SetTime()
```

With the input as 10 10 10, the time would be set as 10:10:10.

All the member names in a function definition are specialized to the name of the calling class. So, this function call is equivalent to the following (provided all three member variables are public):

```
void main()
{
    Time Now;
    cin >> Now·Hour >> Now·Minute >> Now·Second;
    Now.DisplayTime();
}
```

A.4.2 Class Members: Public and Private

Consider Program Code A.11. Here, the class definition `Time` has one new feature that is designed to ensure that no programmer who uses this class can ever directly refer to any of its member variables. Note that the class contains the keyword `private`. All the member variable names that are listed after this line are private members, that is, they cannot be accessed directly in the program except within the definition of a member function. If you try to access any of these members in the `main()` function of the program, the compiler will generate an error message.

PROGRAM CODE A.11

```
// A sample C++ program with Time as a class
class Time
{
   private:
      int Hour;
      int Minute;
      int Second;
   public:
      Time();
      void SetTime(int, int, int);
      void DisplayTime();
};
Time Birth_time;
Birth_Time·Hour = 6;    // illegal
Birth_Time·Second = 45;    // illegal
BirthTime.SetTime(10, 10, 10);    // legal
```

Any reference to these private variables (or member functions) is illegal except in the definition of member functions. Let us consider another class definition as shown in Program Code A.12.

PROGRAM CODE A.12

```
// A sample C++ program with Time as a class
class Time
{
   private:
      int Hour, Minute, Second;
      void SetTime(int, int, int);
   public:
      Time();
```

```
    void UpdateTime();
};
Time Birth_time;
BirthTime.SetTime(10, 10, 10); //   illegal as SetTime
is private
```

Note that in this class definition, the function `SetTime()` is declared a private function of the class `Time`. It is also possible to make a member function private. Similar to a private member variable, a private member function can be used in the definition of any other member function, but not elsewhere, such as the `main()` function.

```
void Time :: UpdateTime()
{
  SetTime(2, 30, 45);         // valid
}
void main()
{
  Time BirthTime;
  BirthTime·SetTime(2, 30, 45);     // illegal
  BirthTime·UpdateTime();           // valid
}
```

The keyword `public` is used to indicate public members the same way that `private` is used to indicate private members. For example, consider the following class definition:

```
class SampleClass
{
  public:
    void AAA();
    int aa;
  private:
    void BBB()
    char bb;
  public:
    double CCC();
    double cc;
};
```

A public member can be used in the main body of a program or in the definition of any function, even non-member functions. We can have any number of occurrences of the labels `public` and `private` in a class definition.

Every time a label `public:` is encountered, the list of members changes from private to public.

Every time a label `private:` is encountered, the list of members following the label becomes private members.

Let us consider the following class `Date`.

```
class Date
{
   int Day, Month, Year;
   void DisplayDate();
   void SetDate();
};
```

All the members in this class are by default private. Hence, the statements in the following function `main()` are illegal.

```
Date Today;
Today·DisplayDate();    // illegal
Today·Month = 3;    // illegal
```

By default the members of a class are private, and hence it is a good practice to always explicitly label each group of members as either public or private. The concept of public and private members can be better understood by the pictorial representation in Fig. A.1

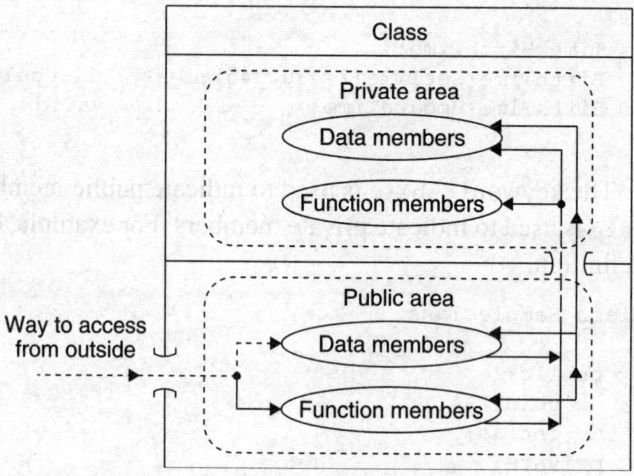

Fig. A.1 Access specifier

A.4.3 Objects

Once a class is defined, an object, which is just a variable of the class type, can be declared in the same manner as variables of any other type. Object is an instance of a class. It has physical existence.

```
Time BirthTime;
Date Today, BirthDay;
```

These declarations create a variable `BirthTime` of type `Time` and two variables `Today` and `BirthDay` of type `Date`. These class variables are called *objects* in C++. No storage space is allocated when a class is declared. The storage space is allocated only when an object of the class is declared.

A.5 STATIC CLASS MEMBERS

Both functions and data members of a class can be made static. Let us discuss each in detail.

A.5.1 Static Data Members

When a member variable's declaration is preceded with a keyword *static*, the compiler understands that only one copy of that variable exists and all objects of the class share that variable. The characteristics of a static variable are listed as follows:

1. In the case of static variables, only one copy of that variable exists and all objects of the class share that variable. Unlike regular data members, individual copies of a static member variable are not made for each object.
2. All static variables are initialized to zero when the first object is created.
3. When a static data member is declared within a class, storage is not allocated for it. It needs to be defined globally outside the class, and only then is memory allocated to it for storage.
4. Although a static variable is visible only within the class, its lifetime spans the entire program.

Consider Program Code A.13 with a class for a website with a static member variable that keeps track of the number of visitors for the site along with other member

PROGRAM CODE A.13

```
// Demonstrating static variables
class Website
{
   private:
      ...
  public:
      Website()   // constructor
      {
         No_of_Visitors++;
      }
      static int No_of_Visitors;
};
// define static variables
int Website :: No_of_Visitors;
void main()
{
   Website V1, V2;
   ...
}
```

A static variable can be accessed either by using an object or by using the class name and the scope resolution operator. By using static member variables, the need for global variables can be eliminated. Since static variables are associated with the class itself rather than the class object, they are also called *class variables*.

A.5.2 Static Member Functions

Similar to a member variable, member functions can also be declared as static. There are some restrictions on member functions to be static, which are listed as follows:

1. They can access static members of the same class.
2. They do not have 'this' pointer.
3. There cannot be a static and a non-static version of the same function.
4. They can be called using a class name as class_name :: function_name.

Program Code A.14 demonstrates the use of a static member function. For a particular company, the record of all its salesmen is maintained as name, city, total sale amount, etc. The company has branches in Delhi, Cochin, Akola, and Nashik. The program reads information about its `N` salesmen and computes the sales amount in each city and also the total sales amount.

PROGRAM CODE A.14

```
// Sample program with static member function
#include<iostream.h>
#include<conio.h>
#include<string.h>
class sale
{
   static int Delhi_Sale, Cochin_Sale, Akola_Sale,
   Nashik_Sale;
   static Total_Sale_Amount;
   char name[10], city[10];
   public:
      void get_data()
      {
         cout << "\nEnter name, city, & sale amount
         for a salesman:";
         cin >> name;
         cin >> city;
         cin >> sale_amt;
      }
     void display_data()
      {
        cout << "\n" << name << city << sale_amt;
     }
```

```
    void add_saleamt()
    {
       int x;
       x = strcmp(city, "Delhi");
       if(x == 0)
          Delhi_Sale = Delhi_Sale + sale_amt;
       x = strcmp(city, "Nashik");
       if(x == 0)
          Nashik_Sale = Nashik_Sale + sale_amt;
       x = strcmp(city, "Cochin");
       if(x == 0)
          Cochin _Sale = Cochin_Sale + sale_amt;
       x = strcmp(city, "Akola");
       if(x == 0)
          Akola_Sale = Akola_Sale + sale_amt;
       Total_Sale_Amount = Akola_Sale + Cochin_Sale
       + Delhi_Sale + Nashik_Sale;
    }
   // static member function
    static void display_saleamt()
    {
       cout << "\n Total sale amount in Akola = " <<
       Akola_Sale;
       cout << "\n Total sale amount in Delhi = " <<
       Delhi_Sale;
       cout << "\n Total sale amount in Cochin = "
       << Cochin_Sale;
       cout << "\n Total sale amount in Nashik = "
       << Nashik_Sale;
       cout << "\n Total sale amount of a company in
       all cities =";
       cout << Total_Sale_Amount;
    }
};   // end of class
//define static variables
int sale :: Delhi_Sale, Cochin_Sale, Akola_Sale,
Nashik_Sale;
int SALE :: Total_Sale_Amount;
void main()
{
   ...
   sale :: display_saleamt();
}  // end of main
```

Note that as static variables are created before any object of its class, the fundamental use of static member functions is to initialize private static data before any object is actually created.

A.6 OBJECT AS FUNCTION PARAMETER

Similar to other parameters, objects may be passed to functions. They may be passed by value or by reference. The following sections explain this concept in more detail.

A.6.1 Passing Objects to Functions

If functions are invoked according to call-by-value then the function arguments are copied to the stack through copy constructors. For larger objects, this affects the performance. Hence objects are normally passed by reference. This avoids costly duplication and allows other functions to use the same object as the calling function.

A.6.2 Returning Objects from Functions

A function may return an object to the caller. Program Code A.15 adds two complex numbers.

PROGRAM CODE A.15

```
// Adding two complex numbers
#include<iostream.h>
#include<conio.h>
class complex
{
   int Real, Imag;
   public:
      void GetNo(int a, int b)
      {
         Real = a;
         Imag = b;
      }
      void GetNo()
      {
         cout << "\n Please Input Real = " << Real;
         cout << "\n Please Input Imaginary = " <<
         Imag;
      }
      complex AddNo(complex.C2)
     {
        complex C3;
```

```
        C3.Real = Real + C2.Real;
        C3.Imag = Imag + C2.Imag;
        return(C3);
     }
     void DisplayNo()
     {
        cout << Real << "+i" << Imag;
        cout << endl;
     }
};   // end of class

void main()
{
   complex C1, C2, C3;
   C1.GetNo(10, 20);
   C2.GetNo(30, 40);
   C3 = C1.AddNo(C2);
   C1.DisplayNo();
   C2.DisplayNo();
   cout << "\n Sum of these two numbers is ";
   C3.DisplayNo();
}

Output:
10 + i20
30 + i40
Sum of these two numbers is 40 + i60
```

A.6.3 Arrays of Objects

Similar to any other variable, an array of objects can be created. Program Code A.16 demonstrates the use of array of objects.

PROGRAM CODE A.16

```
// Array of objects
#include<iostream.h>
class sample
{
   int a;
   public:
      void GetA()
```

```
        {
            cout << "\n Enter a = ";
            cin >> a;
        }
        void PutA()
        {
          cout << "\t" << a;
        }
};    end of class

void main()
{
    sample S[5];
    int i;
    for(i = 0; i < 5; i++)
    {
        S[i].GetA();
    }
    cout << "\n You entered the following values: ";
    for(i = 0; i < 5; i++)
        S[i].PutA();
}

Output:
Enter a = 1
Enter a = 2
Enter a = 3
Enter a = 4
Enter a = 5
You entered the following values: 1 2 3 4 5
```

A.6.4 Pointers to Objects

Public members of a class can be accessed through the dot (.) operator. Members of a class can be accessed through a pointer to the class. When accessing members of a class using a pointer to the object, we use the arrow (→) operator instead of the dot (.) operator as in Program Code A.17.

PROGRAM CODE A.17

```
// Pointer to class
#include<iostream.h>
class student
```

```
{
   int RollNo;
   char Name[];
   public:
      void Getdata()
      {
         Cout << "\n Enter RollNo = ";
         cin >> RollNo;
         cout << "\n Enter Name = ";
         cin >> Name;
      }
      void Putdata()
      {
         cout << "\nRollNo = ";
         cout << RollNo;
         cout << "\n Name = ";
         cout << Name;
      }
};
void main()
{
   student S1, *p;
   P = &S1;
   p->Getdata(); // This is the same as s1.Getdata()
   p->Putdata(); // This is the same as s1.Putdata()
}
```

A.7 'THIS' POINTER

When a member function is called, it is automatically passed an implicit argument that is a pointer to the object which called the function. Such a pointer is called the 'this' pointer. Program Code A.18 uses this pointer.

PROGRAM CODE A.18

```
// Use of 'this' pointer
#include<iostream.h>
class sample
{
   int a;
   float b;
  char c;
```

```
    public:
      void Getdata()
       {
          cout << "\n Enter integer value = ";
          cin >> a;
          cout << "\n Enter float value = ";
          cin >> b;
          cout << "\n Enter a character = ";
          cin >> c;
       }
       void Putdata()
       {
          cout << "\n Integer = " << a;
          cout << "\n Float = " << b;
          cout << "\n Character = " << c;
       }
       void main()
       {
          sample S1;
          S1.Getdata();
          cout << "You have entered the following
data:" << endl;
          S1.Displaydata();
       }
}

/* Here, 'this' pointer points to the object 'S1';
'this->a' refers to object S1's copy of 'a'. So the
functions get_data() and display_data() can be written
as follows */

void Getdata1()
{
   cout << "Enter int, float, char values = ";
   cin >> this->a;
   cin >> this->b;
   cin >> this->c;
}
void Displaydata2()
{
  cout << "Integer =" << this->a;
  cout << "Float = " << this->b;
```

```
    cout << "Char = " << this->c;
}

Output:
Enter integer value = 5
Enter float value = 7.8
Enter a character = g
You have entered the following data:
Integer = 5
Float = 7.8;
Character = g
```

A.8 FUNCTION OVERLOADING

Function overloading is the process of using the same name for two or more functions. However, each function should have either different types or different numbers of parameters. Through this difference, the compiler knows which function to call in any given situation. Program Code A.19 illustrates the use of overloaded functions.

PROGRAM CODE A.19

```
// To add two integers or two float numbers
void main()
{
    int iNum1 = 5, iNum2 = 6;
    float fNum1 = 5.5, fNum2 = 6.7;
    void AddNo(int, int);
    void AddNo(float, float);
    AddNo(iNum1, iNum2);    // calls version 1
    AddNo(fNum1, fNum2);    // calls version 2
}

void AddNo(int i1, int i2)    // version 1
{
    cout << "Addition of integers = " << (i1 + i2);
}

void AddNo(float f1, float f2)    // version2
{
    cout << "Addition of float nos = " << (f1 + f2);
}
```

A.8.1 Types of Polymorphism

Polymorphism is one of the important features of OOP. There are two types of polymorphism—compile-time and run-time. Compile-time polymorphism is achieved using function overloading and operator overloading, whereas run-time polymorphism is achieved using virtual functions.

A.9 CONSTRUCTORS AND DESTRUCTORS

Let us discuss about constructor, destructor, and overloading.

A.9.1 Constructors

Constructors are methods used to initialize an object during definition. Consider the following class definition:

```
class Car
{
   int mirror;
   int colour;
   public:
      Car()    // constructor
      {
         mirror = 0;    // no mirrors
         colour = 0;    // colour 0 means a white colour car
         cout << "A car is created\n";
      }
};
```

Here, the function `Car()` is a constructor.

Constructors have the same name as that of the class. They have no return value. However, similar to other functions, they can take arguments. For example, we may want to initialize a car to coordinates other than the default (0, 0). We, therefore, define a second constructor taking two integer arguments within the class as follows:

```
class Car
{
   int mirror, colour;
   public:
      Car()
      {
         mirror = colour = 0;
      }
      Car(const int M, const int C)    // Parameterized constructor
      {
         mirror = M;
         colour = C;
      }
      void setMirror(const int M);
      void setColour(const int C);
      int getMirror(){return mirror;}
```

```
    int getColour(){return colour;}
};
```

Thus, constructors can be overloaded in this manner. Constructors are implicitly called when we define objects of their classes:

```
Point WhiteCar; calls Car :: Car()
Point RedCar(2, 3); calls Car :: Car(const int, const int)
```

To create a `Point` from another `Point` by copying the properties of one object to a newly created one, the copy process needs to be taken care of. Let us consider the class `Point` in the following code. In the class `Point`, we add a third constructor that takes care of copying values from one object to the newly created one.

```
class Point
{
    int _x, _y;
    public:
        Point()
        {
            _x = _y = 0;
        }
        Point(const int x, const int y)
        {
            _x = x;
            _y = y;
        }
        Point(const Point & from)    // Copy constructor
        {
            _x = from._x;
            _y = from._y;
        }
    void setX(const int val);
    void setY(const int val);
    int getX(){return _x;}
    int getY(){return _y;}
};
```

The third constructor takes a constant reference to an object of class `Point` as an argument and assigns `_x` and `_y`, the corresponding values of the provided object.

This type of constructor is important and is known as the *copy constructor*. It is highly recommended that each class includes such a constructor, even if it is as simple as the one in the example. The copy constructor is called in the following cases:

```
Point Apoint; calls Point :: Point()
Point Bpoint(apoint); calls Point :: Point(const Point &)
Point Cpoint = apoint; calls Point :: Point(const Point &)
```

The syntax for writing a copy constructor is as follows:

```
classname(const classname & 0)
{
    ...
}
```

Here, o is a reference to the object, which is used to initialize another object. A constructor is called once for global objects and for static objects. For local objects, the constructor is called each time the object declaration is encountered. With the help of constructors, one of the requirements of ADT implementation, namely initialization at definition time, is fulfilled. We still need a mechanism that automatically destroys an object when it gets invalid (for example, because of leaving its scope). Therefore, destructors are defined.

A.9.2 Destructors

Consider a class `List` for a linked list. The elements of the list are dynamically appended and removed. The constructor helps in creating an initial empty list. However, when we leave the scope of the definition of a list object, we must ensure that the allocated memory is released. We, therefore, define a special method called *destructor*, which is called once for each object at its destruction time.

Destruction of an object takes place when the object leaves its scope of definition or is explicitly destroyed. The latter happens when we dynamically allocate an object and release it when it is no longer needed. Destructors are declared similar to constructors. Thus, they also use the class name, but are prefixed by a tilde (~).

```
class Point
{
    int _x, _y;
    public:
        Point()
        {
            _x = _y = 0;
        }
        Point(const int x, const int y)
        {
            _x = xval;
            _y = yval;
        }
        Point(const Point & from)
        {
            _x = from_x;
            _y = from_y;
        }
    // destructor definition
    ~Point(){/* Nothing to do!*/}
    void setX(const int val);
    void setY(const int val);
    int getX(){return _x;}
    int getY(){return _y;}
};   // end of class declaration

void main(void)
{
    point appoint;   // constructor point :: point()
```

```
    : // called automatically.
    :
};    // here destructor for appoint is called automatically
```

Destructors have no arguments, and it is even improper to define one. As they are implicitly called at destruction time, a user has no need to specify actual arguments. Destructors are the complements of constructors. Local objects are created when the respective block is entered, and destroyed when the block is exited from. Hence, the object's respective constructor is called on block entry and the destructor is called on the block exit. Global objects are destroyed when the program terminates. So, their destructor is called automatically on program termination.

A.9.3 Constructor with Default Arguments

C++ allows a function to assign a parameter a default value when no argument corresponding to that parameter is specified in a call to that function. Program Code A.20 shows a constructor with parameters.

PROGRAM CODE A.20

```
// Constructor with parameters
class Initialize
{
   int A;
   public:
      void Initialize(int A = 10)    // constructor
      {
         cout << A;
      }
      main()
      {
         Initialize();    // displays default 10
         Initialize(5);    // displays specified 5
}

Output:
10
5
```

All parameters that take default values must appear to the right of those that do not, as follows:

```
Initialize(int A = 10, int B);    // incorrect
Initialize(int B, int A = 10);    // correct
```

Program Code A.21 is an example to find the volume of a cube.

PROGRAM CODE A.21

```
// To find volume of a cube
#include<iostream.h>
class cube
{
    int x, y, z;
    public:
        cube(int i = 0, int j = 0, int k = 0)
        {
            x = i;
            y = j;
            z = k;
        }
       int volume()
       {
           int volume;
           volume = x * y * z;
           return volume;
       }
}

int main()
{
    cube A(2, 3, 4); B;
    cout << A.Volume() << endl;
    cout << B.Volume() << endl;
    return 0;
}

Output:
24
0
```

Writing a constructor with default parameters is advantageous. For the class `Cube` if, by default, the constructor is not written, then two constructors are to be defined: one with parameters for object `A` and other without parameters for object `B`.

A.10 INHERITANCE

Inheritance is one of the key features of object-oriented languages. Reusability is achieved through inheritance wherein instead of creating a new class that is similar to the already existing one, we can reuse the existing one. The mechanism of deriving a new class from an existing one is called *inheritance*.

We can define a general class that has common features related to a set of items. This class is called *superclass* or *base class*. A derived class inherits some or all the features of the base class. The superclass can be inherited by other classes, which can add their own unique features to it. These classes are called *subclass* or *derived class*. The syntax for a derived class is given as follows:

```
class derived class name: access right Base class name
{
   ...
}
```

The phrase 'inherits from' is replaced by a colon in class definition. As an example, let us design a class for 3D points using the already existing class `Point`. Access right is also referred as *visibility mode*. The visibility mode is optional and if present may be either public or private. Visibility mode specifies whether the characteristics of the base class are privately or publicly derived.

```
class Point3D:public Point
{
   int _z;
   public:
      Point3D()
      {
         setX(0);
         setY(0);
         _z = 0;
      }
      Point3D(const int x, const int y, const int z)
      {
         setX(x);
         setY(y);
         _z = z;
      }
   ~Point3D(){/* Nothing to do */}
   int getZ(){return _z;}
   void setZ(const int val){_z = val;}
};
```

A.10.1 Types of Inheritance

In the definition, the keyword `public` is used in the first line of the class definition as its signature. This is necessary because C++ distinguishes two types of inheritance, public and private. By default, classes are privately derived from each other. We need to explicitly instruct the compiler to use public inheritance.

The type of inheritance influences the access rights to the elements of the base class. Using public inheritance, everything that is declared private in a base class remains private in the subclass. Similarly, everything that is public remains public. When using private inheritance, the features are quite different as shown in Table A.1.

Table A.1 Access rights and inheritance

Access rights of base class elements	Type of inheritance for sub/derived class		
	Private	Public	Protected
Private	Cannot be accessed	Cannot be accessed	Cannot be accessed
Protected	Private	Protected	Protected
Public	Private	Public	Protected

In Table A.1, the leftmost column lists the possible access rights for the elements of a class. It also includes a third type, protected. Protected access right is used for elements that are directly usable in subclasses but are not accessible from outside. In other words, we can say that the access rights of protected elements lie between private and public elements such that they can be used within the class hierarchy rooted by the corresponding class.

The first, second, and third columns show the resulting access rights of the elements of a base class when the subclass is inherited using private, public, and protected access, respectively.

A.10.2 Multiple Inheritance

C++ allows a class to be derived from more than one base class, as already mentioned briefly. One can easily derive from more than one class by specifying the base classes in a comma-separated list, as follows.

```
class Son:public Mother, public Father
{
   ...
   public:
      Father(...):
      Mother(...),
      Father(...)
      {
         ...
      }
      ~Son(){...}
      ...
};
```

A.11 ABSTRACT CLASSES

An abstract class is one from which no objects are created. It is designed and used merely as a base class. Abstract classes are defined similar to ordinary classes. However, a few of its member functions are designated to be necessarily defined by subclasses. We just mention their signature including their return type, name, and parameters, but indicating nothing in function body. This is expressed by appending '= 0' after the method signatures.

```
class Baseclass
{
   ...
   public:
      ...
      virtual void MemberFunction() = 0;    // Pure virtual function
};
```

This class definition would force every derived class from which objects should be created to define a method `MemberFunction()`. These method declarations are also called *pure methods*.

A.11.1 Pure Virtual Functions

A pure virtual function is a virtual function that has no definition within the base class. This is illustrated in Program Code A.22.

PROGRAM CODE A.22

```
// Demonstrating inheritance
class BaseClass
{
   public:
      virtual void VirFunc()
      {
         cout << "From Base class virtual function
         named VirFunc()\n";
      }
};

class DerivedClass1 : public BaseClass
{
   public:
      void VirFunc()
      {
         cout << "From Derived class1's virtual
         function named VirFunc()\n";
      }
};

class DerivedClass2 : public DerivedClass1
{

}
```

```
void main()
{
   BaseClass *p, b;
   DerivedClass1 d1;
   DerivedClass2 d2;
   p = &b;
   b→VirFunc();
   // access Base class's virtual function
   p = &d1;
   p→VirFunc();
   // access derived class1's virtual function
   p = &d2;
   p→VirFunc();
   // As derived class2 does not have VirFunc()
}    // It will therefore access the derived class1's
     //VirFunc()

Output:
From Base class virtual function named VirFunc()
From Derived class1's virtual function named VirFunc()
From Derived class1's virtual function named VirFunc()
```

As observed in Program Code A.22, when a virtual function is not redefined by a derived class, the version defined in the base class will be used. In many situations, there can be no meaningful definition of a virtual function in a base class or all derived classes would override a virtual function.

To handle these two cases, C++ supports pure virtual functions. A pure virtual function is one that has no definition within the base class.

```
virtual type func_name(parameter_list) = 0;
```

When a virtual function is made pure, any derived class must provide its own definition; otherwise it results in a compile-time error. Program Code A.23 illustrates pure virtual functions.

PROGRAM CODE A.23

```
// To draw different shapes
class shape
{
   public:
      virtual void Draw() = 0;
};
class line:public shape
```

```
{
   int x1, y1, x2, y2;
   public:
      void Draw()
     {
         x1 = 10;
         y1 = 10;
         x2 = 100;
         y2 = 100;
         line (x1, y1, x2, y2);
      }
};

class circle:public shape
{
   int x1, y1, r;
   public:
      void Draw();
      {
         x1 = 100;
         y1 = 100;
         r = 50;
         circle(x1, y1, r);
      }
};

class rectangle:public shape
{
   int x1, y1, x2, y2;
   public:
      void Draw();
      {
         x1 = 100;
         y1 = 100;
         x2 = 200;
         y2 = 200;
         rectangle(x1, y1, x2, y2);
      }
};

void main()
{
   shape *p;
```

```
    line L;
    circle C;
    rectangle R;
    int gd = detect, gm;
    initgraph(&gd, &gm, " ");
    p = &L;
    p→Draw();    // draws a line
    p = &C;
    p→Draw();    // draws a circle
    p = &R;
    p→Draw();    // draws a rectangle
}
```

In Program Code A.23, since each derived class should implement its own `Draw()`, it should be pure. Pure methods must also be declared virtual because we only want to use objects from derived classes. Classes that define pure methods are called *abstract classes*.

A.12 OPERATOR OVERLOADING

The mechanism of giving special meaning to an operator for the data type is called *operator overloading*. It helps to assign additional tasks to an operator and specify its meaning to a class to which the operator is applied. The general syntax for operator overloading is as follows:

```
return type class name::operator op(arguments list)
{
...
};
```

Here, `op` is the operator being overloaded, which is preceded by the keyword `operator`, and `operator op` is the function name.

Let us consider the ADT for complex numbers, `Complex`, as follows:

```
class Complex
{
   double Real, Imag;
   public:
      Complex()
      {
         Real = 0.0;
         Imag = 0.0
      }
      Complex(const double real, const double imag)
      {
         Real = real;
```

```
        Imag = imag
    }
    Complex Add(const Complex op);
    Complex Mul(const Complex op);
    ...
};
```

We can now add two complex numbers by making a call to the function `Add()` as

```
Complex A(1.0, 2.0), B(3.5, 1.2), C;
C= A.Add(B);
```

Here, we add two complex numbers `A` and `B` and assign the sum to `C`. This expression can also be written similar to integer or real number addition, that is, `C = A + B`. C++ allows this expression also. In C++, we can overload almost all operators for the newly created types. For example, we could define a '+' operator for the class `Complex` as

```
class Complex
{
  ...
  public:
    ...
    Complex operator + (const Complex &op)   // member of a class
    {
        double real = Real + op.Real;
        imag = Imag + op.Imag;
        return(Complex(real, imag));
    }
    ...
};
```

In this case, we have made the operator '+' as member of the class `Complex`. An expression of the form `C = A + B` is now allowed. Here, this statement is translated into

```
C = A.operator + (B);
```

Thus, the binary operator '+' needs only one argument. The first argument is implicitly provided by the invoking object (in this case `A`). However, an operator call can also be interpreted as a usual function call, as in

```
C = operator + (A, B);
```

In this case, the overloaded operator is not a member of a class. Rather, it is defined outside as a normal overloaded function. For example, we could define '+' operator as follows:

```
class Complex
{
  ...
  public:
    ...
    double real(){return Real;}
```

```
        double imag(){return Imag;}
};

Complex operator + (Complex &op1, Complex &op2)
{
    double real = op1.Real() + op2.Real();
    imag = op1.Imag() + op2.Imag();
    return(Complex(real, imag));
}
```

In this case, we must define access methods for the real and imaginary parts because the operator is defined outside the scope of the class. However, the operator is so closely related to the class that it would make sense to allow the operator to access the private members. This can be done by declaring it to be a friend of the class `Complex`.

A.12.1 Comparing Function Overriding and Overloading

Let us compare function overriding with overloading. In function overriding, the prototype for a redefined virtual function must exactly match the prototype specified in the base class, whereas in function overloading, the prototypes must differ either in the number or type of parameters.

In function overriding, if we change the prototype while redefining a virtual function, then the function will be considered overloaded by the C++ compiler, and its virtual nature will be lost.

Virtual functions must be non-static members of the classes that they are a part of.

Virtual functions cannot be friends. Constructor functions cannot be virtual, but destructors can be virtual.

A.13 FRIEND FUNCTION

Friend functions can be used instead of member functions for overloading binary operators. We can define functions or classes to be friends of a class to allow them direct access to its private data members. For example, in Section A.12, we would like to have the non-member function for the '+' operator to have access to the private data members `Real` and `Imag` of the class `Complex`. Therefore, we declare the operator '+' to be a friend of class `Complex`.

```
class Complex
{
    ...
    public:
        ...
        friend Complex operator +
        {
            const Complex &,
```

```
            const Complex &
        };
    };

    Complex operator + (const Complex &op1, const Complex &op2)
        {
        double Real = op1.Real + op2.Real;
        Imag = op1.Imag + op2.Imag;
        return(Complex(real, imag));
    }
```

The only change in using friend functions for operator overloading is that they do not have 'this' pointer. They cannot access the class members directly. They access class members using objects that are passed as arguments to them. They can be declared in the public or private sections of a class without any consequence.

A.14 GENERIC PROGRAMMING: TEMPLATES

A stack of integers is often defined as follows:

```
class Intstack
{
    int Top;
    int Data[20];
    public:
        Intstack()
        {
            Top = -1;
        }
        void Push(int);
        int TopElement();
        Pop();
} S1, S2;
```

This class can be used as a blue print for creating objects, which are stacks of integers such as `S1` and `S2`. The class has private data members, such as `Top` and `Data`, and member functions to operate on. When we need to create a stack of real numbers, we need to define a separate class as follows:

```
class Floatstack
{
    int Top;
    float Data[20];
    public:
        Floatstack()
        {
            Top = -1;
        }
```

```
        void Push(float);
        float TopElement();
        Pop();
} S3, S4;
```

Here, S3 and S4 are stacks for storing real numbers. To avoid defining two similar stacks, which vary only in the type of data being processed, templates are used. When we need to perform the same operations on different data types, we can use function templates. Template is the most powerful feature of C++ that enables software reuse. Templates help in defining generic functions and classes. They allow the user to specify the type of data as a parameter.

Using templates, the two classes Intstack and Floatstack can be defined as a single class as follows:

```
template <class T>
class stack
{
    int Top;
    T Data[20];
    public:
        stack()
        {
            Top = -1;
        }
        void Push(T);
        T TopElement();
        Pop();
};

stack <int> S1, S2;     // integer stacks
stack <float> S3, S4;    // float stacks
```

INDEX

RELATED TITLES

Data Structures using C
Reema Thareja, Institute of Information Technology and Management (IITM), Delhi

Data Structures Using C is designed to serve as a textbook for undergraduate engineering students of computer science as well as postgraduate students of computer applications. The book balances the theoretical aspects of data structures with their practical implementation.

Contents

1. Introduction to C; 2. Functions; 3. Pointers; 4. Introduction to Data Structures; 5. Arrays; 6. Strings; 7.Structures; 8. Linked Lists; 9. Stacks and Queues; 10. Trees; 11. Efficient Binary Trees; 12. Heaps; 13.Graphs; 14. Sorting; 15. Hashing and Collision; 16. Files and their Organization *Index*

9780198065449 | 668 Pages | January 2011 | Indian Original

Data Structures Via C ++: Objects by Evolution
Michael Berman, Vice President for Instructional and Information Technology, California State Polytechnic University, Pomona

This text is designed for a CS2 data structures course using C++ as the base programming language.

The author introduces object-oriented programming concepts in the context of traditional data structures and algorithms, emphasizing encapsulation from the beginning and gradually bringing in generics, inheritance, and polymorphism as the book progresses. Real-world examples illustrate the material in a way that makes it accessible to readers with no more than a basic background in the subject. All supporting materials, including source code, will be available to interested individuals via the World Wide Web.

Contents

Software Engineering and Computers; Designing Software: Two Approaches; Software Reliability; Abstract Data Types, Classes, and Objects; Efficiency; Recursion; Lists; Stacks; Queues; Tables; Trees; Graphs; Appendix A: A Brief Review of C Appendix; B: C++ for the Pascal Programmer Appendix; C: C++ for the Programmer; Bibliography; Index

9780195685787 | 496 Pages | May 1997 | Indian Reprint

Other Related Titles

1. 9780198075103 Thareja: *Data and File Structures Using C* (GTU Edition)
2. 9780198061793 Dey & Ghosh: *Computer Programming and Data Structures* (JNTU Edition)
3. 9780198065302 Sahay: *OOP with C++*, 2/e
4. 9780195690378 Trivedi: *Programming with ANSI C++*
5. 9780198063087 Trivedi: *Programming with ANSI C++*, A Step-by-step Approach (Anna University Edition)
6. 9780198070047 Thareja: *Programming in C*
7. 9780198065289 Dey & Ghosh: *Programming in C*, 2/e
8. 9780198063582 Malhotra & Choudhary: *Programming in Java*